THE CORE OF LEARNING

THE CORE OF LEARNING

The Philosophical Writings of N.F.S. Grundtvig

Edward Broadbridge
(translator and editor)

Introduction: Kim Arne Pedersen & Anders Holm
Afterword: Anders Holm

Introductions by Niels W. Bruun,
Kim Arne Pedersen, Kim Steen Ravn,
Jon Tafdrup, Vanja Thaulow, Steen Tullberg

"Philosophy is an expression of the human endeavour for wisdom" (1816)

"Philosophising without Faith is the same as looking without eyes" (1817)

Aarhus University Press |

The Core of Learning. The Philosophical Writings of N.F.S. Grundtvig

Illustrations selected and annotated by Edward Broadbridge
Language Consultant: Hanna Broadbridge

Typeset by Narayana Press
Cover design by Jørgen Sparre
Printed in Denmark by Narayana Press 2021

A recording of all the texts is available free at www.unipress.dk

This book is number five in the series 'N.F.S. Grundtvig: Works in English'
Series editors:
Niels Henrik Gregersen, Ove Korsgaard
ISBN 978 87 7219 237 6
ISSN 2246-7025

Published:
vol. 1. *The School For Life. N.F.S. Grundtvig on Education for the People* (2011)
vol. 2. *Living Wellsprings. The Hymns, Songs, and Poems of N.F.S. Grundtvig* (2015)
vol. 3. *Human Comes First. The Christian Theology of N.F.S. Grundtvig* (2018)
vol. 4. *The Common Good. N.F.S. Grundtvig as Politician and Contemporary Historian* (2019)
vol. 5. *The Core of Learning. The Philosophical Writings of N.F.S. Grundtvig* (2021)
vol. 6. *Denmark's Catalyst. The Life and Letters of N.F.S. Grundtvig* (2022)

Published with the financial support of Danish foundations. For a full list see p. 10

Aarhus University Press
Finlandsgade 29
8200 Aarhus N
Denmark
www.unipress.dk

INTERNATIONAL DISTRIBUTORS

Oxbow Books Ltd.
The Old Music Hall
106-108 Cowley Road
Oxford, OX4 1JE
United Kingdom
www.oxbowbooks.com

ISD
70 Enterprise Drive, Suite 2
Bristol, CT 06010
USA
www.isdistribution.com

Contents

Translated and edited by Edward Broadbridge

Published by Aarhus University Press

Illustrations

Cover: P.C. Skovgaard's drawing of Grundtvig. The handwriting is Grundtvig's own, taken from Illustration 3.

Foreword

Katrine Frøkjær Baunvig

N.F.S. Grundtvig (1783-1872) is a founding father of Danish democracy and a church father within the Evangelical Lutheran Church in Denmark. Furthermore, he is the architect behind the modern-day Danish school system as well as a romantic reviver and scholar of pre-Christian Nordic religion. This at least is the mainstream, self-reaffirming representation of Grundtvig's life, work, and cultural imprint dominating public discourse in Denmark anno 2021. Remarkably, this widely distributed representation leaves out entirely the important strands of philosophical reflection nested within the body of Grundtvig's works. The present volume seeks to take the first steps in making up for this situation. This is the first ever to gather Grundtvig's most important philosophical works in a single volume.

The Core of Learning is the fifth in a series of six translations of Grundtvig's work into English. *The School for Life*, containing a group of Grundtvig's texts on educational ideas, was published in 2011; *Living Wellsprings,* offering a sample of Grundtvig's vast number of hymns, songs and poems, was published in 2015; *Human Comes First,* comprising highlights of Grundtvig's theological writing, was published in 2018; and *The Common Good*, containing a group of Grundtvig's political writings and writings on contemporary history, was published in 2019. Forthcoming is volume 6, a biography and translations of 60 or so of Grundtvig's letters.

The Grundtvig Study Centre at Aarhus University is the instigator of these translations. The series is an extension of the centre's ongoing critical edition of Grundtvig's Works (in Danish) as they were published in his lifetime; see www.grundtvigsvaerker.dk. The Centre undertakes and supports research focusing on all areas of interest in Grundtvig studies, including comparative research initiatives that offer new perspectives on Grundtvig's work and the reception hereof. Furthermore, the centre fosters and supports knowledge exchange, teaching in, and dissemination of this research.

The texts for *The Core of Learning* have been selected by a committee comprising, in alphabetical order: Edward Broadbridge, Niels Henrik Gregersen, Hans Raun Iversen, Uffe Jonas, Ove Korsgaard, Michael Schelde, and Ole Vind.

Kim Arne Pedersen and Anders Holm are the authors of the comprehensive introduction to Grundtvig as a philosopher covering the stages in his philosophical reflection and the (overlooked) reception of it.

Members of the staff of www.grundtvigsvaerker.dk – Steen Tullberg, Jon Tafdrup, Kim Steen Ravn, Vanja Thaulow – as well as Kim Arne Pedersen, Niels W. Bruun and Edward Broadbridge have generously offered their expertise in aiding the individual Grundtvig texts with introductions; Anders Holm has contributed with a rich afterword on the enigmatic relationship between Grundtvig and his contemporary, Søren Kierkegaard.

As with the previous volumes in the series, Edward Broadbridge has been responsible for the translations and editing of the book. The language consultant has been Hanna Broadbridge.

This publication has received financial support from the following foundations, whom the Grundtvig Study Centre cordially thanks:

Aarhus Universitets Forskningsfond
Svend Grundtvig & Axel Olriks Legat
N. F. S. Grundtvigs Fond
Carlsen-Langes Legatstiftelse

Katrine Frøkjær Baunvig,
Director of the Grundtvig Study Centre, Aarhus University

Editor's/Translator's Note

Edward Broadbridge

Grundtvig is both a philosophical theologian and a theological philosopher, which means that certain articles could have been placed either in vol. 3 on Theology or, as here, in vol. 5 on Philosophy. One such is *On Religion and Liturgy*, which appears here because the first quarter, 'What is religion' is decisively philosophical in tone, and the liturgy takes up only the last part of the article.

Grundtvig's Philosophy of Education

Readers who are interested in this particular aspect of Grundtvig are referred to the illuminating essay by Ove Korsgaard in vol. 1 in the series, *The School for Life* (2011) pp. 13-35. Its very title, 'Grundtvig's Philosophy of Enlightenment and Education' makes the salient point that a single Danish word, *oplysning* (lit. 'uplighting'), includes both these aspects. Education is not fully education unless it also creates enlightenment, i.e. insight. The last two chapters in this book, an essay and three speeches of Grundtvig's, bring this translation series back to its outset in the School for Life. Outside Denmark, Grundtvig is primarily known for his educational ideas. Inside Denmark these vie for influence with his hymns and songs.

Paragraph length

On Human Beings in the World begins with a single paragraph of 1,296 words. In the original edition from 1817 this runs to 6½ pages without a paragraph *break*. But this is small beer compared to Paragraph 11, which in the original Gothic script runs to 2,685 words, (pp. 143-56) without a break. The translation makes room for 13 paragraphs for this single unsparing block of words.

Use of italics

During his lifetime all Grundtvig's works were printed in Gothic script. Until 1875 this was the custom in Denmark. But already by 1877 his lectures from 1838 had been collected and published in Latin script by his son, Svend Grundtvig, under the title *Within Living Memory* (*Mands Minde*). In Gothic script italics were indicated by a double-spacing between letters. Thus the first line of *On Human Beings in the World* reads, in Danish Gothic: "At Mennesket er sig selv en G a a d e ...", where the spacing in 'G a a d e' indicates a stressed word. In this particular case, my translation follows Grundtvig's indication of emphasis: Thus, human beings are "a *riddle* to themselves".

However, as in the previous four volumes in the series, I have taken the decision occasionally to ignore Grundtvig's italics, while finding it necessary to italicise a number of *other* words and add exclamation marks to make for easier reading. Grundtvig's original Danish – even in Latin script – is so complex that Danish university students in the second half of their Theology degrees, aged 25 or thereabouts, still find his works a daunting prospect.

Use of capital letters

To help readers through this, the most intellectually difficult, book in the series I have regularly used capital letters for major abstract concepts, such as Truth, Experience, the Finite and the Eternal – as well as subjects such as History, Theology, and Philosophy. However, when a *particular* 'truth' is in question the lower case is preferred: "The history of Denmark constitutes a minor part of World History."

Translation of Mennesket

The Danish word *Mennesket* is gender-neutral. Until the late 20th century, it would have been translated into English as 'Man' or 'Mankind'. In Old English a woman was known as a *wif* or a *wifmann*! 1,000 years later, in Pope's poem from 1734, *An Essay on Man* (i.e. humankind), we find the immortal words: "Know then thyself, presume not God to scan;/The proper study of mankind is man."

Within the last 50 years or so, the use of 'Man' to include all females has understandably come under increasing pressure. I used 'Man' throughout in *The School for Life* (2011), but I now realise that 'Man' can no longer be defended to cover anything other than the male of the species. In this and the last two volumes I have therefore switched to the gender neutral 'human beings', 'humankind', or simply the first person plural – except in the case of 'Natural Man'. Unfortunately, there is still no alternative to hu*man*kind or the hu*man* species.

Translation of Vidskab/Viden/Videnskab/Videnskabelighed

Another concept that confronts the translator is Grundtvig's use of the above four words, all of which derive from the root-word *vid*, meaning 'know'. The word is Germanic in origin and originally denoted the mind, as the seat of consciousness. With the Saxon invasion of Britain following the end of Roman rule in 410 CE, the word comes into the Old English language as *wit*. It survived the Viking and Norman invasions and is used to this day, e.g. a "quick-witted person", "to lose one's wits", i.e. one's sanity. Grundtvig himself explains his usage thus:

> As we know, Philosophy is an expression of the human endeavour for wisdom, for absolute knowledge, for immediate intuition, and, in the highest Christian phrase, for contemplation 'face to face'.[1] The Danish word that we can best employ to describe this endeavour in all its vitality is without doubt 'Learning' (*vidskab*) (p. 271).

To this can be added Jon Tafdrup's comment below:

> Learning, for Grundtvig, is thus an *ongoing endeavour* in this world, with its foundation in the Christian belief that full knowledge will only come when we meet our Maker 'face to face'. (p. 280)

I have reserved the word 'Learning', deliberately capitalised, as a translation of *vidskab* (used 38 times here by Grundtvig), alternating occasionally with 'scholarship'. The word *videnskab* (used 15 times), which once did service as an alternative, now means 'science', and is a cause of confusion when translating texts that are 200 years old. The word *viden* means knowledge pure and simple – as it does to this day; but Grundtvig uses this form only once in the entire Danish text of the book. On the other hand he uses *videnskabelighed* (70 times) regularly, and often in the sense of *vidskab*; for want of an alternative I have again used 'Learning' to translate the Danish word. Grundtvig himself is aware of the possibility of misunderstanding:

> 'Learning'... on the other hand is an endless endeavour towards an unattainable goal on earth. Any claim that it is actual 'knowledge' is empty boasting. Against this we have 'scholarship', which is closely connected to 'Learning'. In general usage, 'scholarship' allows for this, since it has chiefly functioned as a secondary usage. As the goal of Learning is indubitably full scholarship, there is no need to create new words such as 'learningable' and 'scholarshipable'.[2] They may have a similarity with 'companionable' and 'amicable', but they seem to jar the ear and would at the very least mislead rather than guide our readers (p. 272).

The title of this book, *The Core of Learning*, does not originate with Grundtvig, but is my attempt to render his belief that Learning is progressing towards a final goal in

1 1 Cor 13:12.

2 Here Grundtvig invents two new words *vidskabelig* and *vidskabelighed*.

History. He seeks to encourage this movement in ch. 6, *The Advancement of Learning*, which deals with how to promote this movement actively. Grundtvig believed that Learning was indeed advancing, and that he himself was actively advancing it.

Volume 6 (forthcoming)

From the preliminary work on volume 1 to the final publication of volume 5 (i.e. 2008-21) the idea of a possible sixth volume comprising a biography and selected letters has made its presence increasingly felt. At the time of writing, this will become reality in the coming year or so. The biography will make constant reference to the five published volumes, and the letters will illustrate many of the aspects of Grundtvig the man.

Notes on Contributors

Translator and Editor

Edward Broadbridge (b.1944) BA London, MA Aarhus, taught English and Religious Studies at high schools in Denmark 1967-2008. Among his many theological translations are books on Ruth, Luke, Paul, and Titus of Bostra, as well as translations of 50 Danish hymns, *Hymns in English* (2009). He is also a librettist for Danish composers, and a writer/director of children's musicals. His translations of Grundtvig began with *A Grundtvig Anthology* (1984) and include the first major appraisal of Grundtvig in English, *Tradition and Renewal* (1983), as well as *Grundtvig as a Political Thinker* by Ove Korsgaard (2014) and most of the essays in *Building the Nation. N.F.S. Grundtvig and Danish National Identity* (2015). He is the translator of Anders Holm's *The Essential N.F.S. Grundtvig* (2019), and editor of the quarterly *Grundtvig Newsletter*. He is the translator and editor of the 6-volume series 'N.F.S. Grundtvig: Works in English' (2008-22).

Language Consultant

Hanna Broadbridge (b.1945) MA Aarhus English & Japanese, married Edward in 1967 and has been a teacher of English in Denmark 1971-2009 and lecturer in English at the Royal Academy of Education 1978-2003. She has been an external examiner in English at all the Danish universities 1998-2015, and is an official interpreter for the Danish legal system. She is chair of the Diocesan Council of Aarhus, and chair of the LWF Committee of the Council of International Relations in Denmark.

Introductions

Anders Holm (b.1973) MTheol Copenhagen (2002), PhD Aarhus (2007) on Grundtvig and Kierkegaard. Associate Professor at the Faculty of Theology, Copenhagen University. Editor since 2011 of of the annual scholarly journal *Grundtvig-Studier*. Visiting Fulbright Professor at Samford University, Birmingham, Alabama in 2016. Publications include *To Samtidige. Kierkegaards og Grundtvigs kritik af hinanden*, (*Two Contemporaries. Kierkegaard's and Grundtvig's Critique of One Another*) Copenhagen: Anis 2009, and *The Essential N.F.S. Grundtvig*, Aarhus Filo, 2019. Translated by E. Broadbridge.

Kim Arne Pedersen (b.1957) MTheol Aarhus (1987), PhD Aarhus in Grundtvig's philosophy (1995), Associate Professor, Aarhus, Centre for Grundtvig-Studies (1996-2003),

Leader of the Grundtvig Academy, Vartov (1998-2000). Pastor of Odder Independent Church (2004-15). Has published articles on all facets of Grundtvig's work.

Kim Steen Ravn (b.1963) MA Aarhus Comparative Literature (1985). Former head of Philological Department at the Søren Kierkegaard Research Centre, which produced the complete works of Kierkegaard in Danish (1993-2009). Member of the digitalization and annotation staff of 'Grundtvig's Works' at the Grundtvig Centre since 2010. Has primarily written articles on the Danish author, Poul Martin Møller. Published the Danish poet Johannes Ewald's *Selected Poems* (Borgen Copenhagen 1996) and the Norwegian scientist and diplomat Fridtjof Nansen's diary from 1905 (unipax Oslo 2005).

Niels W. Bruun (b.1944) MA Copenhagen (1970). Philologist for *Thesaurus Linguae Latinae* in Munich (1986-89), and for the digitalization and annotation of the works of Søren Kierkegaard at the Søren Kierkegaard Research Centre (1998-2009). Member of the digitalization and annotation staff of 'Grundtvig's Works' at the Grundtvig Centre (2011-12). Author of books and articles especially in the fields of classical philology and the history of medicine.

Jon Tafdrup (b.1975) MA Copenhagen (2009). Philologist for the digitalization and annotation of the works of Søren Kierkegaard at the Søren Kierkegaard Research Centre (2010-13). Member of the digitalization and annotation staff of 'Grundtvig's Works' at the Grundtvig Centre since 2013.

Vanja Thaulow (b.1977) MTheol Copenhagen (2005). Pastor of Majbølle-Vigsnæs parish on Lolland 2007-11. Member of the digitalization and annotation staff of 'Grundtvig's Works' at the Grundtvig Centre since 2011. PhD Aarhus (2018): 'Warrior of the Lord. Rhetorical Criticism of N.F.S. Grundtvig's Theological Polemics in the Period 1810-1825'.

Steen Tullberg (b.1968) MTheol Copenhagen (1999). Former head of Philological Department at the Søren Kierkegaard Research Centre which produced the complete works of Kierkegaard in Danish (1997-2013). Member of the digitalization and annotation staff of 'Grundtvig's Works' at the Grundtvig Centre since 2013. Has primarily written articles on the Danish and German reception of Kierkegaard, including 'Denmark: The Permanent Reception – 150 Years of Reading Kierkegaard' in *Kierkegaard's International Reception, vol. 1, Northern and Western Europe* (Ashgate UK 2009).

1. Grundtvig 1822

The earliest depiction of Grundtvig is the 1820 painting by the little-known artist, Christian Christensen, reproduced in *The School for Life* (2011) p. 73. In 1822 Johann Walther (1799-1860) made this copper engraving of the painting, reflecting an intense, intelligent man, whose eyes have unusually large pupils. It was advertised for sale on 3rd August 1822 in the newspaper *The Day* (*Dagen*) at the price of 3 Rigsmarks. Vilhelm Saxtorph wrote in his *Portraits of Grundtvig* (1932) that "it is turned in relation to the painting, and the posture is wrong ... It must have been printed in a very large number, since it is still easily available, and that is probably the reason why it is so well-known ... It should never be reproduced or be accepted at face value as a likeness."

"Time will Tell the Truth": Grundtvig as a Philosopher[3]

Kim Arne Pedersen & Anders Holm

1. Introduction

From the outset, philosophical considerations play a significant part in Grundtvig's writings. They are very much contingent on the role of philosophy in contemporary academic and public life, and they form part of his dialogue with the age on spiritual life – particularly in his earliest works.

Even as a child away from home in Thyregod aged 9 to 15,[4] Grundtvig is reading avidly and acquainting himself with the philosophically-based 'natural theology'. This argues that humankind, by observing itself and the universe through its naturally-given abilities, can acknowledge that the world has come into being through a divine act of creation. Aged 17-20 and studying theology at Copenhagen University (1800-03), Grundtvig comes under the influence of Professor of Logic and Metaphysics, Børge Riisbrigh (1731-1809), whose teaching inclines to the pre-critical metaphysics of the German, Christian Wolff (1679-1754). Wolff is inspired by Gottfried Leibnitz (1646-1716), but is also influenced by late scholastic philosophy, and, following the tradition and Leibnitz, emphasises that faith and reason, i.e. theology and philosophy, can in fact be united.

Also while studying at university Grundtvig comes into contact with the works of Immanuel Kant (1724-1804),[5] most likely through Professor of Moral Philosophy, Anders Gamborg (1753-1833). Gamborg is his 'preceptor', meaning his supervisor and guardian, since like most students of the day Grundtvig has not yet come of age.[6]

3 "Time will tell the Truth" was one of Grundtvig's favourite proverbs. He listed it in his alphabetical collection of *Danish Proverbs and Sayings* (1845), and wrote a whole essay on that subject, translated below as ch. 11. He used it as the motto on the title page of his *World History* (1817), below the original Greek version in lines 33-34 of the *First Olympian Ode* by Pindar (c. 518-c. 445 BCE): ΜΕΡΑΙ ΕΠΙΛΟΙΜΟΙ ΜΑΡΤΥΡΕΣ ΣΟΘΩΤΑΤΟΙ (the days that remain are the wisest witnesses).

4 From September 1792 to summer 1798.

5 Immanuel Kant (1724-1804) is best known for his 'critical philosophy', which argued that human beings are 'autonomous', and his duty-based ethics, which meant, in consequence of this autonomy, that it is one's duty to follow the formal moral principle common to all people, the so-called 'categorical imperative'.

6 By Christian V's Danish Law of 1683, boys under 18 were 'minors' (*umyndige*), boys between 18 and 25 were 'underage' (*mindreårige*), and not until they were 25, were they 'of age' (*fuldmyndige*). The age of majority was reduced to 21 in 1922 and to 18 in 1976.

In addition, Grundtvig probably studies the works of a number of Kantian-inspired Danish thinkers outside the university. In his early teenage years Grundtvig has also read the periodical *Jesus and Reason*,[7] known for its French-inspired, deistic approach to enlightenment.

Lastly, he hears about Romanticism for the first time. The source is his philosopher cousin, the natural scientist Henrik Steffens (1773-1845). Between 1802-04 Steffens gives a number of lectures on the subject at Copenhagen University, with those on Goethe and poetry leaving the deepest impression on Grundtvig. He admits that at the time he did not register much of what his cousin said, but he now has a vague idea that something *new* is in the air. More significant than Steffens, however, is the high standing of philosophy in the academic education of the time, which ensures that Grundtvig is well-trained in philosophical thinking, when he makes his debut as a writer in the first decade of the 19th century.

Philosophy as a Social Issue

From 1805-08 Grundtvig works as house tutor at Egeløkke Manor on Langeland to Carl Steensen de Leth (1798-1889), the 7-year-old son of the lord and lady of the manor. To sublimate his secret passion for the lady of the house, Grundtvig turns to a study of Nordic mythology, but more importantly he also turns to the work of Kantian philosophers such as Friedrich Schiller (1767-1805) and idealist thinkers such as Johann Fichte (1762-1814) and Friedrich Schelling (1775-1854). Grundtvig returns to Copenhagen in 1808, and until late 1810 he teaches History and Geography to 14 to 18-year-old boys at the Schouboe Institute, the most modern private high school in the country. In a farewell poem to his pupils he exhorts them to "Turn away from this world's vale of tears/to the Holy One upon the cross!/There alone the soul's true health is found".[8] The poem reflects Grundtvig's return to traditional Lutheran orthodoxy after his religious crisis in 1810, with his philosophical writings now marked by a defence of Christianity. In Grundtvig's approach to Christianity, to human life, and to all scholarly work, philosophy is an *elemental* concern. In the present book, examples of this first phase of his work (1805-10) are presented in the second and third sections: *On Religion and Liturgy* (1807) and *On the Advancement of Learning* (1807).

During this period Grundtvig takes spiritual life as a single entity, an *interaction* between theology, community life, and academic life. His philosophy is to be found in the conclusions he draws from this interaction, which is conditioned by our human

7 The periodical, *Jesus and Reason (*Dan: *Jesus og Fornuften)*, was founded in 1795. From 1797-1801 it was edited by Otto Horrebow (1769-1823).

8 Cf. 'Farewell to my Pupils', no. 134 in *Living Wellsprings* (2015).

citizenship in the eternal world of the Spirit, characterised, like Plato, as our "original home".[9] He emphasises that "only a truly religious mind, an unshakable faith in heaven, and a glimpse of its glory,"[10] can promote the flowering of philosophy and science. A successful spiritual life depends on religion giving *direction* to society.

Throughout his life Grundtvig holds firm to two fundamental ideas that derive from this tenet: that philosophy is a social issue, and that human beings consist of both spirit and body. As regards philosophy as a *social* question, *On Historical Learning, or the Concept of History* (1816) reveals how the broad cultural philosophy of his earlier writings finds a powerful and significant form in the idea of "mutual dependence"[11] between social classes in their collaboration on learning. *On Human Beings in the World* (1817)[12] opens with a powerful poetic image of this division between spirit and body in a quotation from Edward Young's *Night Thoughts*, where the human being is seen as both 'dishonour'd' yet 'divine'.[13] There is a perpetual tension between our physical temporality and our longing for eternity. Grundtvig notes disparagingly how "every other writer in the previous century took... a trip into the maze that makes up the human grove,"[14] i.e. the labyrinthine paths that constitute our human relations as "anthropologists, psychologists, and educationists".[15] From 1805 onwards Grundtvig is critical of Enlightenment thinking; yet, as is often the case with spiritual life, he has been shaped and governed by what he now repudiates. The three branches of learning mentioned above are broadly identical with the three areas he centres on throughout his philosophical work. In the same year, 1817, he also publishes *On Revelation, Art, and Learning*, which bears the hallmark of his Platonic-inspired 'spirit and body' philosophy and "the clash of two worlds, of contending powers loosely linked within us in a mighty ferment".[16] Any philosophy that fails to take into account this transcendent relation "does not deserve to be called a philosophy."[17]

There are thus clear threads from Grundtvig's thinking in the period 1805-10 to his more thoroughly worked-out philosophy in the years 1815-23. In between, 1811-15, the years he calls his "theological" period, he works first as curate to his father in Udby parish and then as a writer in Copenhagen, primarily in his advocacy of the Gospel and

9 *On Religion and Liturgy* p. 139.

10 *On the Advancement of Learning* p. 249.

11 *On Historical Learning, or the Concept of History* p. 292.

12 *On Human Beings in the World* p. 68.

13 Edward Young (1683-1765), *The Complaint: or, Night-Thoughts on Life, Death, & Immortality*, London, 1742. A pioneer book of the Romantic movement, *Night-Thoughts* was immensely successful, influencing the young Goethe and the whole *Sturm und Drang (Storm and Drive)* movement in late 18th century Germany and characterised by extremes of emotion and a rejection of Enlightenment classical norms.

14 *On Human Beings in the World* p. 78.

15 Ibid.

16 *On Revelation, Art, and Learning* p. 192.

17 Ibid.

his polemical deployment against contemporary rationalists. In 1813 he comes to an understanding of the human being as three-dimensional: Spirit, Body, and Mind. He links imagination to the Spirit, feeling to the Body, and intellect/reason to the Mind, as can be seen in the later essays included here. It is also in this 'theological' period that he attacks German idealism in general and leading intellectuals in Denmark in particular, most notably H.C. Ørsted (1777-1851), the discoverer of electro-magnetism.[18] Ørsted, who is influenced by the German idealists, especially Schelling, had attacked Grundtvig's publication of an eschatologically-oriented writing from his late father's papers and his attempt to turn the clock back to pre-Enlightenment times. Grundtvig responds with the claim that the biblical prophecies are in the process of being fulfilled! In *Against the Little Accuser* (1815)[19] Grundtvig calls Schelling "unChristian, ungodly, and untruthful" and contends that he can deliver a logically watertight proof that this is the case: God is transcendental, Christianity and the Bible are the only means of salvation, and the end of the world is approaching, beliefs in which he is far from alone in holding. Ørsted's stinging response claims that God is *immanent* in creation and identical with nature and matter. The controversy eventually dies down, though neither antagonist changes his viewpoint. Ørsted regards Grundtvig's apocalyptic Christianity as obscurantism, while Grundtvig holds firm to his apocalyptic expectation of the coming of Christ. By the end of 1815, however, Grundtvig is setting aside his preaching mode and moving on to what he calls his "historical period" - 1815-23.

Danne-Virke, a One-man Journal

Between July 1816 and January 1819 Grundtvig publishes his own one-man journal, *Danne-Virke*[20] - 16 editions in all, containing essays, obituaries, and poems, and including articles on *Beowulf*[21] and his own magnificent poem 'The Easter Lily'.[22] Grundtvig divides his content of *Danne-Virke* into 'flowers' (poems), 'leaves' (source criticism) and 'fruits' (philosophical essays on history, literature and myth). The last-mentioned genre, philosophy, is repeatedly drawn on in Grundtvig's contemporary work, *An Account of*

18 H.C. Ørsted is often spelt 'Oersted' in English. Oersted's Law and the oersted (Oe) are named after him. His Christian names, Hans Christian, are not used in Denmark - as indeed is the case with H.C. Andersen, the writer of fairy-tales.

19 Danish title: *Imod den lille Anklager.*

20 English title: lit. *The Dane-Work*, named after the rampart along the southern Danish border with Germany.

21 Being a largely self-taught scholar of Old English (Anglo-Saxon) Grundtvig took great interest in the epic poem, *Beowulf* (8th-9th cent). In 1820 he published the first modern translation (into Danish, revised in 1865), and in 1861 he published a new edition of the poem. For further comment see the English summary by Andreas Haarder in *Grundtvig Studies* 1965 (also online).

22 Grundtvig's 30-page drama-poem (Danish title: *Paaske-Lilien*) depicts Christ's resurrection as experienced by imagined bystanders at the grave on Easter morning. It was first published in *Danne-Virke* (1817) and was included as a hymn version in Grundtvig's *Song-Work for the Danish Church* (1837). In 1910 Carl Nielsen wrote a new tune, and the 6-verse hymn is now among the most popular in the Danish hymnbook.

World History, Primarily in the Lutheran Era (1817).[23] His readers include the Copenhagen literati and university students, as well as provincial church leaders, and a handful of Norwegians, among them Professor of Philosophy, Niels Treschow and Professor of Greek, Georg Sverdrup. No fewer than 9 of the 14 chapters in the present book date from the *Danne-Virke* period. Grundtvig is now less combative and more reflective than before – yet none the less impassioned.

The distinguished literary historian, Flemming Lundgreen-Nielsen, calls this historical period one of "*Danne-Virke* patience",[24] meaning that Grundtvig is willing to wait for History to show future generations that his Christian world-view was right in the end: "We only become wise by experience, and therefore we all need to know our history, which alone embraces, connects, and illuminates all human experience." This thought leaves its marks on his philosophical thinking after 1815: He calls this period

> … my *historical* one, as most will agree. Everything I have written since then is concerned with my claim that also at the *universal* level we only become wise by experience. We should all learn from History as best we can, for History alone embraces all human experience and can connect and clarify it.[25]

Grundtvig will no longer preach the Gospel directly, but will see "whether the eye is as blind to human beings… as it is to our Saviour".[26] Fundamental to his thought is that historical experience is the best teacher to help us understand ourselves. This conviction is expounded in a much calmer tone than in the hectic discharges of the preceding theological period. With an allusion to his prophecies during the controversy with Ørsted, Grundtvig will let time be the judge of who was right and who was wrong: "All such clarification I therefore leave to posterity."[27] His task is not so much to prophesy as to present his History-based observations on humankind and our relationship to the world and to God, whom he regards as the core of all learning. Hence the phrase "human condition" is constantly in use.[28]

In turning his attention to our shared human condition and to "the great concerns of the human race: the enlightenment of past generations and thus of humankind itself!"[29] Grundtvig is putting words to the universalist aims that are consolidating in

23 Danish title: *Udsigt over Verdens-Krøniken fornemmelig i det Lutherske Tidsrum.*

24 Flemming Lundgreen-Nielsen (1980) *Det handlende ord. N.F.S. Grundtvigs digtning, litteraturkritik og poetik 1798-1819 (The Word as Agent, N.F.S. Grundtvig's Writing, Literary Criticism and Poetics 1798-1819).* Copenhagen, p. 681.

25 *An Exchange of Letters between North Jutland and Christianshavn*, 1824, quoted in *Grundtvig's Memoirs and Memoirs of Grundtvig (Grundtvigs Erindringer og Erindringer om Grundtvig)*, eds. H. Høirup & S. Johansen, Copenhagen 1948 p. 64.

26 *On Human Beings in the World* (1816) p. 70.

27 *On the Philosophical Century* (1816) p. 271.

28 See pp. 73, 79, 90 etc.

29 *On Proverbs* p. 331.

him through his studies in the history of philosophy, as formulated by the German polyhistorian, Johann Herder (1744-1803). Thus he writes:

> The chronicles of the world, which depict the interaction of the various peoples and the links between the ages, are by their very nature a 'common' that none can justly arrogate to themselves.[30]

The 'common' in question is the *village* common in Danish peasant society, a stretch of uncultivated land on which everyone can graze their livestock. Similarly, history is the shared experience of humankind, to which all should have free access.

The title of Grundtvig's journal, *Danne-Virke*, signals his intent to protect the Danish reading public from the encroachment of German idealism and culture south of the border, but not from the whole wide world in general. On the contrary, he considers it a specifically *Danish* task to philosophise over *world* history, and over the relationship between the individual and the universal. We see how the individual is placed in the same relation to his or her people as to humankind in general:

> Individuals occupy the same relationship to their people as to the entire human race; whatever they are able to comprehend therefore depends first on how much their people can *comprehend* of the present moment, and second, on how much they are aware of the *ideas* of their people.[31]

In the same article Grundtvig argues that "wherever the body is divided among warring members, nothing can thrive," and "the more limited a people's idea of, and feeling for, the human race, the more limited their idea of the human being."[32] The aim therefore is for the individual nations to work together, with world history as their point of origin, to *explain* the human being – including the circumstances of our origin and our destiny.

In this philosophising over history, Grundtvig sees a major role for Christianity, but treats it primarily as a cultural force – especially in the first two volumes of *Danne-Virke*. Already in 1816 he anticipates his later dictum, "Human comes first, and Christian next,"[33] when, with reference to the European nations, he argues that "how they are as a people, so do they become as Christians."[34] Down the ages, Christianity has always interacted with each people's distinctive stamp in the illumination of

30 *On Historical Learning, or the Concept of 'History'* (1816) p. 290.

31 Ibid. p. 283.

32 Ibid.

33 Cf. The poem appears as no. 91 in *Living Wellsprings* (2015).

34 *On Historical Learning, or the Concept of 'History'* p. 287.

its history and understanding of both itself and humankind in general. Grundtvig's gradual transition from Christian polemicist to historically-based anthropologist does not affect his fundamental beliefs. He continues to hold his Christian world-view, but his approach now is to expound this in a successive unfolding of philosophical arguments in *Danne-Virke* to persuade his readers of the truth of Christianity. This move from knowledge towards faith corresponds on a smaller scale to what history offers us: the future will prove that the Christian claims regarding our human circumstances and our destiny are credible and reliable. Indeed, in the detailed position he takes towards contemporary philosophy in *A Brief Account of World History* (1812),[35] he uses the very motto from the Greek historiography, Pindar: "What Truth is Time will tell."

As Grundtvig turns away from a direct proclamation of the Gospel in the years after 1815, it is in this 'historical period' of his authorship that his philosophical observations weigh most. We find here the foundation for his thinking much later, called by one theologian "prefaces to all Grundtvig's later ideas on history and doctrine".[36] He continues to write philosophical texts and to work with philosophical elements right up until his death in 1872. Although they are no longer a main concern, this does not weaken their importance. The 'prefaces' that are the fruition of this period operate with a series of concepts that are fundamental to his maturing view of anthropology, history, society, education, and theology, positions which for the rest of his life he justifies with *philosophical* arguments. Like his contemporaries, he does not define 'philosophy' in its narrower sense but includes both "cultural education and upbringing".[37] However, we must note that although he continues to diverge from the path that philosophy takes in the 18th and 19th centuries, he remains, as in his youth, under its *influence*, including that of German idealism. Inspired by Fichte's concept of *Wissenschaftslehre* (epistemology) but with reference to an older biblical usage, he speaks now of 'learning' (*Vidskab*). In alignment with Fichte's belief that human reflection is an unfinished process, Grundtvig characterises learning as "an expression of the human endeavour for wisdom, for absolute knowledge."[38] In contrast to the specialised sciences, 'learning' is thinking *in progress*, an "endless endeavour towards an unattainable goal on earth".[39]

Fichte and Grundtvig also agree that this awareness of an unattainable goal in this life is the foundation of consciousness. However, where Fichte posits a unify-

35 Danish title: *Kort Begreb af Verdens Krønike betragtet i Sammenhæng*, otherwise untranslated.

36 Bishop Henning Høirup (1909-95) *Grundtvig's View of Faith and Knowledge (Grundtvigs Syn paa Tro og Erkendelse*, 1949).

37 *On Revelation, Art, and Learning* p. 203. Grundtvig's words here are *dannelse* and *opdragelse*. *dannelse* is a central word in the Danish language, and denotes *cultural* education, now including life-skills, while *uddannelse* denotes formal education and training.

38 Ibid. p. 271.

39 Ibid. p. 272.

ing consciousness between God and humankind, Grundtvig honours the traditional distinction between creator and creature. Thus, for us as *created* beings in Time, "all true learning must in every sense be *historical*".[40] The apostle Paul is right to say: "For we know in part and we prophesy in part, but when completeness comes, what is in part disappears."[41] Only in eternity will we understand the riddles of life: where we come from, where we are heading, and what is the meaning of it all. Grundtvig underlines that "all knowledge about an eternal independent existence is impossible for us."[42] At the same time, in *On the Philosophical Century* (1816) he agrees with Wolff that ontologically, "like all the essential basic concepts of existence (p. 273)", God is beyond our understanding. Yet although direct knowledge of God is not possible in this life, his existence can be *proved*, and as Paul says, in eternity "we shall see face to face", and "shall know fully."[43]

These observations are summarised into two major declarations in the following year in *On Revelation, Art, and Learning* (1817). First, "we cannot understand a jot more about humankind than what has been developed and illuminated in us over time."[44] And second, everything in the world, including all phenomena in space and time "is simply an effect of the almighty power of eternal Truth, mirroring His thought as created by His Word."[45] Human beings "reflect God Himself, as the work of His hand with a gleam of His light and a spark of His Spirit."[46] Philosophy therefore reaches its fulfilment and achieves its goal in a knowledge of God. Human beings, created in God's image, "are at the head of it all,"[47] meaning the totality of Time and Space, the world as Nature and History. This idea that human beings are the crown of creation – and a microcosm of it – is the pillar of Grundtvig's philosophy of nature and his philosophy of history. He adds, wittily, "their lives are set on a historical course, at the end of which, like Professors of History, they are created Doctors of Theology."[48] The 'historical course' leads eventually to an indirect knowledge of God on earth, and a direct knowledge, face to face, in eternity.

For Grundtvig, philosophy thus occupies the role of a servant; it provides services on the overriding level for specific purposes. Philosophy is an instrument for the two disciplines within the area of 'the School', i.e. education and the human acquisition of knowledge. In 1819 he calls education a sphere "which our whole life constitutes,

40 Ibid. p. 275.
41 I Cor 13:9-10.
42 *On the Philosophical Century* p. 273.
43 I Cor 13:12.
44 *On Revelation, Art, and Learning* p. 176.
45 Ibid.
46 Ibid.
47 Ibid. p. 199.
48 Ibid.

corresponding to revelation and experience."[49] To this can be added Grundtvig's belief that "knowledge is only of help to put doubt to shame and to strengthen Faith,"[50] a relation to which he gives pointed expression in the same article: "Philosophising without Faith is the same as looking without eyes."[51] According to Grundtvig, our view of humankind and our concept of God illuminate each other. His claim that history is a goal-oriented process directed by Providence – a belief that under the influence of German idealism is central in 1811-15 and still much in evidence in the '*Danne-Virke* period' (1816-19) – is no longer so convincing from our present-day perspective. What speaks to us rather is his view of humankind, which is central to our understanding of creative education and creation theology.

2. Reception and Research

On the basis of the controversy with his contemporaries in the years 1811-15, Grundtvig is widely regarded as a Christian opponent of philosophical thinking. Judgement against him, though sporadic, is harsh. In the monthly journal *Athene* (1813-17), which was influenced by German idealism, the literary critic Peder Hjort (1793-1871) calls Grundtvig's philosophy "suffocating smoke" (1817), a metaphor that Grundtvig borrows and, with an image from hunting, turns to positive effect for his riposte: "What else should I do with my philosophising other than smoke out the foxes that theology has failed to do, or otherwise smoke them into their foxhole-graves?"[52] He hereby demonstrates that his philosophy, also after 1815, remains *in the service of* his theology, a position which confirmed for his critics, like the later champion of democracy, Dr J.J. Dampe (1790-1867), that Grundtvig should simply be written off as an obscurantist and his philosophy as an opaque attempt to undermine free thought. The criticism gradually fades after he moves into his 'historical period' in 1815 and reins in his aggression towards other thinkers. Not least his defeat in a libel trial in 1825[53] makes him a wiser, less combative philosopher in the 1830s. But his ideas remain out of step with his contemporaries, with the sole enthusiast in his lifetime being the philologist and educationist Christian Flor (1792-1875) – the first principal of the first people's high school in Rødding from 1844. In the 1870s Professor of Philosophy Rasmus Nielsen (1808-84) also acknowledges Grundtvig's contribution to theology and education, but he leaves Grundtvig's philosophical ideas to themselves.

Not until 1909 is Grundtvig seriously acknowledged as a philosopher of value.

49 *On the Church, the State, and the School* p. 231.

50 *On Human Beings in the World* p. 75.

51 Ibid. p. 76.

52 *On Revelation, Art, and Learning* p. 174.

53 The 'Clausen Libel Case' is dealt with in vol. 3 *Human Comes First* (2018).

In *Danish Philosophers*[54] Professor of Philosophy Harald Høffding (1843-1931) outlines Grundtvig's controversy first with the Danes: H.C. Ørsted, and the Kantian-influenced poet, Jens Baggesen (1764-1826). Grundtvig represents faith, Ørsted and Baggesen the religiosity that can be combined with free, scientific research. Høffding ends his section on the quarrel with Ørsted by arguing how the aging Grundtvig, "in the midst of the Hegelian dominion [i.e. the 1830s and 1840s] spoke up... for a philosophy of experience on the English model" (p. 64). Following Høffding, Grundtvig is now regarded as a philosophising writer in a number of works, presented below in chronological order on Grundtvig's own broad understanding of what constitutes 'philosophy'.

The next major publication to deal with Grundtvig as a philosopher comes in the form of a doctorate in 1923, written and defended in Swedish by Sven Bergentz. In *N.F.S. Grundtvig's Religious Idealism: with Special Attention to his Ethical Standpoint*[55] Bergentz concentrates on Grundtvig's ethics in relation to the liberal theology of the 1920s.

Before Høffding, the Danish philologist Frederik Rønning (1851-1929) has already written a chapter entitled *Grundtvig, the Man of Learning* in the centenary book commemorating Grundtvig's birthday, *A Hundred Years* (1883).[56] In the same year Rønning also publishes *Grundtvig, the Aesthetic*,[57] in which he demonstrates how in his poetics Grundtvig sets content above form. In *Grundtvig as a Thinker* (1927)[58] Rønning characterises Grundtvig's reflections on culture in *Nordic Mythology* (1832) as a philosophy that seeks to "understand existence" (p. 164). Rønning calls Grundtvig a "dream-thinker", meaning a philosopher who "works unremittingly to untie himself from the dreamer, and his thought from the image" (p. 165). In Rønning's portrait we can see the influence of contemporary life philosophy and German intellectual history (*Geistesgeschichte*).

In 1947 the theologian Carl Immanuel Scharling (1879-1951) publishes a pioneer work, *Grundtvig and Romanticism*, with the subtitle, *Illustrated through Grundtvig's Relation to Schelling*.[59] He analyses in depth Schelling's influence on Grundtvig, pointing out that Grundtvig's Christianity always maintains the distinction between creator and created, between God and humankind. This tends to fade out of sight in Schelling's idealism. Two years later another pioneer work appears on Grundtvig's philosophy and theology: in *Grundtvig's View of Faith and Knowledge* (1949)[60] Henning Høirup (1909-95) shows how in both his philosophical and theological writings Grundtvig argues on

54 Danish title: *Danske Filosofer*. Nb. All the books subsequently mentioned in this section are in Danish only, unless otherwise stated.

55 Swedish title: *N.F.S. Grundtvigs religiøsa idealism: med särskild hänsyn till hans etiska ståndpunkt.*

56 Danish title: *Hundrede år.*

57 Danish title: *Grundtvig som Aesthetiker.*

58 Danish title: *Grundtvig som Tænker.*

59 Danish title: *Grundtvig og Romantikken: Belyst ved Grundtvigs Forhold til Schelling.*

60 *Grundtvigs Syn paa Tro og Erkendelse.*

the basis of the principle of contradiction.[61] More dubious is Høirup's assertion that Grundtvig is also under the direct influence of the English philosopher, John Locke (1632-1704), but of lasting value is his proof of how the principle of contradiction plays a role in Grundtvig's 'matchless discovery' in 1825 of the Apostolic Creed as the Church's foundation.

An important but often overlooked study of Grundtvig's teaching on human consciousness is *Psychological Ideas and Theories in Grundtvig*,[62] which the theologian Villiam Grønbæk (1897-1970) published in 1951. Grønbæk notes how Grundtvig's thinking builds on what was known in his time and within the domain of philosophy as 'psychology' – meaning the theory concerning human abilities. Among Grønbæk's many insights is how Grundtvig's concept of human feeling is actually *pre*-Kantian, in that it encompasses our sense perceptions as well as our emotions. Thus Grundtvig explicitly counters Kant's distinction between human will and human emotion as a dichotomy between spirit and nature.

The literary historian, William Michelsen, introduced an important philosophical text by Grundtvig in his article 'On Our Human Conditions' – a group of manuscripts in the N.F.S. Grundtvig archive.[63] In his doctorate, *The Genesis of Grundtvig's View of History* (1954) Michelsen also treated Herder's philosophy of history.

In *The School for Life. Studies in Grundtvig's Educational Ideas*[64] from 1965, K.E. Bugge (1928-2020) discusses how Grundtvig's educational ideas are influenced by 18th century thinking on the subject, which develops in tandem with philosophy. Bugge singles out the phrase "living interaction" as the defining figure in Grundtvig's educational thinking, and he systematises the *forms* of interaction using the concepts of freedom, life, and naturalness. Bugge's work on Grundtvig's educational philosophy has determined all subsequent research in the area. The literary historian, Erik M. Christensen, treats Grundtvig's dispute with Ørsted in 'The golden age in the history of ideas: H.C. Ørsted's optimistic dualism' in *Studies in the Golden Age. A Festschrift for Gustav Albeck* (1966).[65]

From around 1970 and into the 1980s, a number of minor but significant works on Grundtvig's philosophy are published by older and younger Danish literary scholars.

61 When Grundtvig argues philosophically, he links the principle of contradiction to the human knowledge of our self-consciousness. In his theology after 1825 he therefore insists on the retention in the Creed of the renunciation of the Devil before the confirmation of the Trinity: one cannot say yes without first having said no. The Danish Lutheran Church is one of the few Lutheran Churches to have retained the renunciation.

62 Danish title: *Psykologiske tanker og teorier hos Grundtvig.*

63 *Nordisk Tidsskrift för Vetenskap, Konst och Industri.* Stockholm 1946/6.

64 Danish title: *Skolen for livet. Studier over N.F.S. Grundtvigs pædagogiske tanker.*

65 Danish title: Erik M. Christensen, 'Guldalderen som idehistorisk periode: H.C. Ørsteds optimistiske dualisme' in *Guldalderstudier. Festskrift til Gustav Albeck* (1966).

In *N.F.S. Grundtvig. Image and Echo – Grundtvig's Imagination in the Danne-Virke Period*[66] Poul Behrendt analyses the relation between the power of imagination and conceptualization in Grundtvig's thinking, which he wittily characterises as a "smallholder philosophy of distinction" (Behrendt 1968, 88). In *The Dispute Between Grundtvig and H.C. Ørsted 1814-15*[67] Erland U. Jessen describes a conflict between their two "interpretations of the world" (Jessen 1971, 72). Henrik Fibæk Jensen also publishes an important contribution with his essay in *Grundtvig Studies* 1979: 'Grundtvig's Theory of Knowledge – On the Relation between Faith and Reason in the 'Danne-Virke' Period',[68] which elucidates the systematic thinking intrinsic to Grundtvig's writing following his realisation in 1802 of the transitoriness of human life. Fibæk Jensen's essay draws on the inspiration of William Michelsen, who published a series of articles during the 1970s and 1980s on Grundtvig's *Danne-Virke*-philosophy, based on the belief that Grundtvig's thinking is substantially different from that of his contemporaries. In her essay in *Grundtvig Studies 1980*, 'Science and everyday language. Grundtvig's View of his Native Tongue in Theory and in Practice. As Illustrated by his Article, 'On Proverbs' (1817),[69] Bodil Schmidt praises Grundtvig's appeal for the use of everyday language in philosophical writing.

1983 is a seminal year in the history of Grundtvig philosophical studies, being the celebration of the 200th anniversary of his birth. All four volumes of *Danne-Virke* are published in a photographic reprint of the original Gothic script, thus attracting greater attention to Grundtvig's philosophy. The general interest in this side of his authorship is further bolstered in the same year by the publication of a scholarly edition of *On Human Beings in the World* (1817) by the literary historian Knud Bjarne Gjesing, who draws broadly on the work of the above-mentioned Villiam Grønbæk. Of critical importance is Regin Prenter's weighty appraisal of Grundtvig's trinitarian theology in *The Church View: an Introduction to N.F.S. Grundtvig's Basic Ideas on the People and Christianity*.[70] Despite his approach being dogmatic rather than philosophical, Prenter observes that from around 1815 onwards Grundtvig's theological-philosophical world-view follows a 'system' based on his differentiation of the human being into spirit, body, and mind.

In the final years of the 20th century there is a flurry of books and articles by Danish theologians on Grundtvig as a thinker. Birgitte Grell publishes a brief but significant article entitled *Grundtvig's Anthropology of the Word and its Position in a Meta-*

66 Danish title: *N.F.S. Grundtvig. Billede og efterklang – om fantasien hos Grundtvig i "Danne-Virke"-perioden.*

67 Danish title: *Striden mellem Grundtvig og H.C. Ørsted 1814-1815.*

68 Danish title: *Grundtvig's erkendelsesteori – Om forholdet mellem tro og fornuft i tidsskriftet "Danne-Virke" (1816-19).*

69 Danish title: *Videnskab og hverdagssprog. Grundtvigs betragtning af modersmålet i teori og praksis, belyst ved hans afhandling Om Ordsprog.*

70 Danish title: *Den kirkelige anskuelse: en indførelse i N.F.S. Grundtvigs folkelige og kristelige grundtanker.*

physics Embracing more than Human Beings (1984), in which she is among the first to note that in *Danne-Virke* Grundtvig actually works out a cosmology.[71] Helge Grell had already written a study of Grundtvig's criticism of Schelling seen from a consistent, theological angle in *The Creative Word and the Pictorial Word* (1980);[72] in *The Creative Spirit and the People's Spirit* (1988)[73] he analyses Grundtvig's concept of a 'nation' in the light of contemporary philosophers such as Herder and Fichte. In *Grundtvig Studies 1989-90* theologian Kim Arne Pedersen writes a substantial article on *Grundtvig's View of Nature*[74] as an overlooked theme of his authorship, and proceeds in *Studies in the Relation between Metaphysics and Faith in Grundtvig's Writings 1812-15* (1995)[75] to delineate the historically-generated conditions for Grundtvig's philosophical concepts through a comparison with pre-critical, Kantian, and idealist thinking. In *On Grundtvig's View of Knowledge* (1989)[76] theologian Bent Christensen presents a systematised reading of Grundtvig's philosophy in *Danne-Virke* which shows both that its philosophical articles are borne by an inner coherence, and that its four volumes form the basis for his later ideas concerning humankind and the concept of a 'people'.

In the anthology *A Worm – a God* (1997)[77] Grundtvig's understanding of humankind in *On Human Beings in the World* is treated by various Danish writers. Among these are the literary historian Hans Hauge, who had previously analysed Grundtvig in the light of post-modern philosophy in *Transtheology: Religion (subject) and the Gospel in a Post-modern Context* (1989).[78] Other contributors include Ove Korsgaard, Uffe Jonas, Bosse Bergstedt, and Niels Buur Hansen, writing mainly on the cosmology, psychology, and philosophy of Grundtvig's articles. The literary scholar, Uffe Jonas, has written other articles on Grundtvig's '*Danne-Virke*-philosophy', while his study *The Sun at Midnight. Grundtvig's Song to the Cosmos* (2015)[79] compares Grundtvig's world-picture with both pre-modern cosmology and a number of modern natural science theories. Under Jonas' inspiration among others, the educationist and historian Ove Korsgaard has written a number of articles on Grundtvig's philosophy of humankind and cosmology, most recently in *A Guided Trip Round Grundtvig* (2018).[80] In the clash with philosophical dualism, literary historian Niels Buur Hansen sets Grundtvig between Descartes and modern philosophy in *The Divine Mirror – from N.F.S. Grundtvig to Gregory Bateson and*

71 Danish title: *Grundtvigs ordantropologi og dens placering i en metafysik, der omfatter mere end mennesket.*

72 Danish title: *Skaberordet og Billedordet.*

73 Danish title: *Skaberånd og Folkeånd.*

74 Danish title: *Grundtvigs Natursyn.*

75 Danish title: *Studier i forholdet mellem metafysik og tro i Grundtvigs forfatterskab 1812-15.*

76 Danish title: *Om Grundtvigs Vidskab.*

77 Danish title: *En Orm – en Gud.*

78 Danish title: *Transteologi: religion (subjekt) og evangelium i postmoderne regi.*

79 Danish title: *Solen ved Midnat. Grundtvigs sang til kosmos.*

80 Danish title: *Grundtvig rundt. En guide.*

Jacques Lacan: an Attack on the Nightmare of Dualism (1993).[81] In the same year theologian Niels Henrik Gregersen publishes an article with a similar theme, *The Formation of the Self in Grundtvig and Kierkegaard,*[82] in which he distinguishes between "Grundtvig and the growth of human life" and "the formation of subjectivity in Søren Kierkegaard" (p. 263). Educationist and philosopher Ole Vind publishes *Grundtvig's History of Philosophy*[83] in 1999, a doctorate study which to date is the most detailed attempt to portray Grundtvig's concept of 'history' in relation to his time. A critical angle on Grundtvig's view of life and the world marks the work of the German Scandinavist, Inga Meincke, in her dissertation *The Living Voice: The "True Enlightenment" of the Dane, Nikolaj Frederik Severin Grundtvig* (2000).[84] In his article, 'Herder and Grundtvig – Soundings' in *Grundtvig Studies 2001* the historian of religion Johannes Adamsen also illuminates Herder's and Grundtvig's view of history.

The first major work of the new millennium is theologian Anders Holm's analysis of Grundtvig's hermeneutics in *History and its Echo. A Study of N.F.S. Grundtvig's periodical 'Danne-Virke'* (2001),[85] followed by a study of Grundtvig and Kierkegaard in *Two Contemporaries* (2009).[86] Holm's views have also appeared in two English articles in the *Kierkegaard Yearbook*: *The Contemporary Grundtvig. An Addition to Climacus' Critique in Concluding Unscientific Postscript* (2005) and *N.F.S. Grundtvig: The Matchless Giant* (2009). In the anthology *Existence and Life Philosophy* (2002)[87] the intellectual historian, Jørgen Carlsen, subjects Grundtvig's philosophy of life to a critical examination, while the following year sees the doctoral dissertation by theologian Erik Kelstrup, *The Concept of Truth in N.F.S. Grundtvig* (2003),[88] an evaluation based on theories of Truth in 20th century analytical and hermeneutical philosophy.

Also worthy of mention is Niels Jørgen Cappelørn's article from *Grundtvig Studies 2004*, 'The Image of God and the Fall. Aspects of Grundtvig's and Kierkegaard's View of Humankind in the Light of Irenaeus',[89] even though its approach comes more from dogmatics than from philosophy of religion. Theologian and philosopher of religion Troels Nørager criticises Grundtvig's use of the principle of contradiction in a theological context in his article, 'The Pastor and Loki – Grundtvig's Apologetic Dialogue

81 Danish title: *Det guddommelige spejl – fra N.F.S. Grundtvig til Gregory Bateson og Jacques Lacan: et opgør med dualismens mareridt.*

82 Danish title: *Selvets tilblivelse hos Grundtvig og Kierkegaard.*

83 Danish title: *Grundtvigs historiefilosofi.*

84 German title: *Vox viva: die "wahre Aufklärung" des Dänen Nikolaj Frederik Severin Grundtvig.*

85 Danish title: *Historie og efterklang. En studie i N.F.S. Grundtvigs tidsskrift, Danne-Virke.*

86 Danish title: *To samtidige.*

87 Danish title: *Eksistens og livsfilosofi.*

88 Danish title: *Sandhedsbegrebet hos N.F.S. Grundtvig.*

89 Danish title: *Gudbilledlighed og syndefald: aspekter af Grundtvigs og Kierkegaards menneskesyn på baggrund af Irenæus.*

in *On the Truth of Christianity*' in *Grundtvig Studies 2012*.[90] In *Danish Idealism: 1800-1880* (2016)[91] the philosopher Carl Henrik Koch also discusses the dispute between Grundtvig and Ørsted, calling Grundtvig's arguments "metaphysical humbug" and ignoring Grundtvig's use of the principle of contradiction and his *Danne-Virke*-philosophy. Koch also deals with Grundtvig's philosophy in *Danish Enlightenment Philosophers: 1700-1800* (2017).[92] Both books allow us to gain an overview of Danish philosophy in Grundtvig's time and the preceding years. Finally, mention must be made of theologian Vanja Thaulow's work, *Warrior of the Lord. Rhetorical Criticism of N.F.S. Grundtvig's Theological Polemic in the Period 1810-25* (2018),[93] which shines a critical light on Grundtvig's attacks on his contemporaries.

There remains a need for a major study of Grundtvig's thinking which identifies the works he was responding to, and where his philosophy is placed in relation to contemporary philosophical movements.

3. Grundtvig's Place in the History of Philosophy

Grundtvig's philosophical horizon is bounded by Danish intellectual attitudes in the decade spanning 1796-1806. As we have seen, at Copenhagen University the philosophy of the period is dominated by Christian Wolff's metaphysics, but there is simultaneous influence from French philosophy, François-Marie Arouet, aka. Voltaire (1694-1778), not least in the radical enlightenment journals circulating *outside* the university. Around the turn of the century both Kantianism and to a certain extent Fichte-inspired idealism begin to play a determining role in spiritual life, with the jurist Anders Ørsted (1778-1860), brother of H. C. Ørsted, being a central figure, while in 1802-03 Schelling's version of German idealism is introduced into Denmark by Grundtvig's cousin, the above-mentioned natural scientist, Henrik Steffens. Until 1803 Anders Gamborg, while still under the influence of deism, represents Kantianism in the Faculty of Philosophy. Among theologians, Professor Peter Müller (1776-1834) seeks to unite Kantianism with supra-naturalistic revelation theology. To some extent Schelling for his part influences the periodical *Athene* (1813-17), to which Grundtvig regards his own *Danne-Virke* as an alternative. From the 1830s and into the 1860s the idealist philosopher G.W.F. Hegel (1770-1831) also plays a significant role, partly mediated by the theologian Hans Martensen (1808-84).

However, even though the philosophical climate in Denmark sets the agenda for Grundtvig's thinking in the *Danne-Virke*-years, he mostly refrains from his earlier

90 Danish title: *Præsten og Loke – Grundtvigs apologetiske dialog i 'Om Christendommens Sandhed'*.

91 Danish title: *Den danske idealisme (1800-80)*.

92 Danish title: *Dansk Oplysningsfilosofi 1700-1800*.

93 Danish title: *Herrens stridsmand. Retorisk kritik af N.F.S. Grundtvigs teologiske polemik i perioden 1810-1825*.

attacks on specific contemporary Danes. Only in the first pages of *On Revelation, Art, and Learning* (1817) does he outline the development in Danish thought in his *own* time, presenting it as an image of "the universal relationship between Time and the Schools of Philosophy."[94] Thanks to Grundtvig's allusions to specific philosophical works his contemporary readers may have been able to set names to the works and their philosophical standpoints, but Grundtvig refrains from personal polemical attacks on them, preferring instead to paint with a broad brush and to summarise widely differing conceptions under a common denominator.

Similarly, in his programme declaration in *On the Philosophical Century* (1817) Grundtvig regards his thinking as an alternative to the attempt in the 18th century to *explain* humankind without taking history as its point of origin. He identifies a common path in such dissimilar philosophers as Wolff, Kant, Fichte and Schelling, and considers Schelling's "pure speculative philosophy"[95] as the culmination of this movement *away* from history. We shall return to this in the section on why Grundtvig turns *to* history. Neither here nor elsewhere in *Danne-Virke* does he mention the works he is *specifically* referring to, which makes it difficult to contextualise his philosophical observations. It is nevertheless possible to identify specific philosophical concepts, philosophical positions, and to some degree the contemporary philosophical texts he references in *Danne-Virke*. For instance, when he speaks of "the observation of nature, the immediate perception, or such-like,"[96] he is referring to Schelling's natural philosophy and the pure, immediate perception (*Anschauung*) which for this German philosopher constitutes the basis of thought. Grundtvig builds his concept of the intellect and its foundation in opposition to Kant and his idealist successors. Kant, he says, has made the intellect "the henchman of practical Reason;" Fichte has made it "the schoolmaster of Reason"; and Schelling "under the name of Intelligence called it 'a god'".[97] In Grundtvig's opinion, each of these appellations is the ultimate consequence of the false premises of transcendental philosophy.

In contrast to Schelling, Grundtvig's concept of the intellect is also presented as an unfinished process in this life, a polemical position he has already adopted during his 'theological period'. However, the major figure to whom Grundtvig refers in *Danne-Virke* is Kant. He complains about how "the philosophers" have treated "Truth", arguing that "they assert that Truth has no infallible hallmark except the demonstrable agreement between the object and the concept! In their version this means that knowledge can be acquired only of sensory, tangible things."[98] (p. 341). The hidden reference here

94 *On Revelation, Art, and Learning* p. 298.
95 *On the Philosophical Century* p. 277.
96 Ibid. p. 279.
97 *On Revelation, Art, and Learning* p. 301.
98 *On the Word and the Mother-Tongue* p. 341.

is to Kant's concept of Truth in *Critique of Pure Reason*,[99] whereby cognition's agreement with the transcendental prerequisites in the forms of intuition and intellectual categories is the condition for characterising anything as 'true'.

A similar point is made in *On Truth, Greatness, and Beauty* (1817) where Grundtvig attacks a philosophy which practises its "sophistry on Time, Space and Falsehood."[100] He has in mind Kant's teaching on both Time and Space as well as on truth in *Critique of Pure Reason*. Again, when he wishes to criticise "the greatest philosophers of our time" he argues that reason "knows *nothing*", and that "even when it is working at its very best by its own unaided efforts, it can never get further than a goal and a timeline that stretch into infinity". Here he is thinking of both Kantianism and idealism.[101] The criticism is thus aimed at Fichte's teaching on the endless striving of the conscious 'I' towards total knowledge, as well as at Kant's idea that the forms of perception are empty transcendental frames for empirical feeling. Grundtvig is not completely negative towards Kant, however. When he agrees that "Reason has always gone so far astray when it has walked alone in the kingdom of the Spirit,"[102] he is freely reproducing the main point in Kant's criticism of Reason: when Reason exceeds its limits, it faces insoluble contradictions. Grundtvig's approach to criticism here is based on Kant's argument in *Critique of Pure Reason* that he must (freely translated) "make room for faith by uncovering the limits to human knowledge".[103] The wording gives rise to Grundtvig's use of Kantian thought as a philosophy with faith as its *point of origin*. In his early works Grundtvig can therefore generally approve of Kant's demonstration that there are limits to the work of reason and Wolff's ontological proof of God's existence.

Yet we cannot call Grundtvig a rationalist philosopher by any stretch of the imagination, for human consciousness is forever dependent on experience. Drawing on the broad lines of English empiricism he reminds his readers how "even in Germany"[104] empiricism was a strong presence in the 17th century. In his attempt to link sensory experience to philosophical faith he comes closer to a tendency in German philosophy in the second half of the 18th century than to the English tradition. As we shall see below, his thought is remarkably similar to the theory of knowledge elaborated by the Danish-German Professor of Philosophy, Johann Tetens (1736-1807). This is true both of Tetens' overriding concern to unite rationalism and empiricism and of his theory of what were then known as "the intellectual faculties" of the conscious human

99 German title: *Kritik der reinen Vernunft* (Kant, KrV B, 81).

100 *On Truth, Greatness, and Beauty* p. 113.

101 *On Revelation, Art, and Learning* p. 187.

102 *On the Philosophical Century* p. 274.

103 German original: "das Wissen aufheben, um zum Glauben Platz zu bekommen" (Kant 1787/1956 KrV B XXX (AA III 19).

104 *On the Relation between Learning and Experience* p. 296.

being. For both Tetens and Grundtvig the most important of these are imagination, feeling, and intellect/reason.

Added to these influences comes Grundtvig's wrestle with German idealism, whose philosophy of subjectivity is of radical importance for his thought. In particular, we can trace the influence not only of Fichte's concept of philosophy but also his theory of the dialectic relation between the "I" and the "not-I". Like Fichte, Grundtvig's point of origin is the "I", but not in a transcendental sense. For Grundtvig, consciousness of self is a question of *experience*, the basic knowledge upon which the fundamental principles of formal logic rest. He rejects the "High German 'I-ness',"[105] but when applied to "sensory limits" (i.e. the physical boundaries as a basis for the 'I's' consciousness), Fichte's idea of human consciousness makes sense. As Grundtvig says, "...our body's specific criterion of separation in space" and its consequent "sensory independence"[106] (i.e. the individual's experience of independence and separation from all else) are essential to our basic sensory *experience*. This is central to all Grundtvig's thinking: "I am truly alive, I am truly 'in' time, I am witness to the Temporal: this is the self-conscious truth like I myself."[107] On this irrefutable certainty of the self Grundtvig builds his logical argument: "What we call the foundation of identity is clearly the foundation of Truth in us. And what we call the principle of contradiction is not really a separate principle but the *consequent* principle of Truth. From the statement of identity that "I am I" it follows that "I am not what I am *not*", i.e. the principle of contradiction.[108] He links this philosophical certainty about the self to his conviction that humankind can only ever live with "hints and snatches"[109] of the complete construction that history ultimately constitutes – as opposed to the castles in the air constructed by 18th century rationalist philosophers.

4. Grundtvig's Approach to Philosophy: the Spiritual Syntheses of History

Grundtvig's criticism of Wolff, Kant, Fichte and Schelling as being distanced from real life is countered by what he himself understands as his own more earthbound philosophy. Grundtvig wishes to write so that not only professional philosophers understand him, but all those with "Experience and Common Sense", as he speaks "plainly and intelligibly about things and expressions that are known to everybody."[110] It must nev-

105 Ibid.
106 *On Revelation, Art, and Learning* p. 197.
107 *On the Philosophical Century* p. 275.
108 *On Revelation, Art, and Learning* p. 115.
109 Ibid. p. 182.
110 *On the Philosophical Century* p. 271.

ertheless be added that Grundtvig's ideal supersedes his reality. In practice, his writing is dense and difficult, marked throughout by figurative language and occasionally by a somewhat strained humour. His inclusion of formal logic, his inclination to synthesise, and the very length of his sentences (averaging 120 words) add to the complexity, which must surely have challenged even his contemporary readers. He refers not only to widely differing oppositional views but also to a variety of philosophical disciplines and different areas of spiritual life – all under a common denominator: namely, that the vast majority of contemporary thought shows an overriding tendency to ignore all philosophy based on *history*. This is consistent with how Grundtvig regards philosophy in relation to other areas of human life – and thus to his understanding of his own thinking. On the surface this seems 'philosophical', but beneath it lie layers of what he and contemporary philosophy understood as 'psychology', meaning "a depiction of the soul in its manifestations, in its stamping of the spiritual on the sensory."[111] In accordance with his tripartite division of the soul, Grundtvig regards history as a developing course with three separate periods, into which he weaves a number of layers or 'processes'.

The first and fundamental layer is the path to human knowledge, which is linked to our mental faculties. Grundtvig sees the path to knowledge as a process or movement from one's sight to one's feeling, and on to the formation of one's intellect/reason. This triad is repeated in the subsequent levels, in that the areas of Church, State, and School[112] and each of the scholarly disciplines to which they are linked, i.e. Theology, Aesthetics, and Philosophy, rest on one of these mental faculties. Theology and the Church are linked to the imagination; Aesthetics and the State are linked to feeling (since Grundtvig, somewhat surprisingly, sees art as contributing to the social structure); and finally, the intellect/reason are the foundation of the School. In this context Grundtvig emphasises that our mental faculties – and thus the link between various areas of society and scholarship – were shattered by the Fall. This, in Grundtvig's view, has consequences for the human possibility of obtaining knowledge about the *invisible* world on which the visible world and human life depend. He argues that "the Revelation of Nature"[113] – meaning humankind's knowledge of God *independent* of his self-manifestation in Christ – had been possible *before* the Fall, but that afterwards we only had limited access to it. Even though this realisation through faith is truer than any disbelieving philosophy, Grundtvig imagines the Fall into both his theology and his philosophy, primarily in the transition from Antiquity and the Middle Ages – the eras of Imagination and Feeling – to the Age of Reason, which for Grundtvig

111 *On Human Beings in the World* p. 104.

112 For Grundtvig 'School' is synonymous with education, especially Higher Education, the pursuit of Learning, and human cognition in general.

113 *On Revelation, Art, and Learning* p. 199.

stretches from the Age of Reformation right up to his own times. He interprets the theological and philosophical development since Luther as a movement of universal spiritual history, in which "18th century Reason", as an active agent in the various areas of human life, loosened itself from its dependence on imagination and feeling and thus from faith itself. Grundtvig sees a parallel between reason reaching out for sole independence and Eve reaching out for the fruit of the Tree of Knowledge – with the same disastrous results. The hand's touch is our most sensitive sense, and it is also the outer image of reason. The Fall is in fact replicated in the 18th century, when "personality has sought to take possession of Feeling" but in the process has become "a wretched slave to *sensory* Feeling."[114]

With his dry sense of humour Grundtvig likens this lapse of German idealism – taking thought rather than feeling as its starting-point – to a form of philosophical madness, in which "Reason, fearing History, lost its mind and like a mad tyrant declared all its helpers, the senses, to be traitors! It turned itself into a spider's web just to have something left *of its own*."[115] When German idealism precludes knowledge based on the senses, it merely allows the inner sense – corresponding to the hands as the prime external sensory instrument – to lead an independent existence. The delusion is that reason believes *itself* to be the source of its sense perceptions and has thereby usurped the Creator role which belongs solely to God.

This becomes clear when the history of philosophy in the 18th century is weighed against what happened in the childhood of the human race. Human sense perception in Eve's fall focused on the hand that took the fruit from the Tree of Knowledge "for its own purpose" and "disturbed" the relation that should have held sway between creator and creature, whereby humankind was "the earthly image of eternal Truth... from the beginning".[116] Human beings were made in the image of God, just as the rest of the world was made in the human image. In *On Revelation, Art, and Learning*, Grundtvig writes: "Reason went beyond its limits, dislocated our necessary human standpoint, attempted to gather forces around it as the common core, and thereby unsettled the entire arrangement... Instead of seeing God's image in themselves" – as depicted in Gen 3:8-13, where, after the Fall, Adam is afraid to meet God – "they realised they were naked, [and] lowered their eyes when they heard the voice of the Almighty."[117]

Here Grundtvig interprets Adam and Eve's fear of God in the Garden of Eden as a first example, and thus a lasting image of how fallen reason reacts to God's revelations throughout history. Adam "hid behind a tree, peeped out from behind its leaves and naturally could no longer see far or see clearly." Grundtvig sees Eve's fall as upending

114 Ibid. p. 197.
115 Ibid. p. 188.
116 *On the Philosophical Century* p. 276.
117 *On Revelation, Art, and Learning*, p. 190.

the divine order when her hand "served itself".[118] Adam and Eve's fall is reproduced throughout history, and thus also in Grundtvig's own times, where reason has loosened itself from feeling, going "beyond its limits" and taking the step that Kant warned against. Idealism speculates independently of any constraint to sense perception. In Kant's philosophy sense perception derives from transcendental prerequisites for consciousness through forms of intuition and intellectual categories, but in Grundtvig's philosophy it derives from experience alone. In a series of complex comparisons between the Fall and its repetition in German idealism Grundtvig seasons his argument with illustrations and allusions to show how knowledge came into being.

The abundance of Grundtvig's imagery has led many readers to dismiss his thinking here as no more than a chain of metaphorical associations, but in truth his synthesising of biblical thought with a host of differing philosophical perceptions is a well-argued strategy. In *On Revelation, Art, and Learning* he contends that his scholarship maintains "the utmost regard to the words of Scripture" even though he is writing *philosophy*. With reference to the division between faith and thought, theology and philosophy, which has informed spiritual life since the Reformation, he asserts that "only what melts together in the heart *truly* coinheres, and its gathering together in the brain is merely a loose connection, an idea of what *ought* to coinhere in the heart."[119]

Similarly, when his essay *On Truth, Greatness, and Beauty* moves *across* the Kantian division into theoretical, practical, and aesthetic philosophy, it is a conscious strategy on Grundtvig's part. Despite the increasing philosophical divisions in recent times these areas belong fundamentally *together*, inasmuch as they are inseparably linked by Christian faith and human feeling – and they moreover reflect human history and experience.

With this in mind Grundtvig can best be described philosophically as a *historian of the spirit*, or, in current terminology, an *intellectual* historian. Much of Grundtvig's philosophical originality lies in these spiritual syntheses of history. As is the case with the German *Geistesgeschichte*, he regards the movements in the collective consciousness as determinant for the direction that manifests itself within the spheres in which humankind moves and has its being. Thus, Grundtvig's expositions in *Danne-Virke* progress from the bringing together of historical knowledge and metaphysics as the foundation of philosophy as he sees it, to an ever more specialised account of the human spheres of activity, primarily here the Church, the State, and the School.

118 Ibid. p. 198.
119 Ibid. p. 178.

5. Grundtvig's Orientation towards History and Metaphysics

In the present volume Grundtvig's philosophical writings are organised in accordance with the classic genres of the discipline. They begin with a number of texts gathered under the *first philosophy*, i.e. metaphysics. The texts that follow, which are equally central to Grundtvig as a thinker, encapsulate his thoughts on religion, aesthetics, history, language, and the education of young people, though this order is at variance with Grundtvig's own. This is to give the reader an overview of his writings from a distance of over 200 years. We must remember that Grundtvig never thinks of his philosophising as being 'systematic', only of it being *consistent*. Preferring the journal form of his monthly *Danne-Virke* (1816-19) and the later weekly journal *The Dane* (1848-51) he himself steers well clear of any systematisation. He insists that he does not think or write "as if I were sewing threads into a frame,"[120] meaning that he is not weaving a fabric like Christian Wolff, whose "sewing cotton had to snap". According to Grundtvig, Wolff's systematic construction of his works in paragraphs and sub-paragraphs, held together by syllogistic argumentation, broke under the pressure of experience and common sense.[121] Grundtvig is possibly inspired by Fichte's approach in *The Vocation of Man*[122] from 1799, using its essay form, and explaining in a headline the theme of each article. He regards his articles as "observations",[123] his intention being to present his inner sense of sight – the ability to form ideas, which is the first element in his threefold anthropology from the 1810s onward. He establishes the inner link between these 'visual observations' – and thus the articles – with the aid of accumulating *summaries*, e.g. "All this is a repetition of what I have said before."[124] In the same essay he points out that in previous articles in *Danne-Virke* he has discussed "our wealth of philosophy and its first principles" in the first volume and "the human condition and destiny" in the second.[125] In this context he states that:

> only perfected human beings can completely and clearly understand themselves, and that only through *history* can we get to know the human mystery in all its depth and breadth, and grasp as much of it as Time has revealed and clarified in its passage.[126]

120 *On Human Beings in the World* p. 77.
121 *On the Relation between Learning, Experience, and Common Sense*, p. 296.
122 German title: *Bestimmung des Menschen*.
123 *On Human Beings in the World* p. 71.
124 *On Revelation, Art, and Learning* p. 199.
125 Ibid. p. 221.
126 *On Human Beings in the World* p. 69.

With these *summaries* as connecting links, Grundtvig moves from a study of the fundamental characteristics of human knowledge to "the historical manifestations of human life",[127] meaning the history of what has actually happened, which develops down the generations with branches into the lives of the individual peoples. By "historical manifestations" Grundtvig means what he elsewhere calls "human beings in History and our own Experience",[128] i.e. the ever more specialised observations in which the past and its history are increasingly drawn upon as an example of the path and the disabling effects of the Fall. In the course of the first two volumes of *Danne-Virke*, Grundtvig becomes progressively more direct in the presentation of his Christian standpoint. From the third volume onward he speaks openly of the *truth* of Christianity, making it clear that he now finds himself at a fork in the road: "we can either follow the Christian revelation with justified confidence, seek to develop a cohesion between its parts and its relation to its believers..., or we can let Christianity stand in its historical setting".[129] In accordance with his more *indirect* 'ministry' in his 'historical period', Grundtvig chooses the latter path, believing that history testifies to Christianity as being the key to insight into the human condition, a view which increasingly infuses the articles that follow and lays the foundation for his social philosophy in *On the Church, the State, and the School.*

However, before he gets that far, Grundtvig feels the need to defend his line of reasoning. In the *Danne-Virke* articles he begins with what in philosophy is known as *cognitio historica*, historical knowledge. As the German historian of concepts, Arno Seifert (1936-87), has shown, before Kant *cognitio historica* was widely identified with the human sense perceptions and regarded as more unreliable than intellectual thinking based on the principles of formal logic. Grundtvig turns the relation around, emphasising that historical knowledge is *fundamental* to philosophy and therefore takes precedence over metaphysics; simultaneously he aims at "merging general truths with the historical life of humankind."[130] He therefore develops his metaphysical reflections in organic cohesion with his emphasis on sense-based experience: this is the foundational approach to knowledge for humankind. Just like the experiences which the human race has undergone throughout history, so do the individual's sense perceptions testify to *God* as the source of all existence. Proofs of God's existence and the knowledge that human individuals gradually *acquire* in their time on earth, are two sides of the same coin.

In accordance with tradition Grundtvig designates this form of knowledge as being 'historical'. But he also calls it *universally* historical, inasmuch as it operates with the modern understanding of the *concept* of history as covering a coherent course over

127 *On Revelation, Art, and Learning* p. 175.
128 *On Human Beings in the World* p. 75.
129 *On Revelation, Art, and Learning* p. 177.
130 Ibid.

time. He uses this in his appeal to his contemporaries to turn away from idealistic speculation and to take experience as their starting-point instead: "All true Learning must in every sense be *historical*."[131] This is so, because in the first place "Reason finds nothing in itself without a yardstick for temporal Truth and must seek the content of learning itself"; in the second place, "because the human being develops in *Time* and can only be understood thus"; and in the third place, because learning is historical, *pace* St. Paul: "it must be piece by piece and can only be *ended* with Time."[132] Finally, learning is historical because world history thereby becomes a knowledge-*process*, a development *path*, in which plants gradually blossom and bear fruit. Philosophy "must be respected and loved for its insight into History, for its judgement in its own cause, and for its philosophy of History and its history of Philosophy."[133]

The philosophical fruits from the course of history grow in the process, but will not ripen until the end of time. Under the influence of Schelling's theory of symbols, Grundtvig explains that "in the human race, as in the individual, Reason is the concept and expression of spiritual growth and development."[134] Reason comes to a knowledge of humankind and therefore brings about an "indirect, *figurative* cognition" of God,"[135] inasmuch as the goal of all human learning is "truly to understand oneself,"[136] which, as in Jn 14:6, Grundtvig regards as being analogous to Jesus. History is identical to "the revelation of eternal Truth in time,"[137] and he consistently asserts that this goal is "the Son of Humankind, transfigured in the Son of God."[138]

This is not to say that Grundtvig regards history as the mere realisation of human potential. Human beings are interwoven with their divine origin. As in Gen 2:7, at the dawn of Creation "eternal Truth", i.e. God as Logos or the Son, "breathed life into us and allowed us to hear His voice in the Spirit."[139] Grundtvig is moving on from his line of argument for the indissoluble link between a knowledge of history and the truths of logic to his own 'onto-theology'. The term, which constitutes his legacy from Kant and Wolff, refers to the linking together of the philosophical accounts for the grounds of existence with the natural-theology accounts for the concept of God. These he learned from his teacher at Copenhagen University, Børge Riisbrigh, in the early 19th century. For Grundtvig, as for Wolff, a knowledge of the grounds of existence and of God are one and the same thing. As we have seen, Grundtvig speaks of the "general truths",

131 *On the Philosophical Century* p. 275.
132 Ibid.
133 *On Historical Learning, or the Concept of 'History'* p. 291.
134 *On the Philosophical Century* p. 274.
135 Ibid.
136 Ibid.
137 Ibid. p. 276.
138 Ibid. p. 277.
139 Ibid. p. 276.

i.e. truths which like "the irrefutable certainties of Reason"[140] in a metaphysical sense are universally true at all times. For him, these truths are in the first place the basic principles of formal logic, including the principle of contradiction and the principle of sufficient reason.[141] Secondly, they are not just closely linked to, but are in fact *identical* with, the classic proofs of God, which, following Wolff, he assigns to formal logic. In doing so, Grundtvig affiliates himself with the Leibnitz-inspired 'substance ontology', as he has learned it through the metaphysical system that Wolff elaborated. Indeed, Grundtvig owned four of Wolff's Latin volumes, including those on ontology and natural theology.

Fundamental to philosophy, says Grundtvig, is the concept "of being one's own father and life-foundation,"[142] i.e. the concept of God. He seeks to merge the ontological and the cosmological proofs of God and on that basis he elaborates his criticism of the German idealists' philosophy of religion for not distinguishing between God and humankind. Against their idealism he insists on an "eternal, independent existence,"[143] a substantial *being*, which "of its own accord"[144] is outside and above humankind – in contrast primarily to Fichte's doctrine of the divine as a basis in consciousness.

Merging universal truths into history is in keeping with Grundtvig's wish to merge a knowledge of history with his metaphysical, ontological observations. They are like a pile-driven foundation on which his subsequent thinking builds, as well as being the basis of his specialised, and occasionally hard-to-fathom, explanations of the forms that human life takes in history. "Concepts that we ourselves cannot conceive... must be a Higher Being's concepts," he argues, adding that they are only available to us "through faith."[145] This happens in connection with the transition from sight via feeling to hearing, which is a precondition for the formation of concepts in general. For Grundtvig the process begins with feeling *assimilating* the visions or images of the imagination by taking hold of them as a hand takes hold of an object it desires, which is what enables us to convert images into concepts. However, although over time human beings become capable of conceptually embracing increasingly large areas of their lives and the rest of Creation, they will never be able to *conceptualize* God. They will always have only an *indirect* knowledge, since the object cannot be described exhaustively.

140 *On Revelation, Art, and Learning* p. 178.

141 The principle of contradiction, attributed to Leibnitz, states that everything must have a reason, or cause, which cannot be both true and false at the same time.

142 *On the Philosophical Century* p. 273.

143 Ibid.

144 Ibid. p. 275.

145 Ibid. p. 273.

6. Trichotomic Anthropology and Trinitarian Theology

Grundtvig's conviction that reason is incapable of making God the object of conceptual knowledge is loosely linked to his trichotomic anthropology, in that he does not allow all the mental faculties the same possibility for knowledge of the super-sensory. With regard to the distribution of human *faculties* he follows the European platonic tradition of dividing the human being into three, but Grundtvig's trichotomy follows just as much the development of Wolff's philosophical concepts as those of Tetens.[146] In *Philosophical Inquiries into Human Nature and its Development* (1777)[147] Tetens, who lived in Copenhagen as a high-ranking civil servant from 1789 to 1809, divides consciousness into ideas, feelings, and thought – operating with the same mental faculties that we meet in Grundtvig's work, where he speaks of "concepts, feelings, and ideas."[148] Tetens' ambition to create a synthesis of rationalism and empiricism has its counterpart in Grundtvig's anthropology. In his attempt to merge sensationalism with metaphysics Grundtvig constructs a psychology in which the fundamental faculties of human consciousness are imagination, feeling, and intellect/reason.

The essential point is that the mind – the conceptualizing faculty in the human being – cannot embrace anything higher than itself, despite being able indirectly to acknowledge God's existence as a logical necessity. Reaching "higher than itself" is possible for imagination and feeling, but not for reason, for "human beings are a union of spirit and body" only.[149] There is no place for a separate consciousness here as the third element, for this is nothing *in itself*, according to Grundtvig. Spirit and body alone are the bearing elements in the structure of the human personality. However, although Grundtvig emphasises that the imagination – the capacity to form ideas and images – is important, it is *feeling* that is constitutive for human consciousness, since it opens up the possibility for intellect/reason to conceptualize knowledge: Feeling is "the beginning of life," he says.[150] Since our physical limits are therefore the basis of self-consciousness and logic, Grundtvig goes on to argue that "our true personality is the impression that the idea of our measured existence makes on our body."[151] This reflexive movement is justified by a pre-reflexive one: the feeling of being a 'self' must lie "deeper" than all the ideas of which the mind is aware, but at the same time he

146 German title: *Philosophische Versuche über die menschliche Natur und ihre Entwickelung.* Johannes Tetens (1736-1807) was a German-Danish philosopher, statistician and scientist. This, his major work, studied the origin and structure of human knowledge and was influential on Kant's *Critique of Pure Reason* (1781).

147 German title: *Philosophische Versuche über die menschliche Natur und ihre Entwickelung.*

148 *On Historical Learning, or the Concept of 'History'* p. 284.

149 *On Revelation, Art, and Learning* p. 178.

150 Ibid. p. 196.

151 Ibid.

points out that this feeling can sequentially develop into conceptual knowledge and thus into consciousness.

Grundtvig argues that "philosophy is nothing but the detailed evidence that the transfiguration of existence by the poetry of light is true and absolute."[152] Philosophy is "the illumination of feeling."[153] Through its internalising activity, ideas are absorbed by the human 'I' and can be worked on by reason. In the same place, he regards "depth, force, and clarity,"[154] i.e. the qualities that apply respectively to feeling, imagination, and reason, as being equally valuable elements in the possession of true knowledge. For Grundtvig, human beings cannot be understood without God, nor God without human beings. As mentioned, like Plato, he divides human beings into three, and maintains that they consist of spirit, body, and mind – both the super-sensory (metaphysical) and the sensory (physical), and with a consciousness of both. "Our self-consciousness is mixed,"[155] he says; and it contains both spiritual and sensory experiences. The mind therefore has two sides: consciousness is fundamentally both equal to the individual's knowledge of their own physical existence and to their knowledge that the self is both spirit and has its roots in a higher reality than the sensory, i.e. in a transcendent world which is the object of our intimations and longings. It is not that our consciousness is *divided* in two. The spiritual side of consciousness, which Grundtvig regards as foundational – both in 1807 and later in his 'historical' period (1815-23) and also thereafter – is indissolubly connected to the feeling of *dependence* that the sensory self-consciousness must inevitably come to by virtue of its physical limitation in space and the constraints on its ability and knowledge that follow from this.

Like the almost contemporary theologian, Friedrich Schleiermacher (1768-1834), Grundtvig works with the idea that the human being feels a dependency on God, which builds a bridge from our human view to the theology in his universe, from temporality to eternity. Human consciousness is finite, whereas divine consciousness is infinite in its activity. For Grundtvig, our human dependency on a creating divinity means that both have their entire being and reality in a mirror of this divine creator's thought.

Grundtvig's philosophy is therefore a transcendental philosophy in the broad sense used by the historian of philosophy, Aron Gurwitsch (1901-73) in his book on Leibnitz.[156] For Gurwitsch 'metaphysical' or 'transcendental' refer to the fundamental idea that what is real has its reality in what it exists *for* and in its indissoluble link to a consciousness, but in this case it is a *divine* consciousness. Here Grundtvig shows

152 *On the Word and the Mother-Tongue* p. 347.

153 *On Historical Learning, or the Concept of 'History'* p. 286.

154 Ibid.

155 *On Revelation, Art, and Learning* p. 306.

156 Aron Gurwitsch, *Leibnitz. The Philosophy of Panlogism* (untranslated from the German: *Leibniz: Philosophie des Panlogismus*, Berlin/New York, Walter de Gruyter 1974).

himself to be a pupil of Leibnitz, though we do not have to assume that the connection is via Wolff. Grundtvig owned Leibnitz's major philosophical work in both a French and a Latin edition and is known to have read it.[157]

For Grundtvig the world's reality rests on its creation in, through, and for the concept of God. Our temporal dependency on the eternal God's divine consciousness corresponds to God's eternal consciousness of himself, known as his 'self-affirmation', a concept Grundtvig has absorbed from Schelling, but whose history goes back further. God "is an eternal *Being*, which affirms itself and expresses its self-consciousness."[158] For Grundtvig, this self-affirmation is linked to "a living, self-conscious, trinitarian God[159] in a relationship which he interprets with the help of our human consciousness faculties. As in Gen 1:27, humankind is "created in God's image and according to His likeness,"[160] and for this reason we can draw the conclusion that the human trichotomy reflects the divine Trinity. What Grundtvig calls "the Eternal", i.e. the divine self-consciousness,[161] is identical with God the Son in the Trinity, i.e. Logos, or the Word. The eternal *power* is the Holy Spirit, which "expresses Greatness as omnipotence,"[162] while eternal *love*, i.e. God the Father, is "eternal Beauty".[163] Grundtvig describes this inner Trinitarian process as "an eternal experience,"[164] being "synonymous with the eternal introspection which with God is the same as self-consciousness".[165] Grundtvig thus defines God's Trinitarian being as an inner love relationship and a timeless manifestation through language. Through the Holy Spirit, this eternal predication of the Father's being in the form of Logos, the Son, constitutes the connecting link to his philosophy of language. Grundtvig's reflections on the spoken and written word have their basis in his theological anthropology.

7. Philosophy of Language

In thinking about language Grundtvig does not begin with its basis in humankind and theology. In accordance with his view of history he seeks primarily to demonstrate how language provides us with access to the past:

157 No. 8227 G. W. von Leibnitz: *Theodicæa*, 2. Aufl. Amsterdam 1726, and no. 8228 G.W. v. Leibnitz *Tentamina Theodicæa*. Latin versa a M.D. I. Francof. 1719 in *Registry of N.F.S. Grundtvig's Library (post-mortem)*. Kbh. 1873.

158 *On Truth, Greatness, and Beauty* p. 113.

159 Ibid.

160 *On Revelation, Art, and Learning* p. 119.

161 *On Human Beings in the World* (*ubique*).

162 *On Truth, Greatness, and Beauty* p. 117.

163 Ibid. p. 123.

164 *On the Relation between Learning, Experience, and Common Sense* p. 305.

165 Ibid.

> everything that is capable of spiritual interaction is also spiritually related. We contemporaries are not only one another's spiritual kin, but also the kin of past generations, for their words can affect us, and the spirit that was spontaneously at work among our forefathers has undoubtedly affected us all. Once we realise this, we must also admit that there is a spiritual development at work in the human race and in the individual which enables us to understand the *same* things that our forefathers understood in the days of the Valdemars[166] and Christian III,[167] *plus a little more*.[168]

In saying this, Grundtvig anticipates one of his most famous aphorisms (from 1832), that humans are not apes but a "divine experiment".[169] In the unprinted draft for a *Danne-Virke* essay (1819), he states:

> Even the most casual of glances reveals that the Word is the highest expression of human life; and the most exhaustive studies can only testify to this from all sides. Just imagining the entire human race as being without speech reduces us to a kind of ape, identical in a thousand particulars and without heroic deeds and a history.[170]

It is thanks to *language* that humankind has developed. It is through *language* that the past is preserved. The very *words* of history are a legacy from our predecessors, right back to the first significant era in Antiquity, i.e. from the ages when God revealed himself to humankind through the visions that their inner sight received in connection with their perception of the outer world and then internalised in their feelings: "in our various languages we hear the living voices from days of old. They speak to us as uncorrupted memorials of the spirit and acts of previous generations."[171]

As background for his argument that the legacy passed down by language builds a bridge to the future, Grundtvig speaks of "a *knowledge* of the Word... philosophising about the various languages, literature, eloquence, and style."[172] This takes the form of a detailed account of the relation between sense perception and language, based on his trichotomic anthropology. It is essential for him that language has both a *vertical* and a *horizontal* dimension. Through the *vertical* dimension language allows access to the super-sensory, transcendent world; through the *horizontal* dimension it allows access to the past. Through the language that has been preserved and transmitted

166 The Valdemars include Valdemar I (reigned 1146-82) and his two sons Canute VI (reigned 1182-1202) and Valdemar II (reigned 1202-41).
167 Christian III (reigned 1534-1559).
168 *On Historical Learning, or the Concept of 'History'* p. 285.
169 The famous line is from the Prologue to *Nordic Mythology*, translated in vol. 1, *The School for Life* (2011) p. 66.
170 *On the Word and the Mother-Tongue* p. 345.
171 *On Historical Learning, or the Concept of 'History'* p. 291.
172 *On the Word and the Mother-Tongue* p. 341.

from generation to generation, the past acquires a kind of "spiritual immortality".[173] In other words, in the horizontal dimension language has the ability to preserve the visions, actions, and thoughts of the past in a form that survives down the ages and can be processed by future generations. In the *vertical* dimension Grundtvig speaks of the Word as "the wonderful and mysterious bond between spirit and body, and between Time and Eternity, … as a bodily spirit and a spiritual body."[174] Elsewhere it is "the medium between God and the world."[175] Language is a bridge-builder between the two worlds that come together in humankind.

Grundtvig thus takes issue with the so-called 'onomatopoetic theory' that language has come into being as an imitation of natural sounds in the environment which the first humans met on their path. This explanation may have been popular in the 18th century, he says, but it reduced language to humans merely copying "the impressions made on their senses by their surroundings and their circumstances."[176] Grundtvig regards this theory of the origin of language as materialistic, and his comment on the medieval dispute between the Nominalists and Realists[177] suggests that he links the nominalist position precisely to that theory. The Realists had maintained that universal concepts had their basis in *reality*, whereas the Nominalists took the opposite position. Grundtvig seems to consider the 18th century's understanding of language as nominalist with regard to the super-sensory world, arguing that the theory implies that any language about what lies *beyond* the world of the senses only comes about when humankind has left its original animal instincts behind. According to the theory, in the course of human development certain "appellations" were designated "super-sensory objects… once a people had acquired a sufficient degree of culture to form such an idea."[178] In such cases the connection between the appellation and the super-sensory was merely one of 'chance', with no basis in the image-status in relation to the eternal world that Grundtvig avers; thus it is merely nominalist.

Grundtvig rejects this line of thought and lays out the alternative as it appears "among several semi-biblical theologians in the *previous* century, with traces even in Schelling."[179] According to *this* theory, the relation is quite the opposite: the use of 'the transcendent' and the designation of objects in the physical world as 'images of the transcendental' – as well as the labelling of language as merely a designation for sense-perceived objects – is the result of cultural *decay*. Language must therefore

173 *On Revelation, Art, and Learning* p. 205.
174 *On the Word and the Mother-Tongue* p. 340.
175 *On Revelation, Art, and Learning* p. 199.
176 *On the Word and the Mother-Tongue* p. 342.
177 Ibid. p. 351.
178 Ibid. p. 342.
179 Ibid. p. 344.

originally have come from the transcendent world itself. This could have happened in two ways: either through a form of divine intervention or through a divine facility inborn in humankind. In the first instance, "a god or an angel had taken the role of 'parent' of the first peoples and through intercourse with them had taught them a language, which then degenerated."[180] In the second instance, "humankind is divine as an earthly image of the divinity,"[181] in which case language is, so to speak, *natural* but still God-given, in that its conditions progressed from a divine core that was laid down in human nature.

Naturally, Grundtvig is more attracted to the theory that language is of *divine* origin: "History," he says, "forces us to admit a *super*-natural source for the Word."[182] Yet still he is not satisfied, for in his opinion, it is not enough just to demonstrate that human language is granted by super-sensory powers. The Word must have God himself as its home, i.e. it must be "'divine' in the *true* sense". At the end of his draft he states that a "revelation" of what "we cannot grasp" with our own thought has helped him to understand this, and he closes by quoting Jn 1:1: "In the beginning was the Word, and the Word was with God, and the Word was God."

From this point of origin Grundtvig presents a theory of language which in his view is better than both the belief that it was established through *human* attempts to imitate their surroundings and Schelling's theological teaching that language was *granted* by transcendent powers. The Word is *God*, and human language therefore rests on the belief that humankind is created in God's *image*. On one point, however, he follows the German idealists in rejecting the theory that humankind is a *product* of a successive development from the lower to the higher. This was the common theory among the forms of natural science which, at the same time as the *uniquenesss* of humankind was being emphasised in the late 18th and early 19th century, regarded human beings as no more than a higher species of animal, thereby paving the way for the evolution theory later formed by Charles Darwin (1809-82). Grundtvig disagrees. The relation is the precise opposite, he says, introducing his *horizontal dimension* to the philosophy of language:

> Human beings were appointed to walk *down* the hill. First they were meant to stand on its highest point to gain an overview of their estate and name what they saw with its proper name;[183] then they were to link together in words what they felt was related;

180 Ibid. p. 344.
181 Ibid.
182 Ibid.
183 Ex 2:19.

> finally, when they came down to the fields, they were to show demonstrably that the world was just as they had seen and said it would be![184]

Humankind cannot be explained by *nature*. Nor can God be *explained* by humankind. Language is not the result of humankind developing from an animal existence to the articulate, self-conscious being that we know today. Nature must be explained *through* human beings, whose bodies contain all that is found in the rest of creation, for they are "a small-scale world (microcosm)."[185] Thus, a knowledge of the physical world is a *self*-knowledge with language as the *spiritual* world which *explains* the physical. Human history is destined by God's hand to be a path from "the hill" (the age of the imagination) down to "the fields" (the non-human nature). For Grundtvig the knowledge of history – through which we come to understand ourselves – comes *before* a knowledge of natural science.

Grundtvig's figurative description of the way in which we come to understand ourselves and our surroundings is woven together with our use of speech, testifying to the way in which his philosophy of language is inextricably linked to his theory of knowledge. It also demonstrates the consistency of his thinking in merging his exegesis of the Creation and Fall in Genesis with his philosophy of history. The Bible tells how Adam named all the animals (Gen 2:19), but Grundtvig makes this process include the whole of human history as a prototype of our human destiny. As we have seen, in so doing he divides human knowledge into three: the perceptions of sight; the internalising and establishment of the link between these perceptions in the hand; and finally their conceptualization into expression by the intellect/reason. He insists that we can reach "the tangible Truth,"[186] provided that we verify the information of the perception through our conceptualizing powers of reason. Reason and the intellect are the inner expression of the outer feeling of the hand. Knowledge rests upon "what falls into its hands."[187] The faculties of human consciousness correspond to, and interact with, their physical facilities in an ongoing interplay between inner and outer cognition.

It is precisely this movement which is the basis for language, says Grundtvig. First comes sight, but the moment it is internalised in us through feeling, it becomes speech. Even though linguistic expression, by pointing to the super-sensory, always transcends conceptual knowledge, an inner link remains between speech and conceptualization and thus between language and reason. This link is further connected to the interaction between sight and feeling – the power of the imagination and the development of

184 *On Revelation, Art, and Learning* p. 198.

185 *On Human Beings in the World* p. 80.

186 *On Historical Learning, or the Concept of 'History'* p. 290.

187 *On Revelation, Art, and Learning* p. 189.

feelings into what Grundtvig calls the "hand-feeling";[188] the word hovers between an image and a concept – a thought that recurs in German idealism, for instance in Hegel.

The movement from "the hill" down to "the fields" is a figurative description of the movement from our creation in God's image down to nature created in our human image. It is our path of knowledge from sight through feeling to the intellect/reason, and, according to Grundtvig, it is a path repeated in our development of language. He reiterates his belief that our Fall has prevented us from fulfilling God's original plan:

> most proverbs... have a wealth and a depth that far surpass the intellectual development that the people had acquired at the time they were written down. Proverbs must simply have had their basis in a *poetic understanding* of the early days of our people.[189]

The gap between the loftiness of the imagination's visions as expressed in proverbs and the level of human development when they actually came to be written down is a result of Adam and Eve's guilt. If we had continued our growth in the Garden of Paradise in accordance with God's will, the three periods of sight, feeling, and intellect/reason would have resembled each other, i.e. they would have retained the same high level, since they would have constituted a harmonious, successive development. It is equally important for Grundtvig to assert that *despite* the Fall there is a relic, or legacy, of God's image in us, his human creation. This means that, even after Eve's sin, vision goes before concept. That is why poetry is older than prose. It is significant that here Grundtvig anticipates his "matchless discovery" in 1825 that the oral word precedes the written word also in the very early days of Christianity.[190] This is also true of proverbs: "Among every people aware of its spirit its proverbs are the living hedge between poetry and prose. From another side they are also the gateway between writing and conversation."[191] Giving expression to his trichotomic anthropology, he argues that "proverbs are the closest connection to the *spirit of a people*, to their language and their way of thinking,"[192] corresponding to sight, feeling, and the intellect/reason. Danish proverbs have therefore arisen "in the heart of Denmark" as a poetic product of the people. Grundtvig's belief that perception or sight precedes intellectual activity also chimes with his definition of myth as "an inspired Word in all its power,"[193]

188 *On Human Beings in the World* p. 83.

189 *On Proverbs* p. 329. Grundtvig was a great believer in proverbs, which he argued contained 'the wisdom of the people'. In 1845 he even published a collection of 3,000 well-known, as well as rare, Danish proverbs entitled *Danish Proverbs and Sayings (Danske Ordsprog og Mundheld)*. These formed part of the daily discussion in several of the early people's high schools.

190 cf. vol. 3, *Human Comes First* (2018) p. 91.

191 *On Proverbs* p. 327.

192 Ibid. p. 329.

193 *Selected Works (Udvalgte Skrifter)* (1909-14), V, 421.

and poetry as "the spiritual Word which gives living expression to a spiritual relation when we attribute to life something sensory in which it reflects itself".[194] Moreover, Grundtvig anticipates the definition of 'myth' that he delineates in *Nordic Mythology* (1832): "A myth is a spiritually-infused story in all its power, and as such the fruit of poetic inspiration." Again he divides by three: "Poetry," he says, is "the spiritual Word which gives living expression to a spiritual relation," but there are three forms of poetry that follow upon one another in a successive chain", where "the second two presuppose the first and the third presupposes both the others."[195] On this basis Grundtvig shows how the poetic view, and thus also poetry, comes into being in the early days of a people – or of humankind in general:

> The foundation of poetry is the supremely spiritual *Song of Songs*,[196] which speaks of spiritual matters in similes by naming sensory things that indicate and depict them, just as their Creator ordained earthly images. We can also call such poetry 'the poetry of power', since it transforms the entire sensory world into an image of the Spirit and creates a sensory language in which the Spirit can demonstrably and animatedly express itself.[197]

The poetry which follows may be called 'historical', in that it "celebrates the impact of the Spirit in the course of time, whether it be in spiritual interaction or in spiritual effect on the sensory world."[198]

Finally comes the "poetry of the light", which is "approaching philosophy" and "seeks to illuminate the previous direct contemplations of indirect observations of sensory things in space and time; it sets out to present them as witnesses to the spiritual relation in which they are viewed and in which they have their true foundation; in so doing, it transfigures them in their context and consequence."[199] He further argues that "poetry of the light" has "two areas, dependent on the two preceding subjects which it is to transfigure: in descending order, the historical and the natural. Of these two the historical must of necessity come first, since the lower must be transfigured by the higher, and the Spirit which reveals itself in its effects must be transfigured *by* them."[200] "The Word," he says, "is an effect of the Spirit, and the sensory world is an

194 *On the Word and the Mother-tongue* p. 347.

195 Ibid.

196 The OT *Song of Songs* is of uncertain date, some time before the 2nd cent. BCE. The title shows its superiority to all other songs (cf. the holy of holies). It is unique in its celebration of sensory and spiritual love, interpreted as an allegory of the love between God and Israel.

197 *On the Word and the Mother-Tongue* p. 347.

198 Ibid.

199 Ibid.

200 Ibid.

effect of the Word. The Word must first be transfigured,"[201] before light can be cast on the physical world. This involves an elucidation of the relation between the three major areas of human life, "the Church, the State, and the School", corresponding to the imagination, feeling, and intellectual/rational power of consciousness in Grundtvig's trichotomic anthropology.

8. Social Philosophy

In the above sections we have seen how in *Danne-Virke* Grundtvig moves from a synthesis of historical knowledge and metaphysics to an even more specialised account of human life. In volumes 3 and 4 of the journal we find three essays with three subject-titles in which he gives concrete form to abstract concepts in the areas of life that correspond to the concepts. In the third volume the concepts of the essay *On Truth, Greatness, and Beauty* correspond respectively to those on Learning, Revelation, and Art, while in the fourth volume School, Church, and State replace them. Parallel with this transfer of the abstract to the concrete, and from *On Revelation, Art, and Learning* (1817) onwards, Grundtvig increasingly clarifies for his readers his Christian world-view as expressed in *Danne-Virke*. He hoists his colours to the mast in *On the Church, the State, and the School*, depicting them as three *actual institutions* that correspond to the path to knowledge that we have seen – from sight via feeling to intellect/reason – on the basis of his version of the Christian view of humankind as a self-evident entity. Thus, in *On the Church, the State, and the School* we meet his castigation of the 'Enlightenment' thinking which dominated the 18th century and which relegated Christianity:

> Even when the 18th century accepted the *existence* of the Church, it nevertheless pushed it aside as the lowest of the three in the dispute regarding the paramount status of the School or the State.[202]

Grundtvig is raising what he calls a "war-cry" against the powerful influence exerted in the 18th century by Enlightenment theology, contract theory, geometry, arithmetic, and mathematics. He is in a "pitched battle" against "the 18th century's view of the Church, the State covenant, and the School tables."[203] He then looks for an alternative to Voltaire's 'Church', Paine's 'State' and Basedow's 'School'.[204] Temporal earthly life

201 Ibid.

202 Ibid. p. 211.

203 Ibid. p. 212.

204 Ibid. 1) Voltaire was the pseudonym of François-Marie Arouet (1694-1778), a French philosopher and writer in the Age of Enlightenment. He was a supporter of social reform (including the defence of civil liberties, freedom of

sets the agenda for these philosophers, says Grundtvig, whereas he himself, on the basis of his Christianity, thinks in the platonic tradition: far from being finite beings, bound to a material life and a temporal existence, we have a spiritual, super-sensory side. He contrasts the Enlightenment view of the human being as no more than a highly-developed animal with his own belief "that we are *spiritual* beings, destined for eternal life," and that the true Church on earth is "a community of faith in a Word that reveals the eternal destiny of humankind and the path towards it."[205]

The revelation in question is first of all the Old Testament assurance that we are "created by God in His image," and... "it is our undeniable destiny to obey Him unconditionally and be transfigured into His image."[206] Next comes the resurrection of Christ, as the sign of God's grace and our restitution, but where the goal still remains in what has found expression in the Old Testament, primarily in the Creation story. Theological anthropology is thus the task of the Church. But what is the task of the State? "Human beings are creatures of reason," he says, "destined for eternal life." This means that "our entire earthly life can quite justifiably be called no more than a School, a development leading to a transfiguration":

> ... what goes by the name of 'Church' and 'School' in the world is in fact only the two major divisions within the latter which our whole life constitutes, corresponding to each other like revelation to experience.[207]

Here Grundtvig links his Bible-based anthropology to his historical orientation. Where he spoke earlier about the Church as the life-sphere that should be above all others, here he gives priority to the School as the sphere that covers human life in its forms of Church and State and calls "education the prime concern of the State."[208]

Already in the years before 1810 Grundtvig had made it clear that education was a joint project for all members of society. Now he repeats the view that "the prime

religion, and free trade), and his ideas influenced important thinkers of both the American and French Revolutions. He regarded the Church as oppressive and self-serving. 2) Thomas Paine (1737-1809) was born in England but emigrated in 1774 to the New World, where his writings inspired the settlers to declare independence from Britain. His ideas of free thought and the pre-eminence of reason also influenced the French Revolution. While in prison in Luxembourg he wrote a pamphlet, 'The Age of Reason', in which he castigated organised religion. 3) Johann Basedow (1724-90) was a German educational reformer, teacher, and writer. From 1753-61 he was Professor of Moral Philosophy at Sorø Academy on Zealand, Denmark. His school, the *Philanthropinum*, opened in Dessau, Germany in 1774 with the philosophy of 'everything according to nature'. Basedow pioneered child-centred practical education, in which he focused on learning through play and competitive games.

205 *On the Church, the State, and the School* p. 221.

206 Ibid. p. 220.

207 Ibid. p. 231.

208 Ibid.

purpose of the State is to ensure the growth and security of the School."[209] The State has its outward public expression in the School, which is the only one of the three spheres with a form that makes it accessible to human sense perception. Just as the true Church exists on earth "*invisibly through faith*," so does the proper State exist "*invisibly through love*".[210] Both "express themselves through word and action for the education and upbringing of the human race. (...) Nor can we call the external area in which they express themselves through word and action for the education and upbringing of the human race anything other than a School,"[211] in practice "from the Church Gallery" on the first floor[212] - meaning from Grundtvig's Christian standpoint, where he has a good view of the Church. Thus his acknowledgement of the School as a designation for human knowledge in its broadest sense is seen from a theological perspective: "The State must always have an interplay with the Church, while the School is generated and raised by both."[213] In Grundtvig's division of roles we again recognise his threefold exposition of the path of human knowledge as a movement from sight to feeling to intellect/reason. His philosophy is marked by consistency, contingent on anthropology at its core, and his view of humankind is therefore the key not only to his social philosophy but also to his aesthetics and natural philosophy.

9. Aesthetics

In Grundtvig's time aesthetics played a decisive role in philosophical thought. Aesthetics occupied a central place in the theory of knowledge as well as in social philosophy and education. In *Critique of (the Power of) Judgement* (1790)[214] Kant had sought to assert the independent character of the judgements of taste, and simultaneously make a distinction between taste and knowledge itself. This moved the experience of beauty centre-stage in German idealist philosophy. A major work in the area and a source of inspiration for many was *On the Aesthetic Education of Man* (1794)[215] by Friedrich Schiller (1759-1805), doctor, poet-philosopher, and historian. In turn, Schelling followed Schiller in merging the concepts of *the sublime* and *the beautiful* to express the conciliation between the 'finite' and 'infinite' which happens in the perception of the intellect. He points to art as the place of healing of the split between spirit and nature that characterises Kant's moral philosophy.

209 Ibid. p. 252.
210 Ibid.
211 Ibid.
212 Ibid.
213 Ibid. p. 234.
214 German title: *Kritik der Urteilskraft.*
215 German title: *Über die ästhetische Erziehung des Menschen.*

In *On Truth, Greatness, and Beauty* Grundtvig carries out a similar conciliation. On the basis of this synthesising approach he thinks theoretical and practical philosophy together in the same breath, i.e. knowledge and morality with the sense of Beauty as the connecting link. As regards the concepts that form the title of the essay, Truth is linked to knowledge, Beauty to aesthetics, and Greatness to morality. At the same time, each of the concepts can be illustrated with the aid of the above-mentioned philosophical disciplines, philosophy, theology, and aesthetics. Grundtvig's point of origin is a theoretical and philosophical problem-complex. He endeavours to rehabilitate the belief of pre-critical metaphysics that the super-sensory world also provides evidence for these three concepts and disciplines. He argues that not least Kant and Herder have tried to "cut down the oak-tree of what *they* call 'dogmatism', but what is in fact the tree of Certainty and Faith."[216] But the tree remains unshaken.

For Grundtvig's contemporary reader, *On Truth, Greatness, and Beauty* could not have helped them to understand his disagreement with Herder on transcendental philosophy, as set out in Herder's critical writings against Kant, such as *A Metacritique of the 'Critique of Pure Reason'* (1799).[217] For Grundtvig fails to indicate his shifts between the three forms of 'judgemental power' which Kant deals with separately. The concept of Greatness is linked to both the human observation of size and dimension in the physical world as well as to the aesthetic theory of *the sublime*, e.g. in the experience of Greatness in nature, which for Kant depicts our human response as spiritual beings. *On Truth, Greatness, and Beauty* is carried along by Grundtvig's belief that knowledge, morality, and aesthetics can be traced back to a number of propositions: first, the principle of contradiction;[218] next the principle of cause and effect;[219] and finally the principle of unity.[220] These three propositions constitute a formal logical foundation which reflects divine reality in a logical-ontological way. Simultaneously, Grundtvig's philosophy becomes a defence of the bearing idea in Christian theology since the time of the Early Church that there are traces of God to be found in his creation, including love between the sexes.

Grundtvig places the abstract concepts of truth, greatness, and beauty in the realm of *aesthetics*, which depends on sense perception. "Beauty reaches its zenith in nature, in humankind, and primarily in woman,"[221] he says, and goes on to speak of the relation between man, woman, and child, i.e. marriage and family, as a "passage from the natural to the historical beauty". Thus is developed the highest natural Greatness

216 *On Truth, Greatness, and Beauty* p. 112.

217 German title: *Eine Metakritik zur Kritik der reinen Vernunft.*

218 "one cannot say yes without first having said no."

219 Ibid. "there is no effect without a cause".

220 Ibid. "the effect is the image of the cause".

221 Ibid. p. 126.

(man), fused with the highest natural Beauty (woman) and a historical Beauty (a child) who unites both."[222] With his belief in the beauty of natural experience, Grundtvig synthesises education and social philosophy with the art of poetry, and thus with language and words as the connecting link.

This finds expression in *On Revelation, Art, and Learning*, where he gives concrete form to his series of abstract thoughts in *On Truth, Greatness, and Beauty*. In this regard he singles out feeling as our fundamental faculty of consciousness. For Grundtvig art is, primarily and in its broadest form, "the Art of Poetry," which he characterises as "the fusion of sight and song" – and thus of the sublime and the beautiful. Here his aesthetics become a teaching on gender, in that he defines the internalising of Sight through Feeling as a process between "Man and Woman... the head and the heart in union and in constant interaction... The visions should begin in the head, be inspired in the heart, break into song, and call down the Spirit, which again descends in new and great visions."[223]

Here Grundtvig is under the influence of Schelling's philosophy on the relation between man and woman, a relation he presents in *On Human Beings in the World*, which at several points anticipates *On Truth, Greatness, and Beauty* and *On Revelation, Art, and Learning*. In *On Human Beings in the World* he writes with a sarcastic distance about the synthesis of 'polarity thinking' and the teaching about the sexes that characterises Schelling's natural philosophy and also plays a role for the romantic poet and philosopher Friedrich Hardenberg, aka. Novalis (1772-1801). The dialectic of German idealism, with contrastive relations as its fundamental form of thought, is transferred here to the relation to nature. Grundtvig distances himself from explaining nature and the human species by using "Sun-power and Earth-matter, Osiris and Isis,[224] Odin and Frigg,"[225] meaning the gender-defined contrastive couples in nature which recur in both Egyptian and Nordic mythology.

10. Cosmology and Natural Philosophy

In 1865 the 82-year-old Grundtvig writes a draft for an article which he calls *History and Naturalism, or the Illumination of Time and Space*. It provides strong evidence that he maintains the standpoints he has reached in his younger days. Again he is taking sides in the conflict between naturalism and historical revelation, for naturalism had

222 Ibid.

223 Ibid. p. 206.

224 In Egyptian mythology Osiris is god of the afterlife and regeneration. He is married to his sister Isis, goddess of health, marriage, and wisdom.

225 In Nordic mythology Odin is among the leading gods and is associated among others with victory in battle, royal and runic power, and wisdom. He is married to Frigg, goddess of foreknowledge, wisdom, and marriage.

long ago taken the form of partly the 'natural sciences enlightenment' and partly the German 'fundamental enlightenment', i.e. an ontology that argued only a material explanation of humankind and an ontology that rests on humankind's self-worship. As in the *Danne-Virke* articles from 1816-19, Grundtvig chastises an 'enlightenment' that made light of the eternal life from which we had come and to which we longed to return, and argues instead for a *historical* enlightenment of humankind as an alternative.

15 years previously, he had enjoyed reading some articles written in Uppsala, Sweden by Professor of Medicine Israel Hwasser (1790-1860),[226] a distinctive representative of German idealist philosophy in Sweden's spiritual life. In the years 1848-50 Grundtvig again publishes a one-man journal, this time under the title, *The Dane*. In an article entitled *Youth in Our Time* (1850) he takes Hwasser's writings as his starting-point as he unfolds his own philosophy of youth, appealing to their spirit of self-sacrifice. Grundtvig shows that despite his criticism of idealism he still sympathises with the ideas that pervade its world. The order that we find expressed in his philosophy of language also makes its presence felt here. His starting-point is "the history of human life as an expression of the "powerful drive" that humankind possesses and on this basis he embraces "life's true nature, as from effect to cause."[227] Yet he realises that logically the order could be reversed: "we can also *begin* with natural human life as the true source of all human matters, and embrace the historical as a consequent development of the human life-force, which, like every effect, must correspond to its cause." This 'path' is the one that Hwasser has chosen.

In *Danne-Virke*, written over 30 years earlier, Grundtvig had not only asserted, but had more or less canonised, the order time-space and history-nature. In this regard he had begun the section on natural philosophy in *On Human Beings in the World* with his 'observations' on the concepts of the world, time, and space, which lie ahead of what can be learned about 'human experience'. Such observations can only be verified through their accordance with what is perceived through the senses. Grundtvig opposes the understanding of transcendental philosophy and German idealism that Time and Space "only exist in our human conception". In arguing that "the Temporal only exists in and through its relation to the Eternal, as its revelation,"[228] he constructs an alternative theory in accordance with the transcendental philosophy of Leibnitz and Gurwitsch as outlined above (p. 45). And he adds: "Time is a real

226 Dr Israel Hwasser (1790-1860) was Professor of Medicine in both Finland (Turku and Helsinki) and in Sweden (Uppsala). He wrote studies *On Marriage* (1841) and *On the Youth of Our Time* (1842). Hereafter Grundtvig refers to him affectionately as 'The Old Man'. At the time of writing, Hwasser is 60, Grundtvig is 67.

227 *Youth in Our Time* p. 361.

228 *On Human Beings in the World* p. 72.

idea in a *self-dependent* Truth,"[229] i.e. in God as Logos, the creating Word. On this basis he builds a cosmology that draws inspiration from both the Early Church and from Schelling's thought in *Religion and Philosophy* (1804), where Time and Space are perceived as elements in the break-up of the original, harmonious entity and unity that run through nature and history and culminate in a reconciliation that embraces the divisions. Grundtvig is inspired by Schelling but not inevitably in *agreement* with him. In his controversy with H.C. Ørsted he had directed a head-on attack at Schelling's identity philosophy in his pamphlet, *Against the Little Accuser*, whose very subtitle proclaimed, "with proof that Schelling's philosophy is unchristian, ungodly, and untruthful". Pursuing the principle of contradiction Grundtvig had argued that light and dark, life and death, truth and falsehood cannot be mediated, or dissolved in a single, undifferentiated entity that precedes the dialectical division between the "I" and the "not-I" that Fichte speaks of.

In his second world-history book, *A Brief Account of World History in Context* (1812),[230] Grundtvig had returned to the theology of the Early Church which taught that a Fall in heaven had taken place before the Fall on earth. This was an 'event' in the spiritual world which was the precondition for God's creation of the world. The Church fathers drew on Isa 14:12-14, Lk 10:18, and Rev 12:7-9 among others to justify the pre-existent Fall, and in continuation of this Grundtvig works with a form of spiritual corporality which preceded the Creation depicted in Gen 1-3. On this background Grundtvig asserts that Time and Space have their cause in

> ... a Fall, a falling away from Eternity, in which (...) [the Liar, i.e. the Devil] sought to carry out a transgression, a banishment of Truth, against which he rebelled, an expulsion of Light, which he sought to rob, and thus an imprisonment in Time and Space in chains of Darkness.[231]

According to Grundtvig, humankind and the physical world, with their reality in Time and Space, have come into being as a link in God's reconquest of the world lost through the angels' fall into the hands of the Devil. The divinely-created reality that was under the control of "the Liar" should be "reunited with Truth in a renewed self-consciousness, in a new *soul*, and for this new soul human beings were created."[232]

This new creation, the human being, fell from grace during the process through which it was intended to reconquer the reality stolen by the Liar, and, therefore, the process that should constitute the cognitive side of the reconquest is thus incapable

229 Ibid.

230 Danish title: *Kort Begreb af Verdens Krønike betragtet i Sammenhæng.*

231 *On Human Beings in the World* p. 74.

232 Ibid.

of fulfilling this task. What was lost could now only be won back by God's direct intervention in history through his incarnation in Jesus of Nazareth. Christianity therefore becomes the prerequisite for human activity in the sphere of learning and thus of philosophy. Philosophy presupposes faith, says Grundtvig, and in accordance with its historical manifestation, faith testifies to the truth of Christianity. If right-minded philosophers are not Christian from the start, they can become so in their thinking, in the same way that the "serious people" mentioned in Grundtvig's address to his readers in *Danne-Virke* can become so through reading the journal's reflections. When Grundtvig begins to move towards serious observations of natural philosophy, he builds on his Leibnitz-inspired view of the world as an idea in the divine consciousness and its image of the human as an actual being, limited by Time and Space – as a divine experiment to separate 'purely sensory human beings' from 'the animals'.[233] He does so by identifying how the human body is a composition of what is distributed in non-human nature, and again he attempts to bring his thought into line with the Bible. The human being is God's "point of unity," as he puts it:

> The Creator's Word in Time first prepared a point of unity over which it hovered, as it gathered the scattered forces into a life, one which was now fit to advance, with the Spirit hovering above it, gently wafting its breeze. It is beyond dispute that this point of unity is humankind, created in God's image and according to His likeness.[234]

Here, Grundtvig's characterisation of humankind raises us to being "the instrument within which the Spirit works."[235]

As we have seen, according to Grundtvig, through their bodies human beings are in connection with

> all sensory things – from the Light to the Earth from Water and Air to Stones – is the reason why we call human beings a small-scale world (microcosm) even though we ought rather to call them a joined-together (organised) or *united* world.[236]

In the context of the microcosm theory Grundtvig cuts back to the natural science of the Renaissance in which alchemy and astrology were acknowledged. Despite Grundtvig's declared intention to formulate his philosophy in a language accessible to non-philosophers, he not only depends here on the concept of 'microcosmos', which from Antiquity until the 19th century was the foundational figure in European cosmology;

233 Ibid. p. 81.
234 *On Revelation, Art, and Learning* p. 199.
235 *On Human Beings in the World* p. 80.
236 Ibid.

he also employs the terminology of natural philosophy as he knows it from among others Schelling and Steffens. He translates its fundamental concepts from German, and like them he thinks in terms of the 'organism', i.e. the theory that the parts can only be understood from the whole and its purpose. Like his contemporary idealists, he therefore rejects a materialist view of nature, arguing that the human body can, just as little as nature itself, be explained by deriving its constituent parts from *matter*. Natural science, says Grundtvig, must take as its point of origin "the living, self-conscious body, not the soulless body of a corpse, which has no 'conditions' it can call its own,"[237] but is merely a collection of elementary connections. Taking the human body as his starting-point Grundtvig then formulates his version of the *scala naturae*, as European natural philosophy is traditionally regarded, i.e. as a chain of forms of being. As established by the American historian of ideas, A.O. Lovejoy (1873-1962) in the tradition from Plato and primarily Aristotle, this is called 'the great chain of being'. Like the Swedish natural historian Carl Linné (1707-78) and the French biologist Georges Buffon (1707-88) Grundtvig aims at "a *scientific* division and a *system* in natural history,"[238] even though he believes it is still not possible in his time to offer more than an outline.

He nevertheless considers himself able to "trace the transition from lifeless to life-filled, and thence to animated beings, and through the degrees of animals to the human being."[239] On the basis of the concept of the 'microcosm', he argues that "the *same* characteristics... inform the stone, the plant, and the animal."[240] With regard to the transition from the plant-world to the animal-world Grundtvig chooses the 'flower', rather than the 'polyp' (e.g. the sea anemone) that contemporary natural science saw as the intermediate form between a plant and an animal. In this natural 'staircase' Grundtvig concludes that the human being is "the union... of what is divided in animals and the main advantages that stem from this union: namely, the body's ability to imagine and conceive of itself."[241]

In this connection the "hand-feeling" is again determinant, being the human ability to grasp with our hands objects in the surrounding world and, first and foremost, place ourselves in an independent role in relation to them. The hand-feeling is the physiological foundation of self-consciousness, the human ability to think *of* ourselves, which for Grundtvig is the foundation of philosophy. It is, he says, a condition for "the human being's self-consciousness, which animals lack." The hands:

237 Ibid. p. 80.
238 Ibid. p. 81.
239 Ibid.
240 Ibid.
241 Ibid.

> are not just sense-instruments which stand on the border of a certain self-dependence; they are in a way *outside* our body; at a certain distance they can, as it were, *force* things to be sensed and can themselves sense the whole body. Yet as an instrument for the most developed sense – without which no sense-perception is complete – they give total certainty and create specific ideas. Sense-perception begins with a vague, indefinite feeling and concludes in the hand with the clearest and most unequivocal feeling, a feeling that has become *active*, a feeling of *touch*.[242]

In addition to the influences discernible from the Renaissance and German idealism, a major source of inspiration for Grundtvig's natural philosophy comes from a work on natural history by the Danish theologian Esaias Fleischer (1732-1804), *Experiments towards a Universal History of Nature I-IX*, (1786-1804).[243] In singling out 'the hands' as the body's foundation of the human ability to think, Fleischer draws on the natural philosophy of Aristotle. By himself drawing on Fleischer, Grundtvig stands in a tradition stretching back to Antiquity. In the first instance it is the hand that distinguishes humans from animals. Like Fleischer, Grundtvig develops his image of the sensory hand as the basis for the uniqueness of humankind compared to animals, such as the elephant and the snake, whose physical attributes approach those of the human hand. As in *On Revelation, Art, and Learning* Grundtvig strives to bring his scholarly observations into line with the Bible, first and foremost with the creation story. The snake is "the natural enemy of humans,"[244] who at the Fall "dislocated our necessary human standpoint"[245] in order to "sense the whole body,"[246] which is only vouchsafed to the human, and even then only as a "mere sensory being". Precisely this side of human life is at the heart of the first section on natural science in *On Human Beings in the World*. This section, 'On the Human Being's Physical Conditions', sets out to expound what distinguishes "humans, limited as they are to the sensory world,"[247] but in the course of the attempt, Grundtvig makes it clear that it is doomed to failure. This does not come as a surprise to his readers. At the beginning of the section on natural history, he has pointed out that "At most, we can understand the sensory in the human being in connection with the spirit, for it is only thus that it has entered into our consciousness and become the object of our experience."[248] The section ends with Grundtvig emphasising that the natural side of the human being cannot be separated from the

242 Ibid.

243 Danish title: *Forsøg til en almindelig Naturhistorie.* The book also appeared in a German translation.

244 *On Human Beings in the World* p. 84.

245 *On Revelation, Art, and Learning* p. 190.

246 *On Human Beings in the World* p. 81.

247 Ibid. p. 85.

248 Ibid. p. 80.

spiritual side. In keeping with God "breathed life into the nose of humankind"[249] – our highest clear concept is our *body* – and thus do we acquire "a vague concept of our Creator through whom we inhaled super-sensory life."[250] This is a logical continuation of Grundtvig's definition of "Spirit" as a "super-sensory idea".[251] Any insight into human beings as a species is inextricably linked to their consciousness of their divine origin; anthropology is theology.

11. Conclusion: Grundtvig's Philosophy Today

Grundtvig's most important philosophical texts are now a little over 200 years old, so we no longer have *immediate* access to them. We must first try to reconstruct the 19th century world and the currents that were moving in his times, as we identify the influences that can be traced in his thinking. This is a laborious assignment, since Grundtvig's philosophical works are among the most difficult of his entire authorship. Nonetheless, they are worth the effort for three reasons.

In the first place, we come to understand better the rest of Grundtvig's vast corpus, when the philosophical elements of especially the *Danne-Virke* period are laid bare. Grundtvig's threefold anthropology provides his theological, historical, and educational writings with a logical, consistent thinking, which helps us to find clarity in his dense prose.

Secondly, on the basis of historical reconstruction we no longer have any excuse for reading the thinking of our own times back into his conceptual universe. This is always a looming hazard with any writer from a previous century, and not least with Grundtvig, whose entire authorship is so full of existential and political messages. Theologians, educationists, politicians, and scholars are wont to extract and quote isolated sentences and maxims from his work to confirm their *own* world-picture and to argue their case in a very different environment. This is not necessarily in conflict with Grundtvig's thinking, but it can be at the risk of ignoring the complexity of his world-view and can impede further thinking along these lines. Not least in his early thinking on the philosophy of temporality, i.e. his emphasis on cognition being provisional, we must be on guard against a simplistic use of his ideas.

Thirdly, we are enabled to see similarities and differences between Grundtvig's thinking and that of our time – not least in its complexity! In his strong emphasis on human experience throughout history in contrast to the speculative theories of his day, we find the rudiments of an early phenomenological philosophy. At the same

249 Gen 2:7.
250 *On Human Beings in the World* p. 86.
251 Ibid. p. 91.

time his hermeneutic studies and his observations on the relation between image and concept in the *Danne-Virke* articles may be compared to those we find in the 20th century in Hans Georg Gadamer (1900-2002) and Paul Ricoeur (1913-2005). It is equally clear that Grundtvig's biblical world-picture and his embryonic cosmological thinking are pre-critical. On this point his ideas cannot be transferred into the present without considerable integration.

Nonetheless, these philosophical-religious studies are key to understanding thought-structures which recur in the educational, poetic, theological, and political writings that constitute the first four volumes of this series. The visionary historical-poetic thought, often seasoned with ideas from the Bible and history, are a distinctive form of *knowledge* for Grundtvig, a form of orientation, as he seeks to understand human beings in Time and Space. When compared with the stringent academic thinkers of his time such as Kant and Fichte, it is here that Grundtvig reveals his originality as a philosopher.

I

ANTHROPOLOGY AND METAPHYSICS

1. On Human Beings in the World (1817)
2. On Truth, Greatness, and Beauty (1817)

2. The lightning-man, Henrik Steffens 1813

Henrik Steffens (1773-1845) was Grundtvig's 10-year-older cousin, the son of his mother Cathrine's sister, Susanne. Born in Norway, Steffens moved to Copenhagen aged 14 to study Theology and Natural Science. He lectured at three German universities, Kiel, Jena, and Freiburg before returning to Copenhagen, where in 1802 he gave a series of nine lectures at Eler's Hall of Residence. These introduced Romanticism to Denmark and influenced the poet, Oehlenschläger, and Grundtvig, who both attended. Grundtvig was at first luke-warm, but he nevertheless acquired Steffens' book *Introduction to Lectures on Philosophy* (1803), since he listed it as an item in his library in 1805. Later he began to burn with Steffens' fire, and on his death in 1845 Grundtvig wrote a praise-poem calling him the "lightning-man" (no. 145 in *Living Wellsprings*, 2015). From 1811-32 Steffens was Professor of Physics at Breslau University, where he can be seen in inspirational action in 1813 in the painting by Arthur Kampf from 1891. Steffens' main principle was 'individualisation', which argues that as organisms develop, they acquire sharper outlines and greater individualities.

1. On Human Beings in the World (1817)

Introduction by Steen Tullberg

On Human Beings in the World first appeared in the second volume of *Danne-Virke* in March 1817. It has been seen by commentators as a key to understanding Grundtvig's philosophy, anthropology, cosmology, and psychology, no less! After the Introduction, the three sections reflect his division of the human being into Body, Our Physical Conditions; Spirit, Our Spiritual Conditions; and Soul, Our Relation to Ourselves through our self-consciousness. At the centre of Grundtvig's Christian philosophy and this study stands the concept of Learning (*vidskab*).

In Grundtvig's definition Learning comes from the endless endeavour towards wholeness in this earthly life, whose ultimate goal is our transfiguration into God's revelation. This can be partially reached on earth, but only finally fulfilled in the afterlife or at the end of time. All true Learning in *this* sense derives from the observation of humankind in History, over all the time in which humankind has developed. Through a study of History, and thus of human experience, we can gain a gradual insight into our human conditions and effects as they develop, but since the process is unfinished, we can never systematise it. However, the fact that we are made in the divine image (Gen. 1:27) enables us to *understand* ourselves, i.e. to be self-conscious – to know and reflect on what we think and do. This is part of God's plan for all humankind.

In his introduction Grundtvig finds his definition of the world, of time, and of space first in a rejection of Kant's idea of Time and Space as mere modes of perception, and then in an assertion that Time and Space, and thereby volatility and flux, derive from the Fall from Eternity. The Fall brings about the clash of opposites in Time and Space, and for human beings this entails the battle between light and darkness, good and evil, truth and falsehood.

Grundtvig's anthropological observations take the body as their point of origin, i.e. our physical conditions. The fundamental experience of the body's reality is reflected in the principle of contradiction, which guarantees the polar opposites listed above. Thus we *know* there is right and wrong, and all historical experience testifies to this. Our physical self-consciousness points above and *beyond* our material selves; it allows and enables us to *embrace* ourselves and thus to acquire *spiritual* self-consciousness.

In the second sub-section Grundtvig looks at our spiritual conditions. Spirit is here defined as "a vital, powerful, and active concept that neither in itself, its power, nor its effect can be sensed but can only be experienced in self-consciousness" (p. 90). Spirit is given primarily through "the Word and language" (p. 87), which again have been enabled by our being made in the image of God. The relation between body and spirit is now such that "over time the body had to be transformed in order to grasp the Spirit" (p. 88).

The final sub-section, on the soul, or our self-consciousness, is the longest of the three, yet self-consciousness is treated only briefly before Grundtvig tackles the psychological concepts of will and conscience, both a consequence of the Spirit's activity in the body. He also detects traces of Spirit in specific peoples, which must therefore be considered of historical significance. In a people's poetry, art, and learning – corresponding to its imagination, feeling, and intellect – there are traces of the Spirit working on the body.

Important to the study are Grundtvig's ideas concerning cosmology and natural philosophy, particularly in the section, 'Our Physical Conditions', where we can trace the influence of romanticism and especially Schelling's natural philosophy, as mediated in Denmark by Henrik Steffens.[252] In a larger historical context, many of Grundtvig's ideas of our place in the cosmos can be referred back to some of the oldest, most tenacious ideas in European thought. They have their origin in Plato, Aristotle, and Plotinus and their medieval transformation in the *scala naturae* or The Great Chain of Being. This descends from God to spiritual beings such as angels and demons, then to the sun, moon, and stars, and from there to humans, animals, plants, and the lowest form of minerals. Human beings occupy "a small-scale world" (p. 80), a 'microcosm' idea that receives its fullest treatment by Grundtvig in this study.

How complicate, how wonderful is man!
How passing wonder He who made him such!
Who centred in our make such strange extremes!
From diff'rent natures marvellously mix'd!
Connection exquisite of distant worlds,
Midway from nothing to the Deity!
A beam ethereal, sully'd and absorp'd!
Though sully'd and dishonour'd, still divine!
Dim miniature of greatness absolute.
A worm! a god! – – – –
O what a miracle to man is man!

Young's *Night-Thoughts*.[253]

252 cf. p. 66.

253 Edward Young (1683-1765), *The Complaint: or, Night-Thoughts on Life, Death, & Immortality*, London, 1742. A pioneer book of the Romantic movement, *Night-Thoughts* was immensely successful, influencing the young Goethe and the whole *Sturm und Drang* movement. Young's later book, *Conjectures* (1766) introduced the concept of 'genius', of *innate* originality. In freeing poets from having to study the classical tradition before they could put pen to paper, the book was a milestone and a signpost in European literary criticism. Grundtvig's quotation here (without a translation) omits 5½ lines of the original.

All the poems of classical times concede and proclaim human beings to be a *mystery* to themselves. It was not really until the 18th century that philosophers fancied they had *solved* the *mystery* of the concept of the 'human being'. Here they made an obvious mistake – for which no other evidence is really needed than what they themselves provided simply by asserting what they could not prove! Furthermore, we have seen that only perfected human beings can completely and clearly understand themselves, and that only through *History* can we get to know the human mystery in all its depth and breadth, and grasp as much of it as Time has revealed and clarified in its passage. From this it is self-evident that even if an individual person or an individual age could understand themselves, the human being *as such* would in no way be 'understood'. In fact it would be even more indisputable proof that the person or the age in question had lost the highest and deepest, i.e. the truly *mysterious*, fact about us human beings. This lies undoubtedly in our relation to the Invisible, our link to the past and the present, our longings and forebodings, and our fears and hopes, which surpass the sensory world and exceed the chains of Time.

We know that it will not do for us to see ourselves as *independent* of the Invisible, unless it be in our brutish lethargy or thoughtless intoxication, when the body dominates or overwhelms the soul and disturbs or devours all self-consciousness. In no other condition can we regard ourselves as being *independent* of the Invisible, for even if all desire were quenched, all foreboding dispelled, all conscience destroyed, and all fear and hope dissolved into indifference, the indisputable fact remains that we *are born* and we *shall die*, that our life in this world is *temporal*, and that it begins and ends in the Invisible and the Unknowable. As true as this is, it is equally true that we human beings have also sunk deep, almost inconceivably deep! It is almost literally only our gift of speech that separates us from the dumb animals when we claim to have *understood* ourselves, or at least what our prime concern is, without *first* acknowledging our conception and death, our beginning and end in Time. Plainly, one does not need to be a Christian but only a thinking, feeling child of humankind not only to dread the blindness, the lethargy, and the indifference which prevailed throughout the previous century all over Europe, but also to feel an incandescent resentment over the blind guides who diverted human beings away from their concern for the Eternal and from solving the great mystery in which we all are of necessity enveloped.

We cannot possibly avoid the *solution* to this mystery. At most we can only forget about it, until an invisible hand demonstrates its ascendancy and its powerful presence by severing the bond that links all of us – the wonderful creatures that thought and felt – to our dwellings and our possessions! The hand which severs that bond lets dust become dust, and leads us, we who both animated and moved that dust, – whereto now, I ask? How does the human heart *beat* in that dust which has received a deep, indelible impression of this 'whereto now'? Here is the great mystery into which all human thought must gather, and before which it must stop and be silent. Who has not felt it, and who does not wish with all the weapons of Truth, with thunder and lightning, with disputes and laughter, to do battle with the Troll[254] whose sorcery blinds the eyes of all mortals so they fail to seek the goal and the end? They allow this Troll to numb the heart in the cradle of senses so that it forgets itself, its deepest yearnings, its weightiest questions concerning all things, and its eternal life or death! Must not we strive with all that we have to arouse our kin from the lethargy of indifference into which they have sunken, and first and foremost awaken those who have been created to think, to enlighten, and to speak for the multitude?

I for one think so, and while the pen rests and the tongue is silent, having been employed in vain, I call it a 'duty' to see whether the eye is as blind to us human beings and our conditions and desires as it is to our Saviour! Is the ear equally deaf to the voice of Truth that rings out over the graves and echoes in our heart of hearts as it is to Him who rings down from above and melts away the thunderous voice of Truth in the life-giving birdsong and harpstrings of Love? I call it a 'duty' to see whether the Troll's bewitchment is creeping in unnoticed – or is being *summoned*! Was it only in an unguarded hour of sleep that a film grew over our eyes, or did the hand itself *deliberately* tether the cord? Did the heart conceive a mortal hatred of the light, or was it lured by wilfulness and illusion to succumb to the encroaching darkness, constantly trembling, occasionally longing for the light, and often feeling oppressed by the heavy chains of gloom? I hope the last-mentioned is the case, at least for every heart that is Danish in origin and lineage, for I have felt such a dread of the dark within and without, even when my longing for the deeds of darkness was strong – such a dread and wistful longing for the light that can illumine the moon and the stars, and warm one through and through! I have felt such a fear of going into the dark, and such a longing to bathe in the radiance of the sun. I have found them in my *heart*, even when the darkness enveloped me and was dearest to me, and I seem to glimpse them wherever in days gone by Danish folk walked the paths between fields and woods.

I know well that it was not only in the physical world that our merciless longing for land felled the lovely, shady beeches and hid the fear of the dark behind the plough; not only where the monuments to the past were smashed into cobblestones and fences around our native land; not only where so many field-tracks and narrow

254 According to popular belief in the ancient North, trolls were supernatural creatures, more or less with human features, but invariably ugly. They lived in the countryside, in mountains, hills, and woods, as well as in the ocean and underground. They were useful to the gods; for instance, they made Odin's spear and Thor's hammer, but if forced to make something for a *human*, they would put a secret curse on it, rendering it dangerous to the owner. There are stories of them stealing children and of kidnapping women in order to force them into marriage. Little wonder that the 'troll' has surfaced again in Internet slang, as one who sows discord by posting inflammatory messages in an online community with the deliberate intent to provoke an angry reaction.

church-paths were surrendered in order to lay down paved country roads; not only where consolation for the lack of sunlight and warmth came from the self-made light and heat within the four walls of one's own tumbledown hut. All this I know well, much too well, unfortunately! But I also know that the howl of the storm over the barren fields, and the roar of the waves along bare coasts, are just as frightening as the shadows of the forest when we long for the beeches with their new shoots, for the nightingale, and for the sun with its warm clear rays. 'The day lengthens as winter strengthens', we say, when fire and light go out at midnight, and feather and down can no longer warm frozen old bones! I know well that round and about in the country many a heart sighs in secret and longs for its memories of childhood, for the good old days with the beech in bloom and the long, mild summers that old folks still talk about. I am well aware that such misgivings and longings will one day reawaken in Denmark's heart – and the heart will surely sense that their home is elsewhere than in the childhood days of the nursery! It would have to defy the truth to put these misgivings and longings to flight!

It has been my intention in previous articles to encourage this awakening as best I could, and that is no less the case here. On the borderline between general observations of the goal and conditions of true Learning and the specific ones of my individual articles, the articles endeavour to consolidate what lies behind us to protect us on our onward journey. I do this by presenting a picture of humankind in the world that is undeniably faithful and apposite, despite it lacking so much that we do not understand – yet cannot possibly allow to be a matter of indifference. It would be both rash and inexcusable of us to renounce our noble legacy from our praiseworthy forefathers! We stand or fall by this, and our unborn generations have the right to demand it as their historical inheritance. If I am successful in giving this important study all the stability, substance, and clarity it can receive under the conditions of time and my own ability, then I venture to hope that no truth-loving reader will regret the attention that I hereby request of them.

It is perhaps not irrelevant to note that the reader must not expect to see the human mystery *solved* here, but only to see it presented as far as possible in all its wonder. Where I myself consider the solution to be well-known. I have attempted to show, as previously, that it will not be found quite naturally until we approach the end of the world; and that again will be confirmed in what follows.

~

When we say 'Human beings in the world', we are referring to two wondrous things. For what *is* 'the World'? What *is* 'Time'? What *is* 'Space'? It has been said that Time and Space correspond only to the human imagination, but anything more topsy-turvy could hardly be conceived, for if that were the case, Time and Space could not possibly *confine* us, and we would simply be *of* ourselves and conscious of ourselves as being eternal! On the other hand, if we have *come into being*, then Time existed *before* us, for only *in* Time can *anything* come into being, develop, be created. The reality of Time and the World becomes one and the same, and cannot be denied unless we are willing to deny their effect on us, in which case we are denying our consciousness.

A quite different question is how far Time and the World exist *in themselves*, i.e. how far they are *self-dependent*. To this we must simply answer in the negative, for the Temporal only exists in and through its relation to the Eternal, as its revelation. It has only a *borrowed* reality, since it is neither the cause *of* itself nor contains that cause *within* itself; it is only real as an *effect*, whose activity ceases as soon as its cause is no longer active. Just as in the visible world Light controls Time, and Time is only active in the battle between Light and Dark, so in the Kingdom of the *Spirit* does Time only have reality in the *spiritual* battle between Light and Dark, between Truth and Falsehood. From this vantage-point we clearly see that Time *itself* must be Temporal; it must have begun and it must end, for *Falsehood* must have begun and must end, since it is a denial of Truth. It must cost its purveyor all its invested power, and with the full loss of this power the battle necessarily ceases; for 'battle' is indubitably a counter-activity presupposing contrary powers, or powers employed by contrary wills.

There is also another vantage-point from which we can be convinced that Time must cease when its contrary ceases – or, more precisely, that Time is no more than the relation between active oppositions. For without Change there is no Time, and Time in itself is only unchanging when there is a contending duality, a duality which is not *one* in the Spirit. One of these mutually conflicting powers must therefore be emptied of its power before Change and Time can exist. As soon as this happens and all Reality is one, all Change and Time *cease* to exist. If Time is the mutually conflicting relation between genuine opposites, between Truth and Falsehood, it follows that Time is a real idea in a *self-dependent* Truth, i.e. Truth's idea of its relation to the conflicting Falsehood – and after the Revelation, the Son's idea of His relation to the Devil as the *Father* of Falsehood.[255]

Truth's idea of its relation to Falsehood is precisely its *own* image, for that relation constitutes its personality, which is as temporal as the battle is temporal. We are now surprised to find ourselves suddenly back where we started, for we began with human beings as the temporal image of independent Truth; now we can see that human beings actually express the real idea of their *self-dependence*, or of their relation to Falsehood. It is absolutely within the human being that Time has its spiritual reality, but, please note, in human beings as the *image* of Truth, i.e. in Truth's idea, not our human idea.

255 Jn 8:44.

As regards Space, its reality for human beings is clear from its *effect* on us, for Space confines us in *extent*, just as Time does in age. Whatever its limits, Truth's *image* must necessarily be real in Truth's *idea*, otherwise its idea is limited to human beings coming from nothing and Truth coming from Falsehood! This is just as impossible as Nothing being able to confine and limit Everything. This becomes clearer when we consider what Space actually *is*; for if, as we must admit, it is the *condition* for all contraction and expansion, for all measurements in the sensory world, then it undoubtedly constitutes the relation between Light and Dark. This relation must in turn be just as real as that between Truth and Falsehood, whose visible and sensory (i.e. temporal) side it precisely *is*. Light is Truth's body, as Darkness is Falsehood's body. In Light there is no confinement, and in Darkness it is not acknowledged; only in their relation does it come into view. Darkness is Space *in itself*, just as Falsehood is Time in itself, and both are nothing *in themselves*! They have their finite reality in their contrary relations to Light and Truth as a result of their separation. This is a battle in which Truth and Light consume what Falsehood and Darkness have usurped, a battle whose first scene was the Creation of the World, while its second scene was human life. The first saw the destruction of Darkness, the second will see the destruction of Falsehood. When God's Truth created the World, He revealed His power, and when He created the human being in His image,[256] He revealed Himself in Time and Space, with a temporal and finite *purpose*. In this purpose Time and Space and all that they have consumed have their reality. If they are real in Truth's eyes, then they are also truthful; and insofar as they can conceive of it, they have not only a sensory but also a true and spiritual existence in humankind, for among humankind Truth's idea of Time and Space is bound to a joint transfiguration in Truth.

Out of this came our threefold relationship: to Time, to Space, and to living, creating Truth. All three were clearly one in their relation to the creation of the human being as a creature, for there is no denying that Creation was the ground of our whole being and the event at which life was breathed into all human conditions. It is equally obvious that we are subordinate to Time and Space in what must be called our sensory relations, for we are created *within* Time and Space and out of dust,[257] through which we have a relation both to things in the world and to Darkness and Falsehood. Our dust and all the Earth were freed from their chains through the power of Truth, thanks to Light. Of necessity we therefore had a relation to Time and Space *of our own*, in other words to Falsehood and Darkness. This relation has proved to be hostile, but ends in victory. Our human dust is transfigured by Light, and Light is transfigured by Truth, whereas the activity of Falsehood and Darkness ceases and loses

256 Gen 1:27.

257 Gen 2:7.

itself in infinite impotence. We can reach a fairly clarified idea of human beings and their purpose, if we add that Falsehood is a denial of Truth. Falsehood presupposes a Liar, a spirit that changes itself and produces in, by, and for itself, an established time, a time which is not actually possible, yet which is a *real* time in relation to itself. It does so as follows. The change in question is of necessity a Fall, a falling away from Eternity in which it sought to carry out a transgression, a banishment of the Truth against which it rebelled, an expulsion of the Light which it sought to rob, and thus an imprisonment in Time and Space in chains of Darkness.

Lastly, nothing that is *of the Truth* can perish. Consciousness of self, i.e. the soul, can fall *within* Truth, but it falls in a changeable capacity which ends its life in death, in a separation from what it sought to depend upon, its power and means. When we reflect on these things, we realise that Time in its reality is only the *change* whereby a fallen spirit, a lost soul – the original Liar – is separated from its accoutrements of power and means. When it is reunited with Truth in a renewed self-consciousness, in a new *soul*, and for this new soul human beings are created. They are necessarily exposed to the temptations of the Liar, whose heir they were supposed to be for ever, even though they fought the fight and finished the course,[258] gained their inheritance as the agent of Truth and united it within themselves. All that Truth had created was exceedingly good, and the creature's self-consciousness – the Light, the soul, the intellect – was also good for as long as it let itself be ruled by the spirit of Truth. For like every subjected self-consciousness, it could be tempted by *itself* to rebellion, by the desire for self-dependence outside Truth, and could not stop the temptation from the spirit of Falsehood that demanded such.

It is time to break off from these reflections. As likely as not they will seem strange and obscure to most people and completely unfounded to many, but I needed to present them as the background for what is to come. I cannot possibly speak about human beings in their Experience without being sure of their origin and destiny, so I had to present this brief comment on these in order to be understood. If I should now make any false statement on human beings in their Experience or withhold something truthful in order to conjure up a show of agreement, it will be the readers' business to pay close heed! If they fail to find anything of this nature, then I venture to hope that in the end they will note attentively that my comments can only tally with Experience if they are basically *true*! I say 'basically' because I myself have found it difficult to speak precisely and cogently about such matters, and I do not believe I have successfully covered them in detail. Several other reasons have moved me to add such detail to my reflections, one of them being the insight that either we allow Time and Space to stand as they are, or we pursue them right to their obscure origins; to

258 2 Tim 4:7.

stop half-way only confuses the issue. Another reason is that I had to pay attention both to the few who take the Bible literally and who, if they are used to reasoning and tempted to doubt, will be gratified by the above-mentioned, as well as to those, no longer so few, who know something of Natural Philosophy, for they will find it easy to understand me. If they love Truth, they will enjoy the flashes of light on the chaos into which Natural Philosophy has inveigled itself and its believers!

~

Wherever we find human beings in History and our own Experience, we find them involved in all manner of relations. A host of these are allowed to run freely through the world, while a number rest on the belief in one essential and simple *cause of all things*. It is to the latter that we now turn our attention, and even if we cannot say that they have chosen the best part, we must admit that they follow a middle way which at a certain point divides into two; it is in this direction that we can follow them without danger, if we have the love of Truth in our hearts. We live in a time when the few scholars who seek to understand Truth cannot completely avoid it, in a time when Faith, even where it exists, is so weak that it dare not defy the doubters – until it realises their insignificance in solving what seem to be our biggest problems. It may be that with every step on the path to knowledge new doubts arise that appear to be even stronger, but whoever has once stood before a mountain that with honest regret they considered insurmountable, and whoever has watched them sink into the dust before the Light, will never again forget those mountains without feeling conscience-stricken. What loomed before them proved merely to be a "speck of dust in their own eye,"[259] which prevented them from seeing the Light that is undoubtedly no more obscured by the mountain than the speck of dust. This observation, which is based among other things on my own experience, should help those of my readers who have *not* faced it, to temper their troubled, insatiable appetite not for the Light *itself* but for its *appearance*, its *rays*, and for a broad, uninhibited insight which with every step forward on the path of knowledge endeavours to consume the open, inexperienced heart, and most especially that of the bright-eyed apprentice!

We cannot therefore ever do enough to remind ourselves that the prospect for all mortals – except the saints before the Rock of Faith – is obstructed by a mountain, or by an unfathomable, immeasurable gulf. In that regard the difference between the longest and the shortest, or the sharpest and the weakest, view affects the matter just as little as the intervening space makes any difference to the distance from Earth to Heaven, and to its Light. Knowledge is only of help when we do not covet it for its

259 Mt 7:3.

own sake but only to put doubt to shame, to strengthen Faith within and around us, and to let the Light over Truth's honour penetrate our eyes so broadly and clearly as its construction and our level allows – as our Creator and Providence so wish. For this to happen, we need a composure and an equanimity, a fundamental security and a satisfaction with what we have. Faith alone can grant us this, for Faith is completely incompatible with all the roaring desire and intemperate greed that only cloud the eye and disturb our stance. Philosophising without Faith is the same as looking without eyes; to seek to *grasp* one's faith is like wanting to tear out one's eyes in order to *see* them! On the other hand, to compare one's faith with one's own and one's family's experience is like seeing our reflection in a mirror,[260] with the premise that we can neither see God nor see *through* ourselves! Yet without doubt we can see many marks of our Eternal God's finger, many a trace of what Faith proclaimed, and many a mystery which we feel is *solved* by Faith, even though we cannot say how. From such a reflection we can truly learn why we *need* Faith, since we both own and can use our common sense, just as through a constant use of the mirror (usually the tool of vanity!), we can learn why we *must* see if we are able and willing to use our eyes.

This is how I engage with Knowledge, not as a goddess but as Church soil. Its crops I would sacrifice on its altar, and its profits would help a copper roof withstand the unbridled winds better than tiles! Before I take responsibility for how others engage with Knowledge, I would not wish to have written a jot of my frequent exhortations, for I would rather saddle my readers' patience with such exhortations than my conscience with a guilt which the world laughs at, but Christians dread. I must never doubt that I am a simple, believing Christian, who stands by every word he has written in praise of blind Faith in the Word of Truth in the Bible and in the testimony of the vanity of all Knowledge and Learning when they seek to claim even the very smallest independence in themselves. These are matters that I must never allow anyone to doubt; and without a constant reminder, that could easily happen these days. For we live in a time which prefers not only to believe that one cannot think rationally without losing one's faith, but also to see its delusion strengthened by my present efforts, whose link to my faith and sustained thought I have not infrequently sought to develop. As far as I can ascertain, however, this has been without noticeable success. People will not believe me until they take Faith into their *own* hands! But that is not my fault either, for, to be honest, my conduct must be as my teaching proclaims, whether I am wearing my coat or my cassock![261]

There is one more matter that I consider appropriate to mention here: namely, the playfulness in my use of words and idioms. This regularly comes into play in my

260 1 Cor 13:12.

261 i.e. whether I speak as a layperson or as a priest.

discussion of serious matters, and has irked a number of my dear readers. Let me begin with the admission that by and large this playfulness comes unexpectedly: "*naturam pelle furca ex*, here she comes again, the witch!"[262] When readers open their eyes again, they will see that my nature is so far from all 'fantasies', and that, on the contrary, it is far too prosaically dry and tame! Without otherwise making any comparison to Holberg,[263] I venture to say that I share the same natural taste for poetry, passion, and all such things as he has, which is why, until my twenty-third year, he was my model of a true poet and complete writer. After this confession, which must excuse what I cannot defend, I shall explain why in such studies as this I mostly refrain from expressing this natural desire of mine, for various reasons.

In the first place, it is tiring for both myself and presumably many of my readers to think and write as if I were sewing threads into a frame! And when one is tired, one neither writes nor reads well. Secondly, like most people I feel that when I am at the height of my thought and looking out into the world, I can be tempted to stand on tiptoe to see a little further and a little higher above the heads of the others in the field. This is in itself shameful, and it can easily end with my falling flat on my face. My only advice is instead to go *down* the mountain, for that is where we can best notice the difference between the height one has and the height one was on! The thrill passes, and on level ground again we are better able to distinguish between appearance and reality; we are forced to express ourselves far more carefully, since we can no longer rise above laughter and criticism! It is therefore my firm conviction that in all their talk of common sense both the writer and the reader are best served with a plain, playful style. This should both claim and convey the balance and the cheerful calmness that are absolutely indispensable to thinking sensibly, to drawing proper conclusions, and to making deep-seated assertions. Many writers imagine that concepts requiring strict thinking, seriousness of tone, and dignified expression cannot be combined with wit, jest, and bluffness. Such a projected imbalance would lead me to suppress or delete what seems doubtful or superfluous, but not what is, for me, suitable and necessary! Why should I do *that*? It will be a pleasure for me to frighten away anyone who does not wish to *read* my studies; and whoever reads them for fun has nothing to complain about! But in all seriousness, those who read them as they are written – in *deadly seriousness* – do grow accustomed to them. Not infrequently they discover a deeper seriousness under many a *playful* surface than is often the case under the most *serious* of surfaces! If I occasionally am somewhat free with my jesting, then, believe me, I am meticulously on guard against *overdoing* it; jesting is too precious, too risky. In

262 Lat. 'one can drive nature out with a pitchfork' is the first half of a proverb in Horace which concludes with the words '*tamen usque recurret*', meaning 'but she always comes back'. Grundtvig's reference is based on its use in Jens Baggesen's *Kallundborgs Krønike eller Censurens Oprindelse*" (1786), which adds the words, 'the witch!'.

263 Ludvig Holberg (1684-1754) was a famous Danish-Norwegian playwright.

general, readers can be assured – and close scrutiny will confirm this – that the words which seem most casual are the firmest and weightiest. For when our thoughts are gathered, we do not stand on shaky ground if we know where there is a firm footing!

I am well aware that readers would prefer this lengthy parenthesis to have been placed in a prologue rather than here, where it confounds all artistic rules. However, I also know that it is here that it best reaches my *true* readers, and it is here that it has the greatest effect. Out of this consideration it is my custom to confound all artistic rules! In minor as in major matters, Beauty must surrender to Truth, and the only real loser is *appearance*. Truth can never harm true Beauty, and in Truth's eyes all that is true is also beautiful, whereas what *calls* itself Beauty seeks to fool us into believing that, even in defiance of Truth, it remains 'true' Beauty.

I shall return to this subject when we are finished with human relations, where we stopped in order to set our minds and feet on a path that is not so easy to pursue as one would think. Let us first see how every other writer in the previous century took that path, as the anthropologists, psychologists, and educationists smoked their pipes and wore their slippers and their nightcaps. From the physical side these habits are also mine, but they are far from being universal. On the outside there were those who wore their wigs rolled up with curls beneath, brushed-up cockscombs, artificial hair-tots, Hungarian boots, French coats, Prussian hats, and all manner of German caps! On the inside, however, it was their forefathers' everyday wear that was on show. It is a habit I dislike, for it is basically a kind of extortion! The *best* preparation for a trip into the maze that makes up the human grove is on the outside to don slippers and a nightcap, and on the inside to don night-thoughts and genuine morning-dreams, plus a little morning-prayer and morning-reading. Even if we then see far from everything that we *wish* to see, and do not understand everything that we *do* see, we cause no offence. Nor do we easily violate convention, lose our way, or find ourselves up to our knees in mud or up to our necks in water! Those who trust their high boots and their ability to swim will have to leave their boots stuck in the mud and walk home in their stockinged feet. The swimmers may not sink to the bottom, but then nor do they *catch* much, and what they take home with them is only the desire to be washed and dried! We others would prefer mud to stay as mud, and only measure the depth with our rod as best we can. Above all, we let water *remain* water and only look as far down as we can in the calm weather at sunrise; we must let Time manage the rest.

Instead of jumping up high like many writers, including the youngsters around us who are really only playing somersaults and cartwheels, we would be well advised to look at our slippers, at the new air balloons,[264] and at our oldest feathers. Then

264 The first free-floating hot-air balloon flight was successfully achieved by Jean-François de Rozier and François d'Arlandes outside Paris on 21st November 1783, the year Grundtvig was born.

we should swim a few inches on the surface of the water! We do not need to aspire to the sun, the moon or any stars, let alone the Spirit whose power lights them up! Instead, we should regard everything in which life moves and has its being *amiably*. And we should not imagine that we do not *hear* the singing bird, or will not *run* from the buzzing bee, or let the forget-me-not hide itself away *unheeded*! With these resolutions, which are worth more than all the trip itself, let us embark upon it and make it as brief as possible, since our only intention is to see the Troll-Wood[265] and examine it step by step to the best of our ability.

Parcelling out such small plots so that no one can live off them is just as foolish here as anywhere else, but nowhere is a well-calculated sub-division more necessary. However, we must note that living fences are the only enclosures that can be used here, since it is living people who are to be sub-divided, not a corpse that is to be dismembered. Whoever wishes to see the human being *in effigie*,[266] with a head stuck on a pole, and a brain dissected, must go to a psychological slaughterhouse, for I believe it is only the brain's skull, water, and flesh that can be thus treated. To sell this instead of the whole human head may have been the custom, but it has not proved to be correct! We are not seeking to cut the human being into pieces, for there is never any purpose in separating "what God has joined together"![267] We undoubtedly hang together far too well for that to happen, however finely woven the threads may seem. We are only endeavouring to distinguish our basic conditions from one another in their best-known characteristics, and to look for the boundaries between town and country as they have been from time immemorial, without becoming involved in an endless argument in the attempt to replace the collective with the individual. That is quite beyond my intelligence! And yet it is also the development that spiritual geometry has undergone, where it is no longer enough to use the tape-measure and calculate correctly; now it depends on an 'assessment' or an 'evaluation', which only leads to a poor result if we just measure the surface. So, in proceeding with caution, we discover only three basic human conditions that we can clearly distinguish – less *from* each other than *within* each other: the body, the spirit, and the self. These three not only affect each other, but fuse with, and sink into, each other. This is their sign of life, though death teaches us that they can be separated.

The Body: Our Physical Conditions

We begin here with the body not because its conditions are the clearest, for like the body itself, its conditions are the most obscure elements in human beings and the

265 A metaphor for what both attracts and repels. For 'Troll' see note 262.

266 In effigy, i.e. symbolically.

267 Mt 19:6, and the wedding ritual.

hardest and last things to explain about them. We start with these conditions because they are the first and best-known elements, the instrument within which the Spirit works, and the image in which it reveals itself. Even someone who has acquired the entire physical and mathematical learning of our time, which I most certainly have not, would be unwise to undertake an *explanation* of the body. For it is quite clear that an *analysis* of its elements is not an *explanation* of them, otherwise death would be our greatest triumph instead of appearing to be our destruction. Death is of course a *physical* annihilation, as the body disappears little by little instead of melting into the light. It sinks back into its elements, instead of fusing into an indivisible unity, which is clearly its destination.

When we therefore speak of 'the body's conditions', we mean of course the living, self-conscious body, not the soulless body of a corpse, which has no 'conditions' it can call its own. In animals, we can see before us the concept of a living, conscious body *without* a spirit, i.e. without an extra-sensory imagination. Yet it is quite difficult to define the difference between sensory *humans* and sensory *animals*. We know and see there is an important difference, but since a *purely* sensory human being cannot be found in the species – and even if it were, it could least of all *understand* itself – it all comes down to how we distinguish the sensory from the spiritual *in the human being*. This is well-nigh impossible for us unless we *understand* the body, for otherwise we cannot work out *what* the spirit actually affects in its link to the body. At most, we can understand the sensory in the human being in connection with the spirit, for it is only thus that it has entered into our consciousness and become the object of our experience. However incomplete our self-knowledge may be in this regard, what we *can* have is neither insignificant nor uncertain, for it is undeniable that all that connects us to sensory *things* belongs to sensory *human beings*, and our self-knowledge can and should increase with every step we take in our acquaintance with the external world and our relation to it.

From this point we can see that although dissection of corpses cannot teach us about *living* bodies, nevertheless, for living beings who know how to apply them, our observations of the dissection and the decomposition of the body contribute a great deal to the knowledge about which we are speaking. For they tell us about the *elements* in our body and show us that these really do contain components for a *temporal wonder*, for the composition of an instrument that works throughout the world. It cannot be sensorily present in its own right without the invisible power of the spirit that works within everything! This connection to all sensory things – from the light to the earth, from water and air to stones – is the reason why we call human beings a small-scale world (a microcosm), even though we ought rather to use the phrase a 'joined-together' (organised) or *united* world. We might also mention in passing that both Alchemy and Astrology and many other things are built on this sure connection and are therefore far from being so unreasonable as they are merely presumptuous. Of course such attempts represent an *abuse* of the spirit, and such a connection would, in and of itself, barely distinguish purely sensory human beings from the animals, or otherwise, in order to do so, would need to be explained by means of a comparison which it completely lacked the ability to make.

The difference becomes clearer and more important when we compare the living body of an animal with our own. I do not mean by this the advantages that internal and external creation give our body as an instrument for the spirit, partly because I know far too little about its internal construction and partly because it is irrelevant in the context. On the other hand I wish to point out the *union* in the human being of what is divided in animals and the main advantages that stem from this union: namely, the body's ability to imagine and conceive of itself. Once we begin to observe the human being's ability to *sense*, then the hands immediately attract our attention. They are not just sense-instruments which stand on the border of a certain self-dependence; they are in a way *outside* our body. At a certain distance they can, as it were, *force* things to be sensed and can themselves sense the whole body. Yet as an instrument for the most developed sense – without which no sense-perception is complete – they give total certainty and create specific ideas. Sense-perception begins with a vague, indefinite feeling and concludes in the hand with the clearest and most unequivocal feeling, a feeling that has become *active*, a feeling of *touch*. All the other senses may seem to become aware of an external thing which is not there, but what is *tangible* is truly as present as the body itself.

I cannot determine how deep such a feeling goes in the many animals with fore-paws, but it cannot possibly be compared to human touch. This is the distinctive characteristic and expression, indeed the *condition* of our self-consciousness, which animals lack. Nor do I know how far we can trace the transition from life-less to life-filled, and thence to animated beings, and through the degrees of animals to the *human* being. What I do know is that not until we begin to examine the relation of *all things* to life, and to organise them accordingly, can we speak of a *scientific* division and a *system* in natural history. A division built on anything else might be useful and often correct, but it would frequently be confused by appearances and would be laughable if it called itself a 'system'.

We should begin by defining precisely the characteristics shared by *all* bodies in Space, and then seek to discover their highest temporal cause; only then would we probably be able to work out little by little that it is the *same* characteristics which inform the stone, the plant, and the animal. With my great ignorance of Physics, Mathematics, and Natural History, I am not tempted to answer questions which I cannot understand and which will anyway not be answered fully before the end of Time. But I am permitted to *ask* them, since this is undoubtedly one of the instances where one cannot ask too *many* questions, but can come with too many *answers*. So I ask simply: Are not measurement, connection, and size the properties which inform all earthly bodies, and can they not be distinguished in thought, though inseparable in idea? Moreover, can we not rightly say that the idea comes into being through the thought that came from the image created by the properties which reveal it as a form? I then ask: Is not this form the only thing we can say that lifeless things have *in themselves*? Other properties appear to reveal themselves in their treatment, whereas a plant has *in itself* the active element that can create its form and the ability to demonstrate in its growth what before was only its weight; indeed, without being touched it can reveal a trace of its reality in its scent. Finally I ask: do not the growth and scent of a plant presuppose a certain sense-perception in human beings, albeit involuntary, and is not the scent, though equally involuntary, a genuine life-utterance? Whatever people say about such questions does not matter to me, since they are for the most part a hint to think more deeply and are no more than a preparation for, not a proof of, the following discussion on the animals and humans. Nor should I conceal my claim that I have weighed these questions in the balance and found that they cannot be refuted.

When we look at the animal kingdom – where I prefer to take the flower as an example rather than the polyp – there is far more to see than I can either take in or work out! What I *can* see is that the animal's form is an image of the animal itself, whereas the forms of the stone and the plant are merely images of an effect and an activity which they themselves cannot appropriate. In brief the animal is an animated body that can feel and touch itself; it finds itself set free and in need of differentiating itself from all others. If we could decide the *degrees* in the animals' consciousness, we could divide them into series scientifically and determine whether the sensory human being belonged among them. But this would be difficult, not to say impossible, since sense-perception and all life-utterances constitute a faithful image of consciousness which of necessity expresses itself *through* them. It follows that such a system cannot be built up swiftly, any more than Rome can be built in a day. Yet such a system must *gradually* be made possible, provided that we can find out how it relates to sense-perception and the entire sensory life-utterance at its highest point as well as what *order* this development follows. We can discover this, if sensory life has reached its zenith in the human being; for even without the information we can gather about the foetus in the mother's womb – which is mostly used to illuminate plant-life – a close scrutiny of the child, from the moment of birth until it recognises itself in a mirror and says 'I' to itself, will teach us how sense-perception develops.

Here we can see that we learn about the earth from the plants, about the plants from the animals, and about the animals from humans. However topsy-turvy this may seem, it is how science has been driven for the most part, since it seeks to explain the greater by the lesser, the higher by the lower, the living by the lifeless, and reason from the dumb animals. The world of the senses thus drives us back on ourselves, and Nature rejects all our questions with a dry, "Ask yourself! If it is beyond your comprehension, ask my butler! He is also yours!"[268]

It is a well-known fact that in every way I prefer to do the latter, and we are compelled to follow this advice if we truly wish to know about *ourselves*. Indeed, if our forefathers had not sought the truth and rested in the answer, we should not have been able to speak of Learning at all. We also know that the only question is: Does the only and essential Word of Truth, despite it containing *all* truth, give us a clear and distinct *message*? It follows from this that not everything in the Bible serves the cause of Salvation; it will remain obscure to us until, with the truth before our very eyes, we have come so far in human Knowledge that we see what that message means in our own selves. It is far from being my intention to make people believe that I *myself* have understood it, or have only studied the extraordinary image of creation revealed in the new-born child. Rather do I see myself as possessing a few general observations which I am unable to reveal but only to point to.

The sense of *hearing* is undoubtedly the first that reveals itself in the child, and a glance at the animal kingdom seems to confirm that real sense-perception in Nature *begins* with this. Yet I dare not say for certain that sense-perception develops in the following order, which seems most probable: general feeling, or rather sensing, hearing, smell, sight, touch (hand-feeling), and then taste. However, we do know that the nose is not set between the eyes in vain, and that the hands and mouth have more in common than any one of us knows – as every man knows who has kissed a girl's hand! In other words, smell has a special subordinate role to sight, much as air has to light, and that the special feeling that develops in the hand already plays upon the lips and seeks its clarification in the tongue. It is thus a quite common observation that the child often puts into its mouth what it has watched and touched – for the deep reason that the tongue has the finest feeling, and the purpose of *all* sense-perception is to unite the sensed with the self, though one is not always aware of this.

This union is effected *wherever possible*, particularly between smell and taste, through which we receive more than we recognise. Hearing, sight, and touch, on the other hand, are the senses we best can *distinguish*. Touch distinguishes itself in that it is least suited to receiving, but under sight's condition it is best at recognising. Without drawing any further comparisons we can say that it is only girls and thieves who receive with the hand! What we can learn from this is that the hand – which cannot easily be bribed with nothing! – is, for guaranteed sense-perception, a limb we cannot do without. 'A

268 The response, "Ask my butler!" is repeatedly used in the play *The Pawned Farmboy* (*Den pantsatte bondedreng*, 1726) by the Danish-Norwegian playwright, Ludvig Holberg (1684-1754).

bird in the hand is worth two in the bush'[269] is not only true in that it is *tangible*; it also gives a kind of *knowledge*. In other words, what can be taken and touched affects our whole body; but we cannot say the same about everything we see and hear. In particular we must note that it is not until we grasp something with the hand that we are able to sense our whole *body* and persuade ourselves of its *coherence* – the quality that separates bodies from shadows. So it is to the sense of touch that we owe the very *concept* of 'myself', and the intelligence not to fear our own shadow as though it were a foreign body! This is more important than perhaps it seems, for this clear *I-concept* is precisely what we call the 'sensible self-consciousness', without which all self-observation and all clear concepts of things in relation to one another and to ourselves would be impossible.

Here we have arrived at the point where humans raise themselves *above* the animals. There is no need to argue that all animals lack physical self-consciousness; all we can say is that if this exists in any animal, it must be in one that can sense its whole body and recognise its shadow! We might also add: it must be in one that has sought to disturb Nature's order and thus itself, and has not won but lost its natural advantages by thinking only of itself! Following the Bible's direction, I believe this to be the case with the snake, the natural enemy of humans, which Scripture calls "the craftiest of wild animals",[270] and which undoubtedly can sense its whole body, even though in order to do so it may disturb its place in Nature's order. I shall speculate no further on this but proceed to the undeniable observation that no faculty has been found in any animal whereby the sense of touch could perform that of the human hand! In the animal kingdom it is the elephant's trunk that most resembles the hand, being the hand and the mouth in one, so there is no doubt that the elephant has long been regarded as one of the cleverest, most self-conscious animals. Nevertheless, it cannot think of itself any more than a 1-year-old child can; and if any *other* animal can, it can probably think about nothing else, but sits imprisoned in itself.

On every point, what is obvious to many will surely be confirmed for all: that the stronger one particular sense is in a certain kind of animal, the weaker are the others, just as we see that it takes a long time for a child to use more than one sense at a time. It is also a well-known fact that no animal has all five senses – or even the three recognition senses[271] – to the same degree as humans, so animals are unqualified to register any complete experience or to acquire any clear concepts. Even with our limited

269 Grundtvig was a great believer in the power of proverbs, which represented the collective wisdom of the people. He scattered them throughout his writings, as well as publishing a collection of 3,012 of them in 1845 under the title *Danish Proverbs and Sayings* (*Danske Ordsprog og Mundheld*). The Danish version of this particular proverb translates as 'A bird in the hand is worth ten on the roof'.

270 Gen 3:1.

271 i.e. hearing, sight, and touch.

knowledge we could say much more about animals here – such as their experience, their memory, and the like – but now we must move on to human beings. We shall merely note in passing that as regards the elements or components in the human as a natural creature there is nothing new, but only a union of everything which in the highest degree is shared among animals. It is from this union and the consequent possibility of total sense-perception that the body's self-consciousness is derived on the path of experience, and thus can generate human intellect or reason.

Whoever has some knowledge of books on philosophy will at this point probably ask: Can matter *think*? Does the soul emerge out of *Nature's* organisation of its elements? and more things of that kind! However, I did not promise to unravel what has become entangled by people talking in ignorance in order to prove that the soul was in and of itself a 'king'! Moreover, matter is no more than things in their lifeless state. And just as assuredly as life is not generated by death, light by darkness, truth by falsehood, and everything by nothing, so are all lifeless things *bereft* of life, and all creation *quickened* by life. If lifeless matter can be quickened, it can also learn to *think*, since thought is no more than a development of life-feeling. As soon as the body, through the power of thought, can *comprehend* itself, it is *conscious* of itself and has a reasoning, thinking soul. Nature's organisation does not *create* the intellect, but develops it naturally in the same relation as to life, whose instrument it is. In its service to life, Nature at its highest point *awakens* the intellect, and through this our sense-perception shows, among the other images, one image that it must acknowledge *as its own* and take into its possession. Now it has its *own* yardstick for its ideas and feelings, a hand with which it can grasp and weigh all that it can contain, all of which it is itself the *essence*. It grasps all that is sensory in relation to its body and measures it with *this* yardstick. Through this fundamental experience of the body the human being thus comes to the law of non-contradiction and the basic law of conceptualisation.[272] By applying these we develop our intellect, and our concept capacity increases.

The great question now raises itself as to what degree human beings could come into being *merely* as sensory creatures. This is not easy to answer, but nonetheless worth thinking about with regard to what we could thereby conclude. It is clear that humans, limited as they are to the sensory world, see *themselves* as their highest conception, and must indeed also *be* their highest concept. A sensible conclusion would be that our limbs and sense-instruments undergo a development which enables us to recognise in a unity *inside* ourselves what experience showed us to be scattered *outside* ourselves. Everything thereby became clear to us, on the assumption that we could *explain ourselves*! If we wished to do so, we would have to use our senses to make ourselves 'our selves', i.e. our fundamental idea of ourselves. If we as humans realised

272 The classic law of non-contradiction is that any judgment which contradicts itself cannot be true.

that this had already been done by Mathematics, which is a reproduction of the law of non-contradiction, we would find that the entire explanation depended on our self-consciousness being an undeniable reality because it could not be contradicted without thereby being affirmed!

[273]If we could remain at this point, we would try to use Physics and Mathematics to appropriate all the powers of the world and through them change everything *into our own bodies*, i.e. swallow up everything; but we know that we as humans could not possibly remain where we were and set this play in motion without defying *Truth*, for by understanding our irrefutable self-consciousness, we understand Time and Space, both temporal and dependent and we also realise that we can no longer call ourselves *independent* without contradicting ourselves and that such a contradiction, were it to be activated, could only *destroy* us, and we would then realise that we are not entire 'of ourselves' but only of what we knew: what we did *not* know *must* be known by One *other*, since a dependent self-consciousness presupposes a higher self-consciousness in which all that it encompasses has its being and thus contains the cause of all that is temporal, so it must therefore be eternal, for only in Time can anything *be begun*.

But is not this whole question fundamentally *conceited*? Can sensory human beings ever have their self-consciousness *limited* to sensory ideas? I think not, if the question is of their *origin*, for on the one hand the Creator would have to deny *Himself* (which He cannot), by concealing Himself from his rational, self-conscious creation, and on the other hand human beings could not be conscious of themselves except in Truth, i.e. as depending on something *higher* than themselves. To our highest clear concept, namely our *body*, we therefore had to add a vague concept of our *Creator*, through whom we inhaled super-sensory life. We could not then but strive to *know* our Creator and see His image *in ourselves*,[274] as it is written: "Then the Lord God formed a man from the dust of the ground and breathed into his nostrils the breath of life, and the man became a living being."[275] We became conscious *in the Spirit*, in the creative Spirit of Truth, which hovered over the dust, which had animated all things into the Light, and which now quickened the Light itself in the human being in order to testify to the Truth and transfigure everything within Him.

The Spirit: Our Spiritual Conditions

Quite possibly a number of people would wish for a more *detailed* presentation of sensory human beings, but whoever feels the Spirit within themselves and feels that the Spirit truly *belongs* to the concept of the human being will have felt it onerous to

273 To demonstrate Grundtvig's sentence-structure, in each of the 5 volumes I have allowed a single sentence to follow his syntax precisely. The original Danish sentence here comprises 158 words; the English sentence 173.

274 Gen 1:27.

275 Gen 2:7.

represent humans as something they cannot be: self-conscious, tractable beings, lacking the Spirit for whose instrument and dwelling they were created. We are the animated dust of Paradise! We know that the Spirit of the Godhead is waving from the Tree of Life,[276] ready to flow in and impress all our ideas with the Great Seal which transforms us into stamped images of the power and glory of eternal Truth. We cannot know all this and yet not inhale the heavenly scent, as if we feared that the dust-image would crumble under the radiance that would purify and transfigure us! If we can finally prove to ourselves that humans could never begin their lives as mere sensory beings, but that their very first breath must have been a reception of the Spirit of Truth, then we need no longer hesitate in regarding human beings in their proper form: the Spirit as their Being, the Body as their Image, and the Soul as the linking consciousness of both in Truth. We had to take the Spirit with us *in every way*, for we stand for the Word and language, the living gate between two groves which run into a single one containing both.

One major question is without doubt whether *without* Spirit humans could acquire any *language*. Since I cannot answer this, I shall only ask what *kind* of language this should be? We cannot say much about this even with a free hand, yet nor is it to be derided; for we *can* say for sure that it must have been extremely unpoetical! It must have had its foundation in the form of things and their external attributes, and very likely it must have changed as we got to know things better from experience and to appreciate their use, for we cannot doubt that humans *named* them according to their relation to them. However, since *birds* can sing, there is no doubt that sensory human beings could also sing, and would have wanted to put *words* to their song. How successful they were I shall leave unspoken! I nonetheless understand why rational sensory human beings would express their poverty of words in *song*, and would feel that words which expressed the sensory properties of things were far from capable of expressing the wonderful tones that dance with the birds high over our heads. They would testify that there is something above us more glorious than everything under heaven, a land where song has its home and where songs are understood. We must admit that song is inexplicable except as an echo of the Creator's "Be!"[277] – an echo of the divine Word that reverberated throughout Creation. First it was imprisoned in ore and stone but then it stirred into being in the breast of bird and human, singing the Spirit into us through whose powerful action the Word for its transfiguration could be generated in our dust.

Whether or not these things will one day speak for themselves, we must consider what our spiritual relation in general actually *means*. As previously mentioned, it is

276 Gen 2:7.
277 Gen 1.

basically our consciousness of Spirit, our link to the eternal living Truth in the Spirit, or in other words, our original conscience. A necessary consequence of this was that human beings saw themselves and everything else as being *within* the Spirit, in the light of the Truth with themselves created in God's image[278] and all things God's work. Here we see the origin of poetry, for in its true figure it is nothing more than the imaginative contemplation of things in their created, spiritual relation, in their relation to the creating Truth. To what extent this contemplation can, so to speak, *generate* words and language of its own accord I do not know, but I assume this to be so. However, it is definitely what makes language become figurative, as well as making speech become song – as is demonstrated each time a verse issues from the inspired poet's lips. If we ask whether human beings *understand* their visions, their words, and their speech, it is like asking whether the body 'understands' the Spirit. The answer cannot be in doubt, any more than it can in this case. The former was impossible, yet the latter was certain! This is the origin of the pure understanding of historical *Learning*, for over time the body had to be transformed in order to grasp the Spirit as we gradually understood ourselves and became convinced of the truth of our visions. We expressed this knowledge in ever clearer words and ever greater activity until even the eyes of the body saw the glory of the Eternal and lowered their gaze over Time and Space in the unbounded sea of light.

To ask why this development had to happen gradually and had to be 'historical' is to ask why development should *ever* come about! Why should 'Time' and 'a world' *exist*? For the world is no more than a historical development over time that presumes a complexity which is hard to define, and a kind of knot which is hard to undo; nevertheless, we can more or less deduce it from taking a hard look at ourselves!

The Soul: Our Relation to Ourselves

As we have seen, the 'self' or soul is originally our integral consciousness of our *twofold* relation: our temporal relation, which the body expresses, and our divine relation which the Spirit attests. The former relation is as a king, the latter is as a servant, so that in their *union* the two constitute a vice-regency.[279] To implement this union and to embrace the twofold relation with gratitude and gradual comprehension in Love is undeniably *our basic law*. Any attempt to violate this law will cost us our crown! Obviously, we can be *tempted* to do so, for we can please ourselves in our royal position and thus be tempted to reject our servanthood and strive for *independence*! But we must regard our *apparent* independence in the world as mere appearance, and we

278 Gen 1:27.

279 i.e. subject to the King but master of one's own estate as granted by the King. See Allchin: 'The Holy Spirit in the Teaching of N.F.S. Grundtvig' in *Grundtvig Studier* 1998 p. 180.

must seek our reality in the union with our Saviour, realising that, separated from Him, we are nothing. Conversely, we can *accept* our dependence as *real* and our independence merely an *appearance*, for we are made in God's image yet find in ourselves an appearance of what seems to claim *independence* of God! However, if we do indeed *claim* our independence, then we lie and sin and fall again, and with us falls everything that we are endowed with, even if it does *not* sin, for the mendacious soul becomes entangled in its own consciousness: it crucifies its Spirit in the body, and it usurps its throne. As a result, Truth must inevitably *cut* the knot, dissolve the body, release the Spirit, and destroy the soul. It cannot but make the soul *feel* its nothingness, like an emptied consciousness that contains nothing except itself, or an evil will that curses itself. It is inconceivable how a development should come about whereby the soul is *saved* and *restored*; we can say no more than that it was a great and mighty wonder, for to human eyes it was an impossibility!

Here we come to the major question which in recent times has been passed over with the greatest irresponsibility, or treated as a triviality: Are we human beings *fallen* creatures? The question is not difficult to answer, yet if the answer is in the affirmative, it is terrible to contemplate. Should I then take great pains to *prove* the Fall of humankind? I think not, for if it is not demonstrable to every human being, if there is no *certain* evidence, then we are *not* fallen, then it is only me and a few other limbs that have fallen off humankind! And if we are *so* blind, then we cannot see how day by day we are gaining an ever-increasing *clarity*. In short, if anyone exists who is *not* going to die, then they are not *fallen*! And if there are any alive who from birth have *denied* their own selves and sought their reality and joy in God alone, then *they* are not fallen either! Indeed, I can promise them that if they do not fall, then nor shall they die!

Truth does not build up in order to tear down. It does not join together in order to put asunder what is true. What is *in Truth* can just as little be deprived of life as Truth itself! Anyone who is *in* Truth could at most give themselves over as a sacrifice to death, but they could not be bound by it. Such a wondrous person *can* be found in history, but He claimed precisely that human beings *were* fallen – and only through Him could be resurrected. Nor will I ever deny that I believe Him to be right, until I see another go and do as He did and not say the same thing.

However, it is not my purpose here to *wish* my faith on anyone, and I do not envy the choice of any who consider it better to die *without* hope than to believe in the wondrous resurrection. If they cannot demonstrate their power over death, then their fall is a proven fact, and if they claim to be, or to know, or to do something *entirely of their own accord*, then they are undeniably confirming their fall and generating their own shame.

Nevertheless, among ourselves no one has yet been so bold as to *deny* the Fall. Indeed, people have actually helped themselves by employing the *double* contradiction that we *are* fallen and yet we are continually falling *of our own accord*, and are continually restoring ourselves until we finally fall once and for all into the grave – where we remain buried! In short: nothing is anything and anything is nothing! It is therefore no use disputing with these goodly people, for whoever *contradicts* themselves cannot be convinced, and *contra negantem principia non est disputandum.*[280]

What I therefore shall now attempt is simply to portray our present human condition, as I know it from my own experience, and compare it with what I take to be our *original* condition. Then I shall let the experience of the human race down through History judge between the 18th century and myself.

We began with our physical conditions as being the original ones, but this time we shall begin with our spiritual conditions as being the *clearest* – and what we have seen will illuminate everything. I am well aware that there are not a few nowadays who doubt that they *have* a spirit, not to mention those who doubt that they have a *soul.* The mistake is easily made, for they confuse soul and spirit. Whoever doubts whether they are conscious of themselves or not, should either be made to laugh at their doubt or go to the madhouse to think about it! I am also well aware that it is difficult to *prove* to anyone that they actually *have* a spirit if they are not aware of it themselves, since it is only through our self-consciousness that we *have* anything. But I think it is possible to convince anyone who has a consciousness that their first forefathers[281] must have had a spirit, and that if they indeed have *no* spirit, then they are extremely deficient! However, instead of producing lengthy and superfluous evidence to this effect, I shall settle for stating what *I* understand by 'Spirit': namely, that it is a vital, powerful, and active concept that neither in itself, its power, nor its effect can be sensed but can only be experienced in self-consciousness. I claim it to be undeniable that the human will is such an *effect* of the Spirit.

We must all admit that the human will cannot be sensed, and we all learn that it has neither power nor ability from the fact that we can have a *powerless* will; that it is not moved by anything that can be *sensed* is obvious. For *nothing* that can be sensed can compel even the weakest will, if one is conscious of it. An *unconscious* will, i.e. a passion, can enthral us as it does an animal, but we must admit that it is not *human* and therefore, unlike the animal, does not produce an orderly but a *disorderly*, deranged emotion. If we survive this and come to ourselves again, we find again the *same* will, which cannot be altered except by a super-sensory power. Despite many people not knowing *what* they want in most regards, and despite their being unconscious of their

280 Lat. 'One cannot dispute with those who negate principles'.

281 i.e. Adam and Eve.

will, there is always one or other example where they *are* aware of it. Everyone can learn from their experience.

Above all there is one situation where things do become clear, namely when people ask themselves: Do you want the lie or the truth? Do you wish to be honest or dissemble? For here we are speaking of super-sensory ideas which presuppose a super-sensory imagination, a fundamental *will*-power. Unlike its offspring this is not entangled in sensory ideas and desires whereby it often seems as though the will is *derived* from them because it flows out *through* them! Everyone feels that they ought to be *aware* of this fundamental will-power as a super-sensory effect that can be united with power, but can also be exposed to it, in which case we merely call it a 'wish'. Moreover, in our human self-consciousness there is something that we quite rightly call 'conscience', something which could be called 'consciousness of the will'. This has the peculiarity that it is not only *aware* of the fundamental will but also how it ought to *function*. We may well say that many people *have* no conscience, but just as we know that this means they do not *care* about it, and in a sense have expelled it from their self-consciousness, so has Fichte[282] among others admirably demonstrated that no one has ever managed to actually *do* this. He observes that even the most unscrupulous villains know very well what their conscience demands of *others*, which would be impossible if they did not possess one themselves! If we now consider that conscience is undeniably an effect which we cannot *sense* and which we cannot ourselves *alter*, and if it is true that conscience challenges us both to *want* and to *do* the truth, then this can only be a consequence of the *Spirit* of Truth. This presupposes that there is a spiritual connection between us and Truth, and that there is in us a vital and powerful idea of Truth which calls forth a will that can express Truth in all human relations. If the Spirit of Truth therefore testifies that it *exists* in our conscience, then it must also be *our* fault if it does *not*, for otherwise Truth would be Falsehood. And if it testifies *through our consciousness*, then it must already *be* there every time our conscience makes its presence felt. Moreover, it must be there *as a friend*, since our true self-consciousness cannot be the enemy of Truth!

Thus, no one can ever say that their conscience *reproaches* them for having a body, for possessing reason, and for feeling their advantages over the animals, only that they do not regard or use these as the property of Truth, i.e. that they will behave as if they were *not* the custodians of Truth on earth. In our self-consciousness, conscience is the witness of either an existing or a lost link with Truth, a link both of Love and Spirit. If the link is lost, the conscience is guilty; if it exists, the conscience is clean. If the link is lost, it shows itself in our refusal or inability to do what we *should* do, and we can only

282 Johann Fichte (1762-1814) was a German philosopher and founder of the German idealism movement, whose work on self-consciousness has been influential.

have lost that link through another spiritual link to the spirit of *Falsehood*, through letting that work its will in us to *deny* Truth. The question is only whether or not that will was an unconscious passion or a conscious resolution; the natural consequence either way is that we fall into the hands of Falsehood. The first thing we then can do is to repent our sin – without being able to see what benefit that will give us!

There is no need to develop this any further, since anyone can see that it must inevitably lead to God's wonderful mercy and to the Christian faith. I shall only note that whoever ventures to claim that they have a *pure* conscience, is neither a fallen creature nor in need of mercy. On the other hand they must not deny that they possess the Spirit of Truth, for otherwise they betray themselves as liars! Furthermore, they must *prove* this by never deviating from the Truth either wilfully or unwilfully, and by being able to tell the Truth about all human spiritual relations and the nature of things! For if they deviate even a hairsbreadth, or speak a single word about spiritual matters which we can prove to be false, then they must accept that they are liars. I know of no one who has submitted to this test other than Jesus. I also believe that he has *passed* this test, for I have experienced that His word *is* Truth. In my view, whoever believes otherwise does so at their own expense; they cannot act as our teacher in spiritual matters unless with the Spirit and Power of Truth they can demonstrate their authorisation.

There is one more spiritual question that is not so *common* as the question of the will and the conscience but which might very well be so; it is too evident to be denied and concerns the nature of *Faith*. We do not need to *prove* that Faith neither reveals itself through the senses nor has its source in them. It must therefore be an effect of the *Spirit*. What is in dispute is whether it is accompanied by any *power*, since in its weakest form it often seems to be present, and yet powerless, like the will. Without denying that History is full of proof of the opposite, it is nevertheless indisputable that it *can* demonstrate its spiritual origin by defeating the senses and creating a *new* will-power, in other words it *can* be a vital force. Such a faith with *power* may take two forms, either faith in Truth or faith in Falsehood, i.e. superstition. The hallmark of true Faith is its unity with the conscience, while the effect of true living Faith is a holy and powerful will, which comes of its own accord and needs no further comment here.

We have now seen that it is the will and the conscience which make our spiritual relations undeniable. The fact that they are questionable in so many people and impotent in the majority is sufficient proof that the natural link to Truth has been lost. If we require any further proof that it has been broken, we shall find it unmistakably in the impression it has left on our human abilities and conditions. I say 'we' here deliberately, for it is only for those of us who are actually *aware* of History and who are participants in historical developments. There is a knot here that is difficult to untie – namely, the enormous differences between human children and the numerous peoples from one generation to the next, who, despite all progress, continue a life of animal senses above which neither faith nor thought, poetry nor language, art nor learning appears to raise them. At the same time there are certain areas of the globe where human life twinkles through all these images, like a star that has fallen to earth yet stares up at heaven and glimpses in all things a trace of its spiritual origins.

As we know, the attempt has been made to *cut* the knot by claiming that all people are born with the same aptitudes, and that it was only the soil, the sky, and Chance that separated the races without and within. Yet who does not see that this is taken out of the empty air? It solves nothing, and nothing can be learned from it except the self-appointed sages' rough ignorance about everything to do with God and humankind. What kind of answer is this other than another desperate order by which conceited sensuous reason is accustomed to rejecting every question it cannot answer, leaving everything to 'Nature' (which it knows nothing of) and fooling itself into believing that the problem is solved because it has got rid of it! We cannot deny that it is easy enough to appeal to what no one knows – to 'chance' or to 'Nature', but to explain what is *wonderful* by what is *unknown* appears to be no little a contradiction! It is worth noting that those who have no faith in God and Providence do have faith in the enigmas of Nature and Chance, and boast with a vengeance that they have banished superstition, promoted illumination, and liberated Reason, presumably with regard to the eternal laws of thought. Consequently, Reason is now allowed to *gainsay* both Truth and itself as much as it likes, in fact the madder the better, for the more freely it can then operate!

As we know, 'Chance' is our word for what we cannot explain as an unavoidable effect of known causes. It is clearly madness to claim that something has been explained by saying that it can *not* be explained! But we must also admit that for anyone who knows *every*thing, nothing happens by 'Chance'. If that were so, there would be effects without genuine *causes*, which is a gross contradiction. Now, imagine that no-one knew *every*thing! Then basically nothing would happen by *Chance*, i.e. be inexplicable. Everything would have had to come out of *nothing*, and yet no one would *know* that! Learning would have had to have come out of madness, i.e. the loss or denial of Learning. Anyone who claims this is guilty of self-contradiction! We are obliged to conclude that *some*one knows *every*thing, including the eternal cause of all things temporal, which that 'someone' either must *be*, or must embrace, as a living concept, i.e. as the eternal Truth that unites itself with God. So if we are not to give *God* the glory, we must shun 'Chance' like the plague! We must either pretend that we know everything down to the tiniest detail, or we will be next to the one that does! We must pretend that we really *are* God, or are walking around with the licence in our pocket, waiting for the special birthday that will validate it! In other words we must be like those natural philosophers who, when they are not in the unpleasant situation of being in dispute with Truth and gradually dying out, will doubtless themselves become gods in time.

Those good people who have only *one* bad 'chance' soon realise that this cannot be 'Chance' in the light of divine Learning. Neither the soil of the earth nor the air of the skies explains the matter. The alternative is to have the *planets* create the world's peoples exactly as they wish them to be from the very start: Sun-power and Earth-matter, Osiris and Isis,[283] Odin and Frigg,[284] and the powers of nature with their all their fractions and multiforms. Some will play walk-on parts, others will be chorus dancers, still others solo dancers, and finally a few of them will be heroes and demi-gods in the great world drama – which of course ends with a total catastrophe! Then the Spirit of the World, despite the fatal wound he suffered as Achilles,[285] will invade the Troy[286] of Truth and after a long wander with Odysseus[287] and his brothers-in-arms through all forms of the Eternal finally, make his appearance as a *deus ex machina*[288] for Penelope, sitting on her golden throne. Cold and prudish on the outside but burning and highly tractable on the inside, like a Norn[289] she has been weaving Odysseus' entire journey. She resembles the perfect whore, who makes herself precious for a while but when her time comes unites with inner lust and her beloved husband together with his mortal enemies in her whore's embrace. Naturally, he has to accept this magnanimously for harmony's sake, i.e. for the sake of domestic peace!

The memory is doubtless still fresh as to what I have previously called this kind of poetic drama, and I hereby repeat my incontrovertible opinion that it is the Devil's work! Here I shall settle for a single engaging comparison, borrowed from the good people themselves, to show what happens to God, Truth, and History when one attempts to explain intellectually the conditions of such peoples on the basis of their soil, their air, and the 'Chance' that comes their way. In other words, what happens when we try to grab the Spirit out of the air because the sun's rays are shining through it straight into our eyes! For then, like the ancient heathens, we must seek to explain humans and their world through the sun and the planets; then we must seek to serve

283 In Egyptian mythology Osiris is god of the afterlife and regeneration. He is married to his sister Isis, goddess of health, marriage, and wisdom.

284 In Nordic mythology Odin is among the leading gods and is associated among others with victory in battle, royal and runic power, and wisdom. He is married to Frigg, goddess of foreknowledge and wisdom.

285 In Greek mythology, Achilles is the greatest of all Greek warriors in the Trojan War. He is the central character in Homer's *Iliad*, just as Odysseus is in Homers' *Odyssey* (both from the 8th cent. BCE).

286 Troy (aka Ilium, present-day Hisarlik in Turkey) is the site of the Trojan War immortalised in Homer's *Iliad*.

287 Homer's *Odyssey* tells the story of Odysseus' return from the Trojan War to his home on Ithaca, where he is reunited with his wife Penelope, who in his absence has been plagued by suitors claiming his death and their right to marry her.

288 *Deus ex machina*. Lat. lit. "God from the machine" – a god introduced by means of a crane in ancient Greek and Roman drama to decide the final outcome. E.g. in *Philoctetes* (409 BCE) by Sophocles (496-06 BCE), the play appears to end with Neoptolemus consenting to take the wounded Philoctetes back from Troy to an angry reception in Greece, but as they are leaving, Heracles (a deity) appears above them and tells Philoctetes that if he goes to Troy, he will be cured and the Greeks will win. So they return to Troy – and the Greeks win!

289 In Nordic mythology the Norns are the goddesses of human and divine destiny.

the heavenly bodies instead of their Lord; then we must seek to make Truth a Fool and Falsehood the Truth.

However, our purpose here was to see if we could find traces of Truth among the peoples without doubting that they exist in places where we cannot find such traces. Let us note only one thing when discussing the soil of the earth and the air of the skies: that the same internal difference between the most animalistic and the most spiritual of peoples also exists between the individual members of the most spiritual people we can name! In my view, that ought to be enough to upset the castle in the air with which these natural philosophers seek to protect themselves from heaven! However, such comments are useless against their 'dynamics of Nature' with their 'magnetic stones'; together with their inverted self-consciousness this must be strangled at birth. If it manages to escape with its life, then it has made its point, but that is all it has achieved; for it will never win in eternity so long as Truth lasts for ever.

Actually, I gladly accept the great difference between peoples and individuals for what it is, a hitherto unsolved, but not necessarily insoluble, mystery. I have never doubted that all members of the human race living on earth are of one and the same blood, and I can also see *where* the knot throughout History will be loosened, namely in the dissolving of the bonds that link parents and children. These bonds are visible, but I have no wish to untie them; nor would I, even if I could, for they are the tender spot of our race and would barely survive examination. They may be almost outdated, but they have not yet expired. It is enough to note that no people ever existed who were devoid of will and conscience, nor any whose will was both pure and powerful and whose conscience testified for them that they were in loving community with Truth. This is evidence enough that they all belong to the human race, raised in Spirit but fallen into Sin, and this is the pattern everywhere that the Gospel is preached. As for Christians, I shall further note that just as the Word assures us of the unity and continued cohesion of the human race, so will Christians also understand that the peoples who with a muddy will and a dull conscience have abandoned all traces of Spirit-life have only a sensual language and sensual concepts left; these, more like animals can only regenerate and not develop. They are incapable of receiving the only means of spiritual rehabilitation, namely the Word,[290] before it is so fused with the nature of more spiritual peoples that it can be depicted in a sensual language and comprehended by a sensual understanding without losing its truth and power; clearly, the time for this is fast approaching – on the assumption that we are indeed Christians!

Nonetheless, I see the snake, and I know the peoples who seek to inculcate into the wild and tame alike a sensualised Christianity as a 'Gospel of Nature'. Thus, in order not to include our civilised society by mistake, I must add the following. In my

290 Jn 1:1-18.

opinion, as soon as 'will' and 'conscience' – two concepts of spiritual origin that are inseparably linked to sensual self-consciousness – are clarified for us, we can refer all truth to them, like power to effect. For they are then qualified to convert even the coldest, dimmest heathens, if they are so willing. For this is a practical propensity of Christianity, one which has vaunted so much, understood so little, and demonstrated even less.

I shall not pursue this further here; but the inseparability of conscience and self-consciousness is an important matter! And since I can present it with greater clarity than in the above, I shall seize the opportunity to note that sensory self-consciousness, which is the immediately self-evident basic truth about human beings, must be regarded as a transfiguration of the arcane basic willpower that governs animals. This basic willpower is in turn an effect of the basic power that was set in action by the living Word of Truth. The basic Truth about human beings must therefore contain the basic will to sensual independence (individuality), which originally is the *will* of Truth. This in turn must enter into such a close association with the will that the spirit of Truth spontaneously ensured in human beings that the obligation to be both spiritually and corporally *in* Truth could never be forgotten in self-consciousness. If the soul in the basic Truth does not rebel, the will to be *in* the Truth cannot disappear either, for it only disappears when the will to be *in Falsehood* is admitted into the self-consciousness – and then we are irremediably lost.

Thus, so long as this deadly sin is not committed, the soul has not denied Truth! For in the soul's innermost being there is still a trace of the will to be *in* Truth, even if the will to tell a lie is in control. Of course, conscience, our witness to guilt, never disappears. In every person we shall therefore find the feeling that truth, will, and conscience should be linked into one, so that if we fundamentally have the *will* to truth, and we have the *will* to clarity, then we can make these concepts absolutely obvious – on this all Christianity builds. I shall leave aside to what degree there are peoples who, as in the days of Christ and the Apostles,[291] need to see signs and wondrous deeds before they can wake up and open their eyes. But observing the missions of recent times, especially the Greenland mission in the days of Egede,[292] we would be likely to believe what is in no way improbable: it is clear that it does not help much to send bibles to those who can neither read nor understand them.

After this digression – which dissatisfied readers can skip – we return to the traces of the Spirit that are found in certain peoples and in individuals among them, traces which in every regard we must call 'historical'. They can assuredly be expressed in the

291 Acts 2:22.

292 Hans Egede (1686-1758) was a pastor whose missionary efforts in Greenland led him to be called the 'Apostle of Greenland'. He was the first Bishop of Greenland and also founded the capital city, Nuuk.

three words: Poetry, Art, and Learning. These in turn are equally impressed in the basic human concepts: imagination, feeling, and the intellect. We can also separate them into language, state, and literature, which correspond to the former, but are further linked by common forms and instruments. A broad field opens up here for deep observations – which normally is offered only cursory attention. Nor on this occasion can we continue *our* journey, which is already a lengthy one. Whatever it has done to the reader it has taken the stuffing out of me! I feel like Jean Paul[293] in Levana and would like to take a chapter as respite here. We find ourselves on the border of the precincts of Poetry, where at present there is a stormy blast. It is doubly tempting to dwell here a while, but I look at the hour-glass and see that that is not possible. I shall therefore be brief with the matters that are to be treated separately. If the worst comes to the worst, the reader will doubtless allow me a breathing-space in the following.

I said before that the spiritual traces we mentioned presuppose an *impression* upon us, and that is undoubtedly the case, since we are neither of our own making nor of our own volition. We are *created* beings, and therefore all activity *on* us and all works *by* us presuppose an *effect* upon our component parts. This includes all *spiritual* activity on us and all *spiritual* works by us that are the impression of the Spirit on our body and consciousness. Sensory activity presupposes a sensory impression, and spiritual activity a spiritual impression. All that is presupposed of us is that we have the capability to *receive* this 'impression'. Again this is neither of our own doing nor of our own volition, but it does presuppose a readiness to *be* impressed. In other, irrefutable, words: in order to be 'something in ourselves', we must be conscious *from the very first*; for if we only become conscious *in the course of time*, then we would be 'nothing *in* ourselves'; we would be no more than an *image* which the eternal self-consciousness has created of its own accord.

It follows from this that our fundamental human activity is a *passive* one, a reception of impressions which we call a 'sensing'. Such a 'sensing' sets our sensual life in motion and develops along the path mentioned above. Through this 'sensing' we come to a specific subjective feeling and sensation whereby what belongs to the body is truly united with it. The same is true of our spiritual life. The fundamental sensing of the Spirit, which is coincidental with our self-consciousness, is our will and our conscience. These are like our hearing, which alerts us to sound. Our 'sensing' of something is like our intake of breath, or our sense of smell, sight, and touch, and what we call this 'sensing' to *be*: that is, the idea that this is what it covers. Thus 'taste' covers 'tasting'; it is one with eating and drinking, and in agreement with the whole body.

This is where it becomes clear to us what is meant by the historical *development* of

293 Jean Paul, pseudonym for Johann Paul Richter (1763-1825), German author of *Levana or Pedagogy (Levana oder Erziehungslehre,* 1807).

human beings, namely, the development of the soul towards spiritual consciousness of itself in Truth and the body's gradual acceptance of this. It is a gradual transfiguration of the sensual in Truth as its image, as true beauty. Here on earth we cannot grasp why, with regard to the sensual, there should be more than *one* man, why it was "not good for the man to be alone".[294] But we can grasp it in our understanding of *Love*, and we can feel it when the sensual development which takes place in the individual is found spiritually in our families and down the generations. They must therefore have an inner link to one another, and spiritually they must constitute 'one human' over whom in the beginning there is a Father of humans, from whom we all derive, and in the end a Son of humankind, in whom we are all transfigured. Thus, we are not all transfigured in ourselves, but in *Truth*; for we are 'of' the eternal living Truth, and what is 'of' something else cannot be transfigured in itself but only by what is *within* it. Spiritually therefore, it must be possible for a subsequent generation to absorb the previous one into itself and to develop a new one.

This is not so strange to us, for the human race has reproduced itself with the same consciousness with which, for example, one writes a book. There can be no doubt that human beings wish to reproduce all their merits in their children; and we realise that in itself this is not impossible. What we cannot understand is that it can happen without our *knowledge*, just as it is impossible for us to understand that we exist without knowing that we *do*! On the other hand, we can grasp that just because we cannot understand its origin it would be madness to *deny* our existence. Indeed, we realise that in order to understand it we must *already* exist! We have never *not* been, but must have *always* been! Similarly, in order to self-consciously reproduce our self-consciousness we must be fully able to *grasp* this. We must therefore either *be* the eternal Truth ourselves, or we must be clearly conscious of ourselves as being *in* that Truth, of being one with it. If History is a reliable witness of human spiritual development – as in our own existence it is a witness *of* that existence – then both facts are equally undeniable. It is simple logic that in order to be as certain of one's own development as one is of one's existence, it must have *entered* our self-consciousness. In other words, we must be able to understand that we could not possibly be what we are *conscious* of being, unless such a development had taken place; we must be spiritually aware that we are children of our 'fore-parents', the previous generations.

However, if we are ever to come to an end with all this, then here again I must interrupt myself! I can do so without risk, since my previous studies have been occupied with demonstrating how indisputable our historical development has been and the obvious necessity of taking a breath in the spiritual world before we can see that it is only our sight which, through our feeling, can be developed into clear *concepts*. These

294 Gen 2:18.

form our true taste, which forces us to unite with the Truth. Setting aside whatever extra might be said here, let us as swiftly as possible take stock of our *spiritual* sight, its impressions on our feelings, and its development into concepts as the foundation of Poetry, Art, and Learning.

The eye is the instrument of sight and must be regarded as a mirror. In this mirror at a certain distance forms are reproduced with the aid of light; the soul's ability to *receive* these images we call 'sight'. On the other hand, the ability to gather and recall them and create similar images according to our impressions through the other senses is what we call 'imagination'. 'Sense' is our expression for the passive in us, and 'energy' for the active, so that the latter always presupposes the former. The sensory imagination presents to us things in their sensory form, and other states to the extent that we know them. But if the Spirit has made an impression on the imagination, we see things in a new light – more or less clearly and exactly in their *spiritual* relation. Only then does this capacity deserve the name of 'energy', for if we are to speak precisely, what is spiritually active we must call 'energy' and what is sensorily active 'power'. Since we cannot draw a sharp line around 'activity', and since it is impossible to change our usage of it by force, we shall retain the common expression and call what creates our conceptions the 'imagination', distinguishing between the sensory and the spiritual imagination as best we can.

Now we can better understand that our last genuine sensory conceptions are light, air, and sound, and that the transition happens *in ourselves* through our mixed conceptions that have a sensory origin but a spiritual stamp. This discloses itself in the fact that these conceptions only have a *figurative* form and appear under an *image* of the corresponding sensory object. We ourselves, i.e. our souls, cannot imagine ourselves except as images of our bodies, as their fundamental image (concept). We cannot imagine our senses except as images of their instruments, or imagine life except as an image of air, and words as an image of sound. Here we can clearly see how discomforting it is to crave pictorial images of God, which are the only things that we can have! He lies so deep in us that at our highest point and in our deepest significance we *ourselves* are a pictorial image of God, a work of divine poetry, God's spiritual creation. Our very call and duty is to seek God's image in us, to see in ourselves a living, pictorial image of God, and this insight is the only true human poetry.

We shall leave it to each person to expand on this, but here, for the sake of clarity, we shall note that these various impressions – the insight of our innermost being in sensory images – is the foundation of Poetry, formed as a series of images. Poetry itself, however, is the sight of the sensory objects as creations of the Spirit, as well as the sight of our own innermost being as an image of the *eternal* Truth. In this Truth the sensory finds its meaning and its transfiguration – seeing body, soul and spirit in unity, seeing what exists as the work of the Spirit, and seeing that what happens by way of spiritual consequence is also the work of the Spirit. This way of seeing can be confused when the spirit of Falsehood gains a footing in humankind, and for this reason it can just as well create a false as a true poetry. Indeed, it is clear that no poetry can be completely true unless the soul is in undisturbed unity with God and the Truth. Both history and daily experience also confirm from this side the human being's undeniable Fall.

Hands are our instruments for the sense of touch. When we see something that diverts the eye, we seek to reach out for it in order, given the circumstances, to link it to, or unite it with, ourselves. This wish for another *thing*, though often qualified, is a wish for a closer relation that we call an 'attraction', figuratively speaking, and the reaching out for it is what we call 'desire'.[295] It comes naturally from inside us, but it may be renounced from outside us. Both are expressions of our sense of touch, of feeling – the soul's sense of a certain connection between something external and something of its own.

What is true of immediate conceptions acquired through the eye is equally true of the indirect conceptions which the imagination creates from other impressions. The conceptions which the soul takes pleasure in, and reaches out for, are said to be 'taken to heart' and cherished; in other words, it imprints them upon itself and links itself to them. Obviously, the soul can only unite these sensory conceptions with its conception of the body, and the first conception it can associate with itself is the conception of itself. Since therefore 'Love' is our expression of a spiritual link that is a union, we should not really use the word to refer to our attraction to *sensory* things, but the compound cannot be dissolved. We must bear in mind that it only creates confusion to contradict common usage in such cases. The first trace of spiritual feeling in the soul is its feeling of self, but we cannot call this a love of its *conception* of itself, for since it only has a figurative conception of itself, its love of this is only a love of the body. All aspiration towards something at the *expense* of the body clearly shows that the soul has a feeling for itself as being *separate* from the body. So the feeling of 'self' must lie deeper than all the conceptions of which the soul is aware; it must be what gives our conception of our innermost being its spiritual stamp.

When we reflect, we shall also find that the feeling of 'self' cannot be other than the primal spiritual feeling that makes us 'human'; it enables us both to understand spiritual conceptions without sensory images and to love them, i.e. unite them with ourselves. In this feeling, which is a sense that our life is of a higher order and is related to the eternal, living Truth, both will and conscience have their foundation; for they are originally and fundamentally merely a confirmation of a true feeling of 'self' and

295 Grundtvig's Danish here has *Tilbøielighed* (inclination towards) for 'attraction' and *Begiærlighed* (passion towards) for 'desire'.

the resultant union between the soul and Truth in the Spirit. It follows from this that our feeling of self should be inseparably united with a love of Truth, that is, a love of the Spirit's conception of eternal living Truth. This was precisely what animated the soul to *feel* itself and what made it sensitive, made it an image of God's eternal self-consciousness, i.e. Truth. This love of Truth was to be the soul's will, and would be a conception of Truth – as the Father who would reveal himself in human beings by cultivating and transforming His image. We know that this has not *happened* with human beings; instead, what should only be the image under which we imagined our *true* father has become the ultimate object of natural feeling, namely our parents. Yet we see that love of our parents is a *spiritual feeling*, one that is not found among animals, and one which is found to a *lesser* degree, the less spiritual a people are.

Whether this love has any depth can be seen from whether it continues after the parents' death and extends to all our forefathers. For if it does, then it is truly spiritual and reaches beyond them to Truth itself as its true progenitor, being a *remembrance* of Truth. In the closest relation to this feeling is our love of our children, though we realise that in itself this is more sensual and inseparable from our feeling of self. Whether or not it is 'spiritual' is best seen in our *conjugal* love. If that is spiritual, then married people love their children *in* each other before they are actually seen, and love each other *in* their children even though they are dead. Wherever this spiritual feeling in an ascending and descending line is to be found, there we see an inner sense or embrace of spiritual conceptions which we call 'the heart'. That is why we say that whoever lacks such a feeling has no 'heart', or is 'heartless'. Yet we know that this heart – the open, tender heart, meaning the extended, embracing feeling of self – can also be corrupted, infested with lies, and yet in a sense still be 'spiritual', for it also gives us spiritually *false* conceptions; and then we call it 'the heart of a devil'! We find most often that wherever feeling is not true *historically*, it is more or less only sensual, so its highest point is a feeling of its 'honour', which we must call a sense of spiritual feeling of self. We can now see that spiritual Love is a *poetic* feeling which runs deeper than we can imagine; through this alone can we breathe life into our conceptions. It represents an embrace of divine conceptions and awakens a sense of God in eternal life. For it is an image of life's divine source, of God as love,[296] and the mother of our spiritual life within us, just as feeling is that of our sensory life.

Here again we must say that 'to love' is two different things. We can love eternal life as a *conception*, and indeed are compelled to do so when we feel its wondrous power moving our inner being and surrounding us with its heavenly radiance as far as the eye can see. This is the love that impresses the spiritual seal of eternity on our conceptions, so that our dust becomes light and wings its way over Time and Space, so that

296 1 Jn 4:8.

all conceptions melt together into the blessed feeling of eternal life. But what does all this *mean*? It means great, ineffable things, if only we love eternal life in *Truth* – and if only our sense of both this and of the same spiritual and figurative conceptions of it are precious enough for us to deny ourselves and subordinate all our sensual desires. Otherwise it means nothing but spiritual self-satisfaction if we fancy that we are our *own* masters, or overbearingly allow ourselves such spiritual pleasure; here too we must feel our fall.

The path of poetic feeling belongs to a separate study. Here we shall merely note that what has been enabled by means of the mind and Faith has allowed peoples and races both to receive spiritual conceptions and to endeavour to absorb them through the love of Truth. Only thus did Learning become possible.

Strictly speaking, to 'grasp' and to 'comprehend' are by no means one and the same thing. We can 'grasp' (i.e. take hold of) *externally* much that we cannot 'take in', much less 'embrace' and even less 'clasp' by hand. It is the same *internally*. We can only *grasp* a part of what we can *see* constitutes a whole, however small it may be. Yet still we say that we have understood how, through the part that touches our heart, we feel we have understood the *whole*. Nevertheless, we have only grasped the part that has clearly entered our self-consciousness. Thus neither externally nor internally can we embrace more than we ourselves actually *are*, even though we can conceive of something extending much further than is possible for us to have the *overall* view of. It follows from this that we may well be able to grasp the *concept* of 'eternal life' when we feel its effect, but we cannot embrace or comprehend it while we are on earth; we can only embrace its temporal image.

This brings us back to where we began, namely that we cannot conceive of anything greater than ourselves. If we are to hold all our concepts in our *self-consciousness*, then this is clearly an incontrovertible fact. As with our highest 'conception', our highest 'concept' is figurative, and is a *development* of 'conception'. It is our concept of ourselves as the figurative image of eternal Truth, or, in other words, of being created in God's image and according to His likeness. For God is Love, and Truth is His eternal image, which both conceives Him and is conceived *by* Him – as Christianity has taught us and as an incontrovertible truth.

It is as clear as sunlight that to understand something in the sensory sense is to realise its physical connection, its relation to our body. Equally, to understand something spiritually is to realise its relation to our mind, its connection to us as the image of Truth. Since it is certain that we cannot understand our physical body except through our mind, it is obvious that we cannot understand any physical body unless we have understood it spiritually. No creature can be understood in relation to itself, but only in relation to something higher. What we are said to understand in a sensory sense we must find transformed as our body, and only in our self-consciousness can our body be transformed. From this we can see that it is the wrong way round to try to begin by understanding external things before the internal, the further before the closer, the darker before the clearer. Nothing is as clear to us as our self-consciousness. If we cannot grasp that, then we cannot grasp *anything*: first our self-consciousness, then our own world, meaning our conceptions and feelings down through history, then our physical body, then the external things – that is the sequence.

Whether we are *able* to do so is the question! But if we let this run away from us, then obviously we are abandoning all true concepts of ourselves and our world. We can see elsewhere that all wise heads have felt this; here we must simply note that it does not follow that our gathering of knowledge and its organisation, purification, and deliberation is in any way superfluous; for as we are created, these are in part the necessary conditions for us to understand anything. This task, inasmuch as it arises from our desire to know the true nature of things, we call 'scholarly Learning'. With the power of our imagination and feeling we can simultaneously embrace all that is within us, both the seen and the unseen, just as we can see our whole image and touch our whole body surface and yet fail to understand it all with our intellect. It is as if we contained everything of ourselves in our *hand*, and we can only do that figuratively. Since in this case it is not just a matter of embracing, but of *seeing through*, things, it is clear that everything must be meticulously separated before we can reach an understanding. It is worth noting that unless we can grasp the whole in a single image, then we should let the pieces be, for they can only be comprehended in their inter-relation. To hope for anything else would be as foolish as trying to understand the individual works inside a clock without having the faintest idea of the clock as a totality, or feeling oneself with a hand that has no feeling in it!

Here we stand then – on the path of Learning. There are countless things we want to know about, but they can all be referred to two major branches: History and Nature, the spiritual and the sensory world. To the latter we belong in our body, which integrates and disintegrates, but to the former we belong in our soul, which cannot disintegrate; it belongs to the world of the Spirit and makes us who we are. If we had to know everything else before we could get to know our soul – even if it were possible to tread this path, which, as we have seen, it is not – then all past generations have left this world without knowing themselves! Then we too would follow them in ignorance, as succeeding generations would follow *us*, for even if we could measure the abyss and touch the stars, such a development could clearly never happen in the physical world in its own dust. Such a person would have had to have learned everything 'in part' piece by piece on *this* side of Time and Space and thus found their place.[297] On the *other* side of Time and Space – even if we were unsure whether by knowing ourselves

297 I Cor 13:12.

we are led to know everything else – it would be just as certain that we ourselves are the most important objects of our knowledge.

So, there should be no question whatsoever as to where we turn first – namely, to History, for we have *lived* through History, and that is where we can learn to *understand* ourselves. And yet, the past generations are *dead*, and they seem to have taken with them into the grave what it was that helped us develop! Or, if not into the grave, then into that wondrous, unknown land to which all souls wander and are seen no more. This is where we feel the value of the monuments that they have left us, of the ideas, feelings, and concepts that have left such a mark that they can pass their message on from generation to generation through the changing times.

If we turn our glance to History, it is obvious that it can be seen from two sides: a sensory one, in that it produces a multitude of incidents in Time and Space, and a spiritual one, in that it presupposes some kind of spiritual response, some kind of self-consciousness as its source. There must therefore be unity in its multiplicity and development in its consequence. Both viewpoints are united in the observation of *human beings* as the historical self-consciousness and the active agent. The contents of History then become a coherent series of manifestations through which the human mind develops towards a self-consciousness. Into this self-consciousness the mind endeavours to incorporate the body. The first phase must therefore consist of a practical *psychology*,[298] a depiction of the mind in its manifestations, in its stamping of the spiritual on the sensory. The second phase must be an experimental *physiology*, which depicts the effects of these manifestations – the transfiguration of the sensory into the spirit. The entirety then becomes an empirical aesthetic, depicting the unity of Truth and Beauty in human beings.

The first period of Time is rightly called 'the poetic period', i.e. the creative period, since Truth creates and forms what is beautiful in its own image. This spiritually animated image (the human being) becomes aware of itself as such by imitating Creation and depicting itself in the external world. The second period of Time must be termed 'the philosophical period', for then humans *reflect* on themselves and their life's work; they countenance the Truth, and accept all the images within themselves. This *whole* period must be called 'historical', since it is in reality a matter of to what extent and in what way our mind and body, and truth and beauty belong together. In answering this question we become both 'cosmo-logical', i.e. we recognise life's conditions, and, symbolically 'theo-logical', since the transfigured human being demonstrates symbolically what God truly must *be*.

At first glance History does not seem to match up to this great yet justified expectation – indeed, unpardonable *demand*! This is undeniably disagreeable, for it proves

298 Grundtvig's Danish word is *Psychologie* in its original Greek usage, meaning 'study of the psyche'.

that there must have come dirt into the eye and Falsehood into the world. Otherwise we would not – like the fool who only sees the half-finished work – grumble that the half is not the whole. We would see the half-finished as showing good progress and expressing nothing but the Truth; in other words, it shows that we, humankind, are fallen. But just as on the one hand we can grasp that God would not be God if His creatures could circumscribe Him and with their Fall disturb His plan, so is it certain on the other hand that if humans have come so far that they can see themselves in their proper light, History cannot but show that it happened as we said above: namely, that the first phase is truly finished. Even so, this must indubitably have happened in a mysterious, supernatural way. For, as we ourselves act – and as we can see from History how previous generations have acted – if we confuse Truth and Falsehood, we do not learn to *separate* them and compose ourselves within this distinction. It can be proved to any who seek to hear and use Reason that in the course of time there must have been a supernatural revelation of Truth, different from the one that happened when Truth created human beings in His image.[299] This must be the revelation which through the power of Faith has *led* us to Truth. What has also been an object of Faith has historically proved itself to be a revelation of Truth. It must therefore be *believed*, even if it is not *comprehended*, by all those who love Truth and wish us to reach a perception of it. This in brief is the great and irrefutable historical evidence of the Truth of Christianity. When it is made enlightening for all, it will be undeniable – as it truly is for every thinking brain which has a general knowledge of History.

Thus there is absolutely no doubt that within a very short time in the academic world Christianity will be declared the undeniable Truth and the only sure and reliable guide to true Learning. Yet whoever regards such an insight to be a saving *faith* is fooled; it helps those who believe in reaching their goal, but it offers no *living* faith and does not lead to eternal life! It only arouses the *desire* for it by pointing to its image, and it shows the magnificence of Faith by revealing its power to the eye. In contrast, *living* faith is the loving, powerful *effect* of faith on the heart and must be as preternatural as Truth becoming flesh in the fullness of time.[300] It is precisely an adoption of Him *as He came*, and the condition for this is an inner feeling of the Fall and the desire for restoration. This is a matter of conscience, for it has to do with the will, for which Truth and Falsehood are good and evil. To this must we ever return if we possess a genuine Love of Truth and humankind. For, as we know, Love is the life of the will, and, separated from this, the concept is powerless, empty, and dead in a lifeless shadow.

On this point we must assume as a foregone conclusion that Christianity is *abso-*

299 Gen 1:27.
300 Jn 1:14.

lutely true, and that if we regard History in this light we shall find, even *before* Christ, recognisable traces of the path that was shown to human beings – who turned out to be only errant wanderers. Except for a special few they were partly blind, and partly lost. They wandered on the leash of Truth and consoled themselves in the darkness with glimpses of a glory in the distance, full of promise. Among these few, and in the fullness of time, Truth descended bodily.[301] It lit a light in the darkness which cast its radiance back to the *beginning* of the world and shone its rays to the very *end* of the world. We can therefore see, also among the heathens, the time of spiritual visions and their images. But these visions are confusing and often quite false, while the images are easily mistaken and often wrong. We see that instead of it developing, our basic *language* is split into every corner of the world. After acquiring the memory of previous generations and preserving it in writing for posterity, and after depicting the preternatural in bronze and stone, in bone and colour – in other words in traces of the Spirit's impression on the sensory – we come to the Age of Feeling, with its heroic deeds and the desire to *unite* the visions with song and language in verse; this is the Middle Age of humankind.

However, the language cannot embrace the vision or melt into song; the deeds are bloody; the chronicle is cold and uncertain, and its depiction is in the service of idols. Lastly, we see an Age of Concepts, when the soul endeavours to gather and transfigure all its images and to cast out everything that Reason cannot accept or unite with its consciousness. But this consciousness is almost exclusively physical, whereas Reason is sensory; the spiritual is rejected, the sensory deified, and the human being's goal appears totally mistaken. Only in a corner where Truth has symbolically raised a tent among the children of humankind[302] are the visions *part of the Truth*, and only there are they pursued throughout History and impressed on the heart. Only there does the vision fuse together with song and language in a psalm, and only there does the soul develop into spiritual consciousness. Only there is it revealed, transfigured in Truth. As we can imagine, this all happens in a mysterious, preternatural way, so it is only in a spiritual form that the race thereby reaches its goal in the fullness of time – only when all hope seems to have vanished, when the spirit is denied, and when the body is deified in the world by blind, sensory Reason. Christ rose from the grave with a transfigured, spiritual body,[303] whereas Tiberius, as though possessed, had his body deified indecently![304]

---

301 Gal 4:4.

302 2 Cor 5:1-10.

303 1 Cor 15:44-46.

304 Tiberius Claudius Nero (42 BCE – 37 CE), Emperor of Rome from 14 CE, also during the crucifixion of Jesus, to whom he is here compared. However, all the evidence points to Tiberius being one of the few emperors who did *not* wish to be deified after his death. The Senate also refused to vote him divine honours.

Then began a new era in which the eyes of the heathens were to be opened to distinguish between Truth and Falsehood, and according to their hearts' desires, acquire and adopt in their consciousness either Christ or Tiberius, Truth or Falsehood. Time moved on with great vicissitudes of fortune; the ancient days repeated themselves under transformed, more spiritual, forms. Truth and Falsehood were in open conflict over the Word and the Sceptre in the spiritual world. Often the tongue seemed torn out of the mouth of Truth, and the Sceptre twisted out of His right hand. But always the page was turned again, and only with a struggle was the Word imprinted ever deeper into the Church's heart - to burst out ever more clearly on its tongue. The Sceptre only *seemed* to be broken when it was wrapped and hidden in the hand to find its final form and to be extended in the Cross with the Sceptre and the Sword beside it - as a sparkling Sword and a flowering Sceptre - to Falsehood's horror and the triumphant shout of the believers. In more recent days we have seen the Word as never before, chained to Falsehood's triumphal chariot, its wheels arrogantly rolling over the cross and the earthly figure of the Sceptre.

But now we stand at a turning-point, the times are changing. Believing eyes are flashing with joy at the glimpses from on high, the Word is breaking out in song from the melting hearts which feel in the spirit that its Jubilee is near. The Song of Praise is on the tongue and who will stop it from breaking out into holy tones? Who will go to war to raise a barrier against the almighty, living Truth? Who will deride the voice from on high shouting: "Make peace, make an everlasting covenant with me! I am the Truth, the Way, and the Life."[305] Who would be willing? Who would dare? God be praised, not I! And I dare to hope, not the people who arose with me from the heart and loins of pious, Christian, truth-loving Danes!!![306]

305 Jn 14:6.

306 Grundtvig is otherwise reticent to use exclamation marks, so the three added here are noteworthy.

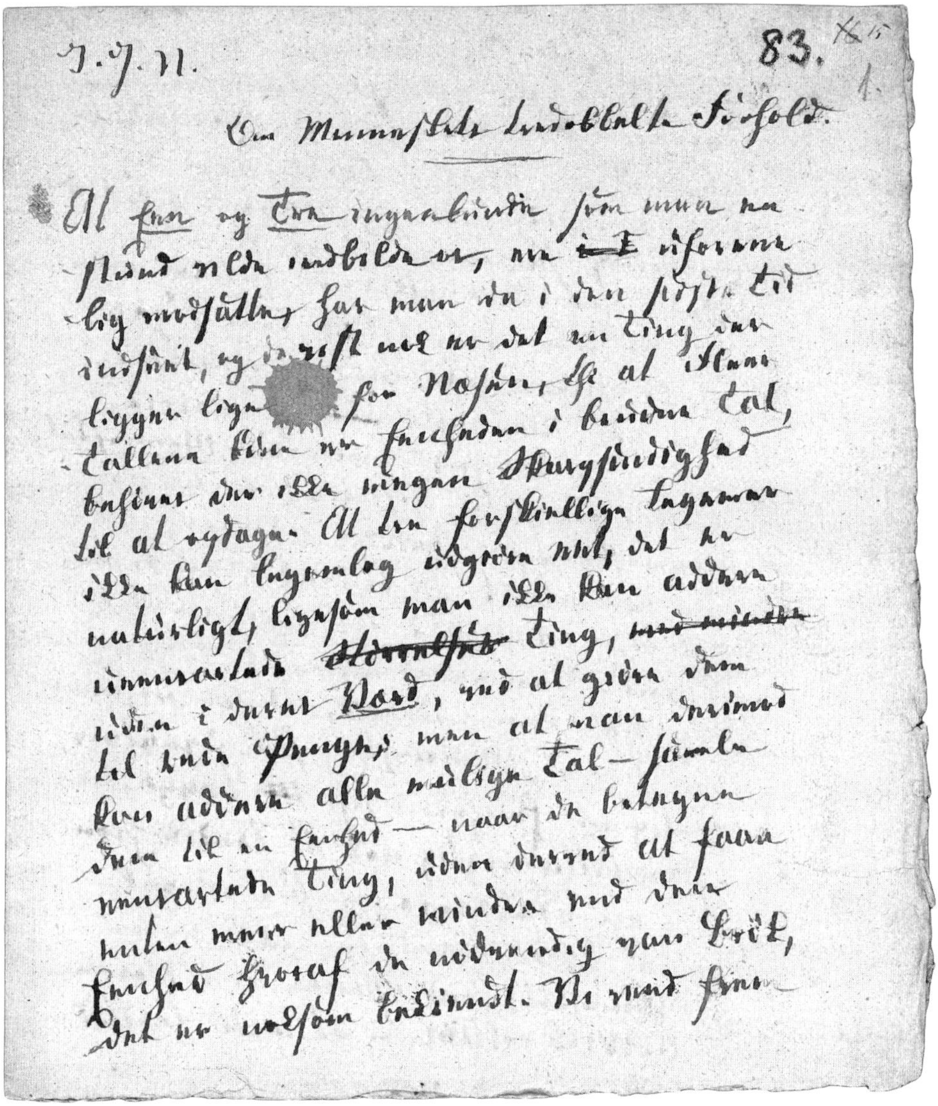
I. J. N.
83.
Om Menneskets Tredobbelte Forhold.

3. Draft manuscript for *On Human Beings in the World* 1814-15

In the Grundtvig archives is a draft (Fasc. no. 159) entitled 'On the Human Being's Threefold Relation' (*Om Menneskets Tredobbelte Forhold*), i.e. to Time, Space, and Truth. It is undated and was not part of the published work; experts place it around 1814-15. In the top left-hand corner are the letters I. J. N., which stand for "In Jesus' Name" (*I Jesu Navn*), a dedication that Grundtvig used to signify that the work was to the glory of God and not himself. The handwriting is bold and regular, and almost entirely *un*intelligible to present-day Danes. The philologists behind the digitalisation of Grundtvig's published works (2010-30) are familiar with such scripts and study them for variants on the published works.

2. On Truth, Greatness, and Beauty (1817)

Introduction by Kim Arne Pedersen

This study, from the third volume of *Danne-Virke* (1817), lies beyond the border between the general observations and expositions of specific sides of human life that characterise the first two volumes. It builds a bridge between the major study, *On Human Beings in the World* in volume 2 and *On Revelation, Art, and Learning* in volume 3. The triads in these titles correspond to each other, even though the order differs:

Greatness and Revelation correspond to Imagination
Beauty and Art correspond to Feeling
Truth and Knowledge correspond to Intellect/Reason

In Grundtvig's philosophy these three human capacities are basic instruments for human cognition. It is through them that we can say we *know* things. From his anthropological starting-point in *On Human Beings in the World* Grundtvig pursues his philosophical pile-driving in *On Truth, Greatness, and Beauty* in an effort to unite logic and ontology with "the historical life of humankind" (p. 177). This means that the abstract expositions in his study constantly lead on to explanations of how the concepts have revealed themselves in human life *in the past*. With *On Revelation, Art, and Learning* as an intermediate station, the same approach is taken in *On the Church, the State, and the School*, Grundtvig's last major study in *Danne-Virke* volume 4.

In the process of demonstrating his own independent philosophical thinking in *On Truth, Greatness, and Beauty*, Grundtvig criticises other contemporary philosophers. Without mentioning names he clearly distances himself from Schelling's attempt to include 'evil' in the divine plan whereby God realises himself.[307] Grundtvig regards this as an attempt to incorporate Falsehood into Truth (p. 113). However, it is first and foremost Herder's philosophy of history and the ideas of Kant that attract his attention. He is aware of Herder's criticism of Kant,[308] but he nevertheless rejects what he regards as Herder's relativisation of Truth, Greatness, and Beauty by virtue of our human dependence on changing historical contexts. Grundtvig regards this as a parallel misconception to Kant's transcendental philosophy – as being the supplanting of God by humankind as the basis of Knowledge. Kant, however, is Grundtvig's main target, and the *Critique of Pure Reason* (1781) is the only philosophical work that he mentions in *On*

307 *Philosophical Inquiries into the Nature of Human Freedom (Über das Wesen der menschlichen Freiheit, 1809).*
308 In works such as *A Metacritique of the Critique of Pure Reason* (*Eine Metakritik zur Kritik der reinen Vernunft*, 1799), *Metacritique of Judgement* (*Metakritik zur Urteilskraft*, 1799) and *Calligone* (*Kalligone*, 1800).

Truth, Greatness, and Beauty. In distancing himself from the 'wise men' of the times who argue that "Truth has no hallmark, Greatness no yardstick, and Beauty no foundation!", Grundtvig also refers to Kant's two other major works.[309] Taken together Kant's three critiques thematise Knowledge, Morality, and Aesthetics – to which Grundtvig responds with his alternative triad, Truth, Greatness, and Beauty, i.e. the solid, the absolute, and the everlasting. He argues that they are to be found not in our limited human imagination but in a *transcendent reality*, prior to, and independent of, the transcendental 'I'. Grundtvig contrasts "our forefathers' simple faith in the Bible" with "the oak-tree of what *they* (the 'wise men') call 'dogmatism', but what is in fact the tree of Certainty and Faith" (p. 112), i.e. the pre-critical metaphysic. Faith and Reason are not opposites, but *support each other*!

Christian Wolff (1679-1754) constructed the framework for the debate on the proof of God's existence outside scriptural or natural revelation – known as 'onto-theology'. Grundtvig accepted such proof but argued that, nevertheless, Revelation is an irrefutable basis for Knowledge. Coupling his trinitarian theology to his trichotomic anthropology, Grundtvig's original thinking differs widely from Wolff. Truth and Being *presume each other*, he asserts. Truth cannot be limited; it comprises an accord of Knowledge with the transcendental prerequisites of human consciousness. The basis for the concept of 'Truth' is therefore God, and not the human awareness of God. In arguing his case Grundtvig states that Truth is "an undeniable affirmation, which in turn undeniably assumes what it expresses. It is an eternal *Being*, which affirms itself and expresses its self-consciousness. In other words it is a living, self-conscious, trinitarian God" (p. 113).

God's trinitarian being is the foundation not only of Truth, but also of Greatness and Beauty. In his elucidation of this concept of Truth, Grundtvig alludes partly to Kant's *Critique of Practical Reason*, and partly to his *Critique of Judgement*. There is much to suggest that his references do not draw on his own reading but on Herder's criticism of Kant, but there are a number of traces of reference to Kant in Grundtvig's study.

At the end of each section of *On Truth, Greatness, and Beauty* Grundtvig alludes to Kant's categorical imperative (from *Critique of Pure Reason*), i.e. Kant's concept that the maxim for human actions should be: "Act only according to the maxim whereby you can, at the same time, will that it should become a universal law". At the end of the section on Truth, for instance, Grundtvig underlines that revealed Truth has been "the great moral principle for past generations" (p. 117), breaking thereby with Kant's distinction between theoretical and practical philosophy. Grundtvig applies the same synthesising principle in the section on Greatness. Here we can trace his response to Kant's moral philosophy, as found in paragraphs 25-26 of *Critique of Judgement*. These deal with one of the core concepts of aestheticism – the sublime (*das Erhabene*). The link to Kant's moral philosophy comes from his idea that Greatness in Nature is an image of the Greatness of humankind as a moral subject, and thus of our citizen status in the spiritual world, but Kant's distinction between the different forms of Greatness fades in Grundtvig's

309 *Critique of Practical Reason* (*Kritik der praktischen Vernunft*, 1788) and *Critique of Judgement* (*Kritik zur Urteilskraft*, 1790).

study: Here he builds on his discussion of Greatness in the physical world as outlined in the above-mentioned paragraphs in *Critique of Judgement*. However, when Grundtvig moves from physical-quantitative Greatness to moral Greatness, the approach is deliberate, for he is working his way towards a philosophy of the human condition that encompasses both morality and aesthetics. The sensory and the transcendental are held together as image and reality respectively. In the section on Beauty, Grundtvig speaks of the relation between man, woman, and child in marriage as a transition "from the natural to the historical" beauty (p. 126), his intention being to link the two worlds, the spiritual and the material, and to show that the latter is an image of the former, a symbol which to a certain degree participates in the reality which it reflects.

Who does not feel that in these three words [Truth, Greatness, and Beauty] we have named everything that *harmonises* with the human mind – everything that has ever been desired, praised, and adored, everything of any consequence that can be owned and comprehended? Who can know the first thing about History without acknowledging that however different our conceptions of these three words may be, they nevertheless express what we have all desired and counted ourselves fortunate to possess? Have we not all considered ourselves enlivened and enriched by observing and admiring what we considered great and beautiful? And even if we did not *love* Truth, we would want its *possession* to be genuine, unfailing, and enduring!

When we ask what Greatness, Beauty, and Truth actually *are*, where they can be *found*, and how they can be *generated* and *sustained*, we are asking a question which encompasses everything and resonates throughout the entire human race. Sages have pondered it down the ages, while others, unaware even of the question, have sought to solve it all their lives. If the question is futile, then nothing is *unconditionally* true, great, or beautiful, and all things depend on arbitrary illumination and an arbitrary connection; meaning that everything under the sun and all that can be thought is mere vanity. It is all a vain game which no one plays, a shadow with no corresponding body, all an impossibility.

Seeing and saying such things, we immediately realise that this cannot possibly be true! It is simply evidence of an indifference and a lethargy that can only astonish and appal every living soul. Without being aware of it, the children of humankind are denying what they themselves prove and confirm with every word they speak, while the sages to whom they listen declare only what brings comfort in the madhouse! Indeed, these sages say that *all* things are in fact madness and a contradiction in terms: Truth has no hallmark, Greatness no yardstick, and Beauty no foundation. We may *feel* the love of Truth spark in our breast, we may *light up* at the sight of past Greatness, and we may be inwardly *touched* by a love of what we cannot even name; but when we pensively turn to the sages of our day to make sense of it all, we fear, we blench, and we shudder to think that this is the sum of their ice-cold, comfortless wisdom. We must *settle* for this muddle, they say, and above all we must never believe that what is solid, absolute, and everlasting exists anywhere else but *in our own imagination*! In other words, it does not actually *exist* out there. In what is limited and replaceable, in what appears and disappears (like ourselves), there cannot possibly *exist* anything that is immutable, absolute, and everlasting, only its image and its shadow – or so they say.

Is there anyone alive who does not realise that with the disappearance of our forefathers' simple faith in the Bible – and with Kant[310] and Herder[311] in full disharmony agreeing to defy the principle of contradiction and make it a feat of Reason to undermine themselves – we have cut down the oak-tree of what *they* call 'dogmatism'? But it is in fact the tree of Certainty and Faith! From their time onwards, Contradiction, under varying names and shapes, has arrogated to itself the chair of Wisdom and Truth, and can only lull people into a magnetic sleep, unless the love of Truth – a living, deep, and powerful Truth – can reawaken them and blow away the delusion that conceals this empty, bottomless abyss from mortal eyes. In their sleep, such people will dream of *light*, even as an Egyptian darkness that the hands can feel surrounds and envelops them! I do not ask: 'Who does not know...?' because I am fully aware that hardly *anyone* will know that this *is* the case. I ask it because it is indisputable that if one does *not* know it, then all knowledge must have been forgotten. People must have lost their reason when a case is proven and yet they reject the proof!

I do not raise this matter because I have any reasonable hope of persuading anyone to take it seriously. The deaf cannot hear any more than ice can be ignited. I have spoken to deaf ears for so long and cast the flames of my heart on so much ice that it is only because I have an unreasonable hope in Him who can make the impossible *possible* for humankind and who can quicken the dead that I leave Truth itself, the owner of the Word, to govern and determine the impact and effect of that Word.

On Truth

If we wish to know how to *complicate* a discussion of Truth and how to use sophistry to strangle true Knowledge at birth, we should read Kant's famous book, which is

310 Immanuel Kant (1724-1804) was a German philosopher best known for his 'critical philosophy', which argued that human beings are 'autonomous', and his duty-based ethics, which meant, in consequence of this autonomy, that it is one's duty to follow the formal moral principle common to all people, the so-called 'categorical imperative'.

311 Johann Gottfried von Herder (1744-1803) was a German philosopher, theologian, poet, and literary critic. He is associated with the Enlightenment, with *Sturm und Drang*, and with Weimar Classicism. His writings were wide-ranging and influential on Grundtvig – in the fields of history of philosophy, language philosophy, aesthetics, metaphysics, biblical criticism, dogmatics, and homiletics.

without doubt the most caustic criticism of Pure Reason ever written.[312] If we wish to see a refutation of the major fallacies which this and other philosophical books of our time have spread, then we should seek to *reject* the contradictions I have pointed out so far.[313] These I shall present more forcefully in what follows; for all fallacy that is dumb must be seen as dead and impotent, whereas there is time enough to answer any objections to Truth, when they are made.

Wherever Consciousness[314] expresses itself, it is irrefutable. *In* this irrefutability we conceive eternal, unconditional *Truth*. For eternal Truth is an undeniable *affirmation*, which in turn undeniably assumes what it expresses. It is an eternal *Being*, which affirms itself and expresses its self-consciousness. In other words, it is a living, self-conscious, trinitarian God. There can be no question that eternal Truth *exists*, nor what it comprises, for it is indisputably the *sum* of Eternal Life. The question here must be whether *temporal* Truth exists, and whether *Falsehood* exists too. Here lies an opportunity to practise one's sophistry on Time, Space and Falsehood, for the only undeniable thing about these subjects is that no Falsehood can be *of* Truth, or *in* Truth. If Falsehood exists, then so do Time and Space, since Truth must of necessity curtail and destroy Falsehood, which is a self-contradiction that encapsulates the denial of Truth. No one can deny eternal Truth without branding themselves a liar, but anyone can *pretend* to do so, if they dare, and if they can avoid contradicting themselves. For the fact that they are born and die proves nothing, provided they simply say that this happens *of their own free will*! If we are willing to defy all Experience, we can deny both temporality and the existence of Falsehood, but if we *allow* temporality, we are forced to derive it from *Eternity*. And if we 'allow' Death, then we have to admit the existence of Falsehood, since Death is a denial of our self-consciousness and must find its origin in Falsehood. In eternal Truth, however, there is neither Death nor Falsehood, since, as a parting from life, Death is a necessary *consequence* of Falsehood, which is a denial of the Truth in which life exists.

If we now agree that we must admit what we cannot deny – without either thereby confirming it or at least contradicting an undoubted *experience* – then we must agree that eternal living Truth *exists*, that is, as an eternal Truth-teller. We must also admit that there is a *temporal* existence in which both Falsehood and Death exist.

The question then arises: Can we conceive Truth and separate it from Falsehood in Time and Space? Here it is important that we first and foremost understand and impress upon ourselves the undeniable certainty that it is not only in *Time* that Truth

312 Immanuel Kant, *Critique of Pure Reason*, Riga: 1781.

313 Grundtvig's own footnote 1: "Such as *The Chronicle's Retort; Against the Little Accuser;* and *Danne-virke*." These were published in 1813, 1815, and 1816-19 respectively.

314 Throughout this chapter the Danish word *bevidsthed* is translated as 'consciousness'. Grundtvig uses it in the sense: 'consciousness of self' or 'self-consciousness'.

and Falsehood are incompatible; also in *Eternity* there is a yawning abyss between them! The fallacy that the separation between Truth and Falsehood is only temporal has of late acquired so many clamorous mouths and eloquent tongues that we must arm ourselves against it – not by stopping our ears but by cleaning them, so that the voice of Truth can penetrate them and resonate in all its power. It is irrefutable that eternal Truth *exists*, for Truth is simply eternal Being's confirmation of itself. If life and Truth were *not* eternal, then that itself would be an eternal Truth; but since it is a denial of the *eternity* of Truth, it brands itself as Falsehood, and affirms the eternity of Truth by denying it! It is equally undeniable that in eternity Truth cannot *allow* any Falsehood without thereby denying its *own* eternity; otherwise it would itself become Falsehood. This too is impossible, since Falsehood would then become Truth; it would become what its denial alone comprises!

On the other hand, *within* time Truth can *bear* Falsehood, can bear to strive against it, for Falsehood does not deny *temporal* life; in fact, it claims that its life is *indeed* temporal – as Time will tell. As the saying goes: 'Only Time will tell what is the Truth'. So a temporal fight can be waged between Truth and Falsehood without Truth thereby denying itself; it will even allow Falsehood to fight it, despite it being obvious that all *power* belongs to Truth, which could only be abused if it *allowed* itself to be! This, to be sure, is quite incomprehensible for us, for we cannot *grasp* eternal Truth. It grasps *us*, so long as we are not one with it; but we *can* grasp that Truth only *permits* the fight because it has a temporal, created work! Truth is actually *promoted* by the fight; and as to this division, only Time will tell, for we are ourselves just such a created work!

Human beings are undeniably a creation of eternal Truth. We develop over Time through struggle. How this struggle actually hangs together is a highly complex question; indeed it is the *mystery of the Word*.[315] However, the question is not relevant in this context; here we are concerned only with the question of how Truth – once it has completed its temporal work and thereby bereft Falsehood of its power – can express itself so that nothing is left except the *will* of Falsehood. This cannot be *ended*, since a finite will is a contradiction in terms – like saying that Love hates and murders itself – as if Falsehood can be incorporated into Truth! And yet this is the equivocation that is argued in order to *protect* Falsehood! We must reject this categorically! For no matter how we turn it, it is unthinkable – unless Truth should stop *hating* Falsehood, and Falsehood Truth. Either way, Truth would have been denying itself throughout the course of Time; and that, we know, is impossible.

We therefore have to acknowledge that the hatred between Truth and Falsehood is eternal, and that the endlessness or eternal *death* of Falsehood is just as undeniable as the eternal *life* of Truth. We know that everything in the world which seeks to

315 'The Word' is God's Word to humankind, as incarnated in Christ and animated by the Spirit into 'the living Word'.

link Truth to Falsehood, or conceal their enmity, belongs to Falsehood. In contrast, everything which seeks to lay bare this eternal hatred and separate what is irreconcilable in this struggle is the *effect and creation* of Truth, in the sense that even the *effect* of Falsehood is governed by the hand of Truth to frustrate the will of Falsehood and transform what it seeks to promote. It is clearly not a problem *in theory* to separate Falsehood from Truth, whereas it can be quite difficult in actual *experience*. This may seem strange to us, if we find nothing in ourselves that loves Falsehood, but if we *do* find something, it is only strange that we should *love* Falsehood; for it is by no means strange but quite natural that Falsehood blinds us, insofar as we love it.

We know in this regard what Christianity teaches us about humankind, how Falsehood gained a footing, how Death is the wages of sin.[316] Nor can it be denied that since Death has power over us by dissolving us, it is because we have *loved* Falsehood, for Death has no power over what exists in Truth, and if we love Truth, then we are *in* the Truth.

We are reminded here of the basic principle of cause and effect, which teaches us that there is no effect without a cause. Just as we found the basic principle of contradiction or undeniability in the universal expression of self-consciousness – I am *conscious* of myself – so does it follow that I am none other than *what I am*; I am not what I am *not*! We thus *conceive* the principle of cause and effect in the specific *expression* of our self-consciousness: I have *become* conscious of myself, I have *found* myself. In saying this we acknowledge that we are not *eternally* conscious of ourselves. However, since an eternal Consciousness indisputably *exists*, and since Consciousness cannot possibly be created by *Un*consciousness – for then Truth would be created by Falsehood – it becomes clear that *our* Consciousness is created by an *eternal* Consciousness, on which it is consequently dependent; for all that is *of* the Eternal is eternally dependent *upon* the Eternal.

Strictly speaking, the latter principle is merely a development of the former, for eternal Truth necessarily presumes eternal Being as its cause, and therefore the principle of cause and effect is eternally true, for it is *within* eternal Truth. If any self-consciousness were to express itself thus: "I am of *myself*!", it would be a falsehood and a contradiction in terms. It would be like saying: "I am not *conscious* of any 'being', but I am a being which originated in the consciousness of *not* being; I am the cause derived from the effect *without* a cause! From the effect we can do no other than endorse the cause.

Next, we must ask: What can the effect *teach* us about the cause? Here we meet the principle of Unity, which also lies within eternal Truth and expresses itself in the essential manifestation of self-consciousness as a unity of Being and Consciousness, of cause and effect, so that the effect is the *image* of the cause. It is obvious that we must

316 Rom 6:23.

conceive a *third* link here, one which links and unites Being and Consciousness, cause and effect, in other words the active effect of the cause – what we call 'power'. Since this 'power' unites what we must imagine separately, it can only be the power of *Love*, for Love is our name for what communicates and unites. Here we have the eternal pillars upon which the basic principles of undeniability, cause, and unity firmly rest.

However, when we apply the principle of unity to cause and effect, we can see that we must also include *temporality* in the equation, in order to stop ourselves from arguing that there is unconditional unity *without* the connecting link of power. Even in consciousness, unity is conditioned by time – i.e. by an ongoing parity. It follows that all effect is an image of its closest cause, i.e. of its power or activity, and only in this is an effect *one* with its basic cause. To what extent this power reflects the basic cause and has connection with it therefore depends on the effect's *partaking of the said power*. Only where self-consciousness is thus *conceived* in every sense is a connection with Truth possible, and even then only to the degree that humankind loves Truth; for only the spirit of Love can unite what is separate and has self-consciousness.

Apart from this, everything which merely *reproduces* power is dead, and is therefore only a shadow. On the other hand, whatever has power *within it* is alive, and is thus an *image* of power. However, only where power is *conscious of itself* is it an image of Truth, and only humankind is therefore created in God's image.

If we then ask what is *temporal* Truth, we can only answer: the true condition of Creation. It is seen in human beings, in whom Creation has its consciousness and in whom can be seen an image of eternal Truth. This Truth expresses Being, *which has reproduced itself*, for this is depicted in the body, which through the senses is reproduced in the mind. In the eyes of Truth, the human being from nature[317] is its direct image. Whether this is so in *human* eyes depends on whether Truth will lend humankind *its* eyes, and whether they will see themselves *through* these eyes, until this process finds its culmination in Love. Thus, the image merges with the Truth and sees physically, with its own enlightened eyes, what before it saw only spiritually; now it sees face to face with what the image *means*.

Here we come to a major question: Has Truth lent us its eyes, and, if so, how have they been used? This is the same as saying: Has Truth lent us its Spirit, and have we thereby *grown*? In the language of eternity, i.e. in the Word of God, the Spirit corresponds to the sensory imagination, which is its image. We then realise that a 'question of conscience' is a question of the relation between Truth and the human will – or the human heart, which is the same thing. To every self-conscious creature we must say:

317 i.e. what in the 18th century was known as 'Natural Man'. I have deliberately avoided the gender-specific 'Man', which nowadays is widely understood as an unacceptable gender limitation.

Follow Truth! And if we human beings have received the Spirit of Truth, the command must be: Reveal Truth! This has been the great moral principle for past generations embracing a love of Truth. Unity should come about through the power of the Spirit; and from the basic principle of unity comes the lesson of every good deed as being an endeavour towards unity with eternal Truth and salvation, i.e. God's eternal life, *in* Him.

On Greatness

Great and Small are known as 'relative' concepts, that is, concepts which presuppose a comparison and denote only an internal relation. This is absolutely true in a sense, nor can it be otherwise in this world. However, if we assume that Greatness is *not* an eternal, sovereign concept, we are making a serious mistake. For Small presupposes Great, of which it is merely a diminution, whereas in its *eternal* concept Great presupposes activity in *Being* and its view thereof. When eternal activity is seen in Truth, then the concept of Greatness is born; and when eternal power expresses itself in Truth, it expresses Greatness as omnipotence. So when God says 'I', eternity announces its Greatness – and *true* Greatness is undoubtedly the Word of God, that is, the revealed power of Truth. We cannot doubt that, at heart, Truth and Greatness are one and the same, since Greatness is none other than Truth revealing itself in all its power. Whoever knows Scripture, knows well how this illuminates Logos. It is important in this context to derive the concept of *temporal* Greatness from *eternal* Greatness, and to hold on to this distinction on earth.

It has never been in doubt, not even in the most faithless days, that a Word from the Almighty is the greatest imaginable experience. This is clear from interpretations of the Pentateuch[318] – even by those grand people who stand on their toes to see above the Mosaic cosmogony! Truth in the Word can be overlooked, but a Word from the Almighty cannot be shouted down. What those grand people do not see is that the only viable transition from the eternal to the temporal lies precisely *in that Word*; only in and through the Word can *anything* be created, and all creation is an effect of Truth through the Word.

Moreover, this shows us where the true distinction between Great and Small lies: everything in Time is obviously either 'greater' or 'smaller', since to some degree or other it clearly reproduces the Almighty's creating Word. The only question is: To what extent are we able actually to *make* this distinction? This is the same as with the principle of cause and effect: To what extent can we *apply* this distinction, since according to this principle the relation between them must clearly be determined on this basis.

318 The 'Pentateuch' comprises the first five books of the Old Testament (i.e. the books of Moses).

Let us now attempt to *make* this distinction this, noting first that Truth is best understood as something 'inner', namely consciousness itself, and its mode of expression. When we speak of 'self-consciousness', as in the above, we cannot define the distinction without continual repetition and needless verbosity; yet we must always bear the distinction *in mind*, so as not to confuse God with the World, and Time with Eternity. For in the Word, which is divisible, Time is *hidden*, and only in the *power* of the Word is the sensory world linked to Truth.

For Truth and *in* Truth, the world only exists as an *effect* of the Word, and truly we can call nothing 'great' which is not seen *in relation to* Truth, seen in its *power*. On reflection, we shall also find that our speech confirms this, for when we call something 'great', we assign to it both power and prestige. If it *lacks* power somewhat, we call it 'striking' or 'remarkable'; if it lacks a little prestige, we call it 'impressive'. We often make the mistake of calling something 'great' which is in fact 'small', and vice versa. This arises not from any disagreement about what *constitutes* Greatness but from an erroneous assessment, which in turn may have many causes. We can either be blinded by its prestige, or have no eye for its true power; or perhaps we are surprised and forget to make the comparison. In other words, we can be blind or blinded in a number of ways. Since everything depends on the eye that sees – and taking into account how much these eyes differ – we cannot expect much agreement in each case on what is 'great'; but this does not stop us from providing many firm definitions of what is *thought* to be great or small in the eyes of all, since our relation to the word of Truth patently gives us an unfailing touchstone which it is our duty to acknowledge and apply. Nor is our difference of opinion nearly so great as it would seem at first glance, for however many people call something great which is in fact small, such as their own little person, it is nearly always a confusion of terms. We rarely call 'small' what is truly 'great' when we are in its presence, for the simple reason that that when Greatness is present, we are *forced* to recognise it. If we have no eye for it, we at least have an eye for ourselves, and whatever makes us small in its presence we are forced to recognise as great, whether we like it or not.

Concerning the sensory world, we often say how great it is in regard to its breadth, but if anyone demurred in the slightest, we would change the expression or be forced to admit that it is only great insofar as we imagine it to be visible and to be *seen* as such. It is truly great in its *own* eyes when it is seen in relation to its *power*, in the light which in the form of the eye has come into consciousness; to the senses it only *appears* great, like a shadow, but it only becomes *truly* great when it is seen as an effect of the Word and *reveals* its power – in other words as proof of God's omnipotence. If we stop to consider for a moment, we shall realise that such things are *as great as they are true*, and that also in this regard humankind is the crown of creation. In itself the sensory world is not great; it only becomes so through the eye that sees what it *means*;

this link to the eye only happens in the human being, in whose consciousness the sensory world of the body is incorporated – or where the sensory world in the body is brought into consciousness. Just as this reveals itself at its greatest in the Word that differentiates us from the animals, so do we realise that the Word is the greatest power in humankind, for it mirrors true greatness itself, as well as expressing what makes human beings an image of Truth in their self-consciousness. In the eyes of Truth, the speaking human being is the greatest creation in the world, being its complete image of Time, an image in which the Word, having first in part reflected its power, now reflects its whole self. Whether human beings can see themselves in this true greatness depends on their ability to regard themselves with the eyes of Truth – as its image.

Here we arrive at the historical question as to whether humankind has received the breath of life though its nostrils[319] and thus acquired a spiritual eye with which it can contemplate eternal Truth, figuratively, in both itself and the world. We know what Scripture says here, and acceptance of it cannot be denied unless we defy experience, both our historical and our daily experience – just as my readers do when they see how I regard humankind and the world in this way. If I *could* not, I would of course refrain from doing so.

We know enough now to realise that it is *through our sight and in the Word* that we are to seek true Greatness, and that no one who understands us will dispute this. Nor will any deny that the temporal *gains* in esteem, when it is seen as an image of the eternal, and that in the expression of such a contemplative thought the Word shows itself in its true power. From this it follows that the Word, though sensory, expresses something *transcendental*, which in turn assumes a transcendental power, whose instrument it indeed is!

However, if this should seem abstruse or questionable, it can be proved through History that at least until now the Word as the expression of a spiritual vision has been the greatest power in the world, for it must have affirmed itself through the *effects* it has occasioned. Who can be so unversed in History as not to know that to deny this is of no avail! Does not History demand of all its adherents that what has had the greatest effect in the world is *religion*, call it what one will, and that according to the principle of cause and effect religion is undeniably the greatest factor of all? How could it otherwise operate except through the *Word* as religion's expressed spiritual vision? The Word *articulates* the link between the sensory and the transcendental, transforming the temporal into an image of the eternal!

Even if it were a consolation to reject all the myths and legends of old, we cannot deny that the words of the Prophets and the Apostles have had an effect without

319 Gen 2:7.

parallel in their Greatness. However we twist and turn, we cannot help confessing that the Word as metaphor has so far been the greatest on earth! If we contend that Christ was even greater, then we know what Scripture says: The Word was made flesh and dwelt among us, and was seen in the glory of the only-begotten Son.[320] This in no way reduces the *power* of the Word, it simply *demonstrates* it through all the miracles that the Word of Christ effected.

What has seemed unreasonable to the many small minds that cannot see human beings above their hands or beyond their teeth is how in days gone by the incomprehensible words which they ridiculed could have left *such* an impression on people! Those words achieved *such* things – beside which the wisest and the silliest words were mere water – that we now consider them *perfectly* reasonable! Pragmatic historiographers can say what they like about the great effects from *small* causes, but we cannot allow them to renounce the eternal principle that *all* effects have a cause, and that the effect is in proportion to the power that caused it. So the many 'effects' of our time have not managed to prove that the pet dreams of small minds have had *any* effect that is a head higher than themselves! It must be even clearer to us now that to us nothing actually seems 'great' that is not in a sense *inconceivable*; for just as we cannot call something that we can hold in our hand 'great', so can we not call any idea or word 'great' if we can *understand* it! Moreover, if we consider ourselves 'great', it is because we do not *understand* ourselves. So it is no surprise that at a time when people led themselves to believe they understood *everything* and yet understood not a jot about themselves, they stood in wonder at their own unimaginable Greatness! Speaking of 'wonder', we are reminded that this is an expression of the spontaneous effect upon us of seeing something Great – unless we are frightened, as can easily happen when we meet true Greatness. What we *understand* does not make us wonder! Here again we realise that whatever characterises Greatness must necessarily contain something inconceivable. If we therefore become completely wise – so wise, for example, that we fully understand the Word with which God created the world – it follows that this 'Word' would no longer be the greatest in the world, and we could simply prove this by *changing* the world, just like that. But we must wait just as long before we set ourselves *above* the Word if we are not to be put to shame when the Word leaves us with our noses in the air!

For as long as we have seen how people consider themselves *superior* to the Word and have refuted eternal Truth, for just so long has there also been Falsehood in the world – and indeed still *is*! People compliantly admit this, if not for the sake of Truth then for their own sake. Whoever denies this must at once declare these words of mine false, and in so doing they are only confirming what they seek to deny, and

320 Jn 1:14.

making not mine but their own words a falsehood. If Falsehood exists, then it has no part in Truth itself, but in some way or other it still has a *share* in this world; so far it appears to have some *influence* over Truth, which is highly significant. For once Falsehood gets someone's mouth rolling, we cannot doubt its desire to use fine words! And once it has a share in the world, it seeks to set no limits until it has gained the whole measure – as in the proverb: If you give the Devil an inch, he will take a mile! In other words, the desire to Falsehood must be to enrich ourselves at the expense of Truth, and usurp its high throne. Once Falsehood has gained a foothold, human blindness is an inevitable consequence, and the foothold is in itself its conquest. Thus has Falsehood become Lord of the World, for, being *in* the world humankind has its share in the Great Word which it has been granted.

We can now clearly see how often human beings are inevitably deceived by what *appears* Great, but is in fact nothing, and how *temporal* Greatness must often be seen to be in league with Falsehood, for that is what happens when people tell a lie and thus place their power in the hands of Falsehood. This is important to note: a lie has no power *in itself*, for in itself it is quite powerless. Nor is any *power* in league with Falsehood; Falsehood is the *vassal* of this power, to which Truth once gave *its* power for a while – in return for its accountability when God commands it. Wherever, to our amazement, this power reveals itself, we must admit to its 'Greatness', for it seems so, at least to our own eyes, and may well actually *be* so, even with the brand of Falsehood on it! But if we *realise* this, we must never *bow down* before such 'Greatness', nor must we think that the power of Truth has retreated merely because it *appears* to be in the hands of Falsehood, or that this power can actually turn Falsehood *into* Truth – which amounts to the same thing. If Truth ever lost a *grain* of its power, it would no longer be Truth, but Falsehood. Through the principle of cause and effect we have the unerring certainty that all power belongs eternally to Truth, that God is *almighty*, and that the commandment therefore follows: Make *Truth* the ultimate power – for all who have their share in Truth.

By its nature all power is a force to be reckoned with: we see it in History, if we have come to an understanding of Truth by that path – and we shall see it face to face when the Light reveals everything. But as for the Will, we all feel that *will-power is our own*. If we wish to *enact* Truth, then that is to our own benefit, for then we retain that power perpetually, i.e. then we *live*. Conversely, if we do *not* wish to enact Truth, then it is to our own detriment, i.e. we die, we are lost. Truth can be indifferent to whether the mendacious will has a branch into Truth. This cannot be prevented, since Truth cannot deny itself – and it would have to do so, if it were to make an ill will good or incorporate a mendacious will. Here we cannot help but recall in astonishment what in more recent times has been discussed in manifold ways – namely the freedom of the Will and the reformation of an ill Will. And we note that emphatically this is a contradiction. We shall merely add here that Kant recognised the contradiction but made light of it. Let us end our discussion of Greatness with a few words about our moral relation to it.

As we have seen, this relation is easily defined, for we must neither deny nor worship Truth; we must *appropriate* it. However, History teaches us that we have great difficulty in carrying out this command, so it is not easy to name a well-known person who retained a *proper* relation to Greatness, whether it was their own or another's. I could perhaps mention *one*, but precisely because he is *so* familiar, he does not actually belong among the famous nowadays. Since this is not my fault, I shall name him as 'Jesus' – the only example I know of a well-known man who is a true and actual appraiser of Greatness and who could point to Himself when he spoke the singularly *great* words to his disciples, "Do not rejoice that the spirits submit to you, but rejoice that your names are written in the Book of Life."[321]

We shall not dwell here on the many examples where the fault lay mostly in the eye and was thus less dangerous; we shall only take note of those in whom the fault lay in their *Will* – when they either bowed down before what they saw as Greatness in a Falsehood, or they despised Greatness in a Truth. In the first case, we know that in the days of heathenism this was widespread, particularly in the deification of the powers of Nature. What is easily overlooked is that the same thing happens every time we extol and glorify a person for their great powers – be they emperor, poet, philosopher, or whatever – despite the fact that they use these powers to *combat* Truth. In the second case, they were mostly stoics, who out of admiration for themselves found nothing else to wonder at.[322] Their race is far from extinct, and we do not need to search far in the books of our time to find people who do not even stand in wonder at the eternal relation between God and humankind; they admit that it exists, but prefer to swoon in wonder at the human intellect! There is of course a simple explanation for this, for they fancy that they can indeed *conceive* the former relation, but they actually find *themselves in*conceivable! So long as we do not wonder at *anything*, we cannot wonder at something we find 'conceivable'. But that does not make it any the less erroneous: it is obvious that we cannot make believe that we understand a relation in which we cannot even grasp the *temporal* aspect, let alone the eternal. Human beings relate to God as creature to creator – as nothing in themselves to everything in Himself. But when that 'nothing' desires to be 'something', calculating that such a relation is to human advantage, this is not just boyish conceit but something we are quite rightly

321 Lk 10:20. Grundtvig actually uses the Danish words 'Livsens Bog' (the Book of Life) instead of 'written in the heavens' (ἐγγέγραπται ἐν τοῖς οὐρανοῖς).

322 The Stoics formed a school of philosophy in Athens in the early 3rd century BCE which taught i.a. the sovereignty of reason. They were influential for the next 500 years or so – throughout most of the Roman period. Grundtvig considers the eternal relation between God and humankind as thoroughly *un*reasonable.

astonished at. This is where we finger the boil, which lies in our desire to ignore the Greatness in the Truth, either through indifference or with empty, cursory wonder, because we wish our*selves* to be 'great' in our own eyes. We seek to counsel *ourselves*, as though we were self-made and *owned* ourselves, when Truth in its Greatness thunders at us: "*Do* the Truth!" It commands us to self-denial in deepest humility and unconditional obedience.

On Beauty

Without doubt Beauty is what we most enjoy in this world, yet least understand, what we praise best, yet treat worst of all. As they say: At Beauty's feet Greatness must lay down its crown, and before its radiance Truth must surrender its sceptre. For *in* that radiance it is perfection itself, and in its smile lies the supremacy of Love. It may be terrible to hear such words about a Greek marble pillar, or a Gothic marble slab, or a Cythera[323] with all her sisters, or even about the ideal of a Madonna.[324] But although the world is accustomed to misdirecting its eulogies, they may nevertheless acquire a certain authority when they find their proper object in the mouth of *Truth*. If this is indeed the case, then there must be an *eternal* Beauty, for to be sure the Word does not yield to temporal power – and even less to Truth! However, when we consider what is meant by 'true Beauty', a light is lit which Art itself has not created; indeed, this light may very well have *created* Art! Since the warmth and radiance of life in perfect union are the ideal of Beauty, it is beyond question that this ideal must be sought in eternal Love, for that is where the all-embracing warmth of eternal Life dwells in all its perfection in an incomparable radiance. We cannot speak too highly of this, for it is no more than saying that Truth itself finds words with which to express eternal Beauty in all its radiance. As we know, this was far from what was worshipped in the past under the names of Aphrodite and Cypris,[325] and later under the Muses,[326] the

323 In Greek mythology (Hesiod's *Theogony*) the islands of Cythera (present-day Kithira) and Cyprus are both associated with the birth of Aphrodite, the Goddess of Love.

324 At the Council of Ephesus in 431, Mary, mother of Jesus, was titulated 'Theotokos' ("Mother of God"), and from then on she was given a central role in worship and church decoration, particularly in Byzantine icons depicting her together with the Christ-child. She is interpreted variously as 'the bringer of victory', as 'she who points the way' and as 'the intercessor'. In medieval art, where the child was often omitted, the Madonna could represent mercy, or perpetual freedom from original sin, or the donator of the rosary. Western Madonnas later aimed to inspire piety through beauty and tenderness rather than worship and intercession. By the mid-14th century in Italy and Germany, the Madonna was even depicted knitting alongside the baby Jesus!

325 In Greek mythology Aphrodite (Roman 'Venus') is a goddess associated with love, beauty, pleasure, passion, and procreation. She was also known as Cytherea (Lady of Cythera) and Cypris (Lady of Cyprus), both locations claiming to be her place of birth.

326 The 9 Greek Muses are: Calliope (Epic Poetry), Clio (History), Euterpe (Music, Song, and Lyric Poetry), Erato (Love Poetry), Melpomene (Tragedy), Polyhymnia (Hymns), Terpsichore (Dance), Thalia (Comedy), and Urania (Astronomy).

Graces,[327] and numberless others. It is not *this* kind of Beauty that Truth promises; it may please 'the world', but when we talk to the world about Beauty without in any way compromising Truth, there is no chance of us reaching agreement!

However, there is *some* Truth at the foundation of what 'the world' claims, even though so much Falsehood has been built on it – and we must truly not deny *a single grain* of that Truth. The world must have the right to retain all the Beauty and all the Greatness that Truth allows; perhaps for its own sake we can even constrain it to permit eternal, incorruptible Beauty to retain its power as *the Word of Truth*.

It is to this Word that we must now turn, if we are to become properly acquainted with the Temporal, for in this creative Word we must assuredly seek the cause of all temporal Beauty and Truth. Just as the power of the Word expresses eternal Strength, so must its Goodness express eternal Love, and just as power creates Greatness, so does Good create Beauty. The only difference here is that where the Effect of Good begins, life too takes its rise, for Good works through warmth. That is why we never think to speak of Beauty in Nature without there being, or appearing to be, life. Greatness begins with Light, but Good begins with the Sun and the Moon; Greatness begins with Esteem, but Beauty with Radiance. Into Light we gather the Word as power, wisdom, and goodness, which separate on their way to humankind – only there to radiate. For just as human beings are the truest and greatest in all creation, so are they undeniably the most beautiful image of the Creator-Word. With warmth in their innermost being and radiance in their countenance, human beings are from nature an image of Love in the eyes of Truth. Here, however, we come back to the two major questions: Have they learned to *see* themselves as such? And have they delved *deeper* into this reflection? The first question more or less answers itself, for Truth would not deny humankind its Spirit to develop all things in the course of time, for this is the Spirit which power, wisdom, and goodness vied to raise as an image of the Eternal in humankind; Truth would not deny humankind the Word to whose temple and tongue it clearly seemed destined!

The second question also strikes at the strings of Conscience, and strikes deepest, since it strikes at the Spirit of Love. No guilt is surer for us than that we have not properly loved Him who loved us before we were born.

So as not to leap from Beauty straight to Conscience – a leap that is not so easy as the other way round – let us recall that Beauty and Virtue are concepts which, despite appearances to the contrary, were considered a unity as far back as ancient Greece. Since the time of Kant, much has been written on this subject.

Beauty is best discussed in relation to the eternal principle of Unity, where it undoubtedly belongs; for where there is no Unity, there is no Beauty either. What

327 The 3 Greek Graces are: Aglaea (Splendour), Euphrosyne (Mirth), and Thalia (Good Cheer).

we find beautiful we naturally wish to unite with, and, where this is impossible, then at least to link it to ourselves. It is obvious that we seek no link except to *what* we love and *insofar* as we love. It is equally clear that Love is the living expression of this union. From this we can conclude about ourselves that we can love nothing without finding it beautiful, nor can we find anything beautiful without loving it! Love and Will, both in our tongue and our heart, are one and the same thing – for Will is only Love in a particular direction and is fully dependent on it. So it is clearly a matter of Conscience as to what, and to what degree, we find *anything* 'beautiful'. Likewise, it is our undeniable duty everywhere to find Truth *beautiful*, since this goes without saying when we love it with all our heart. The wise advice of Truth is: Believe me! His Master's command is: Obey me! His Father's Voice which unites and transfigures all things says: Nurture yourself in Me!

To some extent we could reap the world's praise with a speech that called Virtue and Truth 'beautiful', provided first that they conform to the circumstances, second that they turn a blind eye to the fact that the speech is primarily self-serving, and finally, that they take pot luck with what is left! This may be any of the following: a fine eulogy as an eyewash for a touching theatre-play; a couple of shillings for a new year's gift to the poor; and cold dishes for the rest!

Yet Truth will not be held at bay like this. The consequence is always that many turn *away* from Truth and never learn about it from its noble side. However hard we have tried, we have worked in vain to file away the sharp edges of Truth and make it attractive in the world's eyes or dampen its thunderous voice to make it lovable. Truth will not be robbed, and the law of Truth cannot be deleted without it becoming Falsehood. If it appears otherwise, then Falsehood has been embellished and made itself worshipped as Truth. Then of course, as seems pleasant and altruistic, it seeks to strike a bargain, promises life and salvation for nothing, and gives what it has to offer: an endless empty space and an endless long time. In other words, it offers a bottomless abyss and a hopeless reckoning – in old Danish: 'Hell and everlasting misery'!

In my eyes, and I imagine in the eyes of many others, this is not a pleasant solution; yet whoever refuses to hear it can never appreciate true Beauty! For we cannot deny that the Word is Great – and that in Time true Beauty is no more than molten Greatness. After what we have heard about Greatness, it must be the great and incomprehensible Word of Truth, received with Faith and melted into the loving heart, that will make us participants in this true and everlasting Greatness. The gold lies in the rock; it cannot be picked out with the fingers, nor can it be melted in the luke-warm hand. Beauty lies hidden in the *heart*, which preserves the echo of the great Word that rang out on earth. The rock must be blasted apart and melted in holy flames. Whoever does this has made a masterpiece and will be canonised as a historic artist.

But whoever thinks they have done it 'just like that' has only swept the rock surface and taken dross for gold.

In this we have the hallmark of genuine, temporal Beauty, and this can never fail. It is equally true and equally sad that we are easily disappointed by its appearance, and that we find it hard not to kneel at least in admiration of true Beauty wherever it is found, for that is what follows from Falsehood's dominion in the world and its sway in our hearts. It is of little help that we – as monks, Zwinglians,[328] and Pietists[329] – attempt to deny Beauty or forswear homage to it, for the chronicles of Time teach us on a large scale – and our day-to-day Experience on a small scale – that scorned Beauty exacts a cruel revenge, and forsworn things actually come to pass!

If it is really the case that we find *nothing* beautiful in the world, then that is evidence of a terrible need, the need for Love – or, since it is impossible to draw breath without Love – proof that we love something that does not even have the *appearance* of Beauty. It is also proof that we are ruled by an unnatural love of *ourselves*, in whatever way it finds expression. At its lowest level we notice it with disgust, as in gluttony, drunkenness, and indecency; at its highest level we note it as avarice and pride. If on the other hand we have a sense of *Beauty*, we praise it in our hearts, and only forswear it because we feel that our love is in fact lust. In that case it is an affected and profane insensitivity, which petrifies our heart on its best side, is broken when the waves roar, or, at best protects an impurity that should be swept away. The only advice that works here is to *purify the heart*, so its feelings can follow Truth. Then we shall *find* beautiful what *is* beautiful – as it is already beautiful in the eyes of Truth.

Who would deny that Beauty reaches its zenith in nature, in humankind, and primarily in woman? Who could fool us into believing that he has an eye and a mind for the highest Beauty, if he has none for woman, through whom all temporal Beauty evolves? When we see a beautiful woman gazing with a mother's care at the lovely little boy who emerged from her womb and in whom she recognises his father's features, we are looking not only at the highest Beauty, but also at the passage from the natural to the historical, and thus at the purest sensory image of *eternal Beauty*. Thus is developed the highest natural Greatness (man), fused with the highest natural Beauty (woman) and a historical Beauty (a child) who unites both. Let us now imagine a *prophet* in this boy, who, transfigured in the spirit of Truth, acquires eternal Truth under temporal

328 Ulrich Zwingli (1484-1531) was the most important reformer in the Swiss Protestant Reformation. Like Luther, he accepted the supreme authority of the Scriptures, but he applied it more rigorously and comprehensively to all doctrines and practices.

329 Pietism had its roots in the late 17th century in the work of Philipp Spener (1635-1705), a Lutheran theologian who emphasised personal transformation through spiritual rebirth and renewal, manifested in vigorous, personal devotion and piety. The movement had considerable influence in Denmark, right into the 20th century, where Inner Mission practised a modernised form.

images. Let us hear him express his view to a woman's ear, and let us imagine that her heart is inflamed with an inner love of the Word of the Spirit, so that it melts and gives birth in response in the most melting notes! Then we have the truest image of eternal Greatness and Beauty that can be found in the Temporal. The song of love expressing the power of the Word is the most beautiful thing on earth – *spiritual* Beauty! We shall see it in its fullness, if we can imagine that the woman's song manifests its radiance to a male figure, with its rays of sound transfiguring woman and earth; for in this conception Time and Eternity are historically fused and everything is united in Love, which radiates its eternal life in Truth and Beauty.

Here we can clearly see that Beauty is the great work of Art that History is working on. How far it has come, and whether it can reasonably complete this work itself, we must learn from History, for we too are in its service. Falsehood, which can never be incorporated into eternal Life, is bound to do all it can to hinder the great marriage between Truth and Beauty and entice us not just with brilliant delusion but even with the genuine sheen and sound stolen from the melting furnace of the Word within us. We must accuse Falsehood of theft, and bravely demand that Truth's property be returned. True Beauty itself fights for Truth, for when it is violated, it dies like Lucretia,[330] and from its dead lustre, which lust vainly seeks to resuscitate, the plunder is recognisable. As soon as we lovingly lift the banner of Truth, its radiance flows in upon us and radiates vividly and inimitably – to the indignance of Falsehood and the shame of vice.

Overview

The many observations on humankind and History cogently presented here are so important that they cannot be confined to a few brief remarks. Who does not realise that everything which comes down to us from days gone by is a story about what seemed too great or too beautiful to be forgotten? History is a mirror in which we see what the children of humankind have actively aspired to and lovingly preserved! Who does not feel that in History, word and deed are joined together and that the Word is both

330 Lucius Tarquinius Superbus (Tarquin the Proud, reigned 534-09 BCE) was the seventh and last king of Rome before it became a republic. In 510 BCE he sent his son Sextus on a military errand to the home of Lucius Tarquinius Collatinus, who was away at the wars. At night Sextus entered the bedroom of Lucius's wife, Lucretia, and told her that she could either submit to his sexual advances and become his wife and future queen, or he would kill her. She submitted to the rape. The next day Lucretia went to her father, demanding vengeance; she stabbed herself in the heart, and died in his arms. Dionysius of Halicarnassus (c. 60 BCE – after 7 BC) writes: "This dreadful scene struck the Romans who were present with so much horror and compassion that they all cried out with one voice that they would rather die a thousand deaths in defence of their liberty than suffer such outrages to be committed by the tyrants." Lucretia's husband became the first consul of the new Roman republic. The subject has been painted by i.a. Titian, Rembrandt, Dürer, Raphael, and Botticelli.

first and last? It is preceded by deeds and reflected in them, and from this it flows on and tells us what power it had, what work it wrought, and what outcome it achieved. Who does not see that in the History of every people, be it long or short, certain or uncertain, lies a truthful witness of what in their eyes was great and beautiful, what it meant for them in time, and what gave them the desire and power to act.[331]

We shall not delve any deeper into these observations on the Word and its wondrous passage; we shall only hold a sharp eye with humankind and what has led this Word through History to see whether a light has not thereby been shone on human existence. If so, we can reliably behold our own figure and see the path that leads to the goal of all humankind.

There are also other sensory and temporal truths: for instance, we are conscious in Time and Space, and we are conscious of our bodies having a specific size, cohesion, and form that can be changed. This is a fundamental experience upon which all experience of Truth rests. If we deny this, we are denying the possibility of any experience at all, as well as denying all History; we are unquestionably making liars of ourselves, since our own words bring us down by incontrovertibly proclaiming an existence in Time and Space!

There are further moral truths our conscience must face: we are conscious of our subordinate status; we are conscious of ourselves in relation to eternal Truth; and we are conscious that this has not been so from time immemorial. If with this consciousness we wish to *defy* our conscience, we can deny our dependence on eternal Truth by trying to pass *ourselves* off as that Truth!

History tells us there is also a poetic or symbolic Truth, for humankind can be fully conscious of itself in Time as being an *image* of eternal Truth. Humankind has regarded and felt itself to be so in power and in Love. This would be impossible if Truth were not at their root, for nothing has *no* power!

'Reason' is the central Word, as expressed in the word 'I' – meaning the link by which we carry all that lies in 'I' and all that differs from everything else, both in Time and Eternity. It is in other words our whole personality, in contrast to what it does *not* include. Reason – or, so as not to expose ourselves to empty dispute – *personality*, i.e. our selfhood, has both sensory and temporal Truth, for we exist in Time and Space through our *bodies*, separate from everything else. But Reason does not *possess* eternal Truth, for there is only one *eternal* selfhood, namely the eternal Truth that excludes everything that it does not enclose, thus making it Falsehood. Selfhood possesses only *moral* Truth to the extent that it encloses itself in eternal Truth and lies hidden in our conscience. Once it leaves, it falsely claims independence, and is nothing more than our sense of the flesh, rising against eternal Truth. On the other hand, if selfhood

331 This last sentence is missing in the original 1817 edition, but was printed in a later edition.

remains *within* our conscience, then it possesses poetic Truth, for then it reflects the eternal Truth that lies in Love.

'Intelligence'[332] is the goal of experience. It is sensory to the extent that experience is limited to the body's reality and sensory relation to the body's reality; it is 'moral' to the extent that it relates to conscience, and 'poetic' to the extent that it can grasp the figurative relation between Time and Eternity.

There is another sensory Greatness in human beings, for we have the power to imagine Time and Space as embracing all sensory things, a power that is revealed in our bodies, which can sense it all.

There is a *moral* Greatness which is to be found in all people when for the sake of Truth they deny their apparent independence and thereby raise themselves *above* their senses and their own selves to eternal Truth.

History tells us there is yet another *poetic* Greatness that is granted to the whole human race and belongs to every person, to the extent that they possess moral Greatness; human beings are the image and guardian of the Word, with the power to see God in themselves figuratively and to see themselves as God's son in the world.

The power of Imagination is the ability to conceive ideas; it is sensory to the extent that it imagines things as they may touch the senses; it is moral to the extent that it imagines all that is temporal as being dependent on eternal Truth, i.e. as created; and it is poetic to the extent that figuratively it imagines all that is Temporal as reflecting the Eternal.

There is another sensory Beauty in human beings, for there is a sensory Beauty which in its very radiance pleases them; they find their bodies beautiful and unify them with themselves, incorporating them into their self-consciousness.

There is a moral Beauty which is to be found in all people and which consists of a love of eternal Truth that denies them independence and commands unconditional obedience.

History tells us that a poetic Beauty develops through Love into poetic Greatness; whoever has this moral Beauty will be fulfilled in poetic Truth in an everlasting unity between God and humankind.

Love is the expression of the feeling of Beauty, a sensory love, i.e. love of the sensory in oneself. It presupposes a view of the sensory as something in itself, i.e. a bodily sense, and a denial of the moral Truth, just as it shows disdain for moral Beauty and excludes itself from the poetic in that it separates humankind from eternal Truth.

I should like to see what reasonable objection can be made not against individual phrases but against the general content of the view presented here. I must also point

332 Grundtvig's Danish word here is *Forstand*, signifying the capacity for conceptual understanding, as opposed to sense perception, intuition, and feeling. It is mainly through Kant that the word assumed philosophical value.

out that if it cannot be contradicted, then all who seek their *own* Will are simply excluded from any communion with eternal Truth. They are obliged to follow Falsehood without there being to the human eye any chance of deliverance for them, for a false Will can never be good. Should human Will be divided so that the body is allowed to govern itself rather than seek to make itself independent of it, then such people are admittedly to be pitied - but they are nonetheless *helpless* creatures, for their power has deserted them and their consciences condemn them. They should have appreciated this judgement as the word of Truth, and should have hated their *selves* and changed their ways - but these are complete impossibilities in their eyes.

Each must now conscientiously decide whether humankind needs help from above and beyond, or not. We shall turn to History to see what it can teach us about Christianity from this vantage-point.

History teaches us first and foremost that when we conclude from effect to cause - as indeed we must - then nothing can compare with *poetic* Greatness. It begins as a word hated and spurned, yet with its power it has subjugated the world. History has been believed by the most diverse peoples despite the most ingrained prejudice, and it has outlived all its opponents. Having passed away in the eyes of the world it arose with the energy of youth, and has extended into all human relations with indelible traces. We already know, or can easily convince ourselves, that its ideas of God and humankind are the highest possible. History also teaches us that in consequence of this it must embrace the highest *poetic* Beauty, and that it has produced more of this than of any other idea. However, since this effect depends on the depths to which humankind has allowed this idea into its heart, it belongs more to History's witness to *humankind* rather than to Christianity. For its merger with humankind has clearly yielded the highest form of Beauty. If this has *not* happened or is only gradually happening, that is not the fault of History but of humankind itself. The same is true of *moral* Greatness and Beauty; if Christianity were to lack these, then despite its wondrous effects, we would have to declare it false. However, since it possesses both Greatness and Beauty - as no one would deny - it is simply a shame and a pity for its believers if they have not experienced the two. History also teaches us that it is precisely from this angle that it eclipses everything else that would seem to be Great in this world. In millions of people History effected an unparalleled self-denial and a transcendent Love, which further goes to prove that this Love is the *truest* that History knows of.

This last statement is the conclusive proof, for History teaches us that wherever Christianity is believed and followed, nothing but Truth has come. It teaches us that what we learned to understand only yesterday or today was prophesied in the Bible in the most unequivocal words many centuries ago, indeed many millennia ago! Christianity *must* be Truth, inasmuch as neither centuries nor millennia have been able to find a single undeniable truth that contradicts the Bible, or to discover a single moral or theological error that it did not condemn. Insofar as there is no moral relation between Falsehood and Truth, Christianity *must* be Truth. Nevertheless, it goes without saying that no historical evidence is beyond question for as long as History lasts; it is only irrefutable, i.e. it cannot be refuted without defying one's conscience and experience.

God willing, we shall also see how everywhere Christianity is increasing its reputation and establishing itself with every truth-loving reflection. This is happening as we move forward and endeavour to see what is undeniable Truth and indubitable Experience, and to clarify the relation between Poetry, Art, and Learning as being words that delineate what in History has been called Greatness, Beauty, and Truth.

With this preparatory essay I dare to hope that – if only for a single person – I can break the unfortunate prejudice that, in the directing of their powers, human beings are allowed to lose sight of Truth and to sacrifice it for their own sake, or for what *seems* to them great and beautiful. If this be so, then I have not spoken in vain; and in any case it is not the fault of Truth if no one hears it.

▷▷

4. Front cover of first edition of *Danne-Virke* 1816

"Danne-Virke/A Periodical/By N.F.S. Grundtvig/First booklet/Costs 1 Rigsdaler
Copenhagen, 1816/ Printed by Schiøtz & Mandra, Mønter Street 128"

"Danne-Virke/Et Tidskrift/Af N.F.S. Grundtvig/Første hefte/Koster en Rigsdaler/
Kiøbenhavn, 1816/Trykt hos Schiøtz & Mandra, Møntergaden 128"

Between July 1816 and January 1819, Grundtvig edited and published his own periodical, *Danne-Virke* in four volumes of four paper-cover booklets of roughly 100 pages each. Apart from 4 by another author he wrote all 1,564 pages. The title was taken from the ancient defence work on the Danish border with Germany, figuratively a bulwark against the encroachment of rationalist ideas from the south. This first number was reviewed by the internationally famous philologist Rasmus Rask, to whom Grundtvig wrote a praise-poem on his death in 1832 (no. 142 in *Living Wellsprings*, 2015). Rask noted that despite his antipathy for foreign words Grundtvig employed a number with either German or Greek origin, but he admired the endeavour "to protect the shrines of the fatherland".

Danne-Virke

et

Tidsskrift

af

N. F. S. Grundtvig.

Første Hefte.

Koster en Rigsdaler.

Kiøbenhavn, 1816.
Trykt hos Schiøtz & Mandra, Møntergaden 128.

II

RELIGION AND AESTHETICS

3. On Religion and Liturgy (1807)
4. On Revelation, Art, and Learning (1817)
5. On the Church, the State, and the School, part 2 (1819)

3. On Religion and Liturgy (1807)

Introduction by Vanja Thaulow

On Religion and Liturgy is Grundtvig's first public statement on religious matters, written when he was 23 years old and working as a tutor at Egeløkke Manor on Langeland. The study is a contribution to the liturgy debate that was playing out in the Danish Lutheran Church in 1806-07 after Bishop of Lolland-Falster, Peter Boisen (1762-1831), had proposed a new modernised liturgy, and a more varied and intelligible service. A liturgy commission sent his proposal to pastors in Denmark and Norway,[333] where it created a lively debate, also in the press. The study was published by Lorenz Fallesen in *Theological Monthly* in February 1807. Grundtvig's input differed markedly from all others in disdaining detail in favour of the more fundamental questions: What *is* 'religion', and how do 'Christianity' and the 'liturgy' *relate* to each other? Only when he has treated these philosophical questions does he turn to the bishop's proposal.

Grundtvig's main purpose is to replace the Enlightenment's over-rationalised concept of religion with a more fertile view of his own. Rational thought had sent religion spinning into a crisis, with a widespread indifference to the Christian faith and the reduction of 'religion' to little more than morality. Grundtvig had been influenced by German Romantic philosophy, in particular Friedrich Schelling (1775-1854) and Henrik Steffens (1773-1845), in whose work he appreciated the link between Spirit and Nature, and the concept of 'the Absolute'. *On Religion and Liturgy* is heavily influenced by Steffens' *Introduction to Philosophical Lectures* (1803)[334] and Schelling's *On University Studies* (1803),[335] and is Grundtvig's attempt to formulate a classic Christian teaching in a modern, 'romantic-inspired' language.

On Religion and Liturgy opens with an allegory of human existence. We live in a valley surrounded by a boundless ocean, but we sense that there is a better land beyond – our original home. This romantic intimation is modelled on the platonic idea that our life is but a shadow of a higher, truer reality. We have sought to bridge the Finite and the Eternal through Poetry, whereby it loses itself in the clouds, and Philosophy, whereby it cannot get off the ground. Grundtvig concludes that we must acknowledge our need for instruction from *beyond* the ocean.

In the section 'What is Religion', Grundtvig rejects the general belief that religion consists of a knowledge of the Transcendent. Instead, he defines it as the divine power that raises human beings above all the earth's surroundings to the highest, transcendental pitch. A surer defini-

333 Denmark and Norway were in joint union between 1524 and 1814.

334 Danish title: *Indledning til philosophiske Forelæsninger*. For an illustration of Henrik Steffens, see p. 66.

335 German title: *Vorlesungen über die Methode des academischen Studium*.

tion is to be found in History, says Grundtvig, who draws a line that begins with primordial religion, when God lived in community with his human creation – the Eternal with the Finite. After the Fall came the *decline* of religion, when 'the Eternal' was gradually ousted, 'the Finite' took over, and human beings promoted themselves into quasi-deities. At this historically lowest point, God sent His son to earth, and thus religion resumes with Christianity, for Jesus is the *reconciliation* of the Finite with the Eternal (p. 146).

After a lengthy digression on the fate of the wicked after death, Grundtvig returns to History to describe how in certain periods religion has been downgraded to either Poetry or Philosophy – with unfortunate consequences. In the Catholic Middle Ages religion was reduced to Poetry, and Grundtvig finds that this also applies to many contemporary poets, who wander off into idle contemplation, lose contact with reality, and forget their moral duties. During the Enlightenment religion was next reduced to Philosophy. The human intellect and human reason were elevated, religion was purified of its religious content, and the Eternal disappeared from view. Both the Rationalist and the Romantic philosophers are wrong to believe that we can come to the Eternal through our own powers; this can only be done through God's revelation in Jesus Christ.

Towards the end the study returns to its original subject: the liturgy. Grundtvig notes that the crucial understanding must be that it is the "pure imprint" of the religion of Jesus that should be the archetype of all Christian liturgy. The claim that it should adapt to the times is foolish; for its goal is to raise human beings *above* their finite existence in their "approach to the Eternal" (p. 157). Baptism is the consecration into the Christian religion here on earth, while Holy Communion is the liturgy's culmination, where human beings meet the highest and the holiest above and beyond. Grundtvig suggests that our hymns and prayers should be marked more by poetry and an exalted tone, whereas the pastors of the day should be less moralistic and dogmatic and more open to "the *majesty* of the liturgy" (p. 170).

On Religion and Liturgy had a mixed reception. A number of critics found the study untidy and unclear, but nevertheless praised Grundtvig's zeal and commitment. By his own admission, he would have agreed with them, since he himself wrote the following about the study in his diary in 1815 (unpublished): "It has not been thought through systematically beforehand. It is an enthusiastic eruption of what was fermenting in me at the time. I was teaching myself as I wrote it; that is why it is so uneven." The general opinion was that the young writer was defending the cause of religion with a pure spirit and a warm heart. Everything pointed to him one day becoming a worthy pastor!

In the years that followed Grundtvig's interest in Romantic philosophy cooled, and this study must be characterised as transitional. In his next publication on religious matters, his dimissory sermon from 1810, he returned to a more traditional Lutheran position. Even though *On Religion and Liturgy* is a kind of parenthesis in Grundtvig's authorship, many of its themes continued to occupy him for years to come, such as his critical attitude to Rationalism, his preoccupation with the nature of poetry, and his interest in liturgy, in particular the twin sacraments of Baptism and Holy Communion.

NB. Throughout, Grundtvig uses the inclusive 'we' – meaning 'I' – to involve his readers.

Unter der Hülle aller Religionen liegt die Religion selbst (Schiller)[336]

Once again the liturgy has become the central subject of recent books. This is all the more understandable given that the government has dignified the subject with its particular attention.[337]

Almost all those who have so far pronounced on it have taken as read that our liturgy requires a total renewal, and they have only been concerned with the question of how to achieve this.

It is here that the greatest disagreement has arisen, of course, for they have forgotten to agree on a focus for the more *general* questions: What is religion? What is *Christian* religion? What is 'liturgy'? How we actually *relate to* these questions remains in the background and is either completely overlooked or only regarded with a half-turned eye.

Such behaviour is very strange, as is every judgement passed on the old liturgy, or any other liturgy, without the slightest regard for its fundamental ideas. It is like judging the size of stones without regard for the building into which they must fit! Did they perhaps think that the Christian religion was so well-known that we had *lost sight of* the great revolution that all human ideas have been subjected to in the last ten years?[338] Or did they withhold their view of Christian teachings and a suitable liturgy out of a *caution* which, however justified in certain respects, was out of place here? That the latter appears to be the case for some is borne out by the spirit behind their remarks; but the inconsistency in their behaviour can be seen in their use of the *same* principle on far *less* important subjects in life!

Admittedly people often behave like this in the theatre. If the play is solely calculated towards the fleeting applause of the audience, then it has nothing but a negative effect on the *higher* laws of drama. When it is a question of an unalterable rule for

336 "Under the cover of all religions lies religion itself". The quotation is from the tragedy *The Bride of Messina* (*Die Braut von Messina*, 1803) by the agnostic German writer, Friedrich Schiller (1759-1805), a poet-philosopher and historian, best known for his 'Ode to Joy', which Beethoven employed for the fourth movement of his Symphony no. 9.

337 The liturgy familiar to the young Grundtvig was that of 1685. In 1805 the government set up a liturgy commission, which suggested changes in the Danish Lutheran Church liturgy.

338 This is most likely a reference to the French Revolution of 1789 and its consequences.

the dramas and their stagings that are to be viewed over a considerable period *into the future*, we are hardly likely to settle for what effect they would have on the first and best crowd of spectators called in from the street for the occasion! Indeed, we would not even go so far as to lay down a *single* rule to meet the demands made by more thoughtful persons on the governing taste! Instead we would cast an eye back to the first and highest principle for dramatic writing and then adapt both the material and its formal content into the working process. Neglecting to do so would rightly be called at the very least an unforgivable offence! The offence is as much against both the present generation, whose taste should not be followed unless it has first been proved to come from recognising higher ideas, as against the coming generation, who with the greatest disapproval must see themselves subjected to laws whose motives have long ago crumbled to the dust from which they were taken.

Here and now, however, it is a question of the *highest concern* in life: What raises us above not just *momentary* existence itself, but also raises us up to a contemplation of an *eternal* existence over and above that? And yet these people are content with consulting *our* age as though it were unbiased because it is indifferent!

We have long looked forward to seeing a thorough-going attempt to determine the *foundation* of the Christian liturgy by men who were well-qualified by virtue of their knowledge and their position. But with our expectations disappointed we have taken the somewhat bold decision to place the results of our own honest research before our countrymen.

Of course we know that we are treading a slippery path, one where it is easy to fall; for it guides its wanderers through life itself and allows them to 'hover between heaven and earth', so to speak. But we also know that it is the only path that can *lead* us to the goal and make us feel certain that we shall not become the laughing-stock of the rationalists, even if our foot occasionally slips and our step is shaky! We foresee that the fools who really think themselves wise because they can present everything as being of as little significance as they themselves will laugh out loud; but we must cherish this as much as we would be saddened by the opposite.

Do we need religion?

This must seem a strange question, especially for those of us familiar with History. Yet it is common knowledge that our day and age takes a pride in denying what all past ages have confirmed by confining themselves to this earth only. It is as though the greatest triumph of humankind was to claim the *nullity* of our existence! Here, however, we rightly demand that the question be answered.

Let us seek first to place life and the problem of life on view for all the world to see, not in order to avoid the answer but to introduce readers to our point of view.

We live in a valley, surrounded by an immense, moving ocean. Roused by tradition and driven by an inexplicable desire, we vaguely sense that on the other side of the ocean there must be a land with more beautiful plants and purer air – our original home. Involuntarily we gaze towards it; involuntarily we endeavour to catch a breath of the air that seems to flow from beyond the unknown. Here we could remain standing as though intoxicated by the grapes of the valley, or, being bound to this earth, unable to see an end to it. Here perhaps we might *all* stand, if the waves have not already swallowed us up. But we can no longer be satisfied with this ill-defined feeling – we *will* have *Knowledge*! We dare not venture across the valley for fear of going under in the attempt, and yet we do not even know whether we are allowed to *leave* the valley at all! Nevertheless, we do have two messengers, Poetry and Philosophy, and on them we build our hope. Poetry swings out above the waters and loses itself among the clouds. Only occasionally do we glimpse it in the distance, and despite our gaze, we shall never discover anything except that it is surrounded by a passing lustre. This lustre we sense to be the effect of the beautiful sun's rays from what we call 'the unknown'.

The path of Philosophy is different. First it carefully inspects the valley and follows it through all its ups and downs to see if there is a place from which our premonition flows. But driven by wasted labour, by necessity – it wrongly concludes that it must have *crossed* the ocean. With the greatest care it has equipped its boat to sail across the deep, but it barely manages to move a stone's throw from the shore before it is stopped by cloud-high, rolling waves. Now it must either rise above them and become Poetry, or set anchor before the stormy winds. Or, out of weariness at the vain struggle, it must return to the shore, bid us regard the valley as our home, and settle for giving us the rules for the most convenient path on the winding track that leads to the ocean.

At this point we must either hark back to the premonition which we had and which Philosophy only made all the more concrete, or we must acknowledge our desire for instruction from beyond the ocean.

As soon as human beings have taken their abilities to the level of development where they can see themselves for what they are, the wondrous mysteries of existence confront them. They see how the other earthly animals are content with merely enjoying the moment, yet within themselves they find a desire that goes beyond 'the Finite' – without them being aware of the ultimate *object*. They believe that they have undone a knot by declaring themselves essentially *different* from all other animals, and indeed raised above them. In actual fact they are thereby tightening the knot even more, for unless they see it as their goal to 'eat, be merry, and die',[339] they are abandoned by the whole analogy of life. They have torn themselves away from their only circle of

339 A paraphrase of Eccl 8:15.

acquaintance and are left as a single link with no point of contact. Whether they are perfectly ordinary human beings or wise animals, they will hasten to cut the knot, return to their reasonless friends, and make ultimate enjoyment their highest goal! But not even here are they at one with themselves, for they have only prepared a new battle against the premonition, suppressed but never overcome, of a *higher* existence. The premonition announces itself within them through what is called 'conscience'. Often they can avoid the battle, but they can never end up as its victor, for they must constantly flee from the overpowering army whose attacks become stronger and quicker as age makes them weaker and less equipped for flight. In the end, they are caught between flight and death, and they throw themselves into the cold arms of the latter without daring to hope for release from the pursuing demon.

Human beings, who entertain the premonition that they possess a higher nature, look down proudly on their sleeping brothers and sisters and reproach them for being the cause of their own angst-ridden dreams. They link themselves ever closer to this premonition and hope to realise its wisdom through Poetry or Philosophy. At times they believe that they have indeed reached their goal, but whether or not this is an illusion only later consideration will tell.

Poetry knows how to construct a higher existence from life's most illustrious features, allowing us for a fleeting moment to move with intoxicating pleasure. But it cannot provide us with a *lasting* life in this mode, nor can it assign to existence an independent value as the self-contained condition for a higher form of being. Although its intention is to transport us *out* of this life, it cannot solve its mysteries, which on the contrary encroach all the more, as we approach our goal. Admittedly we know that occasionally, especially in earlier times, Poetry endeavoured to link itself to life. But we also know that it thereby either disdained its nature completely and became the seductive painter of animal pleasure, or it sank beneath the heavy burden of existence that it had thought to lift into eternity.

This is not the place for a detailed criticism of all the philosophical systems, even if that were possible. Let us settle for presenting the highest point which Philosophy by its very nature can and should scale! For this will surely lead us to an awareness of the existential struggle and thus an awareness of our greatest problem. It can motivate its claim that the solution is either impossible, or it can be transferred to human existence. However, Philosophy remains unable to *solve* the mystery.

Philosophy can appeal to the inner experience of all educated people when it claims that our reason acknowledges a higher law than Nature does. But this does not explain the phenomenon of why whatever claims to be 'the highest' cannot manifest itself in life with the same *inevitability*. It cannot explain how this disharmony comes from harmony, nor explain its *return* to harmony. Whoever thinks independently will find that the attempts by Fichte, Schiller, and Schelling – with their unmistakable character of exceptional genius – are nonetheless *failures*. And from here it is only a short step to realising that it could not be otherwise. All the solutions to the great mysteries that Philosophy allows itself to examine must either be a denial of the existence of such mysteries or must rely on a hypothesis that cannot be proved but is occasionally so brilliantly hidden that it seems to be the result of the inward experience itself!

Of the more recent philosophers Schelling is without doubt the one who has most creditably characterised 'the Eternal' and most stringently deduced from this what constitutes the struggle for existence. But only *apparently* so. For what purpose does the most stringent deduction serve, if the very first premise only floats in the air so that without Poetry we cannot reach it? In the hands of Schelling we were given a glorious new creation, but precisely for that reason the connection to the here and now was missing! Lured by our need, we are easily tempted to dismiss the word 'hypothesis' from our contemplation of 'the Eternal'. Yet if 'Philosophy' is to say anything informative about the mystery, it does not become any smaller just because it is shown to be necessary.

We choose Schelling's *philosophy* as an example because we recognise in it Philosophy's admission of its inability to explain the mystery of existence and the consequent referral to an unconditional desire for something higher than this life.[340]

If we cannot connect the highest link of our existence to 'the Eternal', then our knowledge of their mutual relationship must either come from above, or we must do without it. But since we have raised ourselves above animality and feel the need to go beyond 'the Finite', we cannot commit to the latter, and must therefore fervently aspire to the former.

If we succeed, perhaps only partially, in presenting the above ideas with illumination and truth, none of our readers will regard religion as a leash on the ignorant or as a support for the shaky building of our moral system, to be dismantled as soon as it has reached its appropriate solidity; instead, they will follow us with interest as we seek to answer the following question:

What is religion?

The general definition is that religion is a knowledge of the Transcendent. When we consider the existence of a number of religions we must agree with this, since it seems to be the only element that they share. However, if we ignore any single religion in order to observe the concept as it has vaguely drifted into being for all founders of any particular religion, and if, as must be the case, we include the determinative *cause*

340 William Michelsen writes in *Grundtvig Studier* (1948): "Grundtvig made three main charges against Schelling: that he annulled the distinction between good and evil, denied a living, unchanging God, and did so because he wished to evade the doctrines of moral responsibility and judgment after death."

of all religions among more educated people, the answer – 'knowledge of the Transcendent' – cannot satisfy us. The imperfection of this definition cannot be otherwise, since it has come about as a merely logical abstraction from 'a something' that with no evidence is taken to be that which *requires* definition.

If it is at all possible to obtain a satisfactory answer to this important question, it must be looked for in History. For in its calm progress History, being unconcerned with itself, reveals 'the highest' and 'the deepest' of things. If we ask the advice of History, we shall find that although its numbers also include zeros (which though they lack meaning for us were in their somewhat isolated aspect meaningless anyway), religion was generally acknowledged to be the divine power that raises human beings above all the earth's surroundings to the highest, transcendent pitch. Much is gained by accepting this, for religion is now no longer for us mere knowledge, but the golden chain in Jupiter's hand[341] that will lift earth to heaven.

If we go a step further, we shall find that the history of the Greeks, the Jews, and the Nordic peoples loses itself in a golden age, when the gods walked the earth, and heaven and earth coincided in a single idea. Here rests the archetype for all religion, and here we find the answer: religion is the union of 'the Finite' with 'the Eternal'.

We do not equate this expression with the Golden Age of Antiquity, which was only its reflection; nor do we mean by it the new philosophers' idea of eternity;[342] we mean its reality in time and under time's conditions.

In studying the development of this reality, we shall pay no attention to the dull and scattered characteristics of mythology, but concentrate solely on the Bible's pure image in which the figures step forward clearly and fully developed before our eyes.

The Golden Age is depicted in the very appropriate name: the Age of Innocence. All that was here on the earth must have been pure and uncontaminated for it to have flowed together with heaven. The image of God was the name given to this community that we called 'religion', for if it denoted something significant about humankind, then it could not be lost except by human metamorphosis. As such, it could only be lost by eating the Fruit of Knowledge. Community with 'the Eternal' had to cease as soon as we sought Knowledge and could distinguish between good and evil, since this lent us an independent importance to existence. After the first freedom of expression human beings were no longer what they were *of necessity*; now they were the result *of choice*.

In the original state of innocence there was no Death. Eternal life in a state of innocence was *not* death, and eternal life sprang up out of the earth itself; for humans

341 In Homer's *Iliad* 8, 19-27, Zeus (Jupiter) describes the golden chain that hangs from Mt. Olympus with which he can lift the whole earth up to heaven.

342 Among the romantic philosophers (esp. Schelling) 'the Eternal' was seen as the ideal in which all opposites are united and the finite and infinite merge.

expressed their own concept in full. An awareness of death meant the abolition of community, since that could not provide a transition to what already existed. Here we see clearly the meaning of the words: "for when you eat from it you will certainly die."[343]

Human beings were driven out of Paradise and away from the Tree of Life; death stood like a cherub with a gleaming sword between 'the Eternal' and 'the Finite'.

The serpent that seduced Adam and Eve was Existence itself, which lured them into sacrificing themselves for its Knowledge – as though they could thereby become one with God in wisdom. That is why the serpent's punishment is to *crawl* on the earth for ever. Our existence, and the Knowledge of our existence, Philosophy, would never again be able to rise above 'the Eternal'. Thus, with its disappointing promise to humankind, life became a liar from the beginning.[344]

The promise was that the seed of the woman would crush the serpent's head, but that the serpent would also bite the man in the heel. As its main purpose humankind would come to a realisation of the wretchedness of its existence, but would retain enough power to prevent any flight to 'the Eternal'.[345]

There was now no place for religion on earth in the higher sense, only a striving for such, as also the ancient religions demonstrate, for they were all Poetry. By contrast Philosophy was seen as their enemy, and indeed it truly was, given its position.

We believed that we could explain this phenomenon to ourselves thus: The ancients rightly judged that the Knowledge that felled humankind was Philosophy.[346] Fearing the long path ahead, they continually sought back to 'the Eternal', from which they were now cut off. That is why they relied so closely on Poetry, for in the Golden Age it had been one with religion, not in a striving *towards* 'the Eternal', but as an *embrace* of it. Philosophy could therefore find no place in their religions, for the serpent had to be crushed before the community of old could be regained.

The fragmentary depictions of the epic history of the Greeks, which we have from the time of Homer,[347] show that they once believed they had *reached* their goal! We dare not determine whether classical drama was an *expression* of this belief; but it does

343 Gen 2: 16-17.

344 Cf. Jn 8: 44: "(The devil) was a murderer from the beginning, not holding to the truth, for there is no truth in him. When he lies, he speaks his native language, for he is a liar and the father of lies."

345 Grundtvig's own footnote 2: "We realise quite clearly that neither the literal nor the moral interpreters of the Bible's ancient scriptures would agree with us in this understanding, but we declare ourselves willing to exchange opinions as much as anyone, without subtracting or adding anything. This gives us an explanation in which this mythical narrative reveals a deeper meaning and is placed in a closer relation to the subsequent history of religion. This is all that we can say, since so far we have been unaware of any *satisfactory* explanation, and we know of no authority on whom we could rely."

346 Gen 1:3.

347 i.e. omkring 800 BCE.

seem clear that in dramatic art they sought to comfort themselves against disappointed hopes. The illusion could not last, however, for humankind had embraced this life, and could no longer withdraw from it. The Fruits of Knowledge had been cut open and tasted and could never again be whole and untouched, even if they were thrown away to rot. They had to be *enjoyed*, even if they were lethal poison! Already in Greek history we glimpse the transition from Poetry to Philosophy as religion; but it still had to struggle – and it only triumphed under the Romans. Nor was it disdain for the Highest that brought about this change, even though that was truly its origin; instead, it was a vague premonition that a union of Poetry and Philosophy ought somehow to take place.

Yet no *human* spirit could unite these warriors into a harmonious being with a sight of 'the Eternal', for no one has ever gone to heaven except He who came from heaven.[348] Socrates fell as a martyr because the spark of Logos he possessed was too weak and his attempts to use it had the saddest consequences.

Immorality visited humankind with its dirty chains, while the philosophers' auditoria echoed to the praise of virtue and the study of the nature of the gods.

The Art that was born to imprison the fleeing gods on earth was the servant of luxury and vanity.

Life-wisdom wrapped itself in the radiant raiment of Poetry, borrowed its name, and received the homage of the deceived mortals.

Centuries of mutual enmity rolled past, and the mist hiding the rays of 'the Eternal' from the earth became opaque.

The Jews, whose religion as Poetry was lost in the pursuit of nationalism but won far more by its constant allusion to the perfect, gradually lost the ability to see the higher life that had its shoots in their holy books. It seemed that by paying homage to the wise Romans, they had closed their eyes to the last glimpse of 'the Eternal' and confined themselves to *this* life.

If we wish to find vital traces of *Poetry* as a striving towards religion, we must turn our eyes to the Far North and cast a penetrating glance at the deeper truth of the Nordic myths.

Here we find what we have looked for in vain in the mythology of other nations, partly excepting the Jews; namely, the acknowledgement of Poetry's inability to restore to this life its lost fellowship with 'the Eternal'.

From this alone we could explain the marked difference between the Greeks' world of shadows and the Nordic peoples' Valhalla.[349]

The Greeks believed that through Poetry they could regain religion in life, and

348 Jn 3:13.

349 In Nordic mythology Valhalla (lit. the Slains' Hall) is Odin's home, where the slain warriors reside.

therefore they had to regard death as the end of fellowship with 'the Eternal'. So only powerless shadows move around the dark underworld, where Hades, not Zeus, rules. Our state after death is merely a dull reflection of life, and a *return* to life is its highest wish.

The Nordic peoples regarded life as a separation from 'the Eternal', to be used only to prepare their place with Odin on the benches of Valhalla. Their state after death is not a *reflection* of life, but its *empowerment*. That is why the Einherjar[350] stand out so powerfully, imbibe divine power from Heidrun's strong mead,[351] and delight in the loud din of battle and the Valkyries'[352] pleasing songs. They are not *united* with 'the Eternal', for they wish to annihilate death even after overcoming it! Death has become like the bee, which loses its sting by using it, for the heroes who have perished immediately awake as though from a light sleep! But the goal must still be reached, and so the battles of Valhalla are merely patterns for the great battle of Ragnarok,[353] when the gods themselves will perish and make room for the identical 'Eternal'. Only then will a more beautiful, more glorious sun illuminate the reborn earth, and the heroes will live in inseparable community with the All-Father in Gimle.[354]

However reluctantly we must take our leave of the old Nordic holy myths, which in themselves hide the glorious light that permits them the title of the dawn of religion, we must nevertheless now turn our eyes to the golden sun that forever breaks through in the East and whose rays would one day bring warmth to the cold North.

Jesus is born, and with Him religion again descended to the earth, for He was the living expression of the deepest union of 'the Eternal' and 'the Finite':μεγα εστι το της ευσεβειας μυστεριον. Θεος εφανερωθη εν σαρκι.[355]

From this derives the idea of the twin natures in the person of Christ,[356]and from this we could be led to discover the deeper reason as to why the Church Fathers separated λογος into ενδιαθετος and προφορικος.[357]

However, religion in its higher sense could no longer dwell on the earth. With Jesus it again ascended into heaven, after first having wrapped its holy band round

350 In Nordic mythology the Einherjar are the slain warriors who have gone to Valhalla and joined Odin's table.

351 In Nordic mythology Heidrun is a goat whose udders produce mead, the source of poetic inspiration.

352 In Nordic mythology the Valkyries are goddesses obedient to Odin. They select and crown the warriors who are destined to fall on the battlefield.

353 In Nordic mythology Ragnarok denotes the eschatological events that signal the end of the world, when the departed heroes will return from Valhalla to join forces with the gods against the powers of death.

354 In Nordic mythology Gimle is the hall where the survivors of Ragnarok will meet with Odin, the All-Father.

355 I Tim 3:16. "...the mystery from which true godliness springs is great: He appeared in the flesh."

356 The Christian dogma of Christ's two separate natures, both human and divine, was adopted by the Council of Chalcedon in 451.

357 i.e....separated Logos into the 'immanent' and the 'revealed'.

'the Finite', whereby it could raise itself up to 'the Eternal'. That is what the Scripture says: Jesus reconciled humankind with God.[358]

Only now do we have the right to answer the question: What is the *religion* of Jesus? The answer is: The reconciliation of 'the Finite' with 'the Eternal'.

But to deserve this designation it must solve the mystery of existence, and it does so by showing what none had shown before; namely that Poetry and Philosophy linked to 'the Eternal' can be the representative of religion in 'the Finite'.

A comparison with the main ideas of Jesus' teaching will make this plain. Jesus based His teaching on the belief, acknowledged by all religions, that human beings had lost their original splendour and lived at enmity with 'the Eternal' from which they had broken away. Jesus taught that this condition was common to all the race of Adam and that from it arises the simple concept of Original Sin. He taught that human beings did not have the power to raise themselves out of this helpless position, saying that "No one knows the Son except the Father, and no one knows the Father except the Son and those to whom the Son chooses to reveal Him."[359] Paul expresses the same thought with more firmness when he says: "The person without the Spirit does not accept the things that come from the Spirit of God"[360] and: "No one knows the thoughts of God except the Spirit of God".[361] We find Philosophy's endeavour to *be* religion, and the sad consequences of this, painted in the strongest colours in the first chapter of Letter to the Romans.[362]

Thus the first mystery was solved, in that a *light* rose over our human situation. The reason was now known why Nature is in an eternal struggle, and why Moral Law cannot work with Necessity, for it does not belong to this life through its actual *being* but was only conditioned by the Fall of Man, as in Rom. 5 and 7.[363] Now it was seen why humankind had an ineradicable *premonition* of 'the Eternal' without being able to come into contact with it.

One mystery remained which made the coming of Jesus necessary for us, and which showed that its solution must constitute religion: Is reunion with 'the Eternal' possible, and if so, how? That is the mystery.

Jesus answered the first question often and with the fullest clarity; it is therefore enough to refer to such well-known and clear statements as Jn 3:16-17.[364] That the

358 Col 1: 19-20. "God was pleased to have all his fullness dwell in him, and through him to reconcile to himself all things."

359 Mt 11:27.

360 1 Cor 2:14.

361 1 Cor 2:10.

362 esp. Rom 1: 18-32.

363 esp. Rom 5:12-13 and Rom 7:14-25.

364 "For God so loved the world that he gave his one and only Son, that whoever believes in him shall not perish but have eternal life. For God did not send his Son into the world to condemn the world, but to save the world through

Christian religion actually presents the same concept we have assumed concerning this reunion is manifestly clear in the often misinterpreted passages in Rom 8:19-25 and Eph 1:9-10, which say: "He made known to us the mystery of His will according to His good pleasure, which he purposed in Christ, to be put into effect when the times reach their fulfilment - to bring unity to all things in heaven and on earth under Christ." It was the feeling of great bliss at this reunion and its splendour beyond all earthly wisdom that filled Paul with glowing devotion, when he bowed the knee to Our Lord Jesus Christ's Father. Then he prayed that on account of his faith Christ might dwell in his brothers' hearts, so that they could conceive with all the saints - that is, the broad and the long and the high and the deep - and could know the love of Christ beyond all knowledge and fulfilled in all God's abundance.

Jesus' teaching answers the second question thus: Through constant regard for 'the Eternal' and through obedience to the moral law to which humankind subjected itself at the Fall, humans alone can regain the bliss that they have lost. But since humankind was only created in order to descend from concept to individual, it lacks the power to fulfil the law that does not correspond to its entire being. God therefore sent down His son so that by becoming human He should remove the enmity between earth and heaven, and with His holy blood wash away the impurity of 'the Finite', create access for us to the Father, and with His voluntary death fulfil the Law. If 'the Finite' was to be saved from destruction, 'the Eternal' had to briefly let go of His eternality. Jesus had to cut a path through death to life so that *we* could tread it. He had to tear the sceptre from Pluto's hand,[365] as it were, and dry up the Stygian waters so they could no longer confine the dead.[366] Here we have the meaning of the myth of Christ's harrowing of hell.[367]

Thus humankind again stands in a relation to 'the Eternal'. The world of Poetry has gained a reality and become reconnected to Existence, which, as in the sphere of Philosophy, is a significant part of the process of approximation.[368] Poetry and Philosophy appear in the main tenet of Jesus' teaching: Love God above all things, and your neighbour as yourself! Jesus Himself declared this when He said: "All the Law and the Prophets hang on these two commandments."[369] For those who seek entry into the

him."

365 In Greek mythology Pluto is the ruler of the underworld, aka Hades.

366 In Greek mythology the Styx is the river that flows into the underworld, which the ferryman Charon crosses with the dead souls.

367 Grundtvig wrote a powerful hymn on the subject: 'This night came a knock at the portals of Hell', no. 21 in *Living Wellsprings* (2015).

368 The phrase is taken from the philosopher Henrik Steffens' *Introduction to Philosophical Lectures* (1803), where empirical science is described as an "Approximation in the Eternal" meaning a closeness to the true knowledge of nature. Grundtvig transfers the phrase to philosophy, which can approach 'the Eternal' but can never reach it.

369 Mt 22: 37-40.

holy Jerusalem, which shines with the lustre of God's glory and brings splendour to the renewed Tree of Life,[370] these are the commandments they must always have before them. Whatever their faults, they then have the right to kneel with firm hope at the seat of grace which the Lord placed before them through faith in the blood of Christ.[371]

One mystery remains, and it requires so much the more discussion, since it appears unsolved by the Christian religion. Its subject is: the fate of the wicked after death.

For the present we must point out that this is not the *object* of our being, and cannot therefore actually lay claim to being *solved* by religion.

The possibility of Sin was just as necessary as Freedom was; it is the task of religion to show how Freedom can lead 'the Eternal' back. Sin, being the pursuit of a final goal in *this* world, is an expression of our total abuse of Freedom, The riddle of the nature of what results from Sin is of our own making; it is the individual's and not the race's. It cannot lay claim to being solved by religion, which is intended solely for the need of the species for a solution to the first mystery. Put more clearly: religion must show the *path* to 'the Eternal'. Those who do not wish to tread this path deny the goal that religion points towards, a *separate* interest, and cannot accept being taught about a goal whose opposite they have declared to be their *sole* interest. All that they can expect of religion is that it must call their goal the *opposite* of its own, as death does of life. Since they refuse to work towards a reunion with 'the Eternal', they cannot become part of it, and they themselves must *realise* where they are heading, since they wander round unworried and scorn all guidance.

Let us now look more closely at what Christ's teaching states, and set it beside the tenets of philosophising Reason.

Just as Christ's teaching gives no account of the state of 'wicked people' after death, so much the more does it assign a permanence to their misery.

The theologians of old[372] argued that this misfortune consists of everlasting torture and torment of the soul and body by the Devil in Hell. But in addition to protesting at the very singular punishment contained in this dogma, we have the right to argue that it is indeed unbiblical! For nowhere does the Bible say that the Devil will *torture* the ungodly, merely that they will end up in the everlasting fire that is prepared for the Devil and his angels.[373]

From the biblical expression, 'everlasting death',[374] as compared with the idea of

370 Rev 21:1-22.

371 Rom 3:25.

372 In particular, Gregory the Great (540-604), who taught the doctrine of repentance and the concept of purgatory.

373 Mt 25:41.

374 The expression 'everlasting death' is not actually *in* the Bible, only pain, punishment, judgement, and fire are described as 'everlasting'. Grundtvig has probably borrowed the phrase from 'damnation, the everlasting death', found in a theological primer by Bishop of Zealand, Nicolai Balle (1744-1816).

the present human appointment to strive through morality towards 'the Eternal', we might be tempted to believe that Jesus punished the ungodly with some kind of annihilation, such as an inert and painful contemplation of the *bliss* of the godly. This seems to fit the case of the Parable of the Rich Man.[375] The desire for reunion with 'the Eternal' announces itself to him as an unquenchable thirst which burns his dry tongue endlessly. He cannot bury himself in the bottomless abyss at the edge of which he lies, but is tortured by his knowledge of 'the Eternal's' existence, which he is forced to contemplate from the other side of the abyss. Nor can Reason regard this as *unreasonable*; for the ungodly sought in life to *extinguish* the spark of 'the Eternal', which they instead should have *kindled* so as to unite through it *with* 'the Eternal'. They are in a sense *dead*, since the bounds have been set for the sphere within which they have moved. They still lead only a miserable life because they found it impossible with their limited energy to wither the seed of 'the Eternal', even though they did manage to hinder its growth.

There are only two objections of any significance to this.

We can say that this applied only to the *truly* ungodly, i.e. those who went through life with *no* consideration of 'the Eternal', but not to those who, though in premonition, desire, and hope they endorsed it, were nonetheless devoted to some sin or other that carried them away against their will.

It is true that the knot is severed with the words: 'The blood of Jesus washes away the sins of the repentant.'[376] But it would seem like an infection that is often reanimated and makes them unfit to enter into fellowship with 'the Eternal'.

This feeling was what gave birth to the idea of 'purgatory' in its nobler meaning,[377] as a number of the ancients and Origen[378] imagined it. The idea was compatible with the assumption of a higher and final 'life after death', where the concept of pain ceased and seemed to be the only way by which the knot could be satisfactorily untied.

It has been said that this is in conflict with the goodness of the omniscient God – how could He create human beings that He knew from the start would be lost for ever?

This objection seems considerable, but we must realise that it borrows its strength solely from the warped idea that the creation of the world was arbitrary. In our assumption of the eternal existence of God, we also assume the eternal possibility of the creation of the world which under the condition of Time must become reality. The existence of the world and humankind was therefore inevitable. So was the existence of the moral world, on the premise that humankind broke away from the community of 'the Eternal'. And since morality presupposes Freedom, God could just as little

375 Lk 16:19-31.

376 1 Jn 1:7.

377 i.e. before the introduction of letters of indulgence. Luther rejected the concept of purgatory completely.

378 Origen (185-254 CE) was a biblical commentator and Christian philosopher in Alexandria and Caesarea.

prevent humankind from being unhappy as He could prevent its creation or its fall into sin. Whatever still remained was God's doing – in sending down to earth the radiance of His glory and the exact representation of His being.[379] Original sin was thereby effaced, meaning that the transition into the moral world ceased to be sinful, for the way was now shown which led alone to 'the Eternal'. The refusal to travel this road, the intensification of the fall through consenting to the lowest level of existence, and the conscious opposition to the reunion constitute the sin against the Holy Spirit that can never be forgiven.

The new philosophers have defined eternal punishment as the loss of the highest bliss. They believe that after death human beings come to a purer understanding of *duty* and their own true *well-being*. Freed from their sensual bodies they will pursue the path from which they have strayed. These philosophers define wretchedness *after* death as the consciousness of having been *able* to reach another level, if they had dedicated themselves in this life to the service of virtue.

We respect the human heart that first discovered this conjecture of compassion for the wretched, for whom we wish all things well, once they can no longer harm us. But in our hearts we must be indignant towards those who echo these statements, among whom we blushingly must account ourselves for as long as our spirit continues to bow beneath the yoke of authority.

We assume that we can improve ourselves *this* side of the grave! We admit that this is something we desire and do not wish to contradict; the idea that it should be easier to do so in the hereafter rather than here is quite unreasonable, indeed it even abolishes the very *concept* of morality!

So if, after death, we come to a purer understanding of heavenly joy – as we at present assume we shall – and if we gain this by being freed from our bodies, then the temptations that surround us and the difficulties with which we struggle grow by the same token. For it is clear that if virtue has only benefit and beauty on its side, whereas vice has nothing but loss and ugliness, then the concept of struggle ceases to be, and we end up following the same motives in pursuing virtue that we previously followed in pursuing vice. There is no change of *mind*, only an exchange of *names*.

If we were then to believe that our improvement in the next world will be just as difficult as in this one, there is absolutely no reason to suppose that it is more *likely* to occur!

If only the absurdity of this system were realised, it could be forgiven. But the fact that it is inimical to us rather than beneficial, and that it is calculated to confirm people in their blind course on the road to vice, and to prevent their turning back... no honourable person can tolerate that, nor should they keep silent.

379 Heb 1:3.

We must admit that those who are for ever calling for 'morality' are at their most consistent here. Eternity was a thorn in their flesh, since it gave birth to the idea of rewards and punishments, and they wanted virtue to be practised for its *own* sake. They therefore abolished punishment and told us: You ought to be virtuous, for that is the message of your practical reason; but, failing that, you should not fear punishment, for however dissolute you were here, you can always repent in the next life – and it is much easier there, since there are no temptations of the Devil to face!

O what a crowd of virtuous heroes this humane suggestion must have created!

And now they stand in astonishment that the race has not come closer to perfection, since they have been told so many lovely things about it!

Did they never realise that there are sensual, short-sighted people who, even while believing in a *miserable* eternity for pursuing their desires, prefer to postpone their conversion until the approach of death?

Without a trace of venomous satire about the nature of humankind, we dare to claim that in their thousands they followed the temptation to sin, while hoping that having emptied the cup of pleasure to the last drop in this life they could be happy in the next! They had no difficulty in toning down the voice of conscience, and they gently sang what we have already so often heard:

> "I fear not that I shall to Hell be assigned
> by Him who has fashioned both girls and fine wine!"[380]

It might be objected that the philosophers never gave the dissolute any hope of a higher or greater bliss than the virtuous! Is it not true that even those who desire only pleasure count the years, however many millions they be, and measure the distance in degrees between earth and heaven? Do we not see on a daily basis how with an expression of joy on their faces they throw themselves into the jaws of vice, even though it is highly likely that they are thereby burying their fortune, their health, and their life, things that are so much closer to where they actually *are*? And does this happen because they truly value *pleasure* over the loss of these things? Among a few thoughtless people this may well be the case; but in general, vice is successful because its consequences in this life do not necessarily follow, and indeed may even be avoided. If the eternal consequences of vice *also* lose their certainty, it is not much different from the situation of the godly. In which case the entire influence of 'the Eternal' on morality disappears, as does morality itself, for it has no reality without a constant regard for the life beyond.

380. The couplet is from a song by the Norwegian-Danish poet, Johan Vibe (1748-82). It first appeared in *Arias and Songs* vol II (1777).

If the misery in eternity of those who did evil in this life were to consist of an acknowledgement of their loss of the higher bliss that the godly enjoy, it would seem to have its origin in the most disgraceful envy, since in this life they always enjoyed far more than they had deserved. How can such vice ever be *improved*?

It is only in order to create an *illusion* that they have granted to misery such an ambiguous place, since they do not wish to appear to have abolished *all* difference between good and evil - which is what they have actually done. To reach even the lower level of heavenly joy they must consider themselves indemnified when they remember the joyful life they once lived.

The objection could be raised that we know how, *after* death, people do not regard life and all its joys from the same perspective as here on earth; but such conjecture lacks any reason. It is precisely *here* that the triumph of the good endures, and in eternity they find their view of this life confirmed; they acknowledge the reality of their ideas, and they see the reality that is linked to the *possibility* in which they lived. Why then should the opposite be true of the wicked? Because, goes the answer, their view of life was *wrong*. Yet surely the *sounder* view of the good demonstrates that the wicked could *also* have held such a view in their lives, even though they reluctantly rejected it? If their character does not accompany them beyond the grave, they are no longer the same beings. But if it does, they must also close their eyes *there* to the sounder view. The immediate experience of a grievous result can teach them that their path through life was set towards a very different goal than that of the godly. But that is not new to them; they must have already known that in life; they would simply not set any other goal than what could be achieved *without giving up their pleasures*. Since they had no sense of the higher pleasures in life, they could not take any other idea of pleasure with them than what suited such a name as they gave it in this life.

The outcome of the present study is thus that Reason cannot see any means by which to improve 'the wretched' on this side of the grave, and that the Christian religion agrees both with itself and with Reason in assigning their wretchedness to our understanding of eternity. That Jesus did not teach anything more specific about the fate of the wicked after death was essential; for he came to serve not the healthy but only those who needed healing.[381]

The fact that Christ's teaching presents itself as the given identity of Poetry and Philosophy means that it cannot be anything other than a mystery; all those who are misguided by its contents to consider it anything *else* are thereby led astray. One consequence of this is that they believed that they could *reduce* it either to Poetry or to Philosophy.

381 Mk 2: 17.

It was confused with Poetry in the more important period of Catholicism,[382] whose reflection was painted by the poet[383] when he said:

> Raphael composed with love, Buonarotti probed as prophet;
> they raised the Pantheon's dome proudly into the ether.[384]

The signs of the times seem to betoken a similar confusion; but with all their brilliance they are far from being desirable. For the poet this life has lost its interest, and thereby its importance. With fervour he espouses the poetic side of religion, but in so doing he very easily loses himself in idle contemplation, and when he is forced to take part in *this* life, he seems unaware of the limits of moral law. This is infatuation in the wrong sense, but one which often arises in the most innocent way, in that people believe that the religion of Jesus restored a fellowship with 'the Eternal' and that we can be participants in it by moving our gaze from all earthly relations and fixing them on 'the Eternal'.

The present study has shown us that this belief, which is not so very different from that of the Greeks, builds on an obvious illusion; and yet we must never forget that nothing *but* this faith can create the poet. It therefore comes as no surprise that the poet scorns this life and does not even seem to be shot through with the deepest veneration for morality. For in his case it is absolutely necessary to be thus. He cannot rejoice over its fruits, since, in analogy with organic nature, he assumes that the flower must wither before it can produce. Here again he is led astray by his partial view, without which he would not be a poet!

On the contrary, our duty is not to be led *astray* by him. We must not exchange an existence that links us through Jesus to 'the Eternal' for the glossy but deceptive and fast-disappearing offer that the poet makes. For a moment we could follow him and enjoy a foretaste of heavenly bliss; but in wishing to hold firm to it in our lives we make ourselves unworthy of it.

Jesus himself declared that fellowship with 'the Eternal' is impossible in this life when he praised the poet John[385] as the greatest that was born of woman. He nevertheless adds, "yet the least in the kingdom of heaven is greater than he", and so pertinently did Goethe[386] characterise humankind's endeavour to raise itself up to the 'the Eternal' through Poetry when he said:

---

382 i.e. the Middle Ages.

383 August Schlegel (1767-1845) was a leading German romantic and translator of Shakespeare. The lines are from 'Roman Elegy' (1805)

384 The painter Raphael (1483-1520) and the poet, sculptor, and painter Michelangelo Buonarotti (1475-1564) both worked on St. Peter's Church in Rome, which surpassed even the Pantheon.

385 i.e. John the Baptist (Mt 11:11).

386 Johann Wolfgang von Goethe (1749-1832), German writer and statesman. The lines are from 'Grenzen der Menschheit' (The Limits to Man) v. 2.

Even if Man towered up
and touched
with his crown the stars,
he would lose
his firm footing
and the clouds and the winds
would play with him.

In recent times there have been attempts to reduce the religion of Jesus to Philosophy. Although we wish in no way to deprecate the intention behind this – to make it more serviceable for life and more fruitful for morality – we can in no way admire such attempts or wish them to continue. If Philosophy had been able to unlock the mysteries of life, Jesus' teaching would have been unnecessary. But it could not do so, and what else can be the result when the higher seeks to serve the lower?

Philosophy can never forget that it is the wise daughter of Time, and since it does not know its mother's time of birth, it must give her pride of place. The assumption of the existence of 'the Eternal' and its link to this life, by which it seeks to raise itself to religion, is not its own result but merely a yielding to Poetry. They say that earthly life contains all the important numbers and that eternity is only added as a zero, instead of life being a zero which only acquires importance from its position among the numbers of 'the Eternal'.

Without wishing to see the irrationalities and contradictions they fall into, these new theologians showed us neither how this discord entered into human nature, nor how it could come to an end. They prefer to be called, 'philosophers of religion', since they have been educated in the School of Critical Philosophy and suppose that human beings are still fully expressing their character as conceived; that moral law belongs to their original being; and that their only 'fall' lay in their wayward deviations from the path of duty on the flowering way of sensuality.

Instead, these 'philosophers' imposed upon us a 'categorical imperative'[387] to eradicate the elements in our being that stood in the way of their propositions, and thus eventually our true intelligence. However, since this could not immediately happen in *this* world, they promised us a kind of eternity that was really only a continuation of *earthly* time, since moral law would always accompany us with its threatening hand.

They called this 'the purified religion of Jesus', and indeed it *was* 'purified', but only of all the religious elements that *characterise* it! For there is no longer any *higher* life in this origin of time, no yearning for its renewal, no link between earth and heaven

387 The new 'philosophers of religion' take their cue from the German philosopher Immanuel Kant (1724-1804) and the 'categorical imperative' of his moral law: 'Act as though the maxim you act by were a general law.'

without the chain of morality that itself must be raised from below. The idea of the misery of existence and the glory of 'the Eternal' was deemed infatuation, and hardly to be countenanced in the mouth of a poet! Humans became Giants, whose hands could alter the path of the stars if they wished, and, guided solely by their intellect, they could march with steady strides over the arches of heaven. They laughed at the poet,[388] or were irked that he dared to malign humankind and belittle his nobility, so they said of him:

> Even if he stood with firm
> marrow-full bones
> on the solid
> durable earth,
> he would never be tall enough
> to compare himself
> with the oak or the vine.

We too once endeavoured to share the resplendent triumph of the human being! We were drunk on the hope that we could appear to be free intellectual beings on firm ground, and only rarely did we confer the comfort of heaven on our weaker brothers and sisters until their eyes grew as clear as ours. We purified religion of all the irrational things that Jesus and his apostles had taught, merely in order to adapt to their own age – which they were otherwise incautious enough to castigate unsparingly with the sharp double-edged sword of the Word. Soon we were shuddering at the sight of the naked skeleton standing before us without backbone. Life and warmth departed from us and soon we were escaping to the radiant breast of Poetry in order to be made to glow again so that we could see the high meaning of Jesus' teaching with our inner eye.

In consequence we shall hold neither Poetry nor Philosophy in contempt, since we set the revelation of religion as the highest and the only *fulfilment*. For we know very well that every branch of Knowledge has its own specific path to one and the same point which it must pursue with a certain necessity. The duty of Christians is to hinder any confusion that detracts from the excellence of Jesus, and this can best happen by letting it find its total expression in our temples. We know what people *believe*: 'Schools are the places where religious *knowledge* is to be found, and, as the schools improve, our churches will become superfluous.' What nonsense! Children in school should indeed gather the knowledge that they need for their coming position in society, and although they can learn what Jesus has *said*, they will never get to know the religion of Jesus in *school*. We must not forget that there is a touch of 'the Eternal' in children;

388 Goethe, 'Grenzen der Menschheit' (The Limits to Man) v. 3.

they feel no *need* for religion. They cannot possibly take an interest in the greatest truths of life, particularly since these lie so far outside the circle of experience in which they move that they are even regarded as stupid by ordinary intelligence, which seeks to apply the laws abstracted from the physical to the transcendental.

Perhaps this was not an insignificant cause of the scorn for religion which in the last ten years has so plagued people, for all that was holy was made a child's duty and the deepest tones were turned into correct spelling![389] Here is yet another reason why people threw away their religion along with their other dolls as being improper. Thanks be to our Age of Reason! For although it did not always show respect for religion, at least it drove the catechism out of the child's hand! No, no, the religion of Christ is *God's secret wisdom*[390] and can never be generally accepted unless the symbolism brings it closer to our gaze. But just as the religion of Jesus ranks far higher than any of the ancient mysteries, so must its symbolism also be far more consummate, not as any hieroglyphs might obscurely suggest, but as its *pure imprint.* In this lies the concept of the Christian liturgy, or the external divine service. If the identity of Poetry and Philosophy in their striving towards religion is the religion of Jesus, then it must also show itself as such in the liturgy. But if it were to be presented only in its highest power, it would gain nothing from such a presentation. Poetry and Philosophy must therefore appear in their own peculiar clothing but must have an apex at which they are united, a point where they combine to present the religion of Jesus as 'the reconciliation of 'the Finite' with 'the Eternal' in the deepest fellowship between them.

If from this viewpoint we now consider the Christian liturgy as we find it presented in the Book of Acts,[391] we shall see that it agrees perfectly with the requirements we have just made.

Its intention was to teach and to prophesy. What was learning if not Philosophy applied to life, and linked to the doctrine of reconciliation between God and humankind and humankind and Christ?[392] What was prophecy if not a flight on the holy wings of Poetry across this life to the new heaven and the new earth that Jesus promised His followers?[393]

The sacraments of Baptism and Holy Communion make up the lowest and the highest point of the liturgy. At Baptism we are made participants in the given reconciliation; we are accepted as servants of Jesus Christ; and we are thus consecrated into religion. Holy Communion is the culmination of the poetic element in the liturgy,

389 Another reference to Bishop of Zealand, Nicolai Balle (1744-1816), this time to his *Textbook in Evangelical Christian Religion*, widely used in country schools.

390 1 Cor 2:7.

391 Acts 13: 1-2.

392 2 Cor 5: 18-19.

393 2 Pet 3: 13.

for here we touch the Highest and the Holiest towards which we are striving. Here too Philosophy was united with Poetry; for its purpose in the liturgy could only be to make human beings worthy of uniting with the Heavenly.

Only then could we truly see the meaning of Jesus' momentous words to institute Holy Communion: "Do this in remembrance of me!"[394] Addressed to the apostles they can only mean: This must be a powerful remembrance that you have seen what many prophets and kings and wise men wished to see but died in that hope – 'the Eternal' in me united with 'the Finite', 'the Finite' in me reconciled with 'the Eternal'.

The first liturgy is the archetype upon which the Christian liturgy must always be established if it is to be appropriate. Nothing therefore can be more foolish than the claim that the liturgy should 'keep up with the times',[395] since on the contrary it is *independent* of time and should be determined solely by what it is intended to express, namely, an approach to 'the Eternal'. Once it is considered appropriate, it can be altered just as little as religion itself. Could this not be a dim apprehension of the deepest harmony between liturgy and religion that allows the ordinary person to see this change?

The idea of allowing the liturgy to adapt itself to time could only arise once the argument had been followed that Time gave birth to Christianity, which is quite different from saying that Christ came in the fullness of Time. The image can become so tainted and outdated that it requires a complete renewal if it is not to lose all similarity with the original; but that such a renewal could come out of such ruins is indeed a contradiction!

It is true that human beings can grow in Knowledge, but could it not be their highest stage on earth to be able to direct all their Knowledge towards 'the Eternal'? These are not the thoughts of those who see the all-dissolving intellect as our highest attribute; for them the highest goal is to *avoid* 'the Eternal'; so let them do their best in that direction! We believe that the greatest development is when life with all its phenomena and branches of Knowledge is viewed in relation to the eternal archetypal images, in brief, when the whole of life becomes liturgy, for *religion* can only become that in the life beyond.

Although we must never lose sight of the first Christian liturgy in the ordering of our own, we are nevertheless allowed – indeed we are duty-bound – to make of it a progressive unity and to use all the advantages of our times to improve the worthiness of its presentation. Simultaneously, we must always bear in mind what it is we are presenting and never forget the points in Baptism and Holy Communion between which we must move.

394 Lk 22: 19; 1 Cor 11: 24.

395 Grundtvig takes issue with the argument of Bishop of Lolland-Falster, Peter Boisen (1762-1831) here.

To examine the extent to which our present liturgy – in its more extended sense, or as it is practised in our churches – corresponds to these demands is the aim of the following overview.

Even though our churches may not be empty, it is well-known that no one of good repute still visits them except to have their ear itched,[396] or as an example to others, or for less noble reasons. Ordinary people no longer feel the need to meet in the Lord's house, and in many places they come only occasionally, and out of habit. In this connection a number have complimented our age as though it were the increasing enlightenment and acknowledgement of the more important moral culture that was emptying our churches. The age has even asserted its right to the name, 'a vain woman', since it rewards its worshippers with a sweet smile and pretends to protest against flattery.

We do not deny that the steep increase in indifference to all things holy on earth and in heaven that is called 'enlightenment', presumably ironically, keeps many people away from our churches. But we do not need to go beyond these to discover what can persuade the truly religious person to stay away from most of them. We ourselves find it almost impossible to raise ourselves above 'the Finite', for it surrounds and confines us everywhere; it is for ever appearing in portending forms that seem to vie with each other for the honour of our deepest depression in the morass of this life.

But is this caused by the prescribed part of the liturgy, or by the part that is left to the pastor, or by the performance of both of these? Let us look a little closer.

The liturgy is divided into an uplifting part and a teaching part.[397] The former can be united with the latter, but the latter can never be united with the former without doing damage to both.

Let us regard them as we conclude what they *ought* to be, what they *could* be under the present regulations, and what they *appear* to be at present.

In general we reckon the sermon to be the only *teaching* part of the liturgy. Speeches at weddings and on other occasions have a narrower purpose, and following the main principle they must be determined by the situation of the individuals involved. Teaching the catechism is a repetition and continuation of school teaching, which cannot come into consideration here.

At the sermon the pastor moves into a raised position and we must expect to hear from his mouth the great truths concerning: the deep human desire for the guidance and comfort of heaven; God's everlasting decree for our fortune and salvation; the

396 2 Tim 4:3. "For the time will come when men will not put up with sound doctrine. Instead, to suit their own desires, they will gather around them a great number of teachers to say what their itching ears want to hear."

397 The two constitutive elements in divine worship are what Grundtvig calls the 'uplifting' part and the 'serving' or 'teaching' part. He assigns to the former not only Holy Communion ('Lift up your hearts to the Lord') but also Baptism, the saying of prayers, and the singing of hymns.

coming of Jesus in the fullness of time; and what we should do and avoid doing in order to participate in the reconciliation that has taken place. We are permeated by our warm love of God and Jesus, and we feel with Paul that it is far better to leave this world and be with the Lord in the heavenly Jerusalem whose streets cannot be trodden by defiled feet. Or we must expect to hear how we can always show ourselves to be labourers in the Lord's vineyard,[398] labourers who tirelessly plant and water and pray for God's blessing from on high. We must not lose courage when the howling storms break the fragile vines, whose mature grapes we hope to bring to the Lord as a pleasing sacrifice. Or we must be armed with the glorious weapons of faith and hope against the attacks of temptation, so that we learn never to bend the ear to the alluring voice of desire or admire the magical forms that entice us, first with the glitter of the golden flame, then with the flickering, waving robes of pleasure that they present to our eye.

This or something similar we must expect to hear interpreted with dignified words and with the igniting fire of the deepest feeling. That is why the speaker is standing above us – so that his spirit should inspire in us the divine flame with which his own inner self burns and graphically show us that as human beings we should stand between earth and heaven. We should take part in life, but with a constant regard for the *higher* state, so that we do not pay sole heed to this earth and thereby paralyse the wings that should have lifted us up into the glorious regions of light.

The question then arises: Do the majority of our pastors acknowledge these rightful demands?

It is painful for us to have to answer categorically: No! Many could not meet the *majority* of our demands and many refuse to do so. If our wish carried as much weight as it does justification and urgency, we should combine it with the proposal by the noble Fallesen[399] that we should attend to the graduates' proficiency in the preaching ministry and pay close attention to their moral character. For it is an awful thing to listen to pastors who can neither speak nor write Danish, and who have never acquired any concept of rhetorical presentation other than what they once construed from Quintilian[400] and have long since forgotten. It is outrageous to hear the word of the Lord from a cursing hunter who only omits any oaths for as long as he is standing impatiently in a holy place, or from a profligate whose speech outside the temple is full of rotten words and frivolous jests – or indeed from any duplicitous man!

Far be it from us to accuse anyone in particular here, to cast a shadow over a profession that can be so honourable; nevertheless, no one will deny that something like this has been, and may well continue to be, the case.

398 Isa 5; Mt 20: 1-16.

399 Lorenz Fallesen (1754-1824), pastor and publisher of theological periodicals.

400 Marcus Fabius Quintilianus (c. 35-c 98 CE), was a Roman rhetorician whose 12-volume *The Art of Oratory* was a standard work. We know from Grundtvig's library inventory that he owned a copy in Danish of volume II.

Let us return to our true purpose, and characterise the present style of preaching. With the exception of a few who, with educated skills, link diligence to determination and preach the *whole* gospel of Jesus, we must divide our pastors into the dogmatists and the moralists.

The dogmatists talk about the system with no relevant fruitfulness for this life and no relation to 'the Eternal'. Whoever merely rambles on and on about the Trinity and Jesus and the Atonement has no understanding whatsoever of the great significance of these tenets. In such churches we must either stay away or fall asleep.

The moralists all agree that throughout the year they must try to avoid any mention of the *holiest* matters for fear of defiling them with their unworthy presence. But in order not to be one-sided we can separate them into three classes:

Those who lack both talent and active effect.

Those who lack one of these, and,

Those who have both.

Among the first we sleep equally well as with the dogmatists. For they are no more fruitful for our lives by just harping on and on with *dogma*. The difference is only that our sleep is shorter, since these gentlemen seldom have much time to waste in church but must hurry home to look after their horses and cows, their plough and their midden. Even though their numbers are not so small, we believe that the second class are much more numerous, yet we cannot expect much more profit from their sermons either.

Whoever lets his abilities lie dormant because he prefers to sleep, or whoever does not regard the composition of a sermon as a worthy expression of those abilities sinks in the true scales to the level of the above-mentioned, even if his outward expression gives his speech a noble tinge and keeps us awake.

Whoever wishes to have an active effect yet cannot manage to lift himself to the point where he can embrace his sphere of action, and therefore seeks to propagate his knowledge of agriculture and jurisprudence, physics and medicine with a little morality and religion, will also be of little use. But at least he will fulfil the requirements that we in the Church have of him. He will be popular, and he will lower himself to the understanding of the common people. For since they cannot manage any other concepts than those of the stable and the barn, he will, even from the pulpit, tell his listeners, to their great edification "that they should not waste their horse manure on the country road; that the winter has not been so terribly bad, for it has been dry weather for man and beast; and that they ought to thank God for putting earth on the earth, since otherwise we could not live on it". And more of the same kidney.

No one who knows the present method of preaching – even if it is only what we unfortunately can read in print – would call this an exaggeration. Yet nor would anyone wonder why truly religious people stay away from the churches of such pastors!

We now come to those who regard the moral improvement of humankind, at least in the Church, as their sole purpose. Without being led astray by foolish expressions about 'the futility of preaching' they muster all their inner and outer abilities in order to address the intellect and the heart in equal measure. They encourage virtue and berate vice with fervour and feeling; surely they fill the post of Christian pastors just as well as those who give us the complete teachings of Jesus?

We are forced to answer 'no', even though we are fully aware that many respected, intelligent people would answer 'yes' and call our claim 'over-imaginative'. For this reason, and because these spokesmen for morality are the only ones who deserve our attention, we shall examine such words more closely and compare them with the aim of the Christian religion.

Any pastor who believes there is no need to set any store by the most important incentives to virtue that Revelation offers – God's will, a love of God and Jesus, a re-union with the Eternal – and who argues that our human duty, being proportional to our own strength, operates solely on its application, reduces the religion of Jesus to philosophy. If such an approach deprives the religion of Jesus of its greatest benefit by stuffing into us to the riddles of existence instead of solving them as we think we have proved, then despite our admiration for the speaker's singular talent and passion for the good cause we must declare that his speech has nothing to do with religion and does not therefore correspond to its definition.

To clarify this further, let us turn to the motives for virtue that otherwise remain. Either humankind must strive to introduce, as the highest principle for our audience, the rule: Exercise virtue for its own sake! Or we must simply regard certain consequences of any action as being virtuous.

The principle, Exercise virtue for its own sake, has nearly always made an impression through its apparent grandeur, and has been seen as the eternal triumphal arch of Moral Philosophy. But in addition to it forever being devoid of content for the multitude, we have the right to ask: What does 'virtue' mean in this context? The answer will probably be: It is the only absolute, and can therefore claim that everything relative is *subject* to this. We must allow this conclusion a formal correctness, but we cannot be persuaded of the truth of its premise. We think that nothing can be called 'absolute' unless it is raised above the confinements of Time and Space, and unless it includes the determining cause of all things – the eternal identity of that thinking and being – namely, God. Furthermore, we venture to argue that moral principles are limited to *this* life. Admittedly the attempt has been made to overcome this difficulty by calling the Greek gods 'immoral' for standing above moral principles and placing them above God. But since the existence of God, now lacking freedom in the highest sense and being merely relative, was thereby abolished, we must declare the concept to be either too high or too low for our intellect to grasp.

If we grant virtue to be the greatest possible harmony of 'the Finite' with itself – and that must be the case if it is to move forward of its own and not be subordinated to 'the Eternal' – then for it to claim to be unconditionally practised, it must announce itself in humankind as an irresistible natural instinct.

If on the other hand we grant virtue to be the necessary condition for the union of 'the Finite' with 'the Eternal', then it can claim to be exercised without regard for the other conditions of life, though not for its own sake but only for the sake of that by which it is conditioned.

However, there are very few, at least among us, who have employed such an unproductive concept as the basis of their Church teaching. The majority have gone the other way and calculated how much we would gain by doing good, and how much damage by doing evil.

Truly these are the teachers neither of morality nor of religion but only of prudence! They are always seeking to 'guide us through existence' and only have time for a side-look at 'the Eternal', which is presented not for its own sake but as a tangible reward for our desire.

We allow that these interpreters of morality may well deter some from the grosser outbursts of vice, whose grievous and painful consequences they paint in the colours of fire to draw tears from the soft-hearted and to quicken compassionate feelings in their hearts. But at the same time we argue that they cannot infuse their audience with calm devotion in the Lord's hands or the humble acknowledgement of their weakness. Nor could they teach them to use this world as those who do not *need* it, and for the sake of 'the Eternal' give up all that is sweet and beautiful on this earth. Only those who feel that their citizenship is in heaven can do that.[401]

We cannot be asked to provide evidence here that this is a genuine *loss*. For we are not asking whether the religion of Jesus is *true*, as we assume it to be confessed by all of His servants and as it has been the subject of our study. We only ask to what extent, without drawing on those Christian motivations to virtue, we can teach in the *spirit* of Jesus – which is what all our pastors claim to be doing.

It is not inappropriate here to add a few words about self-interest as the motivation of virtue, and about the concept of Transcendence in Christianity. It has been stated many a time that self-interest is an impure motivation of virtue, and on this basis objections have been raised about Christian morality and the call made for the necessity of a higher moral principle. But has the meaning of 'morality' been precisely defined? For morality must express either what is in agreement with our innermost being and our absolute demands on ourselves, or what presents itself to our sensual nature in agreeable form. In the former case it merges with the highest motivation

401 Phil 3:20.

to virtue, while in the latter case it has wrongly been extended to eternity. Those who bid us adapt our behaviour to the consequences of our actions – which only directly affect our lower nature and very much our higher nature – are guilty of the offence of having presented self-interest in its wrong meaning as the motivation of virtue. This is a reproach that Christianity does not deserve. Set against this is the doctrine of prudence, which appears to be a poor substitute for Christianity. We can already see many who would be true and devout Christians if morality had been presented to them in its essential relation to religion, but who now believe that they have fulfilled their destiny once they have observed Knigge's rules for human relations.[402]

In recent years there has been a deep desire to take 'the Transcendent' *out of* Christianity, with the same justification as might be applied to a tree: Take the roots away, since the treetop that we can clearly see in wintertime gathers sap from itself and will undoubtedly offer a far more beautiful view! However, our pastors have been advised good-naturedly to let it stand until it falls of its own accord – and this is called 'pastoral wisdom'! A similar 'wisdom' encourages people to let the old castle walls stand as laughable testaments to the barbarism of the ancients to whom they owe their origins! So it is considered a disgraceful slander to argue that this is because we cannot pull them down ourselves!

We too will attempt to be clever and add a word of wisdom, though we believe that wisdom demands the very *employment* of 'the Transcendent', and we support this belief on the following grounds.

In turning human beings into moral citizens on earth we must place all their abilities at the service of morality. Unfortunately, humans have something called 'imagination', which refuses to limit them to a steady gait on the narrow path of duty. Immediately, we realise that this cannot be part of our rational 'I'. Its Danish equivalent[403] clearly demonstrates that it has to do with the power to make images, and many poets have helped us to contemplate this over and over. It should really be eradicated along with our entire sensual nature through a 'categorical imperative'. But again, how unfortunate! It is much easier to say this than to learn obedience to it, and we must not ask too much of the common people at one and the same time! We had best leave the imagination alone for the time being and simply make sure we occupy it with harmless toys, while we organise the harmony of the powers that are to absorb it. Never did we make a better choice than to hide 'the sensual' in a corner recently. For it is too insignificant to harm morality, and with the present romantic

402 Baron Adolf von Knigge (1752-96) was a German writer who published an internationally popular book on etiquette in 1788: *On Human Relations* (*Über den Umgang mit Menschen*).

403 The Danish word is *indbildningskraft* (= the power to conceive imaginatively).

inclination it will prevent the imagination, confined as it is by existence, from making so many strange leaps to scale the highest walls of morality!

We have spent rather a long time on the sermon, partly because it constitutes such an important part of the liturgy, such that it especially requires improvement in most places.

To avoid the charge of over-specialisation let us now turn to...

Baptism

We do not deny that the formulae for this ritual could be improved, but we acknowledge that the regulations for its administration correspond in the main to its purpose. Baptism must be a consecration into religion and as the first point in the liturgy it should embrace both Poetry and Philosophy. This is truly so, for the child is consecrated to belief in 'the Transcendent' and participation in Jesus' redemption, and as such is committed to renouncing sin and vice, which are the works of the Devil.

It has been considered inappropriate that the pastor addresses the child at Baptism,[404] but it is our belief that the ceremony would lose a good deal of its solemnity from such a change. Unless one is a sworn enemy of poetry there is nothing offensive in this address to the child.

However, since the ceremony of Baptism corresponds by and large to its sacred meaning, why does it generally make so little impression and leave us so empty? We would be making a major mistake if the cause is not thought to lie in the way in which the *actual* baptism takes place! What violence the mention of the Holy Trinity doctrine does to the pastor! What an understandable dislike of superstition is seen in the look on his face when with unwilling finger he must make the significant sign of the cross on the breast and face of the infant! It is so clear that the enlightened teacher wishes to consecrate the child not into faith in the crucified Christ, nor to the inheritance of saints in the kingdom of light,[405] but into citizenship of the moral state which must be able to stand immovable and without Church or religion.

We now move on to the uplifting part of the liturgy, the part that together with Baptism is in the process of undergoing change. It makes a contrast with the Sermon, and includes...

404 The reference is to Jacob Mynster, Bishop of Zealand from 1834-54, whose contribution to the debate on the liturgy in the journal, *Ny Minerva*, argued that the questions asked of the child at Baptism should instead be directed to the godparents.

405 Col 1:12.

Collects, Prayers, and Hymns

It is true that our collects and prayers require improvement, not because the majority of them go beyond this life and deal with 'the Eternal', as they must, but because a number of them lack the fervent and full poetic life that should be expressed *through* them. The question is simply: Who can change them for the better? No one but the true poet, who knows how to exalt the flame of Poetry with the holy fire of religion! If they *are* to be changed, then woe betide us if we leave it to the cold systematist, whatever school he belongs to, or to the prosaist, whose warmth comes from this life only and cannot therefore raise itself above the narrowest circle! We would see the scriptures hopelessly piled up, or the chapters of morality discussed, or meaningless sentimentality court a tear that cannot express the longing for 'the Eternal' but only pity for the *wretchedness* of this life, even in its fairest form. What a miserable contrast would be drawn between our clothing for Sundays and Holy Days and our clothing for the everyday life that entwines them with its dirt-crusted chains!

Then it would be better to retain the less poetic form, which, when it is executed with dignity is nevertheless capable of swinging us up to heaven and dissolving our being in devout and fervent feelings!

The reason why this seldom happens is that in our towns and cities there is an air of general frivolity, while in the countryside it is due to the way in which these things are treated by the pastor.

We now come to singing, the central point in liturgical poetry, in which all that we can produce of sublimity and beauty is united. Poetry must be clothed in harmonious verse and rest on melodic rhyme, and to this is added the intensifying music. We must be raised far above this earth, and a glimpse of eternal life must float over our heavenward gaze.

But dear oh dear! This happens so rarely! – and what is the reason? Is it only in the churches where the *old* hymnbook[406] is used that our expectations are dashed? Not at all! We appreciate the advantages of the new hymnbook[407] especially with regard to the fidelity of the metrical structure and the dignity of the form of expression. We even admit that it contains much poetry, but it is still far from the ideal that floats before us. It would have done well to borrow more from the *old* hymnbook, for it has lost much in being determined by the chapters of morality. Schiller's rightful remark can hardly be unknown to our readers: that poetry should only aid morality through the exalted atmosphere in which it places us as human beings, but that it ceases to be poetry and to exalt us the moment it is put to the service of morality.

406 *Guldberg's Hymnbook*, 1778.
407 *Evangelical-Christian Hymnbook*, 1798.

Much would have been gained if the new hymns had been written not so much to harmonious music (whose beauty only our Catholic brothers appreciate) as to melodic song. But as long as the majority of the singing masters in our church still need to learn much from Bræger[408]and Peer Degn[409], even the most beautiful of hymns lose their power and spread lethargy rather than deep feeling.

Finally we come to Holy Communion, the highest point in Christian liturgy, which expresses the current of the religion of Jesus. Of note are the poet's verses:[410]

1. When earth from heaven severed was,
your spirit sank to earth again;
the heav'nly image pure and clear
no longer in your heart remains.

2. The child within has long since gone
and now you bend to earthly ground;
your harvest you are forced to taste,
who poisoned fruits of Knowledge found.

3. O drink, that you forget again
what arrogance has coldly taught;
the voice of life awakes again
a glimpse of heav'n again is caught.

But why did our so-called enlightened human being prefer to be accused of all evil rather than enjoy Holy Communion, unless it is mainly for the sake of setting an example to others? Indeed why do even the majority who actually partake of it walk away cold and untouched by the holy fire? The reason for their abstinence and coldness must be sought in the corrupt tone of our times, where a disdain for all things holy has taken root. Yet many would still savour its worth, if it were not that most of our pastors *themselves* make little of it. We are not talking here of the despicable perjurers who call themselves servants of the Lord yet join in the scornful tone of the improvident that is used about the holiest rite in our religion. For we dare not believe that such unworthy people can possibly occupy a *teaching* position among us!

---

408 Bræger is the name of the parish clerk in the comedy *Bræger, et Heltedigt* (*Bræger, an Epic Poem*, 1774) by Edvard Storm (1749-94).

409 Peer Degn is the name of the parish clerk in the comedy *Erasmus Montanus* (1723) by Ludwig Holberg, the most famous play in the Danish language.

410 Excerpt from 'The Holy Communion' by romantic poet Adam Oehlenschläger (1748-1827). The poem forms part of the sequence 'Jesus Christ's Life Repeated Annually in Nature', *Poetic Works* (1805).

We only testify to what we have seen, and often we have seen that the distributor of Holy Communion has no idea of the deepest meaning that lies behind this myth, the significance of which transcends the most venerable and holiest produced by classical poetry. For here we see a glimpse of the holy poetry whose creations have a reality. We have seen an annoying boredom in his face, which ought to be glowing with the lustre of 'the Eternal'! Does not such a sight force even the warmest guest back to earth who is seeking to swing up to heaven?

There are two things in the present arrangement that we think people would like changed. We are referring to absolution in the confessional and the wording at the distribution of the sacrament.

The poetic perception of this absolution is a necessary preparation for partaking of Holy Communion, since we humans must be thought to be purified of all earthly things before we dare to approach the heavenly. But purified of religion too? We believe the opposite. As long as we think that Poetry can reunite us with 'the Eternal', so long must purification from the contagion of this life take place; that is also why we see such purifications in all the *ancient* religions. Christ has fulfilled this part of the purification for believers in Him, in that He reconciled the world with God.[411] So nothing is left for us to do except throughout our lives to continue to strive for justice and holiness. Any other 'purification' is specifically in conflict with the spirit of Christianity, and for this reason alone we should ask for absolution. But the further reason is that any other purification is damaging to our true absolution, our moral improvement. It may well be that those who sin but who trust in this would sin anyway;[412] but where is the evidence for this careless phrase, which cannot be confirmed by either outer or inner experience? Have we never seen an offender endeavour either before or after their evil deed to set their mind at rest by receiving absolution from a pastor? And who would dare to claim that even without this comfort or this hope they would have committed the offence? Do we not know that in the hour of temptation we greedily grasp at every means to spare ourselves the heavy battles? Even if there were only one in a thousand who at the thought of absolution was thereby *fortified* in their folly, then it should be abolished as a relic of degenerate Catholicism that has no place in the religion of Jesus.

The second change we should like to see is directed to the words spoken at the distribution of the bread and wine.

No one who has read this far and followed our argument can suspect us of belonging to those who are offended by the holy teaching concerning the sacrament at the altar. Nor would any doubt the union of the believers with their God and Saviour in this;

411 2 Cor 5:19.

412 The reference is to a statement by Bishop Mynster on the liturgy in the journal *Ny Minerva* (1806).

but we think that by declaring the bread and the wine to be the very body and blood of Jesus we are coming close to the blasphemous teaching of transubstantiation,[413] the difference being only one of sophistry.

If all we can do is to capture 'the Eternal' in the works of 'the Finite', and if it is only through the mouth that we can savour the holiest of holies, which can only fall to us through faith, then the profane Voltaire[414] is right to despise us. Were that so, then the meaning of the highest secret of Christ's teaching would be destroyed. For we are then seeking to affix the heavenly to the earthly instead of being *raised* by its divine power to unite with it!

Why can the sacrament not be distributed in silence after the words of institution have been read – as was the custom in the early Danish protestant churches? Or if words *are* to be used, would it be heresy to copy the Reformed church, whose formula 'This means' actually has far more power than ours? Or if we wish for neither of these, what is to prevent us from saying with Paul: The cup for which we give thanks is a participation in the blood of Christ, the bread that we break is a participation in the body of Christ?[415]

Would Paul have spoken thus if he had believed, like those who drew up our Confession,[416] that the body of Christ is "truly and substantially present in, with, and under the bread"[417] that is received into the mouth and – perish the thought! – broken between the teeth?[418]

Did not both Clement[419] and Origen[420] and nearly all the ancient fathers, who did not rest on the surface of religion but penetrated deeper into its being, reject the teaching of the so-called *praesentia realis*?[421]

Before our very eyes Philosophy anticipates itself by turning into religion, thereby casting the most glorious light on its mysteries. Should we then hesitate to grasp their great significance as they begin to grow in classical Christian times? Despite being

413 The teaching stems from the 4th century Church Father, Ambrose; it became a dogma at the Lateran Council of 1215, but was rejected by Luther and the other reformers.

414 Voltaire, François de (1694 -1778), French writer of the Enlightenment who criticised Christianity and the Church.

415 1 Cor 10:16.

416 A reference to Martin Luther (1483-1546) and Philip Melancthon (1497-1560), authors of the Augsburg Confession, a core text of the Lutheran church.

417 Luther taught that at the Eucharist Christ is "truly and substantially present in, with and under the forms" of the bread and wine, which do not *become* the body and blood of Jesus (the Roman Catholic doctrine of transubstantiation) but which exist side by side with them in 'consubstantiation'.

418 An allusion to *manducatio oralis* (eating with the mouth), which Luther employed to underline the real presence of Christ.

419 Clement of Alexandria (c. 150-pre-215), Greek church father.

420 Origen of Alexandria (c. 184-c.253), Greek church father.

421 *Praesentia realis* (the real presence) is accepted by the Lutheran Church under Article 10 of the Augsburg Confession (1530). The condition is that the elements are used according to Christ's institution (consecration, distribution, and reception).

discouraged by meaningless orthodoxy they fought their way slowly forward until like all holy things they were recently threatened with destruction by the intellect.

Should we not acknowledge the truth of the saying: The letter kills, but the spirit gives life,[422] despite it being abused in recent times, like everything else, in order if possible to kill the spirit itself?

Having thus examined the most important elements in the liturgy, we shall turn now to its external administrators, the pastor and the church.

If the pastor knows the religion of Jesus as it can only be viewed *through the highest learning*, if he is both willing and able to *interpret it with power*, and if he is himself a *truly moral and devout man*, it would seem to be a matter of indifference in what *clothing* he came before us. Yet we believe it appropriate that in church he is clearly separated from all his listeners, whatever their rank, and that a change or increase in his clothing should take place during the distribution of Holy Communion. For this is a visible sign that the culmination of the religion and the liturgy is now present.

What happens *inside* the church is of course the most important consideration. Yet the church building itself should be built differently from other houses, just as the pastor should wear specific clothing. For in the temple of the Lord we are quite withdrawn from everyday life, partly in order to raise ourselves above this world and partly in order to contemplate it more impartially when we are outside it, so to speak. In order to achieve these purposes the church should not just have a different building style but also a more beautiful one, a more elevated one than the ordinary house, so that its architecture can be a fixed image of Poetry, which expresses itself thus, and so that we can be helped thereby to view this life not from above but from below.

Everyone knows that this is very far from being the case, and everyone has noted the particular contrast between the tower-high barns of the church owners[423] and the tumbledown church buildings. In most places they have pulled down the humble *church* barns,[424] perhaps because they believed that they broke the harmony of the churchyard wall, or perhaps in order to hinder the false belief that whatever could not be enclosed in these small rooms ought to be used in building up and embellishing the church building.

422 2 Cor 3:6.

423 Country churches in Grundtvig's day were owned by local landowners, who had maintenance duties as well as the right to propose a pastor for a vacant living, until the coming of democracy in 1849. Grundtvig published this article in 1807 during his 3-year stay on Langeland, where all the churches were owned by Count Frederik Ahlefeldt-Laurvig.

424 The corn-tithes were kept in church barns.

We shall doubtless never have cause to be proud of our churches, but it is just as desirable as it is possible that once the price of corn is no longer so low,[425] the time may come when the sight of them no longer arouses the vivid memory of past centuries and long-dead forefathers, or makes us so familiar with the idea of a swiftly approaching and sudden death. When that time comes – and the greenery of hope on the inner walls guarantees it[426]– only then can we talk about suitable indoor adornments. We can forgive them for taking down altarpieces in certain places since their paintings are caricatures of the holiest of holies, but it is clear that a simple table does not elevate the *majesty* of the liturgy. It would be better to put up new altars and make use of the reawakening art of painting to adorn our churches with pictures of the holy story. In that way Art would be given a power that is perhaps the only thing it lacks to raise it to its former glory.

No one believes that this wish arose from a desire to flatter the eyes of the profane and through art to lure those who otherwise lack a sense for the high destiny of the church, even though it was a much greater advantage than can be expected from making worship what is called 'reasonable'. For art is the only creation in life that distinguishes itself by endeavouring to go *beyond* this world!

Even less should people believe that we do not recognise the insane foolishness of earlier Catholicism in worshipping images as though they had their meaning in themselves!

The only reason for our wish lies in the conviction that human beings would find it easier to raise themselves above this earthly life, if, so to speak, they were surrounded by beings from the higher regions who have broken through the prison walls of our dust and appear transfigured by the painter's poetic brush. This heaven-born symbolic presence would give both parts of the liturgy an expression they otherwise acquire only with difficulty, and it would unite the liturgy into a soul-uplifting unity, for we would see those who once wandered in the fear of the Lord and faith in Jesus now in possession of the indescribable bliss that infuses and shines around the holy.

If our forefathers who rooted out Catholicism had allowed the newly-worshipped paintings to remain without thereby fearing any inconvenience, and if more than two and a half centuries had justified their action, how should we who are raised as Protestants with a far purer view of the unity of Protestantism with true Christianity fear that we are creating Catholics by simply exchanging the poor quality paintings for better ones? Seeing that they could encourage devotion or even embellish our God's house and instil in the ordinary people a sense of Poetry without which a large part

425 Although land prices were rising rapidly at the beginning of the 19th century, corn prices were stagnating, to the concern of the landowners who owned the churches.

426 The reference is unclear – perhaps it is to the graves of the churchyard, or even to the fungus growing on the walls of the rotting churches.

of the liturgy is half lost for them, should we not do this? Do we really believe that it is only the good paintings that can do us harm?

We have presented our individual ideas on religion and liturgy in their most important relations without regard for how we, or our intellect, will be judged. It conflicts with our plan to enter into details, and if we are successful in defining the basic concepts correctly, such judgement is unnecessary, since everyone must be able to draw a logical conclusion about our ideas on the matter.

We may have hereby made a mistake, but that is all the more forgivable since we are living in the backwoods[427] and lack nearly all the means apart from our own thinking to rectify our ideas. However, we venture to hope that even the errors do not allow room for any doubt about our warm feelings for religious thinking and in that regard for true morality.

May these pages only show the necessity of a deeper scrutiny of the principles that should be the foundation of our church organisation! May they encourage some of our pastors to make plain to themselves their high calling and purpose as worthy interpreters of the whole of Jesus' teaching! May they arouse some of our brothers, our theology candidates, from their unworthy slumber, in which many of them await a pastoral calling without preparing themselves for it. If that happens, every word of ours may be handed over to oblivion, since that would mean that we had achieved more than our position had led us to hope for.

On the other hand, if readers, apart from a scornful sidelong glance, are unwilling to accept the conclusions that we have drawn on our travels through the higher reaches of the human spirit – because they do not tally with the tone of the times and issue from a person who did not receive a teaching certificate from any faculty, who is not named in any list of scholars, and does not occupy any position, and thus in the language of the times belongs to the absolutely unauthorized – we nevertheless have no regret that we seized the pen with our untrained hand, since it was not our own case we were attempting to plead but that of religion and our species.

Finally we must beg our readers' forgiveness that for the sake of brevity we have called those pastors who set aside religion 'moralists' rather than 'moralisers' – since it was never our intention to say anything about their character.

Egeløkke on Langeland, 1 October 1806.
Nik. Fred. Sev. Grundtvig,
M Theol.

427 Grundtvig was living on the island of Langeland at the time.

4. On Revelation, Art, and Learning (1817)

Introduction by Jon Tafdrup

Textual note

Between "accompanying concepts..." and "What I have so far attempted..." (p. 177) 850 words are omitted, comprising Grundtvig's long-winded defence of his writing-style.

After "... plain black cassock" (p. 207) 3,822 words are omitted. These are summarised at the end of the introduction.

On Revelation, Art, and Learning was published in October 1817 in the third instalment of Grundtvig's journal, *Danne-Virke,* vol. 3. Here he presents a specifically *Christian* view of the nature and purpose of Art, one that has been characterised as "the most detailed contribution so far to Grundtvig's aesthetic vision".[428] Grundtvig himself notes that the study is a turning-point in the *Danne-Virke* series, as he seeks to show how far he has come in "merging general truths with the historical life of humankind" (p. 177).

The essay begins with a retort to the July 1817 edition of the humanist journal *Athene*, in which the critic Peder Hjort called Grundtvig's theology "a dead body", and his philosophy "suffocating smoke." In return, Grundtvig combats contemporary speculative philosophers by "keeping my feet firmly on the ground, meaning that History will not cast off what History itself has contributed". His two major assertions are that History is the path to clarification and enlightenment, and that it is God who determines History: "everything with a time and place in this world is simply an effect of the almighty power of eternal Truth".[429] The *Christian* revelation cannot be reached by Reason alone, nor can Philosophy ever "fulfil its true purpose of restoring and bringing salvation to a fallen people". Grundtvig situates 'Reason' in the body, which is created and exists in History; it can therefore only grasp what is sensory, for otherwise human beings "would have to have a power superior to their Creator" (p. 186). Reason must therefore give up any idea of independence and place itself "under the wings of Faith".

In the second section – on natural and transcendent revelation – Grundtvig reflects on the concepts of Revelation and Learning. The Truth has been revealed to humankind, and with Reason now placed under Faith, we must search the heart for the true, believable Revelation. This will grant the heart peace and unity, in harmony with our conscience, which in turn allows our

428 Flemming Lundgreen-Nielsen, *Det handlende ord. N.F.S. Grundtvigs digtning, litteraturkritik og poetik 1798-1819.* København 1980, p. 760.

429 Eccl 3:1-17.

intellect to grasp what is transcendent. Though Reason is subject to Faith, it is far from inactive. Its role is twofold: to judge what should be included under 'Faith', and to "synthesise what we receive through the senses and the revelation."[430] Grundtvig goes on to describe 'revelation' as the proclamation of a "mystery hidden",[431] from which comes true Learning.

Grundtvig next *distinguishes* between natural and transcendent revelation. We are already granted the ability to comprehend *natural* revelation through the power of our imagination, or "the inner eye", as Grundtvig calls it. Yet this power is somewhat uncertain, since it has been affected by the Fall and may give rise to untrue and contradictory imaginative ideas; it is in need of a transcendent revelation, which enlightens us about the Fall and our possible reparation. In contrast the *transcendent* revelation cannot be grasped: "Faith in the incomprehensible secrets will motivate the intellect to understand the rest." The idea of the sensory is illustrated with the image of a hand, whereas the super-sensory is explained through its effects in time, i.e. in History. If the impression is powerful and positive, then "we strive to reproduce and express it in something sensory; and when we do that, we have taken a step towards its clarification." This is the purpose of Art.

As with Learning we must turn to the heart to comprehend Art. For Art comes into being in the connection between super-sensory ideas and sensory objects, where the conceived ideas are reproduced. To illustrate this Grundtvig turns again to the Fall, and to the image of the hand reaching out for the fruit of the Tree of Knowledge – and thus reaching for *Reason*. In contrast, the feeling heart in us is open to sensory impressions. Reason without Feeling cannot create images or Art, only handicraft.

As elsewhere, the super-sensory is best understood in its presence throughout *History*. Grundtvig therefore turns to the birth of Art and to the oldest work of art, namely God's Creation, including the creation of humankind as divine creatures. What we humans call 'revelation' and 'art' are in fact symbolic reproductions of the divine creative power expressed in the Word of Creation. In the eternal Word, these two are one! And since it is *poetry* that can best depict the spiritual relation of things, it therefore takes pride of place in Art, for it predates everyday language, meaning the use of words to denote the *sensory* relation of things. It is at its best when it sings, for this is an expression of pure sensory activity, a faint hearing of the voice of the Godhead that creates a premonition which bursts spontaneously into song. The Art of Poetry is a merging of sight and song, a process in the heart whose expression returns to the heart and creates ever clearer expressions until the entire revelation stands clearly revealed.

In the omitted section at the end, Grundtvig distinguishes between the three effects of the Spirit: rapture (the greatness of the sensory as an image of the eternal), fascination (the beauty of the sensory as the image of the Spirit), and illumination (the transfiguration of the sensory

430 Sune Auken, *Sagas spejl. Mytologi, historie og kristendom hos N.F.S. Grundtvig.* København 2005, p. 320.

431 Rom 16:25.

in the Spirit). This is followed by a summary of the article, ending with the claim that only true Christian art can "transform and illuminate the sensory, which through the Fall has been subjected to death and corruptibility."

I have long since reckoned that there are readers who, while not being part of my writing audience, nevertheless now and again glance at *Danne-Virke*[432] with half an eye. It is also common knowledge that *Athene's* bird always sees poorly in daylight![433] I would never be surprised to hear this comely little bird singing about the verbosity and obscurity of my writing, for as the cuckoo says in 'Asmus', "Each bird sings with its own beak."[434] I also consider it just as right to be brief when one is making reflections in blindness as to describe in detail what one has seen with open eyes, especially if it is something no one would believe unless they saw it for themselves! As regards 'verbosity', I am always pleased to hear that owls and moles are not at home in my company. Nor have I anything to say to ignorant readers who call everything they do not understand 'nonsense'.

These few lines ought to put a smile on the faces of those who know how philosophers by profession endeavour to employ brevity and clarity when they are unfolding their wisdom! I add one last word merely to demonstrate my humanity and to confirm the proverb: 'A blind hen also finds a grain of corn', for I find the description of my philosophy as "suffocating smoke" to be extremely flattering and rather apposite! What else should I do with my philosophising other than smoke out the foxes that theology has failed to do, or otherwise smoke them into their foxhole-graves?

Since there are good people who have unwittingly given my reflections such a favourable character, I can only feel encouraged to continue with them diligently and to be almost proud to excuse their deficiencies. I nevertheless regard such apologies as circumstantial: they are never superfluous when voiced by someone who wishes to engage in matters far beyond their comprehension, but are necessary in my case only if, after mature consideration, I think it appropriate that I give voice to my view on the

432 Between 1816-19 Grundtvig wrote and published 4 volumes of his periodical *Danne-Virke*, named after the rampart along the southern Danish border with Germany.

433 *Athene* was the title of a rival periodical to Grundtvig's *Danne-Virke*. In Greek mythology the owl was the goddess Athena's pet bird, which whispered words of wisdom in her ear.

434 'Asmus' was the pseudonym of Matthias Claudius (1740-1815), a German poet of the Enlightenment who published 8 volumes between 1775-1812 and achieved some popularity with his deliberately naive questioning of the idealisation of Reason in his day. Grundtvig used the proverb in his song 'A welcome to our greenleaf grove', no. 90 in *Living Wellsprings*, 2015. He included it his own collection of proverbs published in 1845. The full proverb reads: 'Each bird sings with its own beak (said the cuckoo when he heard the nightingale)'. It is now in common use in Denmark, symbolising the individual in the collective.

spiritual history of humanity – for which I have eyes neither to survey nor penetrate, but only to observe with wonder.

It might be thought that when I venture to speak with some boldness about our wealth of philosophy and its first principles, and about the human condition and its destiny, it is hardly appropriate to exhibit embarrassment, as we move towards a description of the historical manifestations of human life. That would seem to testify less to modesty than to the untimely realisation that my previous observations were mirages which History was not persuaded to realise on earth. However, integrity in my use of words is the characteristic which I find difficult to delete or minimise from my calculations, even if I should thereby become the greatest writer in the world! Nor can I conceal the fact that, considering what I am about to write, I have experienced and partly continue to experience great discomfiture.

I believe the reason is not that the above is lamentable, for I rank well below the great philosophers of the times by keeping my feet firmly on the ground, meaning that History will not cast off what History itself has contributed. I venture to hope that the well-informed will understand that my discomfiture is precisely the result of my internal pact with both the history and the truths that I have endeavoured to promote: namely, the noble historical lineage of Philosophy and our short steps on its lengthy path. Where we are to *find* this Philosophy is easy to say, for although there have been a few (and even *one* was far too many!) who fancied that there was more sense in their little finger than in their whole hand and more inside their brains than outside them, that is no more than the remains of a heathen superstition. We cannot expect even animal magnetism[435] itself to repel this in our enlightened time, once Saga[436] with her ruler, her runic staff, has touched only the little finger to show clearly that she has her hand on the shaft and holds the stalk of the Easter lily.[437]

In other words, I am well aware that there are wise scholars who believe that History performed its masterpiece when it produced *themselves*, so they are the ones for whom Athena and Zeus, over the millennia – indeed since the world began – have suffered birth-pangs in their foreheads and have had themselves trepanned in order to create the world![438] If this were true, then I must admit there is no problem in *becom-*

435 Animal magnetism (aka 'mesmerism' after the 18th century German doctor Franz Mesmer) was believed to be an invisible natural force exerted by animals, which could have physical effects, including healing powers. The theory was popular in Grundtvig's day, when practitioners were often called 'magnetizers'; it was discarded in the early 20th century.

436 In Nordic mythology Saga is the goddess of history and storytelling. In Grundtvig's view she has opened his eyes to the meaning and context of Nordic mythology. Her name, for him, is synonymous with History and Experience, as opposed to Reason.

437 These two metaphors denote supreme but hidden power.

438 Around 700 BC, it was said that the ancient Greek god Hephaestus had once performed an axe-trepanation (craniotomy) on Zeus's head to relieve an excruciating headache caused by a tumour growing inside it (which turned

ing wise, and no point in wandering through the *great* madhouse just to feel the loss of what can be found in the *little* madhouse. I shall not deny that in my eyes all those 'miracles' whose workers thereby make fools of themselves are somewhat suspicious, and History would clearly be pulling its *own* leg if it begot a son with the wisdom of all time who became wise by despising it!

Even if I still had a tiny grain of the caustic irony which was once imputed to me but which I have since given away to some good friends, I would make merry to the point of cackling over anyone who found humankind explained anywhere else but in History! On the other hand, now that my pen-sharpener has become blunted by what it has so often tried to cut, I must instead seek to file away crudely at my task, even though I thought the knife could be sharpened on the Philosopher's Stone.[439] Doubtless the opportunity for this will soon arise, since I surmise that it must soon rush out of Saga's mouth.

It is common knowledge that my main contention is that we cannot understand a jot more about humankind than what has been developed and illuminated in us over time. In other words, both spiritually and physically, we are begotten by our forefathers, and must give thanks for their effect and experience as regards both life and philosophy. This is a claim that I think it would be dangerous to deny, and dangerous for any who do not consider themselves capable of winning a duel against Saga and common sense. Whoever might be bold and insolent enough to do so would find me far less daring, since only as an armour-bearer for Saga and only with her gauntlet do I throw down a challenge in her shield-castle,[440] and only there do I find myself safe and secure. There I do not doubt that in her hand Quernbiter[441] will cut flesh like clothes, and cleave every traitor's shield lifted against the Queen of History and our fatherland.

My second contention is that 'the kingdom, the power, and the glory'[442] belong alone to Truth, and that everything[443] with a time and place in this world is simply an effect of the almighty power of eternal Truth, mirroring His thought as created by His Word.[444] At its highest level they reflect God Himself, as the work of His hand with a gleam of His light and a spark of His Spirit. In human beings I see the mysterious creatures who find within themselves the meaning of the world, in that they express what the Godhead *is*. Without gainsaying the truth and making liars of themselves,

---

out to be his daughter, Athena).

439 In medieval alchemy the Philosopher's Stone was a magic substance that could turn base metals into gold.

440 'Saga's shield-castle' (*skjoldeborg*) is Grundtvig's synonym for History.

441 In Nordic legend, Quernbiter (Dk. *Kværnbider* – lit. a 'grinder-biter') was the sword of Haakon I (920-61), so sharp that it could cut through a millstone to the centre eye, according to *Heimskringla* (the chronicles of the kings of Norway).

442 Mt 6:13.

443 Eccl 3:1-17.

444 Jn 1:1-14.

who can belittle my claim or contest my view? Any apology on my part would be improper, for I sentence to death any 'reason' which sought insanely and impiously to climb up onto the royal throne that belongs solely to eternal Truth. I will neither refuse the patent of nobility[445] which the great King graciously granted to our human race, nor will I acknowledge any transcript of it as being valid if it lacks the seal of the Spirit.[446] I will not even admit to any part in the nobility that refuses to be loyal to the King and follow Him in the war against His enemies, the Prince of Lies,[447] who broke his oath and would turn the Temple of Truth into a House of Idols and the House of Prayer into a Robbers' Den.[448] Simply show me that there are no lies in this world, or if that is too difficult, show me the possibility that lying can happen without a will that makes it do so. Or that a lying intention is not a sin and is not a contradiction of Truth!

However, if none of these can be done, it is no use labelling my words 'insufferably long-winded, too obstruse, too sophistic, or too fanciful,' or whatever else the wise men call them! They simply do not realise that in so doing, they are only revealing their own embarrassment and their own awkwardness in dealing not only with my actual language but also with what is the main point here, the thought itself and its accompanying concepts. (...)

What I have so far attempted to develop in *Danne-Virke* I regard in principle as undeniable Truth, which must not be flattered. Now that I shall seek to show how far I have come in merging general truths with the historical life of humankind, I must produce something which in its form is not only imperfect, but in its very content is both incomplete and to some extent contentious. At this point it seems to me that a certain discomfiture is in order. From the title of this essay and from what has gone before, we can see that we are at a fork in the road: we can either follow the Christian revelation with justified confidence, seek to develop a cohesion between its parts and its relation to its believers, and thereby illuminate what is called the 'theological system', or we can let Christianity stand in its historical setting and see what we can find on the path of History about the spiritual beliefs and utterances of humankind. This would be in fragments, like timber in the historical system – as is fitting for posterity to build and complete.

It may seem strange that I do not choose the path most travelled, the one which seems to lead far more easily to the goal. Yet it is even stranger to me that people who wished me nothing but misfortune have reproached me for *not* pursuing that path; whatever else it led to it would most probably lead me to a level where I would

445 i.e. the royal letter raising individuals to the peerage.
446 2 Cor 1:21-22.
447 Jn 8:44.
448 Jer 7; Mt 21:12-13.

be more dangerous to attack and be surer of victory. The reproach demonstrates either their extraordinary self-denial or that they have genuinely laboured under the delusion that I was incapable of presenting the teachings of Christianity in a clearer relation and with stronger references than they have so far appeared in systematic methodology. They must believe that despite my paying the utmost regard to the words of Scripture – even when I am treading the path of scholarship where it is usually rare company – I was still incapable of puzzling out my Christianity when I considered it separately from my faith. However, may my ability to do so be judged on its merits! It is in any case true that any sense that I *lack* the ability would never hold me back, since it would never prevent me from attempting to make advances that are far more difficult. Moreover, were I to find myself in enemy territory, I would think it wiser to drop a hint that there was a small element of ambition here, and I would choose rather to work my way forward than to fear God and follow the beaten path. Of course I do not *say* this, and must avoid doing so, if for no other reason than to conceal the folly I have otherwise committed by constantly placing every emphasis on what one gains by following the *ancient* paths: a simple faith, a childlike hope, and heartfelt love.

While reading the books and papers of the day about all manner of our church teachings I have many a time thought: But that is not *biblical*! Or: That contradicts the irrefutable certainties of Reason! Then my heart beats faster, my cheeks turn red, and I often grab my pen to prove beyond doubt what is so *obvious* to me. Either these people are lying horribly, or they do not *know* what they are saying; they are blind leaders and fools in their 'wisdom'! I have come to realise that there is no point in using *scholarship* to assert 'Christ crucified'; such a concept will forever be folly in the wisdom of the world.[449] Especially in the present age we must beware of using scholarship to take its name in vain, i.e. rob it of its gravity. Only a fool would deny the claim that logic – or, using the far deeper word, 'coinherence'[450] – is a magnificent concept in the right place. But all spiritual coinherence is similar to the mysterious link between spirit and body: only what melts together in the heart *truly* coinheres, and its gathering together in the brain is merely a loose connection, an idea of what *ought* to coinhere in the heart. Just as we die when our heartstrings break[451] – without this affecting our unalterable belief that we human beings are a union of spirit and body – so does Christianity also die unless all our philosophy as regards faith melts

449 1 Cor 1:18-25.

450 Grundtvig compares here the Danish words *konsekvens* (the logical result) and *sammenhæng* (coinherence), whereby the risen Christ *inhabits* believers, enabling them to share the divine interrelationship of the Trinity. God's wisdom is revealed in Christ, who is the source, the model, and the goal of all our earthly endeavour.

451 The Merriam-Webster dictionary writes: "Definition of *heartstring 1. obsolete*: a nerve once believed to sustain the heart."

together in our hearts to become an indissoluble Word of God. Not one jot or one tittle can be taken from this; for only the heart is marked as the sole *living rune*, carved by God's finger and sealed by the Spirit.[452]

Least of all would it help if we were we to draw on the greatest brain to prove that everything in Scripture is true, has been joined together by God, and cannot be separated.[453] This would only lull people to sleep, and encourage them deliberately to *conceal their lack* of a living faith. We also have the sure testimony of History, in that if we go back two hundred years, we can trace this inner coherence everywhere, not just internally between the individual tenets of faith but also between them and all that was being thought, despite the fact that people in those days were unable to link *up* this line of thought. The coinherence was in the heart, ideas were led by the Word, and this in turn united what was one in Truth. If we consult the books a hundred years later, we find the same level of scriptural knowledge and even more prudence, but the inner coinherence is increasingly missing. The artificially constructed loose links in the systems from the days of Wolff[454] clearly augured an imminent breakdown, and, as Pietism showed, this had indeed already begun. The head tried to save itself from death by amputating itself from the body, so to speak! The breakdown has long since come about, but Christianity did not become a *carcass* only – as it did in heathen and Catholic mythology; we did not 'let the holy one see decay'.[455] Its undergarments, i.e. its ceremonies, might be shared and cast aside, but its robe, i.e. its principle, could not be divided; for as we so often have heard, it was woven in one piece.[456] They cast lots for it like the Roman soldiers, but the robe was too long and wide for them. It could be *dyed* in a sense, but it could not be cut to make it wearable, and its base colour shone through. That is why it was left at the cross, where it was found by a robber.[457] He thought it well-suited to be thrown over his head and then to play at 'ghosts'!

Once this is understood, Christians will realise that there are good reasons why I do not make haste to construct a theological system.[458] The *true* system, the true 'church-

452 2 Cor 1: 21-22. This is a striking example of Grundtvig's Nordic heritage – God as a rune-writer.

453 Mt 19:6.

454 Christian Wolff (1679-1754) was a German rationalist philosopher and Professor of Mathematics. Kant called him "the greatest of all dogmatic philosophers".

455 Acts 2: 27.

456 Jn 19: 23-24.

457 i.e. the Catholic/Orthodox Church. Claims to ownership of the original robe are as follows: the whole robe in the Cathedral of Trier, Germany, and in the Benedictine church in Argenteuil, France; portions of the robe in the Cathedral of St. Peter and Paul, Saint Petersburg; in Sophia Cathedral, Kiev; and in the Cathedral of the Dormition, Moscow.

458 This was the task of the movement towards Systematic Theology beginning in the late 18th century – to organise the biblical teachings into categorical systems. These are generally agreed to be 10 in all, as follows: Theology proper – the study of the character of God; Angelology – the study of angels; Biblical theology – the study of the Bible; Christology – the study of Christ; Ecclesiology – the study of the Church; Eschatology – the study of the end

building', is the Bible itself, for that is the Word revealed in flesh,[459] in the spiritual body of Christ. His enemies foolishly believed that they could kill it and bury it, but only those who actively believe this Word and walk in this Church are truly members of this body; they alone are 'Christians', incorporated into the Communion of Saints. Although every thoughtful reader can see what the Bible teachings are, not everyone can adopt its tenets. Added to which come our pastors; if they do what they should, then those who wish to hear (and to read as best they can) will not lack a knowledge of Christianity.[460] They will learn in their *hearts* how it is bound up with the mysterious revelation, and they can prepare their salvation with devout sincerity; otherwise they will never learn, even if they acquire the entire wisdom of the world!

I do not mean by this that a catechism or a public confession of faith is without benefit, for they are in essence the basic Christian teachings. On the other hand, in the face of those who would interpret the Bible according to their *own* ideas the Church community that takes the Bible at its word must clearly demonstrate this by living up to its articles of faith. Nor do I mean that some kind of structure for our teachings is superfluous, for such a structure is a kind of school, and to be sure there are indeed some pastors that need to go to school; all those who *seek* to be pastors need schooling. I cannot deny that what pastors need to learn first and foremost is how to weave homespun wool for the Church, i.e. simple, strong, warm, everyday clothes. That is why Christians put on their Sunday best and go to church; it is in order to repair themselves, i.e. to weave together what has been damaged in their everyday clothing. If a beggar comes along, it is not enough merely to point out that he is wretched and naked; we could also weave him a genuine homespun coat, in which he can live a new life without shame. In other words, we know that there are those who have no ear for the living Word; they call it vulgar, because they themselves let it fall to earth. No one can *teach* them otherwise, not even our pastors and all those who must indeed believe and love their Bible for their own good! At the universities they try to renew the pastors spiritually via the spoken word, but that is where it remains – mere spoken words. Prospective pastors should know their Bible, adopt its teachings, and see them in relation to all the known situations and changes that life brings about; they should be taught quite differently than at present, using the spoken and the written word. It goes without saying that we should answer those who attack the Bible as rationally as we can, but we must remember that only very few understand it, and it is easily

times; Hamartiology – the study of sin; Pneumatology – the study of the Holy Spirit; Soteriology – the study of salvation; and Theological anthropology – the study of the nature of humanity.

459 Jn 1:14.

460 Grundtvig's word here, *Christendoms-Kundskab*, is the name of the compulsory subject currently taught in all Danish schools (6 to 16-year-olds). Since Grundtvig's time it has expanded into the following 4 areas: Life Philosophy and Ethics, Biblical Stories, Christianity, and Non-Christian Religions and other Philosophies of Life.

misinterpreted. So we must never forget to urge upon them that interpretation is merely a side issue, mere 'Latinese'. We do not need to preach this – unless we one day are forced to preach for or against hairsplitting heathens! This is the deeper reason why I have not spent my time commenting on all the many developments – except occasionally and mostly to lay the new German ghost in the churchyard.[461]

There is of course much to say about these developments as to who it actually was walking around in a fog and blowing hot air. Was it Martin Luther and his true successors, or was it the illegitimate children of overblown Reason? Our youngsters must gradually come to the conclusion that Reason ran wild when it banged its head on the Church wall, and they only have shame to show for the dents in their knowledge that it gave them – but that is not on my conscience. As was to be feared, they unfortunately fooled themselves into thinking that through their vitality and their reason alone they could believe in Christ and then find Him! They have forgotten that it is the *heart* which matters most, and that the Bible is the only structure for our teachings which can withstand attack. Even so, this is only when it is allowed to stand on its own two feet – its own firm, invisible foundation; it is useless if it is forced to be regarded as *human* work alone, or is merely carried on top of one's head.

God's Word has much to say that no soul on earth can bear; and what we cannot lift, we must leave alone – without thinking it rubbish! If the Bible contains *all* spiritual Truth, then to be sure we shall not understand it in depth until the next life. To make believe that one can empty its contents through a *system* is even madder than writing about one's personal history and fancying that one has dealt with the *whole* story, including the days to come! The best structure for our biblical teaching is clearly none other than a historical account of how far the human intellect has come *in the Bible*. At its best any *set* teaching denotes a standstill in spiritual development, just as sleep is a sure presage of death. This must not be confused with a set creed, for what we are to confess *must* be set in writing; otherwise we are merely confessing our own opinion about the meaning of something obscure, and in that case we are saying just as little about a Christian teaching as we are about Christianity itself. We must know *what* to believe before we either give our consent or render an account of *what* we believe of the words of the Bible. Either the Bible has not revealed to us what we *should* believe – and is therefore not worth building on; or all dispute concerning the Creed must stem from the fact that we are unwilling to *believe* the Bible, preferring to lean against it or make fun of it, depending on one's degree of disbelief. It is evident that the latter must be true, if the former is false; obviously we have not quarrelled about what we *should* believe in the Bible without knowing what it actually *says*! That would be madness, and anyway Church history does not tempt us to doubt it. It is quite clear

461 i.e. the German rationalist theologians.

that anyone can understand what the Bible wants us to believe simply by reading it seriously. If they do not, then everything else is in vain. Reading the Bible is essential for all who do not wish to be called numbskulls; unless they read it with sincerity and diligence, they are simply playing games with our devotion and our Christianity.

When we separate confession itself from the teaching about it – much the same as separating Luther's *Cathechism*[462] from Balle's *Textbook*[463] – my intentions are clear. Even with genuine scholarship, we must be extremely assiduous, if we wish to propound the semblance of a dogmatic system of biblical philosophy, or write a textbook on biblical knowledge. If we do so with our eyes open – and with our eyes *shut* we can never write clearly or well! – what comes out is no more than a *draft*. This is all the more open to misuse, the better it succeeds, for since it is much easier to copy than to correct and rewrite, a more or less acceptable draft will always tempt us to stand still for a while. For a while it turns into an idol, until it is torn down and then, to its further detriment, it is thrown away as such. This is why I believe that it is both an act of kindness and a true precept of prudence for all who credit themselves with a lighter view of scholarship than most academics of their time never, in any area of philosophy, and least of all in Theology, to present *anything* that resembles a complete system! Hints and snatches are enough for us to weigh up and link together with our reflections before we can use them without shame. I do not mean by this that anything resembling a complete construction will inevitably be inadequate to the needs of scholarship in our present circumstances; it simply needs to be left to those who keep up with the times. It can then be of benefit, provided it is neither exalted nor rejected but is used judiciously, and is adjusted and improved as our philosophy develops, is corrected, and improved.

I would never venture to claim that for anyone who sought to acquire a clearer view and some influence over their times there are not circumstances under which it might be a duty to build something that resembled a philosophical system – including a separate consideration of the Bible's teaching. But such a case could hardly happen more than once, and it could never truly be either a duty or a right to do anything more than construct the building in its broad outline and build a justifiable foundation; but to *complete* the entire structure would be a double offence against Truth. History demands its rights too, and a clearer eye would see how much was missing before the structure was successfully completed and how much of its timber needed testing in a storm before one could have any faith in it. Never, and least of all this year,[464] should

462 Luther's *Small Catechism* was published in 1529.

463 Nicolai Edinger Balle (1744-1816) became Professor of Theology at Copenhagen University in 1772 and then Bishop of Zealand in 1783. He published his *Textbook in Evangelical-Christian Religion Authorised for Use in Danish Schools* in 1791, which became the authorised schoolbook on the Catechism.

464 1817, the year of this writing, marked the 300th anniversary of the Protestant Reformation, which began with Luther's publication of his 95 theses.

we be silent about the laurel wreath which hovers over Martin Luther's tomb – also from this side of the grave.[465] The wreath is far bigger and leafier than if he had set it on a building doomed to be razed to rubble or ruin, for then it would have become a false pretext for those who know full well how to inhabit the various guardhouses that he would have had to build around its borders.

Who actually *knows* Luther? Who has read and reflected on his views in *On the Bondage of the Will*?[466] We cannot but admit that he was minded to construct a *different* sort of building from Melancthon's *Communes*,[467] and to pick holes in Aristotle! We see this in the details, and recall that he did so even before 1517, when he was teaching at the University of Wittenberg. Who can know Melancthon's dryness, his weakness, his vacillation, and not fail to grasp how the blood must have run in the cheeks of Martin Luther when he saw what Melancthon's 'Philipisms' were producing in the universities – like a hobby-horse riding between Faith and Reason? And who is aware of the German love of constructing things and cannot be surprised that Luther, seeing how the academics refused to settle for interpreting the scriptures for general edification, took up his pen and gave them a building to support, one which could withstand a blow and which forced them to stand on biblical ground whichever way they turned? A knowledge of History and a confidential conversation with the departed Luther allow us to make a sketch of the house that he built; anyone who is willing can then see how much we must admire and thank him in his grave for not building a chapel in the churchyard but expending all his energy solely on moving the great Salomonic[468] temple of the Spirit to his fatherland and guarding it like a reborn Nehemiah[469] against heathens and Samaritans![470]

Let us in loving memory venerate this giant warrior of the faith who, despite hordes of enemies, snorted with rage and made ready for the storm. Seeing how his friends preferred to keep vigil over the temple forecourt rather than its sanctuary he was

465 In ancient Scandinavia, a tree was placed on top of a completed building to appease the tree-dwelling spirits disturbed by its construction. Grundtvig uses the laurel-wreath as a symbol of both construction and victory. This ceremony of 'topping out' with greenery of some kind migrated with the Vikings and is now common in many parts of the world.

466 Luther published *De servo arbitrio* in 1526.

467 Luther's friend, Philip Melancthon (1497-1560), was the chief systematic theologian of the early Reformation and principal author of the famous Augsburg Confession of 1530. In 1521 he published *Communes (Loci)*, a system of Christian doctrine based chiefly upon the writings of St. Paul. Luther called Melancthon's various thoughts with which he disagreed 'Philipisms', but he always respected him publicly.

468 King Solomon, son of King David by Bathsheba, reigned from 970 to 931 BCE. Using his father's wealth he built the First Temple in Jerusalem. He is traditionally credited with writing Proverbs, Ecclesiastes, the Song of Solomon, and possible the apocryphal Wisdom of Solomon.

469 Nehemiah is the main figure in the OT Book of Nehemiah. He was governor of Persian Judea under Artaxerxes I of Persia (reigned 465-24 BCE), who gave permission for him to return to Jerusalem and rebuild the Second Temple – from 445 BCE onwards.

470 The Israelites rejected the Samaritans' attempt to help them rebuild the temple; see Ezra 4.

bold enough to believe in the invisible temple guard! He rejected earthen ramparts and built instead a tower in which he hung the church bells that he had cast in the grave of King David of silver from Tarshish.[471] He observed how their ringing brought Christians together and called angels down from heaven on Christmas morning, to the horror of their enemies and the joy of the people, who sensed through the radiance and the holy songs of praise that a saviour was born to them, free of the Pope's power and the murderous Turk.[472]

As always when I am gripped by the memory of Luther and other great priests of Christ, I cannot prevent others from noting that personally I am a curate in this same church and long for my own pulpit, yet nor must I give cause for them to believe that I have forgotten how I am regarded in the eyes of others and what I have promised to remember.[473]

I must remind those who think that what I have just written is no more than a clenched fist aiming to inflict a black eye are making a noticeable mistake. I have merely taken a good opportunity to touch briefly on what I could not let go unheeded; namely, the relation between the Christian revelation and the corresponding scholarship – in the strict sense between Christianity and Theology. For many a century disputes have raged concerning the relation between Religion, Theology, and Philosophy, on the assumption that the Bible was a divine revelation. Since I share this assumption with all Christians, I must declare what I consider it to guarantee: in order to fulfil its true purpose of restoring and bringing salvation to a fallen people, Christianity has no need at all of Philosophy and can only exchange blows with it. Similarly, when Theology takes Philosophy into its service, it runs the same risk as all those princes who surround their thrones with mercenaries: little by little they lose their power and at most retain their name – like the Caliph in Baghdad.[474]

The consequence was that if Theology nevertheless takes Philosophy into its service, it must only be in order to protect its outermost borders against spurious ramblers and to arm itself increasingly against every serious attack from more and greater forces. Once it is a matter of life and death, and the mercenaries have no giant warrior to

471 Tarshish is an unidentified 'far distant land' which supplied vast quantities of important metals to Israel. There are biblical passages hinting that Tarshish was a source of King Solomon's great wealth in metals.

472 'Turk' here, as elsewhere in Grundtvig, is synonymous with Muslim.

473 Between January 1815 and February 1821 Grundtvig was without a church of his own, not least due to his idiosyncratic, aggressive style of preaching. He nevertheless considered himself a 'curate' in Luther's church.

474 Baghdad was a highly cultured city, when the Mongols attacked it in 1258. The Muslim Community in the centuries following Muhammed's death in 632 was known as the Caliphate (under a *caliph*, meaning 'successor'); it grew to include most of Southwest Asia, North Africa, and Spain. When the Mongol leader, Möngke Khan, ordered his brother Hulagu to destroy Baghdad unless the Caliph did homage and paid tributes, the Caliph, Al-Musta'si,m refused – and paid a devastating price. The Mongols killed hundreds of thousands of Baghdad's citizens and destroyed mosques, palaces, hospitals and 36 public libraries. Survivors said that the River Tigris ran black with ink and red with blood. The Caliph himself was wrapped in a rug and trampled to death by horses

support them, they defect to the enemy, especially when they are in a way related. We must seek to unravel this 'kinship' by scrutinising more closely the origin of scholarship/philosophy and other matters.

We have previously noted that all philosophy owed its rise to experience. We did not forget to note how grossly this truth has been misinterpreted and misused, in that the word 'Knowledge' instead of 'philosophy' was used about the internal relations of the sensory matters, despite the fact that Knowledge relates to philosophy as body relates to soul and can only be regarded as philosophy if the soul has dissolved into the body. We also noted earlier that that there must be a higher experience than the sensory and that it was through this experience that History became the source of all true philosophy. Nor did we conceal that these were obscure areas which we had not travelled in but could only point out. Whether what was obscure is now partially clarified only time will tell; but given my previous remarks I believe that I have seen a glimmer of light at the above-mentioned borders, and if my eyes do not fail me, I shall explain here what I can glimpse.

In my view it is Reason that characterises human individuality, or the consciousness which contains what is indubitable. It excludes everything that is alien to our idea of ourselves, and is expressed in our use of the word 'I'. To avoid any futile dispute or sham fight I have stated that 'Reason' may be replaced by the High German 'I-ness'.[475] Having thus explained what I mean by Reason I must also be allowed to use this common word in that sense, all the more so because, as will be seen, this was the sense in which Luther *excluded* Reason from the Church – and yet it has since been canonised![476] Until otherwise disproved, we take the following for granted: that human Reason only has the body on which to build; that only in our senses can we consider ourselves separate from all else; that we are, on the contrary, limbs on the great human body; and that even the whole person must not desire, nor can receive, any spiritual separation except by throwing itself into the arms of falsehood and death. Humankind must regard its sensory limits as an image,[477] and without looking at itself look only at eternal Truth, and seek its transfiguration in Him, the only *independent* being; we assume this to be proven until the opposite is the case.

475 'I-ness' is a reference to the philosophy of Johann Fichte (1762-1814), whose 'Ichheit' or consciousness of self was the basis of all knowledge.

476 Luther writes: "Reason is the Devil's greatest whore; by nature and manner of being she is a noxious whore; she is a prostitute, the Devil's appointed whore; whore eaten by scab and leprosy who ought to be trodden under foot and destroyed, she and her wisdom... Throw dung in her face to make her ugly. She is and she ought to be drowned in baptism... She would deserve, the wretch, to be banished to the filthiest place in the house, to the closets." (*Martin Luther* – Erlangen Edition vol. 16, pp. 142-48).

477 Gen 1:26.

Not only our conscience but every story from days gone by – right up to the great story of how our eyes were opened to see ourselves[478] – testifies to our *originality*. All human children who reach the age of discretion regard themselves with good reason as *individuals* in every sense. According to their various wills they are more or less linked to God and other people, towards whom, at all events, they have a duty. From this and from all else that we know about humankind we can conclude that through an unfortunate transgression we have stepped out of our original relationship and as far as possible our limits. It follows from this that a human creature can only exceed those limits in the soul (through the will) but not in reality (through power or intellect), since in order to be able to do *more* than that, they would have to have a power superior to their Creator – which is a self-contradiction. If we were only 'persons' through our *senses* – through what *they* perceive and record – then by regarding our personalities as our highest achievement we would be limiting ourselves to our sensory selves alone; we would never be able *personally and rationally* to get to know anything other than what was sensory. Within our Reason lies our intellect as a mental capacity; the moment Reason separates itself from eternal Truth, i.e. when we take it into our heads that we are very fine fellows, all our reason becomes sensory. We only *understand* something when we comprehend it in its relation to us through Reason. Being separate, *all things* have only a sensory relation to us, and only through our *reason* can we grasp them. When we think seriously about it, we realise that all things to some extent can be divided into three areas: they are *constant* in that they occupy a certain amount of space; they are *transient* in that they only occupy a limited time; or they are a *combination* of the two. This division is far from being strict, since the one is constantly overlapping with the other; yet in a way this is necessary for us, since to a high degree we ourselves are an expression of this combination and must separate things according to whatever predominates.

This brings us to the well-known division between Nature and History, which is based on the fact that some things have the power to survive, whereas others perish, some things exist, while others come into being. The one corresponds to 'where?' and 'there!', while the other corresponds to 'when?' and 'then!'. Reason must comprehend 'in what' and 'of what' does the one consist that makes it survive, and how and why the other perishes.

From this it is easy to see that all that we are to take note of in History presupposes a form and a stage, i.e. Nature, while all that we are to take note of in Nature – whether or not it undergoes any change before our eyes – comes from creation and form, i.e. History. We are thus compelled to presuppose 'Space', but are forced to conclude from this a previous 'Time' as being the original Time in which all of Nature was created and

478 Gen 3:7.

set in being. Many might call this sophistry, but it was done for their sake and not for the sake of Truth, for it is undeniable that nothing was created before Time existed and that 'there is a time for everything'.[479] The most important thing in this analysis is to begin at the right end; otherwise, instead of *undoing* the knot we create a tighter one which no needle can undo and no sword cut through without the tie going to pieces and the belt of the world being broken. The world must be understood though *History*, if any philosophy is to come of it. But to understand the world historically *in itself*, we ought to have been present – and have been consulted – at the creation of the Earth and the setting of the heavens! To the best of my knowledge this was not the case with human Reason, otherwise it would have looked after its position far better than it has, whatever else it did. Anyone who knows how, quite recently, Reason gave itself off as having *created* the world will not find the taunt undeserved, and all who are willing to use their common sense must admit that never through its *own* aid can Reason advance any further in the world than to grasp that in some inconceivable way it was brought into the world by a far *greater* Reason. Since human Reason does indeed exist in the world, then if we are to follow Truth, we must confess that it was fundamentally foolish of it to get on the wrong side of its superior by shamefully attempting to take a strong line with its Maker.

To what extent Reason has been, and is, master of itself is a historical question, but we have seen that when it uses its intellect best, it comes to the insight that fundamentally it knows *nothing*; in fact it ought to deny itself! We have also seen that even when it is working at its very best by its own unaided efforts, it can never get further than a goal and a timeline that stretch into infinity. It must have read the greatest philosophers of our time poorly if it does not know that in general they are in close agreement here.

With History, however, Reason finds itself in a far different predicament than with Nature, most likely because not only is death a hard nut to crack, but also because if we are to talk about 'philosophy' Reason cannot easily be overlooked. Yet it is hard to employ Reason if one wishes to keep things to oneself. In the case of Natural History, as we etymologically understand it, there is very little problem with its ups and downs, which constantly repeat themselves in a certain order. In this way they can be regarded as a *constant*, as the 'Order of Nature', which gives the intellect a fixed benefit. But whatever goes in leaps and bounds and cannot be fixed and reckoned is an abomination to self-opinionated Reason, because it cannot keep up! The result is a guilty conscience and rheumatism in the feet, which allows it only the sad refuge of tormenting itself with conceiving all manner of objections against the reality which it dreads. No one need consider what I am saying to be an *exaggeration*, for it is only a

479 Eccl 3:1.

mere shadow of the dreadful occurrence *in our times*,[480] when Reason, fearing History, lost its mind and like a mad tyrant declared all its helpers, the senses, to be traitors! It turned itself into a spider's web just to have something left *of its own*, something it could still possess.

However, we cannot assign this question to Saga[481] – noble-minded as she is in her epic poem – merely in order to take revenge on her enemy; at this point we should settle simply for *exposing* that enmity. This is not difficult, since as we know Reason takes a pride in being called 'Saga's enemy' and in its reputation of having proved that History is falsehood! We realise also that this enmity cannot be otherwise, since Reason seeks a reputation for being able to stand on its own two feet, whereas at every turn History impedes this by knocking Reason over and making it hard for it to stand up again. Reason claims that it is 'free' in all its utterances, but History testifies that it is in fact bound to time and place and must be the effect of something else, for Reason has come into being and it cannot have created itself. For as long as Reason demands what it calls its 'rights', it is absolutely impossible for it to comprehend History, for it seeks to understand it through the *senses*; in so doing it not only becomes entangled in the greatest absurdities but hoodwinks itself, and feels called upon to deem History 'inconceivable', despite it thereby again making a liar of itself. It cannot allow any transcendent or *extra*sensory link between successive generations without admitting something it fails completely to grasp; it even denies that power's *independence*! Reason is forced to claim that it *comes of itself* in every human being without that person's awareness – and thus it contradicts itself.

So, however we twist and turn it, Reason either contradicts itself or denies itself the moment we speak of its origin and of transcendent matters; we clearly cannot become wise from self-contradiction, and whether we can do so from self-denial is a moot point. Admittedly, in more recent times the attempt has been made to find a *middle* way – or rather to go both backwards and forwards at the same time, the idea being that in this way Reason can take back with the one hand what it has given away with the other. This would be a masterstroke, if it ever happened; but instead, the only achievement is to contradict oneself twice in one breath, and it would seem difficult to turn two denials into a confirmation.

When Reason surrenders its independence, it places itself under the wings of Faith; and even if it does not lose its common sense, it attempts only what is *credible*. Such an attempt also appears difficult, yet it is not so, provided it is made from the right side (the moral) and in the right place (the heart). The main point is that Reason then

480 Probably a reference to the French Revolution, when reasonable, popular demands somehow ended in the reign of terror and Emperor Napoleon.

481 In Nordic mythology (in both Snorri's *Edda* and *Grímnismál* (st.7) Odin and Saga gladly drink running water from the sunken river (*Søkkvabæk*) to give them wisdom.

denies itself morally, repents its arrogance, and Truth is revealed. If these two things are *verified*, Revelation, in agreement with Conscience, grants the heart peace and unity – in itself an indisputable testimony. It may seem doubtful as to whether the Revelation that makes good on the desires of the heart also produces Learning; at all events it is clear that a revelation which morally proves its own truth can be a reasonable object of faith and thereby develop the intellect so that it can comprehend the transcendent.

We have come now to the historical question as to whether any such revelation has indeed *transpired*, a question which in recent times has been flatly denied by many and declared extremely difficult by the more thoughtful majority. However, as soon as we have agreed on what the word 'revelation' means, it becomes obvious that the question must be answered in the affirmative; what remains is merely a question of whether all revelations are falsehoods, or, failing that, which of them is the true one? We know that 'revelation' actually means the proclamation of a "mystery hidden",[482] and in passing it has been noted, somewhat oddly, how Fichte, in his criticism of *all* revelation, made this a mark of the *true* revelation: that since there was no mystery left to proclaim, there was therefore no revelation. We can well understand why self-conceited Reason must snap its fingers at such a revelation, and the perplexed person be poorly served by it; yet there are other revelations besides the Bible, such as the Koran and various mythologies, all of which proclaim things that are a mystery to Reason. They reveal a specific order that exists *beyond the human horizon* and a particular relation between the temporal and the eternal, the earthly and the heavenly, the human and the divine. So clearly, we must take *some* philosophy from these revelations or give up the hope of doing so. To be sure, if there is a God – as we know there must be – then He must have revealed Himself either in a natural or in a supernatural way.

At face value it would seem most reasonable that the divine Revelation happened in a *natural* way, in other words the Creator furnished humankind with a faculty which in its ordinary function *revealed* the mysterious relationship. We have seen that this faculty could not be Reason, since in its origin Reason is the facility to *comprehend*. In its *ordained order* it is only meant to receive in all stillness what falls into its hands of its own accord, but by concentrating on building up its *own* operation Reason upset the whole relationship and set its face against *all* revelation. Nor could it be Feeling, since by nature it is sensory, and the Spirit must first reveal itself in one of the senses before it can make an impression on the heart. Only Imagination remains, and when did we ever doubt that this is the word we apply to all natural views of humankind and the world when seen in a higher light? From this all revelation comes, in images. We have previously noted that the power of Imagination is the human ability to have ideas, to receive images of itself and other things; it is our inner eye! And just like our

482 Rom 16:25.

outer eye it can differ considerably in strength and vitality, assurance and clarity, and also in colour. The sensory eye sees things as being *within themselves* and detains their shadow; nor can it be denied that human beings have an advantage over animals in the ability to observe things as images of something transcendent. We have evidence in our hands that this has really happened, for we have testimonies to the figurative meaning of sensory things, and myths and legends in metaphors concerning the Invisible; it is understandable that in such matters one wishes to see for oneself! These testimonies are what we call natural or preordained revelation; they are characterised by exposing and divulging what the sensory coverings conceal.

Much has been said about this so-called 'revelation' being simply an absurd comedy and an empty idea which merely nurtured a mysticism and a poetry that was the precise opposite of Truth. Considering the illogical and often contradictory ideas that have entered the world in this manner we cannot deny that it is a task in itself to put one's trust in such revelations; yet that does not make it less true that we stand on the only path where ideas of a higher power can visit us. Eternal Truth, our Creator, cannot possibly have placed a faculty in humankind which in its normal working only hatches lies! Even if we said that the power of Imagination is limited to sensory ideas, it remains equally certain that through the transgressions of humankind it has become disordered and in turmoil. Yet it *cannot* be limited to sensory ideas, since it was determined for a higher order; for obviously whatever is made smaller through such a limitation is *also* out of order. The matter becomes quite clear when we remember that the world's *metaphorical* relation is the true one! It is a self-contradiction to think that the Creator has given us the facility to see His creation in the light of Truth only in order for it not to be used for that purpose! If those visions are distorted and conflicting, it is not because they too elevated, for it is quite certain that even by stretching our neck and sticking our noses in the air we can only become a straw's breadth higher, in other words, by trying to exceed our purpose and our ordained limitations. Even more confusion comes from the fact that our viewpoint has been lopsided and our sight dimmed. The reason is easy to see: Reason went beyond its limits, dislocated our necessary human standpoint, attempted to gather forces around it as the common core, and thereby unsettled the entire arrangement. Instead of seeing God's image in themselves, human beings realised they were naked, lowered their eyes when they heard the voice of the Almighty, hid behind a tree, peeped out from behind its leaves and naturally could no longer see far or see clearly.[483] So from this side our human honour cannot be saved; human beings are sinners, from whichever angle we view them. At the very point where we believed that we had saved our honour, we had openly revealed our shame, the sin and the shame being that we want honour for ourselves! Honour

483 Gen 3.

belongs to the Lord alone, and he has to tell us: "I will not yield my glory to another or my praise to idols."[484]

In passing we must remark that since the days of *Nathan the Wise*[485]there have been whispers growing into loud rumours that *all* revelations in essence end in one and the same thing, and that even though this might remove the guilt of the fathers from their children – and especially from Nathan and those who say good day and good night to such claims – it would make a noticeable difference here. For in that case we could save ourselves the trouble of having to pick and choose among the visions, which are either all false or, since that is impossible, all true! The question here is not about what we can gain from these distorted visions once we have settled on those that are true, nor about how we can use them in our imagination of the Truth, once we possess it; it is about what we can trust as an *image* of Truth and a guideline to it. It seems to me that either we should remain ignorant, or we should imagine that others are ignorant when they claim that Israel's revelation can be matched by the revelation to the heathens.

It is true that we cannot believe *every* spirit, but must "test the spirits to see whether they are from God."[486] As I have said, this is in itself not difficult, since Truth will provide its own proof as soon as Reason retires humbly and respectfully to its proper position in the conscience, and performs its office as thought-collector for the heart. If we still find it difficult to come to terms with our *faith*, then this is only proof of how little desire we have to come to terms with ourselves! If we sit in the mud up to our ears, it is no wonder that we are somewhat hard of hearing; we have to struggle to get to the surface; and in such a state we are reluctant to move into the light. It follows from this that any *true* revelation must be an abhorrence to us, since it can only reveal our shame. No wonder the heathens of old, whose Reason was not so foolhardy as to dismiss *all* vision, preferred what chimed with their heart's desire, concealed their guilt, or presented it as their unfortunate fate. It could either be easily expiated, or as far as possible forgotten and borne. We cannot but imagine that before the Fall humankind had true visions that could hardly be forgotten; but little by little they were muddled up, obscured, and consigned to oblivion. It would have been a miracle if this had not happened *everywhere*, so it comes as no surprise to us to hear that only by a miracle were the true visions saved from destruction and misrepresentation; only by a miracle did fallen humankind continue to exist, to develop, and to come to a knowledge of Truth; and only by a double miracle *after* the Fall did it reach its intended destination!

484 Is 42:8.

485 *Nathan the Wise* is a German play by Gotthold Lessing (1729-81) first performed in Berlin in 1783. It pleads for religious tolerance between Judaism, Christianity, and Islam.

486 1 Jn 4:1.

From the vantage-point where History has indisputably deposited us we can clearly see that the Revelation which claims to have come about by transcendent means, and which Reason rejects, is in no way *suspect*; it is, on the contrary, a good supposition of its credibility. Indeed, if the people[487] which experienced it had *rejected* it – despite their predisposition to revelation – there could hardly be any other justifiable reason for its acceptance than its credibility and veracity. Only the true prophet can be hated in his fatherland; the false prophet strives to inhale the natural and exhilarating attraction of his people to idolatry and, in ethereal garb, produces the favourites of their heart. He of course must be loved and praised like a divine hero subjecting his people to the kingdom of the spirits. Moreover, it has often been noted that in *every* day and age humankind has been strongly disposed to believe in miracles, a trait which appears inseparable from a creature that is conscious of its miraculous mystery.[488] Naturally it feels attracted to a circle from which it seems forcibly detached; the more it feels the miraculous element in human life, the more humankind must listen for the tones from the Unknown, as though they come from its home, and must reach out for every hidden word that might solve the mystery. In Rome in bygone days, for instance, the attempt was made to expunge this attraction to humankind and remove all longing for the land of mystery and all belief in miracles; but this can never be done. For it to happen, the miraculous element would have to be removed from human life, and humankind would have to be turned into gods or dumb animals. As long as a single trace of humankind remains, this inclination will be traceable; it is nothing other than the inevitable feeling that this is the clash of two worlds, of contending powers loosely linked within us in a mighty ferment.

The best we can do in our struggle against what originally belongs to our species is to make it powerless and hardly less unrecognisable in a distorted form. For the inclination to believe in miracles can degenerate into an exclusive preference for a particular kind of absurdity and impossibility, the recent consequence of which was a madness that called itself 'unprejudiced enlightenment'.[489] Obviously, Reason attributes either to sensory things or to itself all the effects which it denies stem from the power of the Unknown. Can there be any *other* difference between believing either that an invisible God has created the world and is at work everywhere within it, guiding every occurrence, or believing that the honour for this should go to the sensory world *itself* or to human *Reason*? There is no other difference than that the former is no more than a mystery, whereas the latter is both an impossibility and a self-contradiction.

Even if one could not quite grasp this and was unable to see that a Reason which op-

487 i.e. the Jews.

488 1 Cor 13:12.

489 i.e. the 18th century Age of Enlightenment.

poses all revelation has lost its mind and can only avoid other madhouses by catching itself in a spider's web of its own making, it is worth noting that this inclination to 'the mystery of things' comes in the most faithless of times, which is beset by a deformed faith far more dissolute than in the most pious of times. When we ask ourselves what do we understand by 'the mystery of things', the answer must be: every effect whose cause we cannot comprehend, either because we cannot *discover* the cause or because there appears to be a strange *anomaly*. Our intellect tells us that an effect requires a force or an activity which we cannot discover in the cause. Let us not dwell here on rational Rome, where sorcerers gained honour when all divinity was derided.[490] Let us instead look to our own times, where we need not emphasise the propensities of the common people in times past, nor the mad desire for novels and plays and all manner of conjuring tricks.[491] We shall concentrate on the most 'rational' of the thousands of childish attempts, large and small, from which precisely those who guffawed at all belief in 'the mystery of things' expected the most mysterious and irrational effects. It belongs to History to set a verbal memorial to the self-contradiction of its most significant claims, examples of which we all have to hand! We merely need to recall the idolatry surrounding words such as: Reason, Enlightenment, Liberty, Human Rights, Tolerance, Methodology, Taste, Cultural Education etc, not to mention the Abracadabra of the Schools of Philosophy! Immediately we recall that a failure to bow the knee for them was as great an offence as a failure to bow the knee in the name of Jesus Christ!

When we recall the extraordinary effects it was believed would follow, as if by magic, every time such words became daily sayings, we can only conclude that superstition and want of Faith are one and the same thing. When Reason appeared to reject all Revelation, it was in fact paying tribute to the most *un*reasonable claim of all: namely, that the senses created the Spirit! This is exactly the same thinking which led the blindest of heathens to kneel before the works of the sculptor and the goldsmith and call them their 'gods'! It would seem irrefutable that in our time there are actually people who have no lack of the naivety which the papist monks, please note, praise

490 When Constantine the Great converted to Christianity in 312 CE, the pagan gods were doomed. In fact it was Theodosius (347-95 CE) who made Christianity the *state* religion. The last pagan public feast, the Lupercalia, was abolished in 494. It honoured Faunus, the satyr-god of the countryside, and was associated with divinely-inspired revelry and abandon.

491 Grundtvig wrote copiously in various genres, and it is worth recalling that among his earliest works were two plays. In 1802 Grundtvig finished the 3-act satirical drama, *The Schoolmasters* (*Skoleholderne)*, which poked fun at the new-fangled pedagogical ideas of the trainee teacher, 'Fichte'. Grundtvig sent *The Schoolmasters* anonymously to the Royal Theatre in Copenhagen, where it was swiftly rejected. The second drama, *The Letter (Brevet)* was finished the following year and featured a modern self-conceited fashion 'peacock'. It was performed by a private dramatic company on 11th September 1803 with Grundtvig himself in the role of the dandy, but according to his journal, "without success" (http://adl.dk/solr_documents/grundtvig-p).

under the name of *credulitas*, gullibility – but in their case only the credulity which drives them to believe a truth which, despite their consciences, warns them of horror, humiliation, and punishment! The superstitious belief in the empty, imageless figment of the brain can never be either methodical or sustained. The flytrap of that spider's web can never become everyman's property; and out of futility and boredom even the most self-satisfied and over-eager must soon yawn themselves to death over the painstakingly-woven web with which they had been infatuated. Whoever kneels before idols of nature in the highest and most sensory sense, i.e. before an *image*, is seeking something to which their belief can fasten itself, in which case we should be able to see which of the two Reason loathes most: 'the mystery of things' or the human conscience.

I venture to believe that even those who do *not* love Truth would find it difficult to reject these main arguments – without obvious contradiction and a lengthy exposition. Nor do I find it gratuitous to summarise them here thus: A philosophy which fails to take into account humankind in its undeniably highest, i.e. transcendent, relation is no *explanation* at all and does not deserve to be called a 'philosophy'. Just as the longing for a transcendent philosophy presupposes a transcendent relationship and the determination to *acknowledge* this, so must such a philosophy presuppose a *revelation* of that relationship, be it natural, mythical, or transcendent, i.e. divinely-inspired. The power of Imagination is the natural ability to receive and link together transcendent ideas. Since it cannot be denied that through Imagination we have received untrue and contradictory ideas, it follows that we have not only 'fallen' from Truth but are also unable to justify a firm faith in *any* mythical revelation. In consequence, we have a twofold desire for a revelation from the divine Spirit or the Spirit of Truth. The first is a universal, inner *desire*, for we are all participants in the Fall and in need of enlightenment as regards both its nature and our possible restoration. The second is a specific or logical desire inasmuch as it is our human species' determination to *come to terms* with itself. If the desire for a transcendent revelation is sure, then its occasion is equally sure, for Truth seeks to make itself known and Love seeks to save; this desire wishes to manifest itself in every human being – if it is allowed to take effect. However, it has temporal Reason *against* it, and fallen humankind does not naturally possess the *will* to receive it; for the Fall can only have happened through the human Will, and for an evil will to become good it must destroy itself and from its nothingness create the opposite of its *old* self – which is a twofold impossibility!

How this conversion and belief in the Revelation of Truth nevertheless became *possible* must be left to humankind to learn. We shall merely remark that one of the hallmarks of true Revelation is to disapprove of the *natural* human being and hold *temporal Reason* to be folly. On the other hand the Revelation must remain a *secret*, since the human mystery is in itself a riddle.[492] At the Fall this riddle became so complex that it could only be solved by a secret – to be comprehended only gradually. On the other hand it was also an *incomprehensible* secret, in that it involved a *restoration*, an untying of the knot which the Fall had tied. The early theologians very wisely divided the secret into two categories which were neither sharply divided nor given definitive expression. The *natural* secrets, which we can gradually comprehend, should not be called 'undiscoverable', for only confusion in the *natural* visions has prevented us from grasping and rightly believing them. Similarly, we must entrust to the *incomprehensible* secrets those which we have not yet deciphered – but only those that have been caused by the Fall. We cannot call 'incomprehensible' the Word of an eternal God and Providence as regards the Trinity, or the Creation, or the struggle between Light and Dark, or Truth and Falsehood, or prophecy and miracles. For these can be understood by humankind *figuratively*, all the more so since humankind *can understand* its Fall and therefore everything it once stood for. On the other hand, conversion and reconciliation and all that lies between them cannot be other than *incomprehensible* for us, since it is an intervention in History whose cause is not so much the *will* of the Almighty as the unfathomable love which saves creation from perdition. What we can comprehend of this is not the issue itself but only its *reality* as being credible, yet incomprehensible.

With regard to Philosophy the main concern is the *comprehensible* secrets, since they are what will enlighten us as to humankind and the world in their original relationship and purpose. We can understand why the transcendent Revelation made not the comprehensible but the *incomprehensible* secrets its main concern, and that all who seek their own good must do the same. For what is the point of knowing what we *should* be, when we cannot *be* it? However, we can also understand partly that the philosophical insight we were destined to gain *will be* gained, and partly that the insight into our created and our fallen state can be active in *arousing* our concern at the loss and our *longing* for restoration. Consequently, the transcendent Revelation often informs us in passing of the intimations necessary for us to purify and fulfil what is natural; and it tells us that faith in the incomprehensible secrets will motivate the intellect to understand the rest. The necessity for this lies in eternal Truth itself, while divine Wisdom and omnipotence vouch for the possibility. Indeed, despite the apparent irrationality, History teaches this to be true, and we can very well see that it is not irrational, only wondrous! For in this restoration the true human being is reborn in us, and in our growth we learn to comprehend everything for which we are ordained. How the intellect develops is a psychological question, whereas in what way the intellect has expanded is a historical question. To what extent the former can be answered depends in turn on how far we have come in History, so we would do best to stick to the second, historical

492 1 Cor 13:12.

question, which in time will serve to answer the former. At the same time, it will do no harm to look *into* ourselves, for it depends on our circumstances what we can see in History – and we cannot comprehend more than what we have.

The first thing to note is that it is as clear as sunlight that the very desire to acknowledge and comprehend a matter cannot arise unless we already have an *idea* about it, however obscure and involuntary that may be. It is equally certain that we shall never manage to *comprehend* an idea unless we conceive a kind of love for it and wish to adopt it in whole or in part. If we do our best to know what we *have*, then we endeavour to *conceive* this idea as lucidly as possible. If we are successful, we become in turn aware of our *self-consciousness*, for then we have comprehended it as we comprehend ourselves. If the idea is sensory, i.e. it signifies a sensory object that exists in space, then it is the task of the hand to explain it; and since, by separating and joining it together in experiment, we can test our idea from all angles, we acquire thereby a sensory concept of the thing that is as clear as the one we have of our own bodies in themselves. If on the other hand the idea is transcendent, i.e. it signifies a matter that cannot exist in space, then we must draw back, for in that case it can only illuminate itself through its effects over time. By contrast, if it makes a powerful and positive impression, then we strive to reproduce and express it in something sensory; and when we do that, we have taken a step towards its clarification. To the extent that this reproduction in others can give rise to the same idea, so to the same extent does the idea acquire a sensory object, by which path it comes into the hands of Reason. We barely need to mention that the discussion here is about Art in its broadest sense; and we can only illuminate this obscure transition from idea to concept in *spiritual* matters, if we ourselves have the necessary clarity. I for my part do not, and must hand over this honour to my masters, whose dwelling is not hard to find; but since they may refuse to be at home for my readers, then I owe it to the latter to offer them the glimpses that I have.

When we want something in its purest form, we most certainly do not look for it in a *fusion*; but if we want something that only exists in a specific compound, then we have to look for it where it actually *is*; and that is how it is with Art. Art is only found in a compound between transcendent ideas and sensory things in which those ideas seek to reproduce themselves. We must turn to the heart to be told about Art, for there lie the mysterious depths from which everything emanates and to which everything returns. Art without doubt is the darling of the heart – and yet far too often its besetting sin. By 'the heart' we mean the *feeling* element within us – our real self insofar as we *feel*, i.e. receive impressions. Since we are not self-created, Feeling is the beginning of life, and our true personality is the impression that the idea of our measured existence makes on our body. Only in our personality, i.e. with our Reason, can we grasp or enfold what there is to be understood of us. Who cannot then see that it is here our heart and personality, our Feeling and our Reason are fused together and seem inseparable? However, experience teaches us that in many areas these two are more or less *irreconcilable*, and we have previously explained the only possible cause of this: namely, that Reason has gone to sleep or taken a bad knock, and that personality has sought to take possession of Feeling and thus make a stance against *spiritual* Feeling – like a 'big man' in his *own* opinion, but in actual fact like a wretched slave to *sensory* Feeling.

We have often noted that the clearest image by which we can imagine Reason is *the hand*. We have also shown how the hand must be the organ that corresponds *visibly* to Reason, since it is Reason's first instrument, and without it we cannot convince ourselves of our sensory independence, i.e. our body's specific criterion of separation in space. It therefore comes as no surprise that the Fall came about from the *hand* as it stretched out for the forbidden fruit, since that was the inevitable expression of what Reason performed internally. From the prohibition of Conscience, Reason declared itself *free*, and sought to act on its own accord. Reason is signified and served by the hand, but like the hand it is only an instrument, miraculously and ingeniously formed to be the most precise instrument of Feeling – and yet *without* Feeling it is nothing but a useless instrument, like a *withered* hand. With only *sensory* Feeling it is like a calloused peasant's hand, which only feels what is observable and otherwise offers resistance, such as to a shovel or a rake, or iron and steel.

Understandably, if all hands were so reasonable, there would be no need of statues or colour-shades in Art, and where Reason failed to *repent* of its madness, there would be no Art whatsoever. If the hand had kept its fingers away from what was not its concern, Feeling would assuredly have benefitted; and if Reason had been pure at heart, it would have illuminated itself in the Conscience, which in turn would have been its life expression for philosophy. Instead, it is now the name of the sensitive hand of Truth, which presses at the tender spot of the heart and makes it feel the folly of Reason. When Reason caught hold and ran wild – as we say of a fire – it became the soul of sensory Feeling, i.e. the soul of the body; it could not possibly take things in their *figurative* sense, which is what Art represents. It did not take the body as the image of the Spirit, but as the image of *itself*, and Art then meant taking *advantage* of everything. Of necessity this only applied to what we call 'Handicraft', since the difference between Art and Handicraft is that the former consists of creating images of sensory feeling for the Spirit, and the latter of creating instruments and conveniences for the Body.

Bearing in mind that abilities are given to be used, and that we can never form or increase our powers by *mis*using them, we realise that humankind is incapable of any activity for which it did not originally have both the ability and the calling. So the difference can only be that sinners *lose* the ability to fulfil their calling, and what they do thereafter is both clumsy and ill-timed. Humankind *before* the Fall would thus have had the same *ideas*, only in a quite different order, namely one of purity and clarity. It would have endeavoured to form the sensory into an expression of its ideas, equally multitudinous, but in a way far more orderly, swift, easy, and dexterous. If the body had not implemented the mad idea of setting up a separate dwelling, we would have managed without one; and if it had not fallen in love with itself, it would not have discovered its nakedness or needed any clothing. If it had not built an arbour in its garden, it would not have needed a house to live in. In brief, there would never have been this distinction between Art and Handicraft, for the hand would never have served itself but would have been led by the eye, and the eye would always have seen the meaning. The greater the role of the hand in a work, the later it was produced, since its sensitivity needed time to be refined, and the tangible element needed time to be clarified before the work could acquire meaning. Only then would what we call 'handicrafts' as well as some of what we call 'art' have been developed as a practical exercise of the Intellect. By this means we would have learned to understand Art without thinking about it, and, together with Art, the Revelation which it depicted.

There are those who say that my observations reveal a certain abstruseness, and that may well be the case here, but I venture to hope and also demonstrate that one needs to be attentive to this if one is not to run over the field like a hare who barely notices the field is there! If we realise that despite human beings at all times loving their bodies as themselves, they have nevertheless preferred to build palaces to the spirit rather than the body. They have begun with what is difficult to copy and ended with what is easiest. Nothing grand has been achieved – except *without* the use of Reason – yet we are supposed to go into a reverie when they take it into their heads that *Reason* is their highest achievement and that humankind developed from animals! They then 'discover' that History accorded very well with this mad idea, and thus they failed to see what they were either running over or walking past. Human beings were appointed to walk *down* the hill. First they were meant to stand on its highest point to gain an overview of their estate and name what they saw with its proper name;[493] then they were to link together in words what they felt was related; finally, when they came down to the fields, they were to show demonstrably that the world was just as they had seen and said it would be! Since this was the preordained course, we can well understand that the *Iliad* had to come long before the Parthenon in Athens,[494] and that even though human beings could be *rolled* down the hill, like the Egyptians,[495] and sought to explain who they were as soon as possible, they never made a single stride, let alone several, back *up* the hill! We can understand how humankind fell over on the hill and could not, or would

493 Ex 2:19.

494 The *Iliad* is dated to the mid-8th century BCE, the Parthenon to the mid-5th century BCE.

495 The ancient Egyptian gods experienced both a finite birth *and* a finite death, after which they could cease to exist. Some could also be resurrected on a cyclical basis.

not, get up again but would remain there until there was firmer footing. We can also understand that once they had repented their false step, they walked down slowly, looked around – especially to begin with – and did not come down to the fields before they had more or less forgotten what they had seen from the *top* of the hill!

What we gradually learn to understand must be pursued back to its source, for only there do we learn the cause of the effect; so we must now turn our gaze to the origins of Art. The oldest artworks are undoubtedly the world and humankind, but they are, we must admit, divine and not human artworks. However, it is here that we gain our footing in the *world* of Art, for the whole of Time opens up to us, like a great new school year where we can learn nothing new – nor does the Master want us to! Instead the artwork has to get to know *itself*, and relate itself to Him. Human beings are at the head of it all and their lives are set on a historical course, at the end of which, like Professors of History, they are created Doctors of Theology. It follows from this that in God's eyes no other study is needed for Philosophy than History. What we call Revelation and Art are only a symbolic image of the Revelation of the Godhead, which the world presupposes, and the created Art, which it expresses, i.e. a figurative replica in humankind.

We have previously pointed out that only the Word can be the medium between God and the world, as between the Eternal and the Temporal; for in origin it is God's eternal, expressed image. By raising and lowering its voice and by sharing its power, it is able to produce many different and temporal effects, which, after circulating, in fact unite and return to their source. We have also noted that for this to happen the Creator's Word in Time first prepared a point of unity over which it hovered, as it gathered the scattered forces into a life, one which was now fit to advance, with the Spirit hovering above it, gently wafting its breeze. It is beyond dispute that this point of unity is humankind, created in God's image and according to His likeness.[496] Our temporal human calling is to understand ourselves as such: we must first *designate* ourselves as such and give expression to this, before we can comprehend it. We must see ourselves *in* the Creator and the world in *ourselves*. After this insight we must *express* the Creator in ourselves, and ourselves in the world. Only then can we understand ourselves as being *in* the Creator, and the world as being in *ourselves*.

All this is a repetition of what I have said before, but I dare not assume that it is ready knowledge. It is therefore here that it must lose its 'obscurity' by being set openly before us. What we have called 'Revelation of Nature' is here designated 'vision',[497] and it should now become apparent why I have been unable to use the word 'poetry'

496 Gen 1:26.

497 Grundtvig uses the Danish word word *syn* here, which has 8 different meanings, including eyesight and an appearance by a supernatural power.

here. Not only has it been badly abused as both a 'foreign' word and a coveted title, but it actually means neither more nor less than 'Art', i.e. 'created through sight'.[498] It is not the sight *itself* – from which it must be distinguished, even though they can only be separated historically. Art lies already in our eyesight and must be created on that basis, just as our eyesight is contained in Art and expressed in its work. 'To see' is not an *action* of the seer, it is the seer's sensory perception; it is not the mirror but the object; or rather, He who produced both them and their relation *creates* what we see, while a spiritual *insight* reveals itself in a sensory mirror as Revelation. Art is an *activity*, an action by the Artist, whereas with sight nothing happens in the sensory world without it physically *existing* therein. However obscure it may seem to us *how* this revelation is received, we must never doubt that the Word is its *body*, because in it and only through it can the Word issue forth and enter the world in the simplest sense *with* a body. Here, with the Word designated as 'sight', we are standing at the cradle of Art, but we dare not call the imagery itself a *human* artwork, precisely because it is divine – and far from *requiring* a human contribution, it actually *excludes* it. We see immediately that we are standing face to face with the great twofold mysterious fusion of the coming of 'sight' and the origin of the Word into humankind. I ask for respect when I state that I can in no way pretend that I understand this; I only claim that Revelation and the Word, which in eternal Truth are one, must also have come together *in humankind*, since the Word is precisely the physical form of Revelation which over time must be glorified. It starts with imagery, ends with Truth, and thus clarifies for us that imagery and Truth are one in the eternal Word.

In passing, we are touching here on something we cannot avoid on a daily basis, i.e. inanimate Nature, which has been given free scope for a while now.[499] I refer to the foolish talk about the *sensory* origin of the Word and the *mechanicalness* of Revelation. I have previously spoken in vain if I have to prove here that this talk has no other basis than the single and sufficient explanation that the souls of these 'chatterers' are wearing corsets, which must be penetrated for their souls to *feel* anything, as well as mittens, whereby all that they can manage to hold on to must be thick and coarse! Let me remind you that if one's imagery is from last year, when one could barely count to five, then one has hardly given the words their meaning according to the thoughts one has *later*. Since spirits are not machines, there can hardly be anything 'mechanical' when a spirit reveals itself to a spirit! The *inactivity* that comes from being *in* the Spirit is the very opposite of the inactivity that comes from being *in the flesh*. It is precisely the condition for the activity which the meat-lump[500] objects to: for this *inactivity* in the

498 The etymology of 'poetry' is Greek *poema*, a thing made or created.

499 A reference to the Romantic movement and its focus on nature both animate and inanimate.

500 Grundtvig really does use this evocative word for a 'dimwit', a 'pudding-head'.

flesh is the condition for all spiritual activity, that is, all Art and Philosophy. Moreover, when we recall those holy men of God who after the Fall 'forgot' themselves *in the Spirit*, we can see that their physical inactivity was the precondition for a quite substantial spiritual *activity* and something very different from an impediment.

It would hardly have been worth touching on this subject, had it not been absolutely essential to touch on the truth that in a twofold way has led to this; namely, that we are *created* by the Word, not just in being quickened by the Spirit, but also in being raised from the dust,[501] not just in receiving lungs and a tongue with which to speak, but also in naming sensory things as such,[502] i.e. in relation to our body and senses. Thus all kinds of starlings, magpies, and polly parrots can jabber away, even though they have no Spirit, and we can learn to sense this language without Spirit, but we cannot learn *imagery*, for that is revealed not by the sound but by the meaning – and only Spirits know what the word 'Spirit' means, for it *expresses* 'Spirit'. If we ask when it was that human beings learned to speak – or in the words of the *Edda*, what was the first word that Mimer's head uttered[503] – that is not easy to say, but it is not difficult to guess without fear of serious mistake that it was literally 'a' and 'b' and the ABC. So we can cheerfully answer with the *Edda* that the first words were runes on the sun's shield, on the bear's pads, on the eagle's beak and on Bragi's tongue;[504] in short, the first human opened his mouth to name what he saw *as he saw it*. And then he had to fall, in order to become conscious that the earth had its own attractive relation to his body. "Whatever the man called each living creature, that was its name,"[505] as he saw them in the Spirit, so he did not call a monkey his 'kinsman'. The names he gave them also denoted his sensory relation to them, and this followed logically from the fact that the Creator *understood* His Art – while humankind was to realise this only gradually. Thus picture-language, meaning the use of words to depict the *spiritual* relation of things, predates everyday language, meaning the use of words to denote the *sensory* relation of things. Moreover, it is striking that from History humankind has always been forced to admit – without realising it was talking nonsense – that humans were in fact animals that spoke the language of the gods! All that was missing was for it to add that humans were themselves gods, but spoke like cattle!

If it is historically true that picture-language, imagery, is older than everyday language, then likewise our sight, which it presupposes, is even older. If in turn both

501 Gen 2:7.

502 Gen 2:19-20.

503 In both the poetic and the prose *Edda*, Mimer (Mimir) is a god of unsurpassed knowledge and wisdom, to whom Odin is indebted. Indeed, even after Mimer is beheaded in the Æsir-Vanir War, Odin carries around his embalmed head, which recites secret knowledge and counsel to him.

504 In Nordic mythology Bragi, son of Odin, is the god of poetry and eloquence, and the greatest of all poets.

505 Gen 2:19-20.

our sight and our picture-language are something we have *yet* to comprehend, then in the beginning humankind was indisputably more than we can as yet comprehend. It seems clear to me that we were not cattle, we were god-like! History thereby agrees with this reflection and understands by what right all historical peoples begin their story with an age of *gods*.

In the revealed or prophetic Word – 'revealed' in that it articulates a secret, and 'prophetic' in that the secret is in time to be discovered – we find what Art is to *form* and especially into what context. But where is Art here? To find it we must not only see the image, we must also hear it, and hear it sing! Song, as the birds teach us, is the most natural of all arts, that is, Art in its most natural form. Song is an expression of pure sensory activity, the winged sound of the Creator-Word which flaps its wings to the heavens and calls sweetly for the Word from which it is separated. Each time the bird sings overhead, it is as if it felt – and would remind us – that in humankind the great meeting has come about and that here the sacred reunion takes place.

All Art has its grounds in the faint hearing of the voice of the Godhead; this creates a premonition which bursts spontaneously into song. Hearing the Godhead thus is an essential consequence of the Creator's Word sounding out to us! Can we not still trace this effect of that solemn thunder-clap – especially in children? Has not Goethe made this expressly clear to us? For of all singers his is the breast that is most like a bird's! Nature's faint perception of its heavenly origins is revealed in its simplest and liveliest form in his mysterious song of the limits of nature for humankind.[506] What a mysterious, moving tremor and poignantly pulsating sensation lightning and thunder can still produce in a sensitive heart that does not dread its own guilt! For the Creator-Word has prepared the innocent human heart to receive the visions revealed in the images, and just as in the sensory world the vague feeling develops itself through the senses to the specific but arbitrary feeling in the hand, so should the same sense develop in a corresponding spiritual line. The picture-language should be the same in the spiritual development as the everyday language still is in the sensory development, from first to last, in the purpose, the means, and the goal.

There is no need to pursue this comparison further; these intimations are necessary for an illumination of the statement that 'the real artwork is formed in the human heart'. Every outward expression comes from a previous inward impression, in consequence of the spiritual elasticity of the heart which, unlike the merely sensory, does not efface the impression but *reveals* it. If our ear were attuned, it would inform us of this in particular – with a glance at the natural history of humankind; here, however, the *intimation* must suffice, since that in itself is enough.

---

506 Johann Wolfgang von Goethe (1749-1832) published the poem 'The Limits of Humankind' (Grenzen der Menschheit) in 1789.

The word 'Art' in itself carries a deep meaningful weight in the mother-tongue. We should not think of it as a kind of 'utterance' or 'contrivance', as when with reference to children we think of cultural education and upbringing. These are deep and heavy words, poorly understood and employed even more abysmally. Least of all when speaking of 'Art' should we mean in particular the poorest, dullest expressions in stone and colour, which for the most part are mere examples of artistic taste and dexterity. Bringing up children must not mean training them in particular utterances and exercises; it means bringing them up *spiritually*, as they are shooting up in height, to be as complete an expression of the great descriptive adjective: 'human'. To form them as such does not mean rounding them off and smoothing them out to move easily and sleekly through the world; it means promoting their development towards unity and clarity, without concern for how children brought up and educated thus will turn out. Do not worry about what they want to say and do – for this depends partly on what we do not know and partly on what we cannot comprehend. On the whole, the better parents and teachers these days bring up and educate children quite differently, and I would not call these truthful words superfluous, even if they do not apply in particular to what is under discussion here. In fact, however, the link is of the deepest and closest kind, not only because in our upbringing of children we show what it means to be 'human' in our eyes, but also because the upbringing of children is the true human art, and therefore in every way the point at which Art and Philosophy meet.

Much emerges from this which is worth consideration, but it is best studied in the university schools together with the Church and the State. Let us settle here for repeating that in their development to becoming intelligent adults children reflect, according to their conditions, the whole of human life, weaker or stronger, dimmer or clearer. In the course of an attentive upbringing – especially one whose aims and practices are of an academic art – the whole of History should in a way be the object of their individual experience. From this genuine historical Art a genuine historical Philosophy should develop, where inner and outer experience meet, the former occasioning the latter, the latter ratifying the former, and both eventually fusing together in a clear conceptual vision. In the previous century there was a realisation of the philosophical importance of such an upbringing and a methodical endeavour to prevent any unpleasant discovery for such an unbelieving and unhistorical time; a *proper* education was on the cards! In fact, I would go so far as to say that there was a feeling that the time had come when children could and should be *studied*![507] However, this resulted merely in a cursory reading and the belief that its lessons had all

507 Grundtvig doubtless has in mind *Emile, or On Education* by Jean-Jacques Rousseau (1712-78), who considered it to be his "best and most important" work. It is the first book on the philosophy of education and contains some wise advice to parents on the nature of education and humankind. It begins: "Everything is good as it leaves the hands of the Author of things; everything degenerates in the hands of man," and goes on to suggest how through educa-

been learned by heart. One only had to get children to memorize everything by rote in capital letters for the picture-book of humankind to be reprinted in their minds and for humanity to be thus summed up![508]

We shall speak further about this, but here we shall merely note that the irreconcilable hatred between the Enlightenment of the 18th century and my humble self, here as in everything, is founded on our totally opposing answers to the great question: Should one try to transform human beings into rational sausages who rule out what they cannot comprehend, or should one try to develop them into intelligent spirits who are advancing towards their home and are leaving aside what cannot follow them to their destination? It is common knowledge that the latter is my unilateral, unequivocal claim – nor can *any* spirit deviate a hairsbreadth from it without contradicting itself. The Spirit asks only what *can* follow it out of the sensory world and what *else* in passing can be employed not to hinder but to promote this advance!

It goes without saying that had humankind *not* fallen, absolutely everything could have followed humankind on its advance, provided it was given time to become refined and enhanced – and that would have been the task of Time. But so long as we must leave the world behind in order to go to heaven – leaving our bodies completely in the lurch! – we are forced to admit that we can take with us only a minimum of the sensory world and that the Art in which we lose ourselves in this world is in sore trouble in the next world. Had humankind *not* fallen, we would not have had to die, for our first parents would have remained with their last children, and they would have had a splendid History of Art merely by studying the History of Nature! But we should have had a hard time, if that had been the source of our Philosophy, for then our sole wisdom would have been: "From dust you are, and to dust you will return."[509] The Spirit protests loudly against this: "I have not *come* from dust and I cannot *return* to dust!" It is History that announces this protest to us in every work, and even every tale, of spiritual activity; for all such activity reveals our higher origins and a future that has no limit on our body. Had humankind *not* fallen, the noblest Art of every generation would have been to breed and raise a posterity wherein humankind continued its development. However, *after* the Fall the bond was broken, and we must imagine that only in very few cases did children naturally *inherit* the Spirit of their parents. Human life was transient now, and even where children *retained* the Spirit, life became ever more divided into two: the holy and the profane, everyday life and Sunday life – both among individuals and among whole tribes. Everywhere in such circumstances spiri-

---

tion 'natural man' can avoid becoming corrupt. It was published in 1762, and in the same year publicly burned in both Paris and Geneva.

508 This was the general experience in Danish schools and universities in Grundtvig's day and one of the reasons why he was home-schooled until he was 16.

509 Gen 3:19.

tual life, rather than advancing, died out gradually – unless the Sundays-only people and their children had learned to 'embalm' their Spirit, so to speak, as the Egyptians embalmed their bodies. This gave them a kind of spiritual immortality whereby as models and teachers they could remain close to succeeding generations.

History will tell us *how* this would have happened and how *little* it would have helped, had Christ not come. And who cannot see that 'the State' is our fixed term for the work of Art that was to unite all others and make them fruitful as an immortal 'artwork of humankind'?[510] Here we shall only note what ought to be the intention of every artwork: that it should vibrantly and clearly reveal its spirit, especially for posterity. This is the reason why all artists have fearlessly acknowledged their intention to *live* in their works, to make themselves immortal through them. The fact that they often wish to be immortal because it makes them *admired* and *remembered* for contributing to the corruption of humankind comes from the evil spirit hovering over them, or the good one being absent from their heart. They happily keep silent about their improper motives and simultaneously announce their ambition to promote unbridled yet self-beneficial activity! Just as assuredly as the desire to become immortal on earth 'for honour's sake' is both sinful and foolish, so is it a proof of lethargy and spiritlessness when, as in recent times, artists declare *all* desire for earthly immortality to be folly! For such a longing is *essential* for every powerful spirit and to a certain extent a condition for all artwork.

Let us now return to Revelation through words, which it must contain for humankind to give expression to it. And let us remember that everything that deserves the name of 'Art' must depend on whether it serves to form a sensory experience into its vibrant and clear image. We shall then realise that the human heart is the *focus* of the senses and must, to a certain degree, be touched and shaped before any further 'education' can take place; and we shall further realise that Art found it easiest and most fitting to express itself in *words*. It is for this reason that we expect the Art of Poetry to precede all others. Moreover, who would deny that the Art of Poetry is not only of necessity the first of its kind; it is also the only form which from a spiritual perspective deserves to be *called* 'Art', since whatever else goes by that name is only art that has the word as its source and as its master!

There has been much dispute in recent times as to what constitutes the Art of Poetry, but from whichever side we look at it in the perspective of 'Spirit', the answer is simple: it cannot be other than the fusion of sight and song – on this there has always been general agreement. What is in dispute is the *nature* of the eyes that see, and on this we can quarrel until the end of time, especially when 'Spirit' is lacking on one or both sides, whereas when 'Spirit' is present, it is merely a question of how the

510 Grundtvig's word here, *Kunst-Menneske*, means literally 'Art-human being'.

fusion should be promoted and completed. Nor does even *this* question seem difficult to answer, when we realise its nature! For if this *casting*, this Revelation of words fused with song, is nothing other than an expression of what has already taken place in the heart, then it is obvious that this work takes *time* to succeed! 'Haste makes waste', as we say,[511] and all efforts to produce a perfect artwork before it is perfected *within* us only serve to impair and distort what we *could* produce, in which case we can at the most produce a clear shell at the cost of the kernel. All warnings against this appear to be limited or useless unless they have their origin in the artist's own heart, since those who are satisfied with producing only a clear shell with no kernel – or a shrivelled one at most – have nothing else inside them! We barely need to mention that such a warning would have been superfluous had humankind not fallen, for it goes without saying that unless artists are willing to go beyond their limits *internally*, they can do so even less *externally*. Whoever loves visions internally will hardly slash and mutilate them externally for the sake of the 'look' of their work, or its 'harmoniousness'. Indeed, whoever sees their work only through spiritual eyes finds nothing attractive about the *sensory* view, and is not even tempted to train it as something in its own right.

If we now ask what is the *use* of the Art of Poetry, we can hardly comprehend its whole purpose! Even what we *can* comprehend seems mere infatuation to many. However, we do know that as the heart's essential expression, Poetry should go *to* the heart; and *through* the heart it should generate ever-warmer and clearer expressions, until the whole Revelation is mirrored unmistakably in the heart, and fully illuminated in the language. We would be mistaken to think that the Revelation must be completed before the Art begins – or that they are constantly interacting, for we cannot be wrong in regarding the ongoing physical Revelation as being an image of the spiritual Revelation which of necessity precedes and gives rise to it, since the body cannot do so of its own accord. Man and Woman represent for us the lasting and truthful memorials of what humankind was in the beginning – and should always be: the head and the heart in union and in constant interaction. The visions should begin in the head, be inspired in the heart, break into song, and call down the Spirit, which again descends in new and great visions, of which the one embraced and illuminated the other.

Finally, in the fullness of Time, Heaven opened, and God revealed His eternal house to human beings[512] and gathered them in the communion of angels. We have retained the shadow of the sacred interaction between the Spirit and the Heart in *the kiss* – but without its power and purity. They cannot fuse together, for in origin the kiss is only a sign which presupposes internal unity in spiritual love and it was dissolved the moment humankind called the body's limit its own. For only at that point did Man and

511 An English variant on the more common 'More haste, less work' which lies closer to the Danish original.
512 2 Cor 5:1.

Woman stand *face to face* with each other as two separate persons who at the most could be *linked*. Whichever *Man* can see this moment as other than a *fall* – when humankind arrogated personality to itself – can never have felt what an inner love for a *Woman* is. He must be incapable of feeling that what is the highest that the human heart in its innermost, noblest stirrings can dream of is precisely that which was God's good will, and His purpose, for humankind. What is particularly horrible and a glaring testimony of how ice-cold the heart has become spiritually is the proclamation that the highest merit of humankind is its personality, its individuality, its I-ness,[513] its rationality – or what we could call the arrogant, vain obsession in us on account of which we detach and sever ourselves in our heart from God and each other.

We praise this merit as the greatest gift of all from our Creator, despite Him having to deny Himself for it to be so! We should be ashamed to call this 'mere infatuation'; otherwise we must demonstrate that it is more than a living expression of what we assume to be true by merely counting on our fingers. It is a truth on which our well-being depends, for if we never come to this central sense that we are fallen and as such seek only ourselves, then no restoration is possible, since all Revelation, Art, and Philosophy are wasted on us – like medicaments for the glazed, callous heart. While there is still hope, what spirit would not prefer to "heap burning coals on his head" rather than that such a misfortune should befall anyone?[514] The doctor does not spare the body a red-hot iron when it is a matter of life and death. I at least do not wish to *become* this spirit or have anything to do with it; for it is Mephistopheles[515] who laughs, when souls perish.

Even if I am not wanted as a pastor, I cannot stop *being* one. I can be silent where I am not contradicted, and I *must* be silent where it is not worth complaining about our times, and what they mock or abuse. But I cannot keep silent when people affirm by *denial*, when what can and must motivate everyone who has not sworn an oath of hatred to Truth is to see what humankind actually is and what it needs. The Gospel is not worthy of our times: either it is not heard, or people are 'sleeping on it'! But the Law runs according to the needs of the times; it has reluctantly placed itself at the disposal of the times, and is partly trying to creep away from them. But just as I whisper about it in its colourful clothing, so would it be what I thundered about if I were wearing a plain black cassock!... ...

513 See Note 475.

514 Rom 12:20.

515 Mephistopheles is a devil found in German folklore, best known as a synonym for the Devil in the Faust legend.

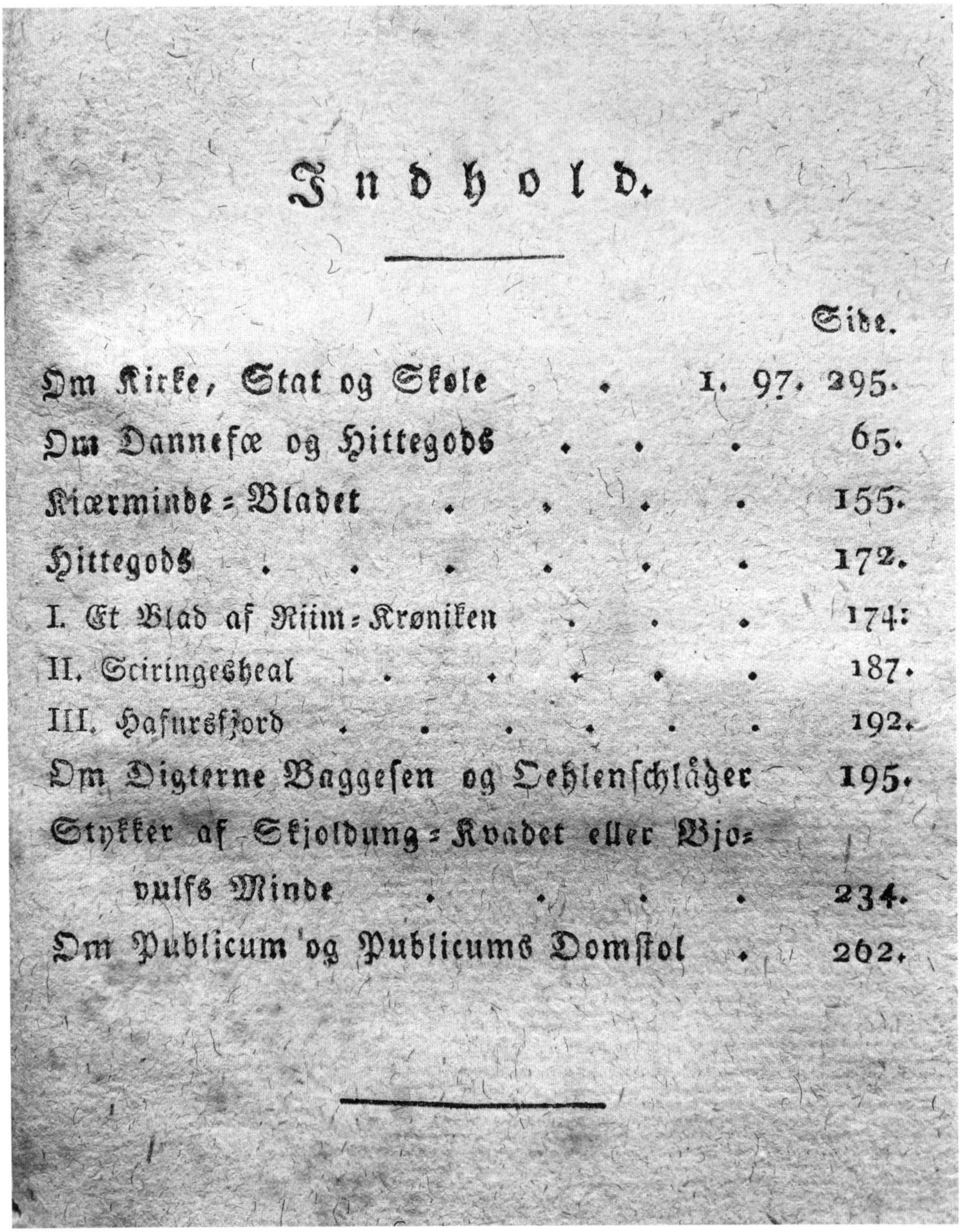

Indhold.

Side.

5. Contents of last edition of *Danne-Virke* 1819

On the Church, the State, and the School / On the Danish Treasure Trove and Lost Property / Forget-me-not Leaf / Lost Property I. II. III / On the Poets Baggesen and Oehlenschläger / Passages from Skjold's Successors or Beowulf's Memorial / On the Public and the Public's Court of Judgement.

There was no indication in the foreword written on 30th December 1818 that the January 1819 edition would mark the end of *Danne-Virke*. Grundtvig simply ends with "With thanks for the old year I wish my honoured readers good luck in the new!" On the back cover he even encourages readers to send in articles with the words: "Contributions in the spirit of Danish history will be received with pleasure." But he was now working on his translations of Saxo and Snorri as well as on *Beowulf*, and in August 1818 he had not only married and settled down with Lise, but had received a royal grant for further historical studies.

5. On the Church, the State, and the School, part 2 (1819)

Introduction by Kim Arne Pedersen

Grundtvig's early thinking on social philosophy can be found in *On the Advancement of Learning* (1807). In the Danish poet Thomas Thaarup's translation of Friedrich Buchholz's *Moses und Jesus* – a work which provoked vehement debate on the role of Jews in Danish society during the 'Jewish literary feud' of 1813 – Grundtvig met a view of 'the state' as no more than an earthly organisation for the promotion of "the security and temporal well-being of humankind" (p. 232). We can see traces of Grundtvig's rejection of this view in *On the Church, the State, and the School*, where he again argues for the eternal transcendent purpose of the State, as set out by the Church. By 'School' Grundtvig means tertiary education including all university work and influence, and ultimately human cognition in general.

On the Church, the State, and the School appears in three parts in the fourth and final volume of *Danne-Virke* (1851). Grundtvig has moved from "our wealth of philosophy and its first principles" to "the human condition and its destiny" (p. 175), and on to the unfolding of human life and thought in triadic structures, determined by the Imagination, Feeling, and Intellect/Reason as the fundamental capacities of human consciousness. Thus Grundtvig's articles constitute a chain of considerations in which their initial general nature gradually becomes concrete, until it culminates in a presentation of "a description of the historical manifestations of human life" (ibid.), i.e. the past. Both in *Danne-Virke* and in Grundtvig's later writings, the past is the source of human knowledge. In History we find "human beings in their Experience" (p. 74), and this concrete life is collected in the triad that makes up the State, the Church, and the School.

Grundtvig links the Church to the Imagination, the State to Feeling, and the School to Intellect/Reason, making *On the Church, the State, and the School* a central pillar of his *Danne-Virke* philosophy. Here, Grundtvig's theoretical considerations acquire flesh and blood in a social context, as he balances the internal relations between the three institutions and assesses which of them is the most important. In the process he touches on Luther's doctrine of "the true invisible Church" and Article 7 of the Lutheran creed, *Confessio Augustana*, which states that the Church is where "the Word of God" is taught "pure and simple" (221). In addition, he takes a stance on the widespread 18th century acceptance of a 'social contract' as constituting the foundation of all society – as formulated in Rousseau's *The Social Contract* (1762).[516] If human beings were no more than thinking animals, Rousseau would be right to argue that human life was better in its 'natural state' (p. 223), for then the State would be characterised by exploitation

516 French title: *Du Contrat Social*.

and repression. But human beings are spirit and body united, and thus the State is needed for them to reach their eternal destiny.

Elsewhere in the study, Grundtvig *defines* the institutions of Church, State, and School: the Church as "a community of believers"; the State as "an actual expression of the relation to the human heart"; and the School as an institution that is to "carry the Church". In the extract here the School is defined as an expression of "the whole life of humankind" (p. 231), a definition that brings it close to philosophy, or learning. In arguing figuratively that the School should "carry the Church", i.e. be its foundation, Grundtvig's intention is the same as elsewhere in *Danne-Virke*, when the subject is reason and revelation or philosophy and theology. They are not at odds with each other: philosophy is a *ministrant* to faith. The School 'carries' the Church, as society's institution of faith, in that it leads human beings to the insight that their relation to God is the most important of the three in which they stand, namely to the Almighty, to their fellow-beings, and to themselves. This explains why Grundtvig begins with an attack on "the errors of the previous century" and thus on the so-called European enlightenment, and then calls instead for "a new and different view of the human condition than before" (p. 212). This refers to the biological-materialist view of humankind, according to which human beings are "incomprehensible animals and spiritless, rational numbskulls" (p. 213). As in *On Revelation, Art, and Learning* Grundtvig yet again emphasises our double citizenship of the worlds of the spirit and body respectively. He argues that:

> ... if we now regard human beings as creatures of reason *in the image of God*, destined for eternal life, then we clearly see that the whole life of humankind can quite justifiably be called no more than a 'school', i.e. a development leading to a transfiguration... what goes by the name of 'Church' and 'School' in the world is in fact only the two major divisions within the latter which our whole life constitutes, corresponding to each other like revelation and experience (p. 231).

Thus the Church reveals what is our human destiny, after which, through the social life of the State, we experience that the Church is telling the truth.

In this relationship between Church and State, Grundtvig links his biblically-based anthropology to his concept of history. Whereas earlier in the study he maintained that the Church should occupy the highest position, he now tends toward regarding the School as the most important of the three, and argues that "like the true State, the true Church is *invisible*. Our senses can only understand their images in the School... and the prime purpose of the State is to ensure the growth and security of the School" (p. 232). As we can see in *On Religion and Liturgy* and *On the Advancement of Learning*, this is a joint task for all members of society. The State has its outward expression in the School, which is the only one of the triad that has a physical form accessible to human sense perception. The true Church only exists on earth "*invisibly through faith*" and the true State only "*invisibly through love*", but both "express themselves through word and action" in the external area that the School constitutes (ibid.).

Making the School the unifying factor in society is nothing if not modern! *On the Church, the State, and the School* argues that in defiance of secularisation, a *transcendent* perspective is essential to social life. Grundtvig links his focus on human cognition to the efforts of political philosophers of the 18th century to *ignore* theology. In the third section of the study not included here, Grundtvig also argues that "each person must give their vote", after which the voting majority must form the basis on which society develops the widest possible agreement between the individual's needs and "the interests of all". This is a clear anticipation of the democratic form that was to come a little later to Denmark. Grundtvig sets himself apart from this organisation of society. Yet we can see from the two sections of the work not included here that he criticises the theocratic tendencies that characterise the view of society by the Lutheran orthodoxy: that Israel alone was a state founded by God, in which the Church, i.e. the religious institution, controlled everything, and directed its citizens to participate in His worship. In the originally heathen peoples, such as the Danes, the Church may well lay down the guidelines for the development of society with regard to education (the School), but at the same time it allowed freedom of worship.

NB. For the sake of clarity, the section divisions in the text into Church, State, and School below have been made by the editor.

Introduction

Even respectable men say that to reject the Enlightenment of the 18th century *unconditionally* is as mistaken and unreasonable as unconditionally to *acclaim* it; but, begging their pardons, this is simply not true! Of course, in the kingdom of the Spirit we must reject nothing unconditionally – except Falsehood; on the other hand it is better to reject than to acclaim a line of thought in which Falsehood is dominant. The problem here is not how many or how few supporters of this view actually *realised* what they were applauding; the problem here is that there were *any* supporters at all! In saying this, I reject the feeble attempt to demand a 'balance' between Truth and Falsehood. For under the guise of combatting the errors of the previous century I argue that the new one is pursuing far more pernicious errors in the attempt to prevent the present generation from learning from bitter experience! Even when the 18th century accepted the *existence* of the Church, it nevertheless pushed it to the bottom as the lowest of the three in the dispute regarding the paramount status of the School or the State.

In the following I shall attempt to demonstrate that this was a completely wrong approach, based on false assumptions. If the attempt is made with a love of Truth and with a judicious hand, I trust that in the circumstances it will be seen as a timely contribution. No one with a sense of our current times can doubt that wherever there is life, there is a *ferment*, the consequences of which must be a new and different view of the human condition than before. All friends of humankind must wish that it should be healthier and worthier, and with this end in mind every honest study must be welcomed, however little it contributes. I am conscious of the word 'honest' and will not be blinded by animosity towards the past, witness the fact that what I have most often and strongly combated is 'the new', in particular the damaging spirit of 'the present', which is so juvenile. People are free to believe what they like, but be wary of any rush either to praise or criticise what I say without sufficient *grounds*. I have thought the matter through, and I am in earnest when I say that I shall treat the subject with as much clarity as I can muster – and if everyone did the same, we would soon come to both agreement and clarity on this important matter.

Finally, I must enjoin the reader to note that I do not raise this war-cry against the 18th century's view of the Church, the State covenant, and the School tables, because I am looking for a pitched battle with them: what can be *blown* away is not worth drawing a sword against! I merely wish readers to know what lies before them. They can set this study aside, if they have sworn allegiance to Voltaire's Church,[517] Paine's State,[518] and Basedow's School.[519] I envy no one such pleasure, honour, or wisdom – yet nor am I in need of any applause. The appreciation of the whole world cannot make a false opinion true – any more than the opposition of the whole world can destroy a grain of sand. It is not a misfortune to be alone with the truth, just because there are many who agree on a falsehood. I shall freely speak my views, which are founded on the Word and Act of God. Hear me those who will; refute me those who can; and turn up their noses, shrug their shoulders, and snap their fingers in their pockets[520] those who know no better and can do no more!

---

517 Voltaire was the pseudonym of François-Marie Arouet (1694-1778), a French philosopher and writer in the Age of Enlightenment. He was a supporter of social reform (including the defence of civil liberties, freedom of religion, and free trade), and his ideas influenced important thinkers of both the American and French Revolutions. He regarded the Church as oppressive and self-serving.

518 Thomas Paine (1737-1809) was born in England but emigrated in 1774 to the New World, where his writings inspired the settlers to declare independence from Britain. His ideas of free thought and the pre-eminence of reason also influenced the French Revolution. While in prison in Luxembourg he wrote a pamphlet, 'The Age of Reason', in which he castigated organised religion, proclaiming that his sole religion was his own mind.

519 Johann Basedow (1724-90) was a German educational reformer, teacher, and writer. From 1753-61 he was Professor of Moral Philosophy at Sorø Academy on Zealand, Denmark. His school, the *Philanthropinum*, opened in Dessau, Germany in 1774 with the philosophy of 'everything according to nature'. Basedow pioneered child-centred practical education, which revolved around learning through play and competitive games.

520 To snap one's fingers in one's pocket *(at slå knips i lommen)* was a hidden reaction to helpless opposition.

If we assume that human beings are created for eternal life, they cannot then be created for temporal life only. On the contrary, temporal life must have been created for *them* – for the sake of Eternity. Knowing that our earthly life is temporal, our relation to it cannot possibly be the highest or the most important. The *purpose* of both State and School is demonstrably temporal, whereas the specific aim of the Church is eternal. It is thus the highest and most important relation of the three, for whoever has *faith* is destined for Eternity.

On the other hand, we could also assume that human beings are *animals* – two-legged creatures who cannot call their souls their own, who come and go in Time, and are begotten and devoured by Chronos.[521] We could then assume that they are not created for eternal life in the image of God[522] but are created in the image of the Devil as temporal monkeys, who copy what they have never seen and covet what they cannot imagine. They could be spiritual ciphers added to a physical number, who mean nothing and whom no God could comprehend. If human beings are a genuine impossibility and a singular contradiction, then it is the *State* relation which is the most important, insofar as any importance can be attached to nothing! In this case, the Church relation is delusional, and the School relation superfluous, since human beings rank far below bees and beavers, who form the best State when no one tries to teach them and they are left to manage their own affairs.

I subscribe to the first of these two views of humankind. This will come as no surprise to anyone; I regard everything in this light, and try to see all human life in this context. It is strange that the majority of those who extol the Enlightenment of the 18th century shrink from recognising the foundation upon which our Temple is built. They will not admit that in their view human beings are incomprehensible animals and spiritless, rational numbskulls, which is what they *must* think if their 'enlightenment' is to be anything other than sulphurous fumes, and their 'wisdom' anything other than post-house gossip.[523] It is as clear as sunlight that if we accept that we are *spiritual* beings, destined for eternal life, but that we also have a temporal life – albeit one aimed either at temporal power and honour, pleasure and happiness, or at Knowledge and Learning... if we accept this, we cannot then believe that eternal

521 In Greek mythology Chronos was the son of Ouranos (heaven) and Gaia (earth). As the god of time he was seen as a devouring force. He deposed his father, but fearing the prophecy that he himself would in turn be overthrown by his own son, he swallowed each of his children as they were born. His sister Rhea managed to save the youngest, Zeus, by hiding him away on the island of Crete. To this day the Diktaeon cave on Crete is claimed to be Zeus' birthplace.

522 Gen 1:26.

523 In Grundtvig's day the post-house was an inn for exchanging post horses and accommodating riders. In Act II:i: 1-2 of his play *The Pawned Farmer's Helper* (*Den Pantsatte Bondedreng*, 1726) the Danish-Norwegian playwright Ludvig Holberg (1684-1754) has the character Christoffer tell his servant: "Run straight to the post-house and collect the gentleman's clothes and cases."

life comes of its own accord; for we cannot be indifferent to whether it is eternal *life* or eternal *death* we are pursuing! Whoever thinks and behaves in this fashion – and the 18th century gives us many notorious examples – is either a sad wretch or a great fool, or an absolute nobody! Either way, we would not turn to them for an *enlightenment* of the human condition.

Therefore, whoever rejects these numbskull beliefs and looks to *the Word* in order to believe in the spiritual and eternal destiny of humankind must seal their lips and swallow their words if they wish to dupe us into thinking that typecasting and conforming are the principal aims in life. If they think that faith is a minor matter, they will be forced to admit that it is the Church alone which can give humankind its *value*! Among wise heads the only *dispute* there can be is over what the Church should be called, what it should preach, and how it should conduct itself in the world. Only in the madhouse can people quarrel about what the true Church should mean for us who confess an eternal life – whether to agree on placing it at the top or the bottom when it is the highest and most important thing we can imagine and desire!

It is the *Church* I am talking about – the house on the eternal mount which stands immovable and defies all enemies. No one can reach out and touch it except its friends; and only heaven-defying titans can delude themselves into thinking they can tear it down from its seat on high! History tells us that the time wasted on building a spiritual tower of Babel which can reach Heaven is even more futile and fruitless than the time spent on the physical tower that people once tried to build.[524] We can lose sight of the Church, but only when we sleep, or run astray, or sleepwalk with our eyes closed. All who feel the longing for eternal life in their hearts, or can even see its image in their spirit, cannot do other than regard it as the first, last, and only thing worth working *on* and *for*. Any State or School that refuses to promote the interests of the Church must be regarded as the enemy of humankind, to be opposed with all the weapons that the Church grants and allows in its defence!

This truth needs no further evidence, least of all in a time when everything points to an imminent universal pledge of allegiance towards it. Yet the Church has always exacted painstaking progress and demanded scrupulous explanation – and never more so than now. For there is now a great fear of those who would seek to abuse it and transform it into a structure on which to build theses and propositions that are far more dangerous than a spiritless (and therefore both impotent and self-contradictory) denial of the Church's pre-eminence and the unconditional importance of church-going.

We live at a time when in many places it will soon be considered objectionable to cultivate the truth that He who cannot be contained by the highest heavens does not dwell in temples built by human hands. The Kingdom of God is *within* us; it does not

524 Gen 11:1-9.

come into being by our *pointing* at it! God does not demand the fasting of our body or the words on our lips, or the sacrifice of a victim, or a meat offering, whatever form these might take. He calls for a sincere, believing, hopeful, loving heart; only *there* will He walk and dwell, as a living tabernacle to the end of our days. In many a place the time is at hand when instead of honouring houses of stone and plaster and those within (with their top hats and their long dresses), people will insist on showing the honour which alone befits the house built without God's hands: the eternal House in Heaven. There He alone dwells whose Word goes out to the ends of the earth in the voice of the Spirit and in the Holy Scriptures. As before, there are those who would craftily confound the only, holy, true, and invisible Church with its earthly shadow – or rather with a synagogue to Satan, who steals its name and pretends to be its lifelike image, fused with the original. We know that this is what happened under the papacy, and whoever is not blinded by appearances and led astray by hot air, realises that almost everywhere that Christ is named, the purpose is to establish a *new* papacy, tarted up to suit the natural inclinations of each and every people.

I have nothing against this writing being called a 'sermon', provided that it is not a sermon which falls on deaf ears, for that would be a pity! People should realise that the only advice against what is being headed towards, namely a hierarchical papacy, is to praise and honour the *true invisible Church* as the genuine, spiritual Mother Mary! She will always appear before us in heavenly radiance above the floating clouds, with the child in her arms who through God's grace will become a perfect man – in other words, just as, in life and spirit, Raphael depicted the shadow in a play of colours.[525] People should realise that the only bulwark against a *self-appointed* vice-regent of Christ on earth is faith in the only *true* vice-regent, appointed by Christ Himself, namely, the Holy Spirit, the Spirit of Truth. Its Word holds good in the Holy Scriptures, whose much-derided sceptre – the letter of the Bible – has proven its power historically to destroy all rebels and self-appointed vice-regents. If only these polly parrots would learn what they screamed themselves hoarse over – that "the letter kills, but the Spirit gives life!"[526] If only they would realise that the letter of the Bible kills only the Spirit's *enemies*, and the Bible's Spirit gives life only to those who bow before its letter. Likewise, the Gospel truly makes no one blessed who has not humbled themselves before the Law – even though the Law cannot make sinners blessed, but can only condemn and destroy them!

525 This is a rare Grundtvig reference to the Fine Arts. Historically, these were painting, sculpture, architecture, music, and poetry, plus the performing arts of theatre and dance. In practice, the Fine Arts are nowadays considered to be the visual arts, none of which seriously attracted Grundtvig. The *Sistine Madonna*, was commissioned in 1512 by Pope Pope Julius II for the church of San Sisto, Piacenza (hence its preceding adjective). It was painted by the Italian artist Raphael Sanzio (1483-1520) and hangs in the Gemaldegalerie Alte Meister in Dresden.

526 2 Cor 3:6.

The Church

Whether or not one should take care not to cause damage, it is nevertheless my duty to set out what I understand by 'the true Church', which alone has the right to govern and rule – and what relation the Church should have to the State and the School.

There can be no doubt that the 'true' Church is the Church that reveals to us the Truth concerning the eternal destiny of humankind, as well as the way in which this can be achieved. Since such a revelation is impossible without *words* – because the Word alone can tell us what the Spirit is and means – it follows that the Church can only reveal itself in words, and that it cannot reveal itself to us in any other sensory way, not in human beings, ceremonies, statues, pictures, or whatever else that is sensory.

From this we learn two very important things: first, in the true Church we need a Word to which we can relate and dare to build on; and second, anyone who speaks and directs in the name of the Church *without a revealed Word* to prove their authority is to be called without further inquiry a rogue or a fool. They give themselves out to be men of the Church, but we know this cannot be so, since we who are of the Church do not recognise ourselves in them.

Many will perhaps think this is of little significance, but it is significant enough! If the validity of the basic principle cannot be contested – that the revealed Word is the only true expression of the Church – then not only is the pope in Rome thereby condemned, so are all those who use their own reasoning to instruct us about Eternity! All are condemned who under the pretence of 'enlightenment' wish to replace the revealed Word with something else. Since their words are *not* 'revealed', they contain no more than one person's opinion about the revealed Word. To build on a single person's own opinion as to matters related to Eternity – which none of us know – is mere superstition and popery, the precise opposite of true faith and Christianity.

Obviously, the question here is whether a revealed Word has been given *by* the Spirit of Truth as a true revelation! If there is no true revelation, then there is no true Church. Similarly, the only possible Church Community on earth exists on the basis of *faith in the Word*. Any idea of a spirit in a revealed word that can be merely *conjectured*, or found in any other way than genuine faith in the Word is either a veiled, covert denial of the truth of the revelation, or it is the fruit of a peculiar misapprehension. This seems to me as clear as sunlight, but there are men whom one would least suspect of still being infected by the 18th century's nebulous use of words who nevertheless proclaim views which Schiller very aptly described as "hounding the truth" – with torches, bowstrings, and swords! In such circumstances, my wish is to clarify the question further, as I shall now attempt to do.

There are many who argue that the Bible is *not* the Word of God but only *contains* the Word of God. It is not in fact a revelation, but it *contains* a revelation. This is the same as saying that the Bible is a book like any other, only with more truth for salvation than in other books, so we must read it carefully to try to find everything that it seeks to preserve! I have nothing to say to such people, for they must admit that if the Bible *is* such a book, there is no point in my trying – or even believing in the Word concerning divine, eternal matters. In that case it is *not* a revelation but the exact opposite – a secret that needs to *be* revealed! Its clarification must either be made intelligible to human reason, which cannot *comprehend* questions of Eternity, or it must be *proved* to be a revelation whose Word can be *believed*.

Others prefer a middle way and say: 'The Bible, or a part of it, is the Word of God, but because it uses imagery, it must often not be taken literally but in a more *subtle* and truthful way.' If this means that when spiritual subjects are designated with words which in everyday speech are used mostly about the corresponding *physical* things, then we should certainly be aware of what we are talking about when using such words. Moreover, this comment is as old as Bible-reading itself, or poetical language, or all discussion of spiritual matters! Whoever regards such things as an objection to the validity of the Bible is making a singular mistake, for to ensure what is truly *meant* we must take the Word in all its literal stringency, otherwise we are just plucking the Spirit out of the air! On the other hand, if it means that when a word seems so strange or unreasonable that we can replace it with another word, or interpret it as we please, and then pass such words off as the Word of God to be believed as revealed Truth, then clearly we are revoking the Church Community, making faith merely a private matter for the individual, and opening the door to all kinds of infatuation. If in matters of faith any of us claims the right to appeal to something 'extreme' – be it with regard to faith, reason, learning or whatever – then that right must be open to all! As soon as we allow the least arbitrariness, then we tacitly take for granted just such a private revelation which claims to illuminate the *universal* revelation! There is not a single teaching in Scripture that we can claim to be universally believed by Christians; we must instead leave it to each individual to follow and maintain their view on their own responsibility. This is the same as saying that there is no true Revelation, but only true mysteries, i.e. myths, whose meaning we must try to guess.

No matter how we look at it, we cannot help arguing that either there *is* no true revelation and no true Church Community, or we must take the revealed Word literally – precisely in order to believe it spiritually! Spirit and its corresponding Word are just as linked as are its content and expression. Where can we find content except in its expression? Or where can we find Spirit except in the Word as it *sounds*? For the spoken Word is the Spirit's only possible revelation!

Since a few specific examples cannot do any damage and may serve to prevent misunderstanding, I shall add them here.

We know that recently a number of 'scribes'[527] have fancied that they were Christian believers and admitted that the Bible is divine revelation without accepting its teaching of Christ's suffering in our stead and our justification through faith in Him.[528]

From every angle this is both unbiblical and unwise, for it draws a line through the whole Gospel and the whole of Christianity! It excludes from 'revelation' what precisely *reveals* God's counsel for our salvation! These theologians nevertheless believe they have spoken out of deep wisdom in telling us how *satisfactio vicaria*[529] is both an illogical and unbiblical teaching. They tell us poor wretches that we have 'gone astray', because we lack a degree of subtlety in our judgement and cannot distinguish between an unmediated and a mediated atonement and justification. If the question were not so important, we would have to laugh heartily that such an empty wordplay could be called 'wisdom'! I shall merely remark what the Bible says and what we take to be true: that Jesus shed His blood for us for the forgiveness of sins, that He died for us, that we are justified undeservedly through faith in Him, that Jesus' blood cleanses us of all sin – as well as everything else that undeniably is written in the revelation that we assume to be true.

This being the case, I argue that there is only one choice: either to preach these words, or to accept the teaching we dread, for that and the words are inseparable! The question is not whether we should call something 'unmediated' when it is proclaimed as happening *through* the mediator and being founded *on* the means of faith. The question is rather: can we assume that those words are true, and yet nevertheless claim that Jesus did *not* bear our sins, that it is not for *His* sake that God will pardon us, that it is not through *faith* in Him that we are justified? Who cannot see that such talk belongs in the madhouse? Who can believe that anyone with common sense could imagine that the proper meaning of a Word of Truth can be the *opposite* of what that Word says? And that it is the nature of imagery to speak directly *against* one's own belief? Clearly, such talk belongs to the Devil and Falsehood and never to the imagery of God and Truth.

We do not really become aware that this must be the case until we realise how imagery works in general, and how it works in particular in this case. 'Justification' is a figurative expression; it does not refer to our everyday usage in the sense of 'acquittal in court for an offence of which we are innocent'. In our context it means an 'amicable' acquittal *for a real offence*. 'Belief' is equally a figurative expression, and should not be confined to our everyday usage of meaning no more than a 'disregard of doubt about something'. In our context it means a spiritual and heartfelt reception of something as

527 Grundtvig uses the biblical word for 'scribe' (Danish *skriftklog*) as a designation for academic theologians.

528 In Lutheran theology the *justification* of humankind is by *faith alone* ((Lat. *Sola fide*), *as* a gift from God *through* Christ.

529 Lit. 'restitution substitute' – the atonement theory for original sin, to restore divine justice through the crucifixion and resurrection of Christ.

being the living, powerful Truth. Every word that we use to describe heavenly matters is and must be figurative, i.e. it must more or less point to this earth, which is a faint depiction of Heaven, for since our tongue is dust and earth, so must our language also be. It is a wretched trick and a gross misunderstanding to make such imagery a shield for unbelief, or a barrier to faith – or to say that just because justification and faith run much deeper, purer, and stronger in the voice of the Bible than in *our* voice, it is not the Bible's intention that we should be justified undeservedly through faith in Jesus, despite that being emphatically what it says!

A further example in this context is the well-known and often disputed directive of Jesus to eat His flesh and drink His blood, if we are to have any part of Him. When we do so, we shall *live* in Him, as He lives in the Father. We can doubt even less that these words are figurative, since Jesus adds that they are 'life and spirit'. We are perfectly well aware that He does not mean His listeners should slaughter and eat Him while He was alive in the world. His intention was that we should *spiritually* eat His spiritual body and drink His spiritual blood, so that in heart and spirit we should sincerely and inseparably be united with Him – just as our body is united in energy through the food and drink by which we live. This is just as assuredly His intention as His statement that in this union He grants His believers the same vital power, i.e. the power of eternal life, as His Father eternally grants Him! We can clearly see here how an image must be taken fairly literally in order to be understood and believed in its true meaning.

On the other hand, when we say, as has often been commented on, that by this eating and drinking Jesus meant the acceptance of His teaching and its application in the improvement of our hearts and our moral conduct, we are in fact saying *nothing*. All we are doing is twisting and turning away from the clear meaning of the words by rewriting them in vague and ambiguous expressions. We fail to realise that in a spiritual sense, acceptance and application, sincere and moral conduct are just as much figurative expressions as eating and drinking. This is because particularly the first two, acceptance and application, are undefined and in everyday speech denote mostly thoughts; however, if we pursue them back to their origins, we find the same figurative meaning as in Jesus' words, only expressed more vaguely, feebly, and rather obliquely. For Jesus' teaching is all the lessons that lie in His words, including those meaning that to 'accept' means to grasp something and to hold on to it. Since spiritual matters can only be grasped and held on to through faith, we come back to the point that we must *believe* His Word. To 'apply' something is to use it for what it was meant. If we believe Jesus' teaching that His Word is able to grant us eternal life, then the proper way to 'apply' it is to acquire eternal life by doing so! Likewise, it is only the power of eternal life that improves our hearts and moral conduct. That alone gives the heart a predominant longing for the good, i.e. God's eternal life, leading us to our destiny, i.e. eternal life in God's kingdom.

It would please me a great deal if this were to *rouse* someone, rather than for them to parrot forth a superficial and frivolous exegesis. I would prefer to open their eyes and compare our new-fangled, enforced darkness and our feeble explanations with the Bible's simple, clear, and powerful Word, which is life and spirit. If this is too much to hope for, I must wish that those who applaud the exegesis I denounce become so angry that they seriously attempt to pick holes in my argument! For then the somniferous lethargy that nowadays cares not a jot or a tittle but just waits for the spirit of the times to fuse fire with water (i.e. for the world to perish), becomes far more painful for a Christian than the hardest attack and the bitterest insults. If there were a *serious* dispute, they would wake up and victory would ensue, with the victor being on the side of Truth; of that I have as little fear as I have doubt. Whoever is affected by such fear and doubt – as must be the case with those I so frankly contradict and provoke – should truly see that these have been overcome, since it is obvious that it cannot be Truth that contributes to such-like!

This was a parenthesis which can be omitted if one so wishes, but I beg no one to do so. I ask them to take it to heart as being far more important than that to which I now return: the concept of *development* in our earthly condition.

We heard that the true Church must be invisible, but revealed in a Word which among all believers engenders one and the same idea about Church and church attendance. This is only possible if this Word governs faith, and yet essential if the idea is to be a spiritual image of the true Church and the human path leading towards it. Oneness is required here, just as God is one and humankind in God's image is one. The meaning of many a word spoken to humankind can be obscure and dubious – sometimes for all, and perhaps always for many – but this cannot be otherwise. The whole of humanity has its own long history, whose major chapters we call 'eras', where the lives of individuals are embraced as genuine strides and transitions. Insofar as the Word is obscure, it is not so much a revelation as a prophecy; insofar as its sense is doubtful, it is not addressed to faith and does not reflect the Church, but points to the School.

However, each person's life is not only part of the human race but also a complete life in itself – with lasting effects; the individual is both a member and a living conscious image of the whole. With this in mind, we should address each person as if this were a revelation and attend to what we presume to be uniform for them all – what makes them human and gives them the faith that human beings are created in the image of God. If we maintain this, we soon realise how the Church Community is possible, how unity is the necessary consequence of its Truth, and how far this unity stretches. If we are all created by God in His image, it is our undeniable destiny to obey Him unconditionally and be transfigured into His image. If we were not sinners, the entire Church Community would consist of this faith; but since we *are* sinners, we have fallen out of this community, which cannot be formed except through faith in a Word which takes the Fall as given and reveals a reparation through faith. In Scripture, as we know, 'revelation' is a specific expression for the gospel of the resurrection in Christ, through faith in Him. Given that we have *received* such a revealed Word, and that the Church Community builds solely on *faith* in that Word, it is obvious that under the provision of faith the idea must be identical with the Word, just as the human condition and destiny with regard to God and eternity are necessarily identical.

The clear consequence is that in the various churches the ideas could be very different, yet the Spirit would be the same among these good Christians, however much their beliefs diverged from one another. Most often it meant precisely the same as when our moral preachers try to make us believe that one can be a very good Christian without believing in Christ! This is the same as when people try to make children believe that one can be a God-fearing person without actually believing in God! There is no other reply to this than to say that all those who believe such things undoubtedly have equally *little* Christian faith! On the other hand, faith in the Word can also mean for us what it meant to our forefathers, namely that we may have widely differing views as regards the truly obscure passages in Scripture, and what can serve our edification – in addition to what Scripture commands; yet we can nevertheless all belong to one and the same invisible Church, provided that we agree on the fundamental truths: Scripture is God's pure Word we must follow; Jesus Christ, as described in Scripture, is our Lord and Saviour; by His merit we can give thanks for God's Grace and the sure hope of salvation; and through His power alone we can comprehend 'eternal life'!

The conclusion is thus that the true, invisible Church is *everywhere* – wherever the Spirit of eternal Truth is found and makes its presence known, and wherever the same Spirit speaks to prove that our forefathers were right when they said that the true Church was wherever the Word of God was taught, pure and simple! Nevertheless, it would be rash to conclude from this that the speaker and the audience were *in* the true Church, for it is possible that only the speaker's *tongue* was present, and in any case its radius must not be judged by its sound but by its faith.

Thus, if we purify our use of concepts concerning the Church, we shall avoid the danger of counselling or applauding any papal or Church rule; for if the Church is present solely in the Spirit, then no other power can lay claim to it except the free-born Word of the Spirit, where it finds faith and resonance.

From this we might be tempted to imagine the Church completely *outside* any link to the State, but this too would be a great error when we consider the Church's area of activity and the conditions laid down by the State. For just as the true Church on earth must be a community of faith in a Word that reveals the eternal destiny of the true Church on earth to humankind and the path towards it, so must the true State be a united endeavour to fulfil that earthly destiny. Since this must of necessity consist of steady strides along the path to eternity, the true State is clearly a creation of the true Church. By the same logic one cannot be in the true Church without following the path laid down within it, and since our Church Community is a unity, church-goers must walk together! In other words, true faith is necessarily a *living* faith. The heart is the source of life, the life of faith is love, and love is perfect unity.[530] The Church Community must be linked through the heart, and thereby constitute a State, for it is impossible to have an identical Spirit and to be one at heart without also being one in the world.

The State

Despite this timely pointer to the true relationship between the Church and the State, pursuing it will hardly promote clarity and precision; there are many reasons why an examination of the State nowadays should begin as far away from the Church as possible. The main reason is that the majority of those who discuss a 'Church-State' understand something quite different by the phrase, while those who *support* a 'Church-State' mean something quite different from what I myself mean!

Let us therefore begin with what we can all agree upon: that a State manifests itself as a society which with united strength endeavours to defend itself in a free position and to initiate what it considers to be most beneficial, i.e. effective, for its welfare. It is not an error to argue that such a description applies equally to an animal state as a human one; for if all peoples agreed to create human states, they could save themselves a lot of trouble by demonstrating in what relationship the State ought to stand to the Church. The only question would be how the State could best serve its purpose and promote its citizens' development according to the Church's revelation. This is far from being the case, however. In the 18th century the human right to be as much of an animal as one pleases has been eagerly defended, with the bold argument that the whole history of the Church's influence on the State has been nothing but a great tragedy which shows *quantum religio potuit svadere malorum*,[531] and that it is essential to begin with the State *in puris naturalibus*.[532]

Prosperity and well-being are the essential aims of every State. We can say this without fear of contradiction; the only disputes are about what *constitutes* prosperity and well-being for a people, and how they can be achieved.

If we regard human beings as rational creatures, i.e. as conscious animals who by nature only look after their own interests, then it follows that by the age of discretion

530 Col 3:14.

531 'To how many evils does not religion persuade!' – from the Latin poem *De rerum natura* (*On the Nature of Things*, c.50 BCE) by the Roman writer Titus Lucretius Carus ('Lucretius').

532 (Lat.) 'in a purely natural state'.

their 'natural state' is one in which they all hate and envy each other! Only out of mutual fear will they allow one another undisputed possession of something that pleases a rational creature; only those who need to chatter and to couple will want company, and only those who are frightened or rapacious will join forces in a state-gang under a kind of leader. If this were truly the case, then Rousseau was undoubtedly right to claim that the State is an unnatural hospital and prison, where the medicine is worse than the disease[533] – a training college for scoundrels, a greenhouse for unnatural vices, and a graveyard for human freedom! However, individuals in their 'natural state' were far more assured of life than in a 'state' where, when the head of state commands it, a hundred thousand hands are willing to deprive them of their lives. Clearly, without 'states' there would be no destructive wars that in a single day cost many thousand lives, limbs, and property; without 'states' there would not be a thousandth of the means whereby they can do damage; in brief, without 'states' the sensible creature would a thousand times better be able to promote and achieve what such 'natural' individuals would call their prosperity and well-being! Similarly, all who in any way were favoured by Fortune would be far better able to claim their assets and take advantage of their beauty, strength, and cunning – or whatever other endowments they possessed.

I dare to defend Rousseau's sentence in all its stringency against any who allege that security, pleasure, or any other physical advantage are worth joining the State for. Indeed, even in any other *extended* form, I would defend Rousseau's sentence on the basis of both Reason and History. We are forced to admit that in this light a *voluntary* link to the State is something that only a cunning brain would trick idiots into accepting! If the right of the strongest[534] and the advantage of the cunning did not make this impossible, we ought to endeavour to have all 'states' dissolved and our 'natural state' returned to us as soon as possible, in accordance with 'rational' human love, meaning love of self.

Moreover, in the 18th century they actually *idolized* this widespread conception of the state as a conspiracy for joint security and other physical advantages! On this basis they made a giant attempt to dissolve *all* states and indeed bring back our 'natural state'. The French Revolution and all that pertains to it was the result – a raucous, glittering proof of this misconception. Oddly enough, many wise heads failed to notice how exceptionally foolish this was.

---

533 Jean-Jacques Rousseau (1712-78), the Swiss-French philosopher born in Geneva, wrote several major works, including *Emile (1792)* on philosophy of education, and *The Social Contract (1792)* on political philosophy. The reference is a passage in *Discourse on the Origin and Basis of Inequality Among Men* (1755) "... however useful medicine, properly administered, may be among us, it is certain that, if the savage, when he is sick and left to himself, has nothing to hope but from nature, he has, on the other hand, nothing to fear but from his disease; which renders his situation often preferable to our own" (translated by G.D.H. Cole).

534 One of Rousseau's arguments is that a person cannot have a *right* to obedience just because they are the stronger – in whatever sense.

'Man's will is not Land's law' runs the proverb. This should be engraved not only over every council chamber but also in the hearts of every subject of the realm; for it is the State's immutable motto. 'The general will of the people alone should be law!', they said. This was the watchword of those 'state' philosophers in the 18th century – and indeed it still is for the most part. But this is the exact opposite of the above proverb, and a manifesto for war against all states! For it is obvious that in a country where it is the general will of the people to care most for the rights of all and to favour their wishes, no law is required! Similarly, a law that expressed the general will could not regard anything but what each person held good. It could not possibly be the *general* will – just for the sake of such a pointless assertion – to dispute the costs which a legislative assembly and all manner of penny-pinching will nevertheless entail. And not only that! It is sheer madness to entrust to a single or several persons the power as the minion of a law which is not required; on the contrary, it would place everyone's self-interest in conflict with that of the people and would invalidate the *general* will which they are appointed to carry out and watch over.

I am very well aware of the multitude of objections which *our* state-subversers have at the ready: I am not taking the phrase 'the general will' seriously; I am forgetting that a people also need external security; and finally, along with much else I am overlooking the fact that human beings are moral creatures who neither merely follow their own self-interest nor yet can be content with the satisfaction of their animal drives.

Are such objections against my argument valid? I think not, and I will tell you why.

It is not I who am making light of 'the general will', it is the state-subversers. With their exaggeration and ostentation they mean something quite different by this phrase than it actually contains. They say it denotes the result of the discussion and mutual consultation among the best and wisest heads in the country! Not, therefore, the *general* will, but the will of the *few*, which they expect everyone to applaud, provided they are good and wise enough to do so. But either they are indeed 'good and wise enough', or they are not, in which case they will have to allow a law of which they disapprove to govern their prosperity and well-being. This is the worst fate that could befall them in their natural state, one that in such a state they would be expected far rather to avoid! This must be true of the vast majority of our people, for they are all governed by self-interest, including their representatives. Those individuals whose will *triumphs* must first and last intend to feather their own nests, and what goes into them is taken from all the others. But – my critics shout in my ear – do you not realise that their representatives must be not only the wisest heads but also the *best* heads? Yes, I hear them, and I assume that they are the brightest creatures in the world, meaning that they understand better than anyone else what is to their own advantage! But nonetheless I say no! They must be full of republican virtues, and must possess integrity, patriotism, and altruism to the highest degree!

That is a quite *different* matter, I add. Nor – with the temporal security and well-being of humankind resting on the mind-set of a few individuals rather than being the whole *purpose* of a state – shall I ask whether a bird in the hand is not better than two in the bush? Or whether it is worth surrendering a guaranteed freedom for a totally unreliable replacement? I ask above all: Is it possible that there exists in all human beings something higher and stronger than our own self-interest irrespective of whether we have an eternal rather than a temporal destiny? Is it possible that on the premise of this eternal destiny, we can draw the conclusion that the object of our human endeavour is purely temporal? That it does not need to subject itself to, or be determined by, our eternal destiny?

This alone should be sufficient to demonstrate that either we must condemn all organisation of the State on the grounds that we are creatures of Reason who would thereby lose out, or we must concede that the State should keep in view the Revelation that we have an eternal destiny and should organise itself in a serviceable agreement to that end. We are forced to make this choice, if we are not foolishly to contradict ourselves time after time!

Let me take this opportunity for a moment to view the matter from several angles, on the assumption that it is *undecided* whether we have an eternal destiny and whether the State is good or bad for humankind. No one denies that at present we do *have* states and cannot do without them, even if it were possible to do so. Let us assume that the sole and undeniable purpose of the State is the maintenance and promotion of general security and physical well-being to the best of its ability. And let me therefore view this from the perspective of the 18th century and ask: Can the State, thus regarded, stand on its own two feet and manage *without* the prevailing Church and be indifferent as to whether it is true or false?

If we also allow the existence of God to remain undecided by the State, then we should begin by examining whether or not the State's maintenance is based on the will of those who *constitute* it. Since this would seem to be undeniable, it only goes to show that the ruling self-interest of the few cannot help but undermine and gradually *dissolve* the State. It follows, as Voltaire said, that if God did not exist, it would be necessary to invent him![535] It would also be easy to show that any God or revelation required by a State would have to be created as a *higher* being, set *above* it, for otherwise it would at most be a theatrical entertainment for the people. It might dispel *ideas* for a while, but it could never unite wills or bend hearts to obedience and sacrifice for the State! I shall not pursue this path, since it is far too great an indulgence to the human animal to call God's existence into doubt; not even the strictest examination

535 'Si Dieu n'existait pas, il faudrait l'inventer', wrote Voltaire (1694-1778) in his verse poem, 'Epistle to the Author of Three Impostors' (*Epître à l'auteur du livre des Trois imposteurs*, 1768).

would demand this. And anyway, we can begin much further down with what no one calls into question, namely, that in the invisible world lies a frightening power whose presence is felt partly in Nature, with floods, earthquakes, crop failure and the like, and partly in History, with all that can be called 'unfortunate circumstances'. One of these alone is often enough to turn a whole State upside-down and for a protracted length of time disturb the general security and physical well-being.

In this connection I am well aware of the advice which in particular the wise heads of the 18th century gave the State as an important suggestion. But to be honest, I think these heads were too dim for us to demand a serious examination of them. Do not misunderstand me. I do not mean that all who gave such advice were dimwits; on the contrary, I regard the man who gave the State the most preposterous advice, Johann Fichte,[536] to be one of the world's greatest philosophers. But when Reason insists on advising itself, it is inevitably at a loss in History; the clearer it understands the dire straits it is in, the more foolish is the advice it gives as it attempts to remain true to itself.

So what *were* the resources that the State was advised to mount against the incomparable superiority of invisible powers? A sedulous cultivation of physique, economy, and politics, alongside a numerous standing army and an almost equally well-manned reserve army, with a vanguard of light troops and strong hounds! With a modicum of awareness of the folly of committing these resources for the purpose, these wise heads would have realised that they were literally comforting people in distress with the consolation that even if they perished, the voyage would not stop! Finally, they learned to scorn both sea and wind and – perhaps on one leg like Ull[537] – confidently circumnavigate the world.

Readers may think I am talking myself *out* of something, but I would actually prefer to speak my mind! On the indisputable assumption that at any moment the State and all those within it risk being maimed, upended, and broken up by an invisible hand, it is quite certain that unless the State is reckless, it cannot consider itself secured by physical weaponry. If there is a blind hand of fate hovering over it as a threat to all things temporal, then the State and all those within it can do no more than seek to emulate the dumb animals, take the beehive as their model, and let fate decide whether a plague of mice, crop failure, or sulphurous fumes end their days! Without repeating what has already been said about the value of the State in

536 Johann Fichte (1762-1814) was the founder of the German idealism movement and a pioneer in the area of self-awareness.

537 In Saxo's *Gesta Danorum* (*Deeds of the Danes*, 13th century) the god Ull (aka Ullr/Uller) is depicted as a cunning wizard who stands on a magic bone to cross the seas as fast as a rowboat. His name is commemorated in the Ullevie Stadium in Stockholm, where Denmark won the European Soccer Championship in 1992 with a 2-0 victory over Germany.

such a case, it is quite certain that in raising the subject of a blind fate which governs humankind we are contradicting ourselves and are naming a specific impossibility, for we are then saying that both a creature of reason (i.e. a created Reason) has issued from Unreason, and that the highest Will and Consciousness can be governed by something that lacks both, which is clearly impossible. If this supremacy presupposes a supreme Will, wherever that may be found, then obviously the State and all within it are poor guardians of their security if they challenge and contend with that superior power. The only good advice is to seek its friendship and attempt to win it over. Thus, if the Church were an expression of precisely our human relation to this superior power, it would follow that merely in order to *exist* the State would have to turn to the Church, and indeed would be seriously concerned to *find* the true Church. That alone can protect the State, since only the true revelation about the invisible powers and human relations to them can teach us how to find the superior power and seek its good graces in a suitable manner.

If this is the case with regard to the *maintenance* of the State, then clearly it cannot be less so with regard to the *purpose* of the State, whatever that may be, for under all circumstances good fortune is required to achieve that purpose, and good fortune inevitably depends on the unquestioned superior power.

Finally, when we delve a little deeper, we soon discover that even though a State which had the will of the people against it could survive at length *on the surface*, it would nonetheless be internally in dissolution and would constitute no more than one big prison. It might be possible to work there, but nothing would thrive or develop that would make people think it *worthwhile* to go to prison! In noting that the presence of such a State Prison would at any moment run the risk of reaching its limits, since every such prison must predict for itself the same fate as in Christianshavn,[538] we cannot conceal the fact that the State is just such a prison in everyone's eyes. It is ruled by self-interest, and gain's nobody's favour unless they can see an advantage in becoming a prison-officer, or at least being good friends with one such, so they have all their needs covered without having to work. If the State wanted the will of the people on its side, it ought not to be a prison but a body whose various parts regard each other as members. If it wants the head to rule, it must be through the people belonging to a Church which the State has *on its side* and whose precepts it follows. Also from this level it would be easy to show how it is only the true Church with whose supporters

538 In 1617, Christian IV established a harbour for the Danish navy at Christianshavn, and the area attracted well-to-do families – until the English captured the navy in the war of 1807. A prison was then built in the area to contain the worst offenders in the country – alongside destitute men and women. In 1817 a riot resulted in a serious fire, but the attempted break-out was contained, and the ringleaders executed. By 1900 the area was inhabited by the working-class, many of them shipbuilders. More recently Christianshavn has become best-known for the hippie colony of 'Christiania', as well as being home to top-class restaurants and, simultaneously, centres for the destitute.

the State is actually served, since only the will that derives from love is powerful and constant. Nothing other than Truth can give birth to the altruistic love which alone is mother of the will which the State needs in its members. This would be easy, but quite superfluous here; for once we agree that the State requires a ruling Church, it follows that the true Church is not only the best Church but the only Church that can come into the reckoning. Truth alone is what humankind, in general and individually, must uphold and pursue, so if the State were best served by a *false* Church, it would only go to show that the State was an ungodly and inhuman organisation.

It is not too soon at this juncture to pose the question: How should the State – or more specifically 'the authorities' – uphold and pursue the true revelation and conform to the true Church? As with all useful questions, it would be easy to answer how people *should* be, given the way they *are*! We would only have to say: The authorities must look after all the members of the State so they have the opportunity to develop in their own particular way, according to the precepts of the Church, and use their combined energies to this purpose as well as to stave off all existing hindrances.

This answer is invariable in every circumstance, yet it is quite inadequate here, for even if the authorities were perfection itself, they cannot *transform* their subjects; and since these are a mixture of good and bad, and even at best fallen, vulnerable people, the task of the State is extremely complex and difficult to solve. It cannot supply its members with the strength they lack, nor can it change their will; indeed even its knowledge of that will is imperfect and inadequate. In consequence, there is on the one hand an unavoidable internal battle between the Law and its violators, and on the other hand a mitigation of the Law according to circumstances, both in the criminal code and all its adaptations. An adequate answer for all states and all times is therefore impossible; indeed this is even true of a particular state at a particular time. The question can only really be answered for the individual state by its *history*, for this reveals the circumstances of the people's spirit and heart at any given time, as well as the stage of development at which they stand. Only by comparing this with the true Church's revelation on the destiny of humankind and its earthly path, can we propose the best course of action without making too many mistakes.

Nevertheless, in committing all such circumstances to a historical examination we should not forget that an overarching view of how the State should view the Church, and how it should act accordingly, cannot be determined with complete certainty. Obviously the authorities should not only ensure that their subjects have every opportunity to develop according to their means in the direction that the true Church enjoins; they should also protect the means whereby this is made possible. On the other hand the State should never involve itself in its members' relationship to the Church, for that is truly a personal matter. Nor should it claim to be able to *change* the Church, for forcing a confession that does not express a personal faith is an injustice that in every way *corrupts* the State, since it can turn people's hearts away and become blind to itself.

Here we see a notable difference between the Church and the State which would undoubtedly be for the well-being of humankind in the eyes of all who wield some influence in these entities. The Church cannot help but be what, with a favoured neutral, is now known as 'in-tolerant', meaning that it must be the irreconcilable enemy of all that deviates from its revelation; nothing can be surrendered of the eternal Truth. This is the role of the true Church. It cannot allow a single word of contradiction without affecting and denying itself; and since every Church must announce itself as being 'true', this must be the case for all of them, despite only one of them being legitimate!

The State, on the other hand, must not be what is called 'tolerant', since that is inconsequential; it must be genuinely 'long-suffering' and 'weaponless' as regards its members' faith. If it is to uphold the true Church, it cannot possibly approve of anything that contradicts the Church's revelation! However, both the true Church and the proper State are ill-advised to *force* anyone to accept this revelation – or punish them for not doing so. All that comes of that is hypocrisy and a secret unrest that can never actually *damage* the true Church, yet can nevertheless banish it from the country and thereby undermine the State.

The consequence is not in doubt. Just as the true Church alone is both entitled and obliged to isolate any who by word or deed exclude themselves from its Community, so is it *unjustifiable* that the Church should demand that the State should attach a temporal punishment to such an exclusion, indeed it is indefensible of the Church at least verbally to *condone* such a punishment!

Of itself the Church has nothing it requires of the State except the freedom to preach its gospel. It must leave to the State any arrangement it makes as a result of this preaching, and it must only request that it be held free of any temporal artillery, since the Word of Truth will surely defend itself and cannot be defended by anything else.

On closer inspection it is clear that not only was it Martin Luther's constant argument that we follow the Bible, it should also be that of all pastors! That indeed is the *very nature* of the case and thus the given relation between the proper State and the true Church. History testifies to what extent this important truth has been changed over the years – without much comfort but with much instructive information.

Let us now ignore the objection that we have provided too little or no information at all about the State, and cast our attention on the School in order to discover its relation to the Church and the State – a relation which will inevitably shed light on what has previously been said.

The School

In everyday speech 'the School' involves what develops and educates us, and most of all its purpose in relation to the State. What then should be the aim of the School in its endeavour to develop and educate the human being?

Everyone would agree on the answer: the School must strive to develop the human being to perfection and to educate every individual to be as capable as possible to achieving this end. This in brief is the work of the School – that is, if we agree on the concept of human perfection, on how humankind came into being, and what we are destined for. However, we must deal with the School in the same way we dealt with the Church and the State: we must make a clear distinction between the two contrary views of humankind and regard the School from both sides.

If human beings are creatures of Reason only, i.e. they have no eternal destiny, it follows that the School in fact has no *real* meaning for human life; it is neither a preparation nor a development *towards* something else. If the human race has no common goal to which all individuals can work with united strength, then their sole task is to make their way through the world as best they can. Insofar as they wish for the fullest instruction in the necessary means to this end, they must also wish that others do *not* obtain it, for the better the others know their advantage, the harder it is for the individual to have any; this must surely be the highest wish and daily endeavour of such creatures of Reason.

I am well aware that most people will regard it as highly unjust, if not downright fatuous, for me to claim that in its choleric 'school-fever' the 18th century attempted to build the School on a swing whose rope would soon snap and bury it in a bottomless morass. In other words, the totally erroneous 18th century, which declared itself the everlasting protector of the School, built itself up on the basic principle regarding humankind and School which deprived the School of its entire human, i.e. historical, importance and ordained it to destruction by setting itself at odds with both the Church and the State.

After due consideration, it will have to be admitted that I am absolutely right on this matter, and if that is so, it is without doubt my duty to continue and develop my claim in all its stringency. I do so because we are still finding in 'the School' so many sad remnants of the madness of the 18th century – even more so because here in the 19th century we are in great danger of either making the School pay for what its bunglers have mismanaged, or, faced with condemnation of its consequences, building on the same totally erroneous principles.

I limit myself to making such a claim solely in order to reserve this development for the historical section of this study where it belongs, and because, without first knowing what is true and right, one cannot have an eye for what is crooked and false.[539]

If we now regard human beings as creatures of reason *in the image of God*, destined for eternal life, then we clearly see that their earthly life can quite justifiably be called no more than a 'school', i.e. a development leading to a transfiguration. Nor can there be any doubt that everything which is rightfully to be called a 'school for humankind' must walk in the reins of the true Church, since it is the Church alone that can reveal what is to be developed, learned, and comprehended in the School. To this end the School must have two major divisions: the one to deal with the common, yet specific, needs of the individual, the other to deal with the needs of the whole of humankind, i.e. with teaching the human race. This is the logical consequence of the fact that we are each a separate entity and must answer for ourselves, yet we are all part of the human race into which we must be incorporated and towards whose goal we must cooperate. The first School is inseparable from the true Church's revelation, and although we cannot say the same about the second School, it must assuredly develop from it, since the true Revelation must embrace temporal humankind in its entirety and fulfil its full destiny in its believers.

Through careful reflection we can see that what goes by the name of 'the Church' and 'the School' in the world is in fact only the two major divisions within the latter which our whole life constitutes, corresponding to each other like revelation to experience. Not just our learning about eternal matters in our childhood but our entire practice of the pastoral teaching role clearly belong to the 'Church-School', just as all scholarship, both written and oral, constitutes the 'State-School' or the School of History. Who would deny that preaching the Word must be the prime concern of the Church, and enlightenment and education the prime concern of the State?

In the proper sense, the School is the highest object of the united endeavours of humankind, for, like the true State, the true Church is *invisible*. Our senses can only understand their images in 'the School', where we learn to know, to love, and to enter into them – to eternal life.

At this stage we can now see that in all circumstances the State is *an essential link*, and its great and glorious purpose is to organise and safeguard the High School of the human race. In a perfect world among the unfallen[540] the State would have fused together clergy and laity, the internal and the external,[541] and there would have been only *one* Church and *one* State on earth. All external compulsion and punishment

539 The historical section followed in the next edition of the periodical.

540 At this point Grundtvig imagines a world without the Fall – hence the use of 'unfallen'.

541 'The internal and the external' refers to Luther's distinction between the two regiments of Church and State, to which the clergy and the laity are respectively attached.

would have been superfluous. However, in the present circumstances, although things are somewhat different, no State has the right to set a lower goal, any more than the individual has the right to lose sight of their eternal destiny, or to subordinate it just because *after* the Fall it is harder to achieve!

The prime purpose of the State is to ensure the growth and security of the School. To this end it is particularly qualified, as we can see from considering any other purpose the State might serve. Whatever that might be, it would already be contained in the prime purpose above; it would be both subordinate and conditional, as well as being far less perfect and far less achievable without the purpose that I consider 'prime'.

No one who thinks this matter through can be in any doubt, for it is clear that the State must maintain itself purely in order to work towards achieving *any* purpose. It must strive as far as possible to promote the security and well-being of all its members, as well as allowing them as free a hand as they rightly demand. All this follows from the need for a constant regard for the School and for the conditions for its prosperity. Similarly, we must admit that the human State would be better served by its dissolution than by its abandonment of the School, just as the School must be willing to sacrifice the individual's security and well-being, if that is necessary for its survival.

Not until we reach this level can we see in what circumstances the waging of war is not only permissible but even a categorical duty for the proper State, when either it or the School of the human race is attacked. Unless something within its borders is attacked from without I dare not therefore say that *every* war which the State wages is unjust. However, most wars of this kind have been so, and I believe that all wars are unjust unless they are waged either for the sake of the School, or for the sake of another State working towards the same goal, or in order to disarm an obvious enemy of the human race who is striving to destroy the Church-School and cut out the tongue of the true Revelation. For like a limb on the great human State, each individual state must regard all enemies of the human race as enemies of their own.

I realise that these words may sound strange in many an ear, since for so long we have been used to regarding the State and the School from their respective sides, rather than from the Church Gallery. That is no fault of mine. If one finds it constrained to use the word 'School' in conjunction with the Church and the State, one must realise that the true Church cannot possibly exist on earth unless it does so *invisibly through faith*, nor the proper State unless *invisibly through love*. Nor can we call the external area in which they express themselves through word and action for the education and upbringing of the human race anything other than a 'School', if we are to be specific! Admittedly in everyday speech we must continue to call them 'Church' and 'State', but if we are to make good sense of them for people, we must call them 'Schools'. This will guard against the dangerous fancy that the Church and the State are basically sensory and temporal, and at the same time affirm the only proper view of what in a stricter, more limited, sense is called 'School'.

In arguing that the School should be the prime purpose of the State, we are saying that its highest concern must be the genuine education and growth of its members towards becoming citizens of Heaven and the limbs of perfected humankind. This must be the highest wish of all individuals both for themselves and for their fellow human beings, and a human State must of necessity be animated and enlivened by the highest human wish. However necessary this may be, we can never believe that *the human heart* should be the object of the worldly arm's activity, for we cannot apply external measures to the heart. And yet these are the only measures the State possesses! So it cannot work more closely for the great destiny of humankind other than to protect and in every way promote the activity of the Word of Truth as the only sensory instrument for the Spirit of all truth and love.[542] It is always an error for the State to employ other means than the Word for the betterment of its members, and it must leave this Word to the Church to advance. If the State takes control of the Word, it will make it its own and thereby deprive it of its authority and activity as the Word of God. Unfortunately, the State cannot do without a prison, but it should not call it a 'house of improvement', for by making 'improvement' the object of its penitentiaries, it would confuse itself with the Church. It would strive through its penal code towards a highly uncertain goal outside its competence, and it would therefore fail in what it could and should accomplish *through* the code. Of course, the jurists and lawyers believe that *they* should be left to decide this, or at least to have some influence over it. In the former case they must study and understand far better than at present both History in general, and the history of the State in particular, of which they are largely ignorant, for they have the means to authorize themselves to decide such questions. In the latter case they will have to deal with a subject they prefer to avoid, even though they have little time to do so.

I shall add only one comment, which is a reminder that there is a difference between Church discipline[543] and State imprisonment. When the Church excludes members for a transgression and after a while admits them again in the hope that they have reformed, there is reason for hope. The miscreants could *repeat* their transgressions, if they so wished, and there is no danger incurred at readmission, since they are not

542 'Spirit of all truth and love' (*Kærlighed og sandheds ånd*, 1837) is also the title of one of Grundtvig's most famous hymns, translated as no. 37 in *Living Wellsprings* (2015).

543 'Church discipline' (1 Cor 5 et al.) is the practice of censuring church members to elicit repentance and reconciliation through a progressively administered procedure of 1) admonition, 2) suspension from Holy Communion, and ultimately 3) excommunication. In Denmark in the late Middle Ages miscreants, whose sin was often of a sexual nature, could be publicly named in church and shamed outside it with the iron collar attached to the church wall; such a collar can still be seen in the bell tower at Varnæs Church in South Jutland.

cut off from supervision; on the contrary, it is sharpened. However, when the State imprisons offenders, it makes every effort to make a repetition of their crime *impossible*, and although this may be successful for a period of time it is no guarantee whatsoever that offenders do not retain the *will* to do so. It is therefore a very moot point as to whether our general security gains *more* through many an offender's imprisonment than it loses with their release, when the State presumes they are reformed.

Perhaps one day I shall write a study of the Penal Code, especially with reference to our country and its legal history. If so, I shall develop this argument in detail. Meanwhile I would dearly love a jurist who has the subject close at heart to precede me and treat the subject from the angle of the history of Christianity, for this is important in maintaining the State.

Yet again the School confronts us with its demands, namely its *historical* demands! None would deny that from the study of History the State must learn to look after both its prosperity and its well-being, and must learn in its legislation to effect what time and place are deemed to be for the best.

The study of History seeks not only to furnish the State with the necessary *knowledge* but also with the necessary *personnel*, people who can understand and *apply* the details and illumination of History. For it is as clear as sunlight that the School of History must be the purpose of every sensible State, even if it had no other goal than its own prosperity and well-being. If, furthermore, its duty is to the human race to cultivate and cherish this alongside the Church-School, then it merely has to say that the practice of this duty is very much worth the while!

In the wake of all the above-mentioned observations regarding the range, coherence, and proper study of History I have no fear of the objection that it is a mere 'play of words' upon which I am building the unity of the School, a concept that is much-needed by the State, whose chief purpose is to cultivate and cherish. However, it never harms a case to make it somewhat clearer, especially since we can thereby gain the opportunity to see how the School *links* the Church and the State.

History comprises the whole of human life. Despite it having the same three divisions as human life, we must differentiate between Church History, State History, and School History, for it is impossible to understand the latter two without understanding the first one! The State must always have an interplay with the Church, while the School is generated and raised by both. Church History cannot be elucidated without accepting the effect of *the Word* on the State and the School, and this elucidation is also essential for the true Church, since the truth of its revelation is thereby clarified *historically*!

Let us assume, without doing the least violence to ourselves, that we regard the School of History as doing both the Church and the State the greatest service possible in mutual interaction by following its own prescribed path. Let us also assume that this service consists of confirming the position of the Church and enlightening and educating the State. Let us further note that by elucidating the historical relations of the Church and the State we not only set aside all dispute between them – or rather, between their servants – but we also dry up the source of strife between them once they wish to be servants of 'the Truth'. Assuming all this, we must say: 'Woe to the Church that the School of History does not hold close to its bosom, for it thereby brands itself as a figment of lies! And woe to the State for whom this too is not the case, for it thereby stamps itself as a prison tower, built from trickery and violence, constructed in blood with the foreheads of death-skulls! And woe three times over to the State that fights the School, for it is like a gang with Satan at its head which is striving to make the earth a nursery for Hell!'

To be sure, there are still many questions to be asked – far more than I can answer, but nevertheless some that I can. My intention here has only been to offer a sketch of the internal relations between the Church, the State, and the School up to this day. To avoid useless repetition I shall leave much to the historical view of the relation until now. In the overview that will follow in the next number, God willing, I hope to elaborate and confirm my view better than the most precise factual advancement, which, even when it is most successful, nonetheless is boring at length and lacks the life and the force that History alone possesses.

▷▷

6. Grundtvig 1842

P. (Peter) C. Skovgaard (1817-75) made several drawings of Grundtvig, including the one from 1847 on the cover of this series, when Grundtvig is beginning to grow his whiskers. By 1857 he is fully-bearded, though without a moustache. In this drawing from 1842 Grundtvig is beardless and in his vestments, as worn at Vartov Church, where he was pastor from 1839-72 and where the Skovgaards were regular churchgoers. Peter Skovgaard knew Grundtvig through Joakim Schouw, whose daughter Georgia Skovgaard married in 1851, with Grundtvig officiating – as indeed he did at the baptism and confirmation of their two children, Joakim and Niels, both artists. Joakim made the drawing of Ernst Trier used as illustration no. 11 in this book, and Niels sculpted the statue of Grundtvig that graces the courtyard at Vartov. Peter Skovgaard himself is best known as a landscape artist, but he was also a skilful portrait artist, and it is most likely that this drawing was a sketch for a painting that never saw the light of day.

III

HISTORY AND SIGNS

6. On the Advancement of Learning (1807)

Introduction by Niels W. Bruun

The full title of this essay, published in 1807, is *On the Advancement of Learning, with Particular Regard to the Fatherland*. It is among Grundtvig's earliest publications – in the periodical *Ny Minerva* (spring 1807) – and circles round the Danish word for 'Learning' (*vidskab*).[544] We must bear in mind that all references to 'the child' and 'youngsters' in the essay refer solely to the male of the species. At this point in his life Grundtvig is a child of the times. Sixty years later he is a *champion* of female education – see his addresses to the young women at Marielyst High School in Text 14. But already here his *concern* for education is obvious, and his pen a potent weapon.

Grundtvig's essay takes issue with the contemporary hindrances to this advancement, based on his own experiences at Copenhagen University and his first two years at Egeløkke Manor as house tutor to the young Carl Steensen de Leth. As we know, Grundtvig fell in love with the boy's mother, Constance, so at this point in his life, aged 23, even love can be a motivator of scientific enquiry. "If his love is rewarded, he will fly to his goal by a shorter route than the one he would have taken with firm steps" (p. 254). In Grundtvig's own case, his passion went unrequited – and he turned to books and writing, including in his own diary: "I must call it good fortune that my love was unfulfilled, since it made me active and contributed to an increase in my knowledge."[545]

In Grundtvig's view, the main hindrance to the advancement of Learning is the universities themselves, and most of all the ignorant students: "I think the most important reason is the increasing irreligiosity and immorality, and the lack of scholarly Learning among our younger students" (p. 249). In caustic, satirical phrases Grundtvig berates students, house tutors, and the clergy for their lack of interest in Learning, and he condemns them for their indulgences and their failure to rescue Danish culture from its imminent death: "I regard our literature as being like a drowned man who for the last time exerts his strength and shouts aloud for help in the language of the gods. But the seashore is almost empty and the few people standing there seriously doubt that he can pay for his rescue with a coinage that they recognise" (p. 244).

What is needed is "a more scholarly training of the students, by which I mean that they are inspired by Love, Learning, and the Arts." Here Grundtvig formulates for the first time his

544 At this earliest stage in his understanding of women, Grundtvig writes that women could be "the *strongest* spur to learning without losing the least bit of their particular character; but in that case their education must be quite different from what it is now: worthless tinsel, with the woman only being formed in the man" (p. 256). The first female university student in Denmark was Nielsine Nielsen (1850-1916), who in 1877 was allowed to study medicine, following which she became Denmark's first female doctor.

545 *Diaries and Journals (Dag- og Udtogsbøger)* vols 1-2, ed. Gustav Albeck, (Copenhagen 1979) vol. 1. p. 383.

educational principle of 'inspiration' – the inspirational teacher and the inspired student: "We need not wait for experience to teach us that the celebration of Learning, a closer relationship between teachers and students, plus the necessity of treating scholarly subjects in both speech and writing, all serve in particular to infuse the students with a respect for scientific enquiry and a desire to pursue it" (p. 253).

It then follows that the inspired student cannot be other than an inspiring professor or pastor, and thus Learning will be advanced. We should also note the first usage in this essay of other principles and practices that form Grundtvig's idea of "the school for life", which crystallises in 'the people's high school'. These include: Danish as the mother-tongue; Danish literature, especially poetry, as its expression; the importance of history as lived human experience; a religious mind that acknowledges a supreme Maker: and the idea that the school should be a *nursery* for the branches of Learning rather than a factory.

Simultaneously, Grundtvig is concerned about the increasing militarism of his age as a hindrance to scientific enquiry: "Are there any who dare to deny that it was the French Revolution that stopped all such enquiry...?" (p. 243). Patriot that he is, Grundtvig is willing to "place my sacrifice on the altar of the fatherland and dare to hope that despite its slightness it will please the all-powerful gods" (p. 245). With Denmark at odds with both France and England, patriotism is the order of the day – also in the sub-title of this essay. Denmark must not be allowed to disappear from the face of the earth but must find an inner strength to combat the outer threat from France (Napoleon) and England (Nelson). Lord Nelson had already defeated the Danes at the First Battle of Copenhagen (*Slaget på Rheden* 1801) and six months after publication of this article Nelson was back to bombard Copenhagen in the autumn of 1807.

Scribendi rede sapere est principium et fons.[546]
Horace, Ars Poetica.

A very useful occupation for 'thinking people' is to pay close attention to the situation of Learning[547] in their time. If they see it flourishing and its many corolla straining toward heaven, and if at its root they see people all around drinking in the juice that

546 'A healthy common sense is the prerequisite for being able to write well.' Horace: *Ars Poetica*, c. 19 BCE.

547 Grundtvig's own footnote 3: "By Learning I understand the sense for the harmonious development of the human spirit without a care for its relationship to everyday life. I regard the ideal of the harmonious human spirit to be a form whose feet touch the ground even though their head touches the stars, whose widespread arms embrace Nature, whose eyes see the past and the present clearly, and for whom even heaven is transparent. But do not misunderstand me and confuse this ideal with the highest degree of development that the spirit can achieve under the limitations of this earthly life." *Videnskab,* the word translated here as 'Learning' and occasionally 'scholarship' or 'philosophical insight' also covers (the spirit of) scientific and spiritual enquiry; in the plural form *Videnskaber*, it refers to the branches of learning. See also Editor's Note pp. 12-13.

in the circulation of the creature's great body alone can prove that it is animated by spirit and gives life meaning, then they have found the pure wellspring of joy whose clear waters in constant flow show them the way into the future whereby a life that is ten times better reveals itself to their sight.

On the other hand, if they see a withered plant whose split stalks appear to beg a miserable appearance of life from the swaggering stems that stole its juices, then, weighed down by anguish they may well lose courage immediately. But they will never be tempted to be like the hired agents who only delay the death of the plant by allowing it to die daily. If they cast an eye back to times gone by, to the intrinsic value of scientific inquiry or Learning, they will also despise the pathetic efforts that dishonour their organs and their times. They will respond with bitter scorn to the poor souls who despise the branches of Learning, and they will ask with true animal naivité whether, since the Philosopher's Stone[548] has been discovered, they might be allowed to learn how to create the almighty metal. Then they will be told that nature concealed the gold in the hard rocks to prevent its rise among humankind, since it envisaged that they would otherwise descend into its emptied bed.

Sceptics acknowledge no other authority than what is dug up before their very eyes, so when they open the scroll of history and regard the Persians, the Huns,[549] and the many who did not owe their elevated position to Learning, they will hear the answer: Without any real respect for Learning in its highest sense and without any intimate knowledge of it, the nations in their masses could roll across the globe and crush all opposition. They could force from their contemporary generation something they themselves call 'admiration', despite it being a mere horror of the same kind as the one that on the banks of the ocean we must all feel at the glimpse of a lava flow that embraced palaces and hovels in its glowing arms and which we would attempt in vain to stop, if it reached us.[550] Yet the Delphic Apollo[551] was stronger than the legions of Brennus,[552] and with true colours the poet painted these scenes from the past and the future when he sang:

548 The philosopher's stone was a legendary chemical substance which according to medieval alchemists could transform base metal into 'the almighty' gold. Used figuratively, it is a giver of deep insight.

549 Grundtvig appears unaware of the widespread learning of the Persians, especially in literature. The three Persian empires stretched from the 7th century BCE to the 3rd century CE. The Huns, by contrast, were fundamentally marauding nomads, whose short-lived empire, admittedly the largest so far seen in Europe, came to an end with the death of the mighty Attila in 453.

550 Probably a reference to the destruction of Pompeii by the volcano Vesuvius in 79 CE.

551 In Greek mythology Apollo is the god i.a. of medicine, prophecy, music and poetry. One of his locations was Delphi.

552 Brennus (d. 279 BCE) was a Gallic chieftain who invaded Greece and attacked Delphi but was driven off by the Greeks and took his own life.

Herds of hailstones hammer down
mixed with driving rain;
frothing mountain waterfalls
fill the valley plain;
bridges, dams are swept away
in this wild descent;
nought can stop their mighty path,
yet their Maker spent
but a moment on their course;
running into sand they lose their way;
only in the whirl can Mem'ry stay.[553]

It is only the spirit of scientific inquiry that can give generations and individuals lasting greatness, and it was this alone that made the Greeks build a temple whose pillars have grown together with the cornerstones of the earth, and on whose altar the greatest geniuses, the chosen of their kind, should sacrifice themselves right up to recent times.[554]

These remarks are far from new, but with disagreeable force they must penetrate every observer of our present-day aspirations. To make the sciences mere vehicles for pleasure is to deprive them of their peculiar character, since they thereby acquire a finality and are limited to our earthly ambition. To place them at the service of politics or any other such service is to drive them off the face of the earth; for they are free as the heavenly spark from which they all stem, and they tolerate no slave-chains but rise into the pure air, pursued by the scorn of the mob and the deep sigh of their friends.

It is not only Fichte and Arndt[555] but all of Europe's greatest thinkers who lament the degeneracy of our time, its blindness to true Learning and to the *nobility* of humankind. Are there any who dare to deny that it was the French Revolution that

553 The quotation is from an English translation of the tragedy, *The Bride of Messina* (*Die Braut von Messina*, 1803) by the German writer Friedrich Schiller (1759-1805). Schiller is best known for his 'Ode to Joy', which Beethoven employed for the fourth (choral) movement of Symphony no. 9.

554 After the fall of Constantinople in 1453 Greece was ruled by the Muslim Ottoman Turks who controlled the entire Middle East, and the Balkans as far as the gates of Vienna. The beginnings of the revolution which led to Greek independence in 1821 can be traced to the French Revolution and not least to the writings of Rigas Velestinlis (aka Rigas Feraios, 1757-98), whose political manifesto was a draft constitution in 1797 supporting a "Hellenic Republic" within the borders of the Ottoman Empire. Revolutionary pamphlets began to circulate anonymously in the first decade of the 19th century, when Grundtvig was writing this article. The identification of the modern Greeks with the ancient Greeks (e.g. by European Romantics such as Byron) became a central doctrine of Greek nationalism in the struggle for cultural regeneration through independence.

555 Johann Fichte (1762-1814), German philosopher. Ernst Arndt (1769-1860), German historian and politician. Both were critics of the morality of their times.

stopped all such enquiry by dragging the eye of enlightened Europe from heaven down to earth in order to witness a new heaven *on* earth?[556]

However, I shall not dwell on the sad sights that Europe affords, but turn my attention to the fatherland – but not because I believe it is of no interest to Skjold's offspring[557] how matters are changing in the rest of Europe, or because I consider it dishonourable to be a cosmopolitan in the noble meaning of the word. For true love of the fatherland can never demand that we increase our restrictions by tying ourselves to the country's border-posts; and like Schiller I believe that it was a great step forward that the citizen again became the human being.[558]

I chose this spot because it was easier for my limited vision, because the powerful history of the North bound me closer to it than birth could, and because I refused to believe that it was a waste of time to tell my countrymen what in my opinion contributes, or *can* contribute, to giving them a higher or lower rank as a people.

Denmark and Norway, or the fatherland,[559] ought to be a safe refuge for Science and Art when the din of weapons and spirits of the dark drive them away. There is peace within our borders, and under our country's peace-loving father, who, as the poet so beautifully phrases it:

> Stand with upright watchfulness unwearied
> for Denmark's Eden, not with vengeful might
> but as an angel's palm-leaf of all innocence
> can wave the child away from deadly fight.[560]

He does not wish to kill the spirit in order to direct machines. But could we instead take pride in being what in this respect we ought to be anyway? It is only a repeat of the claim by the highest in our state when I answer, No, unfortunately! The answer does not rest on any authority, for anyone who knows something of our literature and its predominant tone must give the *same* answer.

556 An ironic allusion to Rev. 21:1: "I saw a new heaven and a new earth."

557 Skjold was Denmark's legendary first king. According to the Old English poem *Beowulf* Skjold (Scyld) came sailing alone to Denmark as a child asleep in a boat, and the Danes made him their king. *Beowulf* begins at the end of his life with Skjold's ship burial.

558 According to Schiller, the study of universal history assists in the humanisation of the individual from mere citizen to full human being: "One destiny you share with everybody in the same way, the one that you brought with you into the world – to educate yourselves as human beings – it is to such human beings that History speaks." Schiller 1792.

559 Denmark and Norway were one kingdom until 1814. In the aftermath of the Napoleonic wars, Denmark lost Norway to Sweden.

560 The quotation is from the pamphlet *Answer to Baggesen on his Letter 'Noureddin to Aladdin'* (1807) by Adam Oehlenschläger (1779-1850), Denmark's greatest Romantic poet and writer of the comedy *Aladdin, or the Wonderful Lamp* (1805).

Strictly speaking, we have no right to draw conclusions about a country's literature from its Learning; for just as the former can flourish over a brief period, though limited to a few individuals, so can it also survive after the latter has been lost. However, we must assume that among a people where good writing is rare, Learning and higher education are either already lost or are in the process of being so. The reason is obvious, for educated people always feel the need to pass on their form of words to others, and only a mighty wall can stop them from doing so. If that wall is indeed too strong, then the sun of the sciences will soon be lost behind it, and the dull glow of its reflection will lose itself in the encroaching darkness.

Learning and literature relate to one another in turn, like cause and effect, in that the one presumes the other and indeed encourages it.

I will not hide my fear that we already stand at a point that presages the demise of both. Nor does that fear fade when I regard with joy some of our more recent poems. Europe ought to get to know these few shoots that bear witness to the vitality of our being. For this life and power did not issue from the bosom of the day, but are intercepted sunrays that still cast light and warmth on a coming time, after our sun has turned in its course. Their lukewarm – I almost said 'cold' – reception and the vulgar curiosity with which they are stared at instead of being *enjoyed*, are for me a sad guarantee that I am speaking the truth. I regard our literature as being like a drowned man who for the last time exerts his strength and shouts aloud for help in the language of the gods. But the seashore is almost empty and the few people standing there seriously doubt that he can pay for his rescue with a coinage that they recognise.

If this contempt for the noble interpreter of scholarship continues, what will be the consequence?

I hear the answer all around me: that no one will any longer be tempted to the folly of putting money into books, which are of no use anyway and continue to lose value, and that people speak less and act more, in brief; that we become such sensible and industrious earth-dwellers that we find better refreshment in good food and the noble grape-juice than in what chronicles, sophistries, and rhymings can offer.

Despite my greatest respect for the golden maxim: 'Wise to heaven's path, but merely fools on earth',[561] and for the whole community that grows rich on it and becomes fat and full of days, no one would blame me for saying roughly the same about my own use of language!

561 Grundtvig's hexameter is his own version of the prose of the great Danish playwright Ludwig Holberg (1684-1754) in the comedy *Erasmus Montanus*: "Rasmus Berg may be a clever man in heaven but he is a fool on earth."

The consequence will be that those fields which, touched by Holberg's magic wand, again produced the wondrous growths that Ewald[562] planted with the holy oaks of classical times,[563] those fields that the great sons of Saxo and Snorri[564] filled with the sound of the Norsemen's rattling shields; those fields that Baggesen[565] dotted with the sweet-smelling lilies of spring yet seem to have no room for Oehlenschläger's harp 'made from sinews of bears and oak trees'[566] for the black shield[567] on which he unfurls the 'richly bursting flower bloom/that eastern airs so light and softly touch'; those fields whose frequent thistles seem to be waiting for the generation of long-eared donkeys; those fields are becoming a desert sand through which only heavily loaded camels trudge to bring to everyday life its meagre ration.

Should we merely complain despondently? Should we be passive spectators to this destruction?

I think not. We should boldly face up to the obstacles that confront the rise of Learning, and if possible defeat them! For such an affliction should work towards its own *cessation*. And such a fight is worthy of all men, and Danish men in particular!

Here I too will place my sacrifice on the altar of the fatherland and dare to hope that despite its slightness it will please the all-powerful gods; for it comes from a heart crushed by the heavy hand of fate but still on fire with feelings for the heavenly sphere – and for Learning and Art, their images on earth.

It is not an uncommon claim that it is our press laws[568] and the impossibility of large sales in a small country that account for the thinness of our literature. So if the desire for Learning were *general* and a warm interest were shown for each rare product that deserved it, then my claim would be far more important than it is at present, when the opposite is the case. But let us look at the question a little more closely.

I know no better than that all the old press laws were abolished by the Act of 27th September 1799, and despite certain points in it being less favourable for the arts and sciences I do not believe they find themselves particularly oppressed by the new Act,

562 Johannes Ewald (1743-81) was a famous Danish poet.

563 In Grundtvig's day the oak tree was wrongly assumed to be the holy tree of the Nordic peoples – an assumption that he appears to have shared.

564 Saxo (c 1160-post-1208), Danish historiographer of *Deeds of the Danes* (*Gesta Danorum*). Snorri Sturluson (c 1178-1241) Icelandic writer of *The Norse Kings' Saga (Heimskringla)* and *Snorri's Edda*.

565 Jens Baggesen (1764-1826) was a Danish poet.

566 Quoted from the prologue to *Aladdin or the Wonderful Lamp* (1805), a play by Adam Oehlenschläger.

567 An allusion to *Aladdin*, in which a black shield is one of the attributes of "the dark poetess of the North, Melancholia".

568 A reference to the Act on the Freedom of the Press (27th September 1799) which introduced a limited censorship followed by increasing government intervention against critical writers.

especially since judges were enjoined by royal decree to abide by it strictly and not apply older laws[569] when scholarly anonymity was allowed.[570]

I use the phrase 'scholarly anonymity' deliberately, for it is not linked to any juridical definition. As it is now, every book publisher is liable to declare the name of any author whose writing is under prosecution. Failure to do so will lose him his Danish citizenship, the hardest punishment of all for the writer, and there is every chance that a whole century will pass before the culprit could ever avoid the punishment of the law. So if there were no other argument against anonymity, then our enlightened and liberal government should at least render its fatherland the *protection of Learning*.

Under the proposed or any similar limitation there will be no opportunity to encourage defamation or flippancy to spread some venomous or immature seed. Whereas under its shelter many a beautiful and fragrant flower that at present does not dare to raise itself from the motherly lap of the earth, would sprout and bloom – to the honour and benefit of the fatherland and to the advancement of Learning. If only those men who are close to the throne would give themselves the honour of being the *champions* of Learning, then whoever sits on the King of Lejre's throne[571] would open his ears to the Muses' prayer; then in our current generation the names of those men would shine alongside those of Christian and Frederik.[572]

In claiming that the abolition of anonymity has damaged Learning and will continue to do so, I argue that the writer is forced to take an extra care that is not based on the nature of the case, and that the shy youth lacks an aegis,[573] which alone during his probation could protect him against the arrows that wound when a well-known individual is their goal. However, I do not believe that literature stands or falls by this, for it is a much higher spirit whose presence propels, and whose absence stops, the printing presses, so long as they are at the service of Learning.

569 Grundtvig's own footnote 4: "Allow me here to raise a question for Denmark's jurists: Under the current law concerning the freedom of the press, to what extent can a writer be regarded as liable for criticising a late Danish king?" This refers to Grundtvig's friend P.N. Skovgaard, whose 1804 work *Descriptions of Bornholm (Beskrivelse over Bornholm)* criticised the late Frederik III for his treatment of the traitor, Corfitz Ulfeldt. The book was confiscated and Skougaard was sentenced to 14 days prison on bread and water and lifetime censorship.

570 The same act forbade anonymous writings. Book publishers had to guarantee the writer's identity; failure to do so meant the publisher was liable. The Act also forbade insulting Christianity, the king, and the government, punishable by exile for life or from 3-10 years.

571 By tradition Lejre, on Zealand, was the first royal seat in Denmark. According to the legend in Saxo, it was created a few years before Christ by Odin's son Skjold (Scyld). Lejre remained a royal seat until Gorm the Old (d. 958) became the first recognised King of all-Denmark, to be succeeded by his son, Harold Bluetooth, who moved the royal seat to Roskilde.

572 With the exception of King Hans (reigned 1481-1513) all the kings of Denmark have been named Christian or Frederik since 1448. On their accessions the current crown prince will become Frederik X, and his eldest son, Christian XI.

573 In Greek mythology an 'aegis' is a magic shield made of metal or skin which grants the bearer total protection.

If our country is too small to have a literature of its own, and if that is the necessary condition for Learning, then despite our deepest love for the Danish language we might be tempted to reject the premise. But that is *not* the case, and indeed Denmark's literature was to experience not so much a noontime as a rose-red morning, when we would see that such Learning could indeed exist!

If we say that poor sales are the reason for the paucity of literary products, it must mean that the nation has ceded its predisposition for literature to 'scholarly Learning'. There is no doubt that more books are being *bought* now than in more fortunate times; but the fact that the writings of those who were educated in that literary atmosphere remain unsold is a logical consequence of the renewed slumber of our higher senses.

Reading has become a way of passing the time; is it any wonder that books which require serious thought, deep feeling, and a greater purpose, are therefore quite unsuitable, are detested even more than following the new orthography?[574]

Disdain for the mother-tongue is also put forward as a reason for the decay of our literature.[575] Clearly I cannot agree with this, since even if such contempt were more widespread, it could never prevent a writer from feeling the call to write in the only language understood by his countrymen, nor would they be discouraged from reading and acquiring his works if only they themselves were sympathetic towards Learning and expected some kind of return.

No one believes that I would *deny* this contempt,[576] or would condone it for a moment, just because it cannot do quite so much damage as it would wish. The truth of the matter is that the enthusiasm for the mother-tongue that awoke with Holberg[577] is an antiquity which like all of its kind is laughed at by the intellectuals and in both

574 In 1805 a commission was set up to standardize written Danish.

575 Disdain for the Danish language was common in the early 18th century. The court, the military, and the administration spoke German, the high schools and university wrote Latin, and French was fashionable especially in Copenhagen.

576 Grundtvig's own footnote 5: "An example of this contempt, motivated by the 'poverty' of our language, can be found in the conversation I once had with a learned philologist. *He*: The Danish language is poor in quality. *I*: So? *He*: Many German adjectives cannot be translated without circumlocution. *I*: Then the Roman language is also poor, for many Danish adjectives such as 'invisible', 'incomprehensible' and so on must be paraphrased in Latin. *He*: Not so, and that is the strength of the Roman language. Moreover nearly all the Danish adjectives compounded with 'in-' are ambiguous. We call both what we *have* seen and what we have *not* seen 'invisible'." You will understand that I was ashamed and silent! But if it is argued that the learned man's argument was illogical, I will answer that it is a *crimen læsorum summorum honorum* (insult to the doctorate), for the learned gentleman was a Doctor of Philosophy. I have recorded this anecdote in particular as a warning to the few who might feel tempted to claim the paradox that nothing/anything at all can be written in Danish that is worth reading. It is truly not the only time that I have been knocked to the ground by such doughty warriors, figuratively speaking, when I was naive enough to defend the Danish language and Danish literature. *Qvod cavere possis, stultum est admittere*." (It is foolish to start on something that is not needed) from Terence's comedy *The Eunuch* (161 CE).

577 The dramatist Ludvig Holberg (1684-1754) is a central figure in Danish literature with plays raising the quality of the language to match its European counterparts.

its life and death is accompanied by a preference for *Learning*, which is the reason why they are sometimes easily mistaken for each other. Even if there are not many books that would publicly fire a salvo at our language, there are nevertheless a large number in whose ear our language sounds as 'abominable' as it once did in Spatzier's.[578] Admittedly there are many houses where Danish is the servants' language, and others where it does not mean so much, just as there are circles where a book that is both foolish *and* Danish means one and the same thing – where the cavalier would blush and the lady laugh if they were surprised by such a book. And there are without doubt many who seek to acquire a certain reputation by being able to spell in German or French but who cannot read Danish! Finally, it is no rare thing that those who in particular can afford to buy books must have travelled south of the Elbe, if not the Rhine, for them to deserve a place on their shelves.[579]

All this is exasperating for every true Dane and doubly so under such a Danish government.[580] But in my view this does not have much influence on the main point, since the opposite could be the case without 'Learning' gaining anything thereby. Those who can scorn a book alone because of its language do not know what books are for, and those who do not care whether they purchase Danish, German, or French books are only interested in praising as deities the distorted effigies of Venus, Bacchus, and themselves as living likenesses of foolishness. Chance circumstances could change this judgement; but the advantage gained from Danish books being purchased but not read would always be small and most significant only for the moths in the provinces, who must now fast while their more fortunate brothers are being nourished by the old and new North in the bookshops.

If after close scrutiny anyone should nevertheless argue that I *underestimate* the obstacles literature faces, they will nevertheless agree with me that the main reason for our present literary situation is the lack of spirit as regards Learning, so the discovery of the reasons for this becomes equally necessary.

578 While a student of theology at Copenhagen University Grundtvig joined an amateur theatre called 'Thalia', where he played Tøraf in *The Virtuoso* no. 2 by P.A. Heiberg (1758-1841). In the course of the play the Danish-speaking German Spatzier says, "I do not the Danish language like; it is an abominable, really an abominable, loathsome language."

579 The River Elbe flows into the North Sea at Hamburg; the River Rhine flows into the North Sea at Rotterdam, 500 km to the south-west.

580 Grundtvig's own footnote 6: "Those who scorn our language should not believe that I mean it as badly as I say. Out of fear of Guldberg and other bad people I dare not publicly make common cause with them; but at heart I agree completely with Father Holberg, who – God be praised and more for this! – called it shameful that any good patriot should be deprived of his name merely because he held the country's language in contempt, provided he did not reject its money, its offices, its corn, and other important things. All this is for them and me far more amusing than reading the Baron's 312th letter." The Baron in question is Ludvig Holberg. When Holstein was annexed into Denmark-Norway in 1806, the state council was divided between the Danish speakers in favour and the German speakers largely against; the latter gradually quit the council.

I think the most important reason is the increasing irreligiosity and immorality, and the lack of scholarly Learning among our younger students.

Perhaps some of my learned friends will smile at my first reason and see the possibility of this being one of the less auspicious signs; but I dare to believe they will judge me otherwise if I am allowed to develop my argument.

I am a Christian, and, for the most part, what is known as a Lutheran Christian. But I do not for that reason believe that any divergence from the Augsburg Confession[581] should be damaging to Learning. On the other hand I hope I am allowed to argue that "if God is their stomach",[582] they could not love the pure daughters of heaven.[583]

What Learning must presume, I believe, is a truly religious mind, an unshakable faith in heaven, and a glimpse of its glory. But under which form our fantasy depicts this seems immaterial to Learning, since only the form possesses the higher beauty. Neither the atheist nor anyone else for whom heaven is no more than the height of morality can possess Learning,[584] since for them existence itself is of such importance that the sciences must, in order for their thoughts to be conceived at all, enter into its service. Those who so often said that the revealed religions hindered the free ascent of the human spirit were right, but only in the sense that those who believe they are walking the only path to heaven are unwilling to acknowledge any other. The genius will always be able to reduce two ways to one, whereas it is impossible for anyone to find a way to heaven if they do not *believe* in heaven! Nor do I think that people will find my claim strange that all the more advanced geniuses who have opened up for us a view into their innermost being were themselves religious. That this is so is undeniable, even by the author of *Nathan*,[585] far more than he himself would like to admit. For this humane soul thought it necessary that we limit ourselves to the *simplest* form; he seized the image of harmony rather than harmony itself, but was a genuine admirer of the latter.

I shall interrupt my flow here so as not to arouse a suspicion even in the weakest soul that I would set a religion like Lessing's alongside the wretched soul's blasphemous admission that "I would like to believe that a God exists!" This carries its own

581 Since 1665 the Evangelical Lutheran Church in Denmark has officially subscribed to the Augsberg Confession of 1530 (unofficially since 1536).

582 Phil 3: 19 (on the enemies of God) "Their destiny is destruction, their god is their stomach, and their glory is in their shame."

583 i.e. the Muses.

584 Rationalist theologians of Grundtvig's time argued against a number of Protestant dogma, such as salvation coming 'only by the grace of God', and often appeared more concerned with public morality than personal faith. Grundtvig initially joined their number, but by 1810 he was returning to the Lutheran tenets of his childhood.

585 Gotthold Lessing (1729-81) was a German philosopher, critic, and poet. In his dramatic poem *Nathan der Weise* (*Nathan the Wise*, 1779), set in Jerusalem during the crusades, Nathan, the wise Jew, argues for an end to all religious intolerance.

corruption within itself, and yet is the most that our falsely-informed age can allow to pass across its contaminated lips. It does not surprise me in the least that such people see 'God' – this 'idea' so interwoven with our very being – as being a somewhat irrelevant, metaphysical semi-nonentity. If from the quagmire in which they joyfully live, nourished by worms and insects, they were to shout "God lives in us!", the bitterest satire would be against themselves. They are not even *clever*, since their highest form of bliss is a *lack* of consciousness; they suffer from a long-established inability to *perceive* themselves.

So as not to tire my readers with the unnecessary question as to whether they believe such people could be open to Learning, I shall merely point out that if the whole nation belonged to this class, this present study would be futile. Fortunately for us, many have not yet reached that 'degree' of culture, and only by *adverse* circumstance are others introduced to the abode where Odysseus's comrades once dwelt.[586] This underlines my argument that the students' lack of scholarly Learning is one of the main reasons for the iniquity that is oppressing us.

Wherever this failure exists, it must have grievous consequences for Learning and for all literature linked to Learning; this failure hardly needs any more proof. If we were to exaggerate, we would claim that three-quarters of our Copenhagen students cannot write Danish and know no other history than the few fragments they learned at school or university. They have no concept of 'philosophy' other than it being something as dry as dust which they have to learn for some exam or other. They know nothing about poetry except that it is something that is most often a lie that rhymes, but sounds beautiful, God knows why. And finally we would claim that they have no higher goal for their studies than the best marks at the first exam[587] – and then a good final exam.[588] This picture is from life as it was a few years ago. Perhaps it is no longer like this, and that would please me, but the sons of the Muses could not have degenerated[589] so much in the few years that I myself have not been acquainted with the university!

586 Odysseus's friends were turned to swine by Circe and therefore lived in a pig-sty (*The Odyssey* 10:230-43).

587 Known as *philosophikum*', this exam in various subjects was taken early on at university to test for university suitability.

588 Grundtvig's own footnote 7: "It goes without saying that I deliberately exclude the students of medicine, who for the most part have begun their doctoral thesis even before their graduate exams and must possess a quite different attitude to Learning. As a layman in medical science I may be a somewhat unauthorized judge; but I believe that this is in the nature of things, and that it explains the phenomenal ease with which medical students come to the most unequivocal view of the great truth: *ars longa, vita brevis*. The only thing I wonder over here is why this legion of theses, which according to my understanding of *summis honoribus*, must surely have created a new era in Learning, is not with all its merited praise mentioned in *Hallische Litteraturzeitung*, alongside the eulogy on Denmark's pharmacists. I do not even recall seeing the name of the first person who on the completion of his work humbly requested that his doctoral thesis be *examined*."

589 The use of 'degenerated' is ironic here.

Fearing, some may think, that I am mixing too much black into my colours, may I ask each and every one who has the desire and the opportunity to take a look at the lending register at the Royal and the University Libraries? They will probably not meet many students in these temples of the Muses, and not much paper is consumed in their name. Find first the one-quarter whom I have indicated in somewhat round figures, and if there are *more* names, then doubtless they represent the loan of a new novel or a play in the strictest sense which was not available in their local library[590] and which the borrower either had to study or acquire for one of his witty girl-friends.

However, let us follow them from the capital city, whose motley throngs may have blinded their eye, out to the country, where a large number of them are dispersed as household stewards, private tutors, sermon assistants,[591] managing clerks, father's and mother's sons, and so on. I wonder if it is here that we shall find them occupied in digesting and increasing all the knowledge that they have gathered?

If I wrote satire I could answer with a clear conscience, Oh yes! But if we are talking about the majority I must answer most decidedly, Oh no!

If they were to become teachers of our youth, they would be serving that call most conscientiously in fear and trembling – without disengaging from the academic reins to guide them to the higher peaks of Learning and without being aware that the young pupil ought to have a different and better education than they had enjoyed. The others, whose numbers are not small, regard teaching as being of secondary importance. They train diligently at dancing, riding, hunting, l'ombre,[592] and whatever the other 'arts' are called;[593] they acquire a young lady, or if they already have one they read Schilling's novels[594] with the women and girls of the area. *Mutatis mutandis*, the same description suits the mini-curates, the waiters in Themis's[595] forecourt, and those who studied so as to be called the family 'scholar'; these latter are conspicuous through their knowledge that Fredriksten Fort is not in Trondheim![596]

How should these hopeful youngsters, who in the capital were blind to the treasures of literature and deaf to the friendly call of Learning, acquire a sense and an eye for such things? That could only happen through their observing their elder brothers in

590 Danish lending libraries, containing popular literature for the most part, began in the 1750s.

591 Grundtvig's scornful phrase for curates!

592 L'ombre is a card game, played by three persons with forty cards, which was very popular in the 17th and 18th centuries.

593 Grundtvig's own footnote 8: "If they have a destination in mind, then they resemble our agriculturalists.

594 Friedrich Gustav Schilling (1766-1839) was a German writer of popular literature.

595 In Greek mythology Themis is a Titaness and goddess of divine order, justice, and reason.

596 Fredriksten Fort was built beside Oslo Fjord in the 1660s and named after the King of Denmark-Norway Frederik III (1609-70). Trondheim, Norway's fourth largest city, lies 500 km to the north.

Minerva;[597] but things being as they are, I doubt very much that such an observation would have such a consequence.

I am neither foolish nor shameless enough to deny that there are spiritual and temporal civil servants who regard Learning with a clear vision, and to grant them the time that their civil occupations allow them. Yet I believe that although there are quite a number of these civil servants, they are nonetheless far from being enough to infuse a scholarly approach into their sleepy-eyed brothers. Indeed I think that in recent times their number has become fewer rather than greater.

I wonder where one would be most likely to meet the majority of our pastors these days – in the field or the stable, in the study at their desks, or at the card table? I should like to compare their book collections with their muck-heaps, and then their bills from the bookseller with those from the grocer and the innkeeper. I wish I had an instrument that could measure, according to the amount of dust or the compression of the pages, how long each book has stood untouched on the shelves; and I wish I could measure the weight of their knowledge on graduating from university and after ten years as a civil servant. The results that could be concluded would hardly be unimportant if we are to answer the questions: Why is scientific enquiry so weak? And why is our literature only a shadow that points to a few individual limbs of a body which in its entirety lies completely outside our field of vision? No one should think that I am hereby reducing the clergy to a position beneath that of the juridical and medical officials. No indeed, in my experience the latter are even *less* scholarly and many would actually be *angry* if they were called 'men of Learning'.

If I am to recommend the most effective means of promoting scientific enquiry, and providing us with the same harmonising literature in the fatherland, then what I have so far written compels me to answer: a more scholarly training of the students, by which I mean that they are inspired by Love, Learning, and the Arts.

We need not wait for experience to teach us that the celebration of Learning, a closer relationship between teachers and students, plus the necessity of treating scholarly subjects in both speech and writing, all serve in particular to infuse the students with a respect for scientific enquiry and a desire to pursue it. This truth has already been partially established in the history of the teacher training college,[598] just as it can also

597 i.e. their academic brothers. Minerva was the Roman goddess of wisdom and sponsor of arts, trade, and strategy. She was born with weapons from the godhead of Jupiter. From the 2nd century BCE onwards, the Romans equated her with the Greek goddess Athena.

598 The first teacher training college (*seminarium*) in Denmark opened in Blaagaard in 1791 as a faculty of Copenhagen University. Among its aims were the professionalization of teachers according to the latest teaching methods and the reduction of the church's domination of education. Brahetrolleborg Seminarium followed (1794-1826), and then between 1802-15 came a series of nine so-called 'vicarage seminaries', founded and run by local pastors. A law passed in 1814 required all children from 7-14 to attend school, the beginning of the present-day *Folkeskolen*.

be seen to have floated before the eyes of the government, when it initiated improvements in the High Schools and their graduation exams.[599]

Much is hereby achieved on condition that when our youngsters leave school they can enter a relationship that can protect their progress; unless this is secured, the new curriculum will hardly be of much benefit to them.

The evidence is clear to me.

The time that is spent in school will be better suited to *enabling* the child to undertake scientific enquiry rather than to generate it in him there and then.

I not only believe, but have the pleasure of knowing for certain, that not even the child is so attached to this earth that its eyes are not raised towards heaven.[600] Even though the outer and inner adult is bound by experience, we are drawn towards the concept of Reason – the higher source of Knowledge that we have within ourselves – and thus in a way we will acquire the appreciation of Learning in its higher sense. But this sense is often imparted rather than awakened, and is therefore unable to put down deep roots in the youngster's *being*. In the face of external opposition it cannot achieve its full independent growth and bear mature fruit, while at the same time it is less equipped to do so in the public system than in private education.

We should not forget here that even the child filled with wonder at the sight of the beautiful, coloured drawing and feeling the desire to imitate it will take a dislike to *repeating* time after time the first strokes and lines, whose strict connection to the artwork he does not easily grasp. In order to awaken this desire – which with every new unexpected difficulty is close to extinction – it is in no way enough merely to point to the *finished* construction, whose brilliance may dazzle the child's sharpened sight but whose unique value cannot be *felt*. Then the teacher is obliged, even against his will, to grant far too much importance to civic life and the influence of the sciences upon it.

Here the youngster is on a false trail, and if he does not belong among the few elevated souls who seem to be born without ties, and who never accept them, then unless he gets active help from outside he will follow this path his whole life through.

If we exclude the few truly great geniuses, who could not be produced through parental upbringing nor, dare we say it, the upbringing of any others than themselves, it is not difficult to predict the path that such people leaving school will follow in the present circumstances.[601]

They have learned the basic elements of a number of sciences and languages, with-

599 Between 1805-09 a new high school curriculum was drawn up (for 10-18-year-olds) which replaced class teachers with subject teachers and Latin with Danish as the formal exam language.

600 Between March 1805 and April 1808 Grundtvig was the house tutor for Carl Frederik Steensen-Leth (b. 31 May 1798) at Egeløkke Manor on the island of Langeland, where he kept a record of his teaching experiences (See *Diaries 1*, 1979, 281-365 in Danish only).

601 Grundtvig follows Kant and Steffens in the contemporary belief that 'genius' was innate and could not be trained.

out having yet adopted the highest goal of humankind, and without calculating the possible steps that could be taken to achieve it. We must already think they have done well if they immediately set a less *distant* goal, such as the ability to fulfil a particular office rather than stagger thoughtlessly towards the next examination. Among the civil servants whose acquaintance they make are a number whom they consider beneath them in Knowledge – and occasionally perhaps not without cause. With this study goal in view they already begin to relax their efforts, for now they can *avoid* the mountains which they once believed they would have to climb and can merely cross the foothills.

If the youngster has set honour and success as the goals of his endeavour, he will soon notice that these can often be achieved more simply; he will then more easily loosen his grip on what for him was only a means to an end, not the end itself, only a duty, not a need. The young man's body grows mature without entering into the willing service of his soul. The latter's higher ability falls asleep and the latter's lower abilities enter into the service of his body. He feels drawn towards the opposite sex and finds it easy to link the warm flow of his blood to a woman's smile and to his own pleasure as being the ideal for earthly bliss. If he regards the sciences merely as a means to an end, he will soon discover that they are not only unnecessary but even harmful when it comes to seeking a woman's favour, since they lend the soul a seriousness and a depth that is not at all suited to a playful fluttering through life. In his view 'Drink wine, be idle, and flirt with the girls'[602] loses its ironic bite and offers him the highest life-philosophy of all!

My heart would be wounded if anyone were to believe that these utterances of mine should be taken as expressing scorn for nature's most glorious gem, or the desire to see the pursuer of scientific enquiry be excluded from the company of gracious women.

If this appears to be even further from my actual purpose, I dare to hope for my readers' forbearance for depriving them of these moments with the pursuance of my opinion.

Scientific enquiry by a genius can hardly be *dangerous*. Baser instincts may perhaps entice but they can never contain him, for they cannot embrace his being. Love may imprison him, but it can never stop him, for though his eye be dazzled, it cannot be closed.

If his love is rewarded, he will fly to his goal by a shorter route than the one he would have taken with firm steps. Exhausted by his supernatural expression of power, by which he was only momentarily able to tear apart the bonds of our dust, he will enjoy a period of slumber in blissful enjoyment and may even mock the lengthy approach to

602 'Drink wine, be idle, and flirt with the girls,' is Grundtvig's slight variation on the source: "My son, if you want to get on in the world, drink punch, be idle, and flirt with girls, but bow!" from the 1790 song 'Rules of Conduct – according to the Occasion of the Times' (*Norma Morum – efter Tidernes Leilighed*) by Werner Abrahamson (1744-1812).

a goal that is only reached by those whom angel wings raised. But his intoxication will evaporate, for despite his 'highness and holiness', it is still an intoxication, and from the bliss he has enjoyed he will only retain the deeply-rooted memory that spurs him to reach out for the glory that he indeed once sensed but then believed that he owned.[603]

If his love is disregarded, he is no longer his own but belongs to fate, and he cannot know whether his muscles will lose their strength in the monstrous struggle between Everything and Nothing. He will sink like a withered flower on Werther's cairn.[604] Or if not, he will survive his crisis, and like Lazarus[605] return from the grave where he sought to hide himself from himself, and he will feel a redoubled need to seek the place to which he can return on the wings of the double being.[606] But the glory of this being which he glimpsed in the midst of the struggle will tear him apart, half lifted by the one wing that his own being granted him.

If all the students were geniuses, then I think we ought to keep quiet, just as it would be pointless to speak up! But since an exception cannot be the rule, I dare to believe that the fair sex would destroy the atmosphere of enquiry among a significant number of our excellent students if left to themselves. I will not even discuss the question, since it is very well known that:

When foolishness and love go hand in hand,
No sillier pair was seen in all the land!

The only use that the foolish can contribute to Learning is to remain passive. See how many noble people have become the prey for this unimaginative love, which imprisons itself in the beloved's body and induces the soul to sleep! Are they not victims of the sensual pleasure that weakens them and deprives them of all higher power? How many have not called this ill-fated flapping around the fair sex a 'pleasure'? And is it any the less demoralizing for that?

It has been said a thousand times that the acquaintance of educated women polishes the man! Who would deny this? Yet it should be said equally often that the youngster who finds pleasure in female company will carry this limitation and inconstancy with him into his more serious occupations, unless he puts them entirely to rest. If he has any spirit, then he will become what is known as 'a gentleman', he will

603 Here Grundtvig speaks very much from his own personal experience of Constance Steensen-Leth, when he himself turned from unrequited love to requited learning.

604 In Goethe's letter-novel *The Sorrows of Young Werther (Die Leiden des jungen Werthers*, 1774) the titular character commits suicide out of unrequited love.

605 Jn 11: 43-44.

606 This is probably a reference to Plato's belief that the two sexes had been divided (by Zeus) and sought to be united again.

speak and write in only a half-alive manner, and he will garnish all that he touches with a certain lightly-flavoured wit. If he has a heart, he will express enough emotion to draw tears from a woman's eyes, but he will lose the deeper feeling and the deeper view; for, being cossetted, he will become exhausted by his unremitting efforts and he will shrink from the more powerful visions.

This is how I understand Addison when he says that he never knew a man of good understanding who was a general favourite of the other sex,[607] and in this sense it is permissible to say such a thing without stretching the truth or arousing the righteous anger of the fairer sex.

I feel with sadness and conviction that women could be not just an innocuous, but indeed the *strongest*, spur to Learning without losing the least bit of their particular character; but in that case their education must be quite different from what it is now: worthless tinsel, with the woman only being formed in the man.

From this it is easy to conclude that I think young students cannot learn anything from women as things are now; let her be, and let her *favour* be, a side-issue, just as social polish, despite the importance that our small-minded times have granted it, is nevertheless no more than that. This is what would happen if he learned to appreciate the times gone by as they present themselves to our eye, to cherish his intimate acquaintance with the immortal sagas,[608] and to distinguish between the heroes of Homer and Lafontaine[609] – in other words, when Learning becomes his highest goal.

If the well-prepared young man really does encounter obstacles that easily stop, divert, or frighten him from the path of Learning, and if these obstacles could simply be removed or reduced by a powerful counterweight, this would precipitate the question as to whether any such counterweight exists among us in Denmark.

If the counterweight really does exist, and if it is true that an unscholarly spirit, or no spirit at all, animates present-day students when regarded in their entirety, then the question is in fact answered. However, the matter requires closer analysis. It may well be beyond my power and my will to offer them what needs to be offered, but forgive me if for a moment I appear to be forgetting the civic and literary heights upon which the professors at Copenhagen University stand far above me, and permit myself to ask certain questions about their activity in the advancement of Learning!

I take it for granted that these highly-learned men are most conscientious in car-

607 Joseph Addison (1672-1719), English essayist, and publisher of the famous journal, *The Spectator*. Grundtvig paraphrases the following: "In all my observation I never knew a man of good understanding (to be) a general favourite; some singularity in his behaviour, some whim in his way of life, and what would have made him ridiculous among the men, has recommended him to the other sex." *The Spectator*, no.156, 29 August 1711.

608 Grundtvig's own footnote 9: "I should perhaps mention that by 'saga' here I understand 'history'.

609 Homer (fl. c. 850-800 BCE), Greek writer of the *Iliad* and the *Odyssey*; August Lafontaine (1758-1831) German popular novelist.

ing for their students *publice*, *privatim*, and *privatissima*.[610] But do they seize every opportunity in their lectures on their particular subject to speak warmly and powerfully about *true* Learning? Do they encourage the young people to make use of our public book collections, and do they show and ease the path that the students should tread?

If that is the case, then it must seem strange that in my time Nyerup[611] could not even attract *five*, repeat *five*, students to his lectures on literary history! And it must seem even stranger for him to see how, behind his back, the genius Steffens[612] sought to awaken the spirit of enquiry and Learning – and indeed did not fail in this aim!

As we know, every student at matriculation among the academic citizens[613] chooses a professor as his private mentor.

However short this arrangement falls from perfection, it nevertheless follows that the wise men of the past fully recognised the need for a closer relationship between students and their teachers. But does any university professor actually *know* which students have chosen him as their guardian and advisor? Or does this imperfect arrangement perhaps overburden the professors to such a degree that they would prefer it to be a shadow? In that case, does each of them go in search of some talented young man to inspire him with a sense of Learning, and to counsel with good advice, instructive conversation, and written assignments? Does the inquisitive young man know that the professor whose advice and guidance he seeks is willing to communicate these and to do even more than is required? Can the poor student longing for Knowledge be sure that, without any other recommendation, he can profit from the academic scholarships?[614] Or is this combination of poverty and a desire for Learning so common that it is impossible to help all who sigh under this double impulse? Is it indeed inevitable that if they are misled as regards student poverty, then the same is the case with the applicants' diligence and aptitude?

These questions are of the greatest importance, but since I have no wish to offend, let alone speak words that fall short of the strictest truth, I shall not even attempt to answer them in full. Only what I know will I actually enumerate, only a few hints will I offer to the experts' assessment.

---

610 Latin: "publicly, privately, and very privately". Professors held public lectures (*collegia publica*), privately-funded lectures (*collegia privata*), and privately-paid lectures/exercises in the professor's home for a very small group of students (*privatissima*).

611 Rasmus Nyerup (1759-1829), librarian and literary historian.

612 Henrik Steffens (1773-1845), Grundtvig's cousin, initiated the Romantic movement in Denmark. See introduction p. 20. and illustration p. 66.

613 From the Middle Ages the university was regarded as an independent 'city' with its own jurisdiction. University staff and students became 'citizens' in this community through an appointment/matriculation certificate.

614 By 1800 there were a number of scholarships available to poor students, mostly from the academic foundation 'The Community' (*Kommunitetet*, founded in 1569), which distributed small grants of 4 marks a week, known as the 'monastic grant' (*klosterdaler*).

It is well-known that in my time the student at Copenhagen University believed he saw a huge gulf between the professor and himself, and dared not inconvenience the professor by asking for advice on how to satisfy his searching spirit – unless minor family connections or other circumstances laid a bridge over the chasm.

I know that *privatissima* exist, and I imagine that for these few lucky youngsters greater horizons are opened up in Learning. But I also know that many of those who visit them are unable to enjoy these horizons. And I know even better that the poor student cannot pay them 10 Rigsdaler every six months, which was the price I was told.[615]

It is true that a number of those trying to making a living out of Learning felt an emptiness which they did not know how to fill, so they endeavoured to forget about it in the madding crowd and to give up on Learning, to whose excellences nature appeared to have determined them. It is equally true that others who tried to develop and grow allowed themselves to be led astray, making them unfit for life as well as Learning – but always it was Time, precious and irrevocable, that robbed them. If this was unavoidable, that is sad; if not, then it is doubly sad.

It is also true that often it is not only the needy and the able, but also the well-to-do and the nitwits that apply for academic grants, and it will not be easily proven that only the former receive them.

How exasperating to hear one of them say that he will apply for the monastic grant, so that he "can go to the theatre a couple of times more a week" – and those very words I have heard! But the annoyance is combined with the deepest sadness when we see, standing beside the wretch, a willing student who despite his fervent love of Learning is forced to leave university with tears in his eyes because he could not obtain a grant: and that too I have seen.

Far be it from me to accuse anyone of bias, but allow me to suggest what I think would better ensure that no *incompetent* youngster was given the help that the *competent* one ought to have, for poverty alone is not a reason for deriving benefit from university foundations.

If, for instance, all the applicants for grants were tested for their aptitude by the professors or other respected scholars, surely the path would be better barred to the incompetent, and all the competent youngsters who needed help would be given it. This would doubtless also provide the groundwork for a closer acquaintance between the professors and the students which would go on to bear the loveliest fruits.

Thus, in the organisation of the university as the regulations are – and even more so when exemption from these takes place – there is much that the friend of Learning would like to change. But who does not hide these wishes in his breast when he lives in a time when *Reason* has supplanted tradition and granted Learning a scientific fo-

615 1 *Rigsdaler* was worth c. 2 modern *kroner* in 1844, and a large farm could be purchased for c. 1,800 *Rigsdaler*.

rum? Who does not see arise from the spirit of the monastery[616] ruins a temple for the Muses, a triumph arch of architecture, and the faculty's ancient tables[617] transformed into glorious altars at which Apollo's[618] young worshippers offer up their spiritual gifts and are initiated into stately worship of the god by his holy priests? Who does not sense and see so much more – which it would be immoderate of me to mention?

When these changes begin to take place, Learning will lift up its head, because its redemption is drawing near.[619] The people will see their radiant geniuses ringed by the jubilant sons of the Muses, who, feeling too weak to be suns, rejoice in its light, and like twinkling stars diffuse the darkness of night that still broods over a large part of the nation. Denmark's nobility will weave itself into the rose garlands of the past, and the sons of Mercury[620] will learn that even though they chose the god Bacchus[621] as their favourite, and sold the melodic lute for the long-horned oxen, eternal peace will nevertheless be thereby concluded between Mercury and Apollo. Then, having led away the spiritless shadows,[622] Mercury will ascend to Olympus to listen to the ravishing notes from the sonorous strings of the father of song. Nor will the peasant forget his plough, but full of awe will order it to stop before the cairns of the forefathers.[623] These stone monuments shall stand as divine guardians in the midst of his fields and no longer be split by the black arts that Loki taught mankind in order to defy the noise of Thor's flaming chariot.[624] No more shall these stones be thrown away among the profane brothers as a transient fence.

Bountiful nature, which the peasant's eye has now discovered, will accompany him to the temple of the Lord, where, harmonically expressed in notes of song and the service of the Word, all the strings of his soul will gather in one heaven-soaring alleluia. Transported by this rolling current of happy feelings I am tempted to forget

616 Poor students had dined at the Monastery of the Holy Spirit until 1736.

617 At the faculty dining tables staff had tested students in the exercises for the day.

618 In Greek and Latin mythology Apollo, among his other attributes, was leader of the muses.

619 Cf. Lk 21:28. 'When these things begin to take place, stand up and lift up your heads, because your redemption is drawing near.'

620 In Roman mythology Mercury (Greek: Hermes) is the son of Zeus and the messenger of the gods, as well as being the god of travel and trade. As a boy he once made a lyre from the shell of a tortoise before stealing 50 of Apollo's oxen. On being discovered he was forced to hand over the lyre to Apollo. Grundtvig sees in this agreement a reconciliation between mercantile and artistic interests in the ideal society.

621 In Roman mythology Bacchus (in Greek, Dionysus) was the god of agriculture, wine and fertility – associated with religious ecstasy, especially at festivals known as 'Bacchanalia'.

622 Mercury also leads the dead souls down to Hades.

623 Grundtvig was concerned that the peasant farmers were removing such cairns in order better to plough their fields. The broken stones were used to build stone fences. In 1807 the first steps were taken to set up a National Museum to preserve all ancient monuments, where possible.

624 In Nordic mythology Loki is a trickster god, who refuses to obey and employs magic and the black arts to get his way. Thor, son of Odin and famous for his hammer, is god of the sky and agriculture; he creates thunder by driving his goat-drawn chariot over heaven.

our present standpoint, which is so different from the one on which I had my premonition as I looked out across the spirited Nordic countries. So, back to the calm path of philosophy!

Once the university has lost all resemblance to a factory and has become a genuine nursery for the branches of Learning, then a worthy literature and a scholarly atmosphere in the nation would be an almost inevitable consequence. Before I expand on this first assertion I shall say a few words in defence of a justified objection that can be made against the latter.

Since a superior manner and substantial wealth are the idols of our time, and since Learning produces an increase rather than a decrease in both, can we expect that their twin temples will be abandoned, or that they place themselves *in the service of* Learning? The former is barely thinkable, but the latter perhaps is; for when the students are minded to *learn*, they must impress upon the younger generation which they are raising and educating a *respect* for Learning, and the generation that has acquired this will not only permit, but encourage, the next generation to be *raised* for academic inquiry.

So, once the first condition is fulfilled, our hope is no longer founded on a possible coincidence of circumstances but on a natural relation between cause and effect! However, just because I consider the interest in academic inquiry to be so remote among the nobility and the business community, despite it being a product of the highest reasonability, I am in no way denying that the goal can be approached already. We must just not expect too much of it right now, since the individual is so easily in danger of being swept off his feet by the current in his natural circles.[625]

Denmark cannot possibly regret such a reputable literature on these conditions; for the students would no longer sleep away the years between their civil service entrance exam and actually taking *up* their post as a civil servant. Instead, as well as training younger men they would spend these years developing themselves, including transformation of the excellent products of other countries. With their senses developed and their language cultivated, they would become true *civil* servants. In addition to the greater aptitude for practical proficiency which they would bring to their sphere of work, they would know how to seize the moments that their business allowed for an intellectual activity corresponding to their desire and strength. And they would do so because such an occupation would become a *necessity* for them, a refreshment of body and mind that they did not need to search for at the card table or in the punch bowl, in the ballroom, or at noisy parties. It is not my intention to make all students *writers*, but so much would already be gained if they were all friends of *Learning*.

625 Grundtvig's own footnote 10: "If I dared to believe that anything from my hand could be of interest in any way, I would develop it more precisely, among others in my own study of private tutors and their situation."

I would not claim that anyone in Denmark could become *rich* by writing; indeed I will not even discuss what would be the case under such circumstances, namely that a number of good writers could live without any *other* occupation. For however desirable this might be, it is not strictly essential. But in this context I imagine that works like Suhm's writings[626] would not be without a publisher, and no good Danish book would lack the necessary sales.

I am in no way counting on a broad academic interest across the whole nation here, only among its civil servants. If external factors have lost their acquired interest and are only respected as being in essence *servants of the body*, then internal factors will become active and strive to extend themselves through the transformation of external things into assimilated matter.[627] Mahogany furniture, guardsman-tall mirrors, English carpets, wine and coffee etc. would be transformed into nourishment and clothing for the spirit, which at present so often sighs with exhaustion and stays in bed to cover its nakedness while the body is close to sinking under its daring attempt to fill the vacuum. Then the subjugated body would never allow itself to intimate that it needed the soft sofa, which so often closes the spirit's eyes to the most beautiful sights, but, satisfied by its nightly rest, would always be a compliant instrument for the active soul.

I am well aware that especially in recent times luxury has found a number of warm supporters; but unless it is claimed that it is *the spirit itself* at work here, enthusing its eulogists, its usefulness will never be obvious to me.[628]

I anticipate an objection that can be raised against the hope that the nation will become full of Learning once its students are! The objection is: will their financial needs not weaken the civil servant's enthusiasm for Learning, or at least hinder its effect on the nation?

The first question here must be: from which of our civil servants could Learning expect its greatest benefits? From the pastors, I think. For if their heterogeneous activities are not increased but if possible decreased, once they continue to be church inspectors of the schools but are not themselves school teachers, then among all state civil servants, excepting professors and sacristans,[629] they will have the most time to dedicate

626 Peter Suhm (1728-98), a Danish historian, himself paid for the publication of his 14-volume *History of Denmark (Historie af Danmark)* from prehistoric times to 1448.

627 This paragraph bears the influential marks of philosopher Henrik Steffens (see p. 20), who used the concept of 'assimilation' to explain how reason takes control of the inner life.

628 Grundtvig's own footnote 11: "There is no need to develop this any further. All will agree with me that when those who are supposed to be men of learning spend what life's necessities offer them on luxury and finery instead of on *thinking matter*, then learning gains nothing. However, it is interesting how they seek to justify the sophisms in defence of this bad practice, which will forever be indefensible as long as the opposite of learning remains humankind's highest goal. – And for as long as *Minerva* does not reject me as an abuser of its good name, I too will endeavour to justify my claim."

629 Grundtvig's own footnote 12: "Few would deny that it would be desirable if the good sacristan posts remained and were filled with deserving men of learning who had no desire for *any* post and could thus live for the highest

to Learning, as well as having the advantage that many tasks in their calling are linked to this. Is it then reasonable to believe that financial concerns would destroy most of the profit that a more scholarly tone among the fatherland's pastors would promise?

It is true that many pastors are at present merely eking out a living, and that in order to support themselves and their family they have to stand behind the plough and forget their Learning; they have as little opportunity to buy books as desire and time to multiply their number!

If the pastors' income is then subjected to tithing,[630] there will be few callings of average size and even fewer small parishes. If even those with a large parish have to make considerable contributions to teacher training colleges and school coffers, then the hope is dashed that their wealth could ever lessen the inferiority of the latter.

All this does not bode well for pastors' circumstances and their consequent ability to be the foster fathers of Learning; but if the farming class and the educational system are to be helped in this way and no other, then even when an involuntary sigh makes its presence felt, we must *credit* a government's wisdom that nonetheless proves to be inspired with a warm fervour for the advancement of Learning. However, while we as good citizens may honour the government's wise intentions, we should as friends of Learning endeavour to lessen, if not replace, the loss that we think they would suffer. In this regard I think it would be useful if a company were set up with the main purpose of publishing all the writing that is sent to them, provided it appeared to have some scholarly value. The well-off writers or the well-paid civil servants would be unlikely to demand, and could not receive, any fee, while the *poor* writer could receive the entire profit of his work or more, in relation to his need and the quality of his writing. No one can deny that much would be gained hereby, but perhaps the proposal will be called a shot in the dark, since it presumes a fund that does not exist!

I do not know for sure but I assume that the Royal Academies[631] that exist in Denmark and Norway do have a Trust Fund; and if that is so, it seems to me that their application in this way and the uniting of these academies, would chime with the goal they must have set themselves, and be of more use to Learning than in their present existence – unless I am unaware of their fruits. Perhaps we might even expect some support from the government, or at least its encouragement and recommendation. This would doubtless have a powerful effect on our rich men, and would it then

occupation of all."

630 In 1796 the government encouraged pastors and their parishioners to replace the tithe with a fixed annual tax; this became law in 1810.

631 The Royal Danish Academy of Sciences and Letters was founded in 1742, followed by the Norwegian equivalent in 1760, and the Royal Danish Academy of Fatherland History in 1745.

be impossible that a present-day or future Brock[632] would have the mind to donate a handsome amount of capital to this in every way *pios usus*[633]?

If this happened, and that first condition for the higher education of the students were fulfilled, then Learning would be as well-prepared in Denmark as any humanly-organised system can be!

The fact that I have not mentioned our reviewers[634] or our prize-givings[635] might lead one to think that either I saw these arrangements as having no *place* in the advancement of Learning, or I did not think they *added* anything to that concept. So in closing I shall offer my humble thoughts on these matters.

There can hardly be any other reasonable judgement on our reviewers than that they are as they *should* be! They represent both a true statement of the relation of writing to the main ideas of Learning and Art under which it has set itself, and a motivated judgement on its inner and outer harmony with itself. If critical reviewing is to exist, it must be instructive, like every other genuine and particular use of universal ideas. But we can hardly claim that this is the case in Denmark, if the critical reviews are taken as a whole. It seems to me that anonymity[636] is absolutely necessary for criticism. For when the critic has to look left and right and behind with every step he takes, he cannot possibly always focus on the point before him; indeed at times he is even forced to lose sight of it. This is what gives rise to all these 'excerpts' and lists of contents which unfortunately correspond far too closely to the word 'announcements',[637] and will never be of use to Learning. But even then, when the path seems freer, our critical reviewers often pursue a peculiar and – if the word is not vulgar – a *staggering* gait.

A number of people believe it their proper duty to inflate every gleam of genius that appears, but they seem to be so full of patriotism that either they encourage even the scribblers to pursue a path that they were in no way destined for, or they must be defended in their rough trudging.

If a critic tore such a poor product to pieces and, despite every effort, found nothing worth praising, but insisted that it was the fault of the writing, not the writer – as if

632 The Randers businessman Niels Brock (1731-1802) left the huge sum of c. 550,000 Rigsdaler to public institutions in Randers and Copenhagen, from which the present-day (Niels Brock) Copenhagen Business College derives.

633 *Pios usus* (Lat.) = good cause.

634 The leading critical reviews of the time appeared in *The Danish Spectator (Den Danske Tilskuer),* edited by Knud Lyne Rahbek, who also published this article by Grundtvig in his journal *New Minerva (Ny Minerva).* In 1812 Grundtvig criticised Rahbek for the leniency of his criticism.

635 Prizes have been awarded by Copenhagen University from 1762-68 and 1791 to the present day.

636 Anonymous critical reviews had been forbidden by law since 27th September 1799.

637 Not until the end of the 18th century did book reviews change in character from being mere announcements to becoming genuine critical reviews.

the former had put pressure on the latter! – could that really be conducive to Learning or a literature that dignifies Denmark? Or perhaps another critic, out of love for the ancient history of the North, wrote with honour and forbearance about a compilation of our forefathers' customs, in which the highly-learned author[638] demonstrated that he did not even know who Stridskøgul was![639] And what if the critic then called him, against his better judgement, an 'honourable' man, despite the author, in admiring the similarities between languages, even translating *fehirder* with *fæhyrde*?[640] I doubt if this was how the younger sons of the Muses should be encouraged to cast a deeper glance at the North and conjure up an illustrious portrait of it!

But what if similar reviews were to be written by men whom we are otherwise *glad* to see sitting in the judgement seat? Is it then so strange that I do not value particularly highly our *Informed News*?[641]

Prize-giving is accepted and is generally used as a suitable means for the encouragement of Learning; but it is also a well-known fact that no such mood is to be found among the students when prizes are necessary, and that those who write in order to receive a prize are as little inclined towards Learning as those who write in order to receive a badge of honour! This was also the experience of our noble friend of Learning[642] when he announced that the postponement of prize-giving was a sad sign of the growing disdain for the Muses' gracious smile, that glorious reward that they themselves bestow on their warm supporters: How should I sing the praises of a measure whose necessity I prefer to avert my gaze from, even though I respect and honour the men who in their station did what they could?

However, I do not think prizes to be entirely ineffective; indeed, they ought to exist, though under a higher form, when Learning itself so enthuses the writers!

In the precise development of this idea I shall try to find the relation between these spiritual rivalries and the Olympic Games, which are the splendid outward symbol of human development. Just as they provided the place to express the strength of everybody, so should the soul also find a free playground here. There is a difference, however, for there is an activity in the body's strength that is bound to *matter*, which is granted from without and cannot therefore be gathered in one point, whereas the soul is its own object and can express its full power once it is conscious of itself. Thus in

638 It is unknown to which reviewer this refers.

639 In Nordic mythology Stridskøgul is one of the Valkyries who decide which warriors are led to Valhalla (the hall of the afterlife) after death on the battlefield.

640 Lit. 'royal treasurer' with 'cattle herder'.

641 *Informed News from Copenhagen (Kiøbenhavnske Lærde Efterretninger)* was a journal edited by Peter Müller (1776-1834), linguist, pastor, and later Bishop of Zealand.

642 It is unknown to whom this refers.

the Olympic Games there are a *number* of disciplines, whereas in the spiritual struggle there is really only one.

The prize must go to the one whose product testifies to the greatest Learning.

However, the day when such an arrangement could exist as a result of the mood of the nation is somewhat distant, and if it came about in any other way, it would be ridiculous.

As long as we still have *branches* of Learning and not just 'Learning' in the singular, the major similarity with the Greek Games can be retained and prizes awarded in these individual branches of Learning. It must seem both by analogy and with regard to the higher goal that the dissertation to be honoured should embrace Learning in the widest sense; the racetrack is not for single wheels. But this was a step too far. It proved impossible to give the prize for the dissertation's contribution to Learning in general, for that would entail the revocation of its existence, and this would take us back to the beginning.

We must start on a lower level and award prizes for dissertations in the individual branches of Learning, since not until all the parts have been gathered into an organized whole, can we clearly see that the whole is in itself only a part. A different question is whether we should prescribe *which* branches of Learning should be treated. I think not, for that seems to me like preparing an art exhibition and wishing to decide beforehand which ideas the painter and the sculptor should carry out; in spiritual work the individual should have all the freedom that is commensurable with the purpose. The purpose of prizes is to advance Learning, and it must be a matter of indifference which subject is chosen so long as it is of interest and is treated respectfully. Moreover the competition would then be greater, more thought would be aroused, and the dissertations would be more adequate. The last-mentioned may perhaps remain undecided, but my duty is to lay out the *premises*, the correctness of which will stand or fall in the result.

In my view, it is impossible for a person whose work is placed at the service of Learning, in order to win a prize, to exchange the thought and the occupation that are precisely his interest for those that are the *conditions* of the prize. And even if he were willing to do so, it would hardly be within his power. For one could hardly claim that just as the shoemaker does not mind whether he sews boots or shoes, so is it of little consequence where the thinker exerts his spiritual power. A good answer to a specific question is dependent on the highly uncertain coincidence that someone who can give the answer has already asked himself the same question.

Furthermore, if the questions are to have an importance and an interest, then they cannot always be answered fully within the deadline appointed; we must assume that the individual has already previously been occupied with them. Yet is it enough to build on such a chance?

Thus, if I remember rightly, the university offered a prize in 1804 for the best answer to the interesting question: "What is characteristic of the epic poem, and which of the more recent poems deserves this name?"[643] What is here taken for granted I have no need to point out.

As far as I know the question remained unanswered by anyone – and is that a surprise?

Recently the Academy for the Advancement of the Noble Arts and Sciences[644] has also partially acknowledged its faith in the usefulness of freedom in this respect, for although it also followed the custom of awarding prizes for products with a specific content, it nevertheless added that the Academy would receive into its collection of writings every aesthetic product that was of value, and those for whom this is not prize enough do not deserve one.

I will not apologise for venturing into a material whose proper treatment perhaps too clearly exceeded my powers; for if I have not said anything that is worth reading or considering, then I deserve no mercy, and if it is not all to be one big black mark, every sensible person will know how much wisdom may be expected of an unauthorised[645] theology graduate who pushes his pen in a corner in order to forget himself.

What I would rather beg sincerely is that if anyone should find an error in these pages he will believe – and this is the truth – that it has its sole cause in my involuntary ignorance!

Nic. Fred. Sev. Grundtvig.

643 In his diary entry for 18th February 1805 Grundtvig comments on this prize question as demanding knowledge of both classical and modern philology that is beyond any student's and even his own grasp!

644 The Academy for the Advancement of the Noble Arts and Sciences *(Selskabet til de skiønne og nyttige Videnskabers Forfremmelse)*, also known as the Academy of Good Taste (*Det smagende Selskab*) was founded in 1759 and incorporated into the Royal Academy in 1966.

645 Grundtvig had no official position at this point in his life.

7. Grundtvig's study at Store Tuborg, Strandvejen 123

On 16th April 1858 Grundtvig married for the third time. His new wife Asta Reedtz, a wealthy widow, was 43 years his junior. On 10th February 1860 Asta gave birth to a daughter, who was baptised with the names of all three of Grundtvig's wives: Asta Marie Elisabeth. In September 1867 Asta purchased the villa, Store Tuborg, on Strandvejen, the prestigious coastal road north of Copenhagen with views across the Sound to Sweden. After living at 31 different addresses in his lifetime Grundtvig moved for the last time. Here he lived happily for the last 5 years of his life - with his library of 6,000 books. And here he died on 2nd September 1872, just 6 days short of his 89th birthday. Grundtvig lived twice as long as the median age of the time, which was 42.

7. On the Philosophical Century (1816)

Introduction by Steen Tullberg

On the Philosophical Century was first published in *Danne-Virke* in August 1816. It comes at the head of a number of Grundtvig's philosophical studies as a kind of programme declaration in his efforts to settle his accounts with the philosophy of the Enlightenment. He was not least averse to the German romantic and speculative ideals, with their emphasis on the power of reason and their neglect or misunderstanding of the significance of History. Nor did the Enlightenment philosophers have anything serious to say about 'the divine' and 'the eternal' as philosophical concepts.

In his alternative, Grundtvig outlines a philosophy based on the Christian *faith*. Faith, he says, is beyond rational *understanding*, and yet it is the testimony of *History*. Humankind is developing in Time and Space and can only be understood in this context, rather than in speculative ideals. Philosophy is quite naturally in a state of constant development, but it will never reach a definitive *conclusion* until the end of the world. In contrast, a faith-based philosophy encompasses both the temporal *and* the eternal.

The determining concept here is Learning (*vidskab*), and Learning only comes in tandem with History! With an allusion to St. Paul, Grundtvig writes that philosophy is "an expression of the human endeavour for wisdom, for absolute Knowledge, for immediate intuition, and, in the highest Christian phrase, for contemplation 'face to face'" (p. 271).[646] Grundtvig traces 'Learning' back to a number of references in the Old Testament and claims that whereas scientific knowledge or scholarship (*videnskab*) denotes "an isolated sphere of certainties" (p. 272), Learning represents our "endless endeavour towards an unattainable goal on earth" (ibid.). It also invites our acceptance of divine Truth. The unattainable goal of Learning is the "illumination of humankind and our existence" (p. 277), which for Grundtvig embraces our foundation and our source, our conditions and our significance, our purpose and our goal.

Scholarship's *instrument* is Reason, but Reason cannot comprehend God, whatever the philosophers say, for there is a truth that is not *accessible* to Reason. Imagination and Feeling can comprehend God, but not Reason, which cannot grasp that which is greater than itself; if it could, there would be no difference between God and humankind. We humans cannot be our "own father and life-foundation" (p. 273) – that is the prerogative of God, who is totally without *dependence* on humankind.

On the other hand, in *support* of Reason, Grundtvig argues that "Reason is the concept and expression of spiritual growth and development" (p. 274), and therefore, assuming it recognises

646 1 Cor 13:12.

its limitations, it can grasp everything that is of importance for our *temporal* existence. When it is 'illuminated' temporally, we have a *figurative* knowledge of the Eternal. Formulated thus, once Reason has understood its limitations, it can begin to judge according to "the eternal basic law of Truth, the principle of contradiction". Only then can and will it "illuminate all things human within itself" (p. 277). The principle of contradiction is classical logic for Grundtvig; it is what enables us to distinguish between truth and falsehood, good and evil, and light and darkness.

If we hold firm to this definition of Reason, says Grundtvig, we shall realise that all true Learning must of necessity embrace History. No philosophical system can ever be *complete*, for in this life we can only ever know "in part".[647] Human beings develop over time, and therefore our understanding of what is 'human' must do likewise. But this in turn must mean that ultimate Truth is already partially *present*, and in bud, as it were; and this can only have come about because Truth has already been partially *revealed*. Humans can bear witness to this revelation by accepting their own partial transfiguration, as the three disciples did beside Christ on the Mount Tabor.[648]

We live in a philosophical century. This is what we all heard in our childhood, and if we ever became men, we found ourselves tempted to regard it as something we might make *children* believe but never reasonable adults! If we regard the 18th century, which like the Anabaptists,[649] christened itself in the world's village pond as 'philosophical', then however we twist it around, we find philosophy written everywhere, and poorly translated from one land to the other. Yet in actual fact it is completely invisible! We must therefore believe that in the 'jargon' of the 18th century, philosophy means *The Jerusalem Shoemaker's Trip to the Moon*,[650] which everybody has heard about but no one has seen.

It has often been said that *Niels Klim*[651] is satirical through and through. But I do not recall seeing anywhere that his account of the journey is an obvious prophecy of 18th

647 1 Cor 13:9.

648 Mt 17:1-13.

649 Anabaptism (lit. rebaptism) has its origins in the 16th century Reformation. The word is rejected by its practitioners, who believe only in believer's baptism. Infant baptism, they argue, has no basis in Scripture, and is therefore invalid, even if an infant has already been baptised. 'Baptists' emerged in the 18th century with similar beliefs. Today there are around 4 million so-called Anabaptists, including the Amish, the Mennonites, and the Hutterites.

650 *The Jerusalem Shoemaker's Trip to the Moon* was a satirical bi-weekly written by Malthe Bruun (1775-1826) and Otto Horrebow (1769-1823). It satirized Denmark (the Moon) as being a despotic land in which the first Article states: "Our regent owns our persons and all that is ours." The utopian counterpart was Oceana, where there was freedom of thought, freedom of the press, and children were raised according to the laws of nature.

651 *Niels Klim's Underground Travels* is a Latin novel published in 1741 by satirist and playwright Ludvig Holberg (1684-1754). Holberg is the acknowledged founder of modern Danish-Norwegian literature, and *Niels Klim* is one of the earliest 'satirical fantasy fiction' works, alongside *Gulliver's Travels* (1726). It describes a utopian society on a distant planet, where, for instance, men and women have equal rights.

century philosophy, theoretical as well as practical. It truly deserved a clearer exposition and the philosophers' attention, especially since Holberg's eulogy over Philosophy was called its funereal oration, which I think is an authentic commentary. However, no one imagines that I am minded to *clarify* such prophecies. Far from it! In the madhouse to which I was banished for a similar attempt and in which I unfortunately find myself, the desire to do so passes away. All such clarification I therefore leave to posterity, which has its own perfectly sensible way of explaining. We shall then gain not only visible proof and faith between our fingers but also a dusted-down jacket and such long noses that if they do not reach the clouds to which they aspire, then at least they reach down to the ground – and all in all we must say that that is a great achievement!

However, I do intend briefly to remind the reader what Philosophy in truth *can* be, and what is has to do with us, and us with it. I shall also add a not unfounded observation on whether the 18th or the 19th century can indeed appropriate the title of 'philosophical'. This may seem like an avoidable inconvenience, what with all the handsome philosophers we have growing up around us, telling us politely how all things lose themselves in allness and nothingness, such as the poetry in Oehlenschläger and the ideas in *Athene*.[652] The point is, it is not difficult to *lose* something; we do not need Philosophy to tell us that. But to *gain* something, that is our first consideration. Moreover, these philosophers' home-made clothes comprise nothing but a little spiritual paper made of foreign rags full of stains, together with some kind of watermark that is their only *Danish* stamp. In other words, their ideas are not only taken on credit but are also hit and miss, and the language is such a demented form of German that it is often painful to see how *mad* the ideas are. We cannot even derive benefit from them as from a decent falsehood, where *cuius contrarium verum est*.[653] So I think it not out of place to say a few words about what we call 'Philosophy', not least in order to remind Danish readers that it is neither the deep thinking nor the impoverished language that prevents self-made philosophers from speaking plainly and intelligibly about things and expressions that are known to everybody. Disordered thought, ignorant language, and a love of humbug are the only true causes of obscurity, vagueness, and the widespread delusion that bombast is sublimity and chaos is profundity.

As we know, Philosophy is an expression of the human endeavour for wisdom, for absolute Knowledge, for immediate intuition, and, in the highest Christian phrase, for contemplation 'face to face'.[654] The Danish word that we can best employ to de-

652 *Athene* was a monthly journal (1813-17), mainly the work of Christian Molbech (1783-1857). Molbech contributed hugely to Danish culture, as founder of the Danish Historical Society and of the *History Journal*, which is the oldest still published scientific historical journal in the world. Among his philological works were the *Danish Dictionary* (1828-33) and the *Danish Dialect Dictionary* (1833-41).

653 'whose opposite is the truth'.

654 1 Cor 13:12.

scribe this endeavour in all its vitality is without doubt 'Learning' (*vidskab*).[655] This is a word which in a number of places in our Danish Bible can be used in this sense,[656] and which can withstand the toughest test with 'know' and 'wit' and 'learn' behind it, 'certainty' alongside it, and 'wisdom' ahead of it. The suffix '*-skab*' is closely linked to the Icelandic '*skap*' (mind) and thus to 'mind-creation'. In our mother-tongue the word *vidskab* therefore denotes fundamental qualities of character in both their internal existence and their living expression.[657] We do not need to tarry here with oral usage but can move up to the highest test of the word: namely, the actual truth that it still exists! For as created beings we must consider *every* human quality, and 'Learning' aims at creating a world of truths in reason and an image of this in language. We might say that 'knowledge'[658] was just as appropriate a word as 'Learning', but against this I would say that one must never develop anything by weakening it, nor confuse things in an effort to clarify them. Even if we could not see how 'knowledge' has come to mean an isolated sphere of certainties, we must guard against giving it any *other* meaning, before it becomes generally clear that it should be either altered or moved. We can rightly say, however, that 'knowledge' means something complete, something concluded. It can only be employed with some justification on a sum of information which, being limited to a delineated sphere, acquires an apparent totality. 'Learning' on the other hand is an endless endeavour towards an unattainable goal on earth. Any claim that it is actual 'knowledge' is empty boasting. Against this we have 'scholarship', which is closely connected to 'Learning'. In general usage, 'scholarship' allows for this, since it has chiefly functioned as a secondary usage. As the goal of Learning is indubitably full scholarship, there is no need to create new words such as 'learningable' and 'scholarshipable'.[659] They may have a similarity with 'companionable' and 'amicable', but they seem to jar the ear and would at the very least mislead rather than guide our readers.

Following this introduction, which may be found superfluous and dry but hardly fanciful and unjustified, we come to the question of the purpose and conditions of 'Learning'. Clearly, the thirst for Knowledge that deserves to be called 'Learning', and indeed *is* true Learning, has to do with the illumination of our very *existence*. It is equally

655 Grundtvig uses the Danish word *vidskab* here and then proceeds to play on it throughout the paragraph, using *vid*, *vittighed*, *vished*, *videnskab*, *videnskabelighed*, and finally *visdom*. This word-play is impossible to reproduce in English – as is the suffix *-skab* ('-ship)' denoting the making of something, e.g. 'craftsmanship'.

656 e.g. Num 24:16; Ps 19:2; Isa 44:25.

657 Such as faithfulness, friendship, foolishness, wildness; further exposition of these belongs with a knowledge of the mother-tongue with consideration for the substantive endings, for which -skab, -mål, and -dom deserve particular attention.

658 Grundtvig uses *videnskab* here instead of *vidskab*.

659 Here Grundtvig invents two new words *vidskabelig* and *vidskabelighed*.

clear that our existence can only be explained when we have clarified our understanding of its foundation and source, its conditions and meaning, and its purpose and goal. The next question is whether its foundation and goal can ever be the object of *human* Learning; in other words, to what extent can we, with our Reason alone, explain our existence and comprehend the foundation and aim of all things – or what in a single word we call 'God'? The premise of all philosophy for this purpose is not to accept as a spiritual truth anything that cannot be grasped by Reason. For just as, physically, we can only grasp what we ourselves comprise, so is it impossible for Reason to grasp what is *beyond* its comprehensive powers. As with the human hand, it cannot understand anything *greater* than itself. Whether or not we can grasp 'the Highest', 'the First', and 'the Last' would seem to depend on whether we *ourselves* are the Highest, the First, and the Last. Imagination and feeling can reach above ourselves, but never above Reason, for then it would have *to stop being itself*. It would stop being our clear, irresistible consciousness, it would stop comprehending and grasping. It would be both Reason and unReason. It would abolish itself, yet function with all its qualities – which is absolutely impossible. The question over which philosophers of the past always had to chew the cud before they passed on their knowledge of divine matters was whether this was indeed actually *possible*. In other words, are divine and human one and the same, and are human beings in fact their *own God*? Are we 'of ourselves (i.e. independent) or are we dependent upon ourselves (i.e. free in the strictest sense)?

This is the sole question to be answered. All our 'knowledge' of God is nonsense if it is proved that we cannot *comprehend* God, since concepts that we ourselves cannot conceive cannot be *our* concepts. True or false, they must be a Higher Being's concepts, which we through faith can acquire. So it is an incontestable truth that if there is only *one single* idea that our Reason cannot grasp, then it is not the Highest, since for the Highest nothing is too high. However, the concept of being 'of oneself', of being independent, of being one's own father and life-foundation, of being God, that is a concept whose reality is irrefutable. Call it what we will, *something* must be eternal; there must be *something* that has never begun. And what has never begun is of necessity unchangeable and must understand itself as such, if any 'concept' otherwise exists. And if it *does* exist, that 'concept' must be either *in* us or *above* us. Yet we know it confronts us and we confront it, and we know we must say stop and declare it incomprehensible to us! Either we must argue that existence has been thoroughly illuminated without its basis being grasped, or we must admit that all *knowledge* about an eternal, independent existence is impossible for us, because like all the essential basic concepts of existence it is beyond our understanding.

All this could be demonstrated far more stringently and clearly, but it must already be clear enough to unprejudiced readers; and anyway this is not the place for a more detailed exposition. I can only briefly remind them of these obvious truths to prevent it being said with some show of Reason that the claim is *fanciful*. An age seeking to understand what to believe, but thinking that something is disproved when it is demonstrated that it is only incomprehensible, such an age is neither 'reasonable' nor 'philosophical' but precisely the opposite! We do not need to examine in detail whether the 18th century has the least claim to be the 'philosophical' century.

The second important question is this: Does 'Learning' have any value or reasonable purpose, if it cannot offer Knowledge of the Eternal and the Divine – of God? I use the word 'important' in the sense of 'urgent', for the question is pursuing every thinking person at the present time. And it cannot be determined by the *history* of Philosophy. When Reason seeks to judge what it does not understand, it makes obvious mistakes, and it misleads those who follow it; it offers nothing in place of its proper use. Even if we can show, as I believe we can, that Reason has always gone so far astray when it has walked alone in the kingdom of the Spirit, this only goes to show how Reason refuses to wait for its hour to come. Like a self-opinionated child who through teaching and discipline can *become* reasonable, so can self-opinionated Philosophy also *become* wise. And when one is wise, one does not *will* what one cannot do, nor does one quarrel with one's superior.

There is no denying that in the human race, as in the individual, Reason is the concept and expression of spiritual growth and development. It is easy to see how it can come to understand what it has not previously understood, and that this must be so unless its path is unfortunately barred. Then the question is whether, by its very conditions, Reason can grasp anything of importance for the *spiritual* person? And the answer is equally simple. Reason must be able to understand itself and all that lies within this concept, that is, the temporal *person* and the temporal *life*. For we human beings are the centre-point of the Finite, and this must be understandable to us! Moreover, just as all Reason must be allotted and prescribed, created and qualified to grasp what it can, so is it clear that although the Finite cannot explain the Eternal, its explanation must have the most decisive influence on human wisdom *regarding* the Eternal, and thus bring about an indirect, *figurative* knowledge. For in truth the Finite can only be an image of the Eternal, and when one clearly grasps a true image, one knows what it characterises and means, even though one does not grasp what is behind the image.

Truly to *understand* oneself is the great goal of human Reason, the apex of human Learning. The first step towards this is the true spiritual self-consciousness of Reason, the acknowledgement of oneself in one's true relationship to the Eternal, to divine Reason and Truth.

I need not expatiate on what is obvious: that the self-consciousness of a people's Reason is just as little spiritually developed in its early stages as the individual's is sensually developed in childhood, before it becomes clear in manhood. Nor do I need to prove that Reason does not become truly *clarified* unless it is previously grounded in truth by means of faith. I shall merely point out that as surely as there is something spiritual, i.e. super-sensory, in humankind, so surely is the Reason that *denies* this spiritual reality completely mad! And as surely as Reason cannot grasp a being's existence of its own accord, so surely is it conscious of the lie when it claims for itself spiritual independence. The same is the case when it claims to be 'sovereign' and to have life *within* itself, for it cannot *grasp* a 'sovereign' Reason, that is, the living truth *within* itself. And what it cannot understand, it cannot itself *be*! Reason is in no way *external* to what it understands. It is for us a temporal concept that cannot possibly comprehend the Eternal and the Unchanging, whereas the *sovereign* is eternal; Truth living within itself is unchangeable. When human reason is true to itself as regards Truth, then it is aware of itself as a temporal, dependent concept, dead in itself and living in the love of Truth. I am truly alive, I am truly 'in' time, I am witness to the Temporal: this is the self-conscious truth like I myself, for this is true *in* and *of* me. However, if Truth asks itself: What is eternal Truth? it answers that it cannot *comprehend* the concept, for *it* includes *me*! But what I *can* comprehend is that anything that excludes me cannot be eternal Truth, and everything that *is* eternal truth for me to exist as I am, that is indeed eternal Truth, for I am the *temporal image* of eternal Truth.

Only when Reason has cleared this up for itself can it bring its spiritual case to court. It can then make its judgement, not from prejudice or appearance, but according to the Truth and the eternal basic law of Truth: the principle of contradiction. Reason judges everything that can be clarified in the light of that Truth, and allows everything to stand on its merits. It is afraid in equal measure of applauding the falsehood and denying the truth, which it understands as being actually one and the same thing. There is no falsehood that does not have a contradictory truth, since the falsehood is nothing other than a denial of the truth. Every 'no' presupposes a 'yes' that is not accepted.

If we hold firm to the clear truth that it is the *temporal* human being that our Reason can and must comprehend, then we realise that all true Learning must in every sense be *historical*. For Reason finds nothing in itself without a yardstick for temporal Truth and must seek the content of Learning itself; 'historical' because the human being develops in *Time* and can only be understood thus; and 'historical' because it must be piece by piece and can only be *ended* with Time. The first consequence of all this is that every study of Learning that does not explain the chronicle of History is false; the second is that every such study that tries to pass itself off as *complete*, i.e. every philosophical system, is one huge falsehood, however much truth it may contain in its individual details. For if it is the human being that is to be comprehended, and if the human being develops in Time, and if Reason is the developing human concept *throughout* Time, then we cannot in the course of Time have any true concept of the human being or human Learning except for what is *in the process of* conceptual development. We cannot truly comprehend more than what has so far developed, since it is the concept itself that is developing! Lastly, it follows that if it were possible for Reason to develop without a prior knowledge of Truth, it would never be able over time to satisfy human beings and give a complete and clear concept of them in all their fullness. Troubled and uncertain all serious persons must wander the world until their days' end, unsure of their most important relation, namely to Eternity, and without a single fully-clarified spiritual concept, for nothing is *fully*-clarified in its *complete* totality.

On the other hand, if this concept is *in development* in the human being, then the *Truth* that is to be developed must be *already present*, however complex. What is to be *clarified* in human beings must be *in* them beforehand, however vague. What they are to conceive they must have already *believed*; what Reason must grasp must already exist! It cannot bring itself into being, any more than the hand can bring into being what it is to grasp. If we are ever to understand ourselves truly as the earthly image of eternal Truth, then we must really have *been* that Truth from the beginning. The eternal Truth must have revealed itself in us right from, and in, our origin; it must have breathed life into us and allowed us to hear His voice in the Spirit, since the living Truth cannot deny itself, nor can it both reveal itself in a temporal life and yet *hide* itself from life, for that is a contradiction.

Reason has been created in order for us to understand the Revelation of eternal Truth in time through History. For History shows us how the Revelation has come about, and expresses itself in temporal images of eternal Truth. It is this image of 'how' this came about that Reason must grasp.

I shall not dwell here on the consequences of a contemplation through Reason of the divine revelations to which History bears witness, for History actually *constitutes* and *describes* this Revelation. I am not speaking here of individual persons or circumstances but of the *irrefutability* of History, of its path and its monuments, of its peoples, their overall feats and events, what they left behind that cannot belong to anyone else and in which they have distinguished themselves as members of the human race. For *as* such they are enduring, whatever the life they have led as separate states, and despite their demise. When we regard History in this way, we realise how it must be precisely questioned by a truth-loving scholar, and how it should be able to offer certain important answers. For it is a *work* in which we humans have been forced to express our true circumstances, and a Word in which Truth has invariably proclaimed its judgement over human impact and human behaviour. Only in History do we find humans as complete as they have so far revealed themselves to be. Only in History do we reveal our reality and our *true state*, which does not allow itself to be hidden from the eyes of posterity. Obviously, philosophers must first ask *themselves*, and thus whether they can *ask* anything of History. But equally, it is spiritual madness for an individual person or a particular era to wish to explain all humankind on the basis of themselves, for they cannot be fully revealed without Him who is the ultimate reward of all human life, the true, transfigured human himself, or in a Christian phrase, the Son of Humankind (Man), transfigured in the Son of God.

It is thus undeniable that the days of old reveal a spiritual imagination and feeling that none can find either in themselves or in others at the present time. Yet these things need illuminating before humankind can comprehend itself, or Reason can understand itself as an evolution of the human spirit, or can illuminate all things human within itself. It is obvious what a self-conscious *Reason* must judge – what has been called pure 'speculative philosophy'.[660] For Folly must then declare the same, unless the philosopher himself is truly the sum total of all History and contains all human qualities in a completely immaculate union at the highest level of development! For to contemplate the human condition independently is the same as examining oneself and finding one's own elucidation to have universal validity. It is like setting one's mind to being the complete and perfect person, and taking one's own experience to be that of the whole history of humankind. And when a single, not unblemished, human child does so before experiencing all that can befall him – before he has experienced death, for instance – then that person is a fool. We may regret his blindness, but we are never tempted to accompany him to the grave unless we ourselves are blind.

When Reason, with its bright eyes wide open and self-conscious, a truly *self-conscious spiritual* Reason, summons the 18th century to its courtroom, as it is in every way entitled and pledged to, then its judgement must be that there has hardly been a *less* genuinely philosophical or truth-loving century! For everywhere Reason declared itself to be 'sovereign', often to be 'independent'. Its philosophers, from Wolff to Schelling, sought to illuminate humankind on the basis of *themselves*! In *this* so-called 'philosophy', History was mangled, distorted, and corrupted – when it was not being completely neglected, despised, and declared invalid. With them, the illumination of History was never regarded as the *highest goal* of Philosophy but as a side-show and a children's game. Their 'philosophy' either left it to the riff-raff in their train, or stooped down for a moment from its transcendental heights merely to enjoy itself, or at the most to silence the rabble and the few level-headed spirits who demanded the human right to see the whole of our great human life transfigured in 'an illumination of humankind and our existence'.

Did Wolff not pretend that History did not exist? Did Kant not claim it was invalid? Did not Fichte try to prove the same thing? Did not Schelling endeavour to turn it into a mere reproduction of the development of Natural Man and a prototype of his self-enlightenment? Where was the philosophy that sought to encourage *History* to

660 Speculative philosophy is founded on intuitive insight rather than demonstrable experience, which is the basis of analytic philosophy. When considering how schoolchildren might be introduced to philosophy, its most famous practitioner, G.W.F. Hegel (1770-1831), proposed three stages: first 'abstract' thinking; next 'dialectical' thinking' and finally 'speculative' thinking.

illuminate humankind? A few, like Herder and Tyge Rothe,[661] attempted spiritedly to ask *questions* of History, that is true. But was it the philosophy of the century that drove them to do so – or did it *prevent* them from doing so? Were they listened to, or were their efforts seen as vain attempts to use History to undermine the failing Church? When they otherwise attempted to explain History, did they allow it to speak for itself or did they put words in its mouth? Did they seek to prove their claims about the conditions of humankind, or did they take these to be given beforehand and only sought as far as possible to fit them into their claims, and to serve *themselves* by denying or doubting the testimony of History, when they failed? And when they took it upon themselves to explain how events had *come about* and were *linked together*, how Poetry and Art had *produced* their wonders, did they prove irrefutably that the reasons they cited *alone* could have had the effect that we all recognise? Did they show a clear understanding of human *skill*? Did they *prove* that the great works of the human spirit could only have been brought about in the way they depicted, or was their sole explanation that they described the way they *themselves* would have set about the task if they were to bring about such events and link them together, and had in fact *made* the works – which of course they had not? Every educated person knows the one and only answer: that History cannot possibly be understood and illuminated by calling the events to be described, in the circumstances, 'inevitable'!

When irrefutable evidence is *not* produced, *nothing* is illuminated; it is all just guesswork. And if guesswork is to harmonise with a claim by Reason of an irrefutable fact in History, then the claim cannot be the valid truth, but is in fact a falsehood until guesswork proves the truth. We know that this was the case every time in the 18th century that the conclusions of Reason were compared with the testimony of History, and that no one can with a clear conscience defend and pursue conclusions that have not paid History their honest debt but only sought to avoid them by equivocation. For it cannot be denied that 18th century Reason claimed that a whole host of events and writings that declared it to be a liar were invented or falsified! And yet it has never proved this of its greatest and noblest accusers: the writings of Scripture. The highest it could prove was the *possibility* of the truth of Scripture's claim, and it went no further than to prove what the possibility itself demonstrated: that it would have had no scruples about such an invention or falsification if it had found it expedient to do so. 18th century Reason never considered the possibility of such inventions; and it was guilty of denying the evidence of reality, of a clear development of an undeniable conflict between itself and the irrefutable truth, as well as being guilty of a failure to

661 Tyge Rothe (1731-95) was a Danish writer, philosopher, and agricultural reformer, in which capacity he argued for a fundamental reform of the Danish feudal system. In his younger days Grundtvig shared Rothe's view that History was a progressive process which, with Christianity as its civilising factor, had reached its provisional zenith with the 18th century. During his spiritual crisis of 1810-11 Grundtvig moved away from this rationalist belief.

produce the undeniable truth of its claims. Until this debt is paid it lies like a rascal in his grave, for it has not redeemed the signature, but has written itself a false receipt. It has copied the handwriting of History and forged its seal so clumsily that every scholar of History must not only testify to the falsification but can prove it by presenting the indisputable handwriting of Reason with the autographic signature of History. This demonstrates clearly that History must have been mad to declare 'already paid' the debt that unborn generations must disburse.

This then is my not unjustified consideration of the philosophy of the 18th century. If, as I think, it can be shown to be the undeniable truth, it follows that the 19th century cannot gain access to the title of 'philosophical' either by accepting or condemning the 18th, but only by doing what that century *failed* to do. For it failed in two things: to acknowledge History for what it irrefutably must be: the real revelation of *Truth*, the real development of humankind, the root, the essence, and the touchstone of all human Learning; and secondly, to cultivate it as such with an open eye and untiring diligence, without allowing itself to be duped into believing that in the observation of nature, the spontaneous perception, or such-like, there is any short cut to the goal of History, which cannot be reached before the end of all days and cannot be other than a *temporal* illumination.

However obvious this seems, however clearly Reason can see the folly of wishing to have its complete conceptual existence *in itself*, while the eye (which the whole of History is still forming and clearing) is still being trained and opened, we must nevertheless confess that the signs of the times seem least of all to promise and announce such a decisive historical direction. We can freely claim, and irrefutably prove, that this is impossible without such a radical conversion and rebirth in the kingdom of the Spirit, which Reason must call *unreasonable*, for humanly speaking it is totally impossible! This can be made evident by presenting what is needed to rightfully consult History and understand its answers, something I shall attempt in a separate study on historical Learning or the testimony of the *Chronicle*. This may seem purposeless, since it is beyond reason that anyone will be up to the task, but it is nonetheless certain that the work must be done, that History much reach its goal, that all things temporal must be illuminated in Truth. The only question is when and by whom it should take place, which people under heaven will let themselves be roused in spiritual battle to take the kingdom, i.e. History, and for which people is that glorious legacy prepared and the boundary lines fallen in pleasant places.[662] It is natural that every man who knows what this is sincerely feels the desire, receives the power, and reaps the blessing. Many a time have I said what I hope for the people from whose roots my eyes took their source, and wherever I turn I am moving among them; otherwise I must repent every word I have spoken here.

662 Ps 16:6. "The boundary lines have fallen for me in pleasant places;/ surely I have a delightful inheritance."

8. On Historical Learning, or the Concept of History (1816)

Introduction by Jon Tafdrup

On Historical Learning, or the Concept of History (from hereon *On Historical Learning*) was published in September 1816 in the third number of the first volume of Grundtvig's self-penned journal *Danne-Virke*. Among the many so-called *Danne-Virke* essays on 'History' in the 4 volumes, Ole Vind considers Grundtvig's attempt to deal with the essence and aim of *On Historical Learning* to be among the most substantial.[663]

'Learning' (*vidskab*) is a central term in Grundtvig's conceptual world. In his view, Philosophy, Scholarship, and Learning had been far too closely interlinked by the Enlightenment thinkers, in particular the German idealist philosophers. They concerned themselves with only *parts* of the world rather than its entirety, and they had no sense of the *historical* origin of humankind or of the importance of human *experience* in the course of History. Grundtvig sought to move on to a deeper, *truer* Learning.[664] In *On the Philosophical Century* in the previous issue of *Danne-Virke* Grundtvig had explained that *vidskab* was a Danish expression for philosophy: "Philosophy is, as we know, an expression of the human endeavour for wisdom, for absolute knowledge, for immediate intuition, and, in the highest Christian phrase, for contemplation 'face to face'.[665] The Danish word that we can best employ to describe this endeavour in all its vitality is without doubt 'Learning'. This is a word which in a number of places in our Danish Bible can be used in this sense" (p. 272). Learning, for Grundtvig, is thus an *ongoing endeavour* in this world, with its foundation in the Christian belief that full Knowledge will only come when we meet our Maker 'face to face'. We find the same thinking in the opening lines of the present essay, where Grundtvig calls the human being "the greatest riddle that human reason can solve" (p. 282).

In *On the Philosophical Century* Grundtvig has already stated that "our existence can only be explained when we have clarified our understanding of its foundation and source, its conditions and meaning, and its purpose and goal" (p. 273). By 'clarified' Grundtvig means transformed into something greater, something *transfigured*. Reason and Philosophy cannot teach us about the divine and the eternal; this can only come about through *faith*. Philosophy should concern itself with History instead, since "all true Learning must in every sense be *historical*. For Reason finds nothing in itself without a yardstick for temporal Truth and must seek the content of Learning itself; 'historical' because the human being develops in *Time* and can only be under-

663 Ole Vind, *Grundtvigs historiefilosofi*. Copenhagen 1999, p. 144.
664 Ibid. P. 138.
665 1 Cor 13:12.

stood thus; and 'historical' because it must be piece by piece and can only be *ended* with Time" (p. 275). This understanding of 'Faith' and the Knowledge gained 'piece by piece' in the course of Time is further developed in *On Historical Learning.*

Grundtvig's condemnation of Enlightenment thinking and German idealism is directed in particular against Immanuel Kant, though he never offers a systematic criticism of Kant. This he reserves for Schelling, who in 1815 was involved in the dispute with H.C. Ørsted on natural philosophy.[666] It is likely that in the same year Grundtvig read Kant's *Critique of Pure Reason*,[667] for whom Time is a mode of perception that cannot be made the object of Experience, but can be understood *a priori* with the aid of Reason. Rejecting this, Grundtvig argues that humankind is limited by Time, which has begun but has not yet ended.[668] He assigns human cognition to Experience, to History, and to what can be understood *a posteriori*. This is true both empirically, in the form of sensory experience, and historically, in the form of transcendent experience, i.e. the traditions handed down by our forefathers in speech and writing.[669]

Grundtvig believes in the spiritual kinship between generations – in the form of a natural and direct link to our forefathers, analogous with our individual kinship to our parents and our imaginative kinship to our children. Central to this, as he notes in *On Historical Learning*, is his belief that "there exist peoples and individuals who with genuine *feeling* can regard all those preceding them to be their forefathers, those contemporary to them to be their brothers, and sisters, and those succeeding them to be their common infant children." The historian who has this "sense of unity" is capable of understanding the development of History "in its origin in unity and its progress to unification" (p. 286).

The foundation of Grundtvig's philosophy of History is the Bible – both in its revealed truths and in its depiction of History: "The same holy book, the Bible, which teaches us how to live on earth in order to be pleasing God and to join Him in the afterlife, also gives us an equally beautiful and true account of the oldest times."[670] Knowledge of the one true God and of the primeval events has been forgotten over time, argues Grundtvig. This separation is part of the human condition until the end times, when human beings will be reunited with God in spiritual unity. As he claims in *On Historical Learning*, we must not forget that "it was the division of the hearts of one people's from another that Christianity sought to break down, not the differences in their spiritual circumstances" (p. 287).[671] The idea of the coming unity, and of our piece-by-piece knowledge, reflects Grundtvig's belief in the progress of the human race through

666 Ibid, p. 139.

667 William Michelsen, 'Grundtvig og hans samtids tænkemåde. Overvejelser over Grundtvigs stilling i dansk åndsliv', *Grundtvig-Studier* 1979, Copenhagen, p. 27.

668 Kim Arne Pedersen, 'Om at læse *Danne-Virke*. Nogle hermeneutiske overvejelser', *Grundtvig-Studier* 1991, Copenhagen, p. 99.

669 Vind 1999, p. 140.

670 *Udsigt over Verdens-Krøniken fornemmelig i det Lutherske Tidsrum*, Copenhagen 1817, p. 2.

671 Rom 12:4-5; 1 Cor 12:12-14.

its historical development. Humankind is advancing step by step towards the fulfilment and object of all Learning, i.e. the complete clarification of the human riddle.

In order to counter any objections to the Bible as a source of universal, eternally revealed Truth, Grundtvig employs what he calls "the basic law of Truth", namely the principle of contradiction, as by the German philosopher Christian Wolff before Kant. The first time that Grundtvig theoretically refers to this principle of logic is in *History's Retort* (1813),[672] its premise being that contradictory statements cannot both at the same time be *true*. Grundtvig takes for granted that eternal Truth *exists* and is to be found in the Bible and in Christianity. This absolute, revealed Truth cannot be grasped by Reason alone, since Truth lies beyond the individual's human horizon.[673]

Is the human being the greatest riddle that human reason can solve? And is it true that the solution to this riddle cannot be reached by the work of a moment, of a single individual, or of any age? That it can only solve itself gradually over time and successive generations? And must this be so until the day Reason can understand what lies beyond the intellect, or an individual becomes the perfect person, or the people of a single age become the most perfect people ever to have existed? And are all such matters in open conflict with the basic law of Truth (the principle of contradiction)?

If the answer to all these questions is affirmative, then it is also true that whoever genuinely wishes to understand the human condition must regard the human being *historically*. No one can comprehend more than what their own times have engendered and illuminated, or what they can gather from past history. For just as we cannot comprehend anything higher than ourselves, so the individual ages and individual persons cannot comprehend anything higher than *them*selves. It must be true of both our inner and outer lives, in physical *and* spiritual matters, that none of us can comprehend more than we can express.

From this it follows how baseless is the objection to Philosophy that it should be 'uncertain'! For not only among different peoples but often also within a *single* people philosophers have held the most divergent views about the human condition. Clearly, when the various schools pretend to be the sole authority, they are all lying – and lying takes as many forms as those schools. The true spiritual reason for the existence of the variety of peoples in a *spiritual* sense is none other than that the human race consists of so *many* spiritual entities, all of whom seek to give expression to human

672 Danish title: *Krønikens Gienmæle.*

673 Vind 1999, pp. 141-43; Henning Høirup, *Grundtvigs Syn paa Tro og Erkendelse. Modsigelsens Grundsætning som teologisk Aksiom hos Grundtvig.* Copenhagen 1949, pp. 122-37.

life. They themselves constitute an incomplete part of it, since they draw more or less sharp border-lines between themselves and other entities, and in spirit and heart these constitute the vast majority of the whole human race. Obviously, the more limited a people's idea of, and feeling for, the human race, the more limited is their idea of the human being, for what we cannot vividly imagine, we can never come to comprehend. Individuals occupy the same relationship to their people as to the entire human race; whatever they are able to comprehend therefore depends first on how much their people can *comprehend* of the present moment, and second, on how much they are aware of the *ideas* of their people.

No thinking person will deny these arguments when they consider how clear and constant is the truth that is at work here; namely, *non omnia possumus omnes*.[674] It is irrefutable that anyone on the path of truth can do no more than see the error of their ways, gather, consider, take into account, and deliberate. Conversely, should they wish to go further than they can actually manage in deep thinking, they go *out* of their minds and truly and literally take leave of all Reason. My contention is that no one can comprehend more than they can actually master, more than what truly exists and lives inside them. It is therefore no longer a surprise that many so-called 'philosophers' who wish to understand not only what lies *behind* them in time but also what will happen in the *course* of time are bound to disagree. Furthermore, they will *claim* all manner of foolish things, since they build their arguments on the folly that the human race is *already* perfect! This folly is only forgivable where it is unconscious – but it is always the consequence of overweening pride. For no one has so little Reason as to be unable to see that it is pride that speaks when someone calls themselves 'perfect' or seeks to go beyond their limits.

Let it be noted that it is not my intention here to pass a hard judgement on anyone who has set out to understand and illuminate humankind, for a number of them have demonstrably less pride than many who are not even *concerned* about the major questions of our existence. Such people, when they lack a divine revelation or a belief in its truth, can easily fool themselves into believing that in all humility it is nevertheless essential to undertake this proud task. They have failed partly because they have lacked a clear understanding of our fundamental spiritual circumstances, and partly because they took the advice of past thinkers without realising how little their ideas could help them, if they themselves could not imbibe them. This in turn proved impossible, unless the ideas came naturally and belonged within the sphere of ideas that their people (and they among them) were qualified and mature enough to

674 'We are not all equal to every task', line 63 in *Eclogue 8* by the Roman poet, Publius Vergilius Maro (Virgil), 70-19 BCE.

embrace in their time. I write here only to enjoin this important truth, not in order to judge any individual.

Having thus done my best to prevent this misapprehension, I turn to the question which thoughtful readers are doubtless asking at this point and which at first glance may seem even more important and difficult to answer than it actually is: Is it possible that any people or individual can arrive at any true and sound *conclusive* ideas about the human being as such and the entire development of humankind? This clearly seems impossible, since, as mentioned, it hangs together with the conditions of the people and the individual in question. History may express human *progress* but not all of it in a single people! Progress comes only in part[675] and only among the various peoples who alongside or after each other have made the life of the spirit available in language or deed. Is not the history of foreign peoples therefore as incomprehensible for another people as foreign ideas are for the individual philosopher? And is this not also true of the history of a specific people? For while it may express the development of an entire people, it is only understood in part among the succeeding generations and individuals. And in a single generation or individual it seems to be unable to make a *common* stand, despite it being only through its individuals that a people can understand itself.

So long as we regard this from only one side, it honestly seems that we must relinquish all hope of *common* spiritual concepts. On the other hand, we can sense that if we turn the question around, that conclusion is over-hasty. For if the *collection* of thought were impossible, then so would be the *division* of thought! The unity that can develop expediently in separate parts must also be able to become a *unity* again, which in the case of the idea presupposes the detail. Indeed, it can do no other, since a development whose goal is not clarity would be inexpedient; it would be no development at all, for development presupposes a goal. So either there is no development of the human race, or its development must have as its goal our ultimate Knowledge *of ourselves*. The only question then is whether to assume that there *is* no human race, but only human individuals, or rather creatures with no spiritual kinship.

This claim has actually been made, or at least presupposed, by *some* thinkers, despite the evidence of Revelation, History, and daily experience. They have even denied a spiritual kinship where it is at its most obvious, between parent and child! They have made the child a mere physical deposit like other bodily impurities. Yet 'spiritual kinship' undoubtedly exists, for one person can most certainly influence another, and can even learn and understand their language. For the *Word*, as the expression of concepts, feelings, and ideas, is a *spiritual* body. If we could imagine two totally unrelated spirits, it would be totally impossible for them to understand and influence one

675 1 Cor 13:12.

another, for they would be totally foreign to each other's concepts, feelings, and ideas. They would constitute two limited autonomies, which is a *double* contradiction. We must also note that the same philosophy which denied all spiritual kinship between human beings strongly argued the impossibility of both spiritual interaction and of one spirit ever *creating* another, if it so wished.[676] It denied that in our upbringing we could in any way give our children either thought or will, whatever their direction, and it argued that the individual was simultaneously both totally *in*dependent and yet totally *de*pendent on others!

Let us now turn from this jumble of contradictions to the pure truth that everything that is capable of spiritual interaction is also spiritually related. We contemporaries are not only one another's spiritual kin, but also the kin of past generations, for their words can affect us, and the spirit that was spontaneously at work among our forefathers has undoubtedly affected us all. Once we realise this, we must also admit that there is a spiritual development at work in the human race and in the individual which enables us to understand the *same* things that our forefathers understood in the days of the Valdemars[677] and Christian III,[678] *plus a little more*, for this testifies to spiritual kinship *and* spiritual development. If such a place with a single people exists, it must be with all its spiritual kin, indeed, with the whole human race to which it belongs. That is what 'kinship' means, that they are part of a spiritual whole designed for interaction, and a harmonised development that ends in unity. This could be proved much more easily through the supposition that we human beings are creatures of God and our life in the world is the temporal revelation of eternal Truth. For God cannot have created or sustained the human race for *no* reason or purpose. Truth cannot reveal itself in time without a progression and a specific goal that must be its *explanation*. Yet however certain these pre-conditions must be, and however clearly they can be proved, they do not *explain* History, but only drive us *towards* it in order to be explained *by* it.

We return now to what History undoubtedly demonstrates: that there is a spiritual development of the human race over time. It follows that it must *reach* its goal, even if we cannot yet understand *how*. We know that *something* was hidden from previous generations and yet they too developed. This is the strongest evidence that where the *reason* for human existence lies, there too lies the force that promotes development. We could deflect the question of the possibility of human Learning by issuing a warning to every people and every individual that if they only sought to imprint and follow the Truth, they or their successors would undoubtedly see *how* it is illuminated in human life. If we do not feel that we constitute a spiritual *unity* with our forefathers and our poster-

676 Gen 1:26.

677 The Valdemars include Valdemar I (reigned 1146-82) and his two sons Canute VI (reigned 1182-1202) and Valdemar II (reigned 1202-41).

678 Christian III (reigned 1534-1559).

ity, then we have no true understanding of ourselves as human beings! All we then can do is to guard against the desire to set our individuality in place of the totality! If we consider such a rejection more closely, we shall find that it even contains a certain *illumination* of the question it was meant to suppress! For just as spiritual unity in the midst of separation and variety is History's secret, so is it clear that if we have a *sense* of this secret, we can develop an *understanding* of it, since understanding is no more than the illumination of feeling. Such a feeling must of necessity exist, if the unity mentioned above is genuine, for it must *influence* us, as it develops our understanding of it.

We can call this spiritual influence a rightful *impression*, and we can call the reception of this impression 'feeling'. This 'feeling' is absolutely natural to all people, though it differs in depth, force, and clarity. We all have a 'natural' feeling of unity with our parents, and even though we may be childless, we can vividly imagine a unity with a coming generation. We do not doubt for a moment that anyone standing in the midst of Time can see a line of their forefathers stretching back to its beginning and a line of their children stretching forward to its end. If their hearts are truly loving they cannot do other than feel a spiritual unity with them *all*. We can clearly see that this depends on whether there exist peoples and individuals who with genuine *feeling* can regard all those preceding them to be their forefathers, those contemporary to them to be their brothers and sisters, and those succeeding them to be their common infant children. For where this sense of unity exists, the temporal will illuminate itself as a clear concept. It will produce generations and individuals within them who 'in part' understand the development of history in general, in its origin in unity and its progress to unification.

Without necessarily joining the wheezing mob who only find room in their hearts for the feelings that beset them via the *senses*, we may now well ask whether this depth of compassion is possible. And we may well question whether the separation of the human race into various peoples with such different spirits and languages raises a barrier that not even all the forces of human feeling can break down even though imagination surpasses it and reason forbids it. When it is a matter of spiritual, unselfish, universal Love, the intellect of every serious person comes to a standstill; they do not wish to be disappointed but only to be enlightened about the human condition as it truly is and as we experience it in ourselves. Whether we are learned or unlearned, with a solid or a cracked brain, we all clearly feel that "Love is the fulfilment of the Law.[679] Wherever we turn in our studies of humankind, we discover that Love alone can *solve* the riddle, and it must therefore be our goal and purpose. But when we genuinely seek it in ourselves, we find it is missing! If we see it in the past or the present, we are tempted to believe that it is the mere *appearance* of Love.

679 Rom 13:10.

In this way many people calm their consciences without considering how little they themselves can be helped, if everyone *else* lacks what alone constitutes true humanity. They must consider how what has actually *happened* could not possibly have come about, if true, deep Love had not many a time stirred the human heart and breathed into our existence a life and a meaning that has often taken centuries to dissipate and forget. I shall merely again remind readers here of the great lack that neither human Knowledge nor tongues of angels can remedy.[680] Just as Love is in itself intangible, so is its conception and growth in our hearts. We must not deceive ourselves into believing that self-love and sensual indulgence are the true *altruistic* Love; rather are they its most spiteful enemy under the mask of friendship. It is my firm conviction that without Christianity Love is impossible, and whoever places in Jesus their unselfish Love for the whole race and sees Him as subject to the same condition as us, must, if they hold to Jesus' positive assurances, either believe in Christ or despair.

These things need to be kept in mind if for no other reason than to recall that when I speak of the aptitude for true spiritual achievement, I am assuming *Christianity* to be the source. Otherwise people are incapable of seeking or accomplishing anything in the world of the spirit that can stand the test of Truth. This universal Love is possible for every Christian, of whatever people they belong to, for Truth belongs to no single person.[681] Moreover, what History confirms is no less certain: that a disparity of spirit among peoples of the world has not been revoked by Christianity. This is a consequence of the argument that how they are as a people, so do they become as Christians. Nor must we forget that it was the division of the hearts of one people's from another that Christianity sought to break down, not the differences in their spiritual circumstances. It wished to make all nations members of one spiritual body, but not all of them one and the same member![682] It sought to unite all human spirits within the spirit of Love and Truth, and to awaken, renew, and sanctify all human qualities and powers *in the service of* Truth. In what lasts for ever, in Love, it wished to make all people equal, though not 'in part' (which would be abolished, when complete Knowledge came), nor in gifts of the Spirit. These are renewed according to the needs of the kin and the eternal basic laws of temporal development, fulfilment, and edification.

In no sense does Christianity wish to *abolish* the Law, only to fulfil it.[683] There are peoples who call themselves Christian yet quarrel over their gifts, their advantages, and their flaws and then lay claim to their own excellence, dispute each other's deserts, and seek to be spiritually independent!. Yet this is not what they were called to do. They end up like the individuals or families who envy and combat each other in

680 1 Cor 13:1.

681 Rom 2:11. "For God does not show favouritism."

682 Rom 12:4-5; 1 Cor 12:12-14.

683 Mt 5:17.

order to be superior. This is what happens wherever the body is divided among warring members, and nothing can thrive.[684] Our world is rooted in altruistic, spiritual *Love*, and in this is revealed all spiritual Truth. So if people strive for the advantage in human Knowledge and regard their flaws as a shame to be brushed off, or at least concealed from themselves and others, the result will be a dismemberment of the body! They will manage all their human relations with a view to doing *without* others and, if possible, emphatically *surpassing* them. But they will end up like anyone who wishes to exhaust every sphere of Knowledge, or run every branch of trade. Everything gets bungled and nothing is completed. A ridiculous vanity, a foolish haughtiness, and an objectionable pride drive their interest and their attempt to prevent all true development and Learning. These are quite impossible without a friendly and humble interaction, a modest satisfaction with one's allotted role, and a loving acquisition of the work and the excellence of others.

History is in no doubt that this is precisely the offence of which the 18th century in particular is guilty, for it sought to detach itself from all previous ages. What we once saw in individuals we now see in all somewhat 'spirited' peoples: namely, an overwhelming desire to cut themselves off from all spiritual dependence and to be a law unto themselves, both spiritually and physically. In all such peoples we saw the same desire making itself known in the individual: in its various guises, 'freedom' is the common watchword and a misunderstood self-interest the common principle! The consequence has been the dissolution of all states and the enslaving of the people. An equally unavoidable effect has been the blackest spiritual darkness and the grossest barbarity, neither of which there has been any attempt to conceal.

However, it is in humanity's greatest interest that dangers are laid bare, so it is high time to pause and consider how to avoid these consequences. For those who know something about the human condition and the course of the world, the propagation of self-interest, the growth of the so-called sense of freedom, and the continuation of spiritual isolation give rise to, indeed conjure up, an exterior disintegration and an enslavement that we saw only the faint contours of in Napoleon's day.[685] Even if this had not been so, it is equally certain that all true Learning will soon perish. Instead, and already in the century which dreamed of universal enlightenment, we see the blackest darkness of ignorance pitch its camp not only over the peasant farmer's cottage but also over the altar, the throne, and the teacher's chair from which 'enlightenment' is trumpeted.

684 I Cor 12:25.

685 Napoleon Bonaparte (1769-1821) was a French military commander who staged a *coup d'état* in 1799 to make himself First Consul. Five years later the French Senate declared him Emperor. He won military victories and made alliances, but Russia defeated him in 1812, and in 1814 he was captured and exiled to the isle of Elba. He escaped and gathered a new army, but he was again defeated at the Battle of Waterloo (1815), and exiled to St. Helena, where he died. His codification of civil French law (the 'Napoleonic Code') was his greatest achievement.

I can only offer proof of this from the confines of my study-room. I am looking at the prospects for Learning at the beginning of the 19th century, and I only touch on this truth in order to remind readers that to find true Learning one should look to *History*. It is equally important that every people that wishes to advance true human development and enlightenment must abandon the conceited desire to do everything alone for itself, or to be the best at everything, and must look searchingly at itself to find out the particular role it has been granted. It should then set to work humbly and untiringly, and not out of envy quarrel with others about the roles *they* have been granted. It should rejoice at the spiritual wonders that generations and peoples can lovingly[686] secure for one another and at the glory of past ages.

If only these peoples possessed the Christian faith and thus a proper understanding of their own good! If only they had room in their hearts for the majestic, blessed feeling that the boundless kingdom of all Truth with its ineffable glory can be ours! If only they realised that this kingdom can through Love be owned by the peasant behind the plough as well as by the most powerful, most learned man on earth! If only they could see how foolish it is to compete and fight about anything other than what lasts for ever, and what alone can give children of the moment heavenly powers and joys that make temporal pursuits truly worthwhile and important. If only the peoples had hearts that would seize this genuinely heartfelt and incorruptible Love, and the sense to understand these pure and mighty truths, they would straightway dedicate all their efforts to developing and illuminating them in deed and truth. The time has come when all hindrances to the great work can be removed, and a living interaction take place. In the past this was almost impossible except through the pious wishes which we, next after God, must be grateful will one day be fulfilled.

Through the art of printing the way was cleared for Learning to spread throughout the lands of Europe. In the days of the Reformation, wherever the peoples were seized by the heavenly truth, the branches of Learning had numerous schools and students; and these were cultivated – as they should be at school, without self-willed differences – only under the wings of Christianity. All they had to do was to proceed onwards until the day when the university arrived of its own accord. By then the students had acquired both years and intelligence to choose, with mature deliberation, the subject and the calling to which through insight and experience they were best suited. But unfortunately their schooldays seemed so stale that they gradually grew bored with their protracted education and their strict schoolmasters. No sooner had they acquired a little down on their chins than they stole away and began on an academic path that had no other goal than to break with school constraints and seek their own counsel.

686 Grundtvig's Danish here (*i Kærlighed*, lit. in love) denotes the preservation of history as an act of love from one generation to the next.

If this had happened all at once and everywhere, all hope of true Learning would have been lost for the European peoples, who were clearly best suited to developing and promoting it. However, to the good fortune of humankind there were peoples who much later than the others *gave up on* this form of education. Indeed there were large numbers who had neither attended nor abandoned the old Latin schools. The former enabled the development of the intellect to realise that all human Learning must be *historical*. The latter nourished the hope that among the peoples there would be *some* families, admittedly fewer and fewer, who would open their eyes to the tangible Truth and their ears to its all-powerful voice. No insight is so qualified to temper scholarly arrogance, envy, and self-restriction than the insight that all true Learning must be historical; it must be gathered 'in part' through historical research, and gradually put together through the spirit of History. This same insight will also encourage the most tireless industriousness, together with the most animated and friendly interaction.

History surrounds us all – including previous generations from the beginning of time to the end of posterity. It is a source of Learning that cannot be exhausted for as long as anyone thirsts for Truth. It opens up a path where there is not only room for all but also a prize for each and every person with the wonderful quality that when it is won, everyone else also genuinely wins in spirit. Every people that has truly been a people in the spiritual sense also has its own history. There is no one better capable of treating and illuminating it if they wish to sanctify themselves in the Truth[687] and not just explain what they do not understand. The chronicles of the world, which depict the interaction of the various peoples and the links between the ages, are by their very nature a common heritage that none can justly arrogate to themselves. Everyone with good cause can acquire them, and since they incorporate the history of all the peoples and steer towards a common goal, it is clear that every step in History towards completeness and perfection is necessarily the fruit of a common labour and, wherever it is finished, a common gain! In the contemplation of History all futile bickering about the superiority of a people or a particular branch of scholarship must cease, for they *all* belong to History. It can be neither understood nor completed without them making its acquaintance. What the peoples have so far achieved, History must teach us. What they may be and what they may achieve, the future will determine. What was good or bad about a people or a culture belongs to those who acquire it for themselves, and it is irrelevant for those who set it aside, even if it has been exercised by their blood relations, for the Spirit testifies that Truth is spiritual.[688] All scholarly diligence asserts its value and

687 Jn 17:17-19.

688 I Jn 5:6. "And it is the Spirit who testifies, because the Spirit is the truth."

significance. What is achieved through working in the service of History is clearly achieved to the benefit of *all* humankind, and the individual branches of Learning receive abundant compensation for losing the appearance of totality by entering into a living connection and interaction with our ongoing human life. Linguistic analysis should no longer be regarded as dry and fruitless, for in our various languages we hear the living voices from days of old. They speak to us as uncorrupted memorials of the spirit and acts of previous generations; even their *corruption* is part of it.

Mathematics and Physics should therefore not attempt to climb the Queen's throne; History refuses their entry to it. They must also be free of all the suspicion and resentment that History throws on their poor, haughty devotees. In the reins of History they should reach the goal and the depth to which they are appointed without losing their way in the clouds or sinking into the abyss.

Poetry should no longer make believe that it can outdo History. It must *survey* it, or run its eye over it, for History has its highest flight and wings in a hiding-place. Poetry must *learn* from History how to understand itself as the voice both of the whole of History and of the individual ages and generations. It must learn to acknowledge its subservient role to Truth, and in its service reawaken the departed. Poetry must gather the qualities disseminated over the ages into a spiritual picture of the path of History and become a model for its illumination. Poetry must enter into a friendly covenant with all true Knowledge and Learning and reawaken them through its spirit. In return it will receive feathers of glory, penance for the clipped wings, and clear mirrors to help the foolish eyes. Philosophy must not be worshipped as an idol which, with empty hands, can enrich its disciples at odd moments and create worlds out of nothing. It must be neither feared nor forbidden, but must be respected and loved for its insight into History, for its judgement in its own cause, and for its philosophy of History and its history of Philosophy. It is forever incomplete, maturing its imperfect but ongoing awareness of humankind as it develops over time.

Revealed Theology must not be queried over the rank which History assigns it. Where History reigns, no other can reach it, any more than true Theology can attract any other kind, since our human development alone must be its purpose and its goal. Revealed Theology is no longer a strict chastener, but a wise counsellor who concludes his teaching and his counsel with the words: "You have now acquired the enlightened eyes of the intellect to realise the distinction between Good and Evil and Truth and Falsehood.[689] You can now see that I did not deceive you when I promised to lead you to Wisdom, provided that you trusted me for as long as your Reason was spiritually blind. If you now think yourself able to ignore my guidance and promises of power from on high, go ahead and try! You know the goal you are to reach and

689 Cf. Gen 3.

the sole conditions thereto obtaining. You cannot ignore them without deliberately closing your eyes and losing sight of them. You know that you cannot judge me until you have comprehended and illuminated me historically! Head towards a harbour of your own choosing!"

It is now easy to see how bright is the light which, in the contemplation of History, rises above the mutual dependence between the poorest, diligent collector and the wisest interpreter – and between reading, thinking, and experiencing. We can also see the significance of our day-to-day pursuits in the eyes of our scholars, and the importance of the scientific spirit in the eyes of our lay people. In the scientist doctors see not only their own eye but also a *legacy* for their children. In the ordinary man scholars see their forefathers and champions of Wisdom. In all useful activity we gradually discover spiritual traces that cast light on areas of our history that otherwise would remain in the dark. These traces also inform all legal activity with an honour and a demand for attention that incorporate it into the indirect scope of the Spirit, turning it into Art.

However, there is no point in painting a portrait which, however attractive the lustre of Truth's own colour-mix, nevertheless demands a sacrifice if it is to gladden and animate inwardly. Few can be bothered to bring this sacrifice to the altar. For Truth shouts out loud at the portrait: 'Give me your *heart*! Acknowledge your own insignificance, not only in the sight of Him whom you cannot comprehend but also in the sight of the entire race of which you are only a single, soon-to-be-invisible link. You may be appointed to a wonderful and everlasting connection to the whole chain, provided that you let yourself be penetrated and governed by the spirit of History, Love, and Truth. But if you seek to stand alone, you are no more than a powerless mortal worm in the clay that the spirit of History crushes in an instant. For History will attain its goal over the dust and decay of you and millions like you – just as easily *through* them as *by* them! This is not a thought that flatters pride or invites sensual pleasure, and many therefore avert their eyes from the serious countenance of History and throw themselves into the harlot's embrace of the moment either to sleep or dream according to the heart's delight.

As for you, Denmark! However much other peoples despise the lessons of History and defy its Learning, it cannot pass your people by just like that. It has its life solely in the sweet and poignant memory of the past and must watch with eyes of its own the dissolution and enslavement of a people who fail to take loving possession of the power and wisdom of their forefathers! You above all others are appointed to show the action of History as a living society in the spirit of our past generations. You above all must show a willing recognition of the precedence and excellence of others alongside your own smallness and impotence. Awake, you true sons of Denmark, awake! In her old age she puts you to the book and reminds you of her forefathers! Awake and work hard, each according to their ability and opportunity, so other peoples may see what History is and what it is capable of. Then they too may be aroused to seek their spiritual freehold and Learning in the only place where it can be found: in the revelation of the Spirit to humankind, in History!

8. Grundtvig's memorial rooms at Udby

It is entirely appropriate that Grundtvig's memorial rooms should be located at his birthplace in Udby, 90 km south of Copenhagen. In Grundtvig's time it took two days to get here – now it takes an hour or so by bus or car. In the large room pictured are Grundtvig's writing-desk (left), armchairs and folding-table (back) and bookcase (right). The memorial rooms are the site of Grundtvig's home in 1811-13 when he returned to Udby as curate for his father.

9. On the Relation between Learning, Experience, and Sound Common Sense (1817)

Introduction by Steen Tullberg

Since *On Religion and Liturgy* (1807) Grundtvig had been working towards the formulation of a Christian-based philosophy on the basis of Learning (Dan. *vidskab*). In a *Danne-Virke* context, this study follows on from *On the Philosophical Century* (1816); Grundtvig now regards Learning as deriving from the open-ended historical observation of people and their experiences down the ages, with the transformation of humankind as its ultimate aim.

In Grundtvig's view, the problem with contemporary Enlightenment thinking was that it brushed aside life's most important questions: where we come from, where we are going, what do life and death mean? If these questions are not answered, this life amounts to no more than "a brutish, craven satisfaction in eating and drinking, and a casting around in spiritual darkness" (p. 297). The remedy against this foolishness is Experience and sound Common Sense, which Grundtvig proceeds to mobilise on behalf of Christianity against the self-willed thinking that Enlightenment thinkers had pursued. He now rejects all misguided attempts to define 'Intellect', and he deliberately sets aside the academic discussion of the difference between Intellect and Reason that had occupied philosophy since Kant. Instead he argues for "assured clear concepts" whose "assuredness and clarity... can be measured by whether ordinary common sense can grasp them" (p. 307). Common sense derives from the Latin, *sensus communis*, and does not condemn faith, but only superstition. Common sense also dictates that self-consciousness is the arbiter of Truth, for no one can deny their own existence or their own experience. In turn, it is from experience that we derive true Knowledge. True *Learning* is neither more nor less than the spiritual application of Common Sense.

Grundtvig goes on to distinguish between inner and outer experience – corresponding to historical Knowledge and historical Learning. The latter *rests* on the former, but a further distinction is necessary – between being sure (*sikker*) and being certain (*vis*). Being *sure* has to do with what cannot go wrong, whereas being *certain* has to do with what cannot be denied. Being sure is based on *outer* experience, whereas being certain is based on *inner* experience. To the latter belongs the agreement or unity of imagination, feeling, and intellect; to the former the agreement of sight, hearing and the "hand-feeling", meaning the sense of touch.

The important distinction that Grundtvig draws between historical *Knowledge* and historical *Learning* can therefore be construed as Knowledge being descriptive historiography, and Learning being an 'inner' digested synthesis of a series of 'outer' facts. The validity of this synthesis is tested by whether all the intellectual abilities harmonise inwardly with each other in their application to the purpose in hand. While historical Knowledge can at the most allow one to be *sure*, true Learning grants *certainty*.

It is common knowledge that at the end of the 17th and the beginning of the 18th century, and after a lengthy pause, people again began to talk about 'real' philosophy. In the opinion of many, this ought to be more than an 'art of thought' (Logic). They argued that Experience and Common Sense were the only sources of Wisdom from which one could draw one's Learning. In Germany this tied the tongue for a while with Wolffish[690] syllogisms, but in England and France they continued to talk away, with Newton[691] and Locke[692] lending them weight – until Wolff's sewing cotton had to snap as soon as it was required to carry them all. In consequence, around the time of the Peace of Aachen[693] it became common even in Germany to refer *everything* to Experience and Common Sense, and to relinquish or ignore anything that seemed to disagree with this.

This lasted for a generation or so – the measured reign of all human opinion – and then along came Kant.[694] In the age that followed, Experience and Common Sense counted for little or nothing in the Schools of Philosophy, where 'categories',[695] pure 'I-ness' (spiritual egoism),[696] and intellectual intuition minted their philosophical coins, or rather, their scholarly bank-checks. The rate of exchange rose and fell with the issuer's personal credit – with the blind faith in his currency as accepted by the bank. The pithy Swiss[697] called this, very appropriately, a 'complete bankruptcy' that

690 Christian Wolff (1679-1754), German philosopher, mathematician, and scientist best known as the German spokesman of the Enlightenment.

691 Isaac Newton (1643-1727) developed the principles of modern physics, including the laws of motion. These were published in *Mathematical Principles of Natural Philosophy* (1687), the single most influential book on physics.

692 John Locke (1632-1704), empiricist philosopher and political liberalist, whose idea of a 'social contract' between government and the people inspired the USA after its Declaration of Independence in 1776. His *Essays on the Law of Nature* (1654) argued that all human conduct is governed by a natural moral law and that all knowledge, including moral knowledge, is derived from experience.

693 The Peace of Aachen (French: Aix-la-Chapelle) in 1748 ended the Austrian War of Succession.

694 Immanuel Kant (1724-1804) was the most influential German philosopher in the Age of Enlightenment. In his *Critique of Pure Reason* (1781), one of the greatest works in the history of philosophy, he attempted to synthesize rationalism and empiricism. He believed that scientific knowledge, morality, and religious belief all rested on the same foundation of human autonomy. In an essay, *Perpetual Peace: A Philosophical Sketch* (1795), he argued that universal democracy and international cooperation was the path to universal peace.

695 In his theory of cognition Kant divides the forms of empirical judgement into 12 classes, or 'categories'.

696 'I-ness' equals individuality in the work of Johann Fichte (1762-1814), the co-founder of the German idealism movement and a pioneer in the area of self-consciousness. He argued that the creative activity of the pure 'I' is the foundation of cognition.

697 Johannes Müller (1752-1809) was a Swiss historian who published the much-admired *History of the Swiss Confederation* (1786-1808).

the intellect had played! In both the West and the North, where Philosophy has never been able to thrive properly, there remained a well-represented 'party' who still adhered verbally to Experience and Common Sense. This was always a party in opposition, whose entire strength and wisdom lay in *denying* things. Theirs was easy idle talk, as when the child says 'No' long before it says 'I', and, while it is still learning to speak, says 'No' to all the wisdom of the world!

If we think about this seriously, we must realise that outside the Schools of Philosophy what was called 'Enlightenment and Philosophical Spirit, Rationality and Independent Thought' was generally expressed most often in the *denial* of things. These included the denial of 'necessity', of 'reality', and of the possibility of a supernatural revelation. To these were added the following three: the denial of Heaven and Hell, and frequently of God; the denial of an interaction between spirit and body; and the denial of the Fall and the testament of History. These philosophers then employed the term 'unprejudiced' to mean much the same as 'enlightened', 'philosophical', and 'thinking for one's self'.

The following questions were put to these enlightened, independent thinkers: What *are* we human beings? Where did we come from, and where are we heading? How are we to understand our strange circumstances? – the inner and outer struggle in which we find ourselves, the discrepancy between our desire and our ability, the undeniable way in which we exceed ourselves, together with History's tale of our determined desire and need for community with the invisible? How could they explain the narrative of that revelation on earth and the wondrous events that seem to prove it, or at least showed how faith in it gave supernatural powers? Can these powers come out of *nothing*?

When these questions were asked of them, how did they respond? Was not their answer that as far as History is concerned everyone knew that it was not to be trusted! All that talk of 'deepest desire' was mere infatuation! The 'soaring flight' that was admittedly found in Poetry was the work of fantasy! We exist with our abilities and weaknesses, our virtues and vices, and our wisdom and folly. To comprehend *why* we are this way, where we come from and where we are going, is to break our brains in vain with 'impossibilities' and to waste the precious time that should be used on useful employment, the fulfilling of one's duties, and the enlightenment of one's fellow-human being. Furthermore, it is quite probable that we *did* come from nothing and that we *do* become nothing! Or, when we are finished here, we go to the moon! Who has not, with quiet attention, coolly considered such responses and asked: Is that an *answer*? Are you any the *wiser* now? Can you now proceed calmly to your post and to your death? Do you know what your post *is*, what life and death *are*?

Is not this 'freedom from prejudice' the most terrifying inanity? The denial of all that our forefathers believed could enlighten humankind about its condition and purpose? There is no *substitute*, no *enlightenment* at all, only a brutish, craven satisfaction in eating and drinking, and casting around in spiritual darkness. And they call this 'enlightenment'! This is to be praised as a work of mature Reason – an effect of the miracle by which human eyes are opened so they become like God![698] This is the 'enlightenment' that you have already begun to convey, as you destroy in the people the Faith that brings them light and peace, in order if possible to lead them to the place where you yourself are sitting in darkness!

I write from memory of the days ten years ago when in the transition to serious manhood I fell to thinking about the wisdom of the times, about my innermost being, my task as teacher of the people, and my occupation as teacher and preacher.[699] The immediate consequence of these lonely considerations became visible in my study of Religion and Liturgy;[700] the latest consequence can be seen here.

It may well be asked, What has this to do with here and now? How does this belong to a scholarly study of Experience and Common Sense? My answer is, Do they think that I write studies in order to win prizes for philosophical style or in order to arouse and encourage especially the young to reflect and to use Common Sense? And is it too much for me to add that in my experience the 'enlightenment' of the times should be judged by Common Sense? Is it too much to urge everyone who has not yet tried this to do so, to then note whether Common Sense makes the same sense in them as it does in me, and to press them to open their ears to the Truth without asking how unpleasant its voice may sound as regards much within it and many around it?

Nor is it too much to warn the young in particular of the mistake that I and many others made, when we came across the folly and delusion of the Age of Enlightenment. These included *blaming* Experience and Common Sense, the very antidotes to folly which would in time have prevented it! There is clearly a sore need for such a warning when we visit the Schools of Philosophy of the times, a visit that we are compellingly drawn towards making when we discover the emptiness of this 'universal enlightenment'. When we do so, we are sure to find at the very least a whole system of pure denials – a complete self-contradiction, like a building made of nothing!

However, before we comment on this 'visit', which I also know about from experience, it seems appropriate to touch on the universal relationship between Time and the Schools of Philosophy. It might be imagined that in a time when Philosophy is claimed to be a substitute for Christianity and to surpass it in simplicity and handiness as much as credit notes surpass banknotes, the liveliest exchanges would be happening between true philosophers and every scholar among the reading public. The philosophers are going to replace the apostles! Surely their greatest endeavour will

698 Gen 3:5.

699 'Ten years ago', in 1807, Grundtvig was teaching privately and occasionally preaching publicly.

700 Grundtvig's essay, 'On Religion and Liturgy' had been published in *Theological Monthly* in February 1807. See ch. 3.

be to present us with a universal enlightenment that is compelling and intelligible! Surely their writings will become the devotional books of all enlightened people and the object of all scholarly research and communication in oral lectures to the man in the street. In brief, we were led to believe that the study of Philosophy would be treated as a matter for universal salvation. For that was how Bible reading and Bible study had been treated, and no one wanted to be known to be taking things *less* seriously as regards their enlightenment and convictions when drawing on their *own* source! All the more did they seek to banish all ignorance and, if possible, make *all* men *equally* wise.

We can be quite certain, however, that at least in Denmark barely one in a hundred scholars – not to mention every other educated person – had actually *read*, let alone *understood*, the works of the most famous philosophers. Nor did they know any more about them than what they had allowed into their reading for the makeshift pattern from which they cut the training cloth for our state civil servants. To put it plainly, this was as good as *nothing*, when it came to knowing not only what the wise masters' intentions were *against*, but most importantly, what their *own* intentions were!

By 'improving' on the biblical passage[701] Kant arrived at a rather smart formula for moral principles that nonetheless did not hold water. It could just as well have been exchanged for 'Fulfil your destiny (and what that *is* you must decide for yourself!), and pursue your analogy with the animals.' That was indeed what we came to hear in due course. Kant was believed to have disproved all the old evidence for the existence of God and to have introduced a new argument whereby Our Lord lost His *sovereignty* but retained a sort of constitutional throne as executor of the Moral Law. However, he had no power to punish even the most spiteful attacks on life, nor, without leave, to interfere in the slightest with the freedom of humankind. Fichte[702] proved that a true revelation could only contain what human reason could grasp, and was therefore superfluous except in a time dedicated mostly to the senses – which of course ours was not. This too we came to hear about in due time. But *how* these good people had gone about producing such improper evidence, and *how* they could have backed Our Lord into such a corner, or *why*, when they had Him there, they did not make Him recreate the world according to their *own* clever brains, or perhaps do so themselves! – how this reflects their *wisdom* is left to each of us to decide!

All our contemporaries know this to be more or less the case with the general knowledge of Philosophy at the start of the 19th century, and is it so very different now? I have no doubt that since then the history of the new philosophers' opinions has become much longer and presumably much more clarified thanks to our university

701 Mt 7:12. 'Do to others what you would have them do to you'. Kant raised this 'golden rule' to the level of 'categorical imperative'.

702 Johann Fichte (1762-1814), German philosopher, who considered 'Ichheit' or consciousness of self to be the basis of all knowledge.

teaching! But can we then conclude that more than one in a hundred scholars, old and young, knows any more than the *history* of the philosophical systems of the time? And are we not tempted towards satire every time we hear of a widespread 'philosophical way of thinking' and all its organisation according to basic philosophical premises? Are we not tempted to ask whether the altar is not being raised to the unknown god,[703] and whether that god is 'Philosophy' as expected and the one whose teaching is to be disseminated? Or perhaps it is the hallmark of the philosophical century that Truth has fallen to *pieces*, so there can be as many 'true' philosophies as there are holes in the level of tolerance? Perhaps every philosopher is good in himself – Kant in himself and the schoolteacher in himself? Perhaps we do not even need to know the greatest thinkers of the age in order to think properly about *everything*, and naturally also about *them* too?

Common Sense becomes exceedingly giddy when it joins the company of such wise people, so let us instead turn to the *Schools* of Philosophy; perhaps it is not their fault that there is so much prevarication. The first thing we come to here is of course the door, above which are printed in large Gothic letters the words, *procul abeste profani!*[704] This means more or less that we should take off our shoes because we are entering a holy place.[705] We must leave *outside* the door our Experience, Common Sense, and our mother-tongue, even if it is Gothic, and crawl in on all fours so as to be transformed from an animal to a human being – and even to a devil of a fellow! Certainly, these are difficult circumstances in which we find ourselves, but what will we not give for a drink of water, when we are thirsty – or at least what will we not promise when we are in dire straits!

Let us be serious, though, since this is not something we should be making fun of – except, in similar circumstances when we would be almost *forced* to laugh or cry. So in all seriousness, there is no doubt that the great philosophers who wished to enlighten the world spoke a language that we first had to learn before they could be understood. Each of them had their own philosophy and their own language. They often used the same *ad hoc* words with different meanings and constantly complained that not even their own sincerest supporters and studious listeners understood them. They all denied the right of our common human intellect and experience to *appraise* their Learning and they refused to answer for each other's judgements. The questions now are first whether it was possible for even all the scholars to understand what they actually *meant*, and second what they ultimately gained from *going* to such extremes? In answer to the first, it is enough to say, No.

703 Acts 17:23.
704 'The profane keep themselves out of sight!'
705 Ex 3:5.

In answer to the second we need to pause for a moment to make an appropriate comment.

Either the major philosophers – Kant, Fichte, Schelling, and their train – really did disagree completely, or they simply *thought* that they did. In either case whoever was to judge their disputes had either to decide who was right, or to see an agreement that was hidden from the philosophers themselves. The said person therefore clearly had to be a greater philosopher than they were – and we can say with the utmost certainty that the philosophers wrote not for their disciples but for their masters!

Whoever did not regard himself as such a master and yet could not accept the irrationality of trusting blindly in any one of them – a practice that would be incompatible with their own philosophy – was none the wiser when he took his leave of them.

In these circumstances we can see that it was perfectly reasonable and indeed quite wise of the majority of scholars to let the great philosophers remain independent minds in the strictest sense. What is so incomprehensible is how Common Sense could allow these scholars to criticise a philosophy they did not understand and to call their own ignorance of the human condition and human relations 'enlightenment'! In fact, it is so incomprehensible that we might cheerfully claim that they never did so! And yet they suffered from a fatally crippled intellect which they called 'sound'! And in a sense, in the jargon of the time it was! They called their 'activity' in everything 'Experience'; they called the measuring-rod by which they evaluated themselves the 'yardstick for God and Human Beings' – and that was their 'philosophy'!

Every sensible person must rightly argue that Experience and Common Sense need to reinstate their offended rights before we can talk about 'true Learning' – or indeed about *anything* at all. It is not *off* the beaten track here but very much *on* it to regard a little more closely what we are actually talking about, so we can find out what has beguiled the majority of our noble thinkers into declaiming against the foundation of all sound thinking. Simultaneously we can see how this foundation is linked to the incontrovertible assertion that History is the only proper source for human Learning.

What is Common Sense, and what is Experience?

To answer this we must first ask: What is 'Common Sense'? For at least on this point the philosophical century has undoubtedly been all at sea and unable to agree on where and what it is. While one philosopher saw it as the tool of practical Reason,[706] another argued it was the schoolmaster of Reason, and a third, under the name of Intelligence, called it a god! 'Common Sense' was turned topsy-turvy until no one could work out what it meant.

706 A reference to Kant's moral philosophy, where Reason motivates action.

In response let us turn straight to Experience, for that is clearly the only thing that can confirm anything. Without Experience all disputes about the meaning of words are empty altercation. And when one man has got it into his head that this word means that and another thinks it means something else, the argument is endless. Let us first ask what the phrase means in ordinary parlance and then see if the meaning holds good for human conditions in general rather than confusing the issue.

We know that people with Common Sense understand it to mean the ability to think properly and conceptualise clearly. For them Reason defines the ability to think in general, whatever age or class one belongs to. So they do not exclude the infant or the insane, only their *intellects*; the first is a minor, the second is a madman. In ordinary parlance Common Sense must designate the ability to think in clear and sensible *ideas*. This is found in everyone who has reached the age of discretion, and it cannot be called 'madness'. We would do well to follow this usage rather than change its meaning according to our *own* thinking. For that is stupid and has caused linguistic confusion[707] in our so-called 'philosophical' books, which in turn has led to the need to have them translated before they can be understood! The philosophers even admitted this by saying their books needed to be 'popularized', and then in all modesty left the task to their disciples! These in turn had to become their masters in order to carry out what the philosophers themselves had declared was impossible: to express their meaning in intelligible words! If we sought to discuss another concept/idea than what is popularly understood as Common Sense', we should require another expression. But as things are, it actually makes no difference, since the philosophers' inconsistency (the best side of their systems!) has allowed Common Sense – which they will have nothing to do with – to retain its validity. This is what ordinary people use on a daily basis. They cannot just let it alone and move on, for that simply unsettles them! So it is now obvious that Common Sense is not only an essential condition for true *Learning*; it is the only condition that can *generate* it. In this regard, the sole difference between the least and the most gifted person is that the latter's intellect is broader, lighter, more penetrative and embracing than the former's.

It might be objected that this too is no more than a battle of words, for the philosophers were not such fools as to disparage Common Sense in *this* definition. When they dismissed its right to pass judgement, they undoubtedly meant only in the *inferior* sense – in what is known as *General* Common Sense, *sensus communis*. We could justly oppose this on several grounds but there is no need to do so. We could admit that the philosophers only ever gave credit to the same intelligence that we all have to some degree. Yet they clearly asserted that General Common Sense is too unqualified

707 Gen II:1-9.

to comprehend and too unauthorised to judge what they called General Universal Truth – and this where their folly lies.

If they had just said that Truth contained facets that General Common Sense could not comprehend, they would merely be repeating an ancient and undeniable truth! But they claimed that the view of Truth which General Common Sense could not comprehend was the *only* one that could guarantee a reasonable certainty. It followed from this that all those who were *limited* by General Common Sense could have no reasonable certainty about spiritual truths and indeed *deserved* none! For any *un*reasonable certainty had of course to be dismissed as idiocy.

However, it is extremely important to realise how in their discussion of universal enlightenment these philosophers undoubtedly exhibited a general lethargy and ignorance. It is common knowledge that they called the belief that rested on History and Experience a prejudice that no sensible person would build on, and they dismissed all forms of authority in spiritual matters. Yet far from *proving* this assertion or what they otherwise called 'truth' in the General Common Sense, they elevated themselves above it in both ideas and language and insisted that either those who possessed only General Common Sense should be completely indifferent to spiritual truths or they should take the philosopher's own words for it.

They were to do so despite their rejection of any divine power with which to guarantee their truthfulness; this led not to the blind belief in authority they had condemned but to a superstition that Common Sense emphatically rejects.

There is no denying that to reach a state of reasoned Learning, sufficient understandable evidence is required; and to reach a state of reasoned certainty, an unmistakable sign of witness credibility is demanded. Otherwise all thinking is guesswork and all belief imagination. But even this is not enough for them. For these 'philosophers' could not even prove their theses on the basis of General Common Sense without committing violence to themselves, and without requiring a far more crass and unreasonable orthodoxy than the one they condemned. They even made the outrageous demand for *acclamation*, using our General Common Sense for arguments that they could not prove to anyone but themselves! This is quite clear when we look at the meaning of the word *proof*.

'Proof' in the spiritual sense is quite clearly the same as *showing, explaining, and presenting* in the physical sense. For something to be regarded as 'proof' it has to be palpable to the Intelligence! Proof that something is true means that it is irrefutable; it cannot be denied without denying oneself. Proof that something is a lie means that it *cannot* be true – unless an incontrovertible truth can be a lie! Everything that is justifiably called 'proof' must be as clear as two plus two makes four, as one is one and I am I!

What we call the foundation of identity[708] is clearly the foundation of Truth in us. And what we call the principle of contradiction is not really a separate principle but the consequent principle of Truth. It is the chain of argument in the great foundational principle which in its totality means Yes is Yes and No is No. Yes cannot be No and No cannot be Yes; they cannot be the same.

The unshakeable foundation for this principle of Truth is self-consciousness, which carries the principle itself and is demonstrated incontrovertibly by it. So if anyone says, 'I do not exist', they are actually *demonstrating* their palpable existence and have convicted themselves of being a liar. For they have said, 'The true 'I' in me hereby declares that it is not real.' In other words what can clearly be referred to self-consciousness (and only to that) has in fact been proved! In this awareness the self - the soul - has its place from which it cannot move without being mentally unsettled and losing its sanity. In self-consciousness it must understand and conceive all that *can* be understood and conceived. It can only infer or conjecture what is outside this.

In the obscure learning of our times I therefore believe that a clear light is shining for Common Sense! We can see how little, if anything, has been proved or disproved in the many books full of so-called 'proof', for these contain only page after page of contradictions, conceits, and conjectures. For the light to shine properly on True Learning we must consider again what 'Experience' actually is.

Experience, people say, is what is gathered down the years if one uses one's intelligence. What has not yet been experienced has not yet been understood, people say. And they are undoubtedly right. For we can hardly express what Experience is more truthfully and precisely than to say that it is an intelligent understanding of specific impressions - which means that one must get to *feel* what one must get to *know*. Obviously what one has not got to *know* one has not yet *experienced*, just as one cannot have experienced something in depth without having got to know it to one's benefit.

Consequently, we cannot understand anything that we have not fully experienced. Experience is therefore the only way for us to *true Learning*, and Learning is nothing more than a spiritual use of Common Sense; or it is when language is used to define the nature of the human being that reveals itself in such an endeavour and with an aptitude for such spiritual experience.

If there is any justifiable objection to this, it can only be that the fundamental principle of Truth, which must be eternal, cannot be an 'experience'. Strictly speaking we should answer that it *is* an experience, but an *eternal* one. We do not need to pursue a study that from here on could acquire the appearance of hair-splitting sophistry, since

708 In Logic, the law of identity states that each thing or being is identical with itself, is one and consistent in itself. The German philosopher, Gottfried Leibniz (1646-1716), formulated the law in its simplest form: 'Everything is what it is'.

by calling the principle of Truth an *eternal* experience, we must use the word '*experience*' in a more exclusive sense than usual, so that it becomes synonymous with the eternal introspection which with God is the same as self-consciousness. Here we are speaking of the temporal human being, who comes to the eternal principle of Truth via the path of Experience. Our self-consciousness is an *experience*, a basic human experience, through which we all come to the foundation of all Truth for the human intellect: the image in our minds of God's eternal self-consciousness, of His eternal Truth.

Only one question remains – but one that is the most difficult to answer. This is not because there is any doubt that it must be answered truthfully, but because it is not easy to see *how* it can be answered in a way that says neither more than can be proved, nor less than is necessary to introduce the subject: How does Learning come from Experience? I shall make the attempt below in the hope that even if I make minor mistakes in the argument, the result will in general be sufficiently clear and unmistakable.

We have seen that all reasonable certainty is only achieved by applying to Experience the basic principle of Truth. It is human Experience generated through History that alone can produce true Learning. Nothing else really needs to be proved, except to demonstrate the unfailing connection between the Experience of the human race and the individual. We must prove the *reality* of spiritual experience and define the conditions degrees of its reliability.

The difficulty of doing so is immediately obvious when we consider that we come to the basic principle of Truth only through self-consciousness. There is no denying that, to begin with, this only assures us of our *physical* existence, then gradually our *spiritual* existence, and only at the end of our days our *full comprehension*. That makes the path of Learning long and hard, and even more difficult to mark out and describe than to find and follow. Perhaps the safest way is to make the wrong side-paths *recognisable*, for if we can avoid them and stay on the *right* path, then with every step taken we will enjoy a greater security than the best guidebook could give us. We ought also to mention the dependable road signs on the noble path of Learning, so that with eyes open we cannot mistake them.

Firstly, everything that has come down to us as Learning, indeed every *concept*, rests undeniably on Experience. The only difference is whether an experience is confused or clear, interrupted or completed. In the light of these experiences our concepts are either well-defined or blurred, singular or universal, firm or shaky, certain or doubtful, true or false. Obviously the next question is to what extent and with what certainty we can experience *spiritual* things; for 'physical' and 'spiritual' are by no means opposites like Truth and Falsehood, despite the bold claim that they are! They in no way cancel each other out, but can be linked through a kindly interaction that assumes a joint reality and a common origin. Anyone who has seriously studied the human condition will undoubtedly aver that we consist of the physical and the spiritual which together make up a whole. They merge in our self-consciousness, which is limited not just to our physical or our spiritual, but to our whole *human* existence – to the reasoning personality, which is a communion of the two!

Day by day we are convinced of this wondrous communion when we speak and when we listen, for then we have the experience that corresponds closest to our compounded consciousness. Through our sense of hearing we experience not only something physical – namely, sound – but also something spiritual – namely, the Word. For the Word is nothing but the spiritual stepping out into the sphere of Experience and revealing itself to spirits.

These remarks are only incidental, however. For the Word is so important and wondrous that it demands a study of its own, not to exhaust it but merely to discover ourselves *within* it. I only mention it here because it is an indisputable witness to the inner link between spirit and body that reveals itself even in the world of the senses. It is an unshakeable wall against all idealism, against all denial of the reasoning reality of the physical. We all know for sure, not just the poet or the individual but everyone who uses their intelligence and their senses, that we can and do experience truly spiritual things, but primarily in connection with the physical body. Whether or not we can acquire true spiritual Learning must depend on our ability to gather it through such mixed experience! For a *purely* spiritual experience seems impossible for earthly beings as such – as the living expression of the communion between spirit and body – as a living soul! We can see that this not only appears to be but actually *is* so, when we consider our sphere of Experience, for this is limited to ourselves, and so our self-consciousness is both our first and our last *experience*. And if our self-consciousness is mixed, then so too is human experience in general. We cannot progress further than we actually are without losing our senses and then the only thing we experience is insanity.

This was how on the road to Experience we came to the insight that in our mortal clay there is no *knowledge*, no *direct* cognition or perception of the Eternal or of God. We can get no further than to understanding ourselves, and from there to embracing God and acknowledging His image in ourselves. This necessarily presupposes a genuine fundamental *being*, which in us humans is a true image, an eternal existence that reveals itself temporally in our clay.

However, the certainty of this is matched only by the certainty of proving the impossibility that temporal humankind can comprehend God, or can proceed beyond a figurative image of Him, or achieve complete fulfilment before the end of our days. It follows of necessity that all true human Learning must be *historical*, and raises the important question as to whether a genuine possibility for historical experience definitely exists. These are questions that can only be fully answered through our *experience*. It is nevertheless already clear that we must distinguish between external and internal experience, not because any external experience can take place without an internal one, or any internal experience can be proved in conjunction with an external one, but because there is a genuine, honest *difference* between them. No true Learning can occur before we have a reliable internal experience of our transcendental existence, before we are spiritually self-conscious, before we can prove that we have a soul, before we can demonstrate the timeless incompatibility of Truth and Falsehood, and before we understand the fundamental premise of Truth so that we can apply it to ourselves and to humankind in general.

It is absolutely certain that thanks to History past generations can be the genuine subject of our experience, both the external experience that grants historical knowledge and the internal that provides historical Learning. Learning must then rest on Knowledge and develop out of it both belatedly and piecemeal. Moreover, it is a proven fact that only a completely internal experience can give assuredness, where imagination, feeling, and intellect make for a total accord. It is the same with a completely *external* experience, a similar accord between the corresponding senses of sight, hearing, and touch. From this we can conclude that what we have experienced through imagination or feeling is still not *certainty*, even though it may be assured enough. It offers no obvious, incontrovertible *concept* and cannot be taken for a universal truth unless its infallibility can be guaranteed by an *external* experience.

Here I clearly distinguish between being assured and being certain. I call 'assured' what is undeniable, 'certain' what cannot go wrong. I shall also note that I am aware that this significant difference requires further explanation and that much of what I have said about History as the great *universal Experience* needs further elaboration. The reason why I stop here is that I need to say a few words to show that we have reached our destination, and that even if there were room, this is not the place to add more.

What I set out to prove in this study was that all human Knowledge and Learning is based on Experience; that only complete experiences provide assured clear concepts; and that the assuredness and clarity of these concepts can be measured by whether *General Common Sense* can grasp them. I believe I have proved this to be so. It was essential to conduct the case from two sides before I proceeded to discuss how History provides enlightenment for the human condition. First, I wished to make plain the folly of discussing human 'concepts' that *exceed* Experience, and of 'proof' that Common Sense cannot grasp. And second, no one can justly argue that the historical view of which I speak is anything *but* Experience, nor is it intended to create assurances that are incomprehensible to Common Sense. I am seeking to help whoever needs it towards the insight that what modern philosophers publish as higher wisdom can only be false and inadequate. It can only stem from unsure and unclear inward experiences, since they cannot prove their claims indisputably nor present their evidence intelligibly.

I have also sought to demonstrate to whoever needs it that when I point to History as the source of all true Learning, I am not presenting anything new beyond the claim that is as old as the solid reflection that I am refreshing and contending to its full extent. It is the claim that Experience is the source of all true Learning, that Common Sense is the yardstick for all our ideas, and that the principle of contradiction is our only infallible measuring-rod. Finally I have sought to show whoever needs it that what made the noble philosophers fearful of Experience and Common Sense was partly the uncertainty as to what these concepts actually mean, and partly the consequent reluctance to settle for assurance where certainty was impossible. Or to settle for the testimony of infallible external experience where the internal could not be clearly felt. Or to admit the credibility of a truth that could not be comprehended and therefore to seek refuge in individual, uncertain, and incomplete experiences. These they attempted to remove from the sphere of Experience and the judgement-room of Common Sense by fancying themselves and others to be of a higher *nature*, and by regarding their conflict with Experience and their scorn of Common Sense to be the mark of higher wisdom.

If I have moderately succeeded in this, then I am delighted and trust that readers are not fully satiated; in other words, that they will question the relation between the Experience of the human race and the individual, that they will ask how they can be merged into one, about the degrees of absoluteness, assuredness, and certainty, and about much else besides. My intention with these studies has been to draw the readers' attention to the many questions that remain to be answered, and to make it clear that Learning is still *in its infancy*, indeed in its swaddling-clothes. It is such a naughty – and in its cockiness – *ridiculous* child when it pretends to be an adult with authority. I also hope, in succeeding studies and on the basis of my own experience, to define and illuminate in every possible way, God willing, the relation between the experience of the human race and of the individual.

So, far from seeking to hide the holes in my own learning, I would much rather point them out so that others can fill them, and those who cannot may learn the limited goals of their own wisdom. Far from attempting to *conceal* the truth that so far Learning has been both rare and unsatisfactory, and is still unavailable to the majority – unsatisfactory for the wisest who genuinely seek certainty – I shall do everything within my power to illuminate this truth. That is what is needed if we are to promote the advance of true Learning – and woe betide those who do not wish to do so!

Whoever seeks to encourage Learning must love Truth, on whichever path they meet it; they will find it in the whole of History and within themselves. So pleasant is the human condition that just as we do not need to have the sun in our hand to be assured of light and warmth, nor do we need to *comprehend* the Truth, the spiritual sun, in order to be illuminated and warmed by it. All we need is to open our *hearts* to

Truth. For the Light has come into the world,[709] since the world did not wish to, or could not, come to the Light. Truth itself came to earth to bear witness to Truth, and whoever believes the witness can experience the power of Truth in their innermost being. Only then will they be qualified to understand its voice and to know and pursue its path through Time.

The conclusion is, as always, that if we believe in Christ, we can manage without true Learning – but we cannot help but develop it! If one rejects this, one is left to walk in the dark. And even if one could steal the *shadow* of the whole Truth, one would not of course thereby gain its power or its salvation; in fact one would gain nothing.

709 Jn 1:8ff; 12:46.

10. History and Naturalism, or the Illumination of Time and Space (1865)

Introduction by Kim Arne Pedersen[710]

In this article Grundtvig, now over 80, confronts Darwin's argument for a materialistic, biological approach to life, and produces a summary of his own anthropology. Since its conception in the first decade of the 19th century Grundtvig's core view has not changed in his insistence on a God-centred universe. There are two reasons why the article is included here. Firstly, despite his advancing years, Grundtvig feels the need to – and is able to – reactivate his criticism of German idealism from the *Danne-Virke* period – demonstrating that it was a lifelong conviction. Secondly, he shows a knowledge of the latest currents in the literature on natural science in his criticism of Thomas Huxley (1825-95), nicknamed "Darwin's bulldog". It is most likely that Grundtvig had learned about Huxley from the *Danish Journal of Popular Accounts in Natural Science*, which in 1865 carried a lengthy article on Huxley's book of the same name: *Evidence as to Man's place in Nature* (1863).[711] Publication had been preceded by a stormy debate in Oxford three years earlier, when Huxley was confronted by the Lord Bishop of Oxford, Samuel Wilberforce (1805-73), who wanted to know whether Huxley was descended from an ape on his mother's side or on his father's side! To this Huxley responded that he would rather be descended from an ape than from a man who misused his great talents to suppress debate.

The *Danish Journal* begins by noting that the question of the human relation to the animal kingdom and specifically to the apes has been "much discussed in recent years, where some have regarded the kinship between humans and apes to be so intimate that they had no hesitation in declaring that humans must descend (given Darwin's hypothetical metamorphosis of species) from some form of ape."

The journal's editor adds that if a natural scientist did not know of "the spiritual and moral superiority of this two-legged animal over the other animals", he would jump to the conclusion that apes and humans belonged to one and the same family. The editor balances between regarding the human being as merely a creature of nature, and – as is the tradition in Christianity – emphasising our special status in creation. This is presumably what Grundtvig is alluding to when he speaks of an anthropology in which the human being is regarded as a "two-legged mammal" (314). Grundtvig is also aware of other relevant works of the time. When he mentions that in the "schoolboys' natural history book" the human being is defined as "a mammal with

710 This article, transcribed by Elisabeth A. Glenthøj, was motivated by, and is partly annotated by, Uffe Jonas, to both of whom the editor is indebted; it receives its first-ever publication here.

711 Danish source: *Tidsskrift for populære Fremstillinger af Naturvidenskaben*, 3. rk., 2. bd., s. 308-336.

an upright walk", he is referring to *The Animal Kingdom. A Teaching Primer for the Upper School*, published in 1855.[712] For good reason its author, the zoologist Christian Lütken (1827-1901), does not refer to *On The Origin of Species*, which Charles Darwin (1809-82) published in 1859, but takes as his starting-point the work of the Swedish natural scientist Carl Linné (1707-78), who in 1758 had designated *homo sapiens* as the only member of the species *homo*.

Grundtvig's approach is to trace a historical link between a non-Christian way of thinking that has its roots back in prehistoric times and Huxley's biological view. From the early days of Christianity there has been a struggle between the historical and the natural view of the world, as well as between the spiritual and the eternal. We distinguish between what we see in Space and what happens in Time. We acquire knowledge of Space through all five senses, but a sense of Time through the Word as *heard*. Here in the 1860s, Grundtvig therefore insists on the philosophical observation that he made already in the 1810s, namely that sense perception and the processing of this through experience is the only source of human knowledge. This does not mean, however, that he accepts a materialist picture of the physical world as the sole form of reality. In protest against the belief that the external senses are the only thing we can be sure of, Grundtvig argues that they can lead to an assumption "which conflicts with the laws which, with our certain knowledge of objects in Space, we have concluded must apply to them" (p. 314). This can only lead to the conclusion that "no person exists except in the empty fantasy of a certain number of two-legged mammals".

We saw in *On Human Beings in the World* how, of all the senses, *speaking* language and *hearing* the Word raise us above the animals, as Grundtvig repeats here:

> ... 'enlightenment' is evidently *impossible* without the use of language, which, though invisible and intangible in Space, yet through its effect via the sense of hearing on the human *body* in Space, proves both its own reality and its power (ibid.).

With 'the Word' (i.e. language) the spiritual enters the physical world. As Grundtvig had already noted in *On the Word and the Mother-Tongue* (1819), language creates the connection between the two worlds. In consequence, he gives priority to Time over Space, and Spirit over Body, and he locates this distinction in two civilisations: Israel and the Far North (ibid.). This is testimony to the emphasis that he places on the Nordic view of life, even though it cannot match the Jewish view of life in the Bible in which spirituality is fully recognised.

Grundtvig points out that the Hebrew view of life has come to the North *via* Christianity. On "the path from Israel to Denmark" it has combatted its hereditary enemy, the purely materialist view of life, and has demonstrated "that historical revelation, both human and divine, is the only possible enlightenment in speech that does not clearly contradict itself" (p. 315). He repeats from memory the words of the German philosopher, Friedrich Heinrich Jacobi (1743-1819), "Na-

712 Danish title: *Dyreriget. En Lærebook til Brug ved Undervisning i de lærde Skoler and Realskolernes høiere Klasser* (1855).

ture *conceals* God," by being an endless chain of cause and effect, whereas "human beings *reveal* God, inasmuch as with the Spirit, they raise themselves above Nature". Grundtvig applies this in a form that suits his own purpose. He describes materialist 'natural science' as containing "fundamental 'human enlightenment'" – and with a minor variation he applies to ontology the Danish word *Grund-Kløgten* (fundamental wisdom), a word that he introduced in his youth.[713]

Grundtvig goes on to explain how German idealism has attempted to reconcile itself with this naturalist view of life, and, starting from Kant's theory of transcendentality, he works his way towards Hegel's "eternal reason".[714] He contrasts the "self-opinionated North Germans" (Fichte and Schlegel) and their idealism with "the worldly wisdom of the South Germans" (Schelling and Hegel), and he offers a mildly sympathetic view of Fichte, whom he calls "the most humane and deepest of German thinkers" (p. 316). Grundtvig draws his views from Fichte's so-called 'popular' philosophical writings;[715] again he shows that he has not forgotten his own philosophical considerations and that he still has a grip on the various positions in German idealism that he criticised in *Danne-Virke*.

Finally, on the basis of his philosophical and historical exposition, Grundtvig depicts how "in Denmark (from 1812) a voice was raised against both the 'scientific' and the German 'fundamental enlightenment'... [which]... pointed to the enlightenment advancing over time through Moses, the prophets, and Jesus Christ" (ibid.). He is referring here to his first world history, *A Brief Account of World History* (1812), with its biblical approach to history, and argues that with increasing clarity the Jewish understanding of life continued into the Lutheran reformation, when the living word became paramount. Grundtvig further believes that this clarity culminates with himself! In this light he then depicts his conflict in 1815 with the natural scientist, H.C. Ørsted, "later a world-famous physicist" (p. 317) and, 10 years later, with Professor of Theology, H.N. Clausen.[716] The remaining 'world history' is covered in leaps and bounds. Grundtvig makes room for the journal *The Corsar*, published between 1840-46 by the Danish Jew, Meïr Aron Goldschmidt (1819-87), which seeks "to hush up as far as possible all further dispute"; by which he means it dominates the public debate to such an extent that "Danish men of Learning" – the representatives of materialism, believed that they had stifled Grundtvig's voice. However, the success of Grundtvigianism in the 1860s testifies to the fact that the non-materialist view that he represents was alive and had a future. With biblical quotations such as "Above all else, guard your heart!"[717] and "Love never fails",[718] Grundtvig ends with the hope that Christianity will be

713 Henning Høirup, *Grundtvigs syn paa tro og erkendelse: modsigelsens grundsætning som teologisk aksiom hos Grundtvig*. Gyldendal. København 1949, s. 22.

714 The German philosopher Georg Hegel (1770-1831) believed that all History is caused by a rational process.

715 E.g. *Anweisung zum seeligen Leben* (1806), *Die Grundzüge des gegenwärtigen Zeitalters* (1806), and *Reden an die deutsche Nation* (1808).

716 For the full story of the conflict with Professor Clausen see Texts 1 and 4 in *Human Comes First* (2018).

717 Prov. 4:23.

718 1 Cor 13:8.

victorious over what he calls the 'world spirit' – in an allusion to 1 Cor 2:12[719] and the Hegelian philosophy's *Weltgeist*, i.e. the materialist world-view of natural science.

For as long as Christianity has existed, there has been a perceptible incongruity between the *historical* view and the so-called *'natural'* view of the world – and indeed of all that we call matters spiritual and eternal. However, since both Nature and History are artificial concepts, and are quite strange, dead, and powerless words in modern Christianity, the so-called 'academic clash'[720] that has revolved around them can only be a confused and futile one. If the incongruity is to be clarified for us, we must first and foremost bear in mind that, call it what we like, there are only two kinds of real-life objects for human regard and consideration, namely *what we see in Space and what happens in Time*. As regards what is present in Space, we can acquire Knowledge through all five senses, whereas what happens and passes in the course of Time we can only ask tidings from the Word itself through our sense of hearing. It goes without saying therefore that we can gain a far clearer grasp of the objects in Space than of the facts in Time.

Our teachers of German, or their Germanised students,[721] would have us believe that in the course of Time they have arrived at an idea that gives them a clearer grasp of the objects in Space than can be acquired through all five of our senses! The senses and all that is sensory are basically nothing, they say! And they make this claim even though the same frightening thought cannot possibly have entered the world except in words and through the sense of hearing! It is obvious that these people either have a screw loose[722] or have no idea what they are talking about!

The same teachers and students, whether in French, English, Latin or Greek, also tell us that since our concepts of objects in Space are the clearest concepts we *have*, our knowledge of them and their internal relations is also the only thing we can be *sure* of. This being so, we must judge all tidings of what *is* happening or *has* happened in the course of Time either from inside ourselves as 'thoughts' and 'feelings', or from outside ourselves as 'events' and 'actions'. Therefore, they argue, we must simply reject

719 1 Cor 2:12: "The person without the Spirit does not accept the things that come from the Spirit of God but considers them foolishness."

720 The reference is to the heated debates on modern empirical and evolutionary concepts of 'natural history' as opposed to the classical concept as meaning primarily 'natural philosophy' exercised in the light of theology, but without the practical and secularising implications of modern science. Grundtvig argues in favour of empiricism, but within his own conceptual frame of 'universal history'.

721 German teachers and German influences pervaded the Danish school system and state apparatus throughout the 18th and 19th centuries. Grundtvig often uses the phrase 'German' or 'Germanised' as a derogative, aimed at the overly speculative tendencies prevalent in German philosophy.

722 This apparently modern phrase is in fact a literal translation of Grundtvig's text: "*skrue løs*".

as *unreasonable*, *unbelievable*, and *impossible*, any information that conflicts with the laws which, with our certain knowledge of objects in Space, we have concluded must apply to them.

Here, then, we have the key to this so-called 'Natural Science', which dominates the world at present and refuses in every way to be reconciled with Christianity or any kind of historical Knowledge of a living God, not to mention human life and its origin, dignity, development, and destination.[723] Even the philistines are outraged when the schoolboys' Natural History book says, "The human being is a mammal'. This is not a printing error for which the typesetters are to blame; it is merely a pacifying expression for the stern statement that no person exists except in the empty fantasy of a certain number of two-legged mammals.[724] For we are only present in Space as a physical *body*, and it is only through acquiring language in the course of time that we have perceptibly raised ourselves above all the dumb animals. And yet we cannot *explain* our superiority over the animals – whether it be sharpness of eye or dexterity of finger, let alone our sensitivity of smell or keenness of taste. In consequence, anyone who allows himself to be educated only about the objects in Space while disregarding the facts in Time must of course rule out completely any concept of '*humankind*' and human *development* from generation to generation.[725]

It is clear to us all that the so-called 'divine enlightenment' of everything is as inhuman as it is ungodly; and yet it is not *available* to any other bodies in Space except the so-called 'human being'. Even then, this 'enlightenment' is evidently *impossible* without the use of language, which, though invisible and intangible in Space, yet through its effect via the sense of hearing on the human *body* in Space, proves both its own reality and its power. This is so obvious to us all that it comes as an astonishing surprise to discover that it is only in Israel[726] and the Far North[727] that this objection is vigorously maintained against the false enlightenment that seeks to obliterate both God and humankind and thereby darken both heaven and earth. No matter how much conflict has been waged in Christian times on the path from Israel to Denmark between naturalism and the revelation of History,[728] nowhere *else* has enlightenment about the times – as communicated by language – found tongues that either dared to claim or were able to prove that historical revelation, both human and divine, is

723 Grundtvig's concept of natural evolution is eschatological, in the sense that human development is naturally predestined to reveal humans as spiritually enlightened beings.

724 i.e. the modern scientists.

725 Grundtvig calls the spiritual development of the human being through History our 'matchless path'.

726 According to Grundtvig, the Jewish tradition is the original source of all historical and embodied thinking.

727 Grundtvig repeatedly uses the 'Far North' to denote Norway, Sweden and Denmark (with its colony Iceland), sometimes stretching the concept to include the United Kingdom with its philosophical history of pragmatism.

728 The 'revelation of history' refers to the development of Christianity which, according to Grundtvig, marks a historical process of enlightenment moving across the European continent from south to north.

the only possible enlightenment in speech that does not clearly contradict itself and thereby prove its emptiness and falseness. As far as I know, it was a German who in a bright moment once said, "Nature *conceals* God, history *reveals* Him".[729] This after all is the case with humankind and all spiritual truth, when we set Nature against History. The spirit of the world is forever struggling with the spirit of Truth over humankind through its instruments of *speech* – as the Rimthurser with the Aesir.[730] And among all the peoples of the world this truth has only been expressed on the tongues and felt in the hearts of the Jewish people and the people of the Far North. It is they, therefore, who may acquire the wisdom to explain and enlighten it.

At this point, however, all reason stops, and words remain stuck in the throat at the monumental, glaring contradiction that this little mammal whom we call a 'human being' has in the course of Time acquired the use of *language* – which alone can reveal thought, and communicate and engender Knowledge! Moreover, this animal has at last come to the absolutely transparent conclusion which *solves* the riddle of all existence by declaring it '*insoluble*'! That is, by declaring the passage of Time – *in* which, and the language *by* which this transparent conclusion has been achieved, as well as the mammal itself who *conceived* this masterstroke – to be perfectly *incapable* of it. Thus, in spite of its insignificance, this mammal has far outrivalled all the imaginary gods, including the so-called 'Omnipotent'. It must settle for doing the best it can, whereas the rational mammal has truly learned, or has picked up from nature, the art of *doing* the impossible, *speaking* the unspeakable, and *brightening* the eternally impenetrable darkness!

Even the Germans, the *shrewdest* of all people, have in vain racked their brains to work out how this so-called fundamental 'human enlightenment' could possibly be combined with Christianity in any shape – or even with *Mathematics* or the fundamental concept of Enlightenment itself – or with the everlasting German *Reason*! However, instead of denouncing Natural Science as representing the *disavowal* of all spiritual truth and promoting the idea of a *progressive enlightenment* from one generation to the next through *Language* (*the Word*) as the only truly *human* achievement, the Germans nobly raised themselves *above* Time and Space as pure sense-forms and indeed above all Revelation and Experience! And they did so on the presumption of their everlasting *Reason*, assuming it to be raised above all discrepancies and contradictions over the course of Time, while working in all secrecy towards "the new heaven and the

729 Friedrich Jacobi (1743-1819) asked: "But is it unreasonable to confess that we believe in God, not by reason of the nature which conceals him, but by reason of the supernatural in man, which alone reveals him and proves him to exist?" (Sir W. Hamilton's *Lectures on Metaphysics*, vol. I. p. 40.) In a criticism of Kant, Jacobi adopted a philosophy of feeling and faith.

730 In Nordic mythology Rimthurser are the frost-giants, the makers of cold winters, frost, and snow. The Aesir are the dominant tribe in the pantheon and are gods of poetry, vision, magic, war and conquest.

new earth".[731] For in *that* world strict German justice dwells under the sunlit clarity of eternal truth.

We learn from the Romans through Tacitus that this, what one might call, 'self-worship' of human breath, is peculiar to the Germans.[732] The most humane and deepest of German thinkers (Fichte)[733] endeavoured to reconcile it with History, with Christianity, and with the human heart. And he did so by beginning with *Love* in heaven and *Faith* on earth as the sources of *light* and *life*, and by presenting the language of the mother-tongue as the *conductor* through which human life has been transmitted and enlightened from generation to generation. Yet since there were no corresponding *realities* whatsoever, but only the shadows of his own making that confronted him, no enlightenment was achieved beyond the clarification of his own thought-processes. Moreover, his imaginary story stopped at a model people (a 'normal people') who had *cultivated* and *transmitted* the light, and from whom the *true* Germans were to be the remnant and core. Indeed Fichte himself, the 'I', was to be the fruit in whom enlightenment had reached the *zenith* of its day, so that, as the last German and the last true human being, he could only end the story with the entry of Time into Eternity!

With Fichte, the vain attempts of the North Germans[734] at genuine human enlightenment also came to a halt (1814). They were replaced by the capers in worldly wisdom of the South Germans (Schelling and Hegel) in order to conceal through reveries and sophistries (mysticism and scholasticism) that human life was handed over to the mercy of the deepest darkness and bottomless abyss.

It was in these circumstances that in Denmark (from 1812) a voice was raised against both the 'scientific' and the German 'fundamental enlightenment' as being solar eclipses of the spirit, one greater than the other. Instead the voice pointed to enlightenment advancing over time through Moses, the prophets, and Jesus Christ. This enlightenment began to reveal itself, after its papal arrest, in Martin Luther. Our

---

731 Rev 21:1.

732 Gaius Cornelius Tacitus (c. 56-117 CE) was a Roman historian whose work *Germania* (98 CE) describes how the German tribes prepare for battle: "they aim chiefly at a harsh note and a confused roar, putting their shields to their mouth, so that, by reverberation, it may swell into a fuller and deeper sound." (tr. by Alfred John Church & William Jackson Brodribb, 1864-77, Book 1, ch. 3).

733 Johann Fichte (1762-1814) was one of the founding figures of German idealism, which developed mainly from the ideas of Immanuel Kant. By distancing himself from Kant's argument for the existence of *noumena*, or "things in themselves", Fichte laid the foundation for a radical philosophical subjectivism, in which the human 'I' sets itself up as a free creative individual, challenged socially only by the offence (*Anstoss*) of other free individuals. Since the publication of his *Addresses to the German Nation* (1808), Fichte is named the Father of German nationalism. Grundtvig began studying the German idealists, Fichte, Schiller, Schelling, and others around autumn 1805.

734 'North Germans' refers to Fichte's appointment as Professor of Philosophy at Berlin University in 1800. Here he associated with the Schlegel brothers, Schleiermacher, Schelling, and Tieck and became Rector of the university, remaining in Berlin until his death.

mother-tongue being well-qualified for the purpose, this enlightenment will win ever-increasing clarity in our Far North!

In Denmark we are inclined neither to speculation nor to brain-racking. On the question of enlightenment we have therefore blindly followed foreigners, especially the German teachers of renown. It was in particular the sharp remarks about these teachers and their Danish pupils mentioned by name in my *World History* (1812) that aroused general astonishment and manifold indignation. Later, a world-famous physicist[735] – on behalf of the prevailing Natural Science and, as he said, of human enlightenment in general – has attempted to strangle this *voice* at birth by calling it an indefinably strident and intolerable echo from the spiritual world's madhouse, disguised as a divine revelation.[736] When his attempt failed and the polemic concerning 'nominal values'[737] ceased, the enlighteners of Denmark calmed down over this voice. Believing it to belong to a single poet with a screw loose, they then closed their ears and allowed it to run on under the name of *Grundtvigianism*.[738] Even when the well-known polemic against a particular rationalist of the second degree[739] alarmed people for a while, the matter was calmly handed over to the city court to judge the scandalous case and, with *The Corsar*,[740] to hush up as far as possible all further dispute.[741] As far as I can discern from

735 The renowned physicist H.C. Ørsted (1777-1851) was the first to discover and describe electromagnetism.

736 Grundtvig's own footnote 13: "Should you require further information about the controversy between H.C. Ørsted and N.F.S. Grundtvig, you must take the trouble to read the former's *Against the Great Prosecutor* (1814) and the latter's *Against the Little Prosecutor* (1815)."

737 The 'polemic' refers to the classical philosophical conflict between 'realists' and 'nominalists'. The 'realists' of the Platonic school claimed that 'The general is anterior to the particular', while the 'nominalists' claimed reversely that 'the particular is anterior to the general'. This classic schism in medieval scholasticism seems to repeat itself in the modern debate as to whether the world has come into being through a conscious process of creation or through an evolutionary unfolding of blind natural forces. In Grundtvig's retrospect of the events, it was this classic theological debate that reflected itself in the heated polemics between himself and H.C. Ørsted. Thus in creation spirituality, ideas or archetypes are *real*, and the idea or 'plan' of the world is anterior to the act of its realisation, whereas in natural evolution there is no idea or plan anterior to the fact, but rather the unfolding of certain *forces* immanent in substances and individual beings which push them to seek a way of progressing through a process of trial and error.

738 Grundtvigianism began to form already in the 1820s and came to fruition as a political and spiritual movement in Denmark and Scandinavia from the 1850s. Grundtvig himself often denounced the term. The Grundtvigians called themselves 'happy Christians', as opposed to the sterner 'pietists'. Among their aims were freedom from the parish-tie, the segregation of Church and School, and the education of the people. The first People's High School inspired partly by Grundtvig's ideas was founded in Rødding in 1844. Cf. *The School for Life. N.F.S. Grundtvig on Education for the People* (2011).

739 Grundtvig's own footnote 14: "The Church's Retort against Prof. Clausen 1825". Cf. *Human Comes First. The Christian Theology of N.F.S. Grundtvig* (2018).

740 *The Corsar* was a satirical periodical founded in 1840 by author and political observer M.A. Goldschmidt. Like Søren Kierkegaard, Grundtvig became an object of its ridicule. In one issue *The Corsar* brought a caricature of Grundtvig blowing a lur with a cock crowing on his head and the following text: "Do not blow your great lur so eagerly. Take your time, while the days of old pass away."

741 H.N. Clausen (1793-1877) was a rationalist Professor of Theology at Copenhagen University from 1822-74. Following his vicious pamphlet against Clausen, Grundtvig was found guilty of libel and placed under publishing censorship

the latest attacks on this so-called 'Grundtvigianism', Danish men of Learning still believe in all innocence that the whole question has to do with the extent to which the pen can prove or disprove the claim that from its earliest days the Christian Church possessed a Word of light and life quite differently pure and powerful from any *alphabetic* writing. And they do so, even though it might be literally a work of '*God's finger*', like the writing on the stone tablets of Moses. It is obvious that this is a question that not all the pens in the world can answer – but only *one* good mouth can!

The obvious fact of the matter is that on behalf of the people's spirit of Israel and the Far North as well as of the people's heart of all Christian and all Danish people, I have raised my voice against all self-constructed, so-called philosophical *systems*.[742] Spiritually speaking, these are merely wretched hovels so low to the ceiling that even the smallest devil could not stand upright inside them. They are only suitable for those beguiled ants and beavers bewitched by *Reason*, or for ravens and magpies. They are not for the *human spirit*, which most of these master builders have consequently and diligently endeavoured to exclude!

"In the beginning God created the heavens and the earth, and God said, Let there be light: and there was light. And God said, Let us make humankind in our image, in our likeness. And he did so, male and female He created them."[743] This is not only the introduction to humankind's Israelite genealogy, it is also the fundamental enlightenment that *human life* under all skies and with its matchless path[744] clearly assumes, since human life – with its Word of spirit and heart, and with its living impression and expression of life eternal and divine – is an undeniable fact that can only be explained on this assumption.

This basic belief in a living *Godhead* bearing the Word, which with the birth of '*Time*' created the fullness of '*Space*' and formed for itself in human beings of both sexes a living mirror and an earthly neighbour, is just as recognisable in the *Völuspa* of the

from 1826-37. In protest he resigned his pastorate in 1826. He was allowed to hold evensong sermons at Christianskirken but forbidden to administer Baptism and Holy Communion.

742 Like Kierkegaard, Grundtvig denounced all attempts to create a rational philosophical system to explain *everything*, such as the Kantian or Hegelian systems. These surrendered the transformative and spiritual potential of genuine philosophical pursuit to mere speculation.

743 Gen 1:26-27.

744 The 'matchless path' is the archetypal spiritual development of humankind, the so-called 'great' or 'grand human development'.

Far North as in Israel's *Genesis*.[745] Moreover the Aesirs' tongue[746] in its entirety is an extraordinary heroic poem that leaves no doubt whatsoever that the inhabitants of the Far North regarded the great stretch of human life from the *beginning* of time to the *end* of the world as a triumphant battle in which the divine life of the human and the human life of the divine, under the wise dispensation of Providence (the Norns), was to annihilate the icy, heartless, god-hostile giants' power and doggish reason, until at Balder's resurrection from the dead new heavens and a new earth could be created with eternal life and light and joy.[747]

Above all, I say, look after your heart, for life issues from the *heart*! People may take the apparent for the real, but God takes the *heart* into account, and a light has been sown for the true at heart.[748] For everything else shall perish and cease to be, but Love will never cease. As we well know, these are Israelite and Christian apothegms, but they are equally basic Danish ideas from time immemorial. For the truth is, that just as Freya here in the North made a pact with Odin to share his death on the battlefield yet continued to weep tears of gold for her lost husband until he returned at the end of the world,[749] and just as the woman led Hadding, hidden under her cape, past Valhalla to the insurmountable wall of the Land of the Life of the Heart,[750] so was it the *Danish* heart, which in a virtually innocent way glorified itself with its memory of Paradise, and thus sustained an open heart to the Gospel of the Heart that is Christianity.

Just as surely as the Christian revelation sets its great seal upon the Israelite seal and opens a new great human path through the birth of God's only-begotten son as the human son of a woman, so must Christianity seek its transfiguration in a life path as much human as divine. This is a path that unfailingly confirms and illuminates the

745 Grundtvig sometimes calls this basic creational assumption 'the Mosaic-Christian view'. He regards it as a sort of spiritual common denominator for all the Abrahamic religions, in fact, for all authentic human wisdom traditions, including the Old Norse. The *Völuspa, or Prophecy of the Seeress,* is the first poem in the Poetic Edda (12th cent.), which tells the story of the creation of the world and its approaching end. The Norns are female beings who rule the fate of humanity, much as the Fates do in Greek mythology. They predict that when the fairest of gods, Balder, is killed, he will be resurrected in a new paradisical world.

746 i.e. the divine poetic language of the old Nordic myths.

747 Grundtvig's own footnote 15: "Thus it is evidently the enlightenment of Time and Space, the historical and the natural enlightenment, which in Odin and the giant Vafthrudner make a wager for each other's 'heads'; the giant loses his because he cannot explain 'the word of the spirit'." See the poem 'Vafthrudnismal' in the *Poetic Edda*, where Odin's poetic and integral world vision is confronted by the giant's drier, more fragmented, type of knowledge.

748 Ps 7:10.

749 The reference is to Snorri's *Prose Edda*. Weeping tears of gold, Freya searches for her husband Od, who is often away on his travels. Similar narratives are found in other ancient creation myths and fertility rites, such as when the god Osiris is condemned to the underworld, while his mourning spouse, Isis, searches for him. The same basic scheme is reflected in the story of Mary Magdalene weeping at Jesus' grave (Jn 20:11). As a mythologist Grundtvig was aware of these parallels, cf. his poem 'The Woman's Gospel' (*Kvindeevangeliet*, 1855).

750 In the legend of Hadding the ride ends at the insurmountable wall of death. The mysterious woman rips the head off a rooster and throws it over the wall. The rooster's head crows on the other side of the wall, confirming the triumph of life after death.

truth of the Israelite revelation by actually overcoming with the Word the refractory spirit of this world, and by creating a heaven of the spirit and the heart on earth, one of righteousness, peace, and joy in the spirit of Truth and Love.

The proof that Christianity has truly had the courage to venture this temporal (historical) struggle against the world's spirit lies in the baptismal covenant. Through this it overtly challenges all the powers of spirit and all the inclinations of man's heart, which like all devilry oppose the Christian faith. The power of Christianity to continue this struggle over eighteen centuries is as obvious as the fact that the Christian baptismal covenant and creed still ring out freely and vitally somewhere or other on earth. Whether this is the case elsewhere than in Denmark and Norway is a statistical topic that we shall leave open for now. But in Denmark and Norway it is a proven fact that we have freedom of belief. Consequently it is here first and foremost that we shall see whether the power of Christianity has withered, as the world's spirit claims, or whether it is actually from here that this power can triumphantly continue its struggle towards its own transfiguration and the end of the world.

IV

LANGUAGE

11. On Proverbs (1817)
12. On the Word and the Mother-Tongue (1819)

11. On Proverbs (1817)

Introduction by Kim Steen Ravn

On Proverbs was published in *Danne-Virke*, vol. 3 in July 1817. Grundtvig took a lifelong interest in proverbs, 'the wisdom of the people', as he called them, and 28 years after this essay was written he even published his own collection of 3,012 proverbs. In 1879, Edvard Mau published the definitive collection of over 12,000 Danish proverbs in the two-volume *Danish Treasury of Proverbs* (*Dansk Ordsprogs-Skat* I-II). Proverbs, then, form part of the philosophy of language that Grundtvig was formulating in the period 1807-17, as he developed his ideas of what it means to be Danish, a national interest that was manifest throughout Europe as its various peoples began to define their relation to their history and their language. This is the age of collecting, of preserving and publishing the past, and of building museums.

In the essay, Grundtvig deals first with the actual state of Danish literature and the current view of proverbs, which he defines thus: "proverbs are the closest connection to the spirit of a people, to their language and their way of thinking." In Grundtvig's day only 10% of all Danes were educated to high school level, while the remaining 90% were peasant farmers and agricultural workers. Grundtvig is clearly drawing on his knowledge of the latter: "All manner of things have been said about what constitutes a proverb. But what is almost forgotten here, as in many other similar cases, is that we should ask not the books but the peasant farmers." For "when we speak Danish, what the peasant calls a proverb is what a proverb is!" (p. 328). Grundtvig also draws on previous Danish collections by Peder Laale (published 1506) and Peder Syv (published 1682-88). He explains the importance of proverbs, and he praises the Danes in particular for their practical use and scholarly understanding of them. He concludes by treating their application in both speech and writing.

In Grundtvig's view, proverbs constitute "the open gate between poetry and prose. From another side they are also the gateway between writing and conversation, so we might call them 'everyday poetry and Sunday prose', or 'oral writing and written sayings'" (p. 327). Fundamentally, they are an oral form of communication, which can then be used in writing, as Grundtvig often does. His definition of a proverb is still by and large the one that we use today, with the following three constitutive elements: a proverb is a *closed text* that needs no adaptation to the context in which it is applied; a proverb is *generalising*, in that it can be used at all times and under all conditions; and a proverb is *lexicalised*, meaning that it can be used in any situation by any person who deems it relevant, since it is expected to be known to the receiver. As Grundtvig says: "They are simply any short, ordinary sentence with many or few elements upon which popular usage has set its stamp as passing for ready money" (p. 328).

The 'closed' form of the proverb is explained by Grundtvig's argument: "Whatever becomes a 'proverb' must have left such a deep impression on a people and become so established that only the greatest of changes can eradicate it." Moreover, so 'lexicalised' is the form that "no damage is done if the same proverbs end up in a hundred different collections; that indeed is their virtue!" (p. 334).

Grundtvig shared the view of the early 19th century that proverbs are representative of a specific people, even though they may have similar meanings. Two good examples are the English, "A bird in the hand is worth two in the bush", which, in translation from the Danish, becomes "A bird in the hand is worth ten on the roof." The somewhat abstract English proverb, "Necessity is the mother of invention", in Danish becomes the more imaginative, "Necessity teaches a naked lady to spin". In the previous volume in this series, *The Common Good* (2019, pp. 362-63) there is a list of 24 Danish proverbs that Grundtvig draws on to supplement his political views, as he becomes more involved in politics in the 1840s. They include a number with English-language equivalents, but also such gems as the insult from the nobility: "Were the peasant not bound, he'd be worse than the hound" (p. 163) – a proverb which, Grundtvig adds, is particularly applicable in England; and the wise saying: "Never roll an apple so far that it does not taste of its root".

There are three reasons why proverbs have been coined and survived, says Grundtvig. The first is linguistic: "idiosyncrasy of its proverbs is the most incontrovertible proof a language can provide of its originality" (p. 330). The second is moral: "For in their proverbs we most definitely learn the people's relation to truth and everyday morality... On this point we must take note that there is always some truth at the heart of all proverbs. For they either say what usually happens, or what *ought* to happen" (ibid.). The third reason is poetic: The pithier they are, and the more meaning to be found in them – not contradictory, but gradually increasing meaning – the more their spiritual significance stands out, and the more poetry there undoubtedly was in the people" (p. 331).

With regard to proverbs as a subject for the teaching of Danish in the village schools, Grundtvig had already recommended this in *Education for the State* (1834): "The history of our country – its ancient history, pithy proverbs, and all the language of the people in the mother-tongue – that is what should be the subject of conversation in the Village School!"[751] The publication of Grundtvig's own collection, *Danish Proverbs and Sayings* (1845),[752] paved the way for their wider usage among the Danish people, in particular in the burgeoning people's high schools. When the founder of no fewer than three of these schools, Christen Kold (1816-70), asked Grundtvig for advice on the *content* of his teaching, he was advised to spend some time on the discussion of Danish proverbs.

751 *The School for Life* (2011) p. 90.

752 Danish title: *Danske Ordsprog og Mundheld.*

If I remember rightly, we have *Athene's* word for it that poetry can be drowned![753] Indeed, shame on me that I myself was accused of attempting this evil deed! But I prefer to call it a *heroic* attempt, since it would be like drowning a living eel – which everyone knows is what a Molbo-man[754] tried in vain to do. Seriously though, I think it impossible to drown poetry, however many Molbo-men have tried, and however much their attempts became part of the Golden Age of Molbo-men, which is how we usually designate the enlightened 18th century. I realise that superficially my claim can be countered, since experience appears to teach us the opposite, and to demonstrate that there is nothing in the claim that Poetry is indeed drowning. But it is for this very reason that I have my doubts. For 'nothing' cannot make anything grow bigger, and even little things cannot possibly take the life out of Poetry, which is indisputably the greatest artefact we have seen in the world! The apparent demise of Poetry under water is confirmed by the signatures of numberless hands in both verse and prose. It is as certain as the announcement of the Devil's own blessed death – in the Public Notices section of the daily paper – by his nearest and dearest for his family and friends out-of-town. However, I doubt the demise of both! Indeed, in the case of Poetry I note that the family and friends may have brought the water to the place where Poetry was to be drowned, but they could never prove that anybody actually *saw* it drowning. Even less likely is it that they have had Poetry in their hands – which is essential if one is to take its life. True there was something in the water that was *called* 'poetry', but, to stay with the Molbo-men analogy that fits the bill here, it was obviously not a living eel they were trying to drown but an air-dried flounder, or a salted herring that they had put in the village pond to spawn!

So here we have a telling image of most of those 'reformations' in the 18th century. They fancied they had put to death what nobody had ever seen, except for its shadow! And they came with a novelty that they thought would invigorate everyone, even though it was only a dead herring! They were sure that they had drowned Christianity and all ancient history in the washing-up water which they called 'Criticism', and they believed they had impregnated the entire village pond with German reason and French science – from which they hoped to be blessed with many a fish. They imagined they had drowned the poetic spirit in the peppermint-water they called 'Aesthetics', and

753 In a review of new Danish writing in 1814, the January 1815 edition of the literary journal, *Athene*, wrote: "Grundtvig published a a book called *Roskilde Rhymes*, in which he assuredly drowned a large part of his poetry in numberless rhymes."

754 The simple folk on the Mols peninsula in East Jutland gained a reputation among their neighbours for being stupid. Already in 1780 a book was published entitled, *Tales of the Well-known Molboes' Wise and Brave Actions*. Modern versions of the book sell well in the tourist bookshops of Ebeltoft today. "It's hard to drown an eel" is a proverb used in one of the Molbo stories.

they thought that they could give 'the Scholars' Lake'[755] both life and taste by throwing the names of ancient idols, muses, graces,[756] and other images into it.

We know that the spawning was not very successful; I claim that the attempted destruction was a failure too, though I would never appeal for witnesses from our scholars' new-fangled Christianity, History, and Poetry, which have installed themselves somewhere out there and are known to us through a few of their deserters. For the surest sign of death is that one walks again, and I am in no doubt about these ghosts and their hauntings. We see it here and now too, if not in the notorious witch-dance around Freya's altar[757] or the merely fleeting signs of life expressed in Oehlenschläger's poetry,[758] then in the hope that their cooking-pot does not break. For in that pot they have cooked all manner of royal dishes for any who wish to prevent their tongue from tasting true poetry. I know the man[759] who nourishes a hope that in the hands of Gutfeld and Boie[760] and others there will be a return to what was called 'the Golden Age of Poetry' – the most insipid, unpoetic, spiritless age of cripples that Denmark has ever seen. I know that as far as his assessment of Kingo, Sorterup, Holberg[761] and several others shows, he has a far greater taste for true Poetry than the age that he so innocently extols – as indeed do all the 'dwarves' who so crassly imagine they have surpassed him. But neither this nor anything else can keep me from taking this opportunity to declare myself utterly possessed of the opposite wish and hope.

I hope that however much the times change, we shall no longer go so far in our spiritual blindness in Denmark as to include among our *poets* Gutfeld and Guldberg, Zetlizt and Horrebow, Haste and Lundbye,[762] and other such versifiers, without a loud and deep objection being raised! They may have other merits but that is not my concern here. Least of all can I silence this hope at a time when the false alarms of our youngsters are awakening the widespread wish for a return to the watery taste of the past,

755 Grundtvig's actual word here is 'Peblinge-Sø', one of the Copenhagen lakes. The word '*pebling*' first appears in 1524 to denote a student from the Latin Grammar School, but its appellation to the lake is of unknown origin.

756 The 9 Greek Muses are: Calliope (Epic Poetry), Clio (History), Euterpe (Music, Song, and Lyric Poetry), Erato (Love Poetry), Melpomene (Tragedy), Polyhymnia (Hymns), Terpsichore (Dance), Thalia (Comedy), and Urania (Astronomy). The 3 Greek Graces are: Aglaea (Splendour), Euphrosyne (Mirth), and Thalia (Good Cheer).

757 In Nordic mythology Freya is the goddess of fertility and love, the most powerful goddess of the Aesir.

758 Adam Oehlenschläger (1779-1850) was a Danish romantic poet and playwright who wrote, among others, the national anthem, *There is a lovely land*. The reference here is to his comedy, *Freya's Altar* (1805).

759 'This man' is a reference to Grundtvig's friend, Knud Lyne Rahbek (1760-1830), a Danish literary historian, poet, and critic.

760 Pastor Frederik Gutfeld (1761-1823) and Pastor Caspar Boie (1791-1853).

761 The Bishop of Funen and hymn-writer, Thomas Kingo (1634-1703), was instrumental in promoting music and hymn-singing in the ritual; Jørgen Sorterup (1662-1723) was a pastor and poet; Ludvig Holberg (1684-1754) was a famous Danish-Norwegian playwright.

762 Frederik Guldberg (1771-1852), Danish poet; Jens Zetlitz (1761-1821), Norwegian pastor and poet; Otto Horrebow (1769-1823), Danish theologian and social critic; Peder Haste (1765-1831), Danish poet and civil servant; and Henrik Lundbye (1772-1830), diplomat and writer.

under which the taste for Oehlenschläger's more recent works can also be included. My hope does not rest in any way on the so-called 'school of Oehlenschläger', or on any other school of pedagogical pedants, but on the knowledge that the Truth will be victorious in the end and that the historical testimony of the Danish heart beats for that Truth. It cannot be long before the chaff is separated from the wheat. And I still nurture the hope that Oehlenschläger himself will discover the distance between Aladdin and the Fisherman, Haakon, and Hugo,[763] and put to shame his adorers by shaking the dust off the feet that they have presented as some holy shrine! The hope that Rahbek's 'feeling' would defeat the empty, spiritless, gutless quasi-aesthetic that never satisfies and often runs counter to it is a hope that I once came close to nurturing but which I must now relinquish. That is hard to do. But it would be even harder to applaud again what he calls 'taste'.

There is indignation over the frenzied disturbances in recent literature that seem to portend a headlong fall back into the village pond, out of which we were beginning to lift our heads, to Oehlenschläger's familiar strings. And there is indignation and grief that our glorious poet, bent deep over his harp, has himself given occasion for such a pitiful turn. Such matters have moved me to say more about our poetic seasons than I had a mind to here, and I shall now swiftly turn to the subject I really wish to treat, namely *proverbs*, for which this introduction is not quite so inappropriate as it might seem.

Proverbs have gone more or less the same way as all matters spiritual and grand from the days of old. They were thought to have been drowned in the waters that were called Rules for Eloquence, Dignity of Expression, and Subtlety of Treatment, to be replaced by what were expected to be miracles using the dry sayings of any old Mr Jensen.[764] I do not mean by this that all proverbs are poetic, any more than I would praise the use, or rather abuse, of all manner of proverbs used at random, which is what the last but one age was guilty of. Among every people aware of its spirit its proverbs are the open gate between poetry and prose. From another side they are also the gateway between writing and conversation, so we might call them 'everyday poetry and Sunday prose', or 'oral writing and written sayings'. The so-called 'Enlightenment' showed its true colours both here and elsewhere by presenting as mere sweepings what were priceless grains of gold, often mixed in with dust, which the light should teach us to sift and wash. Far from hiding this, I am happy to note that there is hardly any other country where scholars have so cherished and so long honoured the proverbs of

763 Oehlenschlager's poetic masterpiece is the drama, *Aladdin* (1805), in which the lamp and the ring are made symbols of artistic creation and the poetic imagination. It is far superior to the poetic drama, *The Fisherman* (1816) and the tragic love dramas, *Earl Haakon the Rich* (1807), and *Hugo von Rheinberg* (1813).

764 'Mr. Jensen' is the most common name in Danish, corresponding to 'John Smith' in English.

their land. What other country has a medieval collection to rival that of Peder Laale?[765] Where else before the Reformation was such a book as his printed? And as Peder Syv has noted, what violence did a Latinist like Saxo[766] do to the Roman language in order to translate the proverbs of his fatherland as best he could? Where else were they used so frequently and so neatly as they were by Anders Vedel?[767] Who showed, even in the days of Christian V,[768] such a love of proverbs and understanding of their value as old Peder Syv? And who remembered them with such concern in the worst of times as Nyerup?[769] Since proverbs have always been close to the hearts of the Danes and so frequently on their lips, it is reasonable for a Dane to plead their cause, for 'old love dies hard'[770] and indeed loosens tongues and opens ears.

All manner of things have been said about what constitutes a proverb. But what is forgotten here, as in many other similar cases, is that we should ask not the books but the peasant farmers. For what the peasant calls a proverb is what a proverb *is*, when we speak Danish. However great the differences in our spoken Danish, when we speak Danish they warrant no more than a simple classification. If we take the proverb appellation from any, we are departing from a specific habit of language, and are obscuring rather than illuminating it.

Proverbs, or as the Danish peasant farmer prefers it, 'old sayings', mean neither so much as they did to Peder Syv nor so little as they do among more recent writers. They are simply any short, ordinary sentence with many or few elements upon which popular usage has set its stamp as passing for ready money![771] They used to believe that we put on and took off proverbs like clothes! They even believed that the proverbs they disliked could be eradicated by sermonising and new ones made through intellectual exercise! But they had 'reckoned without the host'![772] For in such matters the peasants are not like geese;[773] they are not willing to exchange their ready money for bank-notes that no one takes for *valid* currency.[774] On the contrary,

765 Peter Laale (14th cent.) and Peder Syv (17th cent.) collected Danish proverbs. Laale's collection was first published in 1506, Syv's in 1682 and 1688.

766 Saxo (c. 1160-post 1208) worked as a scribe for the great Bishop Absalon (1128-1201). Saxo's *Gesta Danorum* (*Deeds of the Danes*) was handwritten in elegant Latin in 16 volumes. The early volumes contain mainly legendary material, but references to documented events become more and more common in later volumes. *Gesta Danorum* was first published in 1514. Grundtvig's Danish translation was published in 3 volumes in 1818-22.

767 Anders Vedel (1542-1616) was a Danish historian and folksong publisher who also collected some 850 proverbs.

768 Christian V (1646-99), reigned from 1671.

769 Rasmus Nyerup (1759-1829) was a literary historian, linguistic scholar, and royal librarian, who also published commentated editions of the proverb collections of both Peder Laale and Peder Syv.

770 'Old love dies hard.' Grundtvig 1845, no. 841.

771 'Words can be as good as ready money.' Grundtvig 1845, no. 960.

772 'Whoever reckons without the host must reckon twice.' Grundtvig 1845, no. 2,144.

773 'The peasant is no goose, even though he is grey.' Grundtvig 1845, no. 263.

774 'Words can be as good as ready money.' Grundtvig 1845, no. 960.

proverbs are the closest connection to the *spirit of a people*, to their language and their way of thinking. Whatever becomes a 'proverb' must have left such a deep impression on a people and become so established that only the greatest of changes can eradicate it. Indeed, what has become a genuine proverb can hardly stop being so until the people perish completely. Minor changes of expression and, much more rarely, occasional corrections, can come about over time or through internal development, just as the number of proverbs must decline if a people become forgetful. The best proverbs – those that are the most unpleasant to our corrupt human nature or refer most obviously to matters spiritual – are often the first to go, while those that are ambiguous or obscure are used wrongly, as the people's spirit begins to weaken. Yet rarely do proverbs die out completely, except through religious change or the demise of the people itself. For most of them are undoubtedly of ancient origin, partly because 'what is learned in youth, old age does not forget',[775] and partly because most proverbs, depending on the people they belong to, have a wealth and a depth that far surpass the intellectual development that the people had acquired at the time they were written down. Proverbs must simply have had their basis in a *poetic understanding* of the early days of our people.

To persuade the reader that there is justification for this claim, may I draw attention to the only literature on Danish proverbs that I know of? Already at the beginning of the 16th century (1506) Peder Laale published his Latin and Danish proverbs. Later (1515) Christen Svendborg re-published them in Paris (1515) with corrections and background information. Who this Peder Laale was and when he lived is unknown, but we can be sure that long before its publication his collection had become an ordinary 'textbook'. We can see this not only from the publisher's trustworthy testimony, but also from the many additional insertions which for the most part announce themselves by disturbing the alphabet. We allow any doubters all they demand by placing Laale's work in the 15th century, but if they make the slightest objection we shall limit ourselves to the cheapest of arguments, namely that the book was written before it was published! This curious book, which truly deserves a new edition, naturally contains a number of proverbs that have never *been* Danish, either because the language never contained such a proverb or because the collector could not find a proverb that corresponded with the mouthful of dog-Latin that he wished to enjoin upon us. Nevertheless there are many proverbs that I myself have heard round and about in the country, some of them word for word, others with minor alterations that can easily be explained. It follows from this that many proverbs have lasted throughout the period in which the Reformation took place, which was clearly the time when foreign matters and books had most influence on our people. We can therefore justifiably deduce that for the

775 'What is learned in youth, old age does not forget.' Grundtvig 1845, no. 2,824.

people's sake such proverbs can be as old as the hills and, to judge by their powers of survival, they cannot be from yesterday.

However, this was only a hint for those who are as weak in faith as they fancy themselves to be strong in doubt, and we turn now to the position from which we shall regard the significance of these proverbs. As we shall see, this is both historical and considerable.

Firstly, they are of far more importance for the language than linguistic scholarship in general acknowledges or adequately underlines. What immediately meets the eye is that in proverbs we find at its most assured 'the mother-tongue of the people'. Rightly understood, they say all that *needs* to be said! Yet what we actually see is never their deeper meaning – unless they are both thin and flat! Only rarely do people seem to realise that in proverbs we hear the very *spirit of the people*. Otherwise proverbs are quite straightforward, and one only has to translate a number of them from recognizably foreign languages to be convinced of this. Yet the obvious consequence has in general been overlooked, namely that the idiosyncrasy of its proverbs is the most incontrovertible proof a language can provide of its originality! The sceptic may believe that he has disproved, or has sought to push aside, the evidence that we can present for the age and originality of *any* language. Let him even be applauded for claiming that every word of the proverbs may have sounded otherwise in the past, or that they were all made up on the same day they were printed! But only children and fools can be duped into believing that two languages whose proverbs are incompatible are at heart one and the same, for it is much rather the case that nearly all languages share *common* ground on this subject.

The other important element in proverbs is the moral one. This may not have been ignored, but it has certainly been passed over lightly. For in their proverbs we most definitely learn the people's relation to Truth and everyday morality; the fewer mendacious proverbs a language has, the more veracious its people. On this point we must take note that there is always *some* truth at the heart of all proverbs. For they either say what *usually* happens, or what *ought* to happen, or they offer a concrete image to express a law from the kingdom of the spirit – and it is here that we discover the differences *between* peoples. No people is 'pure' as such, and nowhere can this better be seen than in a people's proverbs. The more reflective a people is, the less can we build on their proverbs, whereas the more cordial a people is, the more we can trust their proverbs. The important thing about proverbs is that they are incontestable, and their extremes are determinant.

Finally we come to the *poetic* significance of proverbs. To what extent do they express a historical importance that teaches us to understand the *poetic* side of a people? This has so far been largely overlooked, and unwisely so. For when there is any doubt as to whether a work from days of old belongs to the people in whose language it is couched, there can hardly be a more certain or conclusive proof than its proverbs! If we possess *them*, then they will more or less decide the matter for us. In proverbs we can see both the emphasis the people have laid on matters of the Spirit, as well as from which angle they have viewed the link between the sensory and the transcendental. In this regard we find singular differences in a people's proverbs, not only in their imagery but also in the tone in which they are commonly couched. The pithier they are, and the more meaning to be found in them – not contradictory, but gradually *increasing* meaning – the more their spiritual significance stands out, and the more poetry there undoubtedly was in the people. Conversely, the more partial and specific their commentary on the sensory, everyday world, the less poetic they are. Finally, proverbs show how close are rhyme, metre, and other poetic forms to a people; from their proverbs we can draw many important conclusions about the poetic practices that their writers have employed.

Unless I am very much mistaken, even this brief presentation should be enough to demonstrate that proverbs constitute one of history's most important sources. For the spirit, the language, and the mentality of a people are the soul of its *history*, which, in its turn, seeks to explain that people's achievements and significant events. How much lies ready here for anyone who has the desire and opportunity to advance the great concerns of the human race: the enlightenment of past generations and thus of humankind itself! How much can be done here to determine once and for all the many questions concerning kinship and other relationships! And how important it would be, for instance, to have a collection of *modern* Greek proverbs and compare them with those we possess in the *ancient* Greek writings! What an assured bounty lies in comparing them with the proverbs of the *East*. Nor can any theologian fail to realise that it is essential for a proper interpretation of the Bible to compare Hebrew and Arabic proverbs in order to ascertain the spiritual relationship between these two languages! Perhaps this is even the way to prise open the important writings of the Iroquois and the Huron![776] In such a 'proverb-Mithridates'[777] we would have a map of the human world and a spiritual genealogy whose absence no other scholar but the historian can fill!

Let us assume that this is right. Or let us at least allow that to meet every objection in this important matter we agree that proverbs make a substantial contribution to

776 The Native American speakers of the Iroquois language were primarily the Mohawk, Huron, Cherokee, Onondaga, Oneida, Cayauga, Tuscarora, and the Seneca. *The Constitution of the Five Nations* – or – *The Iroquois Book of the Great Law* was written long before the arrival of the Europeans, and may have had some small influence on the writing of the US constitution. The Iroquois constitution can be read online at https://sourcebooks.fordham.edu/mod/iroquois.asp.

777 According to Pliny the Elder's account of famous polyglots, Mithridates (120-63 BCE) could speak the languages of all the twenty-two nations he governed. If this is true, a number of them were most likely dialects.

a people's history that cannot be overlooked without loss. Let us further allow that they constitute the most important question we can ask about a people who lack a *written* language. Either way, it is also appropriate that this branch on the Tree of Learning should be nursed far more carefully than has so far been the case. Travellers in distant lands should make every effort to collect a hoard from these deep mines, and every people that wishes to know its forefathers must strive to make this area of its literature as complete and fruitful as possible. If this is to happen, there is no time to be lost, for under the present lethargy the treasure is disappearing by the day, and many a glorious proverb that no one has collected is to be found on the lips of the old people who next autumn will take it with them to the grave.

Nevertheless, we must leave this task to the separate peoples to decide how much or how little they wish to do for their history, for proverbs are not easily uncovered but must come to us of their own accord, or at least be 'prised out' of the people. We need a new kind of traveller on a new kind of journey to discover what constitutes an 'old saying' in other countries. But let us now dwell on our own land in the North – little it may be, but it is in every way a blessed and vigorous fatherland.

Danes require no real encouragement to collect proverbs, for they carry such a desire in their blood. But as a people we suffer from an excessive shyness, which is a blemish on us. It shows in our reluctance to promote what foreigners either do not like or have not previously praised elsewhere. It is what daunts us in this and other cases; it is what kills the proverbs on our lips and frightens them out of our books. It is this that has given the Germans, who do not know our old Danish books and sayings, the courage to claim that basically we are mere lumps on which they can set the heads. The incentive that we require is really only the courage and strength to show ourselves as we are, as God has created us, whom we trust in for our defence without having to ask what the German or the Norwegian or, for that matter, the Swede will say. It is well-known that I do not entertain any great thoughts about my own role in this. I am from childhood as shy as any Dane, but I have come so far, thank God, that I dare for all the world to stand by my faith and lineage. I say this despite knowing that these are things people turn up their noses at nowadays. So my hope is that many from Jutland and Zealand will come just as far. What turns hope into wisdom is, next after God, the truth of what we say loud and clear in the old proverb: 'the apple does not fall far from the tree'.[778] For as the chronicle of the Danes says, where the shyness that the *Rhymed Chronicle*[779] mentions is called a noble virtue, it was quite often confused with the vice which steals her clothes. When the national modesty or fear of other people that we have been speaking of became so pressing regarding

778 Grundtvig 1845, no. 1,565.

779 The *Rhymed Chronicle* (1495) was the first printed book in Danish.

God's truth and our forefathers' identity, then our hearts turned red with shame, and foreigners called our manhood no more than the 'modesty' that called up the flush on the cheeks of our Danish women!

Assuredly, all that we read nowadays was dear to our forefathers. We have become so small in our own eyes as well as those of foreigners, and our patch seems to them so threadbare and exposed that a puff of wind is enough to break every beech-tree, and a stroke of the pen enough to delete us from the number of existing *peoples*. If our misfortune is to be turned to *good* fortune, we must draw on our forefathers' proverbs! For they assuredly follow the people's spirit and not the spirit them! Only in the spirit's company are they warriors for the mother-tongue and the fatherland. We have to begin somewhere, and here we can draw on the old proverb that 'whoever sits closest to the fire is the first to get burned'[780] – whether we are thinking of the danger facing our finest proverbs, or considering what might justifiably be the first thing to ignite. In this regard we might justly say that what ignites best is what is closest to the fire, for what is the tongue closer to than the *word*, and what reminds us of the Spirit more powerfully than a pithy proverb?

I have endeavoured so often and so eagerly to urge my countrymen to recognise how important and laudable is all true *History*; it cannot be cherished, honoured and supported enough. And what a singular joy that we Danes, despite our small size, can pride ourselves on being its darling! So I repeat here the reminder of what that truth and fortune obliges us to do: namely, with all our strength to raise, illuminate, cultivate, and protect what is our true, spiritual fatherland, as it is here on earth, and thus promote the cause of *all* proverbs, and in particular the Danish. I myself have no regret over having looked after them according to my abilities and opportunities! Because my upbringing, like my origin, has divided me between Zealand and Jutland, my head, which finds such matters easy, has gathered many proverbs of the common people. These have taught me what Danish I know! And I derive benefit and amusement from comparing them with Laale and Syv's and with those of foreign peoples. But one thing is that I am well able to recall where all these proverbs have their origin, another thing is all the proverbs which have passed me by or which I have forgotten. What is important right now is that we acquire as complete a collection as possible and that we learn *how* they are used. For in Denmark as in all the European kingdoms there are various *peoples*, and one of the most essential means to discover their original circumstances is through their proverbs.

It is my prayer to all Danes who love their mother-tongue and their forefathers' memory and who live among the people outside the ramparts of Copenhagen that without asking what their neighbours do, what people will say, and what use it is, they

780 Grundtvig 1845, nr. 783.

will diligently note down every proverb they come across, seek the source on everyone's tongue, and add a note as to where they found it, be it on the lips of an individual or on the general tongue! If they have any reason to conjecture anything about how old or how new the individual proverb is, they would do well to point it out, for they will thereby help to answer the important question of the people's relationship to their proverbs. We shall soon see that no damage is done if the same proverbs end up in a hundred different collections; that indeed is their virtue! Wherever they are found, they must be *captured*, and it is one of our foremost questions as to how *common* they are. Nor would it matter if all the collections were printed without abridgements, for that would make them a witness whom Saga[781] could trust. Although this is more than we can hope for at present, we ought to ensure that the collections receive the broadest usage, so I therefore suggest that anyone who cares to take the trouble should donate his collection to the university library on the sole condition that whoever is regarded as trustworthy should be allowed to borrow them freely and without any special privilege, which is always a private thing and therefore not available to all.

If I had just one wish, it would be that no one would delay donating their collection until it came as a testament, but would give a little and often, for here too in both senses whoever gives immediately gives twice over. Some might raise the objection that there is some *self*-interest here, and insofar as I am Danish and therefore regard my fatherland's interests as being my own, they would be right to do so, as I shall demonstrate in abundance. It is well-known that I have Saxo's book in hand to translate into Danish.[782] This is making slow progress, as they say. But is that not always the case with us? And is it any better if it goes in leaps and bounds? Throughout the ages the decline and fall of the Danish people and their language has often seemed close at hand, and yet we have made slow *progress*, thank God. Moreover, it is doubtless best to follow History when one wishes to serve it. It is not my fault, nor should it be, that the first volumes of both Saxo and Snorri have not yet left my hand; I have exerted as much pressure as I could, but I have not been allowed to *print* want I want!

Without thereby defending my good friend, Mr. Seidelin,[783] and whoever else is involved in printing these days, I cannot deny that here, as with all our failed wishes, no damage has been done. Firstly, it was good that what was also making slow progress was allowed some useful hours to make its way sensibly – I am referring to the

781 In Nordic mythology Saga is the goddess of history and storytelling. In Grundtvig's view she has opened his eyes to the meaning and context of Nordic mythology. Her name, for him, is synonymous with History and Experience, as opposed to Reason.

782 Saxo (c. 1160-post 1208) worked as a scribe for the great Bishop Absalon (1128-1201). Saxo's *Gesta Danorum* (*Deeds of the Danes*) was handwritten in elegant Latin in 16 volumes. The early volumes contain mainly legendary material, but references to documented events become more and more common in later volumes. *Gesta Danorum* was first published in 1514. Grundtvig's Danish translation was published in 3 volumes in 1818-22.

783 Andreas Seidelin (1777-1840), court and university book printer.

joint subscriptions with which I can now gladden Danish hearts with the knowledge that they are almost shipshape. And secondly, it was good that I was allowed the time to collect my thoughts and, for instance, to study last year the *Rhymed Chronicle*, old Laale's proverbs, and the *Vocabularia ad usum decorum*[784] from 1510, from which I learned more Danish than in all the books of *our* time. Finally, I dare to believe that it was also good for my readers to collect *their* thoughts. However, 'moderation in all things'[785] runs the proverb, even when progress is slow. Whatever anyone else wants, I am hopeful that, God willing, both Saxo and Snorri will very soon have their work properly read and find its legs to walk on. And should a number of good old sayings turn up, be they common or perhaps unknown to me, then shame on anyone who does not want this! For I call this alms for the people who deserve them and who can make use of them! For many a proverb is found on the lips of the old artisans that it is not always easy to find the equal of, and in Saxo there is many a turn of phrase which like water *divides friends* if one cannot build a bridge with a proverb, so to speak.

On the other hand many a fine proverb doubtless exists round and about in the country that had been almost forgotten and could never be located than in the Chronicle. For when people read it, it comes to life, and if they do not, then it still has its place – with our forefathers. There are also many words that have been warped or are used awkwardly, just as there are quite a few that are used a lot even though they are not much good but which could with a small change be good. I venture to credit myself with such a cherished relationship with the spirit of these old sayings that at times I shall manage to be beneficial in the matter. I have not forgotten what was recently noted that when we touch the common proverbs we are touching the apple of the people's eye.[786] We must also do this at times when there is dirt in that eye; it is not my intention to be snappish, it is only to see what can happen with a certain 'carefulness', and most of all to ensure that a good saying finds a good place – and a bad word likewise. For many times the best way to kill off bad words is to put them in a bad mouth, which people would blush to say the half of! Moreover, much would be gained if we knew which proverbs that we had gathered were still in common use, for then we would know what we had in our charge and could at our own risk manage as we wished.

However, that is a minor matter. If the worse comes to the worst I can help myself with what I have in my books and brains. It would not be good if my translations were considered too 'classical', so no harm is done, and there is much to improve if only we structure matters as best we can for our successors I have stated my main

784 *Vocabularia ad usum decorum* (*Dictionary of Proper Usage*) by Christiern Pedersen (ca. 1475-1554) was the first Danish-Latin dictionary, published in Paris in 1510.

785 Grundtvig 1845, no. 1,761.

786 God to Israel in Zech 2:12: 'for whoever touches you touches the apple of his eye.'

consideration and will only add that I regard the question as being decided in favour of the mother-tongue, whereas others believe that our runes point to its ignominy. On the question of whether the language we speak was our forefathers' or was a hermaphrodite (the offspring of German and Icelandic), a more or less complete collection of our proverbs will speak for itself. Admittedly the usefulness of this, as of every other collection, would be far more considerable if the people of Iceland, Norway, and Sweden would institute a similar collection. For that would shed exceeding light on the mutual relation between people and language in the North, as well as on the relation of the North to both new and ancient peoples. But there is not much point in speaking of this, for one cannot expect it to be acted on; and such an initiative can never gain any purchase beyond the people in whose heart it arises. That it has now arisen in the heart of Denmark cannot be denied, even if my part in it were to be talked down. For Laale's collection is undoubtedly the oldest and Syv's the most complete in the North. Syv even had the vague idea of comparing and explaining the proverbs of *all* the peoples of the earth, which is what I have had an eye for here.

In closing, I should like to say a word about the use of proverbs in speech and writing, though that is no easy task when one has to distinguish between use and abuse. Nor does that help much, since what I have written here – as with everywhere that is concerned with rules for speech and writing in the mother-tongue – is determined by whether one knows what one wishes to say and is familiar with the spirit of the language. For otherwise no rules can help; and if that is the case, then none are needed.

I shall merely touch on the claim that proverbs should only be used in their lower style of everyday speech. I must urge the obvious truth that any style that does not as far as possible approach everyday speech is wrong and tortured. For public speech must be heard by ordinary ears, and books read by ordinary eyes! To put something into *style*, as our language quite rightly expresses it, does not mean we should endeavour to use *unusual* words, phrases, and ways of speaking – but after reflection to link the commonplace with a higher degree of plainness, clarity, and emphasis that is normally found in oral language. Using all that comes to hand is therefore obvious; never to make a mistake is a miracle; but that a style should by and large minimise the pith and emphasis of proverbs partly by becoming attached to them and partly by weaving them into oneself – that is clearly a ridiculous demand. More on these observations will find their rightful place in a general contemplation of language. May I for the present beg readers to be satisfied with the not insignificant hints that I consider appropriate to offer here. I cannot close better than with the proverb: 'Many a mickle makes a muckle.'[787]

787 Grundtvig 1845, no. 1,791. The English translation is in fact a Scots proverb. The Danish original translates literally as: 'Many small brooks make a big river'.

12. On the Word and the Mother-Tongue (1819)

Introduction by Kim Arne Pedersen

The title covers a number of drafts that Grundtvig made for his journal *Danne-Virke* (1816-19) with language as their theme, but these were not published in Danish until 1940, in *Værker i Udvalg (Selected Works)*.[788] There is a clear link between the first two sections, *On the Word* and *On the Word in Speech and Writing*, so these may well have been drafted for one and the same article, with merely an additional change to the title. If this is the case, the drafts suggest Grundtvig's plan was to produce three and not four drafts, as the headlines might indicate. The difference between these first two drafts and the following also immediately meets the eye. The first two belong in the context of the other articles in *Danne-Virke*, notably *On Truth, Greatness, and Beauty*, and in particular *On Revelation, Art, and Learning*. They are marked by metaphysical observations in an elevated language. With their frank and humorous tone the last two, *On Speech, Language, and Writing* and *On Denmark's Language*, bring us a little closer to the man in the street whom Grundtvig wished to address. We must bear in mind in the following that for the most part 'the Word' is synonymous with 'human language' – both of which are God-given, and are an image of the divine Word of Creation.

In the first two sections, *On the Word* and *On the Word in Speech and Writing*, Grundtvig expounds his philosophy of language "as the wonderful and mysterious bond between spirit and body" (340). He points out that philological research can only be successful on the basis of a "knowledge of language", meaning a *philosophy* of language, and he therefore concentrates on explaining "what the Word in itself actually *is*" (p. 341). His formulation seems to play on Kant's concept of "the thing in itself" (*das Ding an sich*), an observation which he supports with a refutation of the concept of Truth in *Critique of Pure Reason*.[789] Grundtvig argues against Kant's view, which he reproduces with a formulation close to Kant's own: that "Truth has no infallible hallmark except the demonstrable agreement between the object and the concept." Grundtvig likens Kant's concept – which he correctly construes to mean that Learning only applies to "sensory, tangible things" (ibid.) – to a philosophy of language that has no sense of the super-sensory. He thus criticises the so-called *onomatopoeic* idea that language came into being as an imitation of the sounds of the animals and objects that the first humans met on their path towards becoming *homo sapiens* – an explanation that was popular in the 18th century.

In the course of the article, Grundtvig attacks Professor of Moral Philosophy, Anders Gam-

788 The drafts are to be found in the Danish Royal Library: Kgl. Bibl. Gr. Ark. fasc. 171.

789 German title: *Kritik der reinen Vernunft*.

borg (1753-1833), whose work, *Studies in What is Duty. A Contribution to a Metaethic* (1794),[790] had advanced the idea that animals instinctively followed their destiny, and humans could therefore achieve clarity as to their duties by *observing* these animals, i.e. by following the "animals' analogy" (p. 342). The jurist and philosopher Anders Ørsted (1778-1863), brother of the famous physicist, had joined others to criticise this view, so Grundtvig was following suit in criticising Gamborg for likening humans to animals. The same goes for the onomatopoeic theory, says Grundtvig, which reduces language to a copying of "the impressions made on their senses by their surroundings and their circumstances" (ibid.). For him the faculty of speech is proof that human beings are created in the image of God, i.e. Christ, whom he depicts as the divine Creator's Word in the Prologue to John's Gospel. Christ as the Creator's Word is the mediator between God and His world. Similarly, in the following section, *On the Word in Speech and Writing*, Grundtvig distinguishes between the human Word as being "in itself the specific human *thought*" and its living activity, which unites alone with the "sound of the voice" (p. 346). Human speech reflects the Creator's action and His incarnation, whereby the Word becomes flesh (Jn 1:14).

In the third section, *On Speech, Language, and Writing*, Grundtvig adds to the foundations of his linguistic practice in *Danne-Virke* the principle of employing words and expressions that are widely known among the general public. He promises to use a language that in his own words is "good Danish" (p. 349), and with this popular and national aim Grundtvig contrasts himself with the Germans' attempt to "express all kinds of madness 'in the manner of the people'" (p. 348). This latter phrase is a translation of the German word *volcksthümlich*, which was popular among German nationalists of the day and may well reflect Grundtvig's abhorrence at the suggestion among German scholars that the Danish language could be debased to being a German dialect!

Linked to this was the ongoing debate on the relation between the Nordic and Germanic languages, and the question of whether "*our* mother-tongue is original, or is descended from German and Icelandic."[791] In 1811 the pioneering Danish linguist, Rasmus Rask (1787-1832), published *Guide to the Icelandic or Old Norse Language*,[792] in which he argued that Icelandic was identical with Old Norse, and commented on the origin of the Nordic languages and their relation to German. In 1814, at the behest of the Royal Danish Academy of Sciences and Letters, Rask was awarded the university's first prize and a gold medal for his study of the relation, both originally and in the Middle Ages, between the old Scandinavian language and, respectively, Old Norse and German dialects. Building on this, in 1818 Rask published his *Study of the Origin of the Old Norse or Icelandic Languages*.[793] His antipole in contemporary philology was *Germanic*

790 Danish title: *Undersøgelse om hvad der er Pligt. Et Biedrag til en Metetik.*

791 In fact, Danish is a North Germanic language, descended in turn from Old Norse, which has two sub-divisions. Danish and Swedish are assigned to the East Norse group; Norwegian, Icelandic, and Faeroese to the West Norse group.

792 Danish title: *Vejledning til det islandske eller gamle nordiske Language.*

793 Danish title: *Undersøgelse om det gamle nordiske ell. islandske Sprogs Oprindelse.*

Grammar (1819),[794] by the German, Jacob Grimm (1785-1863),[795] in which 'German' covers all the Germanic languages and thus also the Nordic languages.

With its nationalist overtones, the claim that Danish was derived from the Germanic languages did not escape Grundtvig's gaze. In its concentration on the Danish language, *On the Word* is also in part a retort to *Germanic Grammar*, but the main point in Grundtvig's text is the *Danish* language, and his distinction between the Danish word *Sprog*, which "denotes the inner workings of speech", and *Maal*, "the outer workings", i.e. the oral sound of the inner word. Here we can glimpse a philosophy of language that differentiates between 'the thought' as actual reality, and 'the spoken word' as its representation. However, Grundtvig's main aim in this section is not theoretical observation, but a defence of the Danish 'language of the people', in which "even using 'peasant' Danish can demonstrate a very eloquent usage" (p. 350). Grundtvig ends this draft with a call to return to "proper Danish" – using a phrase with which he is always linked: the mother-tongue is "the language of the heart (ibid.)."

In the final section, *On Denmark's Language*, Grundtvig starts with yet another attack on the Enlightenment thinkers – so common in *Danne-Virke*! This gives him the impetus to work with two types of such thinkers, the Nominalists and the Realists, as defined in the medieval dispute on the nature of general concepts or 'universals' (Lat. *universalia*). Realists argued that universals exist in and outside things, whereas Nominalists denied their very existence. Grundtvig uses the term 'realism' somewhat differently, namely as a designation for the educational ideas deriving from the German educator, Johann Bernhard Basedow (1724-90). Without mentioning Basedow's major work, *Elementary Book* (1774)[796] – an illustrated encyclopaedic collection of the material that was to be taught to children from birth to age 18 – Grundtvig explains the principles of education that the work promotes. He builds a bridge from Basedow's realism to an understanding of common nouns as random sounds with time-honoured usage, descending from the time when humankind was developing out of its original animal state. Through this process, says Grundtvig, Basedow's realism actually becomes Nominalism, since the words have no 'basis' in the reality they describe. He thus transposes the Nominalists' claim that general concepts are merely 'names' to the relation between language and the world it describes. With his belief that the Word (language) constitutes *true* reality, Grundtvig turns the relation between designator and the designated back to front; the created world's reality is due to its *dependence* on language. Language has its roots in the divine Word of Creation. We see here that Grundtvig's philosophy of language is part of his general criticism of Basedow. In the 18th and well into the 19th century, Basedow was famed for wishing to remove all metaphysics from Christianity, and his theology, as well as his linguistically-oriented educational practice leads, in Grundtvig's view, to a materialist philosophy of life.

794 German title: *Deutsche Grammatik.*

795 Together with his brother Wilhelm (1786-1859) he is better known as the author of *Grimm's Fairy-Tales* (1812-15).

796 Full German title: *Das Basedowische Elementarwerk. Ein Vorrath der besten Erkenntnisse zum Lernen, Lehren, Wiederholen und Nachdenken.*

1. On the Word

In my previous studies I have often described 'the Word' (i.e. language) as the wonderful and mysterious bond between spirit and body, and between Time and Eternity. The Word is a bodily spirit and a spiritual body, eternal in its foundation yet temporal in its distribution. I have diligently sought as best I could to postpone any publication of my thoughts on this divine wonder, inasmuch as I shrank from the many and major problems I would encounter. Even though a complete solution would benefit Learning, Time, and all good Fortune, I could only promise myself that I would only *half* solve them.

The reason why I am nevertheless making the attempt is that I hope to set up some useful signposts to the *wrong* paths that have so often been trodden in this area, and to send wiser sleuths on the *right* track. In spite of the many miles I have walked, I still cannot expect to reach the hidden *home* of the Word, or even to pursue it down the extraordinary paths where its sounds fly through the air among its peoples. The main reason why all my reservations must nevertheless now yield is the need to say what I think about the Word *in general* before I can make myself clear about not only our mother-tongue but about all that the Word mediates – and thus about all true human activity in the world. Standing where I do at the moment, I think I can make a useful contribution on the subject.

Since philology has flourished for a number of centuries now, and philosophy is also said to have made giant strides, we might expect that in the circumstances there would be no lack of trustworthy guidance to the illumination of 'the Word'. We can clearly see that without a *knowledge* of the Word, philology can never be a branch of Learning, and we can further ask what progress philosophy could make in the illumination of human life if it were not that it was precisely *in* human life that it found itself, and *through* human life that it found expression, viz. the saying, 'the Word was a dark speech to him'.[797] If we accept that it is only through a *scholarly* use of language that Knowledge can be mediated, it should be clear that either have both philology and philosophy so far been merely tottering – if they are not indeed still in their swaddling-clothes! – or we have actually made notable progress in the discovery and illumination of the secrets of the Word!

In whatever way my readers receive this article, for better for worse, I can only tell them this: philologists have treated the Word/language more or less the way philosophers have treated Truth. Fundamentally, they have treated it according to its merits

797 Num 12:8.

as an incomprehensible mystery – and yet they have considered themselves entitled to make judgements regarding the origin, value, and context of the various languages! In the same way philosophers also claim to know what was true *in the particular* with regard to both human and divine matters, yet they assert that Truth has no infallible hallmark except the demonstrable agreement between the object and the concept! In their version this means that Knowledge can be acquired only of sensory, tangible things.

The first question to which I wish to direct my readers' attention is the delusional folly that an explanation exists for something which has its foundation and source in the Word without first explaining what the Word in itself actually *is*! If I were successful in this alone, I would be satisfied, for that would set up a barrier for all the many *wrong* paths which have been thronged with people in recent times. Such paths all too easily tempt and accommodate all the well-equipped travellers on the Path of Learning, who, completely losing sight of their goal, are destined never to achieve it. If it is true that the Word/language in itself must have made our acquaintance before we can think about understanding it in the world and our work, it goes without saying that all philosophising about the various languages, literature, eloquence, and style that do not stem from this knowledge are a mere groping in the dark and an outburst of risible arrogance.

Of course, I do not mean that without a knowledge of the Word/language all pursuit of the above-mentioned goals is empty and fruitless. Others may assert this, I am speaking only of the *illumination* of the Word, which within its set limits is an irrefutable fact – as will be realised on closer consideration.

We know, for instance, that scholars question the relation between Nordic and Germanic languages and ask among other things whether *our* mother-tongue is original, or is descended from German and Icelandic.[798] To decide the dispute, we could, as has already been done, compare the individual elements with regard to their sounds and their other circumstances; we could even, as has not yet been done, compare them with regard to their context and totality. This ought to be resolved through the scholarly approach, but to determine the matter in its entirety is even more essential: namely, to have a clear understanding of the Word *as such*. For when we see two languages which in certain cases appear similar but in other cases differ, the question naturally arises as to what is *essential* to the language, and what is merely *incidental*. We must also ask how far one language can *derive* from another and to what extent such a language can gain independence and its own specific development. Such questions are linked to the

798 In fact, Danish is a North Germanic language, descended in turn from Old Norse, which has two sub-divisions. Danish and Swedish are assigned to the East Norse group; Norwegian, Icelandic, and Faeroese to the West Norse group.

previous statement concerning the first *origins* of all languages, and to the peculiar circumstances of the Word as such.

The same rules that apply to linguistic research also apply to studies of the use and abuse of the Word, its expression and style, its poetry and prose. Drawing on our historical Knowledge we can gather up and make firm conclusions, but we can never pass a scholarly judgement unless we have an insight into what the Word actually *is*, what it is capable *of*, and what is its *place* in the world. So it is no wonder that an unending battle has been waged concerning eloquence, or the correct style in history, poetry, and philosophy, etc.

The problem then arises: Can we actually get to know the Word/language in its very being and circumstances? This is a vital question, yet whatever the answer, it cannot invalidate the truth that we must refrain from presenting a scholar's judgement about something we fundamentally do not understand.

When we consider the problem, the first thing we note is that there are three conceivable ways in which we could gain knowledge of the Word: through reflection, through a knowledge of History, or through Revelation.

The first of these was attempted in the last century, when it was discovered that the Word/language in itself is no more than certain articulated sounds to which human beings in particular were qualified due to their bodily structure. By chance humans developed a form of the Word based primarily on the impressions made on their senses by their surroundings and their circumstances. Since then, as Reason awakened, the wisest heads of every people conceived a number of more or less arbitrary appellations for all manner of things, which were then agreed on. For some reason or other, once a people had acquired a sufficient degree of culture to form such an idea, a few of these words were chosen to designate super-sensory objects.

This was so simple and natural a use of the rule according to the animals' analogy that we might almost think a horse could have understood it and found it just as suitable as human beings did! In fact it was neither more nor less than a continuation of the Egyptian study of the origins of the Word/language which, as Herodotus tells us, consisted of placing two infants in a goat's stall, cutting the tongues of their wet-nurses and listening to the first words that the babies uttered.[799]

If the linguistic scholars of the 18th century had performed the same operation with posterity's wetnurses and separated all the peoples of the world by language, with their infants growing up beside their cattle, they would at least have avoided contradiction,

799 In his *Histories II:2 – An Account of Egypt*, Herodotus relates this experiment by the Egyptian Pharaoh, Psammetichus I (ruled 664-10 BCE), adding: "This is the story which I heard from the priests of Hephaestus' temple at Memphis...". The conclusion was that the Phrygian people antedated the Egyptians, because the child's first babbled word was *bekos* (bread). This is most unlikely! It is of interest in this context that nowadays most babies' first determinable sound is 'mum', which means 'mother' in English but 'food' in Danish!

even if their shrewd supposition had been proved wrong! However, since, despite assiduous attempts, the operation proved unworkable, I fear that posterity's first word to our erudite scholars will be the one they praised in their powerful objection to the 'enlightenment' of the Bible's in this, as in so many other cases, 'Codswallop'!

I am not sure whether it is worth the while to add anything more to this Egyptian 'wisdom', which relates to enlightenment as Egyptian darkness relates to the midday-light in Goshen.[800] However, it will do no harm to remark that the above conjecture regarding a historical fact older than any folk-tale, let alone any trustworthy evidence, cannot possibly be *proved* and is therefore of no use in proving something else! Even if it *were* provable, it would not teach us to *understand* the Word/language but at most to disdain its origins, an effect which also blind faith would achieve. In general we would then have disdained the various languages in the mouths of their peoples and in their older forms; we would have competed with each other to create new words which only our Creator understood; and, relying on the prevailing unparalleled cultural heights, we would have hoped gradually to have produced *new* languages! These would have belonged nowhere except in the wind that blew them in, but they would have expressed the great ideas of the times, the animal origins of humankind, and its divine progress so precisely!

Finally we must note that the only thing which might have made the Egyptian guesswork plausible – namely, an accordance with History – was missing to such an extent that History expressly contradicted it on every other page by presenting the *effects* of the Word, which according to the unshakeable principle of cause and effect allows it a super-sensory origin. Incidentally, the easiest way for most people to understand the lack of reason in the much-quoted guesswork would be to note that if it were true, then the history of all the cultivated languages would be the opposite of what most of them clearly show: if the Word had its origins in sensory impressions and later in reflection, it would be less metaphorical the further back one went, instead of being demonstrably more so. Similarly, imagery would resemble Arabic for us all, i.e. it would be inexplicable, instead of making a deep impression on us and producing a corresponding feeling and effect on even the most ignorant.

If we now leave the Egyptians, which we can do with a good conscience, we meet the Greeks, so to speak. Or rather, if we set aside all guesswork as to the animal origins of language, we come to the idea of its *divine* origins; and it is probably more reasonable to believe that a god rather than a dumb animal has been the language master of humankind.

In classical times, the idea was common that a god or an angel had taken the role of 'parent' of the first peoples and through interaction with them had taught them a

800 Ex 19:21-22. Five of the seven plagues were limited to Egypt and did not affect Goshen.

language, which then degenerated, while still retaining at least a few indelible traces of its high origins. Indeed, the idea was still in existence among several semi-biblical theologians in the previous century, with traces even in Schelling.

Obviously this new conjecture corresponds far better to the wonder and respect that a regard for the Word over the course of History instils in all who have an eye for the great and a heart for the deep. It also explains why the Word in classical times had an image for everything, since a supernatural being could not possibly regard earthly matters without having an image of something higher: in the likeness of what existed in the gods' sphere to which the language corresponded.

As a conjecture, this idea is irrefutable, but as *mere* conjecture it is of no use to us in a scholarly sense; if it is to be so, this cannot come about by simple reflection but only through the illumination of History or through Revelation.

Seen as the course of human life, History seems no more able to prove this idea than any other conjecture on the origins of the Word, since even the genuine myths of the first peoples can only teach us what they themselves *regarded* as their linguistic master, not what that master actually *was*; and if anyone said that the god was also a person, we lack all evidence to the contrary. It might be conceivable that human History could teach us to understand the origins of the Word from the angle where we no longer had the choice between a number of conjectures and a *particular* one as the only one possible, and therefore the necessary, explanation. I say 'conceivable', but it is far from rational; for since History forces us to admit a *super*-natural source for the Word, it must remain doubtful as to *how* it came into the mouths of humankind.

Imagine also that even if History could indeed enlighten us as to the origins of the Word/language in the world, it could not possibly tell us whether the Word is 'divine' in the *true* sense – in any other sense than that humankind is divine as an earthly image of the divinity. At this point, Revelation seems the only means, since "no one knows the thoughts of God except the Spirit of God... which searches all God's depths."[801]

I do not much care that there are many who consider 'Revelation' in this sense to be a folly, since I am not ashamed go to school in Pastor Street;[802] it is *another* question whether the revelation of what we cannot grasp can help us to understand something we otherwise failed to do. Clearly, this question must also be answered in the affirmative, since even in Mathematics we come to an understanding by building on an incomprehensible assumption.

Assuming that we have a reliable revelation in Scripture, what can we thereby learn about the Word?

---

801 1 Cor 2:10-11.

802 i.e. to have trained as a pastor and to believe in the Word of God.

"In the beginning was the Word, and the Word was with God, and the Word was God."[803]

2. On the Word in Speech and Writing

Even the most casual of glances reveals that the Word (language) is the highest expression of human life; and the most exhaustive studies can only testify to this from all sides. Just imagining the entire human race as being *without* speech reduces us to a kind of monkey, identical in a thousand generations and without heroic deeds and a history. 'The Word' is a true Hermes on winged feet,[804] flying down from heaven with wonderful news and beautiful sounds from on high, and bearing messages to all souls. He is invisible even to Argus,[805] and is the great teacher who develops the intellect and whose magic staff even the dead must follow to Elysium, to Orcus[806] and to the silent fame of their writings in posterity.

"In the beginning was the Word, and the Word was with God, and the Word was God. Through him all things were made; without him nothing was made that has been made. In him was life, and that life was the light of all mankind. The light shines in the darkness, and the darkness has not overcome it."

So speaks a divinely enlightened apostle about the foundational Word, which in the course of time "became flesh and made His dwelling among us",[807] and although the human Word is only a weak, dependent image of Him, it can nonetheless only be *grasped* in its very foundation. It is therefore no wonder that the darkness strove in vain to trace and grasp it, in and of itself. If we are to see it in its proper light, we must begin with a deep feeling of our own ineptitude at grasping what God is *in His foundation* and what can only be grasped *in and with Him*.

There may well be those who ask what is the point of trying to comprehend things that have been declared incomprehensible? However, for serious people such a question can only come from a lack of understanding, or from taking the word 'comprehend' in a different sense from the way it is always used in this connection – and must *always* be used according to its established sense in our language, where a difference is always drawn between 'comprehend' and 'understand'. Since it is undeniably the author's

803 Jn 1:1.

804 In Greek mythology Hermes is a son of Zeus and, with winged sandals, a messenger for the gods (the Roman 'Mercury'). Some sources give him a magic staff, a 'caduceus', with which he guides the dead and protects especially merchants.

805 In Greek mythology Argus is a many-eyed giant.

806 In Roman mythology Elysium (the Elysian Fields) was the place where those chosen by the gods lived a happy life after death. Orcus was a god of the underworld, who punished especially oath-breakers.

807 Jn 1:14.

duty to write as 'comprehendably' as possible, our first endeavour must be to present this difference – so often neglected in books – in a clear light.

To *understand* a book is to know what it is saying, but to *comprehend* it is to realise how it came into *being*; it also includes the ability to produce a matching piece which demonstrates that its concept is totally understood. On consideration, we must agree that here on earth we can only comprehend physical things in their *tangible* relation, only very few spiritual matters in their *temporal* relation, and nothing whatsoever in an *eternal* relation. We are said to comprehend physical things when we are as certain of their existence as we are of our own body's existence; and we know their relation, just as we know what we have *done*. We are said to comprehend spiritual things when they are just as certain as our own self-consciousness, and we can link their entire relation precisely to that. If we are to do so, we must allow them to originate in ourselves, i.e. we must be able to *create* them. For example, whoever says that he *comprehends* Homer or Shakespeare must be able to produce a poem which the connoisseurs who understand them declare to be their equal in every sense; whoever *comprehends* their gold must be able to do the same.

~

The human Word is in itself the specific human *thought*; in its power the Word is the living link between spirit and body; in its activity the Word is the spirit's living interaction. The Word/language can only be heard because it cannot unite with anything physical except the sound of the voice; its characters can be seen in letters, and for those who have heard the living Word it not only recalls but also inspires living thoughts – though only in those who themselves are writers.

The Word on the human tongue can be either sensory or spiritual, for although in its foundation and origin it is always spiritual, we must call it no more than sensory when it only expresses sensory things in their sensory relation, i.e. not just when we tell someone what we have eaten and drunk but also when we tell someone what we are thinking, inasmuch as these thoughts are either clearly restricted to the sensory world or originate in a sensory way of thinking – as when we relate History in the form of annals or declare the Trinity to be 'impossible'.

By contrast, the Word is spiritual when it expresses spiritual, super-sensory relations, whether they be solely spiritual, solely sensory, or somewhere in between. An example of the first is when we speak about the relation between God and our soul, and of the second when we speak about the relation between the parts of the world and the parts of our body; or, somewhere in between, when we speak of sensory things as images of spiritual ones, such as light as an image of truth, fire as an image of love, and flame as an image of power.

Just as the Word only exists in speech through its physical power, and in writing through its characters, so is the spiritual Word only present through its power in poetry and its characters in prose, insofar as these are sharply separated, just as the description of the Tabernacle is when compared to Psalm 84.[808]

We could describe poetry as the spiritual Word which gives living expression to a spiritual relation when we attribute to life something sensory in which it reflects itself.

Poetry can be the third kind of Word, which must not be thought of as separate from, or equal to, the others, but subsequent to them, so that the second two presuppose the first and the third presupposes both the others.

The foundation of poetry is the supremely spiritual *Song of Songs*,[809] which speaks of spiritual matters in similes by naming sensory things which indicate and depict them, just as their Creator ordained earthly images. We can also call such poetry 'the poetry of power', since it transforms the entire sensory world into an image of the Spirit and creates a sensory language in which the Spirit can demonstrably and animatedly express itself.

The poetry which follows may be called 'historical' in that it celebrates the impact of the Spirit in the course of time, whether it be in spiritual interaction or in spiritual effect on the sensory world.

The last poetry is poetry of the light, which seeks to illuminate the previous direct contemplations of indirect observations of sensory things in space and time; it sets out to present them as witnesses to the spiritual relation in which they are viewed and in which they have their true foundation; in so doing, it transfigures them in their context and consequence.

Plainly, this kind of poetry is approaching philosophy; yet it would be a mistake to object to the distinction between the two; no true philosophy is possible except as the son of such a mother, and philosophy is nothing but the detailed evidence that the transfiguration of existence by the poetry of light is true and absolute.

Poetry of the light may again be divided into two areas, dependent on the two preceding subjects which it is to transfigure: History and Nature. Of these two History must of necessity come first, since the lower must be transfigured by the higher, and the Spirit which reveals itself in its effects must be transfigured *by* them. The Word is an effect of the Spirit, and the sensory world is an effect of the Word. The Word must first be transfigured, and this must be the foundational Word of God

808 Yahweh's meticulous prose instructions on how to build the Tabernacle to house the Ark of the Covenant are found in Ex 25-27 and 35-40. By contrast Psalm 84, 'How lovely is your dwelling-place,' is a poetic hymn to YHWH of profound beauty – matched by Brahms' famous setting of it in *A German Requiem* (1868).

809 The OT *Song of Songs* is of uncertain date, some time before the 2nd cent. BCE. The title shows its superiority to all other songs (cf. the holy of holies). It is unique in its celebration of sensory and spiritual love, interpreted as an allegory of the love between God and Israel.

in which Spirit and Word are one. This Word cannot be the Creator's Word which brought the world into being, for that acted *apart* from us; it must be the Word which acted on humankind and which is illuminated by its *effects*, and it is these effects that constitute true human life as such. Only when human life is interpreted as an effect of the Word of God can the world be transfigured in that light, for human beings learn that their bodies are instruments of the Spirit. They are a world in small-scale, or rather in large-scale in their close link to the Spirit, for this indubitably exists in humankind, most clearly in the human Word which is produced through and with a bodily instrument, namely the voice.

Poetry of the light must transfigure first the Word and its History and next the voice and its Nature, first what we call poetry and then what we call music: the coherence of History and the harmony of Nature, both as effects of the almighty Word of God.

3. On Speech, Language, and Writing

There was a time in Denmark when one could search long and hard for anything on speech and style but nevertheless came across *writing* in all its guises, apart from biblical language and proverbs. Indeed, there are those who would claim that it was a time when all things were gold-plated, a time that ought to be called the literary golden age, the age when the dominant language – a simple German – came close to replacing our own mother-tongue of pure Danish.[810] We may well wonder whether those days are completely behind us, but in general there is little left to see of German, since 'Each devil has his time and each time its devil'.[811] Only the Devil could keep it upright, even though it was dead from dropsy and is buried in the Common.[812] In other words, the madness of mixing up all sorts of languages and mother-tongues is on the steep, downward slope, both among us and among the Germans. In fact we are beginning to ask if the words – and occasionally the phrases – that we use belong *elsewhere* than in our own writing; are they part of *our* mother-tongue?

A rapscallion might deny that each devil has his time and that the Devil is a devil of a fellow who is plotting his masterstroke to express all kinds of madness "in the manner of the people",[813] but if I am not much mistaken about our mother-tongue, it will put this devil of a fellow to shame. In plain Danish, lies and wickedness will

810 This was still happening in Grundtvig's lifetime, and he dedicated most of his life to shoring up Danish against the invasion of German, not only of German troops but also of German philosophy and language. Only ten years earlier than this essay, during his stay at Egeløkke Manor (1805-08), the Danish family's first language was German!

811 'All devils have their time' is an ancient proverb which Grundtvig also used in his hymn, 'If you are feeling low, dear friend', no. 67 in *Living Wellsprings* (2015).

812 'The Common' is the largest and most popular park in Copenhagen, north of the centre. Grundtvig's reference indicates that this was the most 'Danish' place in Denmark, where no German would be heard.

813 Here Grundtvig uses the German word *volcksthümlich*.

hardly be a success in Denmark, while outside the country any attempt to wield them against us will not be welcome to the Dane. For that reason it is worth instituting a brief examination of what constitutes 'good Danish', and if it is any use, it will be welcomed by all the writers and speakers among us. Whatever we are aiming at, it is always good to know what one is saying and to be able to talk the hind leg off a donkey![814] I have long had it in mind to inform readers of *Danne-Virke* of the annotations concerning our mother-tongue which I as a reader have observed and as a writer have made a mental note of, but since I had no wish to write an entire grammar-book, I have been in doubt as to where I should begin. To tell the truth, that in a sense is where I still remain; but I do see that it can never be out of the way first to say what I intend to say – and then that comment has been coined!

I will begin with *Sprog* (the Danish word, countable, for 'language', ed.). This is doubtless a genuine Danish word, to be sure, but not in the sense in which it is most often used nowadays, when it means both the spoken and the written word and is thus ambiguous in meaning. Unintentionally, it resembles the German *Sprache*, yet the Danish word is quite different in meaning, as we can see when we compare the Danish *Ord-Sprog* (meaning 'proverb' – but etymologically 'word-language', ed.) and the German *Sprüch-Wörter*[815] (also meaning 'proverb' – but etymologically 'language-saying'). Here we can see that if any German word is to correspond to the Danish, it must be *Spruch*. However, this makes the matter no clearer, for when we speak our *Hjerte-Sprog* (etymologically, 'the language of the heart,' ed.) as honestly as we can, *Spruch* is nowhere near *Sprog*, and we must 'let the liver do the talking'![816] On the question of *speaking* language therefore, we must admit that *Sprog* in Danish denotes the inner workings of speech and *Maal* the outer workings. 'He understands the German language' does not mean in Danish 'He is eloquent in German', only that he thinks and speaks *like* a German, a quality he may possess without being able to understand a word of German!

I am well aware that nowadays we have many speakers of foreign languages among us and that many of the books printed here are written in a good Danish which not every peasant farmer understands. After all this, and after all our research into languages, not to mention our linguistic studies (which we may call 'botchings') and even worse after all our language *teachers*, it will take time before we understand the

814 Grundtvig's own footnote 16: "Here I cannot help noting that nearly all our writers confuse 'lay' with 'lie' and even among the better writers we find 'sit' instead of 'set'. I had long thought such writing errors impossible, even when one was scribbling, but experience has taught me that in particular 'laid' for 'lain' is a shibboleth by which one can more or less recognise all our Ephraimites (Jg 12:1-6)".

815 Nowadays spelt *'Sprichwörter'*.

816 Grundtvig's own footnote 17: "'Frisch von der Leber' as the Germans say, which we might be tempted to translate as 'fresh from the liver'. Incidentally, I am inclined to think that the Germans mean in addition that one really speaks one's mind except when one is either angry or seeking to show off."

language properly. Indeed, I cannot even make promises to myself on this account, for 'The less one has, the easier it is remembered'. However, this does not prevent me from declaring open war on this highly un-Danish usage, and when I use such language I know it is understood! Time will tell whether to call this idea good or bad, but everyone who mixes with genuinely Danish people must admit that, even if Danish were the poorest of all languages, it is important to speak *good* Danish, and that even using 'peasant' Danish can demonstrate a very eloquent usage. In my view, this is evidence enough that we give ourselves away if we call a fluent usage 'good' and a highbrow usage 'elevated'. Whoever wishes to write proper Danish should make every effort to rid themselves of *wrong* usage and replace it with good usage or phrasing. After a lengthy misuse of language this can be difficult, but it is far more rewarding, for in this way we can make good strides back towards the language of the heart!

4. On Denmark's Language

After an age that was known to be enlightened and rational, we would expect to find a priceless inheritance. This should have been in every sense the case with the 18th century, when there were so many people of distinction, both physically and spiritually. In fact, however, they were *beggars*, who lived with pouffe-sleeves and decked themselves in stolen feathers. Sadly, the century was a patched-up affair of interest on loans and stolen goods; it died as a scoundrel both on its own terms and in the proper sense of the word, with a legacy by and large of debt and shame. Like the stunted cattle of the Nile[817] the 18th century ate up the fatness of the past and became a skinny bag of bones unworthy even of the knife; it died of cattle disease and lies behind us as carrion for ravens and crows. Its only use is as bait to shoot the foxes that in the winter of our age come swarming out of the ground. I do not intend by this to impugn any honest person, or to deny that among its writings the previous century owned many a sincere person who believed they were doing their best. There are those lying in their graves who deserve our thanks, but in general the spirit of that century was a poor, conceited Devil. Those who refused to be possessed by him, or at least tried to extricate themselves from his attacks, were regarded as outlaws from previous barbaric times. While this was in fashion, the way they treated people, Faith, and Learning was the most mistaken, upside-down, idiotic way yet seen on earth! It might be thought that I owed the kin and friends of these now-departed a proper balance sheet for this accusation, and this would undoubtedly not be difficult to do – not just with words in columns

817 Gen 41:1-4. In Pharaoh's dream seven fat cattle come out of the Nile, followed by seven lean cattle which proceed to eat them up, yet still remain lean. Joseph's interpretation is that seven years of famine will follow seven years of abundance.

but with good old-fashioned *evidence*, with the unpaid bills from previous ages and the autographed writings of the dead. But there is no need of this, for it is as clear as sunlight for anyone who has eyes to see, and I have so much evidence that this has nothing to do with actually *blind* people that I would rather trust the few testimonies that are *un*signed than the many that *are*. I could not help pointing this out, partly to stop people thinking that I would go out of my way for the ghost that still walks the earth – as is the habit of those who moved the boundary line and measured only the number of tricks involved – and partly to prepare a suitable introduction for what I wish to say about language in general and our mother-tongue in particular.

It is common knowledge that in the last century there were in every sense two kinds of people in educated circles. We can conveniently divide them into their titles: Nominalists and Realists,[818] adding only that there was just as little that was 'real' about the Realists as there was about their old scholastic kinsmen! The educational philosophers were called Realists because they led the way for children and made them believe all kinds of things, both with or without picture-books. Their foundational principle was that children ought to learn all manner of things, but that since Art is long and Life is immeasurably brief,[819] and since the time for education is both fleeting and thorny, one should be satisfied with learning – apart from a handicraft such as shoemaking or writing – the names of all kinds of things and thus turning genuine heavy metal into mere names. They then actually become Nominalists, and like all sorts of other things clearly of not much use! Nevertheless, the separation continues, for the Realists answered to their name by working hard at what only had *real* value in the eyes of the world. This included the knowledge as to what we should eat and drink and how we should clothe ourselves; knowledge concerning all manner of current coinage and dealings; agility in the leap-dance and the leap-frog; and cheating in all the arts of success such as at the bedside table, gambling at the gaming table, and at every table and bench where games are played.

When it comes to language, the most important thing is to learn a little of the languages that are in fashion – to one's advantage and pleasure. However, to be certain, and for the sake of the uneducated and one's own honour, it would be wise to forge a *new* word rather than use a word *borrowed* one from other languages. In passing, they believed it was not so important what the words meant or where they came from; they

818 The Nominalists and Realists are the names of the two main movements in medieval scholasticism. Briefly, Nominalism is a type of metaphysical anti-realism. It holds that things like universals, essences, and abstract objects do not exist at all, whereas Realism claims that they do. Grundtvig is thinking in particular here of the progressive work of Johann Basedow (1724-90,) a German educational reformer, teacher and writer, who together with Rousseau was among the first philosophers to consider *child*-centred education.

819 A reference to the famous Greek/Latin proverb: *Ars longa, vita brevis* (*Art is long, life is short*). This was first attributed to Hippocrates (460-c.370 BCE), then translated by Seneca (4 BCE-65 CE).

were simply as valuable as money. In a time that produced words enough for money but cared not a fig for *good* words, the wisest heads looked at their *real* value, let the words manage as best they could, and instead asked what money *cost* and where it came from. In all events one could fool children into believing that people learned first to bray, then to bark, then little by little to speak, and finally in the 18th century, after millions and billions of days, to talk sensibly!...[820]

820 The manuscript, being a draft only, breaks off here.

V

YOUTH

13. Youth in Our Time (1850)
14. Three Speeches at Marielyst People's High School (1866, 1868, 1871)

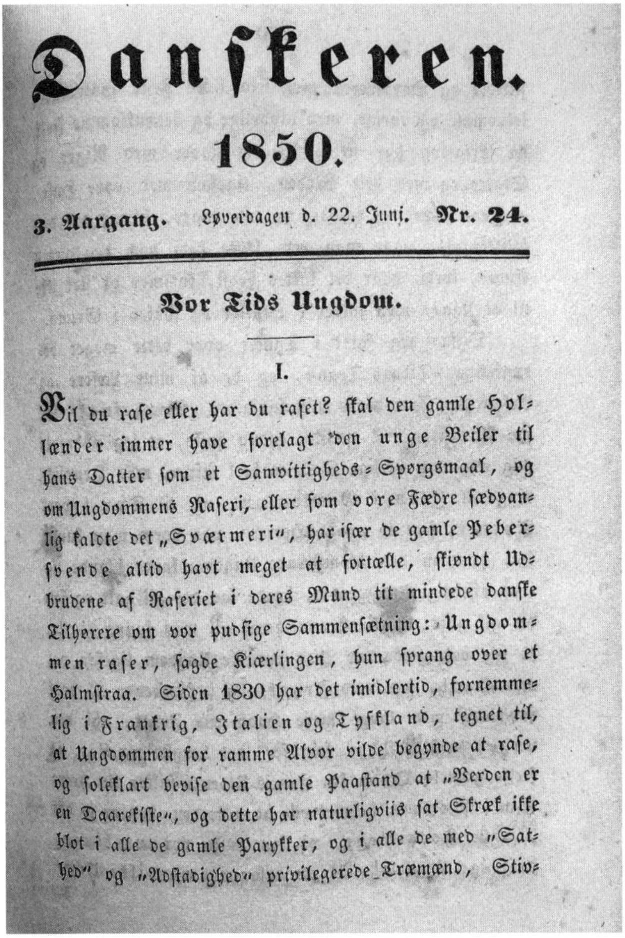

Danskeren.

1850.

3. Aargang. Løverdagen d. 22. Juni. Nr. 24.

Vor Tids Ungdom.

I.

Vil du rase eller har du raset? skal den gamle Hollænder immer have forelagt den unge Beiler til hans Datter som et Samvittigheds-Spørgsmaal, og om Ungdommens Raseri, eller som vore Fædre sædvanlig kaldte det „Sværmeri", har især de gamle Pebersvende altid havt meget at fortælle, skiøndt Udbrudene af Raseriet i deres Mund tit mindede danske Tilhørere om vor pudsige Sammensætning: Ungdommen raser, sagde Kiærlingen, hun sprang over et Halmstraa. Siden 1830 har det imidlertid, fornemmelig i Frankrig, Italien og Tyskland, tegnet til, at Ungdommen for ramme Alvor vilde begynde at rase, og soleklart bevise den gamle Paastand at „Verden er en Daarekiste", og dette har naturligviis sat Skræk ikke blot i alle de gamle Parykker, og i alle de med „Sathed" og „Adstadighed" privilegerede Træmænd, Stiv-

9. First page of *Youth in Our Time*, 1850

From 1816-19 Grundtvig had published his own journal, *Danne-Virke*, from which 8 of this book's 14 chapters are taken. Beginning on 22nd March 1848, Grundtvig wrote and published a weekly newspaper called *Danskeren (The Dane)*. Its purpose, as he writes in the foreword to the first edition, was "to help good Danes understand themselves and each other." The statistics are astonishing. In 1848 he wrote 41 editions running to 658 pages; in 1849, 1850, and 1851 he wrote 52 editions running to 826 pages each year, making a total of 3,136 pages over 4 years. During this period Grundtvig was also drawing up the new constitution, winning election to the new democratic parliament in 1849, sitting on an anti-slavery committee, reviewing the first feminist novel in Denmark positively, mourning his first wife, writing love-poems to his new fiancée, marrying her, becoming a grandfather, and worrying about his two sons fighting in the border war against Germany. Indeed, it was this First Schleswig War (aka Three Years' War) that occupied him most in *The Dane*. The fear of invasion and of Denmark becoming a mere German province drove Grundtvig to produce hymns, poems, and polemical articles to fortify the Danes in their struggle. In the event, the country survived this war, but lost the subsequent one in 1864 – together with the whole of Schleswig-Holstein. *Youth In Our Time* praises the Danish youngsters for risking life and limb for the fatherland and the mother-tongue.

13. Youth in Our Time (1850)

Introduction by Kim Arne Pedersen

This article appeared in the third volume of Grundtvig's weekly periodical, *The Dane* (1848-51), which he published - and for the most part wrote - in the years of the First Schleswig War (1848-50). He takes a critical look at two works from 1842 by the Swedish Professor of Medicine, Israel Hwasser (1790-1860): *Youth in Our Time* and *On Marriage*.[821] The latter had been a contribution to the so-called "It is alright"-debate about marriage as a lifelong institution, a debate set off by a novel of that title by Carl Almqvist (1793-1866), published in 1839. In his criticism from 1841 (with an additional printing in 1842), Hwasser had criticised Almquist's argument that the sexes contract their alliances *outside* the institutions of society. Although the works were thus interlinked, 10 years have passed before Grundtvig takes up a position on them. Throughout, he calls Hwasser "the old man", even though Grundtvig himself is 7 years older, and he draws on the Swedish physician's publications to present his own views in the fields that Hwasser touches on.

En route, Grundtvig refers to contemporary European and Danish politics, as he develops his criticism of the revolutionary tendencies among the young people of his day. He argues, like Hwasser, for youth to be calm and collected. Rather than revolutionise society, as the youth of 1848 were inclined, they should *serve* it. He has seen at first hand how they are willing to self-sacrifice for their country, since his own two sons, Johan (1822-1907) and Svend (1824-83), had volunteered and were sent to the front with Germany on the Danish southern border. Their participation in the war undoubtedly forms part of the background for Grundtvig's appeal to the public spirit of contemporary youngsters, even though he does not mention his sons. Instead he offers a declaration of trust in those youngsters occupied in practical trades and a minor reproach to academic students, who never get their hands dirty.

Grundtvig's admiration of Hwasser comes as something of a surprise, considering Hwasser's support for the German idealists - and Grundtvig's own clash with the Danish physicist, H.C. Ørsted.[822] Yet Grundtvig is not blind to the advances of medical science or to Hwasser's ideas of polarity, inspired by the German natural philosopher and physician, Dietrich Kieser (1779-1862). For Kieser, all courses in nature are determined by contrary poles, by tensions which in the organic world are more complex than in inorganic nature. In the organic world the development of health and justice is dependent on the maintenance of a harmonious balance between the higher/positive and the lower/negative, material poles. In a healthy body the higher, spiritual

821 Swedish titles: *Om vår tids ungdom* and *Om äktenskapet.* Dr Hwasser was Professor of Medicine in both Finland (Turku and Helsinki) and in Sweden (Uppsala).

822 See p. 22.

pole is dominant, and illness therefore occurs only when the lower pole acquires the upper hand. This causes the spiritual pole to increase its power, and unless the conflict ends in the death of the organism, it is the positive power that will end up as the dominant. Hwasser's successful application of small-pox vaccines to young people was a case in point.

The theory of polarity also lies behind Hwasser's description of, in Grundtvig's words, "the richer measure of life" that youth has gained from the smallpox vaccinations that saved the lives of many young people. This was "an advantage in the course of time which previous ages lacked, and thus our common life together is more than ever subject to change" (p. 360)." Under Hwasser's inspiration Grundtvig says that if the positive power to develop possessed by youth is strong enough to dominate, it will lead to "a true and timely change in human life", where the old form can "perish" but "without any real disturbance, since the new form has quietly developed *out of the old.*" But if the activity of youth seeks only revolution, and is more destructive (negative) than constructive (positive), it would be a disaster for all: what if the new-born infant "proves to be a monster!" In contrast, when the *new* form develops peacefully *out of the old*, "the whole movement then proves to be a transition rather than a perdition, a substitution rather than a dissolution" (ibid.). In accordance with Grundtvig's philosophy of the ages of life, it is important that young people realise that their youthful years are years of 'flowering', and that this flowering should bear fruit and benefits for society at large.

In speaking on behalf of "the vitality of the *people*... to put into effect this human policy in a natural and timely way" (p. 371), Grundtvig acknowledges Hwasser's natural-philosophical defence of peaceful change, rather than the revolutionary change that is sweeping through Europe in 1848 – even as Grundtvig was writing this article. Since the people need "illumination from both sides – from the natural as well as the historical – or rather from natural history as much as from popular history" – Grundtvig allows Professor Hwasser to represent the former, while he himself represents the latter. Moreover, he accepts and promotes the wisdom of Hwasser's view of women: "transition and substitution is the only *natural* change in human life, for it is the way whereby every mother is regenerated in her daughter" (ibid.). With this mother-birth-daughter analogy come "the truly human laws of nature" rather than "the physical freedom (the liberation of the *flesh*)" that the youth are fighting for in 1848. Grundtvig is convinced that he and Hwasser are both promoting a development which accords with the fundamental laws of human life that come with humankind being made in God's image. Grundtvig's contrast of revolutionary youth with self-sacrificing youth is not without its nuances. He expresses his understanding for young people's determination to change the existing state of things, so that a more humane society can be established, but there are nevertheless two misunderstandings in their perception. However much our culture has been marked by attitudes that sit poorly with the human laws of nature, it is wrong to think of 'humanity' as something that "can be uniformly grafted onto each individual without regard for a people's characteristics or natural aptitude" (p. 368). The second misunderstanding is the belief that through upbringing and education children can become adults without taking into consideration "the particular nature of the seasons of human life: childhood, youth, adulthood, and old age" (p. 369). Although both these errors have helped to create an inhumane society, revolution is not the way forward, says Grundtvig. With reference to Denmark's experiences at the outbreak of the First Schleswig War (1848-51) he argues that young people must be prepared to give of themselves, "with girls rivalling boys as to who was the more willing to sacrifice what they held most dear in their beloved country" (p. 371).

~

I

"Have you finished kicking over the traces or are you only thinking about it?" said the old Dutchman, as he searched the conscience of a young suitor seeking his daughter's hand. With regard to 'passion' – or what our forefathers used to call 'infatuation' – our old Danish bachelors in particular have always had much to say, even though the 'passion' that issued from their mouths often reminded their audience of our droll proverb: "'Young people rebel,' said the old woman, as she jumped over a straw!" However, since 1830 the signs, particularly in France, Italy, and Germany, are that young people are beginning to rebel in deadly earnest and to prove beyond doubt the ancient claim that 'the world is a madhouse'! This has of course frightened the life out of all the old periwigs and privileged woodentops, the stick-in-the-muds and killjoys, with their 'stolidity' and 'gravity'. Yet even among the majority of wide-awake, quick-witted, free-spirited yet serious and reflective people, experience has taught us that what happens to our houses also happens to our kingdoms, to our states, and to the whole wide world: however crooked and run-down they are, everything goes wrong when we try to turn them upside-down, for at best they collapse and turn to ruin!

I too have been speculating on this very alarming 'sign of the times', and those readers who attended my so-called *Bragi Talks*[823] seven years ago may still remember how I expatiated on this hazardous subject for a whole evening. I referred to Zeus[824] in Greece and Tyr[825] in the North as two 'young men' on whom we could see that

823 *Bragi Talks* (*Bragesnak*). In Nordic mythology Bragi is the god of skaldic poetry. On Mondays, Wednesdays, and Fridays between 20th November 1843 and 31st January 1844 Grundtvig gave a series of 25 talks entitled 'Bragi Talks on Greek and Nordic Myths and Ancient Legends for Ladies and Gentlemen'. For the first time, ladies were present at these lectures, and biographers have noted how Grundtvig repeatedly addressed them in an unconsciously paternalistic, even sickening, manner, as well as complaining of 'worms in my head'. Shortly afterwards he suffered a second nervous breakdown. The talks were collected and published in 1844.

824 In Greek mythology Zeus is the sky god, the king of the gods on Mt Olympus.

825 In Nordic mythology, Tyr (pronounced 'tier') is the god of war, law, and justice. In order to help the gods shackle Fenris, Tyr, the god of war, puts his hand into the Fenris wolf's mouth and has it bitten off. In Grundtvig's symbolism he represents honour and courage – in contrast to self-will. Tyr has lent his name to Danish *Tirsdag* (Tuesday).

when the bloom of youth became involved in public matters, they could do right *or* wrong! Readers may have already concluded that I regard bright young people with both hope and fear, but with regard to our North I do so with far more hope than fear. In order to save ancient Odin from the Fenris wolf for as long as possible the young, intrepid Tyr put his right arm into the wolf's mouth, well knowing that it would be bitten off. He is the most celebrated example we could wish to present for our self-respecting youngsters.

Our Nordic young people are living up to the hopes that I have previously nurtured for them – hopes that are great and extraordinary, yet historically and mythically well-grounded! This has already been clearly proved in my eyes by their bold, honourable, yet equally spirited and willing participation in the 'Jutland War'.[826] The lamentable snail's pace of this war has dispirited and drained them, but it has not yet paralysed or enfeebled our young cubs. Nevertheless, the circumstances are clearly so complex and the temptations of youth to turn everything upside-down so great in our day that human life badly needs illumination from both sides – from the natural as well as the historical – or rather from natural history as much as from popular history. At this point I shall therefore turn to another person's reflection on the 'youth of our time' which, completely independent of me, reaches this same conclusion: Although in general the excesses and blunders that the youth of our time are tempted to commit are frightening enough, we have a youth full of *hope*, one that can therefore 'furnish our house' with far better prospects for the future than our forefathers for many a generation! I realise that most of my contemporaries and even the majority of elderly people would hardly believe this, even though it is being shouted from both sides of the Sound[827] with recognisably separate voices, but this is the fault not of the young people but of our long-standing lack of *faith* in them. The worst enemy of our Nordic youngsters is the irresolution and overconfidence with which they have been systematically raised, and they will doubtless feel strengthened by the good intentions based on the encouragement of experience from both sides.

I feel even more certain of this after one of our young lads recently drew my attention to the elderly Dr Hwasser in Uppsala,[828] whose observations regarding 'youth in our time' I find worthy of note. In the following I shall attempt to present my readers with an 'extract' of his views.

The Old Man begins by repeating previous statements from his study of marriage (an equally notable work), to the effect that thanks to the cowpox, present-day youth is not only more numerous but also healthier, braver, and stronger than youth has

826 i.e. the First Schleswig War.

827 The Sound is the strait separating Zealand (Denmark) from Scania (Sweden).

828 Dr Israel Hwasser (1790-1860) was Professor of Medicine in both Finland (Turku and Helsinki) and in Sweden (Uppsala).

been for a very long time![829] Even though as a historian I cannot possibly allow that this is due to *cowpox* – to which neither our old friend in Uppsala nor I myself can solely attribute our youthful vigour! – I nevertheless thank the doctor for a comment which contains much truth, for cowpox did indeed contribute to producing the promising young people who surround us, and who partly control us! I shall refrain from commenting further on the clear-eyed doctor's observations regarding smallpox as the scourge of the land. For many centuries it not only took away one-tenth of all children, but also disfigured and paralysed numberless people, no less internally than externally. There is no doubt some exaggeration here, and it would take too long to pursue the otherwise well-grounded comparison between the bodily and the spiritual national epidemics over the course of time. However, I cannot help but remark that if we continue to believe that through their immunity to the destructive influence of smallpox the youth of our time have in general considerably more physical strength and a consequent love of life and adventure than those of previous times, then that would most easily explain the latest actions of France's youth, Italy's youth, and partly Germany's youth, which have undoubtedly been far more external than internal and far more powerful in the world of action than of spirit.[830]

The writer has doubtless had *foreign* youth in mind rather than our Nordic youth. It is not his fault that seven years ago our Nordic youth had yet to set out on a new path, and since it is only halfway to becoming aware of its special Nordic character, what he says applies to us too as regards the current unbridled unrest and the great matter of the moment. This is: to create a glorious future with our incomparably rich resources! The task is far beyond the power of our youth and all its gods, because they regard it from the wrong angle and think that merely by breaking down all that stands in the way of their friends, some zealous spirits will of their own accord build a new palace in a single night and wake in the morning with Aladdin's lamp![831]

The Old Man of Uppsala develops this to mean that through its richer measure of life, youth has gained an advantage in the course of time which previous ages lacked,

---

829 Cowpox was an infectious disease often transmitted by dairy maids via the cow's udders. In 1796 Edward Jenner (1749-1823) discovered a preventative 'vaccine' (etym. 'of or from the cow') which made people immune not only to cowpox but also to the much more dangerous smallpox virus. Jenner was hereafter known as 'the father of immunology' and his work is thought to have saved more lives than any other individual's. Cowpox is rare nowadays; in 1979 the World Health Organisation declared smallpox to be eradicated completely.

830 1848 was the 'Year of Revolution' throughout Europe, the most widespread revolutionary wave in European history. It was particularly powerful in Italy, France, and Germany, with youth and the working-class at the forefront. Alexis de Tocqueville (1805-59) wrote in his *Recollections* (publ. 1893): "Society was cut in two: those who had nothing united in common envy, and those who had anything united in common terror."

831 The first known reference to the *1001 Nights* is a 9th-century fragment. The tales appeared in various Middle Eastern collections until they were published in a French translation in 12 volumes (1704-17). Only here does the story of Aladdin first appear (along with Ali Baba and Sinbad the Sailor). With the aid of a magic lamp and a magic ring Aladdin defeats the Sorcerer, marries the princess, and after several trials, eventually lives happily ever after.

and thus our common life together is more than ever subject to *change*. However, since every change involves the destruction of the old and the rise of the new, change will naturally not come about if the activity to secure it is more destructive (negative) than constructive (positive), and if the new-born infant proves to be a monster! Conversely, should the developmental dynamic be great enough to bring about a true and timely *change* in human life, the old form can perish without any real disturbance, since the new form has quietly developed *out of the old*. The whole movement then proves to be a transition rather than a perdition, a substitution rather than a dissolution.

In considering this great turn of the tide in the lives of nations and humans alike – which has happened silently and with no obvious disturbance – there may be certain deviations, since the history of the world has never regulated itself in like manner. The Old Man is nevertheless right to argue that such a calm transition and substitution is the only *natural* change in human life, for it is the way whereby every mother is regenerated in her daughter. However many historical variations from the truly human laws of nature may have been necessary for the sake of our sins, in every life-change that is to be a rebirth the so-called positive force must be stronger and more active than the negative. This means in plain Danish that the life-force must be stronger than the death-force – which goes without saying if life rather than death is to be victorious.

The Old Man is therefore quite right to say that, contrary to what they claim, the French, Italian, and German movements have been far more destructive than constructive, far more disturbing than creative, and far more negative than positive. In so doing, they have revealed not the strength of their youth but its weakness and infirmity! If it seems otherwise to the many who think that in almost every case the street battles in Paris, Milan, Vienna, and Berlin showed the overwhelming *power* of youth, this is clearly because for far too long their scholarly circles have valued the body over the soul, and placed humans in a sub-category of general animals! Consequently, when the intrepid young bodies rise up, crush all before them, and destroy in a few days what took centuries to build and consolidate, they think that youth is demonstrating its *superiority*, despite the fact that everyone who unquestionably supports a *humane* form of life, both externally and internally, dreads the unavoidable consequences of *such* youthful power and superiority.

This is what the Old Man in Uppsala diligently and successfully seeks to demonstrate. It is clear that by fighting for physical freedom (the liberation of the *flesh*) and by taking pride in destabilising all civil society and human thinking, the youth of our time are not pursuing the natural inclination of a *powerful* youth but are wasting their energy in the service of a delusion and a servitude that is as unworthy as it is ill-fated.

"There is no great principle at stake in wasting energy on a stone", said our forefathers. From time immemorial in the ancient North the deeply-felt distinction between rough-hewn giants and wild berserkers[832] should not now require any further proof, but it seems that not only is many an erring soul in our time in need of it, but that it is also the nature of our species to aspire to the clarity that can illuminate our lives when the concord of nature and history see the light.

This can only come about when we pay *human* regard to both Nature and History and refuse to remain stuck in the confusing definitions of 'Nature' as constituting all things present and 'History' as constituting all things past! Instead, we need to clarify their definition, to separate human life from everything else, and to regard it from its *natural* side – as given, present, and real – as well as from its historical side – as past or prospective future, active and advancing. I have followed Old Nordic thought by beginning with the history of human life as an expression of a powerful drive and then turning to life's true nature, as from effect to cause. Yet it goes without saying that we can also *begin* with natural human life as the true source of all human matters, and conclude with the historical as a consequent development of the human life-force, which, like every effect, must correspond to its cause. The Old Man of Uppsala has made this latter choice, since of course it comes most naturally to a 'doctor' and has the advantage that human *nature* carries all human beings along with it, whereas human *history* is more or less unknown to the majority.

For just as the Old Man in his erudite study of marriage notes that woman as 'mother of the living' is the vital expression of the human 'mother-nature', so does he demonstrate here the true and deep meaning of the expression 'flowering youth'; this is on everybody's lips, but is still understood by only a few. He captures the flowering word in flight and says, "Please note: in a higher human sense youth is not the fruit but the flower. The individual may well be at the height of his existence in his youth, but youth is not the *yield* on human life to be enjoyed, but the expression of that power to be used in life's *service*. Thus the flower is sacrificed for the fruit at the great altar of human life, of the family."

As we can see, this is somewhat obscure, in fact almost as obscure as when with my Nordic crow's feet[833] I asked our youth to take Tyr as a model: for the sake of the common good he put his arm in the wolf's mouth even though he knew he would lose it. On the one hand it is the case with human children that either they must shun the depths within themselves, or they must accept that those depths are as murky as the world's ocean. On the other hand thankfully at present we have a youth activity here at hand which sheds light on the above comparison, both with the vibrancy of the myth and with the flowering of natural history.

832 Berserkers (or berserks) were champion Norse warriors who are primarily reported in Icelandic sagas to have fought in a trance-like fury.

833 i.e. poor handwriting.

Two years ago war broke out between Denmark and Germany. Destruction threatened the entire life of our country, our mother-tongue, and our kith and kin – in fact the life of generation upon generation in its Danish form. It was then that we saw how the youth of Denmark, whether or not they were conscripted, forgot itself and the pleasures of the moment in order to express the power of the people and risk its life and blood for the survival of Denmark! They fought with honour, with freedom, and for their ancient preserves. We saw in their struggle the welcome and joyful beginning of a youthful blood brotherhood stretching throughout the North and endeavouring through self-sacrifice to secure for the Nordic kingdoms, people, and languages the security and respect they need in order to develop their distinctive national characters and reach the great goal for which our noble giant spirits of the North have striven from time immemorial. This is an irrefutable fact, and proves that the Nordic youth of our time feel a far greater vitality than for many a generation, as well as a spiritual duty to sacrifice pleasure and self-interest for the common good. They also have the heart and the will to do so, even while the older generation strives to prevent or discourage them rather than embolden them and show appreciation for them.[834]

Such a decisive fact confirms the call and readiness of our youth to surrender the colour and scent of its flowers for their virtue and fruit; it justifies our boldest and brightest hopes for our Nordic youth and for the future to which their vitality is the driving-force. I had hardly hoped to experience this back in 1842, and it would be both unreasonable and unfair to demand that the Old Man of Uppsala should include it in his reckoning. But he has done his best – more profoundly than lucidly – to set out the causes of the fearful excesses of the youth of our time which are quite rightly portrayed as a furious proclamation of the gospel of the flesh and the body. He argues that this stems largely from their poor upbringing – roughly equal in its severity as in its indulgence. Moreover, he argues from the premise of natural science – which I have long demanded rather than hoped for – that wherever the arrogance, aberration, and unruliness of youth prevail, the main cause is the heartless and spiritless misguidance they have been exposed to. This goes back a long way and is due to the 'scientific' enlightenment of human life. It goes without saying that the source of this confused thinking that our body's numbers and figures and weights are the main reason for our human existence lies in an endless confusion that can only be produced by a bold use of all the powers of disruption. The Old Man finds the source to be the spiritless and heartless view of the so-called 'inorganic' (inarticulate, deaf and dumb) Nature, which considers it to be not only the essential condition of human nature but its

834 Grundtvig's own footnote 18: "In passing I should like to ask Danish readers of *Berling's Times* to look up the brief, condensed presentation of 'the Ministry of War and our Volunteers' in No. 127 (4th June) which, whatever its purpose, gives a graphic account of how the young Nordic volunteers have had to fight for the battlefield and see their great sacrifices and noble efforts scorned as folly and rewarded with ingratitude!"

very foundation and living root! Moreover, he has the courage to *assert* this, despite it going against nearly all the natural science of our day, and despite him feeling its pressure to a quite different extent than that of a saga poet who finds simple comfort in the ancient saying: 'He who would be wise to the ways of Heaven soon becomes a fool on earth'.[835]

I am full of admiration for the Old Man's view and for his courage in enunciating it, partly because it confirms a youthful vitality under his grey hairs – the proper mark of Odin both in Lejre and Uppsala[836] – and partly because it predicts a Nordic natural science which neither overlooks nor disputes history's testimony to the nobility of the human spirit and the depth of the human heart; instead it takes these for granted and thus serves to clarify the mysterious yet assured interaction, both glorious and holy, between 'spirit and dust' in our unique human existence.

Here the Old Man makes the well-founded observation that the peculiarity of human nature lies less in its existence than in its formation, and less in its reproduction than in its development. Human nature is misconstrued, shamed, and profaned if it is merely traced back to the universal, spontaneous, and casual activity of the so-called 'natural forces'. Others must judge whether the Old Man is right to say that the flowering of plants according to the Linnean observation[837] is a portent of the distinctive development of *human* nature. With its unique development, human nature is better understood the more we study successive generations in their totality and gain an overview of the continuous development, from obscurity to clarity, in the complete life of a people and the entire existence of humankind. It is as clear as sunlight that with its unparalleled history human nature is sharply distinguished from that of the dumb animals, and since human nature is undeniably uniform in all its forms, there can be no doubt that a thorough study of the *activity* of human nature in the individual will only confirm what is testified to by the entire history of humankind!

The Old Man takes the opportunity to castigate a theological fallacy which has served to promote and confine this profane, spiritless, and heartless view of human nature, and here I give him my full approval. For when our so-called 'Christian theology' strove to explain the gifts of Grace as being *literal, inexplicable*, and even, somewhat conceitedly, *majestic*, then human nature signed off on all the power of the spirit and all the worth of the heart. It did not give a damn for either of them, but sought to press the seal of 'revelation' on the whole spiritless and heartless view of nature, admitting at heart the claim of the Materialists (the body-only believers) that all matters of the spirit and the heart were foreign to it. Only through some mysterious coincidence,

835 This saying appears in the *Danish Dictionary* of 1802 under 'heaven'.

836 Lejre in Denmark and Uppsala in Sweden were centres of Nordic worship.

837 Carl Linné (1707-78), a Swedish botanist and zoologist, formalised the naming of organisms according to the 'binomial nomenclature' i.e. in two names, using Latin grammatical forms.

through a kind of witchcraft and force of habit, did it cling to it and wind itself around it like a parasitical growth; and so it consumed its best sap over time.

This inanity was not confined to theology alone, for spiritual death and impotence were fundamental features of the *Learning* of the time, which sought to pluck the spirit out of the air! It faced a choice between two interpretations of existence: the insubstantial and the substantial. Since the former had the whole of reality against it, it collapsed of its own accord as soon as any faith in it was ridiculed. It was thus the substantial interpretation that triumphed, for the human heart no longer felt the inextinguishable sense of its youthful marriage with the human spirit as a mighty life-power with its living expression in the Word of the mother-tongues of all people. This heart was neither the mother of a flourishing youth which felt itself inspired by the life-force of previous generations towards the people, nor did it find in the Word of its mother-tongue 'the sword of the Spirit', the buried sword 'Skrep',[838] which only had to be swung twice for it to cut down both of its so-called 'spiritual' opponents.

II

The Dane 1850, 3rd year. Saturday 6th July.

I recently sought to draw the attention of the reading circle of *The Dane* to a study of young people by 'the Old Man of Uppsala'. Out of his rich experience as a physician and university teacher he has produced a very lively and notable portrait of the lives of the young people whom he and many others have encountered and observed. I cannot dwell on the study here, as it will deflect our interest from young people in general and the youth of our time in particular and away from the young lads at university whose direction, development, and excesses require special attention as regards the present state and influence of the university. They do not of course constitute the entire youth of our day, or even its main force, which has made its presence very much felt in our time and will continue to do so in the future – to the incalculable benefit or detriment of our civil society. The Old Man's charge that sensuality, unruliness, and arrogance are the characteristics of our young people may well be true of the 'academic' youth of the best German universities, and therefore to a greater or lesser degree of the universities copying them in Uppsala, Christiania,[839] and Copenhagen. But it is in no way characteristic of our own young people in general.

838 Skrep was the legendary sword of the Danish King Vermund, with which, in single combat, his son Uffe killed two Saxons on the Danish-German border.

839 Oslo was renamed Christiania by King Christian IV in 1625 but reverted to its original name in 1925.

Above all it leaves us no wiser as to our young people's vocation, their deficiencies, or their proper treatment.

The fear of violent disturbance that youth poses to civil society and human life in general is not directed at the young *academics*, who for the most part are divided between leading either a wild life or a dull one, and who in adding a little gaiety to their lives only come to a standstill. Very few of them, especially if their university is in the capital, get mixed up with the seriously unruly youth – those who grow up on the streets, in the workshops, behind the hawkers' stalls, and occasionally in an office. No, the youth for whom we have *some* hope is growing up in obscurity – in the cottages of the peasant farmers or under straw roofs in the maternal lap of the countryside and of home living. These young people are generally limited in spirit, are compliant, and are not interested in public affairs and matters of general importance. This in itself makes our times more dangerous than has long been the case, for lying asleep or dormant in these youngsters are the vital forces and the noble heart which nurse a fond affection for the 'opposite sex' as mother, sister, and sweetheart. When put together with the wisdom of experience and trust in divine Providence, which aspires to the best and commands good fortune, this alone can transform our cluttered and rickety state apparatus into a natural gathering of like-minded people and a civil society with the energy, the stamp, and the direction of our people!

Everywhere we sense that this is the task of our time, that 'the hour has come' when the knot must either be loosened or become inextricably tangled. The whole tendency – not just 1830 and 1848[840] but since the beginning of the century – testifies to this movement, be it in a shallower or deeper sense. For such a turbulent popular movement actually stretches to every corner of the world, and even under the most disparate conditions, states, and circumstances we find traces of human life and civil society. Such a movement has a thousand occasions but only a single cause, which can be found not in any of the occasions but only in the common impulse, drive, and destiny of the human race and the universal dispensation of Providence. All attempts to stop or limit by force this universal, popular discontent and dissatisfaction are worse than useless; even if they briefly succeed in suppressing these obvious expressions, and thus concealing them from the short-sighted, they are only storing up trouble that will lead to violent outbreaks in the most pernicious of directions.

As is the case with 'The Brave Soldier',[841] the task for our 'hopeful youth' is therefore to awaken its love of our country and to expand its horizon from the domestic to the national; only thus can youth conceive of fine leaders in its fight for the people

840 1830 and 1848 were years of revolution in Europe.

841 'The Brave Soldier' (*Den tapre Landsoldat*) was a song written to commemorate the Danish victory over forces from Schleswig-Holstein in 1848. After the Three Years War (1848-51) 'The Brave Soldier After Victory' was erected in Fredericia as the first statue in the world to honour fallen soldiers.

towards victory for the common good. In my view the battle is for what 'The Ballad of Holger Danske' calls "the North under Jutland".[842] If the 'brave soldier', i.e. the core of our Danish youngsters in the countryside, continues to fight with a lion's courage for 'the durability of Denmark', he will be led tolerably well to lasting victory. And if these victories are used for a general homage to, and a realisation of, the *Danishness* of our people, then 'Dannebrog'[843] will wave from every house – not just as an image carried in the procession last year but in actual *reality*. Then through the renewed and well-spent energies of the youth of our time, we shall hear that 'the Danes were victorious'; and then our Danish youngsters will be a mirror throughout the North and beyond – wherever else servitude to the state is replaced by the freedom of the people, and wherever a deadly uniformity is replaced by an enlivening unity, breaking out freely like the sun's rays in a profusion of colour.

This may well be 'Hebrew'[844] to most readers, and my efforts to make it 'Danish' will naturally be of no use to anyone unless they understand the language or are willing and able to learn it. That, however, is what I rightly assume to be the case with subscribers to *The Dane*, and I shall therefore in good faith attempt to clarify for the 'Danish-minded' what I think about the great questions of life which are so urgently demanding an honest answer at this moment.

We all seem to agree that 'humanity' in the higher sense – as opposed to brutishness and devilry – should be the goal for which our young people's energies glow with passion and fighting spirit; it is also what should characterise our whole existence, including our efforts to rein in or free up, lead and manage, enlighten and educate, our lives. But this apparent agreement is no more than a mirage unless we look for humanity *within ourselves*, as God's and our own humanity, rather than going astray over it as though it were foreign to us, as something stipulated by Germany or France, Rome or Greece – or even by Israel[845] and heaven itself! If we had no 'humanity' in

842 The ballad 'King Diderik and Holger Danske' (Karen Brahe c. 1580) contains the line: 'The battle is raging in the north part of Jutland'. According to the ballad, King Diderik of Bohemia attempted to invade North Jutland (north of the River Kongeaa) but met with decisive resistance under King Holger the Dane. Only 55 of Diderik's 18,000 men survived. The warrior legend originated in France in early medieval times. Over the years it travelled to Denmark, where Holger Danske became a national hero, especially with the growing nationalism and patriotism of the 19th century. In 1846 Hans Christian Andersen's eponymous story placed Holger Danske in the cellar of Kronborg Castle (also the site of *Hamlet*) and added to the legend that he had fallen into such a deep sleep that his beard had grown fast to the marble table. This accretion took physical form in 1907 when the Danish sculptor Hans Peder Pedersen-Dan (1859-1939) created the present statue in the cellar itself. Danes believe the words that Hans Christian Andersen put into Holger's mouth before he fell asleep: "Remember me, you Danes, I will come to you in your hour of need!"

843 'Dannebrog' is the name of the Danish flag, a white cross on a red background. Legend says it fell from heaven and helped the Danes win the Battle of Lyndanisse in Estonia in 1219. It is the oldest continuously used national flag in the world; it is flown and waved widely and often used as decoration, from birthday cakes to Christmas trees.

844 i.e. incomprehensible.

845 Grundtvig's Danish word here, *Jødeland*, means literally 'Jewland', or 'land of the Jews'.

us, we could clearly never learn to see and love it in others; but if we do have it, and nevertheless overlook it and despise it in its domestic form, we are in danger of failing to appreciate it in all other forms, and of being deceived by appearances. Even when we are *most* fortunate, we cannot take living possession of it under *foreign* forms until we can remove its foreign dress and clothe it in our home-made one – in other words, until the humanity within us comes alive and merges with its partner from outside.

We cannot therefore become true Christians or gain a living likeness with the 'Son of Man', who is also the 'Son of God', unless we have a prior, living feeling of what it means to be a 'human child', with a desire to become *God's* child. Likewise, we cannot become a 'human people' – however much we have the most human of all peoples in focus – unless we have a prior, living feeling of what it *means* to be a 'human' people. Even when we have this prior feeling of humanity both individually and collectively, that which is foreign to us is cold and dead unless a living link is established between it and ourselves. If our own humanity is greater than 'the foreign' then we can adopt it into us; if it is smaller, then it is adopted *by* 'the foreign'.

The fundamental failing in all our so-called 'education', especially in its civic and scholastic sphere, is that we have almost completely forgotten to *open* this living link between the humanity in ourselves and what was presented to us as the highest humanity through foreign sources, be they Christian, Classical, French, or German models. The consequence is not just multiple errors, such as our taking to be an example of 'humanity' what bordered on the *worst* of examples, but that even when the model was the right one, it took the shadow for the body and the depiction for the reality; it learned the foreign 'humanity' by heart, and licked off its colours, instead of taking possession of its power *internally* and allowing it to express itself in our *own* distinctive colours. This endeavour to make us slough off our own skin and creep into a foreign one is the basic error in all our so-called ecclesiastical, civic, and scholarly education, and thus in all our corresponding educational institutions. Unless this basic error is corrected, the state of things remains hopeless, and more brutish at every turn; for if humankind is not allowed to develop freely in each people's distinctive, natural, and therefore only *living* direction, then brutishness cannot but revolt against it as a dead form and unnatural bond, finding it so dead and impotent in every civic and scholastic relation that victory over it is easily achieved.

This, then, is the meaning of the people's fundamental inclination to sever itself from all foreign contact which is moving all races in our century – and not least their young people. It naturally takes different forms of expression, depending on the degree of its initial participation in the human species, but in every case it manifests itself in a fight against the existing state of things and their foreign origins, which are therefore experienced as a yoke of slavery weighing more or less heavily on the people and their culture.

If we now enter the doors of the 'schools' – the educational institutions for our children and our young people – then we find ourselves at a crossroads: we must decide to which side life is to lean and thus which goals we will try to achieve. Here it is quite obvious that it is far more the fault of 'Learning' than of our youngsters that nowadays the two seldom, if ever, go hand in hand. Of course I am not saying that true Learning, in its living core, is at fault; I am saying that either it is not *true* Learning that comes to meet our youngsters or that it meets them in such a deadly and repulsive form that they cannot possibly appropriate it to themselves.

Our entire educational system, even when it is other than a training to control the strange animal in our Lord's garden called 'the human species', and even when it is pursued in the noblest style, nevertheless rests on two false principles of which just the one would be sufficient to turn our whole life in the wrong direction.

The first false principle in our schooling is that 'humanity' in its general form can be uniformly grafted onto each individual without regard for a people's characteristics or natural aptitude; either they are quite unfit for human education or, relative to their strength and diligence, they will reap the blessed fruits of what others have sown, or rather 'grafted' onto them. This at any rate is what makes our so-called 'education' unfruitful for civil life, and wherever there are forces that enter into their service they are destructive of human life, which is not 'civil' in a general, human sense but only in the specific sense of being bound to the forms of an age and a people. Instead of being strengthened and enlightened by a so-called 'general education' these people are opposed, oppressed, and undermined. If there were no longer any Jewish, Greek, Danish, and Nordic people,[846] there would be no people alive with a sense of civil responsibility! At the most there would only be a faded trace of humanity among a flock of monkeys, vainly attempting to copy a human life entirely foreign to them that had either never been led in a civil sense in this world or, if so, only by those for whom it was unfamiliar in this form.

It is therefore not just a love of our country, together with all the conditions for the life of the people to flourish, that our educational system is undermining; it is also a truly *human* life under any form whatsoever, which it is blindly opposing in its fight for a shadow that has never had, nor will ever gain, a human body.

This first false principle is at odds with the history of nations, which manifests an obvious difference between races, peoples, and languages. All of these can express and develop humanity in some form or other, but they cannot exchange their conditions or take one another's place. The second false principle of our general educational system

846 As early as 1810 Grundtvig was redefining the letters to the seven churches in the Book of Revelation as a prediction of the seven great churches in the historical advance of Christianity. In 1860 the idea found poetic form in *The Seven Stars of Christendom*. Grundtvig believed the first six churches to be the Jewish, the Greek, the Latin, the Anglo-Saxon, the German, and the Nordic. He conjectured that the seventh, not yet materialized, would be the Indian church.

also defies the natural law of humanity in paying no regard to the particular nature of the seasons of human life: childhood, youth, adulthood, and old age. It mixes one with the other as far as possible, and in particular it attempts to pack into childhood all the information and cultural education that is needed for an entire lifetime!

In consequence, our educational system sets out to teach children all they need to know in order to lead a virtuous, prosperous, and even godly human life. In the grammar schools they also teach children all they need to lead an academic life and to explain every mystery that exists; and then they assume that, thus clad, the young people can make themselves proficient in all manner of civil occupations which either take their fancy or give them cause to occupy themselves with – even in their youth.

The only living path to becoming human goes through home life and the people's life. Yet even if we were to follow this and limit our academic preparation to a few bright heads, it would be a foolish way of learning to make all children academic! Or rather, foolish to use the black arts to transform childhood into the heart and mind of old age by vaulting over youth and adulthood. Our children would be worldly wise about a human life that they have only just begun to live unconsciously, let alone to *lead*. They would be driven to view something they have never seen and to reflect on something they have never thought or done. In itself this is so backward-looking that even if it failed to nurture a budding youth and a fruitful adulthood, it would always be working to conjure up an equally desolate and spurious old age. Such an education either frightens the life out of the child's soul or lures it into falling in love with its own empty eminence, like an omnipotent prince in a kingdom of shadows. Such thoroughly backward-looking teaching never stands alone, so in such a boys' school it is the backward-looking world that they seek to put in place of the real world. That is why they do not begin by teaching about a single object closest to the eye in order to look further afield and become knowledgeable; no, they begin by casting a sheen over all manner of objects, the more distant the better, and accustoming the eye never to seek rest but continually to seek change.

Particularly in language teaching pupils do not at present begin by mastering their *mother-tongue* as the only means to living communication in their everyday sphere and the living yardstick for all other human languages, for this is considered an aberration rather than an advantage. Better by far to try to *forget* it, so as not to miss out on the *foreign* languages, where all the wisdom is supposed to lie buried![847] Nor does language teaching begin in the only *natural* way, through the ear with coherent speech, but through the eye with incoherent words and changes to the spelling, in other words

847 Grundtvig called the schools of his time 'schools for death'. The emphasis was on classical languages: Latin, Greek, and even Hebrew for 7 to 13-year-olds. Most 'teaching' involved rote learning for the pupils. Grundtvig's revolutionary plan was to give priority to the Danish language, Danish folk-songs, Danish history, Danish geography, and Danish law.

with the grammar-book. This is the place where language is taken apart, and it should never be given to anyone but the language researcher – only there can it be of benefit. It is a torture-rack for all human beings who answer to that name.

As long as this studiously odious practice is regarded as the pinnacle of human enlightenment and cultural education, to be laboriously pursued from childhood in order to be qualified as a student in one's youth, the vast majority of these 'little Latinists' are consequently overburdened and deadened throughout their youth. They are then forced to drag out a miserable existence as their adulthood unravels – with or without the 'assured livelihood' in civil service circles. A further consequence is that all the other youngsters are either completely neglected or obviously warped by this so-called 'general education', which in the opinion of the academics is intended to be a pale reflection of the lustre of scholarly Learning. If it achieves anything, it is only to make all the other youngsters in city and country torpid and incompetent in their daily pursuits and discontented with their position in society.

Added to this is the fact that in such circumstances the education of *women* cannot acquire even that pale reflection of education and knowledge – neither in specific circles nor even among the governesses. It is either completely neglected among the vast majority, or it is totally unnatural, fruitless, or pernicious. So if they have *any* vitality at all, it can come as no surprise that young people kick over the traces and blindly endeavour to *disrupt* civil society; their only view of civil society is that sets limits on their freedom and favours a few at the expense of the many. We always judge whatever we know nothing about by the form it takes when it is close up to us; if it gets in our way we turn against it, if possible. On the other hand, once our eyes have been opened to the *source* of the wretchedness of our times, we can easily despair of salvation for human life and civil society, for they seem to have only apathy in their defence against all the brutishness assailing us and all the devilry undermining them.

However, if we think seriously about Denmark's attitude to Holstein-Gottorp[848] and to Germany a couple of years ago, and to what our young people, both male and female, have risked and sacrificed to save our fatherland – our own human stage and the foundation of our civil society – then we must take courage and regard them with great expectation and ever-increasing confidence! Seen in this light it does not matter whether they are students or not, or whether they are warped or neglected. We must greatly wonder at the high degree of human vitality and nobility which in its popular Danish form has developed among our youngsters and found such expression in great achievements both locally and nationally. Their vitality makes them unparalleled in the history of Denmark! Love, true, self-sacrificing love, of so small a country, one so

848 Holstein-Gottorp designated the areas of Schleswig-Holstein ruled by the dukes of Schleswig-Holstein-Gottorp and not the Danish king.

insignificant and held so cheap in the eyes of the world as Denmark – that is the one human emotion above all others which is most dreadfully assailed by the alien and unnatural deformity on offer to our youngsters in school. It is also the one human emotion above all others that seems most dead and impotent in our neglected youth, who have grown up amid such indifference to, and ignorance of, our country's past that we had no right to expect of them the *least* regard for its future. And yet we have seen the core of both our students and our neglected youth burst into flame over Denmark's peril and indignity, with girls rivalling boys as to who was the more willing to sacrifice what they held most dear in their beloved country. We have also seen our young lads go through fire and water for Old Denmark and dip themselves in their own blood as though in the gentle waves of summer. And we are seeing it still! Despite all that has dampened, drained, and deadened them, they are ready to risk and suffer to the last degree, if only it is of benefit, if only it can *save* Old Denmark!

Speaking of the July victory last year,[849] – the so-called great 'Danish breakfast' – the old captain said: "With such an army everything is possible!" So do I say now, looking at the last two years that have passed: "With such young people everything is possible!" All that is needed is the vitality of the *people*. Nothing else is required for us both inwardly and outwardly to put into effect this human policy in a natural and timely way – and with such a youth as ours it would be cowardice to think otherwise.

849 At the Battle of Fredericia in July 1849 Danish forces defeated a rebel army from Schleswig-Holstein.

10. Grundtvig in his velvet gown, 1872

With his 89th birthday approaching on 8th September 1872 Grundtvig allowed himself to be photographed in his home on 27th August by Adolph Lønborg (1835-1916). According to Vilhelm Saxtorph's *Portraits of N.F.S. Grundtvig* (1932) p. 55, Grundtvig was at first reluctant, but bowed to his wife Asta's argument that "the man can make money out of you"! One of the four portraits taken on that day is reproduced in *The School for Life* (2011) p. 368. Grundtvig is wearing his velvet gown with his Knighthood cross from 1840. This second one is almost full-length, with Grundtvig sitting in the armchair in which he died 6 days later, as his son Frederick was reading to him. Saxtorph continues: "In the picture on the chair the posture is peculiar; it is as if the body has been thrown onto the chair and placed there, more or less unmanageable; the head is supported by cushions; the eyes have almost disappeared; he is without contact to his surroundings, totally turned inwards; he looks as if he is nearly asleep, or seeing visions."

14. Three Speeches at Marielyst People's High School (1866, 1868, 1871)

Introduction by Edward Broadbridge

The inclusion of these three speeches on Grundtvig's philosophy of education – from 1866, 1868 and 1871 respectively – represents the aftermath of the first article in volume 1 in which Grundtvig first announced his new initiative: "my principal idea for Sorø is to set up a People's High School".[850] His hope that Sorø Academy should be the venue of the first people's high school never came to fruition. The first such high school opened in Rødding in 1844. On his 70th birthday in 1853 his friends gave Grundtvig 7,000 Rigsdaler with a view to establishing a people's high school of his own name and making. In 1855 Grundtvig therefore purchased a farm in present-day Nørrebro, which he re-named Marielyst (Marie's delight) in honour of his late wife, Marie Toft. The school opened on 1st October 1856 with Carl Joakim Brandt (1817-89) as its principal. Later, in 1872, Brandt was to succeed Grundtvig as pastor of Vartov Church, where he remained until his death.

The average number of students at Marielyst (including summer and winter courses) was 21, with an age-range of 15 to 37; the majority were around 20 years old, and, exceptionally, came from the whole of Denmark. In addition to Principal Brandt there were two professionally trained teachers, one of whom, Morten Eskesen, was a composer and a musician, and singing was freely integrated into the curriculum. In 1866 girls were allowed into the school. Among the school's attractions was the opportunity to meet Grundtvig himself, both on his visits to the school and, occasionally on the students' visits to Grundtvig and his wife Asta's homes, first at Gladhjem and then at Store Tuborg. As one former student wrote, "I well remember that it was a festive occasion for us at Marielyst whenever the old man came out to his beloved school... He even invited us to a little farewell party (in his own home) on 29th April, a day which for those present will never be forgotten... Grundtvig made a brief, brilliant speech, which though serious still sparkled with life and humour."

Mornings went with discussions on Nordic myths, Danish folk tales, and Danish proverbs, a subject dear to Grundtvig's heart, since proverbs contain 'the people's wisdom'. There was also room for more practical subjects, such as farming, cattle-rearing, and land-surveying. The afternoon curriculum included the 3 Rs: reading, writing, and arithmetic. In accordance with Grundtvig's principles, Homer's Greek and Saxo's Latin were read in Danish translations.

Grundtvig himself attended the opening day of school every six months (with a few exceptions), and gave a speech of welcome to the new students, the last of these being on 2nd No-

850 *The School for Life. N.F.S. Grundtvig on Education for the People* (2011), p. 38.

vember 1871. The new, occasional songs and Grundtvig's welcoming speech would appear in the Copenhagen newspapers the following day. It is worth remembering that throughout his life Grundtvig himself had enjoyed his teaching career, first as private tutor to Carl Steensen-Leth, aged 7, then as history and geography teacher for the students at the Schouboe Institute, aged 16-18, and finally as a public speaker for the lecture series on recent European history (1838) and the Nordic and Greek myths (1843-44). Not to mention his weekly sermons from the pulpit.

The first speech (8th May 1866) calls for "a people's high school for young girls from all walks of life". Grundtvig is well aware of the scandal this will cause: "We must bear the ridicule that follows". He admits that progress has been made with women's education, but it has been mainly in the cities rather than the countryside, and even in the cities the women only learn to draw, play, embroider, and learn foreign languages, with the result that they remain unaware of "our fatherland, our mother-tongue, our songs, and our literature." He then asks the girls to remember the story of Freya and the jewel that was stolen from her, just as "false enlightenment" has stolen the girls' hearts away. Their new high school will give them *true* enlightenment. The past informs the present.

Again in the second speech, we see Grundtvig returning to a Nordic myth – practising what he preaches. This time the myth concerns the kidnapping of the goddess Idun, who bears apples that bring rejuvenated youth. When she disappears, the gods (i.e. the Danish spirit and culture) grow old and grey; when she returns, the people are also rejuvenated and sing songs of praise "to the light and life of our people and of all people". We note again how the rejuvenated spirit inevitably breaks out into song – in every society and community. "May this wish and this hope of every Danish man and woman now resound in the song, 'Welcome, Idun, back from the giants'!"

For Grundtvig the Nordic myths are a cornucopia of knowledge and experience; they underpin Danish society and its community spirit. Having been its advocate since 1829 he welcomes the fact that "throughout Europe popular education in the mother-tongue is the order of the day. The spirit of the people will flourish "when in life, in education, and in the Church the mother-tongue informs all speech, enlivens the people, and regenerates their original mentality."

On 2nd November 1871, in his last speech welcoming new students to Marielyst. Grundtvig emphasises how the educational philosophy of his new school must in practice "come *from the people themselves*". And in this regard he refuses to favour the academic over the practical student, "for just as assuredly God has given us our physical limbs to use for physical work as best we as can, just so assuredly has He given us our *invisible* limbs, our spiritual abilities, to use for our *spiritual* work – and this deserves to share the fruits of our physical work. We are reminded of Grundtvig's great song of equality, 'Is spelling right or wrong a light alone to scholars given?'[851] Of course not, he answers. The academic and the practical must go hand in hand, so "welcome to all the youngsters who are being initiated into this ideal and who will later become its bearers."

851 For a full translation of this song on 'Enlightenment' see Text 10 in volume 1, *The School for Life* (2011), pp. 252-56.

8th May 1866

The idea is new, but not brand-new: we should open a people's high school for young girls from all walks of life. We must bear the ridicule that follows, and when we are asked in earnest to be accountable for this venture, we who have placed ourselves at its head must not be at a loss for an answer.

The fact is that in bygone days women were ranked either too low or too high as regards enlightenment and higher education. Either it was *beyond* them, or it would come *of its own accord* to the woman, as she was by nature a creature of *feeling*. More recently, the big cities have been very busy promoting what they call 'the education of women', whereas in the countryside all the village people of both sexes have been abandoned – except for the boys who were put to study or who were to become clever by reading and racking their brains. The higher education which was available to girls in Copenhagen and the other cities was in our view worse than nothing. On the one hand it made fools of them, so that whether they liked it or not they had to learn to draw, play, embroider, etc. On the other hand, like the boys they had to learn foreign languages and worry their heads about a little of everything and nothing whatsoever, by which they became self-opinionated without becoming wise to themselves!

With no justification this is called 'higher education' – an education which seeks to separate them from their womanly Danish heart. We can see how a *genuine* higher education would teach all those who *have* such a heart to *cherish* it, to take care of what they have, and to let it be fruitful for the benefit and joy of themselves and their neighbour. This will happen when the young girls become aware of what is especially endearing about both them and the entire Danish people: our fatherland, our mother-tongue, our songs, and our literature. I can think of no better way to give them a living idea of the difference between false and genuine women's enlightenment and education than to tell them of the little poem by our ancient heathen forefathers about the beautiful Freya, their goddess of love. She is imagined as a young widow with a little daughter on her lap, every day weeping tears of gold for her lost husband.[852] She is more lovely, more gentle, more cordial, and more faithful than the goddesses of all other heathens. It was said of Freya that she possessed a matchless gold jewel which always hung around her neck and over her breast, and was called *Brisingamen*.[853] Neither she nor anyone else truly appreciated it until it was stolen, causing Freya to lose both her beauty and her loveliness. The thief who had crept in one night and taken the jewel

852 In Nordic mythology Freya cries tears of red gold for her husband, Od.

853 Lit. 'gleaming torc'. In the Prose Edda (13th cent.), Freya wakes up one morning only to find that her necklace has been stolen. She enlists the help of the god Heimdall (see following note), and they find the thief to be the god Loki, who has turned himself into a seal. Heimdall does the same, fights Loki, and eventually wins and returns *Brísingamen* to Freya.

while Freya was asleep was a cunning god named Loki. There was some doubt as to whether he belonged to the gods or the giants, their enemy; but either way he enjoyed deceiving people and, with his fawning and guile, was a constant danger. Fortunately, however, Freya and all the gods had a good friend called Heimdall, who had an eye in every finger and was even cleverer than Loki.[854] He not only discovered the thief but also forced the jewel from him. When he returned it to Freya, she regained her charm and loveliness.

I see this story as a little mirror reflecting both the damage done to the Dane-woman and her daughters by the false enlightenment and education which stole their hearts away, followed by the genuine enlightenment and education which will catch the thief and make good their hearts, so they can show their themselves in all their loveliness. We shall also see in the mirror how it must be the Dane-woman in particular who regains her heart in the right place, where it can be seen in its true light. It is said that the place where Heimdall forced *Brisingamen* from Loki's claws was called the Singing-stone,[855] which points to our songs, the heartfelt, Danish fatherland songs which will enjoy especially good wind here. For this and for everything that can serve true enlightenment and education I wish good fortune and God's blessing.

5th November 1868

My dear young friends! It is only 15 years ago that a number of my good friends deposited a not inconsiderable sum, given our circumstances, so that, having celebrated my 70th birthday, I could try my hand at setting up the people's high school which I had in vain attempted to interest our kings in setting up at Sorø. 15 years earlier most of my friends had regarded such a school and such crackbrained aspirations as no more than a whim of mine. Surely one had to be not just a 'poet' but a daydreamer to seek to share such an idea. Things are quite different now, for not only in Denmark are the people competing to establish and make use of such high schools, but in Norway and Sweden it is becoming a *contest*! Throughout Europe popular education in the mother-tongue is the order of the day, and there is a gradual realisation that it is the Spirit – the vital force with knowledge and consent – that is behind all human undertakings. The *spirit of the people* must therefore awaken, if the life of the people is to be renewed and to flourish. This can only happen when in life, in education, and in the Church the mother-tongue informs all speech, enlivens the people, and regenerates their original mentality.

854 In Nordic mythology, Heimdall is the guardian of the gods' stronghold, Asgard. With his keen eyesight and hearing he can see hundreds of miles and hear the grass grow. When intruders approach, he blows the Gjallar horn, and he will do so again to announce Ragnarok, in which conflagration he and Loki will kill each other.

855 Grundtvig's word *Klangsteen* is linked to *Singasteinn*, Old Norse for 'singing stone'.

This is among the very first lessons that must be learned and encouraged at our people's high schools, for it was not just the Hebrews, the Greeks, the Romans, and the Latinists who had an understanding of the people's spirit and heart; also here in our northern Danish climes, the worlds of the spirit and the heart shone their radiance before the eyes of the people in the form of gods and goddesses. Like the people, they were immortal, but were equally tenacious of life and, like the people, they had in their own way the good fortune as they were growing old to be able to stay young. Our heathen forefathers imagined this constant rejuvenation of the gods as belonging under the goddess Idun,[856] who descended from Yggdrasil, the family tree of humankind,[857] bearing apples that brought rejuvenated youth. This idea was so much the more remarkable in that our forefathers also had a story of the *kidnapping and return* of Idun. This has clearly made its mark, for the people had enjoyed the first story in its mother-tongue, but fell silent at the second one. For when Idun disappeared, the gods turned old and grey, just as the people's life did when the story and the accompanying song in the mother-tongue disappeared. This shut the door to the only 'school' in which our human life can be enlivened and enlightened. The only 'school' which opened in its stead was in every sense the School for Death. It is therefore a delight to see this facing the same fate that struck Idun's kidnapper, when she flew home to the gods as a swallow in spring and he pursued her as a Roman eagle. For we hear how the gods received him with a fire that burned high into the sky and singed his wings, so that he fell to the ground and was killed by some young boys.

Now that the School for Human Life has reopened in the mother-tongue, the people will doubtless also be rejuvenated like the phoenix[858] and sing songs of praise to the light and life of our people, and of all people until it has reached its goal. To this end we wish the School for Life here and everywhere good fortune and heaven's blessing. We also hope that the group of Danish youngsters whom we welcome here today will sincerely give what they can to building the fire on which the Roman eagle will burn its feathers – just like the moth that is blinded by the brightness of the light and finds death in its blaze.

May this wish and this hope of every Danish man and woman now resound in the song, 'Welcome, Idun, back from the giants'!

856 In Nordic mythology, Idun is the wife of Bragi and goddess of early spring and eternal youth. She owns rejuvenating apples for the gods in Asgard. Through the treachery of Loki she is abducted by the giant Thiazi to the land of the giants, but then Loki is forced to die or bring her back home in the guise of a swallow. He chooses to live, but on her flight home Thiazi, disguised as an eagle, pursues her. As she lands, the gods light a fire which burns the eagle's feathers and he is killed.

857 In Nordic mythology Yggdrasil is the immense ash-tree at the centre of the universe.

858 In Greek mythology the phoenix is a long-lived bird that is cyclically regenerated. It obtains new life by arising from the ashes of its predecessor.

2nd November 1871

It has recently been claimed in print that I never intended a new enlightenment and education to be presented as 'the popular' against 'the academic', but only to build a bridge between the light of the learned and the life of the people, so that they could understand each other! This is an extraordinary misunderstanding, for although my first endeavours sought in a sense to build such a bridge between the educated and the uneducated, so that they could influence each other in enlightenment and cultural education in our common mother-tongue, the attempt would have been in vain if there had not been a subsequent interaction to the benefit of *both*. This was what I expected to happen at the people's high school – in our Danish language. What *kind* of enlightenment and education I expected goes without saying, I think, since everything that is to benefit our country and our language must be based on these two factors. Perhaps I should further make it clear that what leads the people's high school towards this goal must come *from the people themselves*, whereas the so-called 'academic' education is based on foreign elements and never comes alive for the people or benefits the country; it only makes the people dumb and spiritually defenceless and further exposed to these foreign elements.

I venture to claim that popular education is the only defence that can combat such a danger – one from which our gaze has long been averted. Now it actually *threatens* us, for the uneducated masses are claiming that only *physical* work is useful and deserving of remuneration. This is the exact opposite of, and partly occasioned by, the view that has been claimed by the other side that only *spiritual* work deserves to be honoured, and that physical work is in fact beneath human dignity and therefore those that undertake it must be regarded and treated as beasts of burden. Both views are reprehensible, for just as God has assuredly given us our physical limbs to use for physical work as best we as can, just so assuredly has He given us our *invisible* limbs, our spiritual abilities, to use for our *spiritual* work – and this deserves to share the fruits of our physical work. For the work involved in such an education to avert the great misfortune that threatens us, I wish every success both for this winter and for all coming winters. Welcome to all the youngsters who are being initiated into this ideal and who will later become its bearers. Even though the intake of young lads is smaller than we could wish this term, let us hope that their work will be carried out all the faster and better that the freer movement allows, and may they go out into life with all the greater warmth and clarity!

11. Ernst Trier speaking at Vallekilde People's High School, 1888

At Grundtvig's request, his friend Ernst Trier (1837-93) established Vallekilde People's High School in north-west Zealand in 1865. Its foundation was national and Christian, so the illustration depicts Ernst Trier in the lecture hall before a famous painting by Christen Dalsgaard. This depicts the arrival of Christianity in the North with the Benedictine monk Ansgar baptising around the year 850 CE. The school had a strong practical orientation; after all Jesus was a carpenter and Paul was a tentmaker. In his 30 years of teaching in the late 19th century Andreas Bentsen reckoned he had trained some 3,000 craftsmen. Other subjects included art, fishing, and in particular gymnastics, which was sweeping the North in the same period. From 1859 onwards Trier became good friends and would, in his own words, "pump the old man" for ideas and knowledge. In *Memories of Grundtvig's Home* (1883) he writes: "On questions that stumped me, I always turned to him for clarity. I have learned much from his sermons and his writings, but even more from conversations with him." As was the case elsewhere, Vallekilde's summer months held increasingly popular courses for girls. The drawing is by Joakim Skovgaard (1856-1933), best-known for his extraordinary decoration of Viborg Cathedral. Grundtvig had baptised him and remained an inspiration for him throughout his life.

AFTERWORD

GRUNDTVIG AND KIERKEGAARD

The Yodeler and the Hairsplitter. On the Enigmatic Relationship between Grundtvig and Kierkegaard

Anders Holm

It comes as something of a shock to read the first remarks that Grundtvig and Kierkegaard make about each other. So much scorn, so many derogatory assessments, and so much personal abuse – from these two great Danish thinkers of the mid-19th century. Kierkegaard, for instance, says that as a hymnwriter "Grundtvig is a hearty yodeler or a bellowing blacksmith".[859] Grundtvig for his part calls Kierkegaard a "hairsplitter", whose sophistry is unbearable.[860] Moreover, Kierkegaard's malicious and misinterpreted version of Christianity is "the work of Antichrist".[861] In other words, they both claim that there is nothing worth looking at in the other's works – if, that is, we are to take these criticisms at face value.

To be honest, posterity has proved them both right – in the sense that the philosophical paths of Grundtvig and Kierkegaard have ever since been regarded as two mutually exclusive ways of looking at the world. Of course, many Danes have made use of ideas and impulses from *both* of them. A present-day people's high school, for instance, might hear a talk on Kierkegaard and then sing a song by Grundtvig; or a pastor might preach a Kierkegaard-inspired sermon, and follow it with a Grundtvig hymn. But there has been very little attempt to draw a fruitful comparison between the two. For the most part, their disciples have followed their master's words, meaning that if Grundtvig is right, Kierkegaard must be wrong – and vice versa. Indeed, their very names have been used to denote wings and to dig ditches in Danish intellectual life – all the way into the political parties. At the same time it is worth noting that their names are used *across* the political divide, so it is hard to characterise who is with whom on which wing!

When we look more closely, however, the case is not so black and white as it would appear. There are indeed certainly irreconcilable differences between the two, but from each we can also find positive statements about the other alongside the insults listed above. Moreover, in speaking in general of humankind, society, and Christianity, the two are not nearly so far apart. They even met and walked down the same street together in Copenhagen!

859 *KJN* 4, 290 / *SKS* 20, 290. For abbreviations see p. 395.

860 In 'Basic Christian Teachings', vol 3 *Human Comes First* (2018), p. 231ff.

861 *Nordic Monthly* (*Nordisk Månedsskrift*), no. 2 1877, 320.

Kierkegaard's View of Grundtvig

The natural place to begin the story of Grundtvig (b. 1783) and Kierkegaard (b. 1813) is with Kierkegaard. Being 30 years Grundtvig's junior, in his formative youth he was far more aware of Grundtvig's presence in Copenhagen than the other way round. Everybody knew about Grundtvig from his persistent attacks on the Danish Lutheran Church and persons of high public repute. Grundtvig (d. 1872) for his part took no notice of Kierkegaard (d. 1855) until shortly before the latter's death at the age of 42.[862]

In the years when Kierkegaard could realistically have been interested in Grundtvig, from around 1830 onwards, Grundtvig was already an established pastor, poet, translator, educator, and budding politician. Yet he had been equally well-known in his youth as a *rebel*, a young man who had been severely criticised for publishing his dimissory sermon in 1810 with the provocative title: 'Why has the Word of the Lord Disappeared from His House?' He became an even more controversial figure in 1826, when he lost a libel case to Professor of Theology, Henrik Clausen, and was placed under censorship, a punishment which lasted until 1837.[863]

However, there was no doubt that Grundtvig was a shaker and mover in the Danish Church, and by the early 1830s he had attracted a number of supporters, many of whom had some standing in society. Thus, in the years in which Kierkegaard was occupied with public life in Copenhagen, years which played such a crucial role in his authorship, Grundtvig was beginning to enjoy public success – not least with his popular lecture series *Within Living Memory* in 1838[864] and his appointment as Pastor of Vartov Church in 1839.[865]

In addition, already by 1833, the 19-year-old Kierkegaard had come into close contact with Grundtvig's supporters, when his elder brother Peter joined what was becoming a burgeoning movement around the man himself. These early 'Grundtvigians' supported Grundtvig's stance in his libel case and were in favour of greater freedom in the Danish Lutheran Church or, failing that, the right to resign their membership and start their own church. This actually happened in 1832, when 83 families signed

862 The average mortality age at the time was 42. Kierkegaard reached it, Grundtvig exceeded it by 46 years! *Befolkningen i 150 år*, Udgivet af Danmarks Statistik Maj 2000, p. 31.

863 Grundtvig's attack on Clausen in 1825, the libel judgement against him in 1826, and his subsequent defence of his actions constitute chs 1 and 4 in *Human Comes First* (2018). The censorship meant that Grundtvig had to submit all manuscripts to the police censor before publication, and permission to publish had to be printed on the title-page. In practice, this hardly ruffled Grundtvig's feathers, but the humiliation shook him to his roots.

864 14 of these lectures are translated in *The Common Good* (2019).

865 Although Kierkegaard died young and published only an eighth of Grundtvig's massive output, he was nevertheless immensely productive, not least in the 1840s. The recently completed commentated Danish edition of *Søren Kierkegaard's Writings (Søren Kierkegaards Skrifter)* contains both published and unpublished works, journals, notebooks, looseleaves, letters and dedications. Add to these 28 volumes another 27 containing commentaries.

a successful petition to hold their own evensong services – theologically outside, but physically inside, the Danish state church, namely Frederikskirken (the Marble Church) in Copenhagen. They were not allowed to celebrate Baptism and Holy Communion, but Grundtvig was a regular preacher here until 1839.

It was in these years that Kierkegaard was forming his opinion of Grundtvig's theology and Church view, but these were coloured partly by his difficult relationship to his brother, 8 years his senior, and partly by the fact that Kierkegaard's references to Grundtvig are out-of-date by their time of writing in the 1840s. This is clear, for instance in his most comprehensive and explicit attack on Grundtvig in *Concluding Unscientific Postscript* (1846)[866] which was based on a draft he had written in the early 1830s.

From Kierkegaard's private notes we can see that he soon came to loathe 'the Grundtvigians' – with their self-glorification and their mutual backslapping; they made a noise in public but looked down on people outside their inner circle, at the centre of which Grundtvig held forth. In 1845 he even nicknamed them "the Ale-Norse",[867] playing on the Grundtvigians' interest in Old Nordic culture and language, and mocking the lack of sobriety in their thinking. The Grundtvigian flock mentality was anathema to Kierkegaard and may help to explain why he went on to become "the philosopher of the individual".

Grundtvig himself was on the receiving end of Kierkegaard's criticism, not least for his uninspiring sermons. There were many fine words and equivocal phrases, but they had little to do with *Christianity* as such, in Kierkegaard's opinion. Having heard Grundtvig preach in Vartov Church shortly after his induction in 1839, Kierkegaard goes home and spontaneously writes the following:

> All of Grundtvig's preaching is nothing but a perpetually repeated exodus of the imagination so that it is impossible to follow along; it is a weekly evacuation. He continually says the reason why the Church until now has not appeared in its full radiance is that it suffers from external pressures; when these are gone, it will be seen – yes, then it will be seen whether this Church of his is the perfect Church or whether in many ways it does not need a preacher like Mynster, who always leads everything back to the individual; that is where the battle must be and it must not lose itself in such historical ramblings. *26th August 1839.*[868]

866 Danish title: *Afsluttende uvidenskabelig Efterskrift.*

867 *KJN* 2, 236 / *SKS* 18, 256.

868 *KJN* 2, 52 / *SKS* 18, 57.

The problem that Kierkegaard seeks to pinpoint here is that Grundtvig's sermons wander off into incomprehensible historical explications and Church politics; they lack a sense of the individual *churchgoer*, who has come to be edified and encouraged. Some years later Kierkegaard again attends one of Grundtvig's services and concludes that "his sermons are not even sermons". They are simply lectures on history, and cannot possibly bring comfort to the individual in the pew:

> In relation to the religious content all historical presentation is a diversion. The listener forgets himself over the papists and the twilight, over Luther and the sunrise, over the matchless discovery[869] which was made in Copenhagen. But in relation to the religious content it is precisely negative to forget oneself. A religious speaker must not be different from his listeners as the teachers *ex cathedra* are different. The richer in spirit and the more knowledgeable the religious speaker is, the greater is the self-possession required in order to achieve unity with the listener. The religious speaker should be distinguished by his having existentially made sure of what the simplest of men also knows. A hawk's-eye view of world history does not replace a sober insight into oneself; the most matchless discoveries, even the discovery of gunpowder, do not compensate as a substitute for a lack of self-knowledge and of maieutic skill in relation to others.[870]

Reading Grundtvig's somewhat cluttered sermons it is clear that Kierkegaard has a point; many a time the preacher fails to live up to his own ideals of speaking plainly to children and the common man. He gets tangled up, and is not always enlightening, though admittedly it is not always easy to distinguish between the written word and the word as preached. The story goes that it was not necessary for his audience to *understand* the sermons, but only to be glad that they had *heard* them![871] There was a special 'atmosphere' in the church when Grundtvig ascended the pulpit to preach in his deep, rumbling tone. Kierkegaard, however, was not impressed; Grundtvig's sermons were anything *but* 'edifying' – to use one of Kierkegaard's favourite words.

In the passage quoted above, Kierkegaard warns, as elsewhere, against Grundtvig's

869 The 'matchless discovery' of 1825 was the phrase applied to Grundtvig's 'discovery' that the first Church fellowship began with the words of institution at Baptism and Holy Communion, as well as the words of the Creed, which came from the mouth of Jesus himself. He believed that the oral tradition that preceded the books of the New Testament took precedence over the written word. Grundtvig never used the phrase himself, speaking only of a 'matchless witness'. The phrase is attributed to Kierkegaard, who intended it ironically. See Anders Holm, *Two Contemporaries* (*To samtidige*), Anis, Copenhagen 2009, p. 26.

870 *JP* I (626), 257 / *Pap.* VI B 11, p. 87.

871 14 of Grundtvig's sermons have been translated in *Human Comes First* (2018), but without Grundtvig's convoluted syntax. To take a single example, his ½-hour sermon for Christmas Day 1843 (Text 14), consists of only 9 printed paragraphs. Each paragraph contains only *one* sentence! Thus the sentence-length in words is respectively: 226, 110, 353, 119, 92, 136, 178, 159, 63 – a total of 1,436 words and an average sentence-length of 160 words. We can only imagine how these were delivered at Vartov Church on Christmas Day in the morning.

talk of *communities*, such as 'the people', 'the Church', 'the congregation', and shared 'history'. We should neither look for, nor be led by, a community in the outer world, such as 'society' or 'world history', over which we have no control. We must realise instead that we *stand alone with ourselves* – with our own tasks to fulfil. Too much focus on 'communities' and what the individual owes to them can all too easily absorb our entire being and lead us to set aside our own responsibilities and tasks. Fundamentally, we must first attend to ourselves before we can attend to others – and this is in the others' *interest*! Kierkegaard's most important concern was 'existence' itself, a concept he continually returned to. However much we must rely on others in our formative years, we are brought into existence as *individuals*; we must manage our lives as best we can as *individuals*, and as *individuals* we shall die.

Few understood this better from personal experience than Kierkegaard, who had lost his mother and five siblings by the time he was 21.[872] When Søren himself was born, his father was 57 – by all accounts a stern man and a powerful influence throughout his son's life. Søren was also plagued by his self-inflicted broken engagement to Regine Olsen and his problematic relationship with his gloomy elder brother, Peter, a supporter of Grundtvig. Life, for Kierkegaard, demanded bitter blows and hard choices – witness the titles of several of his major works: *Either/Or* (1843), *Fear and Trembling* (1844), *The Concept of Anxiety* (1844), *Stages on Life's Way* (1845), and *Sickness unto Death* (1849). All of these point to Kierkegaard's extensive concern with the question of 'existence'.

Kierkegaard published these works under a pseudonym, perhaps in order to protect himself in some way – and yet no one was in doubt who the author was. The works that he wrote in his *own* name were all part of his *edifying* intentions, and none more so than his *magnum opus*: *Works of Love*, which deals with how we can *prepare ourselves* to face life, and how we can be *built up* (lit. edified) through the love that is implanted in us all.[873] We must *work on ourselves* in this existence; this is an assignment that we must *fulfil*. Included in existence are the unavoidable choices we must each make, and the inevitable deaths and the occasional loves that confront us along the way. In relation to Kierkegaard's criticism of Grundtvig, and also of the Church as an institution, it is an obvious conclusion that this concern is not merely a factor in his authorship but is Kierkegaard's own personal attitude to the Church's duty towards churchgoers – to encourage them to work on themselves! It is the task of the Church to enlighten and prepare them for *life in this world*; otherwise, it is neglecting its duty. And it is precisely here that Grundtvig and his circle, as well as the contemporary Church, are failing,

872 Søren (b.1813) had 6 siblings: 1. Maren (1797-1822), 2. Nicoline (1799-1832), 3. Petrea (1801-34), 4. Peter (1805-88), 5. Søren (1807-19), 6. Niels (1809-33).

873 On this point it is possible to compare Kierkegaard's and Grundtvig's ideas on the image of God. The most comprehensive treatment so far is Niels Jørgen Cappelørn's article, 'The Image of God and the Fall: Aspects of Grundtvig's and Kierkegaard's view of humankind on the background of Irenaeus' in *Grundtvig-Studier 2004*.

says Kierkegaard. They do not see our very existence and our lives as Christians as a challenge to make the right *choices*.

Kierkegaard and Grundtvig's Meetings

Despite Kierkegaard's animosity towards Grundtvig, he was often forced to admit, like it or not, that Grundtvig was right to argue that Christianity lives and breathes *in the present*, and is not merely a religion of the distant past. He also agrees that neither the university nor any other teaching establishment possesses any form of special knowledge as to what constitutes 'true Christianity' or the 'true education' of a person. It is perhaps here that we find one of the most important similarities between the two. Despite all the hindrances of our nature and nurture, each of us is ultimately free to learn for ourselves what life is all about; no specific elite or tyrant can ever *dictate* our values and choices. An entry in one of Kierkegaard's journals from 1849 is doubtless not only the nicest formulation either of them made about the other, but also the closest common denominator between them in their attitude to education and authority, two central concepts in both writers:

> There are two kinds of instruction. One is Socratic: to ask questions in order to starve out empty knowledge. The other is the opposite: the learner asks questions. Once, in a conversation, Grundtvig made the really valuable remark that the instruction that asks a child questions is wrong – it is the child who ought to be allowed to ask.[874]

The remark paves the way for a future study in a largely unresearched field – namely the two philosophers' view of culture and education – and indeed of the two together, combined in cultural education (*dannelse*). Both men challenge their readers to define the meaning and purpose of our individual lives. Perhaps Grundtvig is more concerned about the culture of the people and the Church, while Kierkegaard is more occupied with the individual and what is valid for the individual at all times. Yet it is characteristic of them both that they seek answers to the questions that confront us all as we move through our earthly existence.

The words "in a conversation" in the above quotation reveal that Grundtvig and Kierkegaard not only came face to face with each other but also had several encounters on the streets of Copenhagen. Such meetings are recorded first and foremost in Kierkegaard's private notes from 1848-50, but we also have a renowned summary by an eye-witness of just such an encounter:

874 *KJN* 6, 200 / *SKS* 22, 200.

> There was someone who told me that he had once seen Grundtvig and Søren Kierkegaard walking together on Østergade. Grundtvig strode along, big and calm. Kierkegaard hopped about restlessly, now on the one side of his companion, now on the other, all the while engaged in lively discussion. Then they came to the gate at which Grundtvig was to enter. He promptly tipped his hat; Kierkegaard bowed deeply and removed his hat with great deference.[875]

Even though it is tantalising to reflect on this information, we have no way of knowing what actually took place. Some of Kierkegaard's notes nevertheless suggest that it is not entirely unthinkable that for his part Kierkegaard was seeking to make a closer acquaintance with Grundtvig the man, but against 'the Grundtvigians'. In a note he describes how he employs the conscious tactic of attempting to sow discord among the many cliques in the country. After he has described his relation to various persons of standing in contemporary Church life, Kierkegaard states that, faced with such a coterie, he seeks

> to single out one person whom I venerate or draw toward myself, simply in order to weaken the coterie. The most amusing case has been that of Grundtvig. He has been attacked, among other reasons, on account of his party – and so I have succeeded in maintaining a sort of high- spirited relationship with him that very much embitters the party.[876]

The existence of Kierkegaard's "high-spirited relationship" with Grundtvig is intriguing! Since the reference is definitely to a 'coterie' around Grundtvig, it would seem that Kierkegaard's quarrel is more with the Grundtvigians (including his own elder brother, Peter) than with Grundtvig himself. Nor would Grundtvig have particularly minded, it would seem, for he himself was not enamoured with the so-called 'Grundtvigians', as he wrote in 'A People's Identity in Relation to Christianity' (1847):

> I have never been any good at founding a 'party', but then I have never tried... If... one wishes to make the effort to look a little more closely at the subject, one will soon discover the following about the so-called 'Grundtvigians'. The one will praise my sermon or church singing but censure my mythologising, my historicity, and my pure Danish-

875 Kirmmse, Bruce: *Encounters with Kierkegaard*, New Jersey, Princeton University Press, 1996, p. 93/ Koch, Carl: 'Grundtvig og Søren Kierkegaard' in *Grundtvigske Toner*. Copenhagen: Det Schønbergske Forlag, 1925, p. 7. This is Carl Koch's summary of the episode; the eye-witness in question is unknown.

876 *KJN* 5, 38 / *SKS* 21, 40. Here as in many other places Kierkegaard pours scorn on 'the Grundtvigians' as a *quasi* political party. However, although the Grundtvigians held strong opinions they were never organised as a political party in the accepted sense.

> ness, or at the least my do the opposite! So even if I had two half-parties, there would never be a whole one! Even when individual people praise both my Danishness and my Christianity, the end result is most often a reservation that my Danishness must of course be 'christianised' before it is worth mentioning – and that is far from my thoughts.[877]

We meet this same attack on the Grundtvigians rather than on Grundtvig himself in a number of Kierkegaard's journals, for instance in an entry where he complains about his brother Peter's lecture to the Roskilde convention on 30th October 1849. This is perhaps understandable, for Peter had compared Bishop of Zealand, Hans Martensen, to his own brother, Søren, as examples of level-headedness and rhapsodic turmoil, respectively.[878]

> Incidentally, this is curious: I spoke with Grundtvig two days ago; he made quite scornful remarks concerning Peter in connection with his lecture: "his pro and contra and his mediating, without accomplishing anything himself." It does not, however, by any means follow from this that Grundtvig and I are in agreement. Perhaps, indeed, Grundtvig would have preferred that he had attacked me instead of this twaddling mediation, for Grundtvig probably only has the merest notion of my character, my diligence, and sacrifices.[879]

Around the same time, Søren repeatedly accuses his brother Peter of being a ridiculous "copier of Grundtvig",[880] in one of several similarly enigmatic statements about Grundtvig from Kierkegaard's pen.

The admiration which Kierkegaard nevertheless occasionally held for Grundtvig rests undoubtedly on the fact that as a young man Grundtvig too had been brave enough to swim against the current in the fight for his faith. This became ever clearer as the current sought to push Kierkegaard himself back down the river. Thus, in 1855, the last year of his life, Kierkegaard went ahead with his 'Church storm'. In an excoriating yet elegant attack on the Danish Lutheran Church he produced a flood of articles claiming the Church's very existence in Denmark had nothing to do with the Christianity of the New Testament. The pastors of his time ascended the pulpit thinking only of their good salaries and high status rather than in order to bear the cross, he railed. According to the New Testament a witness to the Truth should be willing to be *un*popular for the faith, whereas all that the contemporary clergy wanted was to be praised in life and eulogised in death.

877 Danish title: *Folkelighed og Kristendom*. Quoted from *Human Comes First* (2018), p. 189.

878 The lecture was published in *Danish Church Times (Dansk Kirketidende)* on 16th December 1849, a factor that could only worsen the already poor relationship between the two brothers.

879 *KJN* 6, 415 / *SKS* 22, 409.

880 *KJN* 6, 408 / *SKS* 22, 403.

Back in the 1810s and 1820s Grundtvig had also been an anti-establishment rebel, as Kierkegaard was well aware. Unfortunately, in his later life the old man had become such a conformist that he could not even *break* with the Church that paid his salary and praised his sermons. In a journal note Kierkegaard writes:

> In his younger days he represented old, old-fashioned, ancient, primal-primeval Christianity; now, in his old age, he is decked-out as a truly fashionable fellow.[881]

The word 'fashionable' is a withering criticism of the by now well-established Grundtvig, whereas the 'primal Christianity' (Danish *Ur-Christendommen*) that Kierkegaard champions time and again has long gone missing from the Church. Along with a number of others, Kierkegaard thinks that the aging Grundtvig has lost the Christian passion of his youth, and with it Kierkegaard's respect. The accusation is in dispute, but Kierkegaard's disappointment is not.

Grundtvig's View of Kierkegaard

Kierkegaard took up far less room in the 30-year older Grundtvig's life than the other way round. Only in 1855, when Grundtvig was over 70, did he begin to take Kierkegaard seriously – as a result of the latter's above-mentioned 'Church storm'. Grundtvig's criticism of Kierkegaard was also far more spontaneous and vehement than the younger man's of him. He had of course been aware of Kierkegaard's publications, but he appears not to have taken much notice of them until late in the day. Even then he only refers to them in his sermons, which Kierkegaard is most unlikely to have heard, for he had not only given up on Grundtvig, and but had also stopped going to church altogether in 1853.

Grundtvig is nonetheless shaken to the core by Kierkegaard's attack on the Church, which forces him to rethink his own view of the Church. His sermons in 1855 contain several despairing comments on Kierkegaard, and warnings to the churchgoers (Grundtvigians) not to listen to the mad man. For several years after Kierkegaard's death in 1855, Grundtvig continues to take him to task. His major theological work, *Basic Christian Teachings* (1855-61),[882] is in part a response to Kierkegaard's attack on the Church.

Particularly on two fronts Grundtvig criticises Kierkegaard. Firstly, he rejects Kierkegaard's claim that Christianity should change a person's life completely. With reference to the New Testament Kierkegaard assumes that one can actually *be* like

881 *KJN* 8, 210 / *SKS* 24, 212.

882 Danish title: *Den christelige Børnelærdom*. 15 of its chapters are translated in *Human Comes First* (2018), pp. 239-370.

Christ, the great model. That is not possible, says Grundtvig. The gap between Christ and Christians is insuperable, and Christians can only hope to grow a little wiser on earth through their faith.

Answering a complaint about Kierkegaard from the curate, Nicolai Holten, Grundtvig attacks Kierkegaard's

> ... specifically anti-Christian stance in presenting a claim that the true Christianity is the most impossible human goal under the sun. This not only justifies the world's lack of faith in rejecting the empty name of 'Christian' that proceeds from this claim, it also stigmatises all believers who cannot or will not deny their Lord and their Christian name as open falsehoods. This was recently Søren Kierkegaard's mortal sin, so I am not surprised that that his death caught him unawares. For as long as the days of Anti-Christ have yet to arrive, those who tamper with his masterpiece will always fall flat on their faces – like every false Messiah.[883]

This is a truly vicious criticism, even for Grundtvig, but it does tell us how far he thought Kierkegaard had erred on this point. Secondly, at this stage in his life Grundtvig is refusing to list the necessary criteria to be *truly* Christian or not. In his view, Kierkegaard is demanding that this should be measured by personal suffering – and, since they have not earned it, he therefore denies to all Danish pastors, including Grundtvig, the title of 'Christian'.

Kierkegaard added fuel to his fire in an article in the paper *The Fatherland* on 22nd March 1855 with a claim that everyone should be able to see that the Christianity of the New Testament no longer exists! Grundtvig took umbrage. It is simply wrong to claim that the Christian life *has* to be one of suffering – in a specifically recognisable way. A Christian faith and personal suffering may go together, but this is not necessarily the fate that befalls the Christian. In one of his biblical allusions to Kierkegaard Grundtvig calls him a false prophet:

> ... in no way is this Christian life, this life in the Lord, nothing but sorrow and anguish, pain and torment, as the false prophets claim. Jesus did not live such a life here on earth, and as *He* was in this world, so must *we* be. Which of us can doubt that, despite worldly humbleness, poverty, pain, and death, the life of our Lord Jesus Christ was in its totality the gladdest and happiest human life that can be led in this world...[884]

883 Dated 19th November 1855, the day after Kierkegaard's funeral. First published in *Nordic Monthly (Nordisk Månedsskrift)*, no. 2 1877, 320.

884 Sermon for 8th Sunday in Trinity, 29th July 1855 (Konf. 146).

Is Grundtvig's claim perhaps too much in the *other* direction – as though Christianity should be no more than a *happy* religion? Grundtvig clearly felt himself under pressure to respond to Kierkegaard, and his counter-argument is not exactly crystal clear. However, his general line of argument against Kierkegaard is clear enough: Christians cannot be assessed by their human success – or the lack of it; the very *measurement* is false. We cannot even *see* the result of a Christian life, for the life of the spirit is largely invisible, and anyway, we are not justified by *deeds*, as Luther pointed out. Grundtvig nevertheless took Kierkegaard very seriously, arguing that:

> ... it was no trick when Søren Kierkegaard, to the great applause of the world, described our so-called Christian preaching, Bible-reading, Church worship, infant Baptism, and Holy Communion as an immense tomfoolery and a merry farce![885]

Only where Christians freely *practise* their faith, i.e. through churchgoing, can we *presume* that they are nurturing their Christianity. In prayer, in songs of praise, in listening to the living Word, Christians are responding to God's address to them; and in Baptism, Holy Communion, and the Creed they are in direct dialogue with God. In *Basic Christian Teachings*, Grundtvig nonetheless admits that Christians do have a duty:

> ... it is up to us and the same Jesus Christ whom we confess together with the guiding and comforting Spirit to show the world that such a life does exist, even though it has long been hidden and is hard to recognise.[886]

Grundtvig was clearly aggrieved by Kierkegaard's divisive approach. In the course of two paragraphs in *Basic Christian Teachings* he calls Kierkegaard a 'hairsplitter' no fewer than four times, as well as adding the accusation: "persecutor of priests"!

> Day by day it becomes clearer that if one does not wish to be forced into agreement with the hairsplitter, one must let go of the upside-down idea that the book called the 'New Testament' is the real source, foundation, or rule of faith for true Christianity. The hairsplitter will then stand or fall as a Christianity expert and persecutor of priests and must either refute himself or be seen as the open enemy and denier of Christianity.[887]

Yet despite his antipathy towards Kierkegaard, Grundtvig acknowledges that the younger man's battle with the Church is indeed a form of *Christian* endeavour. He

885 *Human Comes First* (2018) p. 315.
886 *KS* 3, 98. *Human Comes First* (2018) p. 316.
887 *Human Comes First* (2018) pp. 290-91.

understands Kierkegaard's 'Church storm' as a means to understanding his *own* battle against any and every form of forced teaching, or fixed ritual, or indissoluble parish-tie. In an article published in *Danish Church Times* on 2nd December 1855, i.e. only 3 weeks after Kierkegaard's death, Grundtvig suggests two possible ways for the Church to go. Either the bonds between Church and State must be severed completely, or the Church must institute a requirement that only binds pastors to their own faith and conviction "regarding New Testament Christianity". If that is so, as Grundtvig recommends,

> even Søren Kierkegaard could become a pastor in 'the People's Church' without being committed to any other version, practice, or exercise of Christianity than what he found himself inwardly called and driven to, according to the free relation in which he had placed himself with regard to our Lord and the New Testament![888]

Of interest here is not only the skill with which Grundtvig plays on Kierkegaard's entire vocabulary but also how clearly already in 1855 he sees him as a textbook example of what risks coming under pressure in an unfree Church. Kierkegaard is important for his ability to call out hypocrisy, a voice that a healthy Church is always in need of.

What fascinates Grundtvig about Kierkegaard, and vice versa, is his criticism of the lack of *commitment* among Danish pastors. When we read of Grundtvig's reactions to Kierkegaard, it seems as if he is occasionally recognising his own younger self in the junior Kierkegaard, while the later Kierkegaard sometimes appears to identify with the young Grundtvig and *his* attacks on the Church.

Conclusion

Their statements about each other demonstrate that Grundtvig and Kierkegaard crossed each other's paths at various times and in various ways. They undoubtedly differed on crucial points, yet the two together constituted more than the sum of the two parts. Each traced a path through Lutheran Christianity, Grundtvig towards the collective, Kierkegaard towards the individual, the one towards the rewards of joyous faith, the other towards the insights of suffering. They both shared a deep insight into human life, and an eye for where the other went off track: Grundtvig punctured Kierkegaard's impossibly high demands to follow Christ in all things or fail, while Kierkegaard censured Grundtvig for his over-indulgent cultivation of an intellectual fellowship of backslapping admiration. Inasmuch as each tradition continues to this day, it is important to see both paths ahead – and thus carry forward their relevant criticism of each other. Alternatively, one can settle for the unidentified but incisive

888 *Danish Church Times* 1855 no. 49, col. 801. / *Human Comes First*, p. 219.

comment: "How fortunate for Denmark that it had both Grundtvig and Kierkegaard. One of them alone would have been far too much!"

All Kierkegaard quotations in this article are from the following works, abbreviated thus:

Pap: Søren Kierkegaards Papirer (1909-48), bind 1-15. Udgivet af P.A. Heiberg, V. Kuhr og E. Torsting. København: Gyldendal; 2. forøgede udg. (1967-78) ved N. Thulstrup, bind 1-16. København: Gyldendal.

SKS: Søren Kierkegaards Skrifter (1997-2003), bind 1-28. Redigeret af Niels Jørgen Cappelørn m.fl. København: Gads Forlag.

JP: Søren Kierkegaard's Journals and Papers (1967-78), vols 1-6. Ed. & transl. Howard and Edna Hong, Bloomington: Indiana University Press.

KJN: Kierkegaard's Journals and Notebooks (2007-20) vols 1-11. Ed. Niels Jørgen Cappelørn, Alastair Hannay, David Kangas, Bruce H. Kirmmse, George Pattison, Joel D.S. Rasmussen, David D. Possen, Vanessa Rumble, and K. Brian Söderquist Princeton, NJ: Princeton University Press.

Konf.: Konfrontation. Grundtvigs prædikener i kirkeåret 1854-1855 på baggrund af Kierkegaards angreb på den 'officielle' Kristendom (1974). Udgivet af P.G. Lindhardt: København: Akademisk Forlag.

KS: Kirkelig Samler (1862), bind 1-8. Samlet og udgivet af Chr. Kragballe, København: Iversens Forlagshandel.

For further reading on Grundtvig and Kierkegaard see under Special Bibliography.

12. Flyer for course on Kierkegaard and Grundtvig

The wording reads: A week with the fathers on the courage to face life / 26th May - 1st June 2013. In a collaboration between the Søren Kierkegaard Society and Grundtvig's Forum at Rødding People's High School.Numerous courses are held comparing the two great thinkers of the 19th century, here designated as 'fathers' - and with some justification. Kierkegaard is acknowledged as the father of existentialism and Grundtvig as the father of adult education.

Sources

All source material is taken from Grundtvigs Værker (GV) - available at grundtvigs-værker.dk, except ch. 10, transcribed by Elisabeth A. Glenthøj and ch. 12, from *Værker i Udvalg* (Selected Works 1-10) ed. G. Christensen og Hal Koch, II 272-85, which comprises a number of undated drafts for unpublished studies on language c. 1815-19.

1. On Human Beings in the World (1817)
   Danish title: *Om Mennesket i Verden*
2. On Truth, Greatness, and Beauty (1817)
   Danish title: *Om Sandhed, Storhed og Skiønhed*
3. On Religion and Liturgy (1807)
   Danish title: *Om Religion og Liturgie*
4. On Revelation, Art, and Learning (1817)
   Danish title: *Om Aabenbaring, Konst og Vidskab*
5. On the Church, the State, and the School, part 2 (1819)
   Danish title: *Om Kirke, Stat og Skole*
6. On The Advancement of Learning (1807)
   Danish title: *Om Videnskabelighed og dens Fremme*
7. On the Philosophical Century (1816)
   Danish title: *Om Det Philosophiske Aarhundrede*
8. On Historical Learning (1816)
   Danish title: *Om historisk Vidskab*
9. On the Relation between Learning, Experience, and Sound Common Sense (1817)
   Danish title: *Om Videnskabeligheds Forhold til Erfaring og sund Menneske-Forstand*
10. History and Naturalism, or the Illumination of Time and Space (1865)
    Danish title: *Historie og Naturalisme eller Tids og Rums Oplysning*
11. On Proverbs (1817)
    Danish title: *Om Ordsprog*
12. On the Word and the Mother-Tongue (1819)
    Danish title: *Om Ordet og Modersmaal*
13. Youth in Our Time (1850)
    Danish title: *Vor Tids Ungdom*
14. Three Speeches at Marielyst People's High School (1866, 1868, 1871)
    Danish title: *Tre Taler ved Marielyst Højskole*

English Bibliography

Titles are listed alphabetically by author.

1. General Introduction

Holm, A. (2019). *The Essential N.F.S. Grundtvig.* Aarhus: FILO.

2. General

Allchin, A. M., Jasper, D., Schjørring, J. H., and Stevenson, K. (eds.). (1993). *Heritage and Prophecy: Grundtvig and the English-Speaking World.* Aarhus: Aarhus University Press.

Allchin, A. (1997, repr. 2016). *N.F.S. Grundtvig: An Introduction to His Life and Work.* Aarhus: Aarhus University Press.

Allchin, A., Bradley, S.A.J., Hjelm, N. & Schjørring, J. (eds.). (2000). *Grundtvig in International Perspective: Studies in the Creativity of Interaction.* Aarhus: Aarhus University Press.

Allen, E. L. (1947). *Bishop Grundtvig. A Prophet of the North.* London: James Clarke.

Bradley, S.A.J. (trans. & ed.). (2008). *N.F.S. Grundtvig / A Life Recalled: An anthology of biographical source-texts.* Aarhus: Aarhus University Press.

Davies, N. (1931). *Education for Life: a Danish Pioneer.* London: Williams & Norgate.

Davies, N. (1944). *Grundtvig of Denmark: a guide to small nations.* Liverpool: The Bryerthon Press.

Knudsen, J. (1955). *Danish Rebel. A Study of N.F.S. Grundtvig.* Philadelphia: Muhlenberg Press.

Koch, H. (1952). *Grundtvig* (trans. & ed. Jones, L. from orig. Danish by Koch, H (1943). Yellow Springs, Ohio: Antioch Press.

Korsgaard, O. (2014). *N.F.S. Grundtvig – as a Political Thinker.* Copenhagen: DJØF Publishing.

Larson, P.M. (1986). *A Rhetorical Study of Bishop Grundtvig.* Evanston, Illinois: Northwestern University.

Lindhardt, P. (1951). *Grundtvig, an Introduction.* London: SPCK.

Martin, G.O. (1950). *N. F. S. Grundtvig: the Man and his Theology.* New York: Columbia University.

Nielsen, E. (1955). *N. F. S. Grundtvig: An American Study.* Rock Island, Illinois: Augustana Press.

Thaning, K. (1972). (trans. Hohnen, D.). *N.F.S. Grundtvig.* Copenhagen: Danish Cultural Institute.

Specifically on Grundtvig and Kierkegaard

Allen, E.L., 'Grundtvig and Kierkegaard', *The Congregational Quarterly*, vol. 24, no. 3, 1946, pp. 205-12.

Dalsgaard, Mathias Møl, (2015) 'Community and Individuality: Grundtvigian and Kierkegaardian Protestantism in Denmark' in ed. Hall A. et al.: *Building the Nation. N.F.S. Grundtvig and Danish National Identity,* Copenhagen, Djøf Publishing, pp. 300-12.

Høirup, Henning (1955), 'Grundtvig and Kierkegaard. Their Views of the Church', *Theology Today*, vol. 12, no. 3, pp. 329-49 (also published in *Grundtvig-Studier*, 1956, pp. 7-20).

Holm, Anders, (2005) 'The Contemporary Grundtvig. An Addition to Climacus' Critique in Concluding Unscientific Postscript' in *Kierkegaard Studies: Yearbook.* /ed. N.J. Cappelørn, H. Deuser, B. Söderquist. Berlin/New York. pp. 24-36.

Holm, Anders (2009), 'N.F.S. Grundtvig: The Matchless Giant' in ed. Jon Stewart: *Kierkegaard and his Danish Contemporaries*: Kierkegaard Research: Sources, Reception and Resources: Vol. 7. Tome II: Theology. Farnham UK/ Burlington USA: Ashgate, pp. 95-151,

Kvist, Morten (2005), 'N.F.S. Grundtvig's Conception of Historical Christianity. An Introduction to the Relationship Between Kierkegaard and Grundtvig', *Kierkegaard Studies. Yearbook*, pp. 37-52.

Michelsen, William (1983), 'Grundtvig's Place in Danish Intellectual Thought – With Particular Regard to Søren Kierkegaard' in ed. Thodberg, C. et al, transl. E. Broadbridge, *N.F.S Grundtvig – Tradition and Renewal. Grundtvig's Vision of Man and People, Education and the Church, in Relation to World Issues Today*, Copenhagen, Det danske Selskab, pp. 295-302.

3. Essays

Campbell, John L., Hall, John A., and Pedersen, O.K. (eds). (2005). *National Identity and the Varieties of Capitalism. The Danish Experience*. Montreal et al: McGill-Queens University Press.

Korsgaard, O. (2008). *The Struggle for the People. Five Hundred Years of Danish History in Short.* Copenhagen: Danish School of Education Press.

Hall, J.A., Korsgaard, O., and Pedersen, Ove K. (eds.). (2014). *Building the Nation. N.F.S. Grundtvig and National Identity*. Copenhagen: Djøf Publishing.

Thodberg, C. & Thyssen, A. (eds.) (1983) *N.F.S. Grundtvig: Tradition and Renewal.* Copenhagen: Danish Cultural Institute.

4. Websites in English

1. https://www.youtube.com/watch?v=cy2f4RnStlg 2013 (10½ mins)
   Interview with Professor Clay Warren (co-editor) on *The School for Life* and Grundtvig's philosophy of education.
2. https://www.youtube.com/watch?v=_z7-krwFPRw 2019 (29 mins)
   Talk on Grundtvig and the US Folk School by Kerri Hamos, Program Director, The Folk School.

Indexes

1. Biblical references

2. Personal names

3. General

N. F. S. Grundtvig: Works in English

Translated and edited by Edward Broadbridge

Published by Aarhus University Press

"The world and scholarship have been done a great service with this edition of Grundtvig's works."

Linda Woodhead, Professor in the Department of Politics, Philosophy and Religion, Lancaster University

"Scholars and general readers alike will find these translations to be not only invaluable sources for the study of the work of an influential modern genius, but also a very pleasurable reading experience, one that is inspiring and full of surprising insights."

Mark Bradshaw Busbee, Department of English Chair, Samford University, Alabama

Vol. 1. The School for Life. N. F. S. Grundtvig on Education for the People (2011)

"Edward Broadbridge and his dedicated team have delivered a long-overdue English rendition of Grundtvig's educational ideas in a sensitive and highly readable translation that retains the power of Grundtvig's voice and moreover brings the "living word" alive in the accompanying audiobook."

Chris Spicer, Chair, Folk Education Association of America

"How wonderful to welcome Edward Broadbridge's remarkable new translation entitled The School for Life. The book draws together Grundtvig's most important works on education, both prose and poetry, representing a major addition to the English language literature on educational philosophy."

Andrew Buckser, Dean of Arts and Sciences and Professor of Anthropology at State University of New York

"For those English-speaking communities interested in the origins and history of folk education and adult education in Scandinavia, *The School for Life: N. F. S. Grundtvig on Education for the People* provides a charming and much-needed entry point, including an excellent audio recording with the text.

What I have found through this book and its translations is a vigorous, passionate, and inquiring mind fit not only for the transformational times of the 18th and 19th centuries, but one that can inspire the transformations of the 21st century as well.

Dawn Jackman Murphy, Marie Fielder Center for Democracy, Leadership, and Education, Fielding Graduate University, Santa Barbara, California

"This work has been long-awaited: a major translation of the Danish educationist, cultural philosopher, and theologian, N. F. S. Grundtvig. We can follow Grundtvig's theological foundational principle: "Human comes first, and Christian next" through his educational writings, which emphasise the need for a cultural self-awareness along with a radical tolerance for all forms of human expression in a cultural context."

Niels Henrik Gregersen, Professor of Systematic Theology, University of Copenhagen

Vol. 2. Living Wellsprings. The Hymns, Songs, and Poems of N. F. S. Grundtvig (2015)

"I expected a lot from this book and honestly, it is much more than I expected! The Grundtvig anthology of new translations presents the tremendous depth and breadth of Grundtvig's work in a highly accessible way. Songs and poems embracing Nordic sagas, Christian spirituality, education, democracy, wisdom, nature, as well as personal tributes to his wives, children and friends and even more can be found in Living Wellsprings."

Joy Ibsen, Church and Life, May 2015

"Students of historical hymn texts will find this a rich source of material. The translations are well done, reading quite naturally for the most part."

Lydia Pedersen, The Hymn Society in The Hymn, Vol. 67/2, 2016.

"A magnificent book."

Bertel Haarder, Former Danish Minister of Education (Letter to the Editor, 2015)

"One overarching characteristic of the translations becomes very clear after a reading of all the poems and reflecting on their collective effort. Broadbridge has produced translations that recapture Grundtvig's wonder at God's creation and man's place in it. Broadbridge's achievement is that his work bears the mark of Grundtvig's call for 'a plain and cheerful, active life on earth'."

Mark Bradshaw Busbee, Department of English Chair, Samford University, Alabama

Vol. 4. The Common Good. N.F.S. Grundtvig as Politican and Contemporary Historian (20191)

"*The Common Good* should be required reading for anyone interested in the role of religion in politics... Broadbridge's translation is so excellent and elegant that one forgets that it is not the original. Broadbridge has transformed long and long-winded sentences – Grundtvig's "torturous prose" featuring sentences that "approach 300 words" – into an English full of verve!"

Dr Ulrich Schmiedel, Department of Theology, Edinburgh University